Data Engineering with dbt

A practical guide to building a cloud-based, pragmatic, and
dependable data platform with SQL

Roberto Zagni

BIRMINGHAM—MUMBAI

Data Engineering with dbt

Publishing Product Manager: Reshma Raman
Content Development Editor: Joseph Sunil
Technical Editor: Kavyashree KS
Copy Editor: Safis Editing
Project Coordinator: Farheen Fathima
Proofreader: Safis Editing
Indexer: Hemangini Bari
Production Designer: Aparna Bhagat
Marketing Coordinator: Shifa Ansari

First published: June 2023

Production reference: 1300623

Published by Packt Publishing Ltd.
Livery Place
35 Livery Street
Birmingham
B3 2PB, UK.

ISBN 978-1-80324-628-4

www.packtpub.com

To the four females in my daily life: my wife, who supports me every day, my daughters, who keep me grounded in reality, and our dog Lily for the sparkles of love and happiness that she spreads around every day.

To my mother and my late father who through their sacrifices and support allowed me to become what I wanted to be.

I love you all.

– Roberto Zagni

Contributors

About the author

Roberto Zagni is a senior leader with extensive hands-on experience in data architecture, software development, and agile methodologies. Roberto is an electronic engineer by training with a special interest in bringing software engineering best practices to cloud data platforms and growing great teams that enjoy what they do. He has been helping companies to better use their data, and now to transition to cloud-based data automation with an agile mindset and proper software engineering tools and processes, such as DataOps. Roberto also provides hands-on coaching to data teams on practical data architecture and the use of patterns, testing, version control, and agile collaboration.

Since 2019, his go-to tools have been dbt, dbt Cloud, and Snowflake or BigQuery.

I would like to thank my customers and colleagues for all the problems, and discussions to get to a working solution that helped me to become a better software and data engineer and collect a wide array of experiences in software and data engineering.

This book is my little contribution to the data engineering community.

I hope that I have been able to put the core set of knowledge that I would have loved to have in my days as a data engineer in one place, along with a simple, opinionated way to build data platforms using the modern data stack and proven patterns that scale and simplify everyday work.

About the reviewers

Hari Krishnan has been in the data space for close to 20 years now. He started at Infosys Limited, working on mainframe technology for about 6 years, and then moved over to Informatica, then eventually into business intelligence, big data, and the cloud in general. Currently, he is senior manager of data engineering at Beachbody LLC, where he manages a team of data engineers with Airflow, dbt, and Snowflake as the ir primary tech stack. He built the data lake and migrated the data warehouse as well the ETL/ELT pipelines from on-premises to the cloud. He spent close to 13 years working for Infosys and has spent the last 7 years with Beachbody. He is a technology enthusiast and always has an appetite to discover, explore, and innovate new avenues in the data space.

Daniel Joshua Jayaraj S R is a data evangelist and business intelligence engineer, with over six years of experience in the field of data analytics, data modeling, and visualization. He has helped organizations understand the full potential of their data by providing stakeholders with strong business-oriented visuals, thereby enhancing data-driven decisions. He has worked with multiple tools and technologies during his career and completed his master's in big data and business analytics.

I would like to thank my mother, S J Inbarani, who has been my motivation my whole life. I would also like to thank Roberto Zagni for allowing me to review this wonderful book on dbt.

Table of Contents

3

Data Modeling for Data Engineering   105

4

Analytics Engineering as the New Core of Data Engineering   153

5

Transforming Data with dbt   177

Part 2: Agile Data Engineering with dbt

6

7

8

Delivering Consistency in Your Data   275

9

Delivering Reliability in Your Data   303

10

Agile Development   331

11

Team Collaboration   359

Part 3: Hands-On Best Practices for Simple, Future-Proof Data Platforms

12

Deployment, Execution, and Documentation Automation   381

13

Moving Beyond the Basics

14

Enhancing Software Quality

15

Patterns for Frequent Use Cases

Preface

dbt Cloud helps professional analytics engineers automate the application of powerful and proven patterns to transform data from ingestion to delivery, enabling real DataOps.

This book begins by introducing you to dbt and its role in the data stack, along with how it uses simple SQL to build your data platform, helping you and your team work better together. You'll find out how to leverage data modeling, data quality, master data management, and more to build a simple-to-understand and future-proof solution. As you advance, you'll explore the modern data stack, understand how data-related careers are changing, and see how dbt enables this transition into the emerging role of an analytics engineer. The chapters help you build a sample project using the free version of dbt Cloud, Snowflake, and GitHub to create a professional DevOps setup with continuous integration, automated deployment, ELT run, scheduling, and monitoring, solving practical cases that you encounter in your daily work.

By the end of this dbt book, you'll be able to build an end-to-end pragmatic data platform by ingesting data exported from your source systems, coding the needed transformations (including master data and the desired business rules), and building well-formed dimensional models or wide tables that'll enable you to build reports with the BI tool of your choice.

Who this book is for

This book is for data engineers, analytics engineers, BI professionals, and data analysts who want to learn how to build simple, future-proof, and maintainable data platforms in an agile way. Project managers, data team managers, and decision-makers looking to understand the importance of building a data platform and fostering a culture of high-performing data teams will also find this book useful. Basic knowledge of SQL and data modeling will help you get the most out of the many layers of this book. The book also includes primers on many data-related subjects to help juniors get started.

What this book covers

Chapter 1, Basics of SQL to Transform Data, explores the basics of SQL and demystifies this standard, powerful, yet easy-to-read language, which is ubiquitous when working with data.

You will understand the different types of commands in SQL, how to get started with a database, and the SQL commands to work with data. We will look a bit deeper into the SELECT statement and the JOIN logic, as they will be crucial in working with dbt. You will be guided to create a free Snowflake account to experiment the SQL commands and later use it together with dbt.

Chapter 2, Setting Up Your DBT Cloud Development Environment, gets started with DBT by creating your GitHub and DBT accounts. You will learn why version control is important and what the data engineering workflow is when working with DBT.

You will also understand the difference between the open source DBT Core and the commercial DBT Cloud. Finally, you will experiment with the default project and set up your environment for running basic SQL with DBT on Snowflake and understand the key functions of DBT: ref and source.

Chapter 3, Data Modeling for Data Engineering, shows why and how you describe data, and how to travel through different abstraction levels, from business processes to the storage of the data that supports them: conceptual, logical, and physical data models.

You will understand entities, relationships, attributes, **entity-relationship (E-R)** diagrams, modeling use cases and modeling patterns, Data Vault, dimensional models, wide tables, and business reporting.

Chapter 4, Analytics Engineering as the New Core of Data Engineering, showcases the full data life cycle and the different roles and responsibilities of people that work on data.

You will understand the modern data stack, the role of DBT, and analytic engineering. You will learn how to adopt software engineering practices to build data platforms (or DataOps), and about working as a team, not as a silo.

Chapter 5, Transforming Data with DBT, shows us how to develop an example application in dbt and learn all the steps to create, deploy, run, test, and document a data application with dbt.

Chapter 6, Writing Maintainable Code, continues the example that we started in the previous chapter, and we will guide you to configure dbt and write some basic but functionally complete code to build the three layers of our reference architecture: staging/storage, refined data, and delivery with data marts.

Chapter 7, Working with Dimensional Data, shows you how to incorporate dimensional data in our data models and utilize it for fact-checking and a multitude of purposes. We will explore how to create data models, edit the data for our reference architecture, and incorporate the dimensional data in data marts. We will also recap everything we learned in the previous chapters with an example.

Chapter 8, Delivering Consistency in Your Code, shows you how to add consistency to your transformations. You will learn how to go beyond basic SQL and bring the power of scripting into your code, write your first macros, and learn how to use external libraries in your projects.

Chapter 9, Delivering Reliability in Your Data, shows you how to ensure the reliability of your code by adding tests that verify your expectations and check the results of your transformations.

Chapter 10, Agile Development, teaches you how to develop with agility by mixing philosophy and practical hints, discussing how to keep the backlog agile through the phases of your projects, and a deep dive into building data marts.

Chapter 11, Collaboration, touches on a few practices that help developers work as a team and the support that dbt provides toward this.

Chapter 12, Deployment, Execution, and Documentation Automation, helps you learn how to automate the operation of your data platform, by setting up environments and jobs that automate the release and execution of your code following your deployment design.

Chapter 13, Moving beyond Basics, helps you learn how to manage the identity of your entities so that you can apply master data management to combine data from different systems. At the same time, you will review the best practices to apply modularity in your pipelines to simplify their evolution and maintenance. You will also discover macros to implement patterns.

Chapter 14, Enhancing Software Quality, helps you discover and apply more advanced patterns that provide high-quality results in real-life projects, and you will experiment with how to evolve your code with confidence through refactoring.

Chapter 15, Patterns for Frequent Use Cases, presents you with a small library of patterns that are frequently used for ingesting data from external files and storing this ingested data in what we call history tables. You will also get the insights and the code to ingest data in Snowflake.

To get the most out of this book

Software/hardware covered in the book	Operating system requirements
dbt	Windows, macOS, or Linux

If you are using the digital version of this book, we advise you to type the code yourself or access the code from the book's GitHub repository (a link is available in the next section). Doing so will help you avoid any potential errors related to the copying and pasting of code.

Download the example code files

You can download the example code files for this book from GitHub at `https://github.com/PacktPublishing/Data-engineering-with-dbt`. If there's an update to the code, it will be updated in the GitHub repository.

We also have other code bundles from our rich catalog of books and videos available at `https://github.com/PacktPublishing/`. Check them out!

Conventions used

There are a number of text conventions used throughout this book.

`Code in text`: Indicates code words in text, database table names, folder names, filenames, file extensions, pathnames, dummy URLs, user input, and Twitter handles. Here is an example: "Create the new database using the executor role. We named it PORTFOLIO_TRACKING."

A block of code is set as follows:

```
CREATE TABLE ORDERS (
    ORDER_ID NUMBER,
    CUSTOMER_CODE TEXT,
    TOTAL_AMOUNT FLOAT,
    ORDER_DATE DATE,
    CURRENCY TEXT DEFAULT 'EUR'
);
```

When we wish to draw your attention to a particular part of a code block, the relevant lines or items are set in bold:

```
CREATE VIEW BIG_ORDERS AS
SELECT * FROM ORDERS
WHERE TOTAL_AMOUNT > 1000;
```

Any command-line input or output is written as follows:

```
$ mkdir css
$ cd css
```

Bold: Indicates a new term, an important word, or words that you see onscreen. For instance, words in menus or dialog boxes appear in **bold**. Here is an example: "Select **System info** from the **Administration** panel."

> **Tips or important notes**
> Appear like this.

Get in touch

Feedback from our readers is always welcome.

General feedback: If you have questions about any aspect of this book, email us at customercare@packtpub.com and mention the book title in the subject of your message.

Errata: Although we have taken every care to ensure the accuracy of our content, mistakes do happen. If you have found a mistake in this book, we would be grateful if you would report this to us. Please visit www.packtpub.com/support/errata and fill in the form.

Piracy: If you come across any illegal copies of our works in any form on the internet, we would be grateful if you would provide us with the location address or website name. Please contact us at copyright@packt.com with a link to the material.

If you are interested in becoming an author: If there is a topic that you have expertise in and you are interested in either writing or contributing to a book, please visit authors.packtpub.com.

Share Your Thoughts

Once you've read *Data Engineering with dbt*, we'd love to hear your thoughts! Scan the QR code below to go straight to the Amazon review page for this book and share your feedback.

https://packt.link/r/1-803-24628-6

Your review is important to us and the tech community and will help us make sure we're delivering excellent quality content.

Download a free PDF copy of this book

Thanks for purchasing this book!

Do you like to read on the go but are unable to carry your print books everywhere? Is your eBook purchase not compatible with the device of your choice?

Don't worry, now with every Packt book you get a DRM-free PDF version of that book at no cost.

Read anywhere, any place, on any device. Search, copy, and paste code from your favorite technical books directly into your application.

The perks don't stop there, you can get exclusive access to discounts, newsletters, and great free content in your inbox daily

Follow these simple steps to get the benefits:

1. Scan the QR code or visit the link below

https://packt.link/free-ebook/9781803246284

2. Submit your proof of purchase
3. That's it! We'll send your free PDF and other benefits to your email directly

Part 1:
The Foundations
of Data Engineering

In this section, you will get started on your path of learning how to build a data platform by learning the basics of SQL, modeling, and data engineering.

This section includes the following chapters:

1

The Basics of SQL to Transform Data

This book is about engineering data platforms with **dbt**. When working with dbt, you write code in **Structured Query Language** (normally referred to as **SQL**, pronounced sequel or as its letters: es-qu-el), with a spritz of **Jinja** templating.

This means that when we are not discussing architectural and design topics, we will be reading and writing code in SQL, so you should get up to speed with SQL to work proficiently with dbt.

In this chapter, you will review, or learn from scratch, the basics of SQL, becoming familiar with this powerful language that you find everywhere when working with data.

First, we will introduce SQL and walk you through its core concepts, so that even if you are new to this language, you can start building your competence and follow the rest of this chapter and the book.

To complement this introduction, you will quickly be presented with all the main SQL commands, organized by category of use. This will ensure that you know the most relevant parts of SQL and you can use this chapter as a quick reference when you start writing your code.

You will then be guided through how to *create an account in* **Snowflake**, the leading cloud **database** that is very often used with dbt. You will use Snowflake in the cloud, without the need to install anything, and it is free for a trial period.

Once you have a Snowflake account, you will be guided through creating your first role, user, and database.

With your cloud database ready and the basic SQL commands presented, we will look deeper into the SELECT statement and the JOIN clause, as they will be crucial in working with dbt.

Analytical and window functions are presented at the end of the chapter in a simple way, suitable for beginners as well as mid- to senior-experienced SQL users; these advanced functionalities will power up your SQL skills, vastly widening your abilities.

To summarize, in this chapter, we are going to cover these topics:

- Introducing SQL
- SQL basics – core concepts and commands
- Setting up a Snowflake database with users and roles
- Querying data in SQL – syntax and operators
- Combining data in SQL – the JOIN clause
- Advanced – introducing window functions

Technical requirements

This chapter does not assume any prior SQL knowledge and presents information from the basics to intermediate level. If you know SQL well, you can skip this chapter or just browse the more advanced topics.

All code samples of this chapter are available on GitHub at `https://github.com/ PacktPublishing/Data-engineering-with-dbt/tree/main/Chapter_01`.

To run the samples, later in this chapter, we will guide you through setting up a Snowflake account and roles and creating your first database.

Introducing SQL

SQL was created in the 70s and by the end of the 80s, had become the de facto standard to interact with **Relational Databases (RDBs)**, and it now powers most of the data management industry in the world.

Given its huge footprint and powerful abstractions, SQL has become a standard that anyone working with database systems eventually becomes familiar with. The expressive power of SQL is well understood and its knowledge is so ubiquitous that it has been taken into use beyond RDBs, with **Database Management Systems (DBMSs)** of all sorts providing a SQL interface even on top of many non-RDB systems.

Some of the great advantages of SQL are as follows:

- The *core SQL functionality was standardized in the 80s* and yet SQL is still very much alive and well, evolving and adding new powerful functionalities as data management evolves while maintaining compatibility with previous versions.

  Every database has its SQL quirks, but the logic is the same and most SQL code will work on multiple databases with little or no change.

  Learn it now and use it forever, and with (almost) every database.

- At its core, it has a *simple, rigorous, and powerful syntax that reads like English sentences*, so even non-tech people can grasp the basic idea, while professionals can express exactly what they want in a precise and concise way.

Most people can probably get a sense of what the following SQL does:

```
SELECT ORDER_ID, CUSTOMER_CODE, TOTAL_AMOUNT
FROM ORDERS
WHERE YEAR(ORDER_DATE) = 2021;
```

- With SQL, you *work at the logical level*, so you do not have to deal with implementation details, and *it is a declarative language*; you describe in a rigorous way what you want to achieve, not how to do it. The database engine has the freedom to store data, be implemented, and perform the request in its own way, as long as it produces the correct result according to SQL specifications.

- With a single SQL statement, you can *process one piece of data or billions*, leaving the burden of finding the most effective way to the database and giving you some freedom from scale.

SQL basics – core concepts and commands

The SQL language is certainly big and complex, taking time to be fully mastered, but surprisingly, you can get productive with the limited set of features that we will introduce in this book, and you will pick up the nuances when you'll need them while working on real use cases.

The goal of this chapter is not to make you a SQL expert but to get you started with it, getting deeper into the few commands that we will use often to make you quickly productive with dbt.

In this intro, we start with the most basic concepts of SQL and then provide an overview of the SQL commands by their categories of use. In the rest of this chapter, we will dig deeper into the commands that are mostly used when working with dbt: `SELECT`, `JOIN`, and analytical and window functions.

SQL core concepts

The main goal of SQL, as its name implies, is to allow users to query data that is contained in a database; SQL also provides all the commands to fully manage the database, allowing you to add, transform, delete, organize, and manage data and other database objects, such as users and roles.

The core concepts in SQL come from how an RDB is organized:

- A **database** contains **tables**, organized in schemata (plural of **schema**)
- Tables store data in **rows** that have one value for each **column** defined in the table
- Columns have a name and can contain only data of the declared **data type**
- To regulate access to the data, **privileges** are assigned to **users** and **roles**

You can see a database with schemata and tables in the following screenshot, which shows part of the sample database available in any Snowflake account:

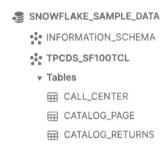

Figure 1.1: Example database with schemata and tables

Let's go through the core concepts of SQL, starting with the table.

What is a table?

The **table** is the most central concept in SQL, as it is the object that contains data.

A table in SQL is very close to the layman's concept of a table, with data organized in columns and rows.

Columns represent the attributes that can be stored in a table, such as a customer's name or the currency of an order, with each column defining the type of data it can store, such as text, a number, or a date.

In a table, you can have as many rows as you want, and you can keep adding more whenever you need. Each row stores in the table one instance of the concept that the table represents, such as a specific order in the following example of a table for orders:

Order_ID	Customer_CODE	Total_amount	Currency
123	ABC	100	EUR
166	C099	125,15	USD

Table 1.1: Example order table

Looking at the previous example order table, we can see that the table has four columns that allow storing the four attributes for each row (order ID, customer code, total amount, and currency of the order). The table, as represented, has two rows of data, representing one order each.

The first row, in bold, is not data but is just a header to represent the column names and make the table easier to read when printed out.

In SQL, a table is both the definition of its content (columns and their types) and the content itself (the data, organized by rows):

- **Table definition**: It lists the columns that make up the table, and each column provides the data type and other optional details. The data type is mandatory and declares what values will be accepted in the column.

- **Table content**: It is organized in rows, each row containing one value for each column defined for the table or null if no value is provided.

- **Data value**: All the values in a column must be compatible with the type declared for the column. null is a special value that corresponds to the absence of data and is compatible with all data types.

When creating a table, we must provide a name for the table and its definition, which consists of at least column names and a type for each column; the data can be added at a different time.

In the following code block, we have a sample definition for an order table:

```
CREATE TABLE ORDERS (
    ORDER_ID NUMBER,
    CUSTOMER_CODE TEXT,
    TOTAL_AMOUNT FLOAT,
    ORDER_DATE DATE,
    CURRENCY TEXT DEFAULT 'EUR'
);
```

> **Tip**
> When we write some SQL, we will use Snowflake's SQL syntax and commands. We will guide you on how to create a free Snowflake account where you can run the code shown here.

In this example, we see that the command to create a table reads pretty much like English and provides the name of the table and a list of columns with the type of data each column is going to contain.

You can see that for the CURRENCY column, of type text, this code also provides the default value EUR. Single quotes are used in SQL to delimit a piece of text, aka a string.

View – a special way to look at some data

If you already have data and you want to make it available with some transformation or filtering, you can create a **view**. You can think of a view like a table, but with the column definition and data both coming from a query, reading from one or more tables.

As an example, if you would like to have a shortlist of orders with *amount greater than 1,000* you could write the following query to create a BIG_ORDERS view:

```
CREATE VIEW BIG_ORDERS AS
SELECT * FROM ORDERS
WHERE TOTAL_AMOUNT > 1000;
```

In this example, we see that this simple create view statement provides the name for the view and uses a **query**, which is a SELECT statement, to define what data is made available by the view.

The query provides both the data, all the orders with a total amount greater than 1,000, and the column definitions. The * character – called star – is a shortcut for all columns in the tables read by the SELECT statement.

This is, of course, a naïve example, but throughout this book, you will see that combining tables that store data and views that filter and transform the data coming from tables and views is the bread and butter of working with dbt. Building one object on top of the previous allows us to take raw data as input and provide as output refined information that our users can easily access and understand.

> **Tip**
> When working with dbt, you will not need to write create table or create view statements, as dbt will create them for us. It is nevertheless good to get familiar with these basic SQL commands as these are the commands executed in the database and you will see them if you look in the logs.

Database and schema

We have seen that a **database** is a container for tables and views.

A DB can be further divided and organized using **schema** objects.

In real-life DBs, the number of tables can range from a few units to many thousands. Schemata act pretty much like folders, but cannot be nested, so you can always identify a table by its database, schema, and name.

In the following screenshot, we see part of the contents of the **SNOWFLAKE_SAMPLE_DATA** database, which is available in all Snowflake accounts:

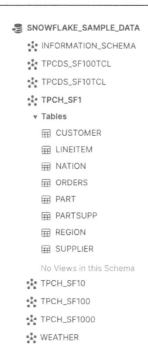

SNOWFLAKE_SAMPLE_DATA
  INFORMATION_SCHEMA
  TPCDS_SF100TCL
  TPCDS_SF10TCL
  TPCH_SF1
    ▾ **Tables**
      ⊞ CUSTOMER
      ⊞ LINEITEM
      ⊞ NATION
      ⊞ ORDERS
      ⊞ PART
      ⊞ PARTSUPP
      ⊞ REGION
      ⊞ SUPPLIER
      No Views in this Schema
  TPCH_SF10
  TPCH_SF100
  TPCH_SF1000
  WEATHER

Figure 1.2: Some schemata and tables of the SNOWFLAKE_SAMPLE_DATA database

The database and schemata, as table containers, are the main ways information is organized, but they are also used to apply security, access limitations, and other features in a hierarchical way, simplifying the management of big systems.

To create the TEST database and the SOME_DATA schema in it, we can use the following commands:

```
CREATE DATABASE TEST;
CREATE SCHEMA TEST.SOME_DATA;
```

The database.schema notation, also known as a **fully qualified name**, allows us to precisely describe in which database to create the schema and after its creation, uniquely identifies the schema.

> **Tip**
> While working with dbt, you will create a database or use an existing one for your project; dbt will create the required schema objects for you if you have not created them already.

A best practice in Snowflake is to have one database for each project or set of data that you want to keep separate for administration purposes. Databases and schemata in Snowflake are soft boundaries, as all the data from all the databases and schemata can be accessed if the user has the appropriate privileges.

In some other database systems, such as PostgreSQL, a database is a stronger boundary.

Users and roles

To control access to your data in SQL, you GRANT access and other privileges to both users and roles.

A **user** represent one individual user or service that can access the database, while a **role** represents a named entity that can be granted privileges.

A role can be granted to a user, providing them all the privileges associated with the role.

A role can also be granted to another role, building hierarchies that use simple basic roles to build more complex roles that are assigned to a user.

Using roles instead of granting privileges directly to users allows you to manage even a large number of users simply and consistently. In this case, roles are labels for a set of privileges and become a way to manage groups of users that we want to grant the same privileges. Changing the privileges granted to a role at any moment will change the privileges that the users receive from that role.

A typical pattern when working with dbt is to create a role for the dbt users and then assign it to the developers and the service user that the dbt program will use.

The following is an example of a simple setup with one role and a couple of users:

```
CREATE ROLE DBT_SAMPLE_ROLE;
CREATE USER MY_NAME;              -- Personal user
CREATE USER SAMPLE_SERVICE;       -- Service user
GRANT ROLE DBT_SAMPLE_ROLE TO USER MY_NAME;
GRANT ROLE DBT_SAMPLE_ROLE TO USER SAMPLE_SERVICE;
```

A more complex setup could have one role to read and one to write for each source system (represented by a schema with the data from the system), for the data warehouse (one or more schemata where the data is processed), and for each data mart (one schema for each data mart).

You could then control in much more detail who can read and write what, at the cost of more effort.

Understanding the categories of SQL commands

SQL commands can be organized into categories according to their usage in the language:

- **Data Definition Language** (**DDL**): DDL contains the commands that are used to manage the structure and organization of a database
- **Data Manipulation Language** (**DML**): DML contains the commands that are used to manipulate data, for example, INSERT, DELETE, and UPDATE
- **Data Query Language** (**DQL**): DQL contains the SELECT command and is the central part of SQL that allows querying and transforming the data stored in a database

- **Data Control Language** (**DCL**): DCL contains the GRANT and REVOKE commands, which are used to manage the privileges that control the access to database resources and objects

- **Transaction Control Language** (**TCL**): TCL contains the commands to manage transactions

In the upcoming sections, we provide more details about these by looking at Snowflake-specific commands, but the ideas and names are of general use in all database systems, with little or no change.

Data Definition Language – DDL

DDL commands do not deal directly with the data but are used to create and maintain the structure and organization of the database, including creating the tables where the data is stored.

They operate on the following objects:

- Account/session objects, which contain and operate on the data, such as user, role, database, and warehouse

- Database/schema objects, which store and manipulate the data, such as schema, table, view, function, and store procedure

The main commands are as follows:

- CREATE: Used to create the database itself and other objects

- DROP: Used to delete the specified object

- ALTER: Used to modify some attribute of the specified object

- DESC: Used to describe the details of the specified object

- SHOW: Used to list the existing objects of the specified object type, with metadata

- USE: Used to select the database, schema, and object to use when fully specified names are not used

> **Tip**
> When working with dbt, we use the DDL and DML commands only in macros.
>
> We do not use the DDL and DML commands in models because dbt will generate the required commands for our models based on the metadata attached to the model.

Data Manipulation Language – DML

DML provides the commands to manipulate data in a database and carry out bulk data loading.

Snowflake also provides specific commands to stage files, such as loading files in a Snowflake-managed location, called a stage.

The main commands are as follows:

- `INSERT`: Inserts rows into a table
- `DELETE`: Removes specified rows from a table
- `UPDATE`: Updates some values of specified rows in a table
- `MERGE`: Inserts, updates, or deletes rows in a table
- `TRUNCATE TABLE`: Empties a table, preserving the definition and privileges

For bulk data loading, Snowflake provides the following command:

- `COPY INTO`: Loads data from files in a stage into a table or unloads data from a table into one or more files in a stage

To manage files in stages, Snowflake provides these file-staging commands:

- `PUT`: Uploads a local file to a Snowflake stage
- `GET`: Downloads a file from a stage to the local machine
- `LIST`: Lists the files existing in a Snowflake stage
- `REMOVE`: Removes a file from a Snowflake stage

> **Important note**
>
> In dbt, we can use macros with the `COPY INTO` and file-staging commands to manage the data-loading part of a data pipeline, when source data is in a file storage service such as AWS S3, Google Cloud Storage, or Microsoft Azure Data Lake file storage.

Data Query Language – DQL

DQL is the reason why SQL exists: to query and transform data.

The command that is used to query data is `SELECT`, which is without any doubt the most important and versatile command in all of SQL.

For the moment, consider that a `SELECT` statement, aka a query, can do all these things:

- Read data from one or more tables
- Apply functions and transformations to the data retrieved
- Filter the data retrieved from each of these tables
- Group the retrieved data on a set of columns (or transformed values), producing one row for each group, calculating functions on the grouped rows, and filtering on the results of those functions

- Calculate for each row one or more functions based on groups of rows identified by a window expression and filter the results based on the results of these functions

> **Important note**
> We have dedicated the *Query syntax and operators* section later in this chapter to analyzing the SELECT command in Snowflake in detail, as you will use the SELECT command in every dbt model.

Data Control Language – DCL

DCL contains the GRANT and REVOKE commands, which are used to manage privileges and roles that control access to or use database resources and objects.

Together with the DDL commands to create roles, users, and other database objects, the DCL commands are used to manage users and security:

- GRANT: Assigns a privilege or a role to a role (or user)
- REVOKE: Removes a privilege or a role from a role (or user)
- SHOW GRANTS: Lists access privileges granted to a role or object

Transaction Control Language – TCL

The TCL commands are used to manage transactions in a database.

A **transaction** groups a set of SQL commands into a *single execution unit* and guarantees that either all the effects of all commands are applied, if the transaction completes with success, or no effect at all is applied if the transaction fails. This can also be described with the **ACID** acronym, which stands for **atomic, consistent, isolated, and durable**.

A transaction succeeds and ends only when all the commands it groups have finished with success; in any other case, the transaction fails, and its effects are rolled back like they never happened.

The TCL commands are as follows:

- BEGIN: Starts a transaction in the current session
- COMMIT: Commits an open transaction in the current session and makes the transaction effects visible to all sessions
- ROLLBACK: Rolls back an open transaction in the current session and undoes all the effects applied since the BEGIN statement

Now that we have covered the basic concepts and commands in SQL, it is time to set up a database to run them. The next section will provide you with access to a Snowflake DB.

Setting up a Snowflake database with users and roles

In this section, you will be guided through creating your own Snowflake account so that you can experiment with the SQL commands from the previous section and use it with dbt in the next chapters.

Once you have created your account, we will help you through a quick setup of users and roles that will be useful throughout this book and in your later projects.

Creating your Snowflake account

To sign up for a 30-day free trial of Snowflake, you can go to `https://signup.snowflake.com/` or look for the **Start for free** button on the Snowflake home page.

On the Snowflake site, go through the following steps:

1. Fill in the registration form with your data and click **CONTINUE**.

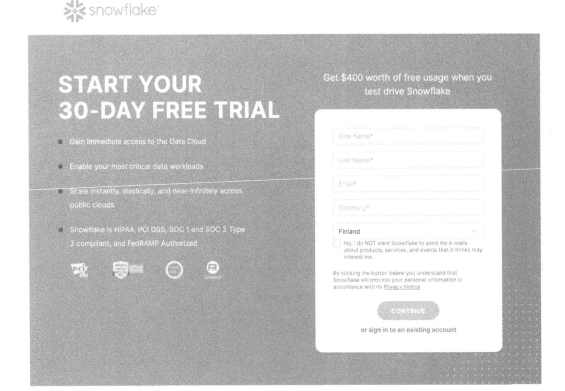

Figure 1.3: Snowflake free trial registration form

2. Select the Snowflake edition that you want to use, pick your preferred cloud provider, and click **GET STARTED** and you will reach a confirmation page.

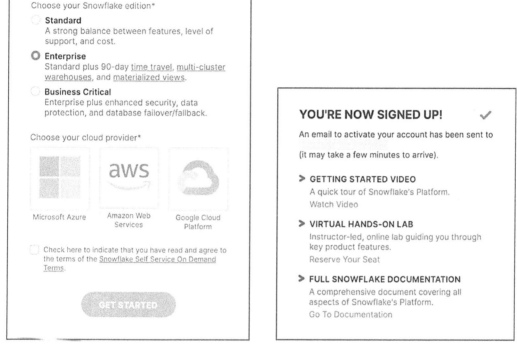

Figure 1.4: Left: Snowflake edition and cloud provider selection form. Right: sign-up confirmation

3. Go to your email client and follow the link from the email that you receive to confirm your email address. It will take you back to the Snowflake website.

4. On the **Welcome to Snowflake!** page, enter the username and password for the user that will become your account administrator and then click **Get started**.

Figure 1.5: Welcome to Snowflake! page

> **Tip**
>
> Later, we will teach you how to create all the roles and users that you want.
>
> Anyway, it makes sense to pick a good name and keep the password safe, as this user has all privileges and can do pretty much everything on your account.

5. After clicking the **Get started** button, you will land on the Snowflake user interface, with an empty worksheet open and an introductory menu with a few topics to get started with Snowflake. If you are new to Snowflake, it is a good idea to go through those topics.

6. After dismissing this introductory menu, you are ready to explore and use your Snowflake account, which in the classical console interface will look like this:

Figure 1.6: The user interface of Snowflake worksheets

If you end up with the new Snowflake interface (called Snowsight) you can work with it or use the **Classic Console** entry in the menu to switch to the older interface.

Setting up initial users, roles, and a database in Snowflake

Now you have a Snowflake account with a user that you can log in with, and your user has been granted the omnipotent role of ACCOUNTADMIN.

That's great, but it is not advised that you use this role for normal work. The best practice is to set up a few users and roles to provide the desired access level and use the lowest level that can accomplish a task.

Snowflake allows you to pick the role you impersonate to execute commands in a worksheet between the ones you have been granted so that you do not have to log out and back in to change the role.

> **Tip**
> You can change your role, the warehouse to use, and the current database and schema with the selector in the top-right corner of the worksheet editing area.

You might have noticed that in the navigation panel on the left, you have two databases:

- The **SNOWFLAKE** database provides you with information about your Snowflake account
- The **SNOWFLAKE_SAMPLE_DATA** DB provides, as the name implies, some sample data

These databases are shared with you by Snowflake, and you can only read from them.

To do something meaningful, you will need at least a database you can write in.

In this section, we will create a database and some roles and users to use it.

Overview of initial roles

In a database a user needs the relevant privilege to be able to perform an action.

A user can have the privilege directly, that is, assigned to the user, or indirectly, through a role that the user can impersonate.

In practice, privileges are assigned to roles, which are assigned to other roles and users, to build the desired security hierarchy, because assigning privileges to users is not scalable.

When you log in to a newly created Snowflake account, you are impersonating the ACCOUNTADMIN role, which has all privileges, but other, more specialized roles are already available.

Snowflake has already set up a few self-explanatory basic roles: ACCOUNTADMIN, SECURITYADMIN, USERADMIN, SYSADMIN, and PUBLIC.

> **Important note**
> To create users and roles, Snowflake provides the USERADMIN role by default, which has the CREATE ROLE and CREATE USER privileges directly assigned. This role is already assigned to the initial user that you created.

The initial user could create new users and roles using the ACCOUNTADMIN or SECURITYADMIN roles, because they have been granted the USERADMIN role; SECURITYADMIN had it granted directly and ACCOUNTADMIN indirectly, having been granted the SECURITYADMIN role.

However, this would not be a great idea, as you will see in the following paragraphs on ownership.

The following is an example of how to create a hierarchy of roles.

You can explore the existing roles and their privileges with these commands:

```
SHOW ROLES;
SHOW GRANTS TO ROLE <role_name>;
```

Ownership is needed for some operations, such as deletions, which cannot be granted.

It is therefore advisable that a user with the role that we want to use to manage an object is the one who creates it, while impersonating such role.

In this way, the user, and all others with the same role, will have the required privileges.

An alternative is to use the GRANT command to explicitly provide the required privileges to a role.

> **Important note**
>
> An object is owned by the role that created it.
>
> When a user has multiple roles, the role impersonated by the user at the moment of the creation will own the object.
>
> Before creating an object, make sure you are impersonating the role you want to own the object.

Creating and granting your first role

Let's switch to USERADMIN to create our users and roles, because this is the role that you will probably grant to people delegated to perform user and role administration.

Being the owner will make all operations, including deletions, simpler:

1. Switch to the USERADMIN role:

    ```
    USE ROLE USERADMIN;
    ```

    Let's create the role that we will use for all users that have to fully manage a dbt project, humans, or applications.

    I usually call this role DBT_EXECUTOR_ROLE because I call the user for the dbt application DBT_EXECUTOR and I like to be crystal clear with my names.

    You can of course pick a name that you prefer for both the role and user.

2. Create a role for users running dbt models:

    ```
    CREATE ROLE DBT_EXECUTOR_ROLE
      COMMENT = 'Role for the users running DBT models';
    ```

    We now have a role that we can shape and use to manage a set of database objects, for example, corresponding to one or more dbt projects.

    The dbt executor user will be used by dbt to run dbt models in shared environments, while dbt will use each developer's own user to run dbt models in their own development environment.

    The simplest setup, giving all developers the ability to manage all environments, is to assign this role to all developers. An alternative is to have a different role for production and other environments that you want to keep protected.

3. Let's keep it simple and assign the executor role to ourselves:

```
GRANT ROLE DBT_EXECUTOR_ROLE TO USER <your_user>;
```

Now, our user has both the account admin and the executor roles. To be able to see and select the role in the user interface dropdown, you might need to refresh the page.

Granting the privileges to create a database

We could create a database while impersonating the account admin role, but this will not help with our plan to use the executor role to manage this database. We must then give our executor role the ability to create a database. To have our SQL commands executed on a database, we need the ability to use or create an existing warehouse.

> **Important Note**
> To manage the structure of databases and the warehouse settings, Snowflake provides the default SYSADMIN role, which has the required privileges.

We can achieve our goal of providing the executor role with those abilities by doing one of the following:

- Granting the required privileges directly to the executor role
- Granting the SYSADMIN role to the executor role, which has the required privileges

What would be the difference?

If you grant the privileges directly, the executor role is totally isolated from other roles, and users with that role will just be able to access what the role allows them to access.

If you grant the SYSADMIN role, users with the executor role will also be able to impersonate the SYSADMIN role and therefore also access any object it can access. As an example, they could access a database created by another user that has created it with the sysadmin role.

Let's assign the desired privileges directly, to keep our dbt objects away from SYSADMIN.

To grant the privileges to the executor role, we need to switch to a role that can grant these privileges and then grant them:

1. Switch to the SYSADMIN role:

```
USE ROLE SYSADMIN;
```

2. Grant the privilege to create a new database:

```
GRANT CREATE DATABASE ON ACCOUNT
    TO ROLE DBT_EXECUTOR_ROLE;
```

3. Grant the privilege to use the default warehouse, named COMPUTE_WH:

```
GRANT USAGE ON WAREHOUSE COMPUTE_WH
    TO ROLE DBT_EXECUTOR_ROLE;
```

Creating your first database

Now that our executor role can create a database, let's do it:

1. Let's impersonate the executor role so that it will own what we create:

```
USE ROLE DBT_EXECUTOR_ROLE;
```

2. Now, let's create our database:

```
CREATE DATABASE DATA_ENG_DBT;
            -- or pick any name you like for the DB
```

To see the new database in Snowflake, you might need to refresh the browsing panel on the left of the user interface, with the **Refresh** button, shaped as a circular arrow, in the top right of the panel.

Tip

Clicking on the new database will show that it is not empty.

The new database has two schemata: INFORMATION_SCHEMA, which contains views that you can use to collect information on the database itself, and PUBLIC, which is the default schema of the new database and is empty.

To reduce Snowflake credit consumption, let's finish by configuring the default warehouse to suspend after 1 minute instead of 10:

```
USE ROLE SYSADMIN;
ALTER WAREHOUSE "COMPUTE_WH" SET
    WAREHOUSE_SIZE = 'XSMALL'
    AUTO_SUSPEND = 60
    AUTO_RESUME = TRUE
    COMMENT = 'Default Warehouse';
```

Tip

To alter the warehouse, you must switch to the SYSADMIN user as it is the role that owns the warehouse; we have granted our executor role only the privilege to use it.

Congratulations! You have now created a role, assigned it to your personal user, created a database owned by that role, and configured the default warehouse. You are almost done setting up.

Creating a user for the dbt application

Let's complete our initial setup by creating a new user that we will use with dbt and grant it the executor role so that it will be able to manage, as an owner, that database.

To create a user, we need to switch to a role with that ability:

1.   Switch to the USERADMIN role:

```
USE ROLE USERADMIN;
```

2.   Create the new user for dbt; I have named it DBT_EXECUTOR, though you can pick any name:

```
CREATE USER IF NOT EXISTS DBT_EXECUTOR
    COMMENT = 'User running DBT commands'
    PASSWORD = 'pick_a_password'
    DEFAULT_WAREHOUSE = 'COMPUTE_WH'
    DEFAULT_ROLE = 'DBT_EXECUTOR_ROLE'
;
```

3.   Let's assign the executor role to the dbt user:

```
GRANT ROLE DBT_EXECUTOR_ROLE TO USER DBT_EXECUTOR;
```

4.   Switch back to the operational role, which we should always be working with:

```
USE ROLE DBT_EXECUTOR_ROLE;
```

Great! You have now performed a basic setup of your new Snowflake account; you have learned the basics of user and role management and you are ready to learn more SQL to query data.

Querying data in SQL – syntax and operators

In this section, you will learn how to query existing data using SQL and the Snowflake example database.

In this chapter, and more generally in this book, you will get familiar with Snowflake syntax, which is modern and very standard. We will also use some proprietary extensions that make your work easier.

Snowflake query syntax

Snowflake supports querying data with the standard SELECT statement, which has the following basic syntax:

```
WITH ...
SELECT ...
FROM ...
JOIN ...
```

```
WHERE …
GROUP BY …
HAVING …
QUALIFY …
ORDER BY …
LIMIT …
```

The only mandatory part is select, so `SELECT 1` is a valid query that just returns the value 1.

If you are familiar with SQL from other database systems, you will wonder what the `QUALIFY` clause is. It is an optional SQL clause that is very well suited to the analytical kind of work that Snowflake is used for and that not all database engines implement. It is described later in this section.

We often use the terms query, command, and statement interchangeably when referring to some piece of SQL that you can execute.

Properly speaking, a command is a generic command such as `SELECT` or `CREATE <object>`, while a statement is one specific and complete instance of a command that can be run, such as `SELECT 1` or `CREATE TABLE my_table …;`.

The term **query** should really only refer to `SELECT` statements, as `SELECT` statements are used to query data from the database, but query is often used with any statement that has to do with data.

You will also often hear the term **clause** used, such as the `FROM` clause or `GROUP BY` clause. Informally, you can think about it as a piece of a statement that follows the syntax and rules of that specific keyword.

The WITH clause

The `WITH` clause is optional and can only precede the `SELECT` command to define one or more **Common Table Expressions (CTEs)**. A CTE associates a name with the results of another `SELECT` statement, which can be used later in the main `SELECT` statement as any other table-like object.

Defining a CTE is useful for the following:

- **Clarity**: You can provide an informative name to a piece of SQL
- **Reuse, maintenance, and efficiency**: You can define a supporting query, whose results you might use more than once in the main query, and the database engine will execute the supporting query once
- **Creating recursive queries**: Defining a CTE that queries itself is the only way to use recursion in SQL
- Break a complex transformation into smaller, simpler steps that are easier to code and understand and limit the scope of future maintenance

The simplified syntax is as follows:

```
WITH [RECURSIVE]
  <cte1_name> AS (SELECT …)
  [, <cte2_name> AS (SELECT …)]
SELECT …
```

We will check out some examples here:

1. Check whether we still have high-priority orders pending:

    ```
    WITH
    high_prio_orders as (
      SELECT *
      FROM "SNOWFLAKE_SAMPLE_DATA"."TPCH_SF1"."ORDERS"
      WHERE O_ORDERPRIORITY IN ('1-URGENT', '2-HIGH')
    )
    SELECT count(*)
    FROM high_prio_orders
    WHERE O_ORDERDATE < '1998-01-01'
      and O_ORDERSTATUS = 'O';
    ```

    Here, you can see that the first expression encapsulates the business definition of high-priority order to be any order with the priority set to urgent or high priority. Without the CTE, you have to mix the business definition and other filtering logic in the WITH clause. Then, it would be unclear whether the status is part of the definition or is just a filter that we are applying now.

2. Calculate some metrics for customers in the auto industry:

    ```
    WITH
    auto_customer_key as (
      SELECT C_CUSTKEY
    FROM SNOWFLAKE_SAMPLE_DATA.TPCH_SF1.CUSTOMER
    WHERE C_MKTSEGMENT = 'AUTOMOBILE'
    ),
    orders_by_auto_customer as (
      SELECT O_ORDERKEY
    FROM SNOWFLAKE_SAMPLE_DATA.TPCH_SF1.ORDERS
    WHERE O_CUSTKEY in (SELECT * FROM auto_customer_key)
    ),
    metrics as (
      SELECT 'customers' as metric, count(*) as value
    FROM auto_customer
    UNION ALL
    ```

```
      SELECT 'orders by these customers', count(*)
      FROM orders_by_auto_customer
   )
   SELECT * FROM metrics;
```

In this example, the CTEs and the final query remain short and very simple. You can start to appreciate that the clear labeling of intentions and the simple pieces of SQL make the full query easy to understand for anyone.

The SELECT clause

The SELECT command can appear in two possible forms: as the central clause of a SELECT statement or used as a clause in other statements. In both cases, it defines the set of columns and calculated values returned by the statement.

The simplified syntax of a SELECT clause in Snowflake is a list of column definitions separated by commas, with the optional distinct keyword to omit duplicates:

```
SELECT [DISTINCT]
   <column_definition_1> [, <column_definition_2> …]
```

The SELECT clause is used to provide the list of columns that the query will return.

For each column definition that is provided, it is also possible to provide a column alias, which will be used to identify that column definition in the results.

When two column definitions have the same name, an alias must be provided for at least one of the two to avoid a name clash in the results.

A column definition can be one of these four expressions:

```
<column_definition> =
   [object.*]            -- all columns in the object
  |[object.col_name]    -- the named column in the object
  |[object.$n]          -- the n-th column in the object
  |[<expression>]       -- the value of the expression
 AS <col_alias>
```

Let's describe in detail these four expressions:

1. The star symbol, *, indicates all possible columns; it means "all columns from all tables" if it is applied without an alias or "all the columns from the aliased object" if applied with an alias.

   • Star without an alias will return all columns from both tables:

     ```
     SELECT * FROM table_1, table_2
     ```

- Star with an alias (or table name) will return all columns from the object with the alias. In this case, it will return all columns from `table_1`, as it is applied to its alias:

```
SELECT t1.* FROM table_1 as t1, table_2 as t2
```

- Snowflake has introduced two powerful extensions to the Star Syntax: EXCLUDE to remove some columns from being returned and RENAME to rename a column while selecting it, as shown in this example:

```
SELECT * EXCLUDE (c3, c2) RENAME (c4 as cx, c5 as cy)
FROM table_1
```

2. A column name, optionally with an alias indicating the object the column comes from and/or an alias to use for the column in the results:

```
SELECT
    O_ORDERKEY,
    ord.O_CUSTKEY,
    cust.C_NAME as CUSTOMER_NAME
FROM SNOWFLAKE_SAMPLE_DATA.TPCH_SF1.ORDERS as ord
JOIN SNOWFLAKE_SAMPLE_DATA.TPCH_SF1.CUSTOMER as cust
    ON cust.C_CUSTKEY = ord.O_CUSTKEY;
```

Note that here, the designers of the TPCH database have gone a long way to keep column names unique between all tables, by adding the table initials as a prefix to column names. This is a pretty old style as it makes it more difficult to recognize fields that contain the same values as C_CUSTKEY and O_CUSTKEY.

Looking at our example query, we can see the following:

- Object aliases are optional if the name of the column is unique in the tables referenced in the query, as it is for all columns in the TPCH database.

- Aliases can in any case be used for clarity, like with cust.C_NAME.

- Object aliases are mandatory when referencing a column name that appears in more than one referenced table. This would have been the case if both fields had been just CUSTKEY, without the C_ and O_ table prefixes.

- Lastly, a column alias can always be used, even just to rename a column with an initial name that we do not like or is not clear, as in the case of a name that would not be clear, so we rename it to CUSTOMER_NAME.

3. A column number after a dollar sign, such as $1 or $3.

This allows us to reference columns that do not have a name, such as when reading out of a CSV file without a header. This is also useful, especially in scripts, to reference columns that we do not know the name of, but we know their position:

```
SELECT $1 as ORDER_KEY, $2 as CUST_KEY
FROM SNOWFLAKE_SAMPLE_DATA.TPCH_SF1.ORDERS;
```

In this case, we read from a table that has column names, and we can always use column numbers instead of column names. But this is rarely done when reading from a table or a view because by using the numbers, the result will depend on the order of the columns in the object, which can change over time if the object is recreated.

4. An expression, like a mathematical expression or a function call, that evaluates to some value for each row:

```
SELECT
    P_PARTKEY
    , UPPER(P_NAME) as P_NAME
    , P_RETAILPRICE
    , P_RETAILPRICE * 0.9 as P_DISCOUNTED_PRICE
FROM "SNOWFLAKE_SAMPLE_DATA"."TPCH_SF1"."PART";
```

The preceding example shows two expressions: a mathematical expression that multiplies a column by a constant to produce a new column and a function call that converts the p_name column to uppercase, keeping the same column name.

> **Important note**
> The ability highlighted here, to write arbitrary expressions and assign a name to the result, is at the core of how SQL is used to transform data and is one of the most common things that we will do with dbt.

In this section, we have seen that the SELECT clause allows us four great abilities:

1. To decide what data from the source tables to keep in the result of a query
2. To calculate new data from source data using arbitrary complex expressions
3. To provide a new name for the data that we want in the query result
4. To keep only one copy of each distinct row in the result, using the DISTINCT keyword

The FROM clause

The FROM clause introduces the table objects used in a SQL statement as the source of data or target of the command.

In the case of a SELECT statement, the FROM clause can list none, one, or more table objects, each with its own alias. The rows in the result of the SELECT statement will potentially have all the columns from all the tables referenced in the FROM clause.

The simplified syntax looks like this:

```
SELECT …
FROM [tableObject1 [AS alias1]]
   [, tableObject2 [AS alias2] …]
```

Table objects, in the context of a SELECT statement, are a combination of the following:

- **Tables** and **views**: Tables and views are the main data objects SQL works with, so most of the time, this is what you find in the FROM clause.

- **Table functions**: Table functions are a category of functions that return a set of rows, with one or more columns. They can be predefined functions or user-defined ones.

- A VALUES clause: This clause allows us to build a set of rows, using constant values. This allows us to create an inline table that can be suitable as a reference table, mapping table, or test input.

- A few other objects that can be read from, such as a LATERAL subquery or a staged file.

When no table is listed, then the columns in the SELECT clause must use constants and global objects such as the current_date function, as in the following example:

```
SELECT 1 + 1 as sum, current_date as today;
```

When we use the VALUES clause, we can define an inline table, like in this example:

```
SELECT * FROM ( VALUES
  ('IT', 'ITA', 'Italy')
 ,('US', 'USA', 'United States of America')
 ,('SF', 'FIN', 'Finland (Suomi)')
  as inline_table (code_2, code_3, country_name)
);
```

When the FROM clause lists more than one table object, the result is the **Cartesian product** of the elements in these tables. To avoid a **Cartesian explosion**, it is important to include a WHERE clause that restricts the combinations, keeping only the ones we want.

> **Important note**
>
> The Cartesian product is the result of pairing the rows of all the objects in the product in all possible ways. This means that the number of rows returned by the Cartesian product is the product of the number of rows in each object in the product.
>
> The expression Cartesian explosion is often used to refer to the fact that the number of rows returned by the Cartesian product increases very quickly and can easily create performance issues.

The following query, thanks to the WHERE clause, will generate a more meaningful and compact set of rows, ideally equal to the number of rows that exist in the LINEITEM table:

```
SELECT count(*)
FROM "SNOWFLAKE_SAMPLE_DATA"."TPCH_SF1"."LINEITEM" as l
    ,"SNOWFLAKE_SAMPLE_DATA"."TPCH_SF1"."ORDERS"   as o
    ,"SNOWFLAKE_SAMPLE_DATA"."TPCH_SF1"."CUSTOMER" as c
    ,"SNOWFLAKE_SAMPLE_DATA"."TPCH_SF1"."PART"     as p
WHERE o.O_ORDERKEY = l.L_ORDERKEY
  and c.C_CUSTKEY  = o.O_CUSTKEY
  and p.P_PARTKEY  = l.L_PARTKEY
;
```

In the previous query, we have used a WHERE clause to keep in the results only the rows that are really related. We achieve this by using equivalence constraints between the fields of the related tables.

The previous query generates a result of exactly 6,001,215 rows, which is the number of rows in the LINEITEM table, instead of the astronomical number resulting from the multiplication of the number of rows: 6,001,215 x 1,500,000 x 150,000 x 200,000, which is pretty much 2,7 x 10^{23}.

I'll let you calculate the exact result…

The consequence is that the full query processes 6 million rows and runs in a few seconds, while the query without the WHERE clause will try to process 10^{18} times more rows, taking very many hours or days to complete, in the process using up a lot of resources for nothing, as the resulting data provides nothing of interest.

The exact correspondence in the count derives from the fact that for each line item, there is only one order, for each order only one customer, and so on.

Providing the relevant WHERE clause will help with reducing the result by many orders of magnitude even if the keys don't match so precisely. We will deal with this topic in more detail in *Chapter 3*, where we talk about data modeling.

This example illustrates well the power of SQL and why it is important to express what we want correctly.

> **Tip**
> As a basic rule, never do an unrestricted Cartesian product unless you know what you are doing and you are fine with the exploded number of rows that you will generate.

The JOIN clause

JOIN is a subclause of the FROM clause and is used to describe in a more precise way how to combine the rows of two tables. JOIN cannot exist outside of a FROM clause.

The simplified syntax of `JOIN` looks like this:

```
SELECT …
FROM tableObject1 AS to1
[<join type>] JOIN tableObject2 as to2 ON <condition_A>
[[<join type>] JOIN tableObject3 as to3 ON <condition_B>]
…
```

The condition in each join is a Boolean expression, often using columns from the base `to1` table and the joined table. It does not need to be an equality check and can use columns from multiple tables or even constants.

It is normal to chain more than one `JOIN` inside a `FROM` clause to pick data from multiple tables at once, and you generally do not need to think too much about the order of the joins, but it is good to know that the order might matter. In the case of Snowflake, the order is from left to right (think of the statement written on one row).

We will look in more detail into the `JOIN` clause in the next section, where we will introduce the different types of joins and some examples.

We have seen that we can combine data from multiple tables, listing them in the `FROM` clause, and that we can use the `WHERE` clause to restrict the resulting Cartesian product to the combined rows that we actually want to keep. This use of `FROM` and `WHERE` is equivalent to the `INNER JOIN` construct, which we will see in the *Combining data in SQL – the JOIN clause* section.

The WHERE clause

The `WHERE` clause specifies the conditions that the rows involved in the command need to match.

The rows for which the expression evaluates to `true` are kept/processed.

In the context of a `SELECT` statement, the `WHERE` clause limits the result of the query to the subset of rows that verify the overall condition set by the `WHERE` clause.

The simplified syntax is as follows:

```
SELECT …
WHERE <predicate>
```

`<predicate>` can be as simple as the literal `true` or `false` or a complex expression, including logical operators and database functions that evaluate to a Boolean value (`true`, `false`, or NULL) for every row that the query processes.

> **Tip**
> An expression that returns a Boolean value is called a **predicate**.

The following example returns only the rows where the order total is greater than 500,000:

```
SELECT O_ORDERKEY, O_CUSTKEY, O_TOTALPRICE
FROM "SNOWFLAKE_SAMPLE_DATA"."TPCH_SF1"."ORDERS"
WHERE O_TOTALPRICE > 500000;
```

The following example does not return any row, but defines two columns with the same name and type as the columns in the source table and two with the name and type that we provided:

```
SELECT O_ORDERKEY,O_CUSTKEY, 1 as an_int, null::number as a_num
FROM "SNOWFLAKE_SAMPLE_DATA"."TPCH_SF1"."ORDERS"
WHERE false;
```

This may be a good trick when you need to define some column names and types. Remember that you do not need a FROM clause if you do not want to use columns from an existing table…

> **Important note**
>
> Be careful when NULL is involved as it might not behave as you expect.
>
> As an example, the NULL = NULL expression evaluates to NULL.
>
> In a WHERE clause, it means that the corresponding row is discarded.

We have seen in a previous example using the FROM clause that the WHERE clause can be used to specify some types of JOIN. We suggest using the JOIN … ON … syntax for joins and the WHERE clause to filter rows. We will look at more examples in the *Combining data in SQL - the JOIN clause* section.

The GROUP BY clause

A GROUP BY clause is used to calculate **aggregate functions** on groups of rows that produce the same value for the *group by expression.*

The simplified syntax is as follows:

```
SELECT …
GROUP BY groupExpr1 [, groupExpr2 …]
```

The group by expression can be one of the following:

- **Column name**: The result of the expression is the value of the column with the given name. All rows with the same value in the column are grouped.

    The following query calculates the sum of all orders by each customer (customer key):

    ```
    SELECT O_CUSTKEY, sum(O_TOTALPRICE)
    FROM "SNOWFLAKE_SAMPLE_DATA"."TPCH_SF1"."ORDERS"
    GROUP BY O_CUSTKEY;
    ```

- **Number**: The value to group by is the value of the column in the given position in the result of the SELECT statement. The value is evaluated at the end of the statement, after applying any function or expression.

  The following query is the same as the previous one, using the ordinal 1 instead of the O_CUSTKEY column name to indicate the column to group by:

  ```
  SELECT O_CUSTKEY, sum(O_TOTALPRICE)
  FROM "SNOWFLAKE_SAMPLE_DATA"."TPCH_SF1"."ORDERS"
  GROUP BY 1;
  ```

- **SQL expression**: Any expression using any combination of data from the query. The value to group by is the result of the expression.

  The following query calculates the total orders by year, using the year() function, which returns the year from a date:

  ```
  SELECT YEAR(O_ORDERDATE), sum(O_TOTALPRICE)
  FROM "SNOWFLAKE_SAMPLE_DATA"."TPCH_SF1"."ORDERS"
  GROUP BY YEAR(O_ORDERDATE)
  ORDER BY YEAR(O_ORDERDATE);
  ```

  We have also added the ORDER BY clause with the same expression as the GROUP BY so that we get the output in a nice order. This is a pretty common pattern.

When more than one group by expression is provided, the rows are grouped together according to the values of all the group by expressions.

In the previous example, you could have used GROUP BY YEAR(O_ORDERDATE), MONTH(O_ORDERDATE) to have the order total split by month (and year), like in the following:

```
SELECT YEAR(O_ORDERDATE),MONTH(O_ORDERDATE),sum(O_TOTALPRICE)
FROM "SNOWFLAKE_SAMPLE_DATA"."TPCH_SF1"."ORDERS"
GROUP BY YEAR(O_ORDERDATE), MONTH(O_ORDERDATE)
ORDER BY YEAR(O_ORDERDATE), MONTH(O_ORDERDATE);
```

The HAVING clause

The HAVING clause filters the rows resulting from a GROUP BY clause according to a predicate:

```
SELECT …
GROUP BY …
HAVING <predicate>
```

The predicate is an expression that returns a Boolean value and references:

- Constants
- Expressions that appear in the GROUP BY clause
- Aggregated functions that can be calculated according to the GROUP BY clause

As an example, we could extend the example from the GROUP BY topic to look at the months where we have less than 10,000 orders.

The following query does it:

```
SELECT YEAR(O_ORDERDATE), MONTH(O_ORDERDATE), sum(O_TOTALPRICE)
FROM "SNOWFLAKE_SAMPLE_DATA"."TPCH_SF1"."ORDERS"
GROUP BY YEAR(O_ORDERDATE), MONTH(O_ORDERDATE)
HAVING count(*) < 10000
ORDER BY YEAR(O_ORDERDATE), MONTH(O_ORDERDATE);
```

In this query, we have used the count() aggregate function to count how many lines, one for each order, there are in one group.

> **Tip**
>
> The HAVING clause is for GROUP BY what the WHERE clause is for the FROM clause.
>
> We will look at the third filtering clause, QUALIFY, in the next topic.

The QUALIFY clause

The QUALIFY clause filters on the results of the window functions, which is the third type of data calculation that we can have in a query after expressions and group by.

We will dedicate the last section of this chapter to window functions.

The QUALIFY clause is an optional SQL clause that proves extremely useful in analytical workloads, so it is implemented in Snowflake.

To recap a bit of what we have seen, these are the three clauses that are used to filter data:

- WHERE applies to the data being read from the sources specified in the FROM / JOIN clauses
- HAVING applies to the data that has been grouped by a GROUP BY clause
- QUALIFY applies to the data that has been calculated by a **window function**

One of the most common usages of the QUALIFY clause together with the simple row_number() window function is to defend against undesired duplicates or select one specific row with respect to other rows that represent different versions of the same object:

```
SELECT *
FROM "SNOWFLAKE_SAMPLE_DATA"."TPCH_SF1"."LINEITEM"
QUALIFY row_number()
            over(partition by L_ORDERKEY, L_LINENUMBER
                order by L_COMMITDATE desc ) = 1;
```

This query selects all fields from a table, just filtering out undesired rows for which the `row_number` window function returns a value different from 1.

The `row_number` window function, assigns a progressive number from 1 onward to all the rows in the same window, following the row order, and then restarts from 1 with the next window.

Picking the rows where it is equal to 1 means keeping only the first row for each window.

The windows are defined by the `over (...)` clause, which comprises a `partition by` part that defines the windows, in a way similar to `group by`, and an `order by` that provides the ordering in the window. We will look in more detail at this in the section devoted to windows functions.

> **Tip**
>
> When using the `QUALIFY` clause, as shown in the previous query, we avoid the need to create a column with the result of the `row_number` window function and then use a subquery to filter on it. That is the normal way of doing this kind of filtering in a database that does not support the `QUALIFY` clause. `QUALIFY` is much simpler to read and use.

Now, let's extend the order example from the previous section to select out the "good months," when we have higher total sales than the average sales for the year they belong to:

```
WITH
monthly_totals as (
  SELECT
    YEAR(O_ORDERDATE) as year,
    MONTH(O_ORDERDATE) as month,
    sum(O_TOTALPRICE) as month_tot
  FROM "SNOWFLAKE_SAMPLE_DATA"."TPCH_SF1"."ORDERS"
  GROUP BY YEAR(O_ORDERDATE), MONTH(O_ORDERDATE)
)
SELECT year, month, month_tot
      ,avg(month_tot) over(partition by YEAR) as year_avg
FROM monthly_totals
QUALIFY month_tot > year_avg
ORDER BY YEAR, MONTH;
```

Here, we have put together a few of the clauses that we have seen so far, using a `WITH` clause to define a CTE named `monthly_totals` with our previous query to calculate monthly totals.

We have then defined a query that reads from the CTE and uses the `avg` window function to calculate the average monthly sales for each month of the full year that a particular month belongs to. Then, we use the `QUALIFY` clause to keep only the rows where the monthly total is greater than the yearly average.

> **Tip**
>
> The previous example illustrates why the window functions are also called analytical functions.

> **Important note**
>
> Please note that the window function calculates a value for each row using the defined windows, not changing the number of rows. In contrast, using the avg aggregate function with a GROUP BY clause would have reduced the number of rows to one per group.

The ORDER BY clause

The ORDER BY clause specifies in which order the query or window function lays out the rows.

The simplified syntax is as follows:

```
SELECT ...
ORDER BY orderExpr1 [ASC|DESC] [NULLS FIRST|LAST] [, orderExpr2 ...]
```

Each order by expression can be made out of three parts:

1. One expression that identifies what to order on. It can be either a column alias, a position ordinal, or an expression, as we have seen for the GROUP BY clause. Please refer to that section for more details.

2. An optional direction for the sorting: ASC for ascending or DESC for descending sort.

3. An optional specification of how to sort null values: NULLS FIRST or NULLS LAST, which are self-explanatory.

Please look at previous sections for examples of ORDER BY in action, in both queries and window function definitions with over().

The LIMIT/FETCH clause

The LIMIT clause is used to restrict the number of rows returned by the query.

LIMIT and FETCH are synonyms, with slightly different syntax.

Let's look at the LIMIT syntax:

```
SELECT ...
[ORDER BY ...]
LIMIT <count> [OFFSET <start>]
```

The count parameter is a number that specifies the maximum number of rows to return.

If the OFFSET part is present, the returned rows are the ones *after* the start position. This allows tools connecting to a database to retrieve all the results in chunks of the desired size. As an example, a LIMIT 10 OFFSET 10 clause would retrieve rows from 11 to 20.

> **Important note**
> If no ORDER BY clause is present, the order of the rows is undefined and could differ in each execution of the same query. In this case, the result of a LIMIT clause is non-deterministic because what rows are returned depends on the order in which the rows happen in the result set.

Query clause order of evaluation

In the previous sections, we have seen all the clauses that can appear in a SELECT statement.

Now is a good time to bring your attention to the fact that these clauses are generally evaluated in the following specific order, as well as what it is important to pay attention to for each clause:

1. FROM and its JOIN subclause, which are used to identify the source data for the query.

2. The WHERE clause, which is used to filter out the source data that we do not want.

    This is probably the most important clause for performance, because the less data a query works on, the quicker it is. Use WHERE whenever possible to just bring in the data you need.

3. The GROUP BY clause, which groups the source data left after applying the WHERE clause and calculates the aggregate functions on the grouped data.

4. The HAVING clause, which filters on the results of GROUP BY.

5. Partitioning of the windows and calculation of the **window functions**.

6. The QUALIFY clause, which filters on the results of the window functions.

7. The DISTINCT keyword, if applied to the SELECT clause, which removes duplicated rows.

8. The ORDER BY clause, which puts the resulting rows in the desired order.

9. The LIMIT clause, which caps the rows returned by the query to the desired amount.

SQL operators

When writing queries, we can perform operations on the data handled by the query.

We do so by building expressions that return the desired value, using functions and operators.

We can perform an operation pretty much everywhere a value is expected: in the SELECT clause to provide the desired outputs by transforming the inputs, in the WHERE clause or ON part of a JOIN clause, HAVING clause, or QUALIFY clause to identify what should or should not be returned by the query, in GROUP BY to decide how to aggregate, and so on.

Let's go through the categories of operators and how they are used:

- **Arithmetic operators**: These are the traditional +, -, *, /, and % (modulo).

  They expect one or more numeric (or convertible to numeric) inputs to provide a numeric result, with the usual arithmetic precedence and meaning, like in the following example:

  ```
  SELECT 1 + '2' as three,  (3+2) * 4 as twenty
  WHERE twenty % 2 = 0;
  ```

  Note that '2' is a string but can be automatically converted to the number 2. Also note that implicit conversions happen, but explicit conversions are better.

  The modulo operator returns the remainder of the division of the first operator by the second, and the val % 2 = 0 pattern is often used to identify even numbers.

- **Comparison operators**: These are used to test two values for equality or other comparisons, and are = (equal), != (not equal), <> (also not equal), < (less than), <= (less than or equal), > (greater than), and >= (greater than or equal).

  They are typically used in the WHERE clause, but can be used anywhere a Boolean result is desired, such as in the following example:

  ```
  SELECT 2 < 1 as nope, '3' != 'three' as yep
  WHERE 1 != 2;
  ```

  Note that the operators can compare all types where the operation is defined.

  I have seen WHERE 1 = 2 used in many places to avoid returning any row, because 1=2 always returns FALSE; it would be clearer to write WHERE false directly and if you do not need to filter any row out, you can just leave the WHERE clause off, or use the WHERE true expression.

- **Logical operators**: These are the traditional AND, OR, and NOT Boolean operators.

  They operate only on Boolean predicates and values and return Booleans.

  They are generally used in the WHERE clause, but can appear anywhere an expression is allowed, such as in the following example:

  ```
  SELECT *,
    (C_ACCTBAL > 7500) AND (C_NATIONKEY = 24) as IS_TOP_US_CUST
  FROM "SNOWFLAKE_SAMPLE_DATA"."TPCH_SF1"."CUSTOMER"
  WHERE (C_NAME IS NOT null) AND IS_TOP_US_CUST;
  ```

In the previous example, we have defined an IS_TOP_US_CUST column using a logical operator to combine two predicates, as we have done in the WHERE clause, also reusing the new Boolean column we created.

- **Set operators**: These operators are used to put together the results from multiple queries, and are INTERSECT, MINUS or EXCEPT, and UNION [ALL].

  The simplified syntax is as follows:

  ```
  query_1 <set_operator> query_2
  ```

  The queries must be compatible, having the same number of columns and of the same type.

  It is also important that the semantics of the columns in the same position are correct, as combining people's names with state codes is possible, as they are both strings, but in general, it does not make much sense.

  Let's describe the set operators:

  - INTERSECT returns the rows that appear in both queries, checking all columns to have the same value

  - MINUS or EXCEPT returns the rows from the first query that do not appear in the second

  - UNION [ALL] returns the rows from both queries, with ALL keeping duplicates

  As an example, the following query returns data for the customers from India (8) and the US (24) and the customers in the AUTOMOBILE segment without duplicates:

  ```
  SELECT C_NAME, C_ADDRESS, C_PHONE
  FROM "SNOWFLAKE_SAMPLE_DATA"."TPCH_SF1"."CUSTOMER"
  WHERE C_NATIONKEY IN (8, 24)
  UNION
  SELECT C_NAME, C_ADDRESS, C_PHONE
  FROM "SNOWFLAKE_SAMPLE_DATA"."TPCH_SF1"."CUSTOMER"
  WHERE C_MKTSEGMENT = 'AUTOMOBILE';
  ```

  In this special case, as both the queries are on the same table, we could have just used a single query with a slightly more complex WHERE clause using an OR operator to compose the two individual clauses. In real cases, you might want to combine similar data from different tables and the set operators are here for you.

- **Subquery operators**: These operators allow us to use subqueries in WHERE clauses.

  A subquery is a query defined inside another query.

  A subquery can be used without any operator as a table-like object, such as selecting a subset of a table we want to use some data, or an expression if it returns a single value, as in the following example:

  ```
  SELECT C_NAME, C_ADDRESS, C_PHONE
  FROM "SNOWFLAKE_SAMPLE_DATA"."TPCH_SF1"."CUSTOMER"
  WHERE C_NATIONKEY = (
    SELECT N_NATIONKEY
  ```

```
    FROM "SNOWFLAKE_SAMPLE_DATA"."TPCH_SF1"."NATION"
    WHERE N_NAME = 'JAPAN'
);
```

In this example, the subquery returns only one value, so we can use the equal operator.

The subquery operators extend their use to other cases, as per their definitions:

- ALL/ANY: Allows you to apply a comparison to all/any rows of the subquery

- [NOT] EXISTS: Returns true if the subquery returns at least one row, false with NOT in front

- [NOT] IN: Returns true if the expression is *not* included in the results of the subquery

The following example extends the previous example to the case when we want customers from more than one country, picking the country by name:

```
SELECT C_NAME, C_ADDRESS, C_PHONE
FROM "SNOWFLAKE_SAMPLE_DATA"."TPCH_SF1"."CUSTOMER"
WHERE C_NATIONKEY IN (
  SELECT N_NATIONKEY
  FROM "SNOWFLAKE_SAMPLE_DATA"."TPCH_SF1"."NATION"
  WHERE N_NAME IN ('JAPAN', 'CANADA')
);
```

We could easily rewrite the same query using = ANY instead of IN, and probably with some changes in the subquery also using EXISTS.

Now that we have been acquainted with the basics of querying data in SQL, let's dive deeper into the JOIN clause, which allows us to put together data from multiple sources, which is crucial to turning raw data into useful information.

Combining data in SQL – the JOIN clause

The JOIN clause, and the equivalent forms of the FROM clause with multiple tables, is used to combine the rows from two tables to create a row with the columns (that you select) from both tables.

Joins are useful when the tables to be combined are related, that is, when the two tables have some columns that represent the same thing, and we want to combine data from both tables.

We express how to combine the rows by providing a join clause, usually with the ON subclause, which compares the rows from one table to the rows of the other table. Most of the time, the relation is that the values of corresponding columns are the same, but any predicate is fine in the ON subclause.

Combining orders and customers

One example of how to combine data might be a web_order table and a customer table.

In both tables, you normally have a column with the customer ID information even if the columns might not have the same name. Let's assume that in the order table, there is the ID of the customer who placed the order in the ORDER_PLACED_BY column, and in the customer table, there is the ID of the customer in the CUSTOMER_ID column. Then, we could write the following query:

```
SELECT *
FROM web_order
JOIN customer ON ORDER_PLACED_BY = CUSTOMER_ID;
```

This query, using *, returns rows that have all columns from both tables, in all the cases when there is a row that satisfies the ON condition.

Let's look at the relevant rows of the input and output tables in the case where we have one order with ORDER_PLACED_BY = 123 in the order table and one customer with CUSTOMER_ID = 123.

Say we have one row with ORDER_PLACED_BY = 123 in the web_order table, as follows:

Order_ID	ORDER_PLACED_BY	ORDER_VALUE
WEB_0001	123	225.52

Table 1.2: Sample web_order table

And we have one row with CUSTOMER_ID = 123 in the customer table, as follows:

Customer_ID	Customer_Name	Address
123	Big Buyer LLP	Nice place road, 00100 SOMEWHERE

Table 1.3: Sample customer table

Then, we get the following row in the result table:

Order_ID	ORDER_PLACED_BY	ORDER_VALUE	Customer_ID	Customer_Name	Address
WEB_0001	123	225.52	123	Big Buyer LLP	Nice ...

Table 1.4: Sample result of the previous query

If we do not have any customer with CUSTOMER_ID = 123, then we will have no row returned (for that order) in the result table.

Say we have the same order table as before, but three rows with `CUSTOMER_ID = 123` in the `customer` table:

Customer_ID	Customer_Name	Address
123	Big Buyer LLP	Nice place road, 00100 SOMEWHERE
123	Another Customer	Some road, 10250 SOME PLACE
123	A third customer	No way road, 20100 NOWHERE

Table 1.5: Alternative example of a customer table with three rows with CUSTOMER_ID = 123

Then, we will have three rows returned, each having the same order information combined with one specific customer per row, as you see in the following table:

Order_ID	ORDER_PLACED_BY	ORDER_VALUE	Customer_ID	Customer_Name	Address
WEB_0001	123	225.52	123	Big Buyer LLP	Nice …
WEB_0001	123	225.52	123	Another Customer	Some …
WEB_0001	123	225.52	123	A third customer	No …

Table 1.6: Table resulting from the previous sample JOIN query, with three customer matches

This last situation is probably not what you want, as it will "duplicate" the order, returning one row with the same order information for each customer that matches the condition. Later in the book, when we talk about identity, we will see how to make sure that this does not happen and how with dbt, you can also easily test that it really does not happen.

Another question that you might have is how do we keep the order information in the results, even if we do not have a match in the customer table, so that we get all the orders, with the customer information when available? That's a good question, and the next topic on join types will enlighten you.

JOIN types

In the previous section about the query syntax, we introduced the simplified syntax of a `JOIN` clause. Let's recall it here with shorter table names and no aliases:

```
SELECT …
FROM t1
[<join type>] JOIN t2 ON <condition_A>
[[<join type>] JOIN t3 ON <condition_B>]
…
```

In the most common cases, the join type is one of [INNER] or { LEFT | RIGHT | FULL } [OUTER].

This gives us the following possible joins with a join condition using the ON subclause:

- INNER JOIN: This is the default and most common type of join, returning only the rows that have a match on the join condition. The INNER keyword is optional, so you can write the following:

  ```
  SELECT … FROM t1 JOIN t2 ON <some condition>
  ```

  Note that the preceding INNER JOIN is equivalent to the following query that uses only FROM and WHERE:

  ```
  SELECT … FROM t1, t2 WHERE <some condition>
  ```

  It is preferable, anyway, to use the JOIN syntax, which clearly shows, especially to humans, which conditions are for the join and which are for filtering the incoming data.

- LEFT OUTER JOIN: This is the second most used type of join, as it returns all the rows from the left table, which is the first to be named, combined with the matching rows from the other table, padding with NULL the values where the right table has no matches

  Of course, you will have one row of the left table for each matching row of the right table.

- RIGHT OUTER JOIN: This is similar to LEFT OUTER JOIN, but it keeps all the columns from the right table and the matching ones from the left table. It is less used than the left as you can reverse the table order and use the left expression.

  The query t1 RIGHT OUTER JOIN t2 is the same as t2 LEFT OUTER JOIN t1.

- FULL OUTER JOIN: This type of join combines the left and right behavior to keep all the rows from left and right, padding with nulls the columns where there is no match.

There are also two other types of join where you do not specify a join condition:

- CROSS JOIN: This type of join produces a Cartesian product, with all possible combinations of rows from both tables. This is also what you obtain if you do not use an ON subclause when using the previous types of joins. The cross join does not have an ON subclause:

  ```
  SELECT … FROM t1 CROSS JOIN t2
  ```

  This is equivalent to what we have seen in the FROM clause:

  ```
  SELECT … FROM t1, t2
  ```

  The difference is just how obvious it is for a human reader that you really want to have a cross join, or that you forgot about the ON subclause or some join-related condition in the WHERE clause. It is not so common to use cross joins, because of the Cartesian explosion we talked about; it is, therefore, a much better style to explicitly indicate that you really want a cross join, the few times when you will actually want it.

- NATURAL <type> JOIN: The NATURAL join is identical to the various types of JOINs that we have seen so far, but instead of using the ON subclause to find the matches between the two tables, it uses the columns that have the same name with an equality condition. Another small difference is that the columns with the same name in the two tables are returned only once in the results as they always have the same values on both sides, because of the equality condition.

Here are a couple of examples of how to write queries with this type of join:

```
SELECT … FROM t1 NATURAL INNER JOIN t2
```

The preceding query is like an INNER JOIN query on columns with the same name in t1 and t2.

```
SELECT … FROM t1 NATURAL FULL OUTER JOIN t2
```

This one is like a FULL OUTER JOIN query on columns with the same name in t1 and t2.

> **Tip**
>
> When talking about JOIN, we use LEFT and RIGHT, but with respect to what?
>
> It is a reference to the order in which the tables appear in a chain of joins.
>
> The FROM table is the leftmost one and any other table that is joined is added to the right in the order in which the join appears.
>
> Writing SELECT … FROM t1 JOIN t2 ON … JOIN t3 ON … JOIN t4 ON … makes clear that the tables will be stacked from left to right like this: t1-t2-t3-t4.
>
> You could rewrite the same example as it is normally written on multiple lines, as follows:
>
> SELECT …
>
> FROM t1
>
> JOIN t2 ON …
>
> JOIN t3 ON …
>
> JOIN t4 ON …
>
> The result is the same, even if it is not so immediate to see left and right as mentioned in the previous statement.

Visual representation of join types

We have defined how joins work through examples and explanations, but I think that for some people, an image is worth a thousand explanations, so I propose two ways to graphically look at joins:

- One that tries to show how the matching and non-matching rows are treated in different kinds of joins

- One that uses a set notation and compares the different types of joins

Visual representation of returned rows in JOIN queries

The following figure visually describes how two rows of tables A and B are aligned to form the rows resulting from the different types of joins:

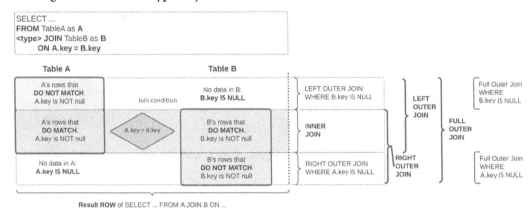

Figure 1.7: Visual representation of different JOIN types between tables A and B

Each table is divided into two: one part where the rows have one or more matches on the other table that satisfy the join condition and another part where each row has no match on the other table.

The rows from the two tables that have a match, in the center of the figure, are properly aligned according to the matching condition so that each resulting row contains the values from A's columns and B's columns where the condition is met. This central part is always returned by all joins, unless explicitly excluded with a WHERE clause requesting one of the two keys to be NULL.

The rows where there is no match, shown at the top for table A and at the bottom for table B, are aligned with columns from the other table padded with NULL values. This produces the somewhat unintuitive result that a query with an ON A.key = B.key clause might produce rows where one of the two keys is NULL and the other is not.

> **Tip**
>
> Please remember that NULL is a special value and not all things work out as expected. As an example, the expression NULL = NULL produces NULL and not TRUE as you might expect.
>
> Try it out yourself with this query: SELECT NULL = NULL as unexpected;.
>
> That is why you test for NULL values using <field> IS NULL and not using equality.

Full outer join

The following figure depicts the result of a FULL OUTER JOIN in terms of the rows of the two original tables:

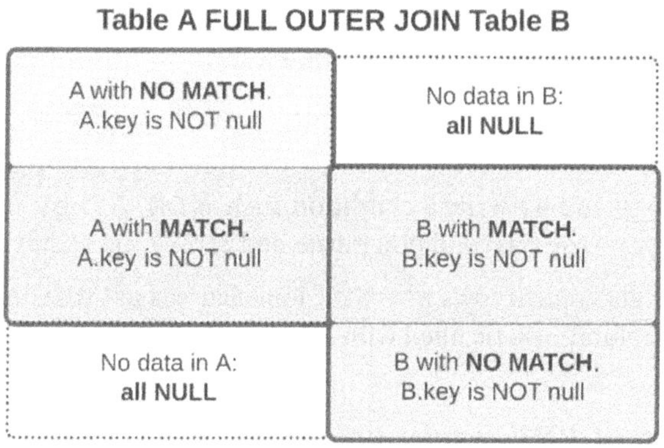

Table A FULL OUTER JOIN Table B

Figure 1.8: Visual representation of a FULL OUTER JOIN

You can clearly identify the central part of the previous picture, where rows from both tables satisfy the join constraint and the two parts where one of the tables has no matching rows for the other table; in these rows, the columns from the other table are filled with NULL values.

Left outer join

The following figure depicts the result of a LEFT OUTER JOIN in terms of the rows from the two original tables:

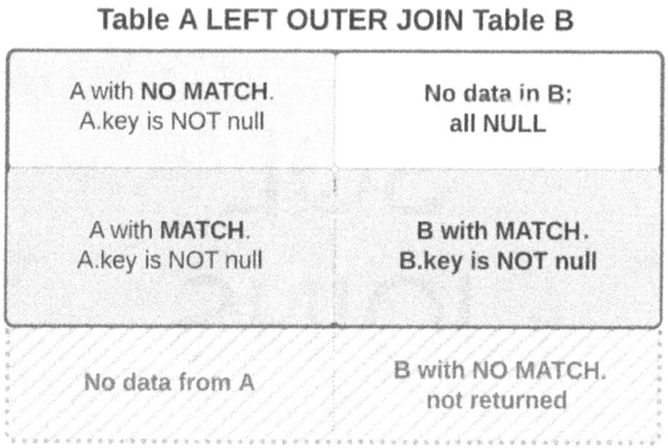

Table A LEFT OUTER JOIN Table B

Figure 1.9: Visual representation of a LEFT OUTER JOIN

You can clearly see in the picture that the result consists of the rows from both sides that satisfy the join constraints, plus only the rows from table A that do not have a match in table B, with the columns from B filled with NULL values.

The rows from table B without a match in table A are not returned.

Another way to express this is that we have all rows from table A, plus the rows from B where there is a match in the join condition, and `NULL` for the other rows.

Important Note

When we join two tables, and we write a condition such as `ON A.key = B.key`, we are expressing interest in rows where this condition is true, and `INNER JOIN` just gives us these rows.

However, `OUTER` joins also return rows where the join clause is not true; in these rows, either the `A.key` or `B.key` column will be filled with `NULL` as there is no match on the other table.

Visual representation of JOIN results using sets

The following figure visually represents the join types that use an `ON` clause, representing, as sets, the rows from tables A and B that match or do not match the join condition in the `ON` clause.

The overlapping area is where the condition is matched by rows in both tables:

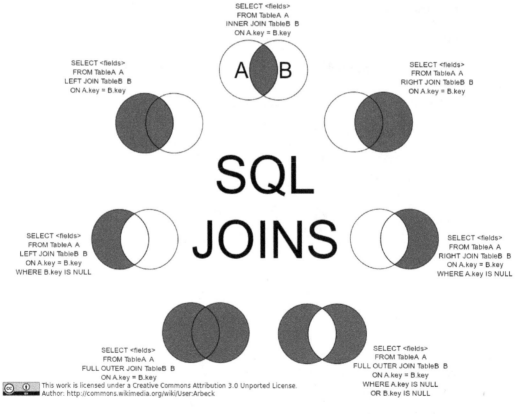

Figure 1.10: Visual representation of SQL JOIN types with an ON clause, as set operations

The preceding figure represents the join types that we have seen in two forms:

1. Using only the ON subclause, showing the results of the pure join
2. Using a WHERE clause on the column used in the ON subclause

    In the figure, this information is used to exclude from the outer joins the rows where the match happens, where A and B overlap, which are the rows returned by an inner join.

This type of query is useful, and often used, for example, to see whether we have orders where the referenced customer does not exist in the customer table. This would be called an **orphan key** in the order table.

Let's see an example using Snowflake sample data:

```
SELECT *
FROM "SNOWFLAKE_SAMPLE_DATA"."TPCH_SF1"."ORDERS"
LEFT OUTER JOIN "SNOWFLAKE_SAMPLE_DATA"."TPCH_SF1"."CUSTOMER"
  ON C_CUSTKEY = O_CUSTKEY
WHERE C_CUSTKEY is NULL;
```

This query should return no rows, as all the customers referenced by the orders should exist in the customer table. Now that we have covered all the basic functions in SQL, let us check out an advanced feature: windows functions.

Advanced – introducing window functions

A **window function** is a SQL function that operates on a set of rows, called a window of rows.

These functions are also called **analytic functions**, as they are mostly used in analytic queries.

A **window** is a set of correlated rows, containing any amount from 0 to all the rows resulting from a query.

Generally, the windows divide the resulting rows into disjointed partitions.

Some window functions can also operate on a **window frame**, which is a dynamic subset of the rows defined by the window, based on the current row.

You can define a **cumulative window frame**, taking the rows of the window before or after the current row, or a **sliding window frame**, going from some rows before the current row to some rows after the current row.

Window functions have a lot in common with aggregated functions, the ones that use GROUP BY, as they both divide the results of a query into groups, that is, partitions, and then calculate the function on the rows in each group.

The big difference is that with GROUP BY, you get only one row per group, while with window functions, all the rows are returned, with the function calculated on the desired subset of rows.

Let's show some examples to make the concept more real.

Assume we have a table with orders, and we would like to know how much each order contributes to the total by day or month. We can calculate the percentage with the following formula:

*monthly_pct = order_total / monthly_total * 100*

Using group by, you could calculate the order total for each day or month, in separate queries, and then you would need to join those results with the original table to be able to apply the formula.

Window functions are here to help, as you can calculate the daily or monthly measures in a single step by defining a window that puts the rows together in different ways, as in the following query:

```
SELECT
    O_ORDERKEY,
    O_CUSTKEY,
    O_ORDERDATE,
    O_TOTALPRICE,
    avg(O_TOTALPRICE) over(partition by O_ORDERDATE) as daily_avg,
    sum(O_TOTALPRICE) over(partition by O_ORDERDATE) as daily_total,
    sum(O_TOTALPRICE) over(partition by
            DATE_TRUNC(MONTH, O_ORDERDATE)) as monthly_total,
    O_TOTALPRICE / daily_avg * 100 as avg_pct,
    O_TOTALPRICE / daily_total * 100 as day_pct,
    O_TOTALPRICE / monthly_total * 100 as month_pct
FROM "SNOWFLAKE_SAMPLE_DATA"."TPCH_SF1"."ORDERS"
QUALIFY row_number() over(partition by O_ORDERDATE
                          order by O_TOTALPRICE DESC) <= 5
order by O_ORDERDATE, O_TOTALPRICE desc;
```

This example uses window functions to calculate totals and averages over different periods and also to limit the returned rows to the five biggest orders for each day.

This query is pretty efficient, executing in a few seconds even after processing million of rows. By changing the schema from TPCH_SF1 to TPCH_SF10, TPCH_SF100, or TPCH_SF1000, you can try out bigger tables in the Snowflake sample data, to see how it works with bigger datasets.

Window definition

A window is defined using the OVER clause, which specifies how to partition and order the rows of the incoming data to apply the window function.

To use a window function, you use this syntax:

```
<function_name> ([<arguments>])
    OVER ( [PARTITION BY <part_expr>] [ORDER BY <order_expr>])
```

The presence of the OVER clause specifies that the function is applied to the windows defined inside the OVER clause. Of course, the function can also take its own arguments.

The PARTITION BY clause defines how the rows are partitioned and <part_expr> is a comma-separated list of columns or expressions calculated on the query data, in a similar way to what we have seen for the group by expressions and shown in the previous example.

The ORDER BY clause specifies the ordering of the rows to be used to calculate the function and it is not visible outside of the window function. The order by clause and <order_expr> work pretty much as they do in the SELECT statement to order the results of the query.

At the syntax level, both the PARTITION BY and ORDER BY clauses are optional, even if some functions require or forbid one of the two. Look at each function's documentation for more details.

The ORDER BY clause has an effect on the **order-sensitive window function**, which comes in two types:

- **Rank-related functions**: These functions calculate values based on the rank of the row, which is the order of the row in the window. They are used to make explicit, that is, crystallized into a value that can be used later, one of many possible orderings of a row in a window.

   One example is the ordering of teams in a championship based on points or medals in a sport: you can have different styles of ordering based on what is decided when you have the same value.

   As an example, if two teams (A and B) have the same score, after another team (C) with an higher score, you can say that A and B are both second or you can say that one is second and the other one third.

- **Window frame functions**: These functions work on a window frame, which is a dynamic subset of rows of a window. As we saw previously, they can use cumulative or sliding window frames. The next section will delve into these.

Window frame definition

Some functions can use a dynamic window frame instead of a fixed window.

You specify the window frame inside the OVER clause, after the ORDER BY clause of the window:

```
<function_name> ([<arguments>])
    OVER ( [PARTITION BY <part_expr>]
        ORDER BY <order_expr>
        <cumulative_frame_def> | <sliding_frame_def>
      )
```

A **cumulative window frame** is a subset of the window that is either growing or shrinking based on the current row inside the window. The frame contains the rows of the window either before or after the current row. The syntax of the cumulative frame definition is the two following lines:

```
{ROWS | RANGE} BETWEEN UNBOUNDED PRECEDING AND CURRENT ROW
| {ROWS | RANGE} BETWEEN CURRENT ROW AND UNBOUNDED FOLLOWING
```

The first expression takes all the rows in the partition or all the rows in the same order range up to the current one, while the second takes from the current row to the end of the partition or range. A better description of ROWS and RANGE follows.

A **sliding window frame** is a subset of rows that extends from a number of N rows before the current row to a number of M rows after the current row. One or both sides can be fixed to the start or end of the partition.

The following are the three possible forms of the syntax:

```
ROWS BETWEEN <N> { PRECEDING | FOLLOWING }
       AND <M> { PRECEDING | FOLLOWING }
| ROWS BETWEEN UNBOUNDED PRECEDING AND <M> { PRECEDING | FOLLOWING }
| ROWS BETWEEN <N> { PRECEDING | FOLLOWING } AND UNBOUNDED FOLLOWING
```

The first syntax is when you want to create a frame that extends from N rows before to M rows after the current rows, while the other two are the cases when one of the two extremities is fixed to be the start or end of the window.

ROWS/RANGE in a cumulative window definition

When specifying a cumulative window frame, we can use either ROWS or RANGE, but what is the difference?

- ROWS: Indicates that the fixed side of the frame extends to the limit of the partition: from the start of the partition to the current row or from the current row to the end of the partition.

- RANGE: Indicates that the fixed side of the frame extends to the previous/following rows that have the same value for the ORDER BY value. The frame operates on the preceding/following rows that are in the same position in the ordering. As an example, you can think of stepping through many teams that have the same number of points in a championship list.

> **Important note**
> Providing extensive information on window functions is beyond the scope of this introduction to SQL used in analytical operations. It is also one area where SQL is not always the same in all databases. We suggest searching for "window functions" in the documentation of your database.

Summary

In this chapter, you were introduced to SQL, starting with the basics and working up to some quite advanced topics. You also got hands-on with working with Snowflake in the cloud.

You learned about the different SQL commands and categories, opened an account in Snowflake, and created your first database with users and roles. You then got into the details of the possible clauses and operators used in writing `SELECT` queries and tried them with Snowflake sample data. You then analyzed in more detail how to use the `JOIN` clause to blend data from multiple tables. We closed the chapter by presenting the window functions, which open up new avenues for our queries and make easy and efficient many complex calculations.

In the next chapter, *Setting Up Your dbt Cloud Development Environment*, we will create our first dbt models, setting up dbt and GitHub in the cloud.

Further reading

In this chapter, we have described the most important SQL topics, but there is much more that you can read if you want to look deeper and become proficient with SQL.

The Snowflake documentation is free to use and provides good explanations and examples, and of course, is the reference source of knowledge for the Snowflake dialect of SQL.

You can start with these pages:

- SQL command reference: `https://docs.snowflake.com/en/sql-reference-commands.html`
- Summary of commands: `https://docs.snowflake.com/en/sql-reference/intro-summary-sql.html`
- Queries: `https://docs.snowflake.com/en/user-guide/querying.html`

2

Setting Up Your dbt Cloud Development Environment

In this chapter, we will start to work hands-on with dbt.

We will start by setting up a **development environment**, first creating a free **GitHub account** with a repository for your dbt project, then creating a free **dbt Cloud account** to host your first project. We will connect the dbt project to the **Snowflake account** that we created in the first chapter.

Once we have **dbt Cloud** up and running, we will have a look at the differences between dbt Cloud and the open-source version, **dbt Core**. In the rest of the book, we will use dbt Cloud as it requires no installation and offers the same experience independent of your operating system, plus a host of extra services and functionalities.

In this chapter, you will start to learn about the **data engineering workflow** when working with dbt and why **Version Control** (**VC**) is important.

We will close the chapter by experimenting with some SQL we saw in the first chapter and then by looking at the default dbt project, which will allow us to introduce two core functions in dbt: `ref` and `source`. These functions are at the base of how dbt works as they create the structure of your ELT most naturally and transparently.

By the end of this chapter, you will be able to navigate dbt Cloud and build a simple dbt project to transform data after covering these topics:

- Setting up your GitHub account
- Setting up your dbt Cloud account
- Comparing dbt Core and dbt Cloud workflows
- Experimenting with SQL in dbt Cloud
- Introducing the `source` and `ref` dbt functions

Technical requirements

This chapter assumes only basic SQL knowledge, which you can get from *Chapter 1* if you are new to it.

You will only need an email address to create a free GitHub account and a free dbt Cloud account.

Setting up your GitHub account

GitHub is an online service that offers free and paid access to VC based on the **git Version Control System (VCS)**.

In this chapter, we will briefly introduce you to what a VCS is and why we need one, then we will guide you on how to create an account on GitHub, and finally, we will guide you through setting up a repository to hold your first project in dbt.

Introducing Version Control

Modern code development is based on VC, which is the ability to store source code in a central server so that multiple developers can retrieve the code, work on it, and send back a newer version to be stored. *VC allows multiple people to collaborate on the same code base.*

The main functionality of a VCS is to allow storing all the different versions of code in the order they are produced and going back and forth to a version of any file at any point in time. *VC also allows easily identifying the changes between one version and the next.*

A key functionality of VCS is allowing developers to *work on parallel code development lines* by creating branches, which are named development lines, where they can develop the code for a period and then merge the contents of a **branch** into another branch, integrating all the changes.

Another key functionality is automating or facilitating the merging of changes from different developers and development lines so that changes to the same file work as expected.

The benefit of VCSs is that developers are able to change their code in a very safe way, as you can always go back to a previous version should the new one turn out to not be as good as you expect.

VCSs also allow developers to create multiple branches to isolate the changes of a development line, allowing them to concentrate on one set of specific changes independently, also making it easy to merge back, in a mostly automated way, the result of these independent developments into the main development line, which is a combined version of all the developments.

The ability to identify changes between versions enables colleagues to review the changes coming from a development branch and discuss them with the author(s) of the change. This is a fundamental best practice that provides better code quality and spreads the knowledge of changes and of what the code does to everyone in the team that participates in the **code review** actions.

In summary, the use of VC is a key enabler for modern software engineering and the keystone for productive teamwork.

Git-based version control

There are many VCSs, but the one that has revolutionized the software engineering landscape in the last 15 years, enabling real agile teamwork, is **git**.

Git was created to support the work on the Linux kernel by Linus Torvalds in 2005 and to allow the quick management of non-linear and distributed work.

The central goal of git is to make branching and merging quick and simple, with a philosophy close to that of dbt: make things simple to do, and even make possible complicated things.

Let's introduce some basic terms:

- A **repository**, often called a **repo** for short, is the *container of the files for a project*. You have your files in a totally normal folder structure, and all the repository information is kept in a hidden `.git` folder under the root folder of the repository.

- A **commit action** is the action of saving the current version of some files and assigning an identifier to that set. A commit action moves the branch pointer one step forward, from the previous commit to the one being created.

- A **commit** represents the state of all files at the specific moment in time when the commit was done, and it is identified by a unique ID. You could think of a commit as storing the selected files, if they changed with respect to the previous commit, and a pointer to the previous commit. Once created, a commit is an immutable object that, by following the chain of previous commits, can produce a full snapshot of the project at the time of the commit.

- A **branch** is used to create *an alternative development line* that can evolve independently from other branches. A branch is a named pointer to commits that can move over time. A branch starts at the same point (commit) of the branch it was started from, but then evolves independently. As the name correctly suggests, a branch looks like the structure of a tree where a branch starts off the trunk or from some other pre-existing branch. Each branch evolves independently of the other branches until a merge operation.

  The sequence of commits designated by a branch indicates a specific version for each file in the repo, representing the state of the project in the branch.

- A **merge** is an operation that combines the changes that happened to the files in one branch into another branch. Just after the merge, the contents of the two branches are equal, but then they can keep evolving independently.

- A **merge conflict** is a situation when a file has been changed in both branches involved in a merge operation and the system cannot determine automatically how to mix the changes. A simple, manual intervention is needed to edit and save the desired final version of the conflicted files.

The interaction between commits and branches is that you create commits to freeze the state of the project at a specific moment and a branch follows the evolutions of snapshots to identify the current state of one of the development lines.

There is plenty of literature on git, and if you want to dig deeper, you can start at `https://git-scm.com/`, where you can also find a great free book explaining all the details of git. I learned a lot from it when I started working with git.

The great news is that to work with dbt Cloud, you do not need to know much more about git, as it has a simplified git flow guided by the UI, making it simple for everybody to just work by following the implicit flow. We will see more about this later in the *dbt Cloud workflows* section of this chapter when we have dbt Cloud in front of us.

Creating your GitHub account

Let's sign up with GitHub so that you can create as many git repositories as you need:

1. Head to the GitHub home page at `https://github.com/`.

Figure 2.1: GitHub home page

2. Click on the **Sign up** button at the top right or enter your email address in the box and click the **Sign up for GitHub** button in the center of the page.

3. Enter your information in the fields on the next page and then click **Continue**.

Figure 2.2: GitHub input form

4. Solve the puzzle to verify you are human and then click **Create account**.

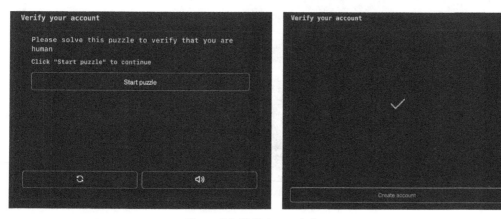

Figure 2.3: GitHub puzzle form

5.   On the next page that appears, you need to enter the code that you received by email.

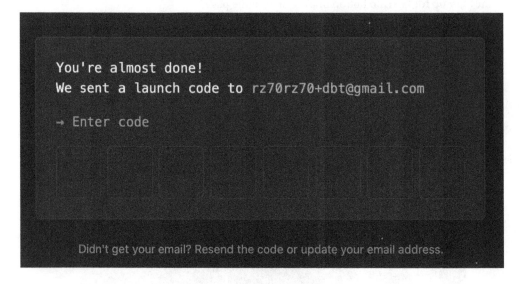

Figure 2.4: GitHub verification form

6.   Welcome to GitHub! The setup is almost done. Pick a range of how many people you will be working with; to start, **Just me** is fine.

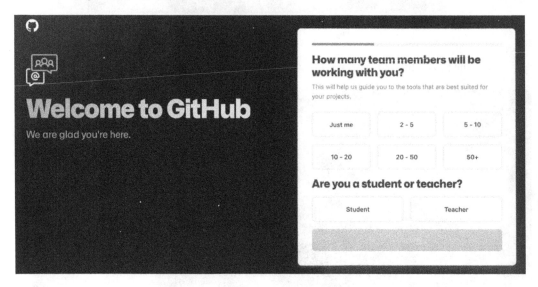

Figure 2.5: GitHub welcome page

7. On the next page, select the tools you want to use, and continue. For now, **Collaborative coding** is good enough.

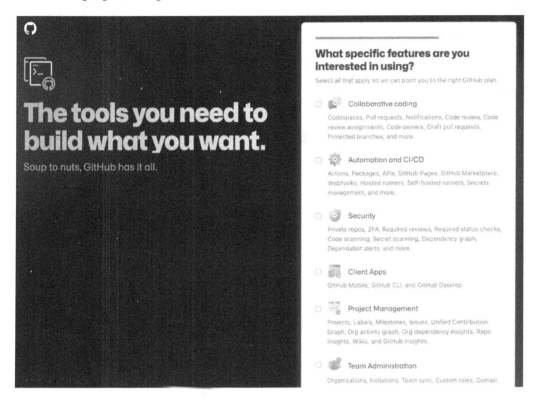

Figure 2.6: GitHub feature selection page

8. Finally, pick the plan you want to start with. The Free plan is fine to start, so you can continue by choosing **Continue for free** at the bottom of the page.

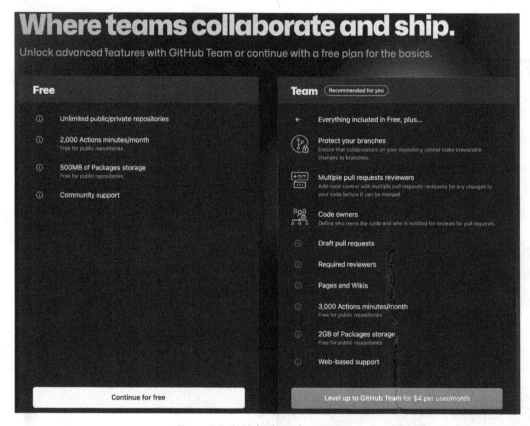

Figure 2.7: GitHub plan selection page

9.   Now you are really done, and you will land on your signed-in home page.

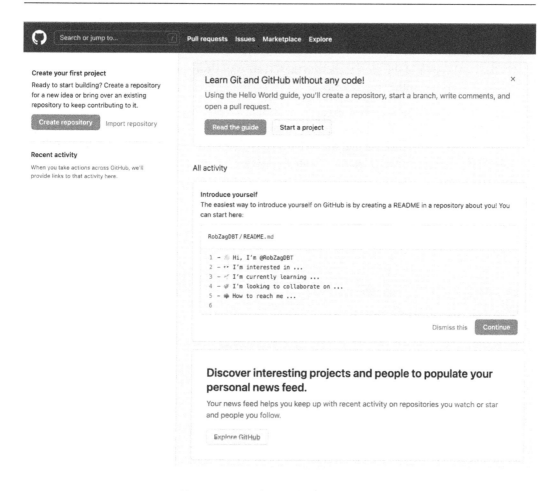

Figure 2.8: GitHub signed-in home page

On your signed-in home page, you can always create new repositories, and now it actively suggests you create your first project. We will do so in the next session, but now, if you want, you can take 5 minutes to complete the README.md file to introduce yourself.

Setting up your first repository for dbt

Whether you have just created your GitHub account or you have had one for a long time with many repositories, it is now time to create a new repository for your first dbt project:

> **Important note**
>
> A dbt project is the main unit of organization for code and configuration that work together to accomplish one goal, and every dbt project is hosted in its own git-based repository.
>
> The good news is that you can have as many projects as you like in dbt, and in GitHub, you can create as many repos as you wish, too.

1. Let's start from the signed-in home page at `https://github.com/`, where we ended the previous section (see *Figure 2.8*).

    In the top-left area of the screen, click on the **Create repository** button, or on the **New** button, if you already have other repositories.

2. Fill in the **Create a new repository** page, providing a repository name and a description and choosing it to be public or private. It is *important that you leave the repository empty* (no files, no README, no license) so that dbt will ask you to generate the default project, so leave the checkboxes empty and click on the **Create repository** button.

Create a new repository

A repository contains all project files, including the revision history. Already have a project repository elsewhere? Import a repository.

Owner *   **Repository name ***

   RobZagDBT ▾   **/**   data-eng-dbt   ✓

Great repository names are short and memorable. Need inspiration? How about special-doodle?

Description (optional)

   My first project with dbt|

○   **Public**
       Anyone on the internet can see this repository. You choose who can commit.

◉   **Private**
       You choose who can see and commit to this repository.

Initialize this repository with:
Skip this step if you're importing an existing repository.

☐ **Add a README file**
       This is where you can write a long description for your project. Learn more.

☐ **Add .gitignore**
       Choose which files not to track from a list of templates. Learn more.

☐ **Choose a license**
       A license tells others what they can and can't do with your code. Learn more.

   Create repository

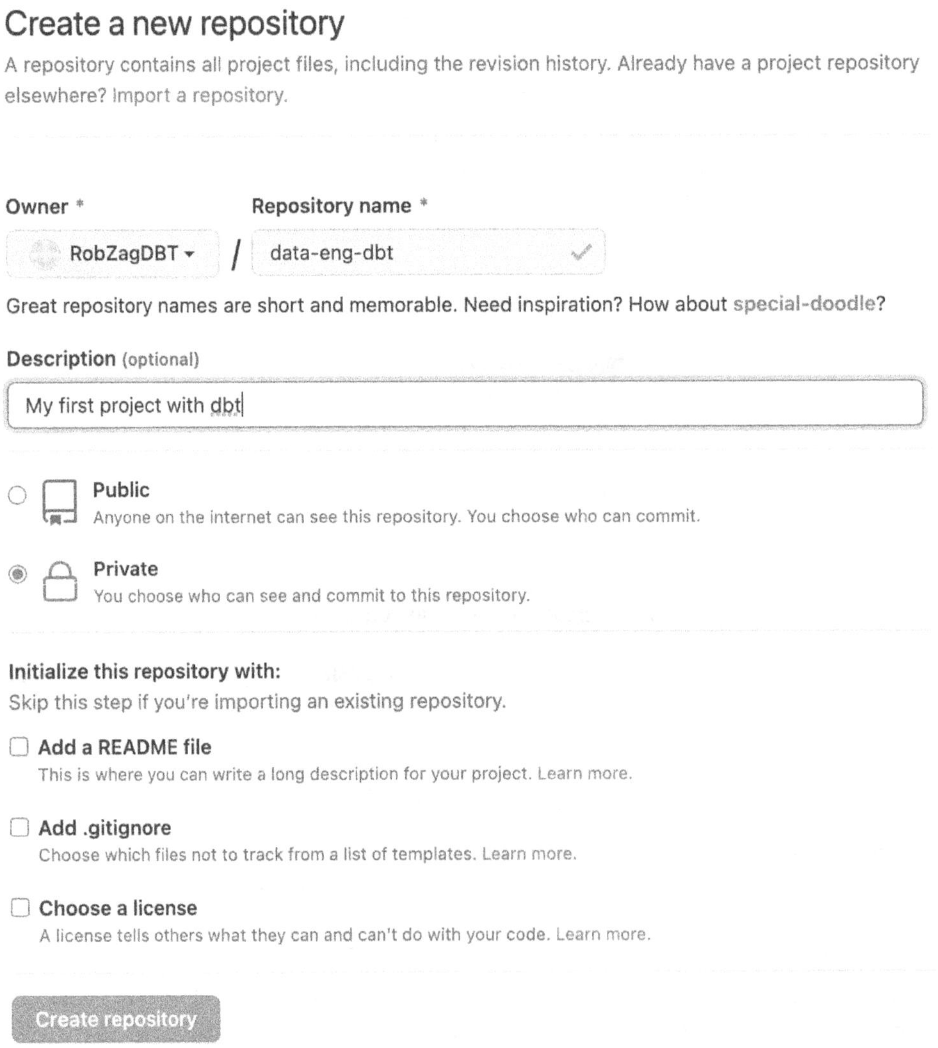

Figure 2.9: GitHub repository creation page

Congratulations, you now have an empty repository that is ready to host your first dbt project, and being an empty repo, dbt will ask you if you want to generate a default project, as we will see later in the *Adding the default project to an empty repository* section.

Setting up your dbt Cloud account

In this section, we will guide you through how to create a dbt Cloud account and then create your first dbt project using the repository you just created on GitHub.

While creating the first dbt project, we will also configure the integration between dbt Cloud and GitHub, so the process will have a few more steps that only need to be carried out once.

Signing up for a dbt Cloud account

You can easily sign up for a free dbt Cloud trial account, and after the initial trial period of 15 days, you will be able to choose between a paid Team plan or the forever free Developer plan.

Let's get started:

1. Go to the dbt home page at `https://www.getdbt.com/` and click one of the two **Start free** buttons.

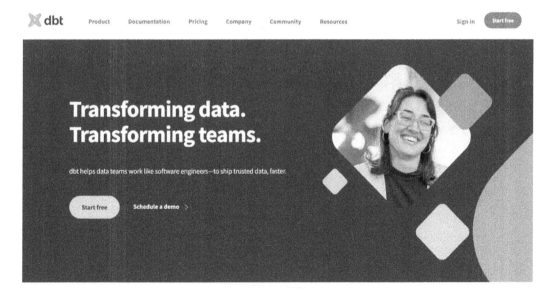

Figure 2.10: dbt home page

2. Fill in your details in the form you land on and then click the **Create my account** button.

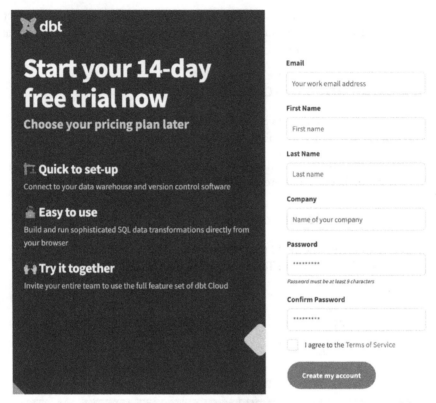

Figure 2.11: dbt subscription form

3. You will land on the **Welcome to dbt Cloud!** page, which informs you that a verification email is underway and where you can request a new one if you did not get the first.

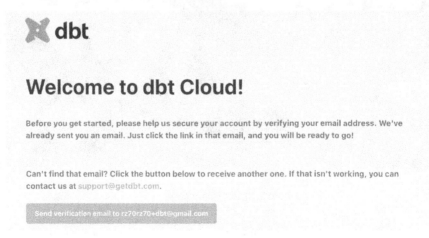

Figure 2.12: dbt welcome page

4. You will receive an email with a button to verify your email address. Click the **Verify email address** button in the email to go back to the dbt Cloud site, verifying your email address.

Welcome to dbt Cloud!

Before you get started, please verify your email address by clicking the button below.

Verify email address

If you have any questions, feel free to contact our support team anytime.

Best,
The dbt Cloud Team

Figure 2.13: dbt welcome email

Upon landing on the dbt Cloud site, you will we able to start the creation of your first project, which we will see in the next section.

Setting up your first dbt Cloud project

To set up a project in dbt Cloud, you have to go through these steps:

1. Provide a name for the project.
2. Select a **Database (DB)** and provide connection details, specific to the DB type.
3. Set up the integration between dbt Cloud and your git system. This is only necessary if this is the first project that you have set up with that git system.
4. Select a git repository to host the source code.
5. Optionally, invite more users to the dbt Cloud account, as part of the initial account setup.

In this section, we assumed that this is the first project that you have set up, so we have also guided you through setting up the integration between dbt Cloud and your git repository provider. This will not be needed for future dbt Cloud projects.

Continuing from the previous section, once you click on the email to verify your email address, you will be automatically directed to the creation of a new project named **Analytics**.

If you already have a dbt Cloud account, or you left the creation of the first project halfway, you can get back to the point you left off by opening the main menu, ☰, in the top-left corner, and then picking **Account Settings** and then **Projects**, which is the first element in the new menu and where you will land by default. Then, click on the **Analytics** project, if you had previously started creating it, or the **New Project** button and provide the desired project name, if you are starting a new project.

Then, follow these steps:

1. Once you land on the **Set Up "Analytics"** page from the confirmation email, shown here, click the **Continue** button.

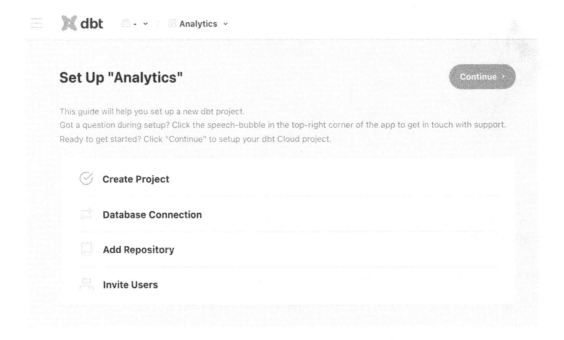

Figure 2.14: dbt setup page for the Analytics project

If you arrive on the similar **Set Up a New Project** page, because you are creating a new project, click on the **Begin** button and provide the project name on the next page, named **Project Settings**, and then click the **Continue** button.

2. On the next page, **Set Up a Database Connection**, click on the DB you want to use.

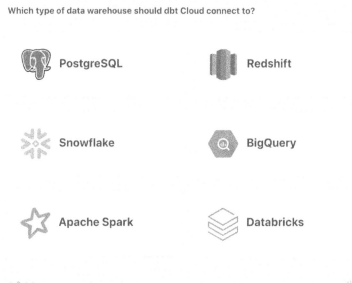

Figure 2.15: dbt DB connection selection page

3. On the next page, also titled **Set Up a Database Connection**, you have to enter the name of the connection and the details of the connection, plus the user details, which we will see in *Figure 2.17*:

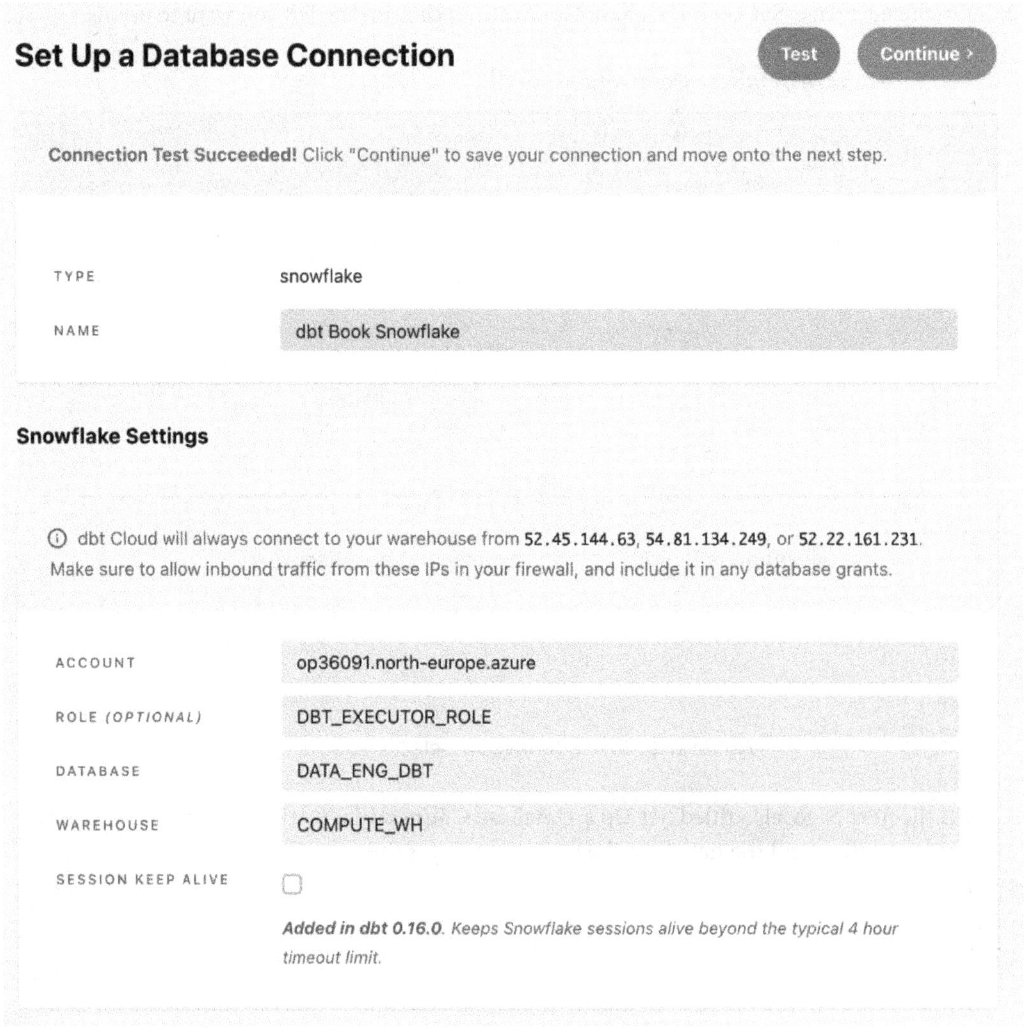

Set Up a Database Connection   Test   Continue >

Connection Test Succeeded! Click "Continue" to save your connection and move onto the next step.

TYPE	snowflake
NAME	dbt Book Snowflake

Snowflake Settings

ⓘ dbt Cloud will always connect to your warehouse from 52.45.144.63, 54.81.134.249, or 52.22.161.231. Make sure to allow inbound traffic from these IPs in your firewall, and include it in any database grants.

ACCOUNT	op36091.north-europe.azure
ROLE (OPTIONAL)	DBT_EXECUTOR_ROLE
DATABASE	DATA_ENG_DBT
WAREHOUSE	COMPUTE_WH
SESSION KEEP ALIVE	☐
	Added in dbt 0.16.0. Keeps Snowflake sessions alive beyond the typical 4 hour timeout limit.

Figure 2.16: dbt DB connection setup page

In the case of a Snowflake connection, it is important that for the **ACCOUNT** parameter, you just enter the account part of the URL that you use to access the Snowflake server, leaving out the initial http:// part and the final .snowflakecomputing.com part.

If you did the setup in *Chapter 1*, then you can enter the **ROLE**, **DATABASE**, and **WAREHOUSE** parameters as shown; otherwise, enter the ones you want to use.

4.   On the same page, after scrolling down, you can enter the authentication credentials for your instance of the *development environment*. You will create other environments in later chapters.

Development Credentials

Enter your **personal development credentials** here (not your deployment credentials!). dbt will use these credentials to connect to your database on your behalf. When you're ready to deploy your dbt project to production, you'll be able to supply your production credentials separately.

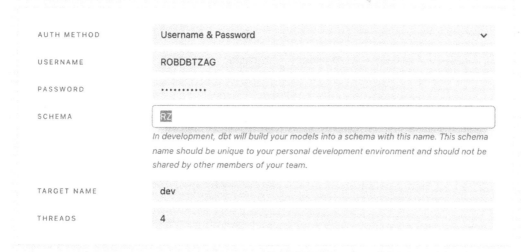

Figure 2.17: dbt DB development credentials entry page

For simplicity, we used **Username & Password**, but you can also pick **Key Pair** from the drop-down selection to use a private key, with an optional passphrase.

You can keep the suggested value for **SCHEMA** or pick a shorter one, as long it is unique for each developer working on this project, as it will be used as the name or prefix for the DB schema to be used in your development environment.

For **TARGET NAME**, you can keep the suggested default or change it to something that better identifies the development environment, such as dev, which is my usual pick.

Pick a number for **THREADS**, with 4 to 8 being good choices.

Once you are done with both **Snowflake Settings** and **Development Credentials**, click the **Test** button at the top of the page to verify that the connection works (you'll get a green message as shown in *Figure 2.16*) and then the **Continue** button.

5.   After setting up the connection to the selected DB, you are taken to the setup of the repository to hold the code for the project.

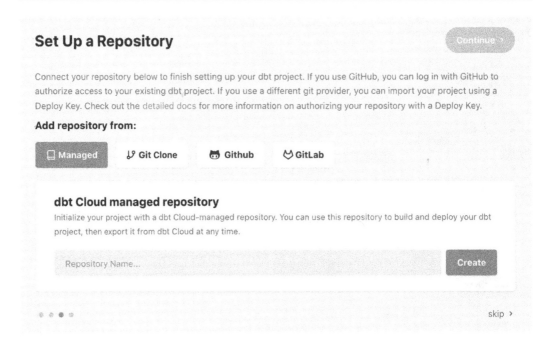

Figure 2.18: dbt repository setup page

You have a few choices of where to host the repository. The default is to use a dbt Cloud managed repo, but to provide you with the knowledge of a more commonly used setup in professional settings, we will go through the GitHub integration setup.

By picking **Git Clone**, you can set up a repository hosted on any other git provider, such as Azure DevOps or Bitbucket, while by picking **GitLab**, you can set up GitLab integration.

Select the **Github** button to start the setup.

6. You will be redirected to sign in to GitHub, so enter your credentials and click **Sign in**.

Figure 2.19: GitHub sign-in form

7. Give permission for the dbt Cloud application to access your GitHub by clicking the **Authorize dbt Cloud** button.

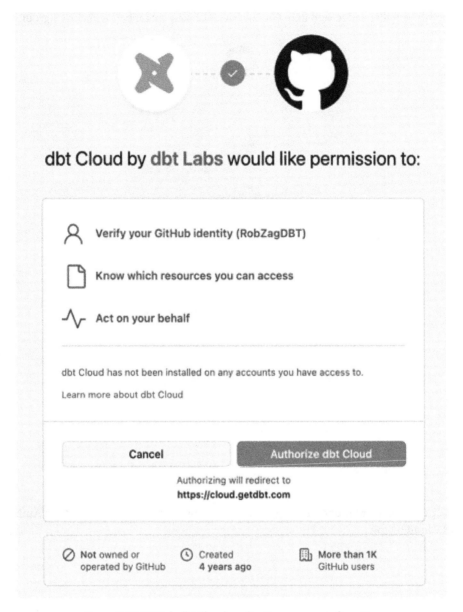

Figure 2.20: GitHub dbt Cloud application access confirmation

8.   Once confirmed, you will be taken back to the dbt Cloud **Set Up a Repository** page.

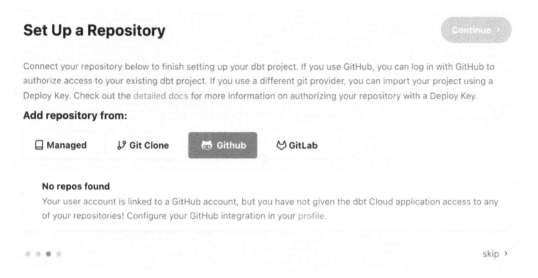

Figure 2.21: dbt repository setup page

Now, you have authorized dbt Cloud to access GitHub, but you have not configured what dbt Cloud can access in your GitHub account. The integration is managed as part of your profile, so let's click on the **profile** link offered in the **No repos found** part of the page.

You can also get there by clicking on your profile icon in the top right and selecting **Profile** from the drop-down menu and then **Integrations** from the menu on the left.

9. On the **Integrations** page, click on the **Configure integration in GitHub** button.

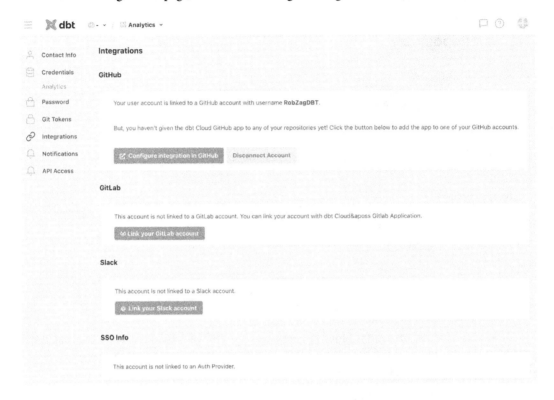

Figure 2.22: dbt integrations page

10. If you have one or more repositories, you can choose the individual ones you want to give dbt Cloud access to, or you can choose **All repositories**, as in the following screenshot:

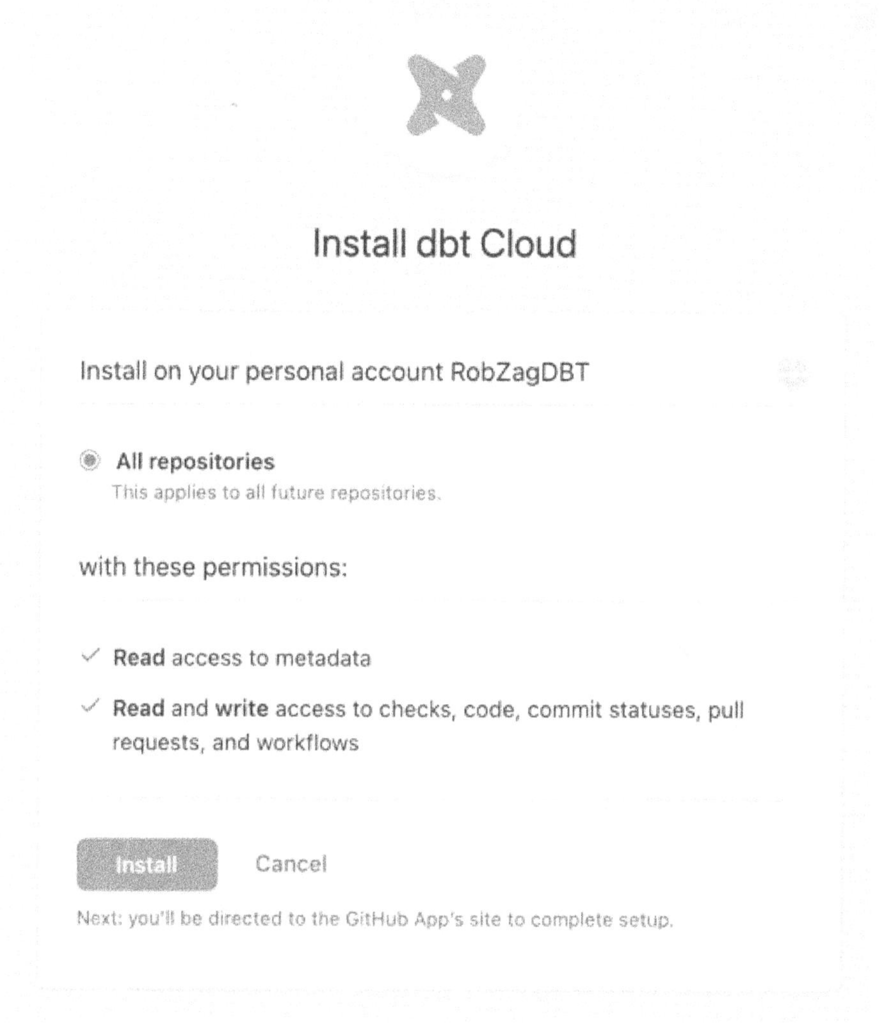

Install dbt Cloud

Install on your personal account RobZagDBT

◉ **All repositories**
  This applies to all future repositories.

with these permissions:

✓ **Read** access to metadata

✓ **Read** and **write** access to checks, code, commit statuses, pull
  requests, and workflows

> Install   Cancel

Next: you'll be directed to the GitHub App's site to complete setup.

Figure 2.23: GitHub repository selection form

Choosing **All repositories** is convenient because you will not have to come back here to give access to other repos in the future, but it might not be the best choice for an account where there are many projects not related to dbt.

11. Once you authorize dbt Cloud to access your repos in GitHub, you will be back in dbt Cloud with your GitHub integration configured. You will not need to configure this again.

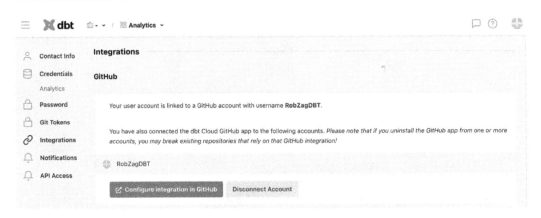

Figure 2.24: dbt Integrations page

12. Now, we can go back to complete the project configuration by choosing **Account Settings** from the menu, ☰, in the top-left corner and then picking the **Analytics** project.

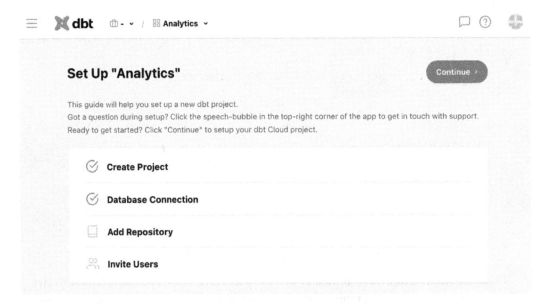

Figure 2.25: dbt project setup cover page

Once you are here, click the **Continue** button to finish the setup by adding the repository.

13. Now that the integration is configured and dbt Cloud has access to your repos, you can pick the one that you want by clicking on it to start the import process.

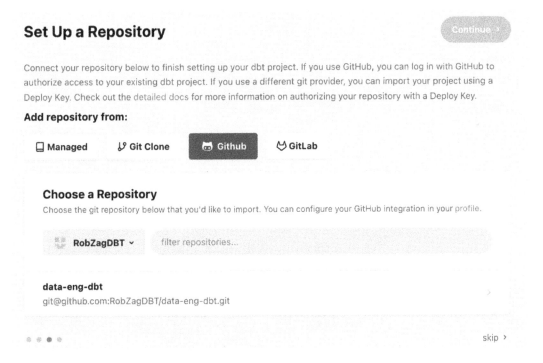

Figure 2.26: dbt git repository setup page

14. Once the import is done, you will get a green **Successfully imported repository.** message and you can click **Continue** to go to the last step.

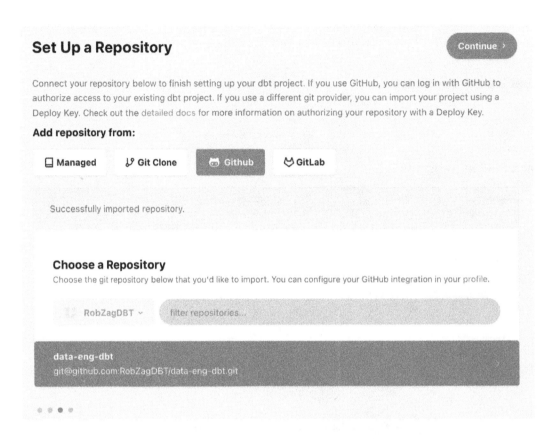

Figure 2.27: dbt git repository setup page after successful authentication

15. When you go through the initial account setup, you will also be asked whether you want to invite more people to the dbt Cloud account. Unless you want to, you can click **Skip & Complete** to finish.

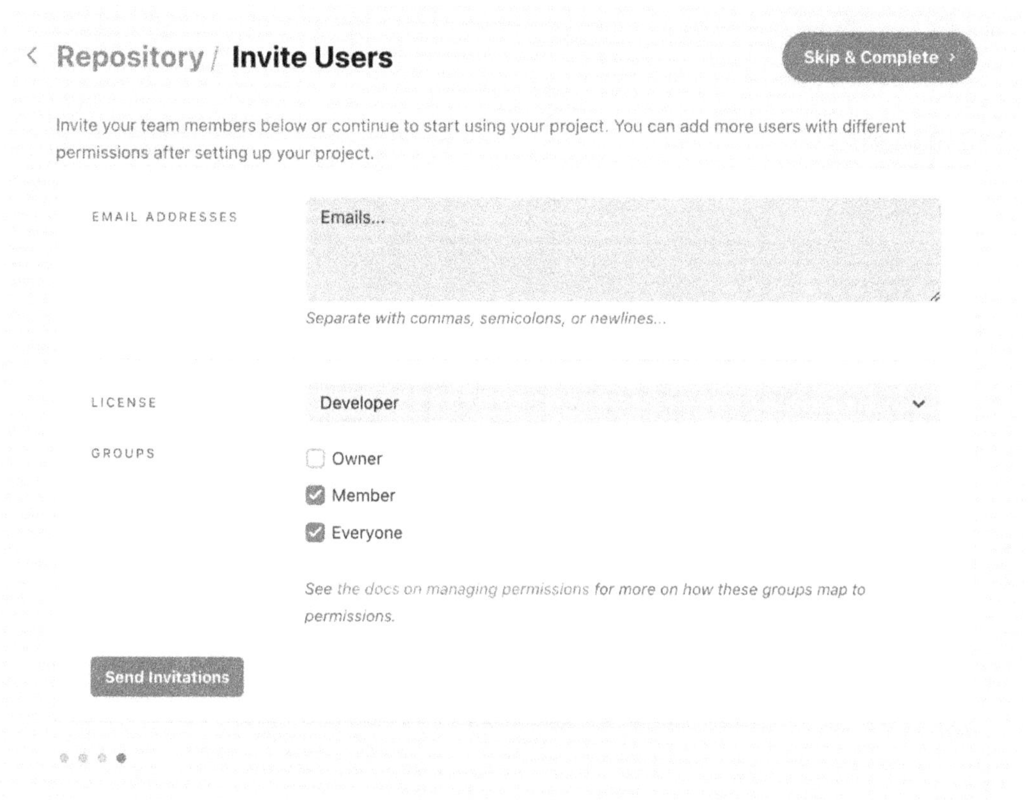

Figure 2.28: dbt Invite Users page

16. You will then land on your signed-in home page in dbt Cloud.

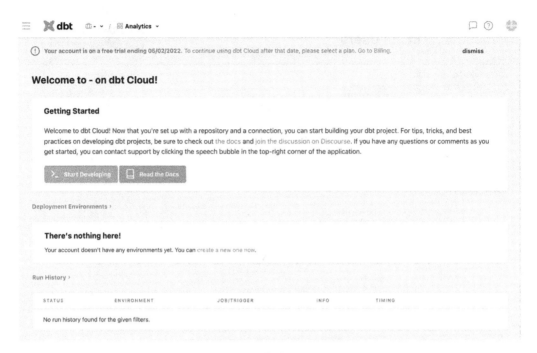

Figure 2.29: dbt home page

In the screenshot here, you can note my lighthearted choice of - as the company name.

Congratulations! You have now set up a fully working professional environment with top-notch components: Snowflake as a data platform, GitHub as a git provider service, and dbt Cloud as a data automation tool.

We still have an empty repository for now, so in the next section, we will see how to create the default dbt project in our repo so that we can start exploring and testing our setup.

Adding the default project to an empty repository

Whether you have just completed the initial setup or you have added a new, empty repository to an account that already had several projects, the default dbt project is a nice way to check that the new project works as expected.

I therefore suggest you always let dbt generate the default dbt project when you start a new project and then delete it once you have checked that all is fine, and you are ready to develop your project. This is what we will do here and in the rest of this chapter.

From your signed-in home page, go to the **Integrated Development Environment (IDE)** by clicking the >_ **Start Developing** button or the **Develop** item in the main menu, ≡, in the top-left corner. Then, follow these steps:

1. After some seconds of waiting on the grayed-out IDE with a popup saying **Loading Analytics** (or the name of your project), you will land on the IDE page with an empty project, as shown in the following screenshot:

Figure 2.30: dbt IDE page for an empty project

You can see that the repo is empty as there are no files in the left area under your repo name, and the repository action button, in the top-left area, reads **initialize your project**.

Do not worry if you see a red **compilation error** in the bottom-right corner; this is normal if you have nothing in the project. Same for the message in the **Lineage** window.

To create the default dbt project, click on the **initialize your project** button.

2. The folders and files of the default project are added to your development environment. You can see them in the file explorer, and you can click on their names to open them.

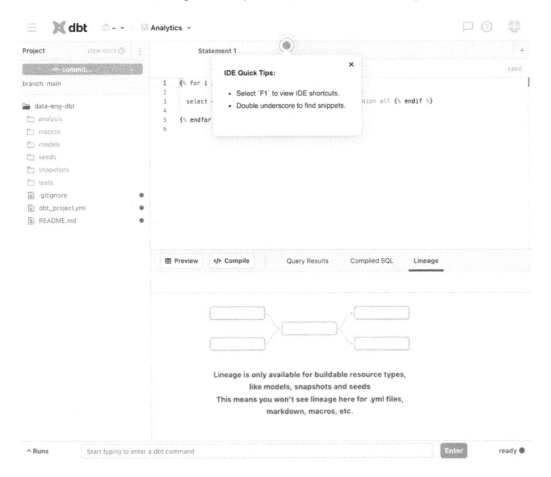

Figure 2.31: dbt IDE page with the default project

If you want, you can explore the files and folders that have been added, but we will come back to them later in this chapter. When you are ready to save the new files in the repository, click the **Commit...** button.

3. The **Write a Commit Message** popup will appear for you to enter a commit message.

Figure 2.32: dbt commit message window

A good commit message explains clearly and in an assertive way what has been done since the previous commit. It is good to start your phrase with a past participle, such as *Added* or *Fixed*, although this isn't obligatory and the important thing is that it makes clear what has been done. Click on the **Commit** button to save the changes to your repo.

4. Once your commit has been processed and synchronized to your git repo, you will be back in the IDE and the files and folders will be in black, as they are not new or changed anymore.

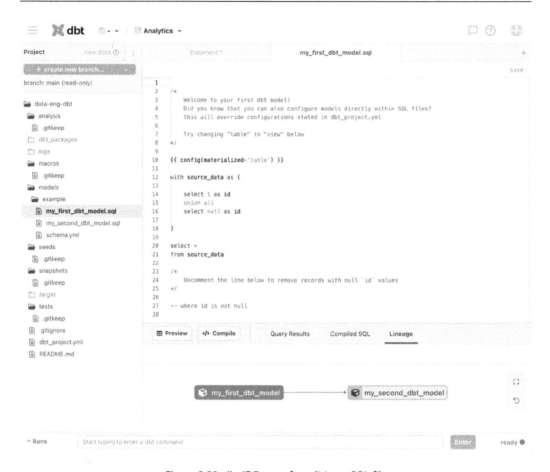

Figure 2.33: dbt IDE open for editing a SQL file

This screenshot shows that most folders are empty and contain only the .gitkeep file, which is an empty file that only exists to force git to create the folder (git skips empty folders).

The only folder with real files is the **models** folder, which contains the two sample models under the **example** folder. We will look into them later in this chapter.

Please note that now you are on the main branch, which is the new default for GitHub (earlier, it was named master), and that when you are in main, you are in read-only mode, so you cannot make changes. This is part of the guided git workflow, as we will see later.

Congratulations, you have now finished the setup of your development environment, including setting up the default dbt project. In the next sections, we will get better acquainted with the basics of dbt Cloud using the default project.

Comparing dbt Core and dbt Cloud workflows

There are two dbt versions that you can decide to use:

- **dbt Core**: This is open source software created by dbt Labs, developed in Python, that you can freely download and use locally from the command line on many operating systems, such as Windows, Mac, and Linux. It provides all the core functionalities of dbt and can also be used for commercial projects.

- **dbt Cloud**: This is a commercial software created by dbt Labs that offers a **Software-as-a-Service** (**SaaS**) experience that includes all the functionalities from dbt Core wrapped in a web interface that makes it easier to use the dbt Core functionalities, adding many features that are useful when running a real-life data project.

The **dbt Core** open source product offers all the features to run a full dbt project, with no differences nor limitations in the core functionalities with respect to the dbt Cloud product, to the point that you can execute the same project under any of the two products.

The features that **dbt Cloud** adds on top of **dbt Core** are designed to make the development, maintenance, and operations of dbt-based projects simpler, quicker, and, in general, more productive or valuable to the wider team. The following is a list of the main additions:

- A powerful web-based IDE, with online compilation and execution of models

- A guided git workflow, integrated into the web IDE, including support for pull requests

- The creation and maintenance of development environments, including the selection of the dbt version

- The creation of execution jobs, to run dbt commands in a reliable way

- The scheduling, monitoring, and alerting of job execution

- The monitoring of data source freshness

- The publishing of generated documentation

In this book, we have decided to use the dbt Cloud development environment, as it makes it easier to work with dbt projects, does not require any installation, and looks and works the same for everybody, independent of the operating system of your computer.

dbt Core workflows

When working with dbt Core, you interact with dbt by issuing commands from the command line standing in the root folder of your project. dbt Core just looks at the local files and folder, without knowing or caring whether your project is also stored in git or some other VCS.

A typical workflow to develop a feature with dbt Core can look like the following:

1.   Before starting a new feature, if you use a VCS and follow the best practices to do new work in development branches, go to the command line and run the commands for your VCS to create a new branch and set it as the active branch in the project folder.

2.   You can then create or edit the dbt model in your editor of choice, saving it inside the dbt project folder structure.

3.   To see whether the current version works, without applying the changes to your DB, you have to go to the command line and run the following command, with eventual switches to just compile what you have changed:

```
dbt compile <eventual switches>
```

This generates or updates the compiled SQL file for each model under the target folder.

4.   If all works and you get no compilation errors, you'll find the compiled SQL file for the model under the target folder. Once you find the file you have to open it, copy its contents, and paste them into a place where you can run them on your DB. In the case of Snowflake, you can copy them into a Snowflake worksheet and run them from there. Some code editors also allow running SQL scripts.

As an alternative, you can replace the cumbersome *steps 3* and *4* and do like in *step 7*, running the model you want to test using the dbt run command, but once you run it, you will change your DB and won't be able to easily go back to the previous version without reverting the code and running the old version again. Note that going back and rerunning does not work for incremental models.

5.   You'll see the result of your model; if you need to make changes, go back to *step 1*, repeating the process of editing, compiling, opening, copying, pasting, and executing until you are happy.

6.   When you are satisfied and want to apply the changes to your DB, go to the command line and run the following command, with eventual switches to run the models related to the current development:

```
dbt run <eventual switches>
```

This generates or updates the compiled SQL file for each model under the target folder and then runs it on the DB enclosing the SELECT query in the code to generate the view or table.

7.   Then, execute the tests that you have declared or written by issuing the following command, with eventual switches to test the models related to the current development:

```
dbt test <eventual switches>
```

8. When you are happy with the development and have completed a set of changes that you want to save to your VCS, go back to the command line and issue the appropriate commands to commit the changes. You need to know the relevant commands.

9. When you are ready to finish the development and ask your colleagues for feedback, before merging your code into the main development branch, go to your VCS and start a new pull request. When the pull request is approved, merge it and you are done.

A typical workflow to run a dbt project looks like the following:

1. Put the code that you want to run in the dbt project folder. This is usually done by checking out the desired branch, but any way you choose works for the dbt product.

2. Run from the command line, maybe using a shell script, a sequence of dbt commands that performs the operations that you want. A typical case is as follows:

    *   Optionally, run any `dbt run-operation` command needed to maintain the DB, set up access to the data sources, or import data into landing tables.
    *   Check the data source freshness with the `dbt source freshness` command.
    *   Run the tests on the source data or landing tables you are going to read from.
    *   Run the eventual `dbt snapshot` command to store the changes in the sources, followed by eventual tests on the snapshots.
    *   Run the dbt models; that is, issue the `dbt run` command.
    *   Then, run the tests on the models with the `dbt test` command.
    *   Generate the documentation with the `dbt docs generate` command.

    This is a simple setup that can get you quite far in real-world usage.

3. Monitor the logging info that is output during the execution to verify that all went well, and at the end of every step, you can decide whether to proceed to the next step until you are done.

    Note that if you use a script to run the commands, you should have checks on the output, as you should stop the run if an error occurs at some point.

4. If you do not need to store the logging info, you are done; otherwise, you need to set up something that captures the logging info and stores it as you need.

5. If you want to schedule the run, you need to set up the scheduling yourself, with whatever technology you have at your disposal. In simple setups, this is often achieved using a scheduler such as `cron`.

6. If you want to store or publish the results of the data source freshness check, you need to capture the result or extract it from the JSON files generated by the execution and publish it.

7. If you want to publish the generated documentation, you need to copy the generated files, which are generated ready to be published, in a place from where to publish them. A simple choice is to copy them to a file bucket in Amazon S3 or a similar service that is then published to your desired audience.

As you have seen in the preceding descriptions of the dbt Core workflows, it is not at all difficult to apply basic edits to your models and run them to execute your ETL process if you are at ease with the command line, a code editor, and a tool to run SQL.

If you do not want to have to do everything manually every time, you also need to know how to write a few scripts to automate the execution, and if you want them to react correctly depending on each step, you also need to code how to decide whether to continue or not.

If you also want to do any of the steps that I labeled as optional, but are normal in a professional setting, such as scheduling the execution, storing the execution results, and publishing the freshness checks or documentation, you need a lot more knowledge and effort than just running the models manually.

Even when you are working alone on a project, it is so useful to use VC and branching; we take it for granted. When you grow your project to two or more developers or environments, using a VCS is the only effective way to keep synchronization between environments and facilitate collaboration between the developers.

Therefore, to move beyond a one-man show, you need to get acquainted with a VCS.

dbt Cloud workflows

Let's go through the same two workflows that we have seen for dbt Core, but using dbt Cloud, so that you can appreciate the main differences.

This is what the dbt Cloud IDE looks like:

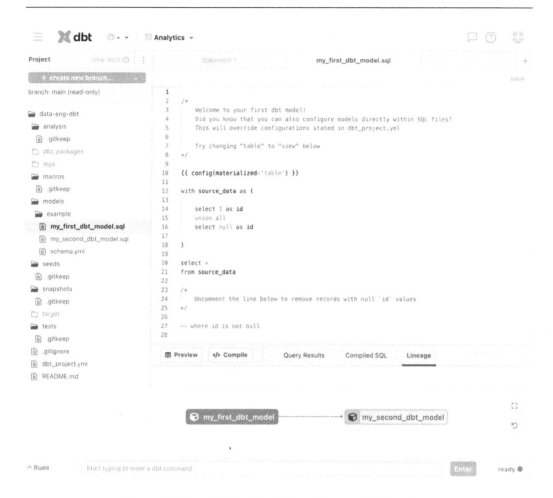

Figure 2.34: The dbt IDE with a SQL model opened in the editor

A typical workflow to develop a feature with the dbt Cloud IDE can look like the following:

1. When you want to start a new feature, you can create a new branch by clicking the **create new branch…** button in the VCS area in the top-left corner of the IDE or move to another branch by selecting it from the drop-down on the right side of the VCS action button.

2. You can then open, edit, and save the files directly in the IDE.

3. Test the model in the IDE by clicking the **Preview** button, and dbt Cloud will compile and execute the generated SQL on your DB and present you with the results in the IDE. You can also look at the compiled SQL, and if you just want to look at the SQL, you can click the **Compile** button instead of the **Preview** button.

4. Keep working on your models, editing, saving, and selecting **Preview** or **Compile** in the IDE until you are happy.

5. When you want to apply any model on the DB, go to the command line at the bottom of the IDE page and enter the same dbt command that you would enter in dbt Core, as follows, with `eventual switches` to test the models related to the current development:

```
dbt run <eventual switches>
```

In the newer version of the dbt IDE you can directly click the build button or one of the run options from the button's drop down.

6. Then, run the tests with the same command as you would in dbt Core, as follows, with `eventual switches` to test the models related to the current development:

```
dbt test <eventual switches>
```

7. When you are ready with your development, click the **commit** button in the VCS area, which is shown once you save the first change in a model, then you can enter the commit message in the popup shown at the top of the IDE, and you are done, without having to leave the IDE.

8. When your development is ready for feedback and eventual release, click the **open Pull request** button in the VCS area, which brings you to GitHub (or your VCS), on the pull request creation page, where you can enter a description and invite the desired reviewers to comment on the new pull request.

If we compare the workflow that we have just described in dbt Cloud against the same one we described before in dbt Core, we see that while the logical operations and dbt commands are the same, the effort to perform them is quite different. In dbt Cloud, you can perform everything from the IDE, without the need to copy and paste any code, look for the compiled files, or edit or run the compiled SQL queries in different tools.

Let's move on to the second workflow, which is how to run a dbt project. In dbt Cloud, you can run everything manually from the IDE, which is what you do in your development environment, or you can define a repeatable job to run in a deployment environment (such as QA or production), which is what you do when you want to schedule the execution of your ETL pipeline.

The workflow to run your project in dbt Cloud would look like this:

1. To select what version of your code to run, define an environment and associate a VCS branch with it.

2. To decide what dbt commands to run on the code, define a job, entering the dbt commands in the order you want them to be executed. The commands are the same as in dbt Core, but some functionalities, such as checking the data source freshness or generating the documentation, are enabled by a checkbox.

When creating or editing the job, you can also define a scheduled execution, and dbt Cloud will run the job according to your scheduling.

3.   When the job is started, on your command or on a schedule, the commands are executed in the order you defined and if there is an error, the job stops executing. You can see the logs in real time, or you can let the job run and come back later to look at the result, with the full logs at your disposal.

The execution results and logs are automatically stored in dbt Cloud. You do not need to do anything to enable them.

4.   If you want to schedule your run, you just define the schedule editing in the job, using the normal `cron` syntax. You can also start a job manually or with a REST call.

5.   If you want to store or publish the source data freshness check, activate the checkbox in the job, and then pick one job that runs the check to be published on the project's data source freshness page.

6.   If you want to publish the generated documentation, just enable the specific checkbox in the job configuration and then decide from what job to publish the documentation.

7.   If you want, you can enable sending a notification from dbt Cloud when a specific job is run, is interrupted, or fails. There is a page to control all the notifications for a project.

Comparing this second workflow on dbt Core and dbt Cloud, we can see again that in both cases, we can accomplish the same result and that the dbt commands involved are the same. But with dbt Cloud, you have a simple web-based tool that provides you with all the features needed in a professional setting.

dbt Cloud also makes these, and other, modern data automation features readily available to smaller teams that do not have all the skills or time to build such features themselves.

We have seen that the dbt commands to execute are the same whether you are using dbt Core or dbt Cloud. In the rest of this book, we will use dbt Cloud and its features, but you can rest assured that you will be able to run the same models with dbt Core, should you prefer that version.

Now that you have an understanding of both dbt Core and dbt Cloud, let's start exploring what you can do with dbt by using dbt Cloud.

Experimenting with SQL in dbt Cloud

Now that you have dbt Cloud set up and connected to your Snowflake data platform, you can use the dbt IDE to issue SQL commands and see the results. The **Preview** feature allows you to easily test models while you are developing them, but it can also be used to just run any SQL on your DB.

In this section, we are going to run some of the examples we saw in the previous chapter so that you can get used to the dbt interface and experiment with SQL if you are not familiar with it.

Exploring the dbt Cloud IDE

Let's start by looking at the dbt Cloud IDE. The default layout of the IDE is vertically divided in two; on the left, you have the VC area and below it a folder structure that is used to organize the files of your dbt project, while on the right, there are the main editing and result areas.

The main area of the screen is again divided in two; at the top, there is the editor, where you edit the source code of your models, while in the lower part, there is a multifunction area that will display the data resulting from your query, the compiled code, or the lineage graph of the selected model. Between these two areas, there is a bar hosting the two main buttons, **Preview** and **Compile**, and the tabs to access the query results, the compiled SQL, and the interactive lineage of the model.

In the following screenshot, we can see that the IDE has opened a tab named **Statement 1** that contains a sample script, which illustrates very well the powerful ability to mix SQL code and Jinja scripting in dbt. You can open more statement tabs with the plus sign on the top right:

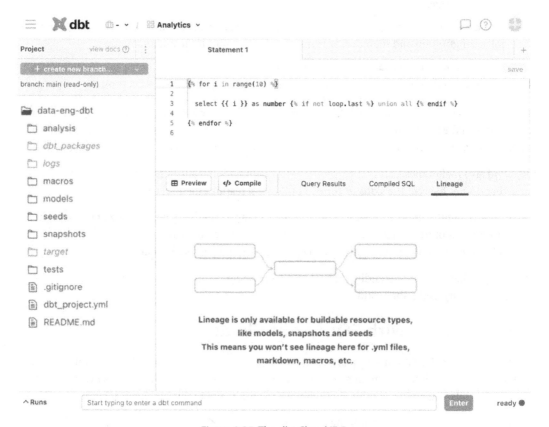

Figure 2.35: The dbt Cloud IDE

In the next section, we will use this area to execute some sample SQL, and you can also try out the samples from the previous chapter.

Executing SQL from the dbt IDE

Let's start running one of the queries from the Select section in *Chapter 1*.

Enter the following code in a statement tab:

```
-- ** SELECT clause **
-- Sample SELECT with alias
SELECT
    O_ORDERKEY,
    ord.O_CUSTKEY,
    cust.C_NAME as CUSTOMER_NAME
FROM SNOWFLAKE_SAMPLE_DATA.TPCH_SF1.ORDERS as ord
JOIN SNOWFLAKE_SAMPLE_DATA.TPCH_SF1.CUSTOMER as cust
        ON cust.C_CUSTKEY = ord.O_CUSTKEY
limit 100
```

Once you enter the code in the IDE and press the **Preview** button, you should see the results of the query after a few seconds, as in the following screenshot:

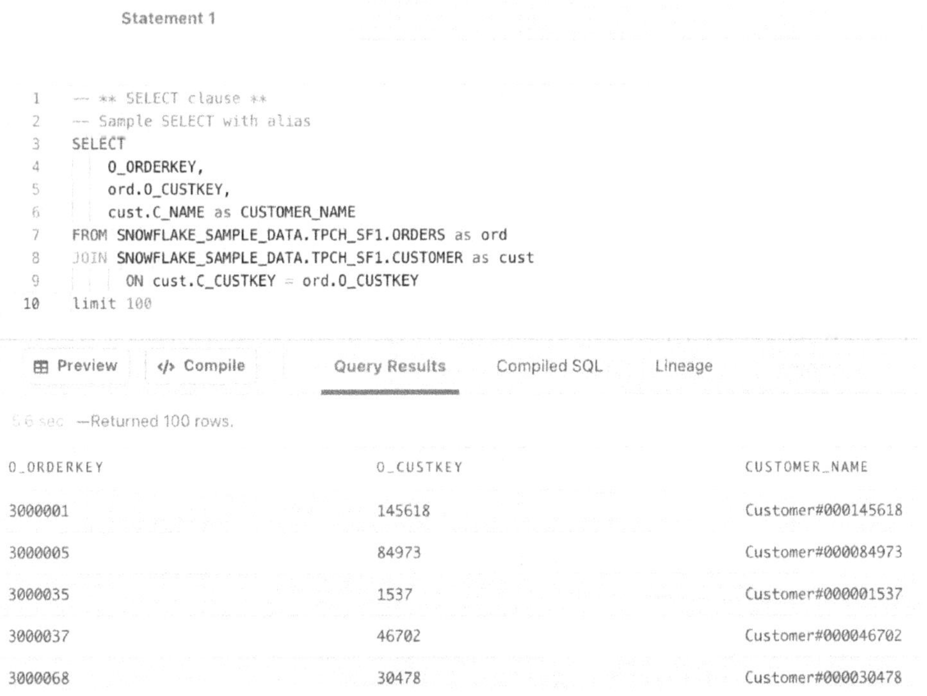

Statement 1

```
1     -- ** SELECT clause **
2     -- Sample SELECT with alias
3     SELECT
4         O_ORDERKEY,
5         ord.O_CUSTKEY,
6         cust.C_NAME as CUSTOMER_NAME
7     FROM SNOWFLAKE_SAMPLE_DATA.TPCH_SF1.ORDERS as ord
8     JOIN SNOWFLAKE_SAMPLE_DATA.TPCH_SF1.CUSTOMER as cust
9         ON cust.C_CUSTKEY = ord.O_CUSTKEY
10    limit 100
```

⊞ Preview   </> Compile   Query Results   Compiled SQL   Lineage

5.6 sec —Returned 100 rows.

O_ORDERKEY	O_CUSTKEY	CUSTOMER_NAME
3000001	145618	Customer#000145618
3000005	84973	Customer#000084973
3000035	1537	Customer#000001537
3000037	46702	Customer#000046702
3000068	30478	Customer#000030478

Figure 2.36: Running a sample query in the IDE

Now that you have run the first query, you can try experimenting a bit by running other queries from the first chapter, changing the fields returned by the previous one, or applying some of the concepts that we saw in the first chapter.

For ease of reference, in the following screenshot, you have the contents from the **ORDERS** and **CUSTOMER** tables in Snowflake:

⊞ **ORDERS**	Preview Data ✕	⊞ **CUSTOMER**	Preview Data ✕
1,500,000 rows 40.3 MB		**150,000** rows 10.3 MB	
Cluster by		Cluster by	
–		–	
Columns	Data Type	Columns	Data Type
O_ORDERKEY	NUMBER(38,0)	C_CUSTKEY	NUMBER(38,0)
O_CUSTKEY	NUMBER(38,0)	C_NAME	VARCHAR(25)
O_ORDERSTATUS	VARCHAR(1)	C_ADDRESS	VARCHAR(40)
O_TOTALPRICE	NUMBER(12,2)	C_NATIONKEY	NUMBER(38,0)
O_ORDERDATE	DATE	C_PHONE	VARCHAR(15)
O_ORDERPRIORITY	VARCHAR(15)	C_ACCTBAL	NUMBER(12,2)
O_CLERK	VARCHAR(15)	C_MKTSEGMENT	VARCHAR(10)
O_SHIPPRIORITY	NUMBER(38,0)	C_COMMENT	VARCHAR(117)
O_COMMENT	VARCHAR(79)		

Figure 2.37: ORDERS and CUSTOMER tables

> **Tip**
>
> When running any query from the dbt Cloud IDE using the Preview function, dbt will append a limit 500 clause to your query to avoid wasting time and resources moving a lot of data around.
>
> To avoid this addition, you can use a limit in your query or append a commented-out limit yourself, adding --limit 100 to the last line of your code.

Introducing the source and ref dbt functions

You have seen that in the dbt Cloud IDE, you can write any SQL and use the **Preview** button to execute it on the DB configured for your project. This is handy when you are exploring a dataset or perfecting a query, but it is just the tip of the iceberg.

In this section, we will look at the dbt default project and you will learn about the source and ref functions that are at the real core of how dbt works.

Exploring the dbt default model

Let's list what the dbt default project contains:

- README.md: This is a text file with some instructions and pointers to the dbt documentation
- dbt_project.yml: The main configuration file
- .gitignore: A git-specific file that lists resources to exclude from VC, such as the dbt_packages, target, and logs folders
- Inside the models/example folder, we have two models and a config file:

  - my_first_dbt_model.sql: As the name suggests, this is the first model, which is just made up of plain SQL that will generate two rows of hardcoded data
  - my_second_dbt_model.sql: This is the second model, and it reads from the first model, introducing the use of the ref function to reference the other model
  - schema.yml: Another configuration file that provides metadata for the models and also declares tests that we want to be run on these models

If you open/select one of the two models and click on the **Lineage** tab on the lower part of the editing panel, you will see the lineage graph, which shows the dependency between the two models that we have in this project, as shown in the following screenshot:

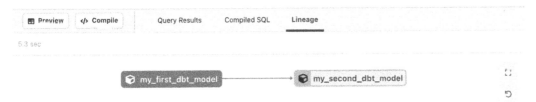

Figure 2.38: Lineage for the dbt default project

Let's analyze the contents of the model folder a bit better.

Analysis of my_first_dbt_model

The first model has the following source code (we have removed a few empty lines and comments):

```
01    {{ config(materialized='table') }}
02    with source_data as (
03        select 1 as id
04        union all
05        select null as id
```

```
06    )
07    select *
08    from source_data
```

We can see that lines 3 to 5 use two very basic queries that just return a value and a UNION ALL operator to generate two rows of data, one with an ID value of 1 and one with a value of null, which is a special value in SQL signaling the absence of data.

The rows from 2 to 6 declare a CTE with the source_data name, used by rows 7 and 8 where we select everything produced by that CTE.

Probably the most interesting row is line 1, as it is not SQL code, but an inline configuration that directs dbt to materialize the result of this query as a table. If you preview the model, you will see the result of its SQL, in the dbt Cloud IDE, but you will generate nothing on your DB. To affect your DB, you need to run your model using the dbt run or dbt build command.

> **Important note**
>
> Doing a preview of a model will run the query in the model as it is, while when *running a model*, using the dbt run command will wrap the SELECT query with the correct DDL to materialize the model in the DB in the desired way, such as a table or a view.

Analysis of my_second_dbt_model

The second model has the following source code:

```
01    select *
02    from {{ ref('my_first_dbt_model') }}
03    where id = 1
```

If you try to preview this model before you have used the dbt run command, you will get an error, as the first model that you reference does not exist on your DB. Most probably, the schema with your selected schema name will not exist either.

We will use the dbt run command in the next section, so for the moment, we can just note that this model just selects everything from your first model that is referenced simply by its name using the dbt ref function.

The curly brackets symbols, { and }, are used to start and end the blocks of Jinja code in our models. We will look at Jinja in more detail in the second part of the book. For the moment, note that double curly brackets symbols, {{, are used to print out values from Jinja expressions.

We then expect that the {{ ref('my_first_dbt_model') }} line will print out the proper SQL name to reference the table or view containing the first model.

Analysis of schema.yml

The first rows of this configuration file are the following:

```
01
02    version: 2
03
04    models:
05        - name: my_first_dbt_model
06          description: "A starter dbt model"
07          columns:
08            - name: id
09              description: "The primary key for this table"
10              tests:
11                - unique
12                - not_null
```

The second line declares the version of the configuration file.

The fourth line declares that in the next rows, we are configuring some models.

The fifth line identifies a model by its name and line six declares a description for it.

Line seven declares that we start configuring the columns for the selected model.

Line eight identifies the ID column (remember that in Snowflake, field names are case insensitive if not quoted) and line nine provides a description for it.

Line 10 declares that we will list tests that we want dbt to run on this column of this model, and line 11 requests a unicity test, while line 12 requests to test that the column is not null.

After these lines, we have a similar set of lines to configure tests and provide descriptions for the second model.

Using ref and source to connect models

We have seen from the lineage graph that this project has two models and that my_second_dbt_ model connects to the first one thanks to the following piece of code: {{ ref('my_first_ dbt_model') }}.

The `ref` function allows you to *reference a dbt model by its name* in a simple yet flexible way. When the model is compiled into SQL, the `ref` function will generate the correct fully qualified name to read from the correct table or view, according to the environment, user, and configuration.

In a very similar way, the `source` function allows you to reference a table or view that has not been created by dbt. By defining a source system, pointing to some DB and schema, and one or more table objects under it in a YAML file, we can then access them in a flexible way using the `source` function, as follows:

```
{{ source('source_system', 'table_object') }}
```

The exceptional power of dbt comes from the fact that when we run a dbt model, the mix of SQL and Jinja code in the model is compiled into pure SQL code for the target platform; *dbt generates all the boilerplate required to deploy the logic in your model to your DB*, so that your logic, or its result, is deployed to the DB as a view or a table with the same name as the model's filename.

The `ref` and `source` functions are the keystones of how dbt works; by using them, we provide dbt with the information needed to build the graph of dependencies of the whole project, and dbt is then able to generate the SQL code dynamically, making it simple to write a model once and deploy it to multiple environments.

When writing your SQL in a dbt project, you must always reference other DB objects by using the `ref` or `source` functions, depending on whether they are managed by dbt or not, so that the model will automatically generate the correct SQL name whenever you change the configuration or deploy it to multiple environments.

Running your first models

Now that we have looked at the models in the default dbt project and how to chain them, it is time to create them in our Snowflake DB. To do that, we need to run the dbt project.

To run all models of a project, you can simply type the following command in the command line, which you find at the bottom of the dbt Cloud IDE, or in the command line with dbt Core:

```
dbt run
```

The result of running the command is that dbt Cloud will open a panel where you can monitor the execution and inspect the results, as shown in the following screenshot:

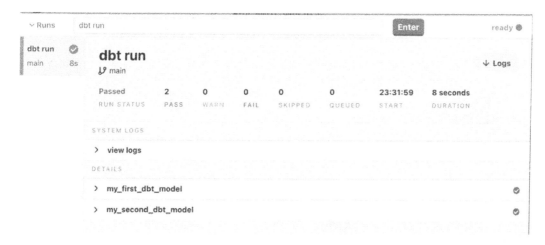

Figure 2.39: The execution results panel of dbt Cloud

You can click on **view logs** or on the name of any model to see the summary and detailed logs for their execution. Try both the **summary** and **details** views inside the models. In the **details** view of the models, you can see the actual SQL executed by dbt toward your DB.

Now that we have successfully run the models, dbt has generated the artifacts in the Snowflake DB. Now is a good time to build your understanding of where the models get generated, by looking at the results in Snowflake. Note that to see any changes, you need to refresh the Snowflake folder structure with the **Refresh now** button located at the top of the folder structure.

The following screenshot shows what you should see in your DB:

Figure 2.40: The artifacts of the default dbt project on Snowflake

Inside your Snowflake DB, named **DATA_ENG_DBT** in our example, you should have a schema with the name that you selected during the setup, **RZ** in our example, and inside that schema, you should have the two models, as shown in the previous screenshot.

Great, we have successfully executed the models and generated the desired artifacts!

Are we done? No, producing working models is one important step, but making sure that they do what you expect is arguably even more important, so it is time to talk about tests!

Testing your first models

Tests are as good as your understanding of the problem and the effort you put into them, so you should put at least the same effort into testing that you put into writing the code.

The ability and simplicity of adding useful tests to your code are the key points that set dbt apart from other ways of building data platforms, but be warned that tests are code and too many tests bring maintenance costs, with a little extra safety, and wrong or brittle tests are even worse than not testing a feature or model.

What should we test? How do we achieve the right balance?

We will discuss testing in more detail in the second and third parts of the book, but for now, note that it is especially useful to test your assumptions about the data that you will transform, such as the uniqueness and non-nullability of keys and fields that you rely upon, and the results of business logic that you feel to be complicated or not well understood.

Let's look at what tests we have in this default project.

This project has declared four tests using the generic `not_null` and `unique` tests for each of the two models. You can find them declared in the `schema.yml` configuration file, which we analyzed at the beginning of this section, where we reproduced the first half, including the tests for the `my_first_dbt_model` model (at lines 11 and 12).

You can now run the tests with the following command:

```
dbt test
```

Do not be surprised if you have an error; this is intentional, so you can see how errors are reported, and it gives us the opportunity to learn how to fix errors.

Figure 2.41: The results of the first test run

From the previous screenshot, we can see that we have an error. You can open the dropdown of the failing test and look at the summary, which in this case tells us that we have only one row that is failing the test. Looking at the details view, you can see the actual query, which is run as a test, and you can even copy and paste it into a new statement panel of the IDE to run the query on your DB.

In this case, looking at the code of the model, also analyzed previously in this section, we can see that it produces only two rows, one of which has null as a value for the id column.

We have found where the error is, so let's fix it.

First, as this is an out-of-context example, we need to agree on what the correct situation is:

- The correct logic is that the id field must not be null, so we need to fix the model
- The correct logic is that the id field can be null, so we need to remove the test
- This is an example of where writing a test that does not follow the correct logic causes more work than not having it

Let's assume that the right logic is the first one, so we want to fix the model. We'll do that in the next section.

Editing your first model

In dbt Cloud, you cannot edit while you are on the main branch so this is what we are going to do:

1. Create a new branch.
2. Edit the my_first_dbt_model model in the branch.
3. Run and test the modified project to check that it now works correctly.

Creating a new branch

The dbt Cloud IDE offers a simplified git workflow, so to create a new branch, all you need to do is click the **create new branch…** button on the top right of the VCS area.

Then, enter a name for the branch, without spaces, such as `fix-first-model`, and hit the **Submit** button. The VCS button will be disabled while the branch is created.

After a few seconds, the VCS button will be re-enabled and change to **open pull request…**. The branch name you selected will be under it and you are now able to edit the project files.

Modifying your first model

To fix the fact that one row has a `null` value in the `id` field, we want to edit the model.

Find the `my_first_dbt_model` model in the navigation panel on the left, opening the `models` folder and then the `example` folder, and click on it to open it in the editor.

Now, you can simply replace `null` on line 16 with any number that you like. Note that it is important you use a number, as line 14 produces a number for the `id` column and therefore, Snowflake will infer the number data type for that column.

When you are done, hit the **Save** button on the top-right side of the editor, or press *Ctrl + S* to save your changes.

Running and testing the updated project

Now that you have made the changes to the model, it is time to deploy it to your DB by running the models in the project and then testing them to check that everything is now working.

As you did before, you can now run the project with the following command:

```
dbt run
```

Run the tests with the following command:

```
dbt test
```

Now that all the tests have passed, congratulations, we are done with the changes!

In a real situation, you should bring the new working code back to the `main` branch, by opening a pull request, as the VCS button suggests, and then completing it to merge the changes back into `main`. For this introductory chapter, we will stop here, as we will come back to the simplified git workflow in the second part of the book.

Summary

Congratulations!

In this chapter, you have completed the setup of a world-class environment completely in the cloud and you have started to use dbt Cloud to edit and deploy your project to your DB.

You opened a GitHub account and created your first repository, then created your dbt Cloud account. Then, we walked through creating your first dbt project by connecting dbt Cloud to the GitHub account you just created and to the Snowflake account you created in the first chapter.

We then compared the dbt Core and dbt Cloud workflows and started to learn how to use the dbt Cloud IDE by trying out some SQL code from the first chapter.

In the last part of this chapter, you explored the default dbt project, learning about the `ref` and `source` functions, and how to run, test, and edit the models of a dbt project.

In the next chapter, *Data Modeling for Data Engineering*, you will learn the basics of data modeling and how to represent data models.

Further reading

If you want to learn more about git and how it works, the best place to start is the git website at `https://git-scm.com/`. You can even download a full book on git from there.

In this chapter, we have used the dbt default project to get you acquainted with both the dbt Cloud IDE and how dbt works, but there is much more to say about it, so you may be interested in the following sources:

- The dbt documentation at `https://docs.getdbt.com/docs/introduction`
- The dbt reference at `https://docs.getdbt.com/reference/dbt_project.yml`

3

Data Modeling for Data Engineering

In this chapter, we will introduce what a data model is and why we need data modeling.

At the base of a relational **database**, there is the **Entity-Relationship** (**E-R**) model. Therefore, you will learn how you can use E-R models to represent data models that describe the data you have or want to collect.

We will present the E-R notation, cardinality, optionality, and the different levels of abstraction and of keys that you can have in a data model, and we will introduce two different notations commonly used in the industry, throughout the different examples that we will discuss.

We will explain a few special use cases of data models, such as weak entities or hierarchical relations, discussing their peculiarities or how they are usually implemented.

We will also introduce you to some common problems that you will face with your data, how to avoid them if possible, and how to recognize them if you cannot avoid them.

By the end of the chapter, you will have had an overview of the most important modeling styles and architectures in use in data engineering projects, discussing the pros and cons.

To close, we have a brief discussion of what our general approach in this book is, with reference to the styles and architectures that we have discussed.

In this chapter, you will learn about the following topics:

- What is and why do we need data modeling?
- Conceptual, logical, and physical data models
- E-R modeling
- Modeling use cases and patterns
- Common problems in data models
- Modeling styles and architectures

Technical requirements

This chapter does not require any previous knowledge of the topics of E-R models.

All code samples of this chapter are available on GitHub at `https://github.com/PacktPublishing/Data-engineering-with-dbt/tree/main/Chapter_03`.

What is and why do we need data modeling?

Data does not exist in a vacuum. Pure data without any surrounding knowledge rarely has any value. Data has a lot of value when you can put it into context and transform it into information.

Understanding data

The pure number 1.75, as you find it in a column of a database, by itself does not say much.

What do you think it represents?

It could be 1.75 meters, kilograms, gallons, seconds, or whatever unit you want to attach to it.

If instead of the pure number 1.75, you have 1.75 meters or 1.75 seconds, you already understand it much better, but you can't really say that you know what this data is about yet.

If you have 1.75 meters in a column called `width`, then you know a bit more, but good luck guessing what that number really represents. If you also know it is in a table called `car`, `product`, or `road`, you can probably understand much better what it really represents.

By following through this very simple example, you should have started to see that to really understand what data means, data alone is not enough; you need to have some surrounding information that puts the data in the right perspective.

What is data modeling?

Data modeling encompasses the activities to provide a clear context for your data, at multiple levels.

In the most common interpretation, a data model is a visual representation of the data, in the context you are analyzing.

An important part of data modeling is naming, such as in the example that we have seen previously, which provides the basic layer of semantics, while another important aspect is to explain how different pieces of data are related to each other.

To be effective at conveying information, a data model must be simple to read, and this means limiting the amount of information to a specific level of detail that is generally inversely proportional to the size of the domain considered. For this reason, it is common to refer to three levels of detail that we will see later in this chapter: conceptual, logical, and physical data models.

The typical components of a visual data model are as follows:

- **Entity**: An entity is a concept that we want to analyze, a thing of interest that we want to collect data about, such as a car, an order, or a page visit

- **Attribute**: An attribute is a property of an entity for which we want to store values, such as a car plate, a customer, or the total amount of a transaction

- **Relationship**: A relationship is a connection between two entities that are related to each other and captures how they are related, such as the ownership relation between a car and its owner, or the purchasing relation between a customer and a product

These three components allow us to describe data and relations between data in a concise way. We will see in the next sessions of this chapter that we can express this information with multiple notations and that we can complement it with other tools to clarify the data semantics.

As an example, we show in the following figure an E-R diagram, which is a common way to represent a data model (which we will describe in the next section). This sample diagram describes two entities (**Owner** and **Car**) and a relation between them (**owns**). The diagram also represents two attributes of **Owner** (**Owner_ID** and **Owner_Name**) and two of **Car** (**Plate** and **Model**):

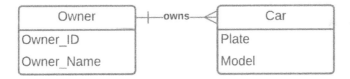

Figure 3.1: A sample E-R diagram

A visual model such as an E-R diagram is a useful starting point, but it is not enough to convey all the information useful to build or properly use a data platform, and many data teams understand that it should be complemented by more information.

Why we need data modeling

Data modeling is all about conveying information so that those that work with the modeled data can better understand it and each other.

Data modeling is generally used in two main contexts:

- To describe what data should be generated or collected by an application or in a project.

    In this case, we build the data model before having the data.

- To describe some data that already exists.

    In this case, we reverse-engineer the data model from the available data.

This distinction is crucial because in the first case, you have the freedom to design a model how you need it to be according to the needs of the use case, while in the second case, the data is given, that is, it already exists, and consequently, the data model can only reflect how the data is, with no real freedom of modeling.

In data warehousing, we always start with the second case, as we get data "as is" from source systems, and if we do not have a data model of the source system, we reverse-engineer one that describes the data to the best of our knowledge.

Usually, we have multiple source systems, with quite different data models, even if they contain similar data, and a goal to integrate data from them. The typical situation is that none of the models from any of the source systems are easy to understand for the analysts nor ideal to answer the business needs.

We therefore end up transforming the source data to build a new target data model that should be simpler to understand and satisfy the business needs as much as possible and makes it possible to combine the desired data from the different source systems.

A good practice is to explicitly design this new data model before coding the transformations, drawing at least one model that represents the business concepts that are the goal of the integration and will form the refined targets of our transformations. This model can be at a high level of abstraction, describing the business and only the main entities, or at a greater level of detail, already representing the technical design.

This is different from the situation in the first case because building this new target data model is a constrained exercise, and the modeler should keep in mind the starting models because the further the new data model lands from the sources, the greater the need for extra information, such as mapping tables and master data, and work to transform the data and the higher the risk of losing or altering the original data, introducing errors.

Having an explicit target model simplifies the collaboration and provides a clear goal for the project. It is also a good starting point to analyze whether we are missing any information or need mapping tables or business rules to go from the source system data sets to the desired target model.

This target model can also be interpreted as the set of all the business concepts and their relations that are needed to power the reports in the desired data marts. In fact, the best way to identify the concepts that should be in the target data model is by going backward from the desired reports to the business concepts.

> **Note**
>
> We will often refer to data marts and reports, as that is the most common use of data marts, but consider that a data mart is just a way to provide a well-thought-out set of tables to satisfy a use case, be it a report an AI/ML model, exporting data, or something else.

The next step is to identify the needed connections from these concepts to the data in the source systems, identifying when we are missing some connection or change keys and need mapping tables, business rules, or master data.

Complementing a visual data model

We have seen that a data model is a communication tool, and the concise nature of a visual data model makes it a great tool to convey some technical information, while other important aspects for data engineering projects, such as the semantics or business rules, are not clearly expressed using only the standard components of a visual data model.

We therefore suggest complementing the visual data model with other kinds of documentation that can better convey these kinds of information.

Descriptive documentation, such as a wiki or a glossary, is a great way to explain the semantics of the entities and attributes that appear in your data model, build alignment on the meaning of the terms that you use in the model, and explain important business rules that are vital to be understood besides the technical implementation details.

Another important aspect is to properly describe how we derive the data in the new destination data model starting from the data sources. This is called data lineage.

When you use dbt, it is easy to keep this information close to the code, and some information, such as the data lineage, is automatically generated from the code itself.

Now that we know what data models are, their purpose, and why they are useful, it is time to dig into more detail. In the next section of this chapter, we will introduce the different types of data models, and in subsequent sections, we will look at notations to express them and some examples and problems. We will close by looking at different modeling styles and architecture that frame the use of data models.

Conceptual, logical, and physical data models

Data models can be designed with slightly different notations, but no matter how you design them, a model that describes everything in your data project would be as complex as your database and become too big to be useful as a communication tool.

Furthermore, when working on a data engineering project, you have discussions with different people, and these discussions focus on different levels of detail with respect to the data, business, and technical aspects of the project.

It is common to refer to the following three types of data models, which differ in the level of detail:

- **Conceptual data model**: This is the most abstract model, defining *what will be in the domain of the project*, providing the general scope
- **Logical data model**: This model provides much greater detail, defining *what the data will look like*
- **Physical data model**: This is the most detailed model, describing exactly *how the data will be stored in the database*

In the following subsections, we will describe these three types of models.

Conceptual data model

The conceptual data model is the least technical of the models, as it is used to *capture the most important entities and relations at the business level.*

This model identifies the core master data entities and their relations, defining what will be in the domain of the project, providing the general scope and naming.

A good starting point for drawing it is to identify all the entities that are needed in the desired reports, clarifying the semantics of the entities so that they become clear to all people involved in the project.

This model must use real business entities and relationships that are relevant for the real-world business and usually does not contain attributes or other technical details, such as system-specific names or attributes.

It is created between data architects and business stakeholders and should be complemented by a collection of the most important business rules and constraints.

Because a conceptual data model describes the real business as it is in reality, with real-life entities, it is expected to be valid across different projects that touch on the same domain.

Example of a conceptual model

The following conceptual data model uses the UML notation to provide a simple, business-level data model of orders and returns:

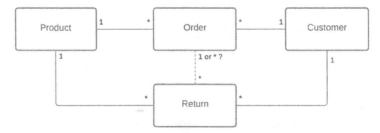

Figure 3.2: Conceptual data model of orders and returns

Despite its simplicity, this model already opens up discussions with the business and captures some interesting information, such as whether there is a data connection between returns and orders or not, or whether a return can be related to only one order or even multiple orders.

While it is true that we might figure out this info by analyzing the source data, it is also true that digging out everything from data is slow and error prone, also because business rules such as these change over time.

Having both the data and the expected rules from the business allows us to spot inconsistencies before they reach the reports and the users.

Logical data model

The logical data model is a technical model that defines how the data will be organized, without yet committing to a particular technical implementation.

This model starts to identify the key attributes of the entities, such as **Natural Keys (NKs)** and **Business Keys (BKs)**, which will be used to identify the entity instances or to connect to other entities or reference tables. It also identifies key measures and categorizations that are important for the use of the data.

This model also includes operational and transactional entities, supporting tables, and mapping and reference tables as needed, depending on the part of the domain that is in focus.

It is usually developed between the data architects and business analysts to provide a detailed map of what needs to be developed and how it will work. It must be complemented with all the non-trivial business rules and data structure specifications.

When a good conceptual model exists, this model can be built and refined incrementally as the project approaches the different areas of the domain.

Example of a logical model

The following logical data model is drawn using the crow's foot notation, which is the simplest and most common for E-R diagrams. The model represents only the order part from the example in the conceptual data model:

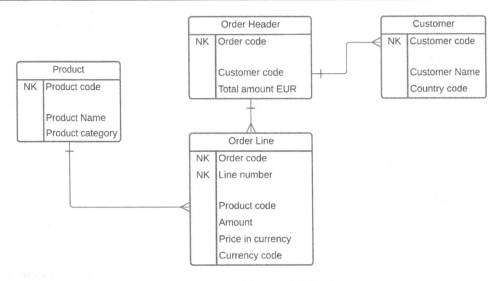

Figure 3.3: Logical data model of orders

You can clearly see that this logical model has much more detail than the conceptual model, providing the natural keys of the entities and some key attributes of interest for the business or developers. It has also split the order conceptual entity into its implementation with a header and a detail table.

If we also had the return part, we would have the opportunity to describe what the relationship between orders and returns is. It could be at the header level only, or a return line might have a reference to a specific order line.

> **Tip**
>
> Consider that changing the cardinality of a relationship can trigger major changes or the need for substantial reworking, so *when in doubt, opt for the most relaxed constraint* that you think you might ever need to accommodate the data (such as one-to-many instead of one-to-one, or many-to-many instead of one-to-many), and if you expect a stricter one to apply, add a test to see if/when it is violated. Taking this to an extreme, the **Data Vault** (**DV**) methodology always uses many-to-many, so you are always ready for whatever unexpected situations may arise, and everything works out the same way.

General considerations on the level of detail of models

The level of detail for both conceptual and logical data models is not fixed at all, so you can have very basic logical models that just identify the entity keys and are very close to conceptual models. You can also have very detailed logical models that split the entities into all the existing types and show the intermediate and support tables. In this example, we could have two types of orders, an order master data table and the two mapping tables to map them to the master data, plus a currency conversion table used to convert from local currencies to the desired common currency.

It is very common to start with a simple, basic version of a data model and then make detailed diagrams for parts that are considered difficult or unclear. Another common occurrence is that detailed diagrams are done for only the first parts to be developed, while they might not be needed if the other parts can be developed with a similar pattern.

Models are a communication tool that is especially used to clarify complex situations, so if in our example the monetary conversion for returns is similar to orders, a detailed diagram might not be needed if all the stakeholders are already clear on the situation.

Physical data model

The physical data model describes the actual implementation of the data model in a specific database. The name physical indicates it is extremely detailed, actually one-to-one with the DB definitions and can often be used to generate the commands to instantiate the database or be created by reverse-engineering of the database.

This model includes the **Primary Keys** (**PKs**), indexes, and everything needed to instantiate the database, including the conversion of many-to-many relations into associative tables.

Such a detailed model used to be much more important in the past when a key part of a data project was to squeeze out as much performance as possible from very expensive machines that had to be accurately dimensioned, bought, and then used for a period of years.

Nowadays, with the advent of SaaS cloud data warehouses with near-infinite scalability and the ability to pay only for what you consume, the focus has moved on to delivering quickly and performance is mostly guaranteed by best practices, coming into focus only when runtimes or costs start to be out of desired ranges.

We are not going to provide an example of a physical model as they are becoming less relevant in data warehousing because of a few factors, such as the increased amount of semistructured data and the ability of modern cloud databases to work well without the need or ability to define constructs such as indexes and relationship or unicity constraints that are core contents of physical data models.

> Important note
> When working with dbt, the physical tables or views in the database will be created for us by dbt at runtime from our code and the metadata in our project. We do not need to write or maintain scripts to accomplish that.

Therefore, it makes no sense to spend a lot of energy on manually creating and then maintaining a physical model that becomes stale at every change in our dbt models, and we will not even use to generate the table/view creation scripts. It is much better to have a stable logical or conceptual model and up-to-date documentation with the details of the generated views/tables.

Tools to draw data models

Many tools exist to help you draw these models.

At a basic level, there are many general-purpose drawing tools that have the ability to draw UML and/or E-R diagrams. They are generally easy and cheap to buy, but they are limited to just the visual aspect of a diagram.

There are also modern, web-based tools such as Ellie (`https://ellie.ai/`) that are designed to help you draw conceptual and logical models in real time, while discussing them with the business stakeholders. They help you collect much more than the visual E-R part, so that you can also gather descriptions, key fields, and metadata and it allows you to generate very useful business glossaries.

There are also tools to assist you in drawing the physical data model or reverse-engineer it from the database, such as SqlDBM (`https://sqldbm.com/`). As we have seen, the physical models are less useful for the part that you will produce with dbt, but it may be useful to collect the models from source systems.

Now that we know that there are different levels at which we can express a data model and how to draw them, in the next section, we will look at a couple of notations to express data models.

In the next sections, you will find some examples to improve your understanding and we will also describe some problems that we face when working with data models. We will closely look at different modeling styles and architectures that frame the use of data models.

Entity-Relationship modeling

In the previous sections, we briefly defined the three components of an E-R model: entity, attribute, and relationship. We have also seen a few E-R diagrams, drawn with different notations such as UML or crow's foot.

In this section, we will define in a bit more detail the E-R models and show how different cases can be represented in these two common notations (UML and crow's foot).

Main notation

We have already introduced the three components of an E-R model. In this section, we explain how they are represented visually in E-R models:

- **Entity**: This is represented as a box with the name of the entity inside

  If attributes are shown, the entity name is at the top and often in bold or bigger and visually separated from the attributes

- **Attribute**: This is represented by the attribute's name inside the box of the entity it belongs, with one name per line

- **Relationship**: This is represented by a line joining the entities involved in the relationship and optionally the name of the relationship close to the line

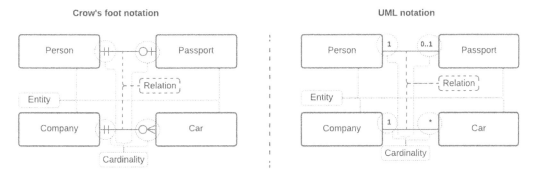

Figure 3.4: E-R notation basics

In the previous figure, we have illustrated two of the most used notations at a level of detail that you generally use to describe a conceptual model. In this example, in fact, we do not show keys and attributes, but you have already seen an example with attributes and keys in the example describing the logical models in the previous section of this chapter.

This example also illustrates cardinality, which is another core aspect of an E-R model, which we will describe in the following section.

Cardinality

The **cardinality** of a relationship indicates how many instances of one entity on one side of the relationship participate in the relationship with how many instances of the entity on the other side.

Let's see the possible cases using the crow's foot notation:

- **One-to-one cardinality**: This is quite a rare case where only one instance of each entity participates on each side.

  An example is the relationship **Person** *has* **Passport**: one specific person has zero or one (active) passports, and one passport belongs to exactly one person. Note that if the **Passport** entity semantic was not intended to record only the current active passport, we would have a one-to-many relationship, as a person can have multiple passports over their life. Also, some countries allow having more than one active passport at the same time, so it is really important to correctly understand and describe the semantics of each entity in the domain.

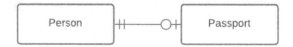

Figure 3.5: E-R sample model for one-to-one cardinality

- **One-to-many cardinality**: This is the most common type of relationship, where one entity on one side participates with many entities on the other side.

  An example is the relation **Company** *produces* **Car**: a company produces many cars, and a car is produced by exactly one company. The **Person** *owns* **Car** relationship shown later might be a good example of one-to-many, depending on the semantics of **Person** and *owns*.

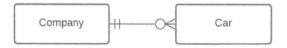

Figure 3.6: E-R sample model for one-to-many cardinality

- **Many-to-many cardinality**: This is a relatively uncommon case where many entities on one side participate in the relationship with many entities on the other side.

  An example is the **Student** *follows* **Course** relationship: a student follows one or more courses, otherwise loses their student status, and a course is followed by zero or more students.

Figure 3.7: E-R sample model for many-to-many cardinality

The following figure illustrates the representation of the cardinality used in the crow's foot notation and the UML notation, including the same **Person** *owns* **Car** relation in both notations.

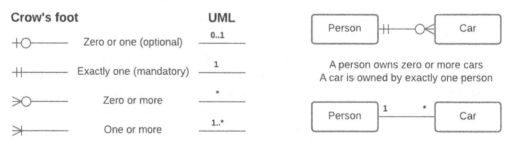

Figure 3.8: Visual representation of cardinality in two different notations of E-R diagrams

Finding out the cardinality

What is the reasoning process to follow to understand cardinalities or find them for your model?

The answer is simple: you think of a generic entity on one side of the relation and with how many entities on the other side of the relationship it will be related in your domain.

As an example, one person uses only one passport to pass through customs, so you would say cardinality of one in such domain, but a person can have multiple valid passports from different countries at the same time, and most people will have multiple passports over their lifetime, with only one valid at a given time. Changing the domain or the time perspective might change the cardinality of a relationship.

On the other side of the same relation, a passport will always refer to a single person.

Now that we have seen the components of the notations, it is time to look at a third dimension that heavily influences the outcome of the model that we will draw: the time perspective.

Primary key, foreign key, and other types of keys

When working with data models, one crucial aspect is how to identify an instance of an entity, such as a specific car, company, or person.

A field or set of fields that can be used to uniquely identify one instance of an entity is called a key for that entity. Examples could be the plate and state or the **Vehicle Identification Number** (**VIN**) for a car or the **Social Security Number** (**SSN**) or a unique combination of personal data, such as name, surname, birthdate, and place of birth, for a person.

Keys are classified with a few names:

- **Primary Key** (**PK**): This is the field or set of fields that uniquely identifies an instance of an entity. Primary indicates that it is the key that is used to ensure a unicity constraint on the entity. It is the main key used to determine whether two rows relate to the same instance or not when storing data.

- **Natural Key** (**NK**): This is a key that has a business significance and uniquely identifies the instances of the entity in the given context. An NK also exists outside of the database world. It is something printed on forms or that a person might use to identify an instance of the entity in the real world. An example could be the plate for a car inside a state or an email for a user inside a system.

- **Surrogate Key** (**SK**): This is a key that has no business significance and is used as a key inside the system that generated it. An old way to generate SKs was to use sequences. A more modern way is to use hash functions. SKs are often used to simplify identification, especially when no good NK exists or when NKs or PKs are made of multiple fields.

- **Foreign Key** (**FK**): This is a field or set of fields in one entity that matches the key of another entity. The field names do not have to match, as long as the content does.

One field or a combination of fields used as a key can fit more than one of the preceding definitions. As an example, a VIN field can be both an NK and a PK for a car entity, and an FK for a trip entity.

> **Important note**
>
> Two instances of an entity with the same key are considered the same instance, or more precisely, two versions of the same instance, and cannot be stored in the entity table at the same time without violating the key definition.
>
> Operational databases usually enforce the unique constraints declared on keys, preventing inserting a new row with an existing key. In contrast, reporting databases Snowflake, BigQuery, and most columnar databases do not enforce the unicity constraints, even if they allow defining them, so you can end up having two instances with the same key in a table, generally called **duplicates**.
>
> Duplicates are usually created because of the bad quality of input data or errors in the SQL code, often arising from a wrong understanding of the data model of the source data. They are a serious problem that should be avoided and closely monitored with tests.
>
> So-called history or historicized tables allow storing multiple versions of the same instance by adding an implicit version identifier, which is often a timestamp, to the original key of the entity.

We have little control over NKs because they exist by themselves and are defined by the business case and the domain. There is, instead, more freedom in choosing a PK for our tables and we can always decide to create a new SK to take the place of another key.

Some good advice is to use the available keys, if possible, but not to hesitate to create a SK when a reliable and simple key does not exist. As an example, when we have a composite key, creating a SK from the combination of the multiple fields of the composite key is often a compelling proposition. This in fact makes a lot of operations much simpler. Never use sequences to create SKs, it has many drawbacks.

Implementing cardinalities

Let's have a look at how the relationships of an E-R model can be implemented in relational database systems.

The simple case is when one of the sides of the relationship has a cardinality of one. In this case, the other entity can have a reference to this one entity. A reference is implemented as a field, or a set of fields, matching a key (usually the PK) of the entity with a cardinality of one.

In our **Company-Car** example, if the PK of a company is **Company_ID**, then the **Car** entity will have a field matching the value in **Company_ID**. That would be an FK in the **Car** entity pointing to the PK of the **Company** entity and the simplest solution would be to give the fields on both sides the same name, but that is not required.

Let's look at some details for the specific cardinalities:

- **One-to-one cardinality**: In this case, both entities could have a reference, an FK, to the other entity, but that is usually not a good idea as you get into the chicken-egg problem, and you also risk having inconsistencies. The best solution is usually to have the FK only in one of the two entities, usually the optional entity. If both sides are mandatory, then you might consider uniting them into a single entity or table.

   In the **Person-Passport** example, a person exists even without a passport, but not the other way around, so having the **Person** FK inside the **Passport** entity is a good solution.

   Note that the two one-to-one entities might have the same PKs or NKs, but that is not required.

- **One-to-many cardinality**: This is the most common cardinality and the simplest case, as the many side will have an FK toward the one side. In our **Company-Car** example, each car will have a reference to the company that produced the car.

   As a note, consider that it would be possible to denormalize the data model and store the one side together with the many side, repeating its data every time that it is needed, such as repeating the company information for every car that is produced. This is almost never done in operational systems, as changing the information for the one side will be very impractical as you need to change many copies, and the size of the data would increase a lot. It is more common in the context of reporting and quite common in some contexts such as marketing reporting on BigQuery and when using Google Data Studio.

- **Many-to-many cardinality**: This is a case where model and reality cannot align. An FK in an instance on any of the two sides can only contain one reference to the other side and cannot therefore correctly contain the multiple references needed for a many-to-many relationship.

   To represent this kind of relationship, we need an extra table besides the two tables for the entities. This extra table is called a join table; it has as the PK the combination of the PKs of the two entities, and it is the many side of a one-to-many relation with both original entities.

   This third table is very often created as a new entity that represents the many-to-many relation and also records attributes of each instance of the relationship. One example is to create an **Order** entity between **Customer** and **Product** or an **Enrollment** entity between **Student** and **Course** that have a many-to-many relation.

Figure 3.9: Alternative representations of a many-to-many relation

While the cardinality of a relationship is the main driver in a data model and its implementation, the time perspective, which we will discuss in the next section, is one of the main drivers behind the semantics of the entities that are part of a context and therefore are used in a model.

Now that we have seen the basics of E-R modeling, it is time to look at a dimension that heavily influences the outcome of the model that we will draw: the time perspective.

Time perspective

Another important aspect that we have not yet discussed is if and how the time perspective will influence an E-R model. The short answer is yes, it will, and often, this remains an implicit assumption, remaining mostly underexplained.

An E-R models a part of reality and expresses the constraints, or business rules, that a system trying to capture that reality should abide by. The role of the system, and specifically its time perspective, deeply influences the semantics of the entities, what rules are in force, and therefore the model that describes the entities and relations in that context.

Consider an application that manages a fleet of taxis. For that application, if you were to describe the direct relation between **Driver** and **Taxi**, you would say it is one-to-one, as a taxi needs a driver and a driver can drive one taxi at a time. This is pretty much the viewpoint of every application that uses an E-R model to describe how live objects collaborate and what they can do at a certain point in time.

Figure 3.10: Relation between Driver and Taxi in a live application

In this case, it is clear that a driver drives one taxi and one taxi is driven by a driver at a time, so the upper bound is one, but what about the lower bound? Well, both **Driver** and **Taxi** make sense without the other, as a driver can have a day off or be available as a backup, and a taxi still exists even when it is not being driven.

The same kind of reasoning can be true for every operational application that has been designed to satisfy the operational needs only, without consideration for reporting.

In some cases, even in an operational application, the time perspective becomes embedded into intermediate entities that the organization already uses, such as shift, contract, performance, and so on. These are entities that have been created to keep track of the individual instances of a relationship over time.

We join the two perspectives to correctly represent reality by having a constraint that these time-based entities should not overlap with respect to the entities that can appear only once at a time.

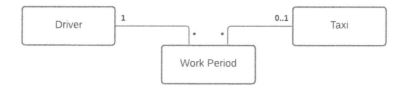

Figure 3.11: Relation between Driver and Taxi mediated by Work Period

When we work in data engineering projects, we usually adopt a lifetime perspective, meaning that we are interested in a relationship over the life of the involved entities.

In this data warehousing perspective, we would probably consider that, over the period covered by our data, a driver will drive multiple taxis and that a taxi will be driven by different drivers too.

The relation between **Driver** and **Taxi** will then be considered a many-to-many relation. This would still be the case even if our data platform captures the changes from an operational table that implements the optional one-to-one relation that we saw earlier in this section.

Figure 3.12: Many-to-many relation between Driver and Taxi

This relationship, like all many-to-many relationships, cannot be implemented directly in a database and it will eventually be implemented with the use of an intermediate association table that will store the period when a driver has been driving a taxi. This will look like the **Work Period** we saw earlier but being generated by us capturing changes happening on an operational table, it will have limited information and will be, at best, as precise as our ability to capture changes to that table. In fact, we risk losing some changes if our replication is not complete, as is the case when we have periodic table exports.

The best situation for a data warehousing project is to have a time-aware entity, such as **Work Period**, in the source system, because we will not risk missing periods and, most probably, we will collect better and more complete data.

An example of an E-R model at different levels of detail

A data model is only one of the many possible ways to represent a real-life situation and as we have seen, the appropriate level of detail of a model depends on the intended use of the model.

In the following example, we show that the same situation of a student that enrolls in **Course** instances can be represented in multiple ways, depending on the abstraction level of the model.

In the case of a conceptual model, a high-level model that just states that a **Student** can enroll in multiple **Course** instances and a **Course** can have multiple **Students** be enrolled might be enough, as shown on the left of *Figure 3.13*. Both sides are optional because a student can be not yet enrolled in any course, or a course can have no students yet.

If we are building a data warehouse, we want to dig a bit deeper, and if this relation is important for the business, we would like to try to record more information about the **Student-Course** relationship. We therefore introduce an **Enrollment** entity between the two original entities with the purpose to record the desired information about the student enrolling in the course.

In this case, both **Student** and **Course** are mandatory in their relations with **Enrollment**, as the latter will not make sense without either of the two original entities.

The simple many-to-many relation of the initial conceptual model has been converted into an indirect relationship, broken down into two one-to-many relationships.

Figure 3.13: The same reality, at two different levels of detail

In the next section, we will look at another common type of relation between entities: generalization and specialization.

Generalization and specialization

In the following figure, we look at another topic arising from representing models at different levels of abstraction to introduce the notation to express generalization and specialization. It is not so widely used, possibly due to a lack of generalized knowledge and standardization, but it is very useful:

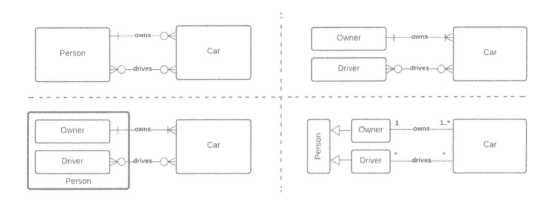

Figure 3.14: Different ways to express the same Person-Car model in E-R diagram models

In this model, we want to express that a person might own a car, becoming an owner, and regardless of whether they own a car, they can eventually drive multiple cars. The two things are independent. A car always needs a person to own it (that being an owner) and it can be driven by multiple people, or just sit there having never been driven.

In the top-left model, we have the most general one, which could be a conceptual model. It makes no distinction between the different roles of **Person** in relation with **Car**.

In the top-right model, we have highlighted the two roles that a person can have, but we have left out the **Person** entity. This could be the starting point for a logical model.

In the lower left model, we have introduced one way to represent generalization relationships, with the general entity containing its subtypes. This kind of notation is used mostly with the crow's foot notation.

In the bottom-right model, we have used the UML notation with the explicit notation provided by UML for the generalization-specialization relation.

Please note that relations involving supertypes and subtypes can be drawn in the way considered to best represent reality. In the same diagram, some relations could be drawn toward the general and some others toward specialized entities.

In our case, the **drives** and **owns** relations were meaningful for the subtypes, but if we also drew a **Person** "is transported by" **Car** relation, it would make more sense to draw it toward the **Person** supertype, leaving the other relations on the subtypes.

Now that you know about data model types and how to represent a basic data model, in the next section, you will find some examples to improve your understanding. Later, we will also describe some problems that we face when working with data models and will give a close look at different modeling styles and architecture that frame the use of data models.

Modeling use cases and patterns

This chapter introduces the use of E-R diagrams to represent conceptual and logical data models in data engineering projects, but we have seen that the same modeling concepts are also used to design data models for applications and everywhere we want to describe how different pieces of data are related.

In the next sections, we will present a few common use cases of data structures and their models, some known problematic cases, and finally, we point to the whole area of data model libraries.

Header-detail use case

One of the ubiquitous cases when working with data is the header-detail data structure. It is so common that I am pretty sure you have already seen it somewhere.

As an example, it is used in invoices and orders, and almost anywhere else where there is one document with multiple lines of detail inside. The common document info goes into the header **entity** with the detail lines represented by one or more **weak entities** depending on the header. A weak entity is an entity that does not have any meaning without the header entity, such as an order line without an order header.

The following models illustrate, at different levels of detail, the **Order-Order Line** case, including the **Order** relationships to the surrounding **Customer** and **Product** entities:

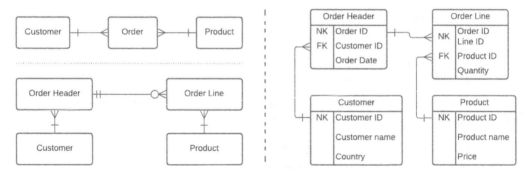

Figure 3.15: Different abstraction levels for an E-R model

In the top left of this figure, we have a very high-level conceptual model where **Order** is just a single entity. In the bottom left, we have a more detailed conceptual model where **Order Header** has been separated from **Order Line** and the connections to **Customer** and **Product** are assigned where they belong.

On the right, we have a logical model that has the same detail as the conceptual model in the bottom left but adds details about the NK of the different entities, together with some important attributes.

Looking at the logical model, it is easy to be tempted to just assume that a line number would be a good addition to the **Order** PK to provide a PK for **Order Line**. This might be the case, but it is important to have a clear semantic for it. The problem that we always have with weak entities is that their key does not have a real business meaning and the assigned key might not be a stable key, meaning one instance of the weak entity might not always have the same key, or the same key might indicate different instances over time.

Let's walk through an example to illustrate the problem. Assume that on the first day, we have one order with five order lines and each line uses the order ID plus its line number as a key. On the second day, we get an update of the same order, and now it only has the first three lines, unchanged; this might not yet be a problem as we get three lines with the same PK and content as the day before and we should just mark line four and five as deleted. On the third day, we get another update and now the order has four lines, with the first three unchanged and the fourth line having a totally new product. If we just use the line number to produce the PK, we would have this new line getting the same PK as the fourth line of the first day.

Should we consider that the fourth line from day 1 is back, undeleted, and changed or is this to be considered a new line?

The best solution would be to have a proper PK of weak entities, such as by having a stable line number as it would be the case if the new line showing up in the third day had a line number equal to 6, as number 4 and 5 were reserved for the now deleted lines that used them first.

It is very rare that weak entities have proper, stable keys as the architects of operational systems are generally not aware of or concerned with these kinds of consequences affecting downstream systems using the data they generate.

The same is almost always the case for weak entities coming from JSON structures, as it is typical for REST APIs that elements embedded into a JSON object often do not have an identifier, let alone a proper, stable key.

Unfortunately, there is not a general way to alleviate the problem if we are not in control of how the data is generated, but we can at least try to carefully understand the semantics of the data that we receive and ensure we are in control of how we model and store it.

Implementation notes

In principle, we could implement **Order** as a single table, with one line for each order line, and repeat the information that we have stored in the order header in each line.

This single table, also known as the denormalized form, would have quite a few drawbacks, such as duplicating the same information many times over, and worse, making it difficult to maintain consistency, as a change in the header information would need to be applied to all the rows of the order. Furthermore, queries such as counting how many orders a customer has placed become complicated.

The header-detail solution provides a few benefits, such as guaranteed consistency and simplified maintenance, plus most queries are easier as you can query the table that holds the information you need or join there if you need data from both tables.

That said, the denormalized form is sometimes used as a final form to run reports on, as it has the performance advantage of not needing any joins. This is also very simple to use by people not skilled in data modeling that would not be able to create a join.

Hierarchical relationships

Hierarchical relationships are very common and generally are a special case of one-to-many relationships. They represent data structures that look like a tree.

The common pattern is that one instance depends on another higher/bigger instance of the same entity, unless it is itself one of the instances at the highest/biggest level.

They are special for two reasons: they are usually built on top of one entity only, which is both the starting and ending point of the relationship, and they are recursive, meaning that they can have an unbounded level of nesting, as you do not have a limit to how many times you can traverse through the relationship.

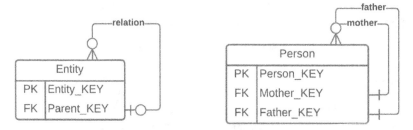

Figure 3.16: Single and multiple hierarchical relationships

While the most common way to represent relationships is a single table, it is also possible to just have one table with the list of existing entities and their attributes, with a second table used to just represent the recursive relationship. This is similar to what we show later for many-to-many recursive relationships, just with a one-to-one relationship between the **Entity_KEY** fields.

The relationship is always implemented with the smaller unit, sometimes called the child, pointing toward the bigger unit, called the parent. The child is the many side and therefore has a field containing the PK to the parent, as it is in all a one-to-many relationship.

Note that in the previous figure, we have left the **Mother_KEY** and **Father_KEY** fields as mandatory, but that will probably only be accurate in theory. While it is true that everybody must have a genetic father and mother, the reality is that some will be unknown, and we certainly cannot trace all the way back to the first human. The given model is correct in theory, but a more pragmatic approach would be to make those two relations optional, as we have done for the generic **Entity-Parent** case where **Parent_KEY** has zero or one multiplicity.

Some common examples of hierarchical relationships are as follows:

- **Employee-manager**: Every employee has one other employee it depends on, which is its line manager, unless it is the CEO or someone else who does not depend on anyone, and an employee might have zero or more people reporting to them.

- **Organizational units in a company or companies in a group**: A company is usually made up of a number of smaller parts, which in turn are split into smaller parts. These are usually called organizational units and they make up at least one hierarchy, even if it is common to have more than one. The same goes for groups that are made up of companies that are then split into organizational units. While the strict legal ownership might not be linear or one-to-many, it is usually the case that there is a simple hierarchical structure implemented to manage the group, so as always, be aware of the semantics of what you are modeling.

- **Categories/subcategory**: This is a very common situation and usually, it is a top-down one-to-many hierarchy, as this makes it simple to roll up totals from the lower level to the upper one by summation. In these cases, be aware of the relations between the items that are categorized and drive the numbers toward the categories.

  If you do not have a simple top-down relation, such as when a product belongs to more than one category, then you are not able to just sum up the numbers, as you have a many-to-many relationship between the categories and the numbers. This is a case of fan trap, which we describe later in this chapter.

- **Bill of Materials (BOM)**: This is a common occurrence in production organizations.

  A BOM represents the lowest-level parts needed to build a finished product; think, as an example, of everything that is needed to build a car or a piece of furniture.

  The parts are products themselves and often make up an intermediate product that needs to be assembled or sourced, creating a multilevel hierarchy.

- **Work Breakdown Structure (WBS)**: A WBS represents all the tasks needed to complete a project. It is usually represented by progressively smaller subprojects, which are tasks themselves, building a multilevel hierarchy of tasks.

In the following figure, we represent some of the cases discussed here, with the others following the same schema:

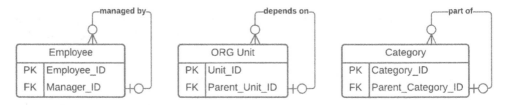

Figure 3.17: Examples of hierarchical relationships

In cases when it looks like an entity might have multiple parents, it is usually the case that we have multiple hierarchical relationships that can be separated into individual singular dependencies.

Examples can be the **Parent-Child** relation, where there are always two parents that exist for every child, a father and a mother; you can then represent these two independently and fall back to the same **Person** entity having two hierarchical relations on itself: father and mother. Another similar example is in organizational units where you might have different reporting lines, such as legal ownership or sales organization.

In all the cases where you are faced with the possibility of multiple parents, I suggest you look hard for multiple parallel relationships. When it is really the case that you can have multiple parents, then you have a many-to-many relationship and therefore you need a supporting table that holds the entity key and its parent, as is normal in many-to-many relationships. The following figure shows this:

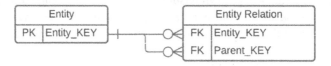

Figure 3.18: Many-to-many hierarchical relationship

Hierarchy exploration

A bit of a confusing aspect of hierarchies in the relational world might be that the relationship is represented from the bottom up, every entity pointing to its eventual parent, but its exploration is usually done from the bottom down, starting from the top-level entities, the ones without parents, and adding one layer downward at every step, attaching to each visited entity its children.

Hierarchy exploration is usually done using recursive code, with a step down in the hierarchy being a recursive step. The following pseudo-code illustrates the process:

```
1. Get the initial entities, the ones with no parent;
   process and store them
```

2. Get the entities that have one of the stored entities as parent;
   process and store the new entities
3. repeat step 2 until you keep finding new entities;

Let's look at an example of creating a table for a recursive entity and querying it to produce the hierarchy.

The following SQL code will create a table with eight rows of data representing people working in a fictional company and their management relationship:

```
CREATE OR REPLACE TABLE DATA_ENG_DBT.PUBLIC.Entity as
SELECT * FROM ( VALUES
  (1, null::Number, 'President'),
  (2,1,'VP Sales'),
  (3,1,'VP Tech'),
  (4,2,'Sales Dir'),
  (5,3,'Lead Architect'),
  (6,3,'Software Dev Manager'),
  (7,6,'Proj Mgr'),
  (8,6,'Software Eng')
) as v (Entity_KEY, Parent_KEY, Entity_Name);
```

The following SQL code uses a recursive **Common Table Expression (CTE)** to navigate the hierarchy and calculate some useful information while walking over the hierarchy:

```
WITH recursive
ENTITY_HIERARCHY as (
  SELECT
      Entity_KEY
    , Parent_KEY
    , Entity_Name
    , 1 as level
    , '-' as parent_name
    , Entity_KEY::string as key_path
    , Entity_Name::string as name_path
  FROM DATA_ENG_DBT.PUBLIC.Entity
  WHERE Parent_KEY is null
  UNION ALL
  SELECT
      ENT.Entity_KEY
    , ENT.Parent_KEY
    , ENT.Entity_Name
    , HIER.level + 1 as level
    , HIER.Entity_Name as parent_name
    , HIER.key_path || '-' || ENT.Entity_KEY::string as key_path
```

```
      , HIER.name_path  || '-' || ENT.Entity_Name::string as name_path
    FROM DATA_ENG_DBT.PUBLIC.Entity as ENT
    JOIN ENTITY_HIERARCHY as HIER ON HIER.Entity_KEY = ENT.Parent_KEY
  )
  SELECT * FROM ENTITY_HIERARCHY;
```

The following table shows the results of the query:

E_KEY	P_KEY	ENTITY_NAME	LEVEL	PARENT_NAME	KEY_PATH	NAME_PATH
1		President	1	-	1	President
2	1	VP Sales	2	President	1-2	President-VP Sales
3	1	VP Tech	2	President	1-3	President-VP Tech
4	2	Sales Dir	3	VP Sales	1-2-4	President-VP Sales-Sales Dir
5	3	Lead Architect	3	VP Tech	1-3-5	President-VP Tech-Lead Architect
6	3	Software Dev Manager	3	VP Tech	1-3-6	President-VP Tech-Software Dev Manager
7	6	Proj Mgr	4	Software Dev Manager	1-3-6-7	President-VP Tech-Software Dev Manager-Proj Mgr
8	6	Software Eng	4	Software Dev Manager	1-3-6-8	President-VP Tech-Software Dev Manager-Software Eng

Table 3.1: Table with the results from the recursive query

By analyzing the code of the recursive query, you can see that the CTE is made up of two parts: the anchor part before UNION ALL and the recursive part after it.

The anchor part uses a query to fetch the initial set of rows and set the initial values of the calculated fields.

The recursive query uses a join between the base table and the content of the previous recursive iteration, accessed by the name of the CTE, to retrieve the next layer of entities and update the calculated fields.

Looking at the results, you can see that with this kind of data structure and query, you can calculate fields over the full path traversed in the hierarchy.

You can refer to *Chapter 1* for more info on CTEs.

Forecasts and actuals

In companies, it is very common to have budgeting and forecasting processes that try to predict some figures in the future and then want to analyze them by matching the different forecasts done over time with the actuals once they become known.

One of the peculiarities of the model in this case is that between the source data model and the reporting data model it is common to create two very different data models even if the entities involved do not change.

Generally, we have one actual value for each period and unit, and many forecasts that have been done over time for the same period and unit. We therefore have a one-to-many relationship between **Actuals** and **Forecasts**.

When we want to analyze **Actuals** and **Forecasts** together for reporting, we want to be able to associate the actual figure, once it is available, with each forecast. We can therefore consider them as two subclasses or specialized versions of the **Figures** entity, which is the common generalization.

In the following figure, we use the UML notation to visualize the source data model and the reporting data model, which uses the generalization-specialization notation. It is important to note that generalization is not a relationship in the E-R sense but indicates derivation:

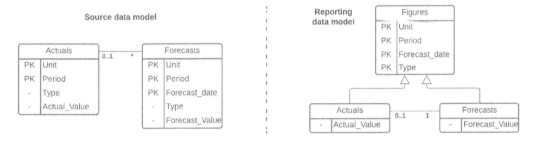

Figure 3.19: Data models for Actuals and Forecasts

The specialized entities are made up of the attributes inherited from the general entity plus the attributes specific to the specialized entity.

While it is possible to implement the reporting model in multiple ways, the most common is to have all specialized entities in a single table with one column for each different attribute of all the specialized entities. Compatible attributes, such as **Actuals_Value** and **Forecast_Value**, in our example, are stored in the same field, to make their use/comparison simpler.

When going from the source data model to the reporting one, we have to take the existing actuals and make a copy of them for each forecast over the same period and unit. This is simply done with a join from the **Actuals** to the **Forecasts** table. If the number and dates of the forecasts are known and reliable, it is possible to produce the desired copies of the actuals using business logic, which can be as simple as making one copy for each forecasting date in a known number of previous months.

Libraries of standard data models

Given the frequent use of data models, there are people who specialize in that field and there are also multiple books describing in detail collections of data models that apply to common situations that companies encounter in general or in specific industries.

These collections are sometimes called libraries of data models, as the idea is to use them to pick the right model for your use case as you pick a function from a code library.

These models are very detailed and very general in their application, not being immediately intuitive given their size, but giving peace of mind that they will be able to capture company data in a correct way. Those models are seldom used "as is," especially in data engineering projects, but can always provide an interesting insight into how different entities interact with each other.

John Gilles, in his book *The Elephant in the Fridge*, introduces a series of 12 general data models that cover most needs of a company.

If you would like to get to know more about data models, I suggest you start with those. Also, you might be interested in reading John's book and it will also provide you with a good explanation of how to collect the information to build a data model. You will also learn the foundations of another data engineering methodology called DV, which we will briefly present in the next section of this chapter as it has many overlapping ways of working with the methodology presented here.

In the *Further reading* section, you also have a reference to the much bigger and more detailed work *The Data Model Resource Book* by Len Silverston, which provides a full library of universal data models.

Now you know about data model types and how to represent a data model.

In the next section, we will describe some problems that we face when working with data models. We will then close the chapter by looking at different modeling styles and architecture that frame the use of data models.

Common problems in data models

Creating a correct data model is only the beginning of providing a good data platform, as users of these data models must also be aware of problems that can arise because of the nature of operations on relational models.

In the following section, we present the most common problems you will encounter.

Fan trap

The **fan trap** is a very common problem that can happen every time you have a join in a one-to-many relationship. It is not a problem of the relationship, but of how you might use it.

The fan trap problem causes the calculations done on measures joined from the one side of the one-to-many relationship to be wrong.

This is only a problem if you use a measure that is on the one side of a one-to-many relationship, when grouping/working at the granularity of the entities on the many side. This happens because the join will duplicate the measures to match the cardinality of the many side.

Let's look at a simple example based on the following data model. In the model, we have company sites where some units are based. Sites have a **Site_surface** measure and units have a **Unit_Budget** measure:

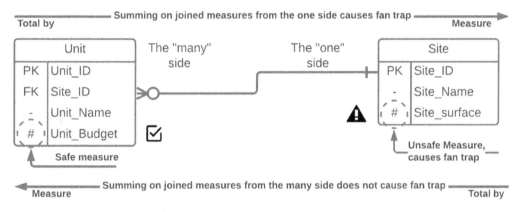

Figure 3.20: Data model with potential for a fan trap

To understand the fan trap, you have to recall that when joining two tables that have a one-to-many relation, the occurrences on the one side are repeated for each instance of the many side that has a match with their key in the join.

At the end of the join, you end up with a table with the same number of rows that you had on the many side, with columns on the one side filled by repetitions based on the matching key.

Let's show an example of joining the following two **Unit** and **Site** tables:

Unit_Name	Site_ID	Budget
Unit_1	Site_1	100
Unit_2	Site_1	130

Site_ID	Site_Name	Surface
Site_1	HQ	2500

Table 3.2: Unit table, many side   Table 3.3: Site table, one side

The result of joining the **Site** and **Unit** tables on the **Site_ID** key looks like the following table:

Unit_Name	Site_ID	Budget	Site_ID	Site_Name	Surface
Unit_1	Site_1	100	Site_1	HQ	2500
Unit_2	Site_1	130	Site_1	HQ	2500

Table 3.4: Unit and Site tables joined by Site_ID

As you can see from the joined table, we now have two measures, **Budget** from the **Unit** table, which has not been duplicated, and **Surface** from the **Site** table, which has been duplicated for each unit matching a site key.

We can therefore have two cases of calculations done with these metrics:

1. **Total on a measure from the one side**: If we try to calculate a total over the **Surface** measure, we are going to have problems. This is because we will sum the same value for every copy that has been created by the join:

     i.   If we group over the one side, using **Site_ID**, we have the wrong values for every total and, of course, the grand total will also be incorrect.

     ii. If we group over the many side, using **Unit_Name** or the ID, we do not really have a sum, as there is one line for each ID, and we cannot say whether the value for the total surface for each unit is really meaningful, but we are sure that the grand total will be wrong, as it will multiply the surface value for the number of units matching the site. Thinking about the meaningfulness of the results, can we say that **Unit_1** and **Unit_2** both use a surface of 2,500? I guess not.

2. **Total on a measure from the many side**: This is the safest bet. In fact, if we try to calculate a total over the **Budget** measure, we are not going to have problems. This is because the **Budget** measure has not been duplicated by the join. We can therefore group by the one or the many side and both the totals and the grand total will be correct.

How can we deal with the fan trap?

The simple, limited use case-specific solution is to group the many side with the one side before joining them. This has the undesired effect to remove all the dimensions with lower granularity than the one side we are starting from, but it allows us to get correct numbers on the measures of the one side.

One example from our sample model could be to group the **Unit** table by **Site**, calculating the total budget by site, and then joining the grouped table with **Site**. This will be a safe operation as now we have a one-to-one relation between **Site** and the grouped table.

A better understanding and a more general solution to deal with fan trap issues is to use the **Unified Star Schema (USS)**, as explained in the book *The Unified Star Schema* by Francesco Puppini.

Chasm trap

The **chasm trap** is another very common problem that we face in reporting.

In essence, a chasm trap is an unmanaged and often unintentional many-to-many relationship.

Because it is unmanaged, it becomes an unintended partial Cartesian product.

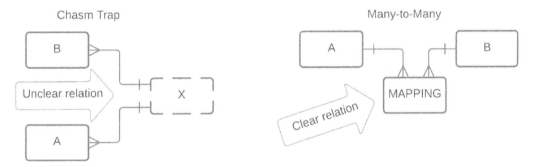

Figure 3.21: Chasm trap and a correct many-to-many relationship model

The previous figure illustrates *the scenario for chasm trap: having two tables with a common key that is not unique in both tables.* Tables A and B both have an FK toward table X, so the key appears multiple times on each table. Please note that table X is not needed for the chasm trap problem to exist. It is there to show that tables A and B have a key in common and also because the "shared dimension" is the most common case where we immediately see a chasm trap.

In a chasm trap scenario, instead of a full Cartesian product, you will have a key-constrained Cartesian product: the rows on one side will be cross-joined with the occurrences of the same key on the other side, de facto making a per-key Cartesian product.

The difference between a chasm trap and a real many-to-many relationship is that in the latter you have the mapping table that limits the Cartesian product to only those occurrences that make sense. In the many-to-many case, you enter the mapping with one key, you have the designated M rows that give the actual mapping, and then you move to the other table where you only have one row, so in the end, you have only as many rows as there are in the mapping table. This make sense because the mapping table is built to represent a specific relationship.

In the chasm trap case, you enter the mapping table with M rows matching a key in one table and you find N rows with the same key in the other table, in the end producing MxN rows joined on that key, but you have no actual relation between the rows of the two tables as the common FK is there to express a relation from the two tables toward the table that has that key as a PK, not to express a relation between these two tables.

The classic case for a chasm trap is having two facts, **A** and **B** in the previous figure, with a common dimension, **X**. The dimension is not needed, but it is often what enables the unintended and unmanaged indirect relationship to be used in a **Business Intelligence (BI)** tool.

The following figure provides an example of the potential usage of multiple unintended relations causing chasm traps between the **OrderDetail** and **ReturnDetail** fact tables. Joining the two tables on one or more of the common FKs is not going to produce sensible results, as there is no information about what instances on one side are related to the other side:

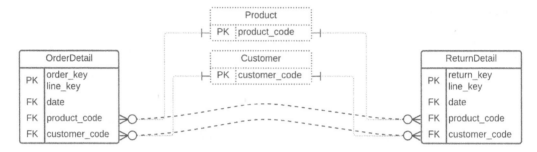

Figure 3.22: Example of chasm traps between facts with shared dimensions

As an example, consider that not every return of a product is related to all the orders of the product, and the other way around, which is what you would get with a join on the product code.

The result is that *the chasm trap causes an exploded number of rows*. The explosion is not as big as the full Cartesian product because the multiplication is on key-by-key counts and not total-by-total counts, but it is generally very significant and generates the following problems:

- **Slow performance**: Taking already-big tables and multiplying their size by a non-trivial factor has the potential to make the calculation very slow. The approximate factor of the multiplication is the product of the average occurrences of a key on each side. If you have on average 10 occurrences of a key on one side and 20 on the other side, you can expect the join to be 200 times bigger than the starting tables.

- **Wrong numbers**: As the measures on one side will be repeated for each occurrence of the same key on the other side, the summation will mostly be totally out. The same is the case for eventual measures coming from the X table, as they will be multiplied too.

- **Missing results**: If one of the two relationships toward the PK is optional, then you will miss some rows, as in the join, you will find only the keys that exist in both tables.

  Tawke as an example the case of orders and returns; if you join them on **Customer** without thinking of the consequences, you will not find any orders for each customer that has not done a return, while you will have every order multiplied by the number of returns for the customers who have done returns.

Why do perfectly good data models generate these problems?

The short answer is that two tables that have an FK in common, such as a customer key or a product key, are probably related in some way, but the common key alone is not enough to express the possibly multiple and complex relations between the two tables. Trying to extract information without enough data in general does not provide meaningful results.

Let's look at an example: take the case of orders and deliveries, but the same would also apply if you also considered related tables, such as returns or payments.

They all have a reference to **Customer**, **Product**, or both, but what would be the point of joining orders and deliveries by customer? Having each order from a customer paired with each delivery to that customer does not make much sense.

It makes sense to match the grouped orders for the customer with the grouped deliveries to that same customer, so you can compare summarized data for that customer and do all calculations you want with the summarized measures. Having a one-to-one match between the summarized tables will provide perfectly good results, without any duplication.

It also makes sense to match a single order with the deliveries done to deliver that specific order, but to do that, you need more data than just the customer and/or product keys. If the delivery has the order key, then you are all set because you have the relation you are looking for.

If you do not have that key, you might be lucky enough to be able to use some logic to try to do some exact or approximate match between orders and deliveries, but you must use more info than just the customer and/or product with the ultimate goal to try to allocate each order and delivery so that you do not have duplicates. A real relation provided by the data is one thing; it's another thing to have an approximate one based on some heuristics.

As always, the semantics of the data that you have and of what you want to do should be your best guide. Refrain from joining two tables just because they have an FK in common.

Now that you know about data model types, how to represent a data model, and its possible problems, we will close the chapter by looking at different modeling styles and architectures that frame the use of data models.

Modeling styles and architectures

In this chapter, we have introduced data modeling and seen how it is used to describe the data we have or how we want it to become.

Data modeling is the basic tool to describe the data but building a data platform is more than describing the data hosted in the platform and the relationships between the various entities. As an example, how you load new data into the tables and how you update all the intermediate tables to keep your data marts up to date is a key point that is not captured by a data model.

In the next chapter, we will look in more detail at the overall data life cycle, but in this section, we want to introduce a few design styles that are heavily connected to how you develop data models for your data platform.

The great news is that with dbt, there are no preferences or limitations, and you can adopt any of these different paradigms and implement whichever will work best.

We will start with the Kimball method, which introduces the star schema, which most of the time will be the model style for the data marts used by your BI tools to access the data.

A word of caution before we begin: each of the following subjects has been explained in more than one book, so we will not try to teach you them in any detail. The goal of the following sections is to give you a starting idea about some of the most common paradigms you might encounter and discuss some of their features and problems.

At the end of this chapter, there is a list of books if you want to look in more detail into these topics.

Do not worry if you do not understand or cannot follow all topics. We will come back to many of them in the rest of the book, as we will try to pick the best out of these approaches.

Kimball method or dimensional modeling or star schema

Probably the most ubiquitous design style in the data warehousing world is the **dimensional model** from **Ralph Kimball**, which is the de facto standard in the BI area.

The signature feature of the dimensional modeling design is to produce a data model structure called a **star schema**, which is the access interface to the data for BI tools.

In a star schema, a **fact table** containing the events or records containing the measures of interest is surrounded by several dimension tables. A **dimension table** is a denormalized table that contains the descriptive data at the lowest level of detail that you want to access and should not contain measures (in the original Kimball definition) to avoid the fan trap issue. A **measure** is a number that you want to use for calculations.

The following figure shows a typical star schema organized around an **Order** fact:

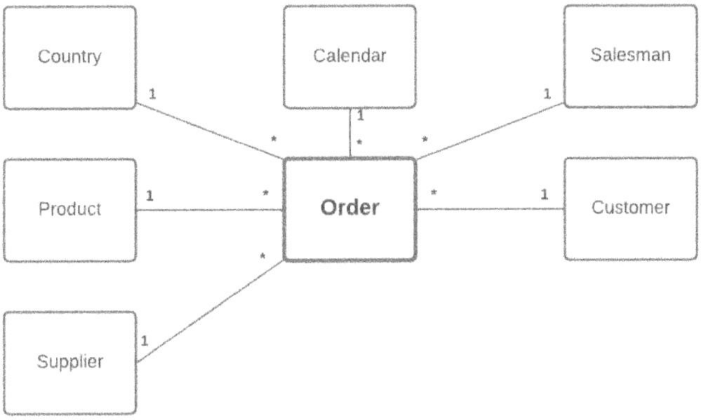

Figure 3.23: Example of a star schema

The main advantage of a star schema is its simplicity, which makes it very simple to query and easy to understand even for non-technical people.

The simple pattern in use is that each row in the fact table contains the FK to the dimensions, such as **Product_ID** or **Country_Code**, and the measures, such as **Amount_ordered**, **Price**, and **Discount**.

The relevant FKs are used to join on the needed dimension to retrieve the descriptive data desired in the specific report, such as the product name, the customer's name or address, or the VAT code.

Given its simple structure and exclusive use of many-to-one relations from the fact to the dimension, it is also very performant to query and therefore well suited to provide data for interactive reporting.

The dimensional modeling design style has the objective to build these facts and dimensions starting from the source data. In principle, each fact might be joined with its own set of dimensions with different keys and columns, but you can see that having a different customer and product for each different fact will create a huge number of similar but different dimension tables.

The concept of **conformed dimension** is used to avoid the multiplication of dimension tables and integrate the data from different systems. A conformed dimension is just a dimension, but it is designed to be used by all or at least most of the fact tables that are interested in such descriptive data. It must therefore be at the smallest granularity needed and must contain all columns of interest in all reports that have to be built on all facts that use the dimension.

The Kimball data warehouse methodology uses a matrix with facts in rows and dimensions in columns to prioritize the addition of conformed dimensions and facts. The matrix describes the content of the star schema that surrounds each fact.

The data processing in a Kimball data warehouse is based on transforming the incoming source data to build the needed conformed dimensions. The transformations are done as directly from the data sources to the facts and dimensions as possible and the facts and dimensions are the structures that store the data. This network of facts connected to dimensions is the central data model of the data platform in a Kimball warehouse.

> **Tip**
>
> A *data mart* is a collection of data, generally a small subset of all the available data, that is selected to satisfy the BI needs of a specific business area, such as a department, or use case.
>
> The idea is to provide a limited number of tables, and often a reduced number of attributes in those tables, which makes it easier for analysts to find the desired data and produce correct reports.
>
> A data mart often comes in the form of a handful of facts and the relevant dimensions to provide one or more star schemas that are used to analyze these facts in the context of the selected subject.
>
> The collection of the available data marts is the only external interface that most users have to access the data platform, so it is extremely important that the names and semantics of the available tables, such as facts and dimensions, and attributes are clear.

We have seen the main concepts of a Kimball warehouse, so let's also look at some of its downsides:

- According to the original definition, there should not be measures in dimensions, because if you have them and you use them for calculations involving the fact, you always have a fan trap. Not having or not using important metrics like the price in a product dimension is very limiting, so in practice, we have measures in the dimensions, then you should be aware when a Fan Trap is triggered.

- Another limitation according to the Kimball rules is that facts are only connected to dimensions, not other facts. But some of the most interesting analyses are built by using data from multiple facts, such as orders and deliveries or returns. Kimball star schemas do not help here, so you can look at other methodologies, such as the USS, or write your own SQL to produce a new joined fact to be analyzed.

- The Kimball method is oriented to report business processes, not build a data view of the enterprise, so the facts and conformed dimensions might not handle other reporting needs besides the ones that the star schemas were designed for.

- The process of loading and storing the data from the data sources is deeply intertwined with the implementation of the business rules because the conformed dimensions and the facts are both the goal of the business transformations and the primary storage for all the data.

This causes the code to have a high level of complexity and many reasons to change, as any change in a data source or a business rule might cause all the transformations between the data source and the final dimensions to be reworked, including fixing the existing data. This can also easily spread to connected facts and dimensions, causing a very high rate of code changes compared to the business needs. This becomes even more acute as the project becomes bigger, because more facts connected to one dimension create more potential for that dimension to change.

- Having the main data storage in the facts and dimensions, which are produced after many technical and business transformations, makes it practically impossible to know what the original data looked like and is risky as it might be impossible to undo the application of a wrong or changed business rule to correct it or apply a new business rule to old data.

- Storing the history of changes for a dimension is not easy when it has also to be integrated with the business rules, so very often, the dimension just stores the current values.

The greatest contribution of the Kimball methodology is the star schema, which is the de facto standard for the delivery layer in the majority of modern data platforms, as most BI tools expect such a model, with facts and dimensions organized in data marts.

Building the core of your platform with the Kimball methodology is a bit surpassed, and it is not commonly done anymore nor the one we suggest.

Unified Star Schema

The USS is an extension of the Kimball star schema that addresses some of its limitations, such as the fan trap and the impossibility to query more than one fact at a time without the risk of a chasm trap.

The USS produces a single star schema with the Puppini Bridge at the center like a super fact and all the dimensions around it. This makes it extremely easy to use for every kind of user as the data model is fixed and trivially simple, while powerful enough to answer more BI questions than a full set of data marts.

The technical solution that allows the USS to innovate and provide more answering power than the usual star schema is that the super fact, named Puppini Bridge after its inventor, uses the UNION ALL operator to produce a single table that has all the facts and dimensions encoded inside it, with every row having and potentially using an FK to all dimensions.

The real marvel is that every row in the Puppini Bridge encodes a full path of relationships between all the tables used to build the USS. Their relationships and how complex they are, independently from being facts or dimensions, are therefore already correctly processed and their measures are stored in the Bridge at the right granularity so that no fan trap or chasm trap occurs.

We can look at an example of the TPCH database available in the Snowflake sample database. The following figure shows the **Oriented Data Model** (**ODM**) from the USS methodology that always represents one-to-many relationships as an arrow going in the lookup direction, that is from left (the many side) to right (the one side) with the arrow pointing to the one side of the relation:

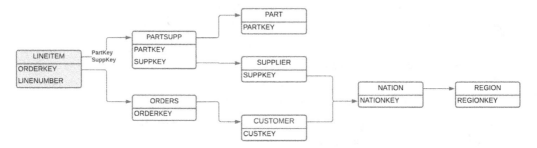

Figure 3.24: The ODM for the TPCH database

The following figure shows the final star schema for the TPCH database with the **USS TPCH** super fact at the center and all existing dimensions around it:

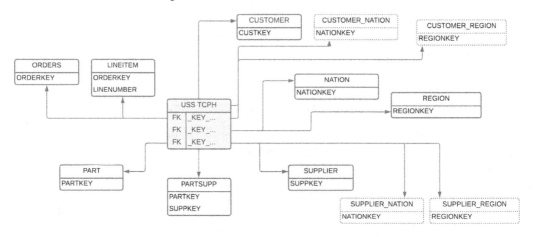

Figure 3.25: The star schema for the USS super fact of the TPCH database

The **USS TPCH** super fact will have one row for each row in any of the facts and dimensions and all keys from all the tables, plus the measures from the facts and dimensions. You can now understand that each row is able to encode a relation between any of the tables.

Of course, a single USS cannot encode all possible relationships between all the tables of interest to a company, as is the case of **Nation** and **Region**, which have two possible paths in the TPCH database, but the ability to decide on and encode a full "preferred" path of a relationship, such as **LineItem** => **Orders** => **Customer** => **Nation** => **Region**, allows having stable and clear semantics for the specific USS and produces correct and consistent results.

In the figure, you can see that there are some dotted dimensions. These are examples of aliases, a technique that the USS can adopt to increase the number of relationships that you can represent while eliminating ambiguity (is **Country** the customer country or the supplier country?).

We have included the following figure to give you an idea of what a classic Kimball star schema could look like in this simple database

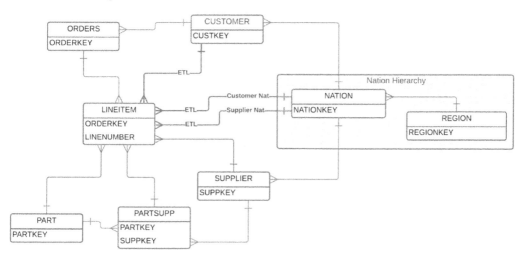

Figure 3.26: A classic star schema for the TPCH database

You can see that many of the existing relationships cannot be directly used or represented in the star schema, such as **Customer-Orders**, but an ETL process is needed to take that relation and turn it into a relation between **Lineitem** and **Customer**.

Similarly, if you do not want lose the relationship between **Nation** and **Region**, you have to build a new dimension containing the **Nation Hierarchy**. Because many of the dimensions are not directly connected to the facts, we need an ETL process to follow the correct relationship paths and store the result in the fact.

As a last note, I want to make clear that the USS can take the place of any normal star schema as it is to all effects a perfectly compliant Kimball star schema, with a few tricks up its sleeve.

The USS is therefore very well suited as the delivery star schema for all situations where there is interest in giving the users the ability to safely query a wide array of facts and dimensions that would be impossible with the normal star schema. This is often referred to as **self-service BI**.

If you want to know more about the USS, I suggest you read the book that introduces it: *The Unified Star Schema* by Bill Inmon and Francesco Puppini, listed at the end of this chapter.

Inmon design style

Bill Inmon is considered the father of data warehousing, and together with Kimball, he has shaped most of the way data warehouses have been built.

The signature concept of the Inmon design style is the goal to create a corporate-wide, integrated, and interoperable data repository. While Kimball was working to satisfy the need for reporting, Inmon tried to build a repository of data that describes the organization and its business processes, providing a company-wide single source of truth.

The goal is therefore to identify the business concepts, that is, the entities, that describe the company and how it works and take the input source data and turn it into homogeneous data under the correct concept. To avoid redundancy and maximize the expressive power, the data is normalized in **Third Normal Form** (**3NF**), and all interesting relations can be captured between the desired concepts.

The delivery of data for reporting needs is done through data marts that are built to satisfy the information need of a specific business area. The business concepts stored in the data warehouse end up being very close to the facts and dimensions or used to produce the facts and dimensions that we find in a Kimball star schema and data marts. You can have a data warehouse built and organized according to Inmon design and then you produce facts and dimensions pretty much as we have seen in Kimball style.

The main difference in this case is that the data warehouse layer stores a richer set of concepts and relations than the minimum required to power the desired facts and dimensions.

As you can imagine, the goal of enterprise-wide data integration requires an enterprise-wide effort with commitment from top management for an extended period of time.

An important advantage of the Inmon model is that the data warehouse founded on enterprise-wide business concepts is very resilient to changes in the business as well as in technical source systems.

Because it expresses the company's business processes, the Inmon data warehouse has the data to answer most reporting questions, even the ones that were not initially identified.

The main drawbacks are the wide scale and complexity of the process, requiring a highly skilled data modeler and experts in data warehousing to code the ETLs, maintain the platform, and create/update the data marts when new reporting needs arise.

Another drawback is that the main storage of the data is in the form of business concepts, after a lot of transformations and application of business rules that make it hard to go back to the original data. This exposes the data warehouse to the need for re-work and makes it impossible to audit the original data. While this is similar to the issue we have seen about the Kimball design style, we have to say that the Inmon business concepts preserve much more information than the simple facts and dimensions of the Kimball style.

Data Vault

DV is a data platform-building methodology invented by Dan Linstedt.

The current incarnation, **Data Vault 2.0 (DV2)**, was released in 2013 and keeps evolving as technology, data platforms, and use cases evolve.

The DV2 methodology encompasses an architecture, model, way-of-working methodology, and implementation, but the most famous and signature element is the DV model.

The most central idea in DV is that *all the information is aggregated around the identified business concepts* and data is integrated by the BK. Concept definition and identity management are two important cornerstones of DV2.

The signature DV model is based on these three core elements:

- **Hub**: Contains all the unique instances of BK for the concept of the hub
- **Link**: Contains all the unique instances of a relationship between hubs, as a tuple of BKs, providing a very flexible many-to-many relation
- **Satellite**: Contains the changes over time of the descriptive information connected with a hub or link

The DV methodology provides an array of specialized versions of these core elements for use in specific situations, plus a few other elements, such as point-in-time and bridge tables.

The following figure shows an example of a simple DV model:

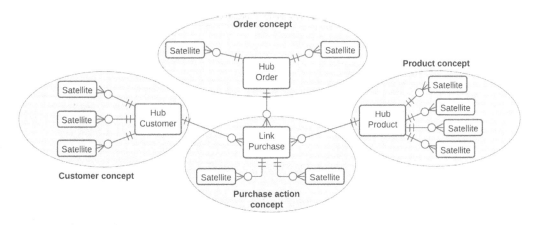

Figure 3.27: Example of a DV model

As you can see from the figure, all the relationships are one-to-many and the side of the hub always has a cardinality of one, as one key tenet is that all keys for a business concept are stored in the hub for that concept.

The link only records the existence of one relationship between the connected hubs, using their BKs, and allows recording a many-to-many relationship between the hubs. This enables us to keep using the same structure for all kinds of relations, even storing data with different cardinalities coming from different sources or allowing a relation to evolve from one-to-many to many-to-many without any changes in the model or the code.

The identities of the business concepts of the domain are stored in a hub dedicated to this concept, the relationships are encoded using links, one for each relationship, and the descriptive data is stored in as many satellites as needed.

As you can see in the figure, the satellites are the descriptive data containers that can be attached to a concept when we need to store some new information. They just depend on the BK of the concept they belong to.

Building and understanding a DV model requires an elevated level of training in data modeling and the specifics of DV, to avoid any possible pitfalls, such as creating source-centric DVs instead of business-centric ones.

The other key element that distinguishes DV from the previous modeling styles that we have seen is the DV architecture, illustrated in the following figure:

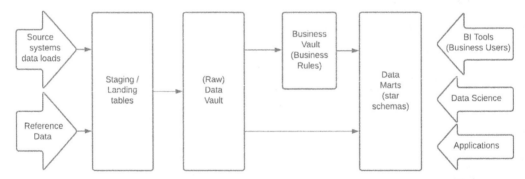

Figure 3.28: DV architecture

The external data from source systems, the reference data and the master data, are loaded into staging tables that are not supposed to alter the incoming data, keeping the good, the bad, and the ugly. We only apply hard business rules that align data types, add metadata, and eventually apply normalization. The idea is that we must be able to audit what came in from source data.

The data loading process takes data from staging and loads it into the DV, where it is stored according to the DV model. The DV is the only place where all the history is stored forever. The load process uses patterns based on best practices, is automated and highly parallel, and is often automatically generated. This ensures speed of delivery and correctness of the code.

The data in the DV is still pretty much the source data, and therefore auditable, but it has been organized and integrated by business concept using BKs. The absence of modifications is a feature, not a problem, as it allows for auditing and gives us the possibility to go back and recalculate everything according to new business rules.

The business rules, that is the most specific part of the data platform, that varies in every use case, are applied in the **Business Vault** (**BV**), which takes the original data and applies all needed business rules to produce the refined versions of the identified business concepts.

The last step is taking the required data from the DV and BV to produce the **data marts**, where the data is usually organized according to the Kimball star schema, the USS, or whatever model your BI tool and users in your organization need to receive the information, that is, data understandable by business users.

The following is a list of logical and technical reasons why I like DV:

- The greatest advancement of DV is the *separation of the storage of the historical data from the application of the business rules*, which gives to each part of the architecture only one reason to change, drastically reducing the need for reworking to add or change a data source or to modify or add a business rule.

- The use of just three model elements, hub, link, and satellite, which are highly standardized, allows fully automating and automatically generating most of the loading logic.

- The use of **natural key** (**NK**), instead of **surrogate key** (**SK**) like sequences, greatly simplifies the ETL as there is no need for SK lookups; this allows for huge parallelism in the processing. Note that NKs can be used "as is", including composite keys, or through hashing or other transformations to build a single key field derived from the NK.

- The use of **Hashed Difference** (**HashDIFF**) fields to check changes between instances of an entity greatly simplifies and automates the loading patterns.

- The adoption of loading patterns that use *insert only queries to store and update a complete and auditable history* is a great advancement and enables the manipulation of billions of rows exploiting the scalability of the new cloud-based platforms.

- The ability to handle bitemporality, as in, when something happened versus when we got that information, is very important in some contexts, such as compliance departments.

The following is a list of reasons why I do not like DVs:

- The creation of a DV platform requires the presence of skilled data professionals with training and experience in DV2, which is a hard requirement to meet in many situations.

- DV models require a huge number of joins to collate all the bits and pieces of data back in the correct form. This is generally beyond the comfort zone of most developers and certainly out of reach for analysts and business users.

- The creation of a proper DV requires a thorough analysis of the business concepts of the domain under development. This requires sponsorship at a high enough level, some time, availability of experts on the business side, and someone who is able to put all that together.

The DV methodology has been able to adopt the best from previous design styles while adding noteworthy improvements: like Inmon, it puts business concepts at the core of the DV organization, but preserves original data; it uses the de facto standard Kimball star schemas to deliver easy-to-use data marts for the users of BI tools; it innovates by separating the ingestion and storage of source data from the application of the business rules, to decouple the two most challenging aspects of building and maintaining a data platform.

Given the common focus on business concepts, the following quote from Bill Inmon will not be a surprise: "*The data vault is the optimal choice for modeling the Enterprise Data Warehouse in the DV 2.0 framework.*"

In conclusion, we can easily say that the DV methodology is extremely attractive in all cases where the size of the development and the complexity of the requirements justify the availability of the highly skilled people required and the high-level sponsorship and visibility.

The good news is that dbt is well suited to support development with the DV methodology. To give you a quick start, allowing you to quickly apply the correct loading patterns, there is an open source dbt library named `dbtvault` that is available for download through the dbt hub at `https://hub.getdbt.com/datavault-uk/dbtvault/latest/`.

Data mesh

The hottest buzzword at the moment in the data world is **data mesh**, so let's have a look at it.

The data mesh approach was born in some of the most tech-heavy companies to obviate a very common problem that affects most of the data engineering industry: data ownership.

The pain is real and widespread: the people in charge of building the enterprise-wide unified data platform have no knowledge of the source data and the business; they receive at best weak support from their colleagues that run the business applications and have little to no opportunity or ability to interact with the key people that really understand the business and how data is used and interpreted on the business side.

In practice, nobody in the enterprise is the end-to-end owner of the data generated by an application or related to a specific business concept or domain. There are no common definitions, and the semantics of the same concept may be slightly different according to the domain you are in. Will you get the same answer if you ask "*What is the definition of a customer?*" in different departments of your company?

No wonder what comes out of this kind of data platform is seldom appealing to the business users that the data platform should have been built to serve. This is unfortunately an often-encountered situation, despite Inmon telling us since the 80s that you need to organize your data according to business concepts and DV being entirely built around the idea of business concepts and BKs.

If the root problem is that different technological teams manage the source systems and the data platforms and that the goals of business departments and the IT department are not aligned, is there a way to fix this?

The solution in the tech-heavy companies that invented the data mesh has been to use the same approach that has worked for application software delivery. They took the microservice architecture and the DevOps way of working and applied it to the data realm creating the data mesh. The data mesh can be thought of in a simplistic way as a microservice architecture where a microservice is a data warehouse.

Instead of trying to build a unified, centralized data platform, a data mesh is built by business unit scale data platforms that can interact through known and well-defined interfaces, with clear semantics, each maintained by a different team.

The interaction of the different parts is managed by the creation of data products.

The key point is that the team providing the data product provided by the units' platform is the same team that runs all the other technological systems for the business unit.

In short, a data product can be one of the following:

- An application that allows doing something using the underlying data that you do not have but is in the system providing the product.

  An example could be the verification that a customer is active or is authorized to place an order of some amount. Another could be a customer-facing application to require the estimation of their house value or a quote for the car insurance.

- An interface that allows retrieving data with a clear semantic.

  An example could be the marketing department providing recent customer actions or touchpoints, a production site making available the status of an assembly line, or the logistics department making available data about distance, fuel consumption, or CO_2 produced by their trucks or associated with their deliveries.

  A data mart is a data product that you are already used to.

The effect is that these technicians have end-to-end control of the data and know well the semantics of the data they are dealing with. You also have proper alignment to deliver good data because it is the whole business unit's responsibility to provide and keep the agreed business products running.

It all sounds fantastic but remember that a distributed system is much more complex than a centralized one and it brings many new problems that do not even exist in a monolithic system.

Furthermore, the required skillset to manage agile projects, provide reliable APIs, and keep running many distributed data pipelines might not be readily available in most traditional industries, even if they are in tech-heavy companies and big e-commerce businesses.

While the available competencies and the maturity level in data management might not match the required levels to start implementing a data mesh, it is possible to adopt some of the insights, such as thinking in terms of data products and designating business units' data ownership to extend to the realm of data warehousing.

The flexibility of dbt also allows having multiple dbt projects interacting through clear APIs, which are the sources for one project and the exposures for the other.

dbt also allows you to easily involve people from all over the company in data projects and to deliver powerful documentation to clarify the lineage, data model, and semantics of the data provided.

Our approach, the Pragmatic Data Platform - PDP

At the end of this overview of the major data modeling styles and data architectures, you might be wondering what dbt is best suited for and what we are going to explain in the rest of the book.

In terms of tool suitability, you can rest assured that dbt is a totally unbiased development tool, and while both the creators and we have our personal preferences, the tool itself works equally well to produce any of the styles we have gone through in this chapter.

Regarding this book's approach, we take a pragmatic approach using what we think is the best from all the available styles and architectures, with the goal to use the full power of the tool while keeping the expertise requirements as simple as possible.

There is a lot to like in the DV proposition, but the sponsorship, the company-wide collaboration, the time to build a conceptual model of the domain to be developed, and the expertise requirements are very high and not always easy or even possible to have.

Our goal is therefore to produce a modern data platform that adopts best-in-class solutions, while skipping the parts that increase the requirements without strong benefits in most cases.

As an example, we adopt an architecture that is very close to the DV architecture, as we think that separating ingestion from the application of business rules is a key advantage.

We also adopt the pattern-based, insert-only ingestion of the full history, which brings many advantages, which we were already using before knowing of DV2.

We also adopt the idea from both DV and Inmon that data should be organized according to the business concepts of the domain. We also focus on clear BK definitions, and we consider identity management an important part of a data platform.

We skip the use of DV modeling, not because it is not useful, but because it is complex and unknown to most people in and around the data community. We know that skipping DV modeling makes the refined layer a bit less resilient to some changes, but it is an acceptable compromise for us.

In most of the use cases, we also chose to deliver the data through data marts containing a few star schemas, but in some cases, such as when we use Google Data Studio or for ML/AI use cases, we might prefer to deliver wide, denormalized tables instead.

We also adopt many of the techniques that we described in the *Data vault* section, such as hashes, even if they are not exclusive or specific to DVs.

All in all, we are trying to be pragmatic, so we decided to name our approach the **Pragmatic Data Platform (PDP)**.

Summary

Congratulations, you are now able to draw and understand simple data models!

In this chapter, you have learned the bread and butter of data modeling using the E-R model at different levels, as well as how to express key ideas about your data.

You now know how to look at some of the most common data model patterns and you should not be tricked anymore by fan and chasm traps.

You have gone through the architectures and modeling styles in use today, learning about their pros and cons, and you have a better idea of the approach we will use in this book.

In the next chapter, *Analytics Engineering as the New Core of Data Engineering*, you will get a full picture of data engineering and then dive into the core of what we do with dbt: analytics engineering.

Further reading

In this chapter, we have introduced many modeling styles and architectures.

The following books are good starting points to learn more about those subjects.

Data modeling:

- A set of books providing a library of universal data models:

  Len Silverston, *The Data Model Resource Book*.

  John Wiley & Sons Inc, 2001, ISBN 978-0471380238

Kimball data model:

- The self-declared definitive guide from the creator itself:

  Ralph Kimball & Margy Ross, *The Data Warehouse Toolkit*.
  Wiley, 2013, ISBN 978-1118530801

Inmon design style:

- The foundational book from the father of data warehousing:

  W. H. Inmon, *Building the Data Warehouse*.
  Wiley, 2005, ISBN 978-0764599446

Unified Star Schema:

- The book that introduced the USS. It is also a good source of information about model issues such as fan and chasm traps. The first part is an updated vision of the Inmon style, from Bill Inmon himself:

  Bill Inmon & Francesco Puppini, *The Unified Star Schema: An Agile and Resilient Approach to Data Warehouse and Analytics Design*. Technics Publications, 2020, ISBN 978-1634628877

Data Vault:

- A great introduction to modeling and the DV:

  John Giles, *The Elephant in the Fridge: Guided Steps to Data Vault Success through Building Business-Centered Models*. Technics Publications, 2019, ISBN 978-1634624893

- A concise, practical introduction to DV, ideal for a quick intro:

  Kent Graziano, *An Introduction to Agile Data Engineering Using Data Vault 2.0*,
  ISBN 978-1796584936

- The DV2 bible, from its inventor Dan Linstedt, even if it is a bit old and does not reflect some of the most recent and important changes in the standard:

  Daniel Linstedt & Michael Olschimke, *Building a Scalable Data Warehouse with Data Vault 2.0*. Morgan Kaufmann, 2015, ISBN 978-0128025109

4

Analytics Engineering as the New Core of Data Engineering

In this chapter, we are going to understand the full life cycle of data, from its creation during operations to its consumption by business users. Along this journey, we will analyze the most important details of each phase in the data transformation process from raw data to information.

This will help us understand why analytics engineering, the part of the data journey that we focus on when working with dbt, besides remaining the most creative and interesting part of the full data life cycle, has become a crucial part of data engineering projects.

Analytics engineering transforms raw data from disparate company data sources into information ready for use with tools that analysts and businesspeople use to derive insights and support data-driven decisions.

We will then discuss the modern data stack and the way data teams can work better, defining the modern analytics engineering discipline and the roles in a data team, with a special look at the role of the Analytics Engineer.

We will then close the chapter by looking at the best practices from software engineering that can help a data team working with dbt on a modern data stack to produce better code, be more relaxed, stop firefighting issues, and provide better data to their stakeholders.

In this chapter, you will learn about the following topics:

- The data life cycle and its evolution
- Understanding the modern data stack
- Defining Analytics Engineering
- DataOps – software engineering best practices for data projects

Technical requirements

This chapter does not require any previous knowledge, but familiarity with data infrastructure and software engineering might make your understanding quicker and deeper.

The data life cycle and its evolution

Data engineering is the discipline of taking data that is born elsewhere, generally in many disparate places, and putting it together to make more sense to business users than the individual pieces of information in the systems they came from.

To put it another way, data engineers do not create data; they manage and integrate existing data.

As Francesco Puppini, the inventor of the Unified Star Schema, likes to say, data comes from "**datum**", and it means "**given**." The information we work on is given to us; we must be the best possible stewards of it.

The art of data engineering is to store data and make it available for analysis, eventually distilling it into information, without losing the original information and adding noise.

In this section, we will look at how the data flows from where it is created to where it is consumed, introducing the most important topics to consider at each step. In the next section, we will look at the professional figures that make this possible in the modern data stack.

Understanding the data flow

At the highest possible level of abstraction, the data flow for an organization is as follows:

1. **Data creation**: Data is born in a **data source** where something work-related happens.

    The data sources, even related to a single subject or concept, can be many and very different across all the units of the full business. This is the **raw data**.

2. **Data movement and storage**: Data from multiple data sources is moved to some place to be analyzed. Let's call it a **data platform**, to be generic and implementation agnostic. We call the data stored here with the desired time dept **historical data** or just **history**.

3. **Data transformation**: The goal of data engineering is to take the data made available on the data platform and transform it to produce integrated, meaningful, and easy-to-consume information for business users. This is the key stage of a data platform, where value is added by producing the **refined data** used in reports and understood by business users.

4. **Access to reports**: The most common interface to the refined data is the **business reports** built with reporting tools that provide simple access to pre-built reports for general business users and may allow varying grades of self-service reporting for power users.

5. **Data write back**: Eventually, business users can interact with the data in the reporting tools to produce data that is fed back into the data platform. Business user input, as well as machine learning insights, can produce data that is even sent back to the source systems.

This flow is so general that it can be applied to pretty much every use case, with the many and big differences being in how the steps are done and what the result of every step is.

> **Note on data meshes**
>
> *Steps 2* and *3* will be different in the case of a data mesh, as there is not a central platform and the steps are performed in a decentralized way, adding some mechanism to allow other parts of the business to access and use refined data born elsewhere. Essentially, the steps are the same, but with a different scope as we are not trying to build a complete data platform and not all data will come as raw source data. In a data mesh, every department setting up their local data platform will replace the same source systems with more refined sources coming from other departments' data platforms.

In the following sections, we will analyze these steps in more detail.

Data creation

Typically, we can identify three main types of data sources where data is created:

- Operational systems, including **Enterprise Resource Planning** (**ERP**) software and all sorts of business systems, without forgetting Excel files, which are still a cornerstone piece of many business processes. The most valuable and easy-to-use data is generally born in operational systems, where operational personnel carry forward the day-to-day operations and generate data that is aligned with the company operations.

- Production systems, including IoT systems that monitor production sites.

  These systems can produce a great amount of very low-level data, often using specialized or industry-specific formats, making this kind of data quite far from the company's business thinking and not very simple to use.

- Online systems, including marketing and websites, potentially producing a huge amount of data. These systems can produce high-level, easily usable data, such as online sales and payments, and huge amounts of lower-level data about user behavior that require sophisticated analysis tools. This is one of the reigns of machine learning, used to understand and predict user behavior.

Understanding the data sources that we work with is essential, as the speed and level of structure in the data is a key driver of how the data can be moved and managed.

You can understand that dealing with high-volume, semi-structured web data, structured ERP data from **Change Data Capture (CDC)**, and flaky IoT data is very different.

In the second and third parts of the book, we will see patterns to manage different kinds of data.

Data movement and storage

If the source systems that we work with do not provide the required analytical tools, or if we need to integrate the data from these systems with data from other systems, the first hurdle that we face is how to move the data from these source systems to someplace where we can do the analysis.

If you are lucky enough that your source system is standard and common enough that is supported by one or many data extraction tools, such as Fivetran, Stitch, or Supermetrics, then you might be set up for an easy ride where you just need to configure the tool to have your data moving.

In all cases where you are not so lucky to have an out-of-the-box tool that can move the data quickly and reliably for you, then you need to design your data movement, considering the following aspects:

- How to extract the data from the source system
- How to move the data from the source to the storage place
- Where and how to store the extracted data in the long term

Inside these three main operations, there are a lot of nuances to be considered, as we will discuss in the following sections.

Extraction from the source system

The happy case is when the source system has been designed to provide external observability of the data or even its state, without the need to deal with the system's internals. This means that the system publishes its changes in a place that is simple to read from (usually a queue). In this case, we do not risk losing any changes and are not in a hurry to get the data, as everything is there for us to read and will remain available for a while.

We can end up in the same situation if we can attach to the logging system of a **Database (DB)**, as that is where the DB itself writes all the changes it is performing.

The extraction of the data from a source system can be straightforward if the system has been designed with data export in mind, but might be difficult if the source system is a complex application, is not built to have external interfaces, and is maybe also scarcely documented.

In all these cases, even when we can perfectly replicate the DB tables, the design of the tables themselves or the application logic might lend well to external observability, as the data itself could be in an inconsistent state if not interpreted according to the application's own rules.

An example is when a system deletes things that are done or no longer valid, such as deleting an invoice that has been canceled but leaving in place the entries in the many-to-many tables that connect invoices to orders.

That is a simple case, once you figure it out, but other cases are more subtle and the business logic to be applied can be very hard to reverse-engineer from the data alone.

Another common example is when subsequent changes overwrite themselves, such as different statuses of a document. If we do not get the changes of the tables (snapshots) often enough, we will miss the intermediate steps. This might not be a problem but should be known, as the data platform will not be able to provide all the historical changes and explain all behaviors observed in the real world.

In the following list, we describe the most common extraction types:

- **Event-based observability**: This is when the system itself publishes the changes that are considered useful for external applications to know. If this is well thought out, we have the guarantee that we do not lose (important) intermediate steps and that there are no logical inconsistencies. A special case is when the events are not just data change events, but *business events*, that is, well-defined events that have business significance, such as an order created or payment accepted. The fact that the semantic of the event is connected to a business process provides additional context for the event data and its information can often also be used for additional use cases that were not initially considered when the event was designed.

- **Change data capture**: This is when we can connect to the DB log or some other event stream from the source system. While we can be sure that we do not lose any intermediate changes, we might still have logical problems as the tables might not have been designed to be accessed by external systems. This is a very common use case that provides good and auditable data, but we must be vigilant for inconsistent data.

- **Application Programming Interface (API)**: Another very common use case is when a system provides an API that we can use to read data from the system. These days, they tend to be REST APIs that provide data in JSON format, while in the past, most APIs provided data in XML format.

  In this case, a lot depends on the quality of the API design. The most common problems stem from the fact that JSON and XML can represent nested structures, and the relation is clear from the nesting, while SQL tables can only represent flat structures. To represent the relation between nested structures in SQL, we need at least two tables and some keys. If we want to be able to manage the relationship over time, we need the keys of both structures in JSON or XML; otherwise, we cannot say what structure in each table that makes up the relation we should add, update, or even delete.

- **Database snapshot**: This is another very common method, where the data from the source system is exported at a specific time (whether at regular intervals or on demand) and might contain all the data (full data export) or only the most recent data (created or changed since a known time). The snapshot name recalls that the data is "as is" at a specific time.

With snapshots, we can have both kinds of problems: we cannot observe intermediate changes that happen and are overwritten between two snapshots and while we have the individual tables as they are at a specific time, we can have logical inconsistencies.

If the export is full, we can track deletions, while we cannot if we export only the changed data.

The temporary storage of extracted data

We have seen in the previous section that there are many ways to retrieve/extract data from the source systems. In some of these ways, the data can be transferred directly to the permanent storage in the data platform, but in many cases, the extracted data is stored for some time in an intermediate storage.

That can happen to keep the data available for multiple attempts to move the data or because the tool moving the data between the systems is different from the tool that is extracting the data.

The following list provides a brief discussion of the most common ways data is stored after extraction:

- **Directly in the data platform**: Storing the data directly in the destination system, whether directly in tables or files stored in a data lake, is the simplest and cleanest way, as the tool doing the extraction is also moving the data between the systems.

- **Files**: This is the most common and oldest way to move data. Many systems, including databases, have a way to export data into files, often CSV files, but also XML or JSON files.

  This is also a common intermediate format when reading data from an API when the tool reading from the API is not doing the movement to the destination. Having different systems doing extraction and movement was common when working with on-premises systems but is becoming less common nowadays and it is rare in the case of cloud applications.

- **Queueing systems**: Storing the data in queue systems, such as Kafka, is very common when the source system is designed to provide external observability, sending itself messages about its state or events. Another common use case of queues to store data in transit is in IoT or real-time use cases, where the data stored in the queue can be accessed by multiple systems, with the data platform being only one of the destinations of this data.

Data movement between the source system and data platform

When looking at the actual movement of the data, we have two dimensions to look at: how the movement is coded and what happens to the data in transit.

These are the common ways the data movement is coded:

- **Data movement/loader tools**: With the move to the cloud of many applications and services and the rise of online marketing, there has been a huge rise in tools that are able to extract data directly from the APIs, provided by a multitude of these cloud applications and databases to move it to cloud data platforms such as Snowflake or BigQuery.

Tools such as Fivetran, Supermetrics, and Funnel are born with the marketing department in mind, while others, such as Stitch Data, approach the data movement topic from an IT department/ETL perspective. They all end up offering easy-to-configure interfaces to retrieve data from hundreds of common cloud services so that non-technical users can easily download the data from them without having to learn their APIs and with close to no configuration besides the access parameters.

- **ETL or data science tools**: The use of ETL-specific tools, such as Matillion, Talend, or Informatica, or data science tools, such as Alteryx or Dataiku, is an effective way to move data using already-available tools, as these tools offer a wide range of possibilities to deal with both files and data in tables. With these tools, someone has to code, or draw using a visual UI, the transformation that is then generated/executed by the tool.

- **Direct coding**: Directly coding with general-purpose programming languages such as Python or Java is a possible choice when there is a strong IT department and no established tool suitable for the purpose. A method still common in on-premises settings is the use of some scripting (such as Shell or Perl) coupled with common Unix-style tools, such as FTP or ad hoc built executable.

We have listed the preceding categories of tools as a modern way of dealing with data movement, but in the end, you can choose whatever way fulfills the need to move your data without errors and manual intervention.

The second dimension in the data movement is about what happens to the data during the movement. The options are as follows:

- **Data is transformed during the move**: This is the "old-school" way, called **ETL**, which stands for **Extract, Transform, and Load**. Transforming the data while moving from the source system to the destination was a reasonable thing to do when the amount of data was limited, databases were row-oriented, slow, on-premises and had limited memory and storage.

  Nowadays, this is not so common anymore when we consider logical transformations, but it is not uncommon that a format conversion is needed when dealing with older systems providing XML or proprietary data formats or even a complex JSON format that is not suitable for easy ingestion in the desired platform.

- **Data remains unaltered during the move**: This is the modern way of doing data warehousing in the cloud age, called **ELT**, which stands for **Extract, Load, and Transform**.

  The logical shift is much bigger than just swapping actions, as the new paradigm is to load the data as is on the data platform and then transform it, making full use of modern, extremely powerful databases that can muster huge amounts of memory, practically unlimited storage, and linearly scalable performance.

When working with dbt, you will start working on data after it has been moved. You can start the transformation of the data with the tool you use to move it, but our suggestion is to keep the data unaltered as much as possible and as close as possible to how it was in the source system.

While it is fine to do any required format conversions, we suggest refraining from applying any business logic during data movement. This will preserve the original data as close as possible to how it was recorded by the operational systems, untampered by business rules that will change over time.

Changing as little as possible is easy and quick and it will provide you with practically unaltered data that is suitable for good auditing of the source system and can be trusted to tell the real story, not how the business rules interpreted it back then.

Keep the facts unaltered and build interpretations later in the process.

Initial and permanent storage in the data platform

After extracting the data from the source systems, you want to move it to some location to make it accessible to your data platform in a simple and organized way, meaning that people can easily find the data they need and that can get the data that they have access to.

When moving the data just after the data extraction, we are still talking about pretty raw data, so people refers to data architects, data scientists, and analytics engineers that will store the data more permanently and transform that data into information.

The good news is that on the technical side, you have many names but pretty much only two options for initial and permanent storage, and they are generally easy, cheap, and not so distant one from the other.

The two options for permanent storage at a tech level are files or database tables.

Here is a brief discussion of the two options:

- *Files* are the go-to choice for data that is semi-structured (such as JSON or XML, where the schema is in the data and is not fixed) or unstructured (images, video, audio, textual documents, or logs where there is little to no schema).

  This kind of data could be stored in a database, but it might not match the database structure well and you will not be able to do much with it using SQL and the typical database code, so it is better to keep it in files that keep the data intact and are the expected format for the tools and libraries that work on that data.

  This approach is often called a data lake, originally named this to describe the lack of a fixed, standardized structure and the ability to contain vast amounts of data. While the lack of a fixed, standardized structure is still the case, nowadays, cloud databases can store the same amounts of data at comparable prices, because in the end, the data is stored in the same cloud storage as your files.

  Modern cloud databses also allow us to manage semi-structured data very well with SQL, making it more comfortable to work with this kind of data with dbt.

- *Database tables*, including non-SQL equivalents, are the place of choice to store structured and strongly organized data that by its nature is easy to manipulate with SQL or the language of choice of the selected DB. Structured data can also be stored in files, but for all practical manners, it will be treated as a table when dealing with the data.

  This is the obvious choice for most business information and is the kind of data that dbt is perfectly suited to manage.

It is important to note that these two are not exclusive but can and should be used together, storing different kinds of data in the place most suitable for it. Also, consider that metadata and data derived from data that is kept in files, such as information extracted from video or audio, can be well suited for storage in database tables, so you might have related data stored in both ways.

Here, we want to briefly distinguish between initial and permanent storage, as the first is about storing the data when moved from the source system and the data platform, while the second is where you will have the permanent storage of your trusted history.

The initial load is almost always done, in modern platforms, by loading the data to the destination as it is retrieved by the source system. One important note is that the data that is retrieved and saved here is often not the full history, but it is at best the current state of the source (referred to as snapshot or full export), while often it is just the part of it that has changed (referred to as delta or incremental export).

Permanent storage is instead the place and format in which you expect to have all the information that you intend to store, for as much time as you intend to store it. As we will see, it can be similar to the data coming in, or it might be quite different.

When storing data for your permanent storage, it is essential to be clear about at what point of the transformation from raw data to refined information you decide to store the data recording the history of changes in your entities.

There are two alternatives, and in the following list, we briefly describe the reference architectures that adopt them:

- **Storing the source data**: In many reference architectures that have the ambition to build long-lasting data platforms, the decision is to store the history by saving the data very close to the RAW format it arrives in on the data platform.

- The layer storing this data can be called the core warehouse, raw data vault, persistent staging or history layer, but the ideas are very similar: save what you get according to some format or organization, but without transforming it or applying business rules:

  - In Inmon-style data warehouses, you store the data that comes in in third normal form, to avoid redundancy while preserving all the information, especially regarding the relationships.

  - In Data Vault, you store the data in as raw form as possible, to preserve the auditability, and you store it organized by business concept, with passive integration centered around well-defined business keys stored in the same hub, even if from different systems.

- The style that we are going to use in this book is to store the data as much as possible in the same form as it comes from the source systems, preserving the data and the relations, and explicitly identifying the business keys, aka natural keys, that will be used in the next layers to drive the integration between systems.

- **Storing the refined data**: In the Kimball architecture, the idea is to transform the incoming data into facts and conformed dimensions, applying the needed business rules to the incoming data to be able to conform it to some agreed way of representing the desired information. While it is almost a norm to produce facts and dimensions as the final layer of a data platform to power reporting, we do not advise using facts and dimensions as your main data store, as advocated according to the Kimball architecture, as the data in those structures can be quite far from the original data, changed multiple times by the application of many and complex business rules. To reiterate, going back to the original data in the case of errors or changes in the business rules can be very difficult or even impossible.

Our advice on this matter is to move and save the raw data as much as possible "as is", performing only the very important tasks of properly identifying the concepts, their identity, by clearly naming and testing the primary and business keys, and their way of changing, as these are three key aspects to store history properly.

In fact, if you want to be able to identify and store the changes of a concept, you need to know what the instances of this concept are and how to distinguish whether two instances of the concept are two versions of the same concept entity or two separate entities.

As an example, it is of paramount importance to be able to recognize whether two rows in a "Person" table are about two different people or two versions of the same person, that is, the same person after some changes.

Data transformation

Once you have moved the raw data from the source to your data platform and stored it in a way to keep all the desired history available, it is not likely at all that the data will already be in the correct format to be used for reporting.

As we have seen in the previous section, most likely, you will land the data on the platform in some initial place and format, store it permanently in some other place and format, and finally, you produce something that is used by the business users through BI tools.

This lets us identify the following three main layers for your data:

- **Raw data**: This is the data as initially loaded on the data platform, as it was at the source or delivered by the tool that moved it.

- **Historical data**: This is how and where you have decided to keep the full history of your data. No business rules have been applied. It is still very similar to the form it was in in the source system.

- **Refined data**: This is data that is ready for reporting/other use cases, such as machine learning or AI. This is the data that you produce by applying all the required general and use case-specific business rules.

The core function of dbt is helping you manage the data transformations between these layers. Here is a description of the two steps:

- **Storage transformations**: Making the landed data ready for persistent history storage.

  These transformations present some technical complexity, but they are pretty common and quite repetitive, to the point where it is possible to automate most of the process. We will see how to do so using dbt and its macros.

  In this step, the column names should be changed to use business names to create a common vocabulary, but the transformations applied to the data should only be technical and should not change the data, only its format, add metadata available during the processing, and add calculated fields.

  Examples are parsing dates and numbers from text, calculating hash keys and hash DIFF fields, plus the actual code to store the incoming data in the history. Actions such as removing padding zeroes and spaces can be done, but in this layer, the original source data should be preserved and stored in the history every time that data is changed.

- **Master data and business rules transformations**: Taking the data from the persistent history and making it ready for reporting.

  This is where we apply most of the transformations on the data, going from the master data mappings to the most varied business rules.

  This is the "creative" part of the data engineer's job, where best practices, guidelines and experience can help you find good solutions and avoid dead ends, but your personal input makes all the difference.

  After all, the discovery and application of business rules is the most complex affair in building a data platform and it is still something where an expert professional delivers huge value.

In this section, we have started to expose the way of thinking that we believe to be best suited to modern tools such as dbt and Snowflake and in our experience, provides the best possible value for a company building a cloud data platform.

One of the key concepts that we will touch on multiple times is that some of the more traditional data warehousing methods must be dropped in favor of simpler ways that are now viable thanks to the power and cheapness of cloud platforms.

One example is the use of surrogate keys built with sequences. When databases were much better at handling keys made of numbers than of text and they were not able to work in parallel, surrogate keys were fine. Nowadays, there is little to no difference based on key type, and cloud databases can exploit parallelism to make your queries unbelievably fast, so it is much better to use natural business keys or surrogate keys built by hashing, which work well with parallelism, and avoid at all costs sequences that kill any parallelism to both generate the keys and look them up.

Another example is incremental loads; they are much more complicated to get right than a simple query providing the required transformation. The difference is that incremental loads depend on the state, on the history – including failures – that happened before the current execution. If something goes wrong, you must fix the data, or your data will be inconsistent as it will be built over the not-fixed data.

When you had to buy your database servers, you often ended up with the smallest and slowest that could fit the bill, so no wonder small and slow databases, coupled with missing parallelism, could not handle all your data at once. Back then, we were forced to use incremental loads as a performance tool, to work on less data at once, making the transformations more complex but quicker.

Nowadays, with cloud platforms that provide extremely powerful setups, we have the ability to avoid incremental loads as a performance tool and we can build simpler transformations that can be built quicker, are easier to understand, have fewer errors, and require way less maintenance. Just think about not having to deal with what happened in any of the previous runs, just caring about what your code does.

Business reporting

The main reason to build data platforms is to make available refined data that can be used to power reports that in turn can drive good decisions.

Nowadays, we have two main use cases: classical business reporting, derived from source data applying business rules, and advanced analytics, where we include the reporting insights generated by machine learning or AI.

In both cases, we will probably have to deliver the data to the final users according to the Kimball dimensional model, which means using facts and dimensions. While we advise against using these artifacts as your permanent storage, they are a standard way to provide data for reporting.

The most common way to deliver these is to build one data mart, which is a collection of tables and views delivering the desired facts and dimensions, for each reporting domain, such as marketing or purchases, and sometimes by country or geography.

To increase consistency and avoid reworking, we suggest you have a general refined layer implemented as tables that store the result of applying the master data and general business rules, while implementing the individual data marts as a collection of views that read from the refined layer and eventually add any business rules specific to that reporting domain.

Machine learning and AI processes can use the full history or the refined data as their input data and produce more refined data, which in this way can be added naturally to the desired data marts.

Feeding back to the source systems

The last potential step in the data flow is about the data generated in the data platform and the desire to use it in other systems.

One common use case is taking some data calculated in the data platform back to some operational system. This is very common in marketing and CRM, where the data platform can be used to calculate customer segments and all sorts of measures that then need to be fed back into the marketing tools and CRM platform.

Another increasingly common use case is when some machine learning process is building valuable data for operational systems, such as sales forecasts or predictive maintenance figures.

In all these cases, we can similarly approach the topic as we have seen with moving the data from the source system to the data platform, with the big difference that many systems come with some way to get data out but offer little to no way to load data in.

Even when the target application does have an API to load back data, it is way less common for data loaders to have the same wide range of abilities to load data back.

Despair not, as there are tools that focus on the "reverse ETL" process, that is, moving the data back from the data warehouse to the business tools/operational systems, such as Census (available at https://www.getcensus.com/).

Another case of data generated in the data platform is when the people using the BI tools can edit data in the reports on the BI tool and have it somehow sent back to the data platform itself. This is often called the write-back feature in BI tools.

Some sample use cases are when people can use their BI tool to enter missing information or to provide updated values in specific reports, such as managing inventory levels or updating forecasts.

In this case, it is much better to treat the new data, written back from the BI tool, as new input for the data platform and integrate it as part of the transformation chain, instead of directly changing the data mart that is powering the report. This is again in the spirit of making the changes to data visible and being able to reproduce the final result from scratch without having to deal with the previous state.

Now that we have explored the data life cycle and its evolution, we will move on to learning about the modern data stack, which has made data engineering much more seamless.

Understanding the modern data stack

When we talk about data engineering, we encompass all the skillsets, tooling, and practices that cover the data life cycle from end to end, as presented in the previous section, from data extraction to user data consumption and eventually including the writing back of data.

This is a huge set of competencies and tools, ranging from security to scripting and programming, from infrastructure operation to data visualization.

Beyond very simple cases, it is quite uncommon that a single person can cover all that with a thorough understanding and good skills in all the areas involved, let alone have the time to develop and manage it.

The traditional data stack

The traditional data stack used to be built by data engineers developing ad hoc ETL processes to extract data from the source systems and transform it locally before loading it in a refined form into a traditional database used to power reporting. This is called an ETL pipeline.

The process included creating some ad hoc integration to extract the data from the source system, find what was to be extracted, and design an extraction logic. Often, it also included the required data transformations, including summarization, before finally loading the "digested" data into an otherwise-normal database to be used for reporting.

Using a transactional database such as MySQL or SQL Server for reporting poses huge issues and calls for all sorts of tricks to make reporting possible. The main issue is that those databases are optimized for many small operations that interact with the whole line of data in a table. They are row oriented.

The fact is that analytics is the opposite: it requires a few queries on a big amount of data that often just use a few columns instead of all the possible ones. To solve the needs of analytical workloads, columnar databases have been created, but in the first decade of the 2000s, they were not widely known, and they were still quite expensive if confronted with "normal" row-oriented OLTP DBs.

One of the most problematic compromises to be done using traditional OLTP DBs was the application of business rules and summarization of data before loading it into the reporting DB. This created a situation where any change in the source data or business rules would affect the whole history of the data. This in turn called for a fix in the transformation logic *and* in the existing data to conform to the new logic. As you can see, this is double work, and scary too, as you had to modify the only copy of your historical data.

Another issue was that size and power of the tools were limited as well as the time to write integrations and then keep them running, so only the really needed data was loaded, often retaining only limited periods of time.

The data analysts would take the data loaded in the database and build reports and dashboards for the end users, plus doing the occasional deep dive into some aspect of the data.

Even in these deep dives, they just had what they had: if something was summarized too much, they could not do anything but ask for a new load, and if some useful data was not available, they could again just ask the data engineers to add it, by creating another ETL pipeline.

No wonder the final users were often left to wait for new data to be added or received half-answers with the available data.

The division of work between the data engineers and the analysts also made it more difficult for the data analysts to develop a good understanding of the data and its limitations, and for the data engineers to understand the use and quality of the data that they delivered.

Usually, little to no tests or data quality checks were in place, leaving the data team exposed to continuous firefighting at both ends of the data life cycle: changing/missing data from the source systems and stale/bad data in the reports.

Another point is that given the technical difficulties of keeping the ETL pipelines working and the distance of the data engineers from the business questions, often, more effort went into making the data flow, a traditional and objective metric no one can dispute, than understanding the data and making sure of its quality.

The modern data stack

Fast forward to the mid-2010s and we find ourselves in a much better situation:

- Analytical data warehouses in the cloud, such as BigQuery, Redshift, and Snowflake, are more and more common and becoming an affordable option for most data teams

- Data movement/integration tools, such as Stitch and Fivetran, make it very easy to move the data from traditional databases and common business platforms to the cloud data warehouse

- Modern BI tools start to provide improved abilities for self-service reporting that power users can exploit

The advent of cloud-based data warehouses is the turning point as it made available a huge amount of storage and processing power without the need to buy capacity upfront.

On the consumer side, this enabled companies to load in these cloud **Data Warehouses** (**DWs**) vast amounts of data and to process it much faster and cheaper, spending a fraction of the cost of on-premises systems.

On the commercial side, this enabled the creation and rise of data movement tools that made it quick and painless to load data to one of these standard cloud DWs from the most used systems, such as traditional DBMS and operational and SaaS software.

Adopting this modern stack made it simple to easily load raw data from the source systems into your cloud DW, reducing the need for the most complex and time-consuming jobs in the data engineering world.

Having a tool that you just set up in a short time and delivers you the data in your DW made it possible for a single person to own all or most of the data life cycle for source systems that can be managed with data movement tools. It also solved the need to study and keep up to date with these rich, but often-changing, APIs, as that is now a problem of the dev team of the data movement tool.

Nowadays, you create ad hoc pipelines as a last resort when no tool exists to automate the data movement.

Having the raw data easily available promoted the development of the next question: how do we improve the transformation phase and make it effective? *This is what dbt was created to help with.*

We will provide more details on this in the next section.

The other big change in the data stack has been a shift into putting as little as possible logic into the reporting tools and keeping it in the DW so that you write and manage it once and it is available for every report and every other use as well. This was made possible by the fact that with less programming and infrastructure needed to run the ETL pipelines, the engineers working on the transformations have better SQL and warehousing skills, and modern tools such as dbt make it easier to write and test the business logic directly into the transformations.

Now that we have described the traditional and the modern data stacks, let's dig into the bread and butter of dbt: transforming the raw data into usable information while working as an agile team. This is the core of analytics engineering, which we will discuss next.

Defining analytics engineering

We have seen in the previous section that with the advent of the modern data stack, data movement has become easier, and the focus has therefore switched over to managing raw data and transforming it into the refined data used in reports by business users. There are still plenty of cases where ad hoc integrations and ETL pipelines are needed, but this is not the main focus of the data team as it was in the past.

The other Copernican revolution is that the new data stack enables data professionals to work as a team, instead of perpetuating the work in isolation, which is common in the legacy data stack. The focus is now on applying software engineering best practices to make data transformation development as reliable as building software. You might have heard about DevOps and DataOps.

With this switch of focus, the term **analytics engineering** has emerged to identify the central part of the data life cycle going from the access to the raw data up to making the refined data available to the BI reporting tools. It is not a coincidence that this is also the part of the data life cycle covered by cloud DW platforms and dbt.

Looking with new eyes at the data life cycle, we can divide it into the following:

- **Data integration**: Collecting all the data in a single place, the cloud data platform, by using as many off-the-shelf tools as possible and resorting to ad hoc data pipelines when needed.

- **Analytics engineering**: Transforming the raw data into refined, usable, trusted data.

  This is what you do with dbt, using your preferred data platform, which is Snowflake in our case.

- **Data analysis**: Using the refined data to build reports, dashboards, machine learning models, and more.

  This is the work you do in your BI tool to make data accessible to business users.

These three phases are not much different from the ones we have seen in the previous section. What is different is that in the modern data stack, we now have clear boundaries that align with the modern tools, and this has consequences on the professional roles that work on it.

The roles in the modern data stack

Having divided the data life cycle into these three steps, these are the professional figures that belong in a modern data team using dbt and a cloud DW:

- **Data engineer**: The "traditional" data engineer, armed with scripting/coding and infrastructure knowledge, is still very much valuable, especially if not all your sources can be covered by modern data-loading tools. Even in that case, complex scheduling, security, and a myriad of other topics might require the expertise and focus of a data engineer.

- **Analytics engineer**: A new figure that is firmly centered around knowing and transforming raw data into useful information. They are less concerned with data movement pipeline development and are instead focused on making the data available, usable, and trusted.

- **Data analyst**: This is an improved version of the traditional data analyst, as now they can understand and even help with the construction of data models and certainly have an unprecedented ability to investigate a wider array of datasets.

While it makes sense to clearly distinguish the three roles, it is important to note that they overlap a lot, with the core competency being around SQL and data literacy.

The modern data stack even makes it possible to have a data team of one, if you can move the data without the need to write and babysit one or more data pipelines and your business logic is not constantly changing, so existing data models and reports do not need frequent changes.

The analytics engineer

We have seen that the analytics engineer is a bit of a data engineer, in collecting and understanding the raw data, and a bit of a data analyst, in being aware of how to create datasets that enable good analysis. But the core of this role is to transform the data into information using the best practices that allow software engineers to produce and maintain reliable software.

The main change from the old to the new stack is the ability, and the need, to move from individual work to teamwork to use the mindset and powerful tooling that has been created for traditional software engineering for data engineering.

The approach to building a data platform becomes more similar to building software, recognizing that even in the data world, you can build modular models and you can compose complex datasets by using general-purpose, reusable models just as you reuse software components and libraries when building software.

The analytics engineer organizes the data transformations and their dependencies just as a software engineer designs an application, using reusable patterns, and applies the separation of concerns to minimize the need of changing a model for many different reasons.

The analytics engineer's job is not just to write the SQL that does the required transformations from raw data to information, but also to apply or discover patterns to break down, structure, and organize the transformations in a meaningful and repeatable way, using clear naming, so that everybody in the team knows what to expect from each step of these transformations.

In the following section, we will discuss the best practices that we can adopt from traditional software engineering to improve data projects.

DataOps – software engineering best practices for data

The fact is that many data teams were, and still are, not staffed by people with software engineering backgrounds, and for this reason, they have missed the adoption of the modern techniques of software engineering that fall under DevOps.

Living up to the hype, the DevOps movement has brought great improvement to the software development area, helping teams to become more productive and satisfied with their jobs.

In short, the core ideas of DevOps are to provide the team with the tools it needs, as well as the authority and the responsibility for all of the development cycle: from software coding to **Quality Assurance (QA)**, to releasing and then running the production operations.

The cornerstones to achieving this are the use of automation to avoid manually doing repetitive tasks, such as releases and testing, the emphasis on automated testing, the reliance on proactive automated monitoring, and, most importantly, the team's shared ownership of the code.

These ideas are exemplified by the **four-eyes principle**, requiring each piece of code to be seen and approved by at least two people (through pairing, pull requests, or code walkthroughs), and the **boy scout rule**, which prompts you to ensure a piece of code you touch is left in better shape than it was before you touched it, independently of the person that wrote it, therefore improving the work over time.

Another important concept is the active management of technical debt. While it is fine and normal that some parts of the code base might get released even if they're not up to standard, this must be for a real contingent reason and the team must repay that debt, fixing the lower-quality code once the contingent reason has passed.

In the following subsections, we discuss some of the software engineering best practices that can help data teams to work in a more satisfying way.

Note that they are very much aligned with the ones that Tristan Handy, the founder of dbt-labs, laid out in a seminal post when starting work on dbt. You can read the 2016 post from Tristan at this URL: `https://blog.getdbt.com/building-a-mature-analytics-workflow/`.

Version control

Having a central repository with all the code stored and organized for everyone to access, with a clear understanding of the succession of the versions, is already an improvement over many situations where SQL files were saved to shared disks and versions maintained by file or folder name.

The ability to create branches to work independently and then merge the changes simply enables the parallel development of features and provides a safe way to experiment with changes.

Anyway, adopting code version control is not only useful by itself but is also the required step to enable many positive processes.

The version control system, such as *Git*, becomes the integration hub that can trigger collaboration and automation processes such as the following ones:

- **Pull requests**: This powerful feature allows the team to look at the changes proposed by a developer and comment on them, asking for clarifications and proposing improvements, all the while getting up to speed with the latest changes

- **Automation**: When new code is checked in, many kinds of automation can be triggered, from code quality tools that analyze the new code to automated tests, all the way to continuous integration and continuous deployment

- **Authorization**: Especially in very bureaucratic or heavily regulated environments, the version control system can work as a recording tool for approvals, making that required step trivial

Quality assurance

The three cornerstones of DataOps, ownership, freedom, and responsibility, heavily rely on the fact that the team has a solid quality assurance process in place.

The best way to be sure that the code that you have in production works as expected and that the data that comes in is as you expect is to have automated tests that are executed every time that new code is released or that new data is loaded.

With such a process in place and good test coverage, it is possible to move away from the reactive/ firefighting stance of most data teams and take responsibility for the team's code.

You should think about tests and quality assurance as your ticket for sleeping well at night.

As a bonus, you will also get a better reputation for providing trusted data and fewer interruptions in your daily work to fix data issues.

Being able to catch bugs and data issues before they hit your production DB is invaluable, as it saves a lot of time for the data team, provides a better service to the business users, and, most importantly, builds and keeps the trust in the data elevated.

You cannot have a data-centric organization if people do not trust the data that you provide.

The modularity of the code base

One of the most problematic things in many data teams is the amount of code repetition to do the same thing. Code is often copy-pasted from one place to another, or even developed slightly differently by different people as they do not work as a team but as isolated siloes.

The most important change in writing code with the modern data stack is the ability to use functionalities that were only available in proper languages, such as functions to encapsulate reusable code, conditionals, loops, and meta-programming that were not possible/easy to do in plain old SQL. Also, the reduction in boilerplate code helps to focus on good business logic code.

Another cornerstone is reducing the use of incremental loads to free ourselves from dealing with the complex state when we can easily recalculate values according to the current business rules and avoid dealing with the effects of past ETL runs and previous business rules.

dbt makes these programming primitives available for you as first-class objects, and the speed, scalability, and massively parallel architecture of cloud DWs make it possible and more efficient to transform huge amounts of data from scratch than updating existing data. When you factor in the huge simplification in logic and the productivity gain for the developers, it is a win-win scenario.

Taking advantage of these new possibilities, offered by dbt and cloud DWs, requires a mind shift in the data team. The analytics engineer needs to aim to write clean, reusable code and produce reusable models that are always up to date with the latest business rules so that all the team can build layer upon layer and minimize rework.

How many times are you going to develop "the" customer or vendor concept and the resulting dimension? What about the invoice or order concept?

Are you going to refine each from the raw data every time, with slightly different rules every time you need one in a report or data mart?

The modern data stack allows you to build reusable models so that you can code the customer only once, maybe composing it by putting together lower level models that represent the online customers, the store customer and the wholesale customer. All of them are useful refined models that can be reused in multiple contexts.

The key here is that technology and business must align to define the relevant business concepts, and the technology then helps to implement them, reducing code duplication and promoting the use of stable interfaces.

We will look more into how to write modular code in the *Designing for maintainability* section.

Development environments

To provide your development team with the ability to quickly iterate over code and develop and test new functionalities, every developer must have their own environment where they can work without the need to wait or synchronize with others and without the fear of breaking something.

Being free to run your code when you are ready, to run tests that give you trusted answers in seconds or minutes, or being able to break and recreate your environment in the same short time are essential abilities that the modern data stack provides. These enable developers to focus on writing good, clean business code and not on support or side tasks, let alone just waiting.

On the contrary, when developers must try out their code in production, they cannot afford to make errors because they cannot fail without causing relevant issues. The result is fear of changing any piece of code and releases taking forever, as every little change has to be thoroughly considered and weighted against consequences.

Even in the case where there is only one shared development environment or a few that are slow or expensive to create and therefore must be shared and well maintained… the result is similar: fear of change and demotivation because of time lost waiting for an environment or from misleading results because the dev environment does not reflect the real environment.

After all, this should not be very surprising as most people do not like waiting in a queue, and are even less keen on taking a walk on a cable suspended high up, with or without a safety net.

Personal development environments are a key enabler for the ability to quickly develop and test new functionalities. How can you release daily or even multiple times a day if each developer waits half a day to try out their code?

Continuous integration is the next step in increasing the speed and trust in the development process, making sure that all the individual features that have been developed are working well together. It provides another, stronger level of confidence, reinforcing the awareness that all the code being released has been reviewed and discussed by the team.

Continuous deployment provides the last step, allowing the code tested in the integration environment to be released to production. That can be done automatically or upon manual code promotion.

Designing for maintainability

We have kept for last the most important of all the best practices: develop being mindful about the future, that is, taking into consideration evolution and maintenance.

Data platforms are some of the longest-living enterprise applications, so while you are writing one, you can be assured it will be in use for a long time. This means that over time, there will be a lot of changes in data sources as well as business rules, and even more, questions will arise about the data managed in the data platform.

That in turn means that a lot of people, including yourself in the next months and years, are bound to come back and reread that code. This makes the case for writing code that is understandable for humans.

Writing code that just works is not enough, just like putting a control half-hidden in a place that is difficult to access is not a good design. Design your code so that the next person to touch it will thank you for putting the control where it is easy to see and reach.

Writing maintainable code means writing code that is easy to understand and change for your fellow human colleagues. Avoid long and complex queries by breaking down your logical steps into individual **Common Table Expressions (CTEs)** so that you can provide proper naming for each step and create clean, readable code. Keep your models under 100 lines and the number of joins to two or three, unless a model has the single purpose of joining many tables.

In this area, the evergreen book *Clean Code* by Bob Martin and the articles by Martin Fowler on architecture, refactoring, and agility will be great guides; even if the code samples and the main discussion may be about Java and application software, the ideas apply to every programming context.

Performance and correctness are a consequence of well-architected code that is also clearly expressed; they are never an excuse to write obscure code or overly complicated logic.

Remember, the less code there is, the fewer bugs will be in it.

The fact that we might be using SQL or some Python-based scripting to express our logic does not mean that we should settle for anything less than good, readable code and clearly expressed business logic. After all, if the code is easy to understand, it is also easy to verify its logic by humans and automatically test that it does what is expected, while that is not the case if the code is obscure or the business logic is not clearly understood.

The other key part of writing maintainable code is making sure that your code does not have to change every other day and that when you need to change it, it is easy to change. For that, we can resort to the whole body of knowledge of software engineering, with special regard to the SOLID principles from object-oriented programming. The following are some principles that are easy to put into use by anyone in data projects:

- **SRP**: The **single-responsibility principle** says that a model should have one, and only one, reason to change. In practice, this means that a model should focus on doing one thing, hopefully doing it well and making obvious what it does. This means the opposite of the huge query that does everything at once and more if possible.

- **OCP**: The **open/closed principle** says that a model should be open for extension and closed for (interface) modification. This means that the models that we use as connecting points between systems and models should be stable in the interfaces they expose and should also be easily extensible. In the data world, this is easily accomplished by picking good, business-proven names that can stand the test of time and using views as contact points to insulate the consumers from potential changes to the tables where the refined data is stored.

- **ISP**: The **interface segregation principle** says that a client should not depend upon an interface it does not use. Seems trivial, but we all have seen customer dimensions with over 100 columns. Again, it is quite simple to adhere to this principle in the data world by using a view that provides access to the underlining refined data exposing only the required information, and not everything available "just because." In this way, we limit the "blast radius" of eventual changes that make some fields unavailable or change semantics.

- **LSP**: The **least surprise principle** says that a model should do what seems obvious it would do from its name and position in a project. You should be able to guess correctly what it does and should not be surprised by it does by reading its code. Without this principle, you cannot trust any piece of code without rereading it every time, making work a pain.

  An example is that you would not expect a view in a data mart to read from a raw data source, nor a model where you apply a master data mapping to also calculate some unrelated metric.

In discussing these principles, we have already tried to adapt the wording and the examples to the data world, so you might find them slightly different from the equivalent definition for application software development.

Besides these overreaching principles, there are other software engineering principles, such as abstraction, encapsulation, and inheritance, that while not directly mappable to the data/SQL world can provide good inspiration, such as using views to define an abstraction (think of a generic interface such as a basic customer or product dimension that can be in many general-purpose data marts that do not need all the details) or encapsulation (by exposing a subset of the columns of a big table with an appropriate name).

Lastly, a lot of the understandability and maintainability of a project depends on very simple actions, such as adopting simple, agreed-upon conventions that make it easy for everyone to figure out where to find a model or what a model does, as the LSP suggests.

Another important topic for maintainability is documentation. Mind that overly detailed, manually created documentation tends to become stale very quickly and thus worthless or even misleading.

Here, we want to stress the fact that most of the documentation should be generated, certainly for technical details that change often, such as the models and their connections.

It is perfectly fine if the stable parts, such as the high-level architecture and descriptions of models or fields, or the general description of a report or dashboard, are created by humans.

Summary

In this chapter, you have learned about the full data life cycle, and you became familiar with DataOps and the modern data platform concepts that make it possible to develop data projects with similar way of working and to achieve the same satisfaction level as software projects developed using a DevOps approach.

Well done!

We introduced the figure of the analytics engineer, who takes the central role of building the core of a modern data platform, and we saw the best practices and principles that we can adopt from software engineering to make our work on data projects more reliable and satisfying for us and other stakeholders.

With this chapter, we close the first part of this book, which has introduced you to the key elements of data engineering and will enable you to better understand how we work with dbt.

In the next chapter, *Agile Data Engineering with dbt*, you will start to learn about the core functionalities of dbt and you will start building the first models of a bigger example that will provide us with a realistic use case.

Further reading

In this chapter, we have talked about the data life cycle, software engineering principles, DevOps, and DataOps. There are many books on these subjects, but none that we are aware of about the modern data stack, so we present here a few very classical references that are written with software application development in mind, but present topics that are of use in every programming context:

- My personal favorite, as it makes clear the benefits of clean code:

  Robert C. Martin, aka "Uncle Bob", *Clean Code: A Handbook of Agile Software Craftsmanship*, Prentice Hall, 2008, ISBN 978-0132350884

  If you like this one, there are a few other books about clean code and architecture written by Uncle Bob. You can also refer to his site: `http://cleancoder.com/`.

- The classical book about keeping your code in good shape, from an author that I deeply respect and that has produced my favorite quote, which could be the title of this chapter: "*Any fool can write code that a computer can understand. Good programmers write code that humans can understand.*" M. Fowler (1999)

  Martin Fowler (author), Kent Beck (collaborator), *Refactoring: Improving the Design of Existing Code*, Addison-Wesley Professional, 2019, ISBN 978-0134757599

  This is the updated version of one of the classical books in software engineering, providing the wisdom of Martin Fowler with the collaboration of Kent Beck, the creator of extreme programming.

5
Transforming Data with dbt

In this chapter, we will start to build a data application in dbt and touch on how to manage the data life cycle and organize the layers of our data application.

After presenting our reference architecture and its benefits, we will introduce the sample application that will serve us for a few chapters, providing the use cases and the context for importing and managing some data and developing the transformations required to implement the use cases with dbt.

By the end of this chapter, we will have started to develop our example application in dbt and will have done all the steps to create, deploy, run, test, and document a data application with dbt, even if this one is still a very simple one.

The content of this chapter is the following:

- The dbt Core workflow for ingesting and transforming data
- Introducing your stock tracking project
- Defining sources and providing reference data
- How to write and test transformations

Technical requirements

This chapter builds on the previous ones, so we expect a basic understanding of SQL, data modeling, and the data life cycle.

To follow the examples, we expect you to have an account at dbt Cloud, connected with Snowflake and GitHub, as explained step-by-step in the first two chapters.

The code samples of this chapter are available on GitHub at `https://github.com/PacktPublishing/Data-engineering-with-dbt/tree/main/Chapter_05`.

The dbt Core workflow for ingesting and transforming data

In this chapter, we will build our first full-blown dbt project, taking data from a source system and making it available for use in reporting, but let's start with the big picture by describing the reference architecture for a modern data platform.

In *Chapter 4*, we outlined the data life cycle. In the following image, we will start to visualize the layers of a modern data platform and start to tie them to how we build them with dbt:

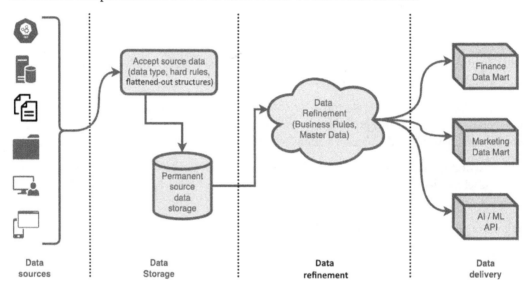

Figure 5.1: Layers of a modern data platform

The layers are as follows:

1. **Data sources**: We will use the full abilities of the underlying data platform to load the data coming from our data sources. In the case of Snowflake, this means being able to load data from files stored on major cloud providers, and of course, data residing in other Snowflake **databases** (**DBs**), whether our own or shared with us by others, such as partners, customers, or other departments.

2. **Data storage**: We will read the data from the data sources, put it in the format we want to use for permanent storage on the data platform, and track the changes in the source data. We want to store data as close as possible to the source data, only applying a few technical steps that do not change the data, such as converting it into the correct data type (numbers or dates received as text), applying hard rules to data (removing padding zeros or spaces, converting to the desired time zone, or managing cases), and eventually flattening out data received as objects (from JSON, AVRO …) into SQL or relational, compliant data structures (as an example, separating invoice headers and invoice rows received as a single object).

3. **Data refinement**: Here is where the real data transformation happens: turning raw data into useful information. The two main parts of this transformation are applying **Master Data (MD)** to convert source system-specific data into enterprise-wide usable data and then applying **Business Rules (BR)** to transform data into usable information.

    While the MD part can follow some guidelines and patterns, the BR part is where experienced analysts and data professionals really make the difference by keeping order and creating reusable data models instead of a spaghetti web of ad-hoc transformations with no organization.

4. **Data delivery**: In the data delivery layer, we will have traditional reporting data marts that deliver data to reporting tools using a dimensional model, other data marts that provide data as wide tables, and other "marts" with more technical uses, providing a simple way to build and manage APIs for external tools, such as AI or ML workloads, or refined information that is taken back to the operational systems, such as updated customer profiles or full-fledged segments for use in marketing tools.

The signature feature of the architecture that we propose is the separation of the source data ingestion from the application of the business logic and the creation of the business concepts.

This core separation of concerns is the basis of our modern data platform idea, as it allows a lot of freedom in the details of the implementation and delivers the following substantial advantages:

*   Decoupling the two most important activities, ingesting and building the business concepts, simplifies the overall development, allowing the use of the best solution for each part of the problem.

*   The extensive use of patterns allows much quicker development, keeps complexity low, makes for easy people training, and offers reliable outcomes and predictable delivery times.

*   The preservation of the source data enables proper auditing, allows for advanced source system analysis and improvement, and guarantees that we are always able to use all our data, as the original data is not changed by the application of BR that might not be valid in future and the source data is not changed in ways impossible to revert.

*   A well-organized refined layer with a simple MD Management playbook, oriented dependencies that are easy to navigate, and a few recurrent types of models with clear roles allows us to build even the most complex business concepts without creating a huge spaghetti ball of code that quickly becomes too complex to manage and maintain.

*   The practice of constantly recreating the refined and delivery layers from the stored historical source data allows you to easily change MD and BR and have it immediately deployed to all of your data, removing any state that needs maintenance.

*   The ability to remove any accumulated state from the refined and delivery layers makes the system simple and quick to change and as easy to maintain as a stateless application, gaining back developer and stakeholder confidence and a lot of human effort previously spent on data repair or fix tasks. This is in direct contrast with legacy data warehouses where changes are

constantly hindered by the need to preserve, backfill, and maintain the complex state caused by incremental loads and the incremental summarization of data.

- The flexible delivery layer provides simple data mart personalization on top of a well-separated refined layer that is always up-to-date with MD and general BR and allows you to provide every department, customer, or external interface with all your data according to the latest data mart developments.

- The external dependencies are easily managed with simple DB constructs such as users, roles, schema, and views, and access is intrinsically limited to the smallest possible surface thanks to the ability to quickly provide data marts to offer any desired API on top of your refined data.

The following image visualizes the main effects on the implementation effort and costs in a modern warehousing project using the workflow we have described in this section compared to a traditional one where the focus is on data mart delivery without any separation of concerns:

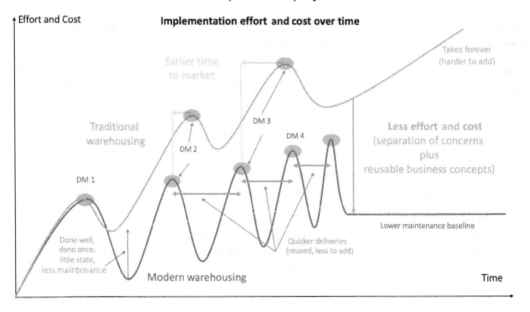

Figure 5.2: The implementation effort and cost over time in a warehousing project

Now that we have a workflow to build our data platform, it is time to start learning how to use the features of dbt and Snowflake to solve real-world use cases.

Through this and the following chapters, we will lead you toward building a complete data platform, from the source data to the data marts ready to serve out reports.

The two main tools that we will use are a stock tracking data platform and the Snowflake sample data provided as a data share to every Snowflake account.

We will start to build a very simple stock tracking data platform and incrementally transform it to incorporate more features to illustrate the dbt functionalities and the power of a modern agile development process.

This sample data platform will provide the core lessons that you can follow step by step using low row-count examples that are easy to analyze and understand. The Snowflake sample data will be used when we want to specifically target big row-count use cases.

Introducing our stock tracking project

We have chosen to build a simple stock tracking platform to illustrate the dbt functionalities, as it can be initially reduced to a simple set of concepts and relations while offering multiple ways to add complexity and interesting requirements to develop in further iterations.

Using an example project that many people will relate to, we hope to provide easier understanding and involvement and maybe provide real value through the ability to start a project to track your stocks.

It is, in fact, quite a common situation that a person or a family ends up having more than one account and that there are tradable securities in these accounts. A common desire is to therefore have a global view of all the accounts.

With the advancement of fintech solutions, this is becoming simpler in modern portfolio applications if your accounts are in a single country, but you have them in different jurisdictions, then I wish you good luck, or you can roll up your sleeves and cook something that fits the bill together with us.

Other common reasons that might make the use case valid are to keep your data independent from your brokers, so that your history will always be with you, or to personalize your reporting and analysis beyond what your current provider offers.

As an example, I find that the attribution of categories such as industries and even countries are often missing or not aligned with the reality for many small and medium stocks, especially outside the US market. What country would you use for a Canadian company with mines in Mexico or Russia? Is that operation in a developed or a developing country? Is it exposed to Canadian dollars, Mexican pesos, or Russian rubles?

The initial data model and glossary

This sample project is about being able to track the value of investments spread across multiple portfolios and analyze them in the ways we prefer. We will start simple, just tracking the current value of the portfolio, and we will add more functionalities along the next sections and chapters.

The starting use case is that an investor has portfolios, potentially at different brokers, where they hold positions in securities. They can buy and sell securities, therefore opening, closing, and changing the positions they have.

They would like to use the data they receive from the brokers to track the daily value of their overall situation and analyze their holdings according to multiple attributes of the securities.

The following conceptual data model illustrates the main entities and their relations, as you could gather from the initial explanation of the use case.

Note that in the data model, we do not have all the entities we named because we are more interested in showing the core "structural relations" and not fully denormalizing the data model, showing all existing entities and all their relations. As an example, we do not show the **Investor** entity, because for now, we can start with an `owner` or `owner_id` column inside the **Portfolio** entity:

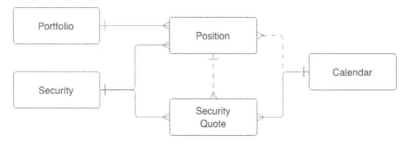

Figure 5.3: The initial data model for the portfolio tracking project

To provide for a common understanding it is good practice to provide a glossary with the description of the concepts of the data model, such as the following:

- **Position**: A position tracks the amount of a specific security hold in a portfolio and comes with a few measures besides the amount of stock owned, such as the cost of the security hold in the position.

- **Portfolio**: A portfolio is a container of positions, usually associated with a trading or custody account at a broker.

- **Security**: A security is an investment instrument that can be bought and sold on a specific market. Securities exist in multiple types, including bonds, stock, options, and many others.

- **Quote**: A security quote is a set of values, such as a bid and an ask price, that describe the market offering for the stock at a moment in time or a set of values that describe the market offering for the stock during an interval of time:

  - **Daily quote**: A daily quote is a set of values, such as open, close, max, and min prices, that describe the market offering for the stock during a trading day.

- **Calendar**: The calendar represents the time dimension at the desired resolution, often a day, providing useful precalculated attributes for all the items in the calendar.

Throughout this chapter and the following chapters, we will start with very simple needs and features first and add complexity and features along the way to introduce more dbt or Snowflake features, and sometimes also to just show alternatives or how initial solutions might have limits.

The idea is to go about it how you would with a real-life project: you start with some needs and by the time you have done half of what your people had in mind, new ideas emerge, and you find yourself steering the project toward new, more promising goals. You get the idea: change is the only constant.

Therefore, bear with us if in some cases, we might change the idea abruptly or introduce a new need that might not be totally logical, but that's done to utilize a dbt feature or introduce an interesting pattern. Here, it might serve as a skill progression but we will try to keep it not too far from what actual projects look like.

Setting up the project in dbt, Snowflake, and GitHub

Now that we have described the project in broad strokes, it is time to roll up our sleeves and start building it.

To get started and have a project ready in dbt, we need to have a repository set up in GitHub to host the code and a database set up in Snowflake to hold the data and deploy the code.

We also need to make a few basic design choices to organize the project. We will briefly discuss them in the next *Portfolio tracking project design* section.

In the following sections, we will quickly describe the steps that you need to do to get your project set up. If you are not sure how to do so yet, you can reference the step-by-step instructions we gave in *Chapter 1* for Snowflake and *Chapter 2* for GitHub and dbt.

Portfolio tracking project design

This is a sample project, so we will keep the setup as simple as possible, but this is the occasion to discuss the alternatives we have for bigger projects:

- **Database and environments**: For this project, we will use the ability of dbt to provide multiple parallel and independent environments in the same database by using prefixes. We will also only use two environments: a development environment for coding and a production environment for the stable release. This might already be overkill for a single-person project, but we want to do things well and it costs close to nothing in terms of money or time.

    In a real-world application, you might want to have all the developer environments in one DEV database, then a **Quality Assurance (QA)** or **Continuous Integration (CI)** environment in its own QA database to integrate all the developments, and finally, a production environment in its PROD database to hold the good data and run on stable releases.

- **Git branches**: As we will only have DEV and PROD environments, we will use feature branches with the names you come up with for each feature in the DEV environment, while main (or master in older setups) will be the branch corresponding to the PROD environment.

If you had QA and PROD environments, it would make sense for the `main` branch, where the developments are merged by default, to be associated with QA and then a long-running `PROD` branch to be associated with the PROD environment. The same pattern can be used if you would like to have more deployment environments, such as release candidates, between QA and PROD. We just advise you to keep things simple and agile.

- **Users and roles**: We are going to use a single role, `DBT_EXECUTOR_ROLE`, for DEV and PROD. We will use our user for the DEV environment and create a user for the PROD environment. They will both use the executor role to run the dbt project.

  In a real-life scenario, you might want to have one writer role for each database or environment, and one or more readers, assigning to the developer's user the DEV writer and the reader roles to the other environments, as you only want dbt to make controlled changes there when acting on manual commands from the developer. You might also want to create reader roles restricted to one data mart to control and manage the delivery of your data better, assigning these reader roles to the users depending on their access needs.

- **Location and format of input data**: We want to give you ample coverage of the dbt-SF combined capabilities, so we will use data in CSV file format as source files included in the dbt source code repository (not always the best choice).

  In a real-life project, the use of CSV files stored in the project repository is useful but restricted to a few cases, and loading files is not manual but automatically done by a piece of data movement code that puts them in a file container, often external to SF, and dbt macros that load them.

Setting up the repository for the portfolio project

We need a repository to hold the data, so let's make a new, empty repository on GitHub:

1. Log in to your profile on GitHub or the Git provider of your choice.
2. Create a new repository with a name you like. We used `portfolio-tracking-dbt`, but you can pick the one you prefer and *leave it totally empty*, that is without a README, `gitignore`, `license`, or any other file.

That's it – we now have an empty repo that we can use with dbt.

We will use the dbt integration with GitHub to do the connection from dbt, so no more work is left to be done here.

Setting up the database for the portfolio project

We need a database in Snowflake and a user to run the production environment, so let's do it.

First, let's recall the setup from *Chapter 1*, where we created a `DBT_EXECUTOR_ROLE` role for all the users that needed to run code in dbt.

We have granted the ability to use the existing warehouse to run queries and create new databases. Then, we assigned that role to our user so that we can use it in the dbt DEV environment and to the DBT_EXECUTOR service user that we will configure to run the PROD environment.

Therefore, we just have to create the database, as we are already fine with the two users we have.

Create the new database using the executor role. We named it PORTFOLIO_TRACKING. If you change it, remember to consequently change all the commands and scripts that will use this name:

```
USE ROLE DBT_EXECUTOR_ROLE;
CREATE DATABASE PORTFOLIO_TRACKING
    COMMENT = 'DB for the portfolio tracking project';
```

Now that we have everything that we need, you can create a new dbt project.

> **Note**
>
> We have decided to create the database with the executor role, but another choice might be to use a different role to create the DBs and give the executor role the ability to create the schemata in that database.
>
> The main difference would be the ability (or the lack of the ability) of the executor role to drop the full database in a single command.

Creating a new dbt project for the portfolio project

We have prepared the things we need, so we will be able to create the new project following the same steps that we have shown in the second chapter, which we will recall here:

1. Click **Account Settings** from the dbt main menu (the hamburger tiles on the top left), click **Projects** in the left-hand menu, and then the **New Project** button on the top right.

    By clicking the **Begin** button (on the top right) you will start the guided setup.

2. Enter a name for the project – we have used Portfolio tracking.

    Once you are done, click the **Continue** button.

3. Select the **Snowflake** database by clicking on its logo or name. You will be taken to the page to set up your connection.

4. In the **Connection Settings** page, enter the **Snowflake Settings** information, which is the general connection parameters that apply to all users, and your **Development Credentials** information, which is related to your user and your development environment.

    Note that you have just created the database you want to use with the role you want to use, so for the SF settings, you just need your Snowflake account (the part of your SF address between https:// and .snowflakecomputing.com) and the execution warehouse name (the default is COMPUTE_WH and we have not changed it).

Then, enter your SF user details, set **schema** to your initials, set **target name** to dev, and use 8 or 12 **threads** in the DEV environment credentials.

Test your connection and click the **Continue** button when it is working.

5.   On the **Set Up a Repository** page, click on the **GitHub** button (or the one for your Git provider) and then select the repository that you want to use (the one we just created). When the import is successful, click on the **Continue** button, and you are done with the setup.

Congratulations – you now have a new empty project set up in your dbt account!

> **Note**
> If you have a newer dbt account and you cannot create a second project for free, use the previous steps to change the first project that we have set up and the following ones to test and clear it from the default project.

From the dbt overview page, select the **Start Developing** button to go to the **Integrated Development Environment** (IDE) or code editor. You can do the same by clicking the **Develop** item in the main menu.

Once in the code editor, click the **initialize your project** button and dbt will generate the default dbt project for you. Click the **commit...** button to save it to the Git repo:

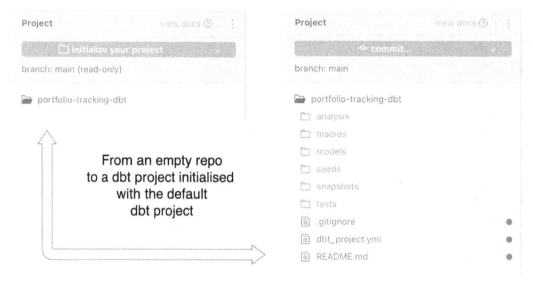

Figure 5.4: The dbt Cloud UI with the project content

Now, check that your project is correctly set up with two very simple checks:

1. Enter the following SQL command in an empty scratchpad and click the **Preview** button:

   ```
   select 1
   ```

   If the preview executes without errors and you see the **Returned 1 row.** result in the **Query results** panel and the 1 value in the results, then this means that you can connect to your database and run queries on it.

2. Run the dbt default project by entering the dbt run command in the command line at the bottom of the code editor. If the run completes correctly, it means that you can create schemas, tables, and views in your DB. If you go to your Snowflake interface, you will find the schema (with the initials you entered in the project setup) and the two models (one table and one view) created in your database.

   This is all we need to be sure we can build our project with dbt and Snowflake.

3. You can clean up the dbt default project by removing the example folder inside the models folder. If you do this, you can also clean up your database by dropping the two models or the entire schema if it does not contain anything else.

Great! We have checked that our project is set up correctly and we are ready to start our portfolio project.

Defining data sources and providing reference data

Every data warehousing project, in theory, can be reduced to finding the right data sources and their transformations to achieve the outputs that you want.

In an ideal world, you can always find the data that you need and produce what you want, but life is usually more complicated, as you might not have all the data sources or information that you would like. The reality is that often you need to adapt your goals and see what you can achieve starting from what you have.

In any case, defining your data sources is crucial, as they are what is provided to you, and by writing proper transformations, you can be the best steward of the information contained therein, unless you are in the rare position to change what the source systems collect or to design your data sources.

Defining data sources in dbt

In dbt, you have two proper ways to designate and take into use external data, that is, data that is not created or transformed with dbt:

- **Sources**: The general mechanism for using external data in dbt is to define the initial data you want to start your transformation as a *source, defined by a source system definition that points to a database and schema, and one or more table definitions that select one table or view from that* *database and schema*. Defining a source system and using a `source` reference is a great way to make the usage of data from a system that you consider born or managed externally to the current dbt project explicit, whether it is a properly external system or data that is managed by another dbt project and practically local.

- **Seeds**: In dbt, you can put CSV files into designated folders and have dbt load them into a table with the `dbt seed` command. Note that this is not a general-purpose CSV data loading mechanism by design.

- **Created data**: As strange as it sounds, in a DW project, some data can be created out of nowhere. A common example is the calendar dimension, but this is true for anything that can be generated by some logic and little starting data. These are treated as normal models, as with any other model where the logic part is overwhelming compared to the input data, even if these have no input outside variables or hardcoded values.

- **Direct hardcoded references**: When you start writing code in dbt, it will be common for you to use direct references to actual database tables, as you do in normal SQL queries, instead of using the `source` and `ref` references. Please resist this at all costs. While this is technically a potential way to refer to external data, it is also a way to completely hinder your dbt project and defeat the benefits of dbt on many levels. We will mention just a few reasons to avoid direct references: making it impossible for dbt to run the project in the correct order, making it impossible to trace and visualize dependencies (lineage), making it impossible for your code to work on different environments managed by dbt, removing flexibility from your code, and making dbt unable to generate proper documentation. You see that it is not a good idea to directly name tables in your SQL instead of using the proper `ref` or `source` syntax.

The proper way to structure a dbt project is to have your input defined in terms of `sources` and `seeds` and build your first layer of dbt models on top of them, then continue the transformation pipeline, referencing the previous models using the `ref` function, as explained in the *Introducing source and ref dbt functions* section of *Chapter 2*.

Understanding and declaring dbt source references

Using `source` references in your code, you can define the boundaries of your dbt project and have its dependencies properly visualized and managed.

As an example, you can declare an SLA for the data freshness on a source system or a specific source table, write tests to define the expectations you have on the incoming data, or be able to manage the external data location in a very flexible way.

A source is declared as metadata in a YAML file and can be defined for any database object that you can query with the normal `SELECT ... FROM db.schema.source` syntax, so it includes external tables and similar database extensions that you can query directly in that form or that you can encapsulate in standard database objects such as views.

The typical pattern to provide and access external data is that all the data from a specific system, real or logical, is made available inside a schema of a database that your dbt code can read from so that you identify the **source system** as the database and schema and the **source table** as a database object (table, view, or other) inside that system (database and schema).

The following code gives you an idea of how a source system and a source table are defined:

```
sources:
  - name: <source system name>

    database: <db name>
    schema: <schema name>
    description: <some description of the system>

    freshness: # system level freshness SLA
      warn_after: {count: 12, period: hour}
      error_after: {count: 24, period: hour}
    loaded_at_field: <default timestamp field>
    tables:
      - name: <name we want to use for the source table/view>
        identifier: <name in the target database>
        description: source table description
```

Let's describe the above definition of a source system and a table inside it:

- The initial name field defines the name of the source system that we are defining and it will be used to access it when using the source function in the SQL code.

- The database and schema fields define the location to read from, as used in fully qualified database names. They are optional, defaulting to the database and schema declared in the project connection, but we suggest making them explicit unless they strictly follow the dbt project location.

- The description field allows us to enter a human-readable description in the documentation.

- The freshness and loaded_at_field fields allow us to define a system- or table-level data freshness SLA, which defines the maximum age for the most recent data in the source system tables before raising a warning or error and the timestamp field to query for the age of the data in the table.

  A system-level SLA or field applies to all tables defined under it and, as always in dbt, can be overridden at a lower level – in this case, at the table level.

- The tables key introduces the declaration of individual source tables inside the defined system.

- The name field under `tables` defines the name of the source table that we want to access and it will be the second element used to access it when using the `source` function in the SQL code. Unless you include an `identifier` field that provides the actual object name in the target database the `name` field will be used and it must match the object found in the source system location.

Under this source table definition, you can declare all the available table properties and configurations, exemplified here by the `description` field, that we will see later in more detail for all models. As an example, this includes tests and tags.

In general, consider that this is a normal YAML dbt file and you can use the general dbt properties and configs that exist and apply to sources.

While you can define multiple source systems with different names pointing to the same database and schema, this is not generally a good idea, as having two names for the same thing creates confusion. One case where I can see good use of this is when you have been provided data from multiple systems into a single database and schema. By defining multiple source systems and picking the right tables, you can effectively separate what table comes from what system.

Special cases involving sources

In general, sources are defined on data that is provided to us and the first contact with dbt is when we start reading that data from the source definition.

While this remains the case at a logical and semantic level, in some loading patterns, we have dbt perform certain operations on the raw data received by a system and then define a source on the result of these operations, which will be the start of our dbt transformations.

The most common example is when we use dbt to ingest data from files into a landing table.

In this pattern, the step of loading the raw data from the files into the landing table is done by a dbt `run-operation`, which invokes a macro that executes the database command, such as `COPY INTO`. The `run-operation` is run before the actual `dbt run` is started and the landing table is defined as a source table so that when the dbt code is run, it properly references this external source with a `source` reference and our transformations start from the landing table, not from the files.

Other common cases are when using an external table that is created by a dbt `run-operation` (or a run-once setup time query) or declaring a view that encapsulates a special database construct, such as federated queries in **Big Query (BQ)**, to give access to non-native SQL data.

> **Important tip**
>
> In general, it is useful to use dbt to manage resource creation with `run-operations` or setup time queries and then define a source on the results of these setup or load tasks. The logic is to define the database object as a source from where you can start writing the SQL transformations that make up our dbt models.

As you become familiar with the power of sources, you might be tempted to define fake sources as results of snapshots on models or models themselves, often to overcome the very sound limits that dbt upholds to avoid circular dependencies. Please refrain from this temptation. Unless you know exactly what you are doing and why, chances are you are putting yourself in a difficult position and maybe you can achieve the same in a different way that is more closely in line with how dbt works.

Understanding seeds

The seed loading mechanism in dbt is not a general-purpose way to load high amounts of data from CSV files – it is only intended as a utility tool to load small amounts of data (up to hundreds or a few thousands of lines) that are strictly connected with the current project and do not make much sense to maintain or load in a different place or with a different tool.

The data suitable to be loaded as a seed has the following properties: changes infrequently, is generally maintained by hand, and is suitable or even required to be versioned inside your Git repository to track changes.

Examples of good seeds are hand-maintained lists of things such as test users or sample products, special mappings such as mapping user codes to internal employee codes, or reference data such as connecting country codes to country names and stats or currency codes to names.

Bad cases for seed loading are big files, as they will load slowly and every copy will stay there forever, cluttering your Git repository, data that changes frequently, and data that contains personal or sensible information, as it will be recorded and exposed in clear text in your repo forever.

To load the data from a CSV file, it is enough to put the file in the folder indicated in the project configuration file, directly or in a subfolder, and then run the dbt seed command. Of course, you can run the dbt seed command with switches to better control what seeds are to be loaded or re-loaded.

The following line shows the seed configuration line inside the project configuration file, where you can name the folder to be searched for seeds:

```
seed-paths: ["seeds"]
```

If you do nothing else, the data will be loaded in a table with the same name as the CSV file and with the data types inferred by dbt and the destination database.

Tables generated by seed loading can be accessed as normal dbt models using the ref function.

For seeds, dbt offers the standard metadata driven approach of defining properties and configurations in a hierarchical way inside YAML files.

Seed can be configured in the main configuration file under the seed key as exemplified in the following snippet, which shows the seed-specific configurations:

```
seeds:
  <resource-path>:
```

```
quote_columns: true | false
column_types:
  column_name: datatype
```

With the configuration, you can decide what database and schema the table are generated in, define which column names from the CSV file are quoted, and most importantly, declare the data type for each column so that you can choose it instead of relying on type inference by the target database, which will sometimes be off.

To document and define tests on your seeds, you can use the usual YAML file mechanism, defining them as you would do on any other dbt model.

In the following sections, we will exemplify the process using our portfolio tracking project.

Loading the first data for the portfolio project

Now that we have a basic understanding of the functionalities of dbt in place, let's see how they come into play in a real scenario by loading the data of our first portfolio that we want to track.

Let's start by loading the data about the portfolio that we assume to have at the fictional ABC Bank. Then, we will try to complete that information.

Loading your first export of portfolio data

Every broker offers a way to download data about the investments we have with them, which we call a portfolio, with each investment being a position.

The following table represents a minimal set of information that most banks will provide when exporting the data related to investments made with them. Many will provide much more data.

In this example, we have three investments (positions) in stocks traded in three different markets (exchanges), two in the USA and one in Canada:

	A	B	C	D	E	F	G	H	I
1	accountID	symbol	description	exchange	report_date	quantity	cost_base	position_val	currency
2	ABC000123	GCM	GRAN COLOMBIA GOLD CORP	TSE	09/04/21	100	559	678	CAD
3	ABC000123	TTD	TRADE DESK INC/THE -CLASS A	NASDAQ	09/04/21	10	5310,45	6925,6	USD
4	ABC000123	STAR	ISTAR INC	NYSE	09/04/21	150	2444	2725,5	USD
5									
6									

Figure 5.5: The data export of our fictional portfolio at ABC Bank

To get our project started quickly, we can save this data as a CSV file – we could load it using the dbt seed feature. However, we explained in the previous section that this feature is not meant to load data that changes often, and it does not make much sense to have one CSV file in our Git repository for each day we update the portfolio, so this would be an abuse of this functionality.

To keep the setup simple and avoid using an external file storage system (such as AWS S3, Google File Storage, or Azure Storage) or installing SnowSQL to load the files from your local filesystem, we will guide you on loading the CSV data in a table using the Snowflake **User Interface** (**UI**). In essence, we will manually execute the process that is normally done automatically to ingest file-based data. We will analyze the file-based loading patterns in detail in the final part of the book.

The plan is therefore the following:

1. Create the landing table that will hold the external data.

2. Manually load the external data from the CSV file in the landing table.

3. Define the landing table as our source table.

4. Read the data from the source table to start our ELT.

The goal of loading the data in a landing table and then defining a source on it is to provide a resilient way to use our data so that our ELT will not have to change if, at some point, we start loading this data in an automated way or from a different file storage system.

Let's get started, then!

1. Earlier in this chapter, we created the PORTFOLIO_TRACKING database that we will use, so let's start by using the executor role to create a SOURCE_DATA schema to hold the data that we load from external sources:

    ```
    USE ROLE DBT_EXECUTOR_ROLE;
    CREATE SCHEMA PORTFOLIO_TRACKING.SOURCE_DATA;
    ```

2. Now that we have a schema, we can create the ABC_BANK_POSITION table where we want to load the data for the ABC Bank portfolio:

    ```
    CREATE OR REPLACE TABLE
      PORTFOLIO_TRACKING.SOURCE_DATA.ABC_BANK_POSITION (
        accountID        TEXT,
        symbol           TEXT,
        description      TEXT,
        exchange         TEXT,
        report_date      DATE,
        quantity         NUMBER(38,0),
        cost_base        NUMBER(38,5),
        position_value   NUMBER(38,5),
        currency         TEXT
    );
    ```

The preceding statement creates a table with the same columns and data types and in the same order as our CSV file so that we can easily load it.

Now that we have the table to hold the data, we can load it using the Snowflake interface:

1. First, create a file with your investments in it, following the format from the previous figure, and export the data in CSV format (follow the US standard or adapt the format), or download the CSV in the picture from our repository: https://github.com/PacktPublishing/ Data-engineering-with-dbt/blob/main/Chapter_05/ABC_Bank_ PORTFOLIO__2021-04-09.csv.

2. To read the CSV without problems, we have to provide Snowflake with the settings for how we exported the CSV file. We can do that effectively by defining a File Format that we can then reuse every time we use files formatted in the same way.

   The following code creates a file format suitable for reading CSV files created by exporting data from Excel using the US locale (the US standard settings):

```
CREATE FILE FORMAT
    PORTFOLIO_TRACKING.SOURCE_DATA.ABC_BANK_CSV_FILE_FORMAT
      TYPE = 'CSV'
            COMPRESSION = 'AUTO'
            FIELD_DELIMITER = ','
            RECORD_DELIMITER = '\n'
            SKIP_HEADER = 1
            FIELD_OPTIONALLY_ENCLOSED_BY = '\042'
            TRIM_SPACE = FALSE
            ERROR_ON_COLUMN_COUNT_MISMATCH = TRUE
            ESCAPE = 'NONE'
            ESCAPE_UNENCLOSED_FIELD = '\134'
            DATE_FORMAT = 'AUTO'
            TIMESTAMP_FORMAT = 'AUTO'
            NULL_IF = ('\\N')
    ;
```

   Note that most of the attributes are optional, as they have the right default, but we provide the same file format that is provided by the **Load Data** wizard if you pick the key values. It is important to note the value for SKIP_HEADER = 1, as this allows us to define the first row as a header (to be skipped when loading data). The FIELD_DELIMITER and RECORD_DELIMITER attributes are important, as they define how the columns are separated in a row and how a row is terminated ('\n' is a new line).

   The FIELD_OPTIONALLY_ENCLOSED_BY = '\042' attribute specifies string-type columns that can be optionally enclosed in double quotes. This is needed if they contain characters with special meaning, such as the delimiters.

3. Now that you have the CSV ready and a file format to read it, go to your Snowflake account in your browser and make sure to select your DBT_EXECUTOR_ROLE as the role you impersonate (in the top-right-hand part of the SF UI).

To load the data from the CSV into the table that we created, click on the **Databases** icon in the top-left-hand corner, and then click on the **PORTFOLIO_TRACKING** database in the list that appears. Then, select the row or click on the name of the **ABC_BANK_POSITION** table and click on **Load table** to start the **Load Data** wizard:

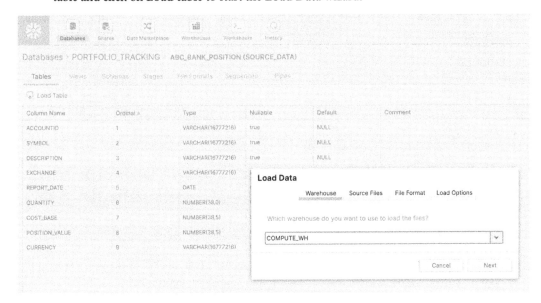

Figure 5.6: The Load Data wizard in Snowflake

In the **Load Data** wizard, pick the warehouse you want to use to load the data and click **Next** on the **Warehouse** page. Click **Select Files**, select the CSV file you have saved, and then click **Next** on the **Source Files** page. Select the file format that we created and click **Load** on the **File Formats** page. You can click **Next** and then **Load** if you want to explore the next page of the wizard.

Once you click the **Load** button Snowflake will load the CSV file into a stage, then parse it in memory using the file format that we specified and then insert the data into the specified table using a COPY INTO command, that is the most efficient way to load big amounts of data.

To check that all is good, go back to **Worksheets** in the SF UI, and then select the database, schema, and table where we loaded the data in the left-hand navigation panel. You should see that the table contains the number of rows that were in your CSV. You can click **Preview Data** to see the first few rows of the data.

Defining the source data

In a real-life project, you will already have the source data provided to you or your team will have built a pipeline to load it. In the last part of the book, we will get into detail on that part.

Let's define the dbt source for the data that we have loaded and then access it from dbt.

A best practice to conjugate project order, ease of editing, and to avoid many merge conflicts is to define a different YAML file for each source system that we get data from.

Create a new file named `source_abc_bank.yml` under the `model` folder in the dbt editor with the following content:

```
version: 2
sources:
  - name: abc_bank
    database: PORTFOLIO_TRACKING
    schema: SOURCE_DATA
    tables:
      - name: ABC_BANK_POSITION
```

You can find the source in our repository in the `05_03_v1__source_abc_bank.yml` file inside the materials for *Chapter 5* in the `dbt` folder.

Let's analyze the preceding file:

- The first line with `version: 2` is mandatory and tells dbt that this YAML file uses the second version of the dbt YAML file specification. Version 1 has been deprecated.

- The next line with `sources:` declares that we are going to describe some source systems in this file under that declaration.

- The line with the `name` attribute introduces the first system with its name.

- Under the system name are a few attributes that better configure the source. The `database` and `schema` attributes indicate to dbt where to look for the tables of this source system.

- The `tables:` attribute introduces the declarations of the source tables that we are going to use from this source system. We can add as many tables as we need.

- The `- name: ABC_BANK_POSITION` line introduces the first system table, using the `name` attribute, as we have done with the source systems.

  Now, we have left it as simple as possible, but we will see shortly that we will use this declaration to add more functionalities such as describing columns and introducing tests.

With this initial YAML file, we have done a minimal configuration of our first source so that we can access the data simply and flexibly.

We can try our source by writing the following query, which is the simplest for testing a source:

```
SELECT *
FROM {{ source('abc_bank', 'ABC_BANK_POSITION') }}
```

Note that the names in dbt are case-sensitive, so use the same casing as in the YAML file. This calls for an agreed upon code convention for table and source names inside your project.

By clicking the **Preview** button in the dbt IDE, you ask dbt to compile and run the query on your database, and then take you to the **Query Results** tab, where you can see the results of the query:

Figure 5.7: Results of a query on a source in dbt's Preview tab

Going to the **Compiled SQL** tab, you can see the SQL that was executed on the database, as shown in the following image. Note that clicking the </> **Compile** button just compiles the code and brings you to the **Compiled SQL** tab, without executing it:

```
1    SELECT *
2    FROM {{ source('abc_bank', 'ABC_BANK_POSITION') }}
3
```

| Preview | </> Compile | | Query Results | Compiled SQL | Lineage |

```
4.6 sec
```

```
1    SELECT *
2    FROM PORTFOLIO_TRACKING.SOURCE_DATA.ABC_BANK_POSITION
3    limit 500
4    /* limit added automatically by dbt cloud */
```

Figure 5.8: Compiled code for the preceding query in dbt Compile SQL tab

We have defined a source system with a source table and checked that it all works fine.

Let's move on to seeing how we can use this to build our first dbt models.

> **Tip**
>
> Note that names, including model names, are case-sensitive in dbt, so 'abc_bank' is different from 'ABC_BANK'.
>
> This might be confusing when working with Snowflake, as all names are case-insensitive and always shown in uppercase unless you explicitly quote the name with double quotes.
>
> We use uppercase for model names (so that it matches what you see in SF and works if you copy and paste table names) and lowercase for other objects, such as macros and system names.

Now that we have some content in the models folder, you can delete the .gitkeep file before we move on to creating our first dbt model in the next section.

How to write and test transformations

Now that we have some data, we can start using dbt to transform that data into the information that we want to deliver for reporting or our other use cases.

Writing the first dbt model

For the time being, we just have one piece of information – the content of the portfolio from ABC Bank that we have loaded in the landing table.

This, in dimensional modeling terms, is a **fact**, which is a table that provides quantitative information about some objects or events that we want to reason about.

To provide more value on top of the data itself, we want to calculate a few other measures for the positions and make them available to our reports.

First, we are going to calculate the profit for each position.

Let's create a POSITION_ABC_BANK.sql file in the **models** folder with this content:

```
SELECT
    *
    , POSITION_VALUE - COST_BASE as UNREALIZED_PROFIT
FROM {{ source('abc_bank', 'ABC_BANK_POSITION') }}
```

Let's discuss it:

- By using * (the star symbol) in the SELECT command, we take all the fields from the source we are reading from, so we stay open for future changes

- We calculate UNREALIZED_PROFIT as the difference between the current value and the cost base of the position

Just a note on the file names: we named the CSV file ABC_BANK_POSITION and the dbt model POSITION_ABC_BANK. Are they good names? Do we risk confusion?

It is common, and logical, to think about the incoming data with the source first and then what the content is, so the name of our CSV reflects this "source first" thinking that is proper for the source and storage layers. When we move to the dbt models in the refined layers, where we convey information, we start thinking in terms of the content (or concept) first and maybe we need or want to recall the source if the data is not of general use or scope. The name of our model conveys that we talk about the *POSITION* concept and that the content is limited to the ABC Bank system.

So far so good, but if you run the query, it looks like the position for "TRADE DESC INC/THE" with the TTD symbol has a large absolute profit, and the others just a small one. Let's add a UNREALIZED_ PROFIT_PCT field to account for the size of the initial investment.

Let's change the POSITION_ABC_BANK.sql file as follows:

```
SELECT
    *
    , POSITION_VALUE - COST_BASE as UNREALIZED_PROFIT
    , UNREALIZED_PROFIT / COST_BASE as UNREALIZED_PROFIT_PCT
FROM {{ source('abc_bank', 'ABC_BANK_POSITION') }}
```

Now we also have the percent of profit concerning the position cost base.

All looks good, but maybe we do not like the long string of decimals from the division.

Let's fix it by using the standard ROUND function from Snowflake.

Change the line as follows:

```
    , ROUND(UNREALIZED_PROFIT / COST_BASE, 5)
        as UNREALIZED_PROFIT_PCT
```

Now we have rounded the result to the fifth decimal digit.

You can find the final version of this source file in the Git repository in the 05_04_v1__POSITION_ ABC_BANK.sql file inside the materials for *Chapter 5* in the dbt folder.

Real-time lineage and project navigation

We have produced our very first dbt model from the single source that we have declared, so it is very difficult to get lost in our project now, but if you have experience with data platforms, you know how complicated understanding which transformations are connected becomes.

Stop despairing and click on the **Lineage** tab of the dbt IDE while you are in the POSITION_ABC_ BANK model.

Lo and behold… you now have a nice, easy-to-read lineage diagram showing the relation of this model with all other models that are related to it:

Figure 5.9: The initial lineage diagram for the portfolio project

While there is not much to see now, as we just have declared one source table (shown on the left with a database icon with an arrow) and one model (shown on the right with a cube icon), when your project becomes bigger and more complex, this diagram will be an invaluable guide to easily traversing models and remembering what you have been building.

The lineage diagram is drawn in real time and it is always up to date with your project.

You can also use it to move around the project quickly by double-clicking to go to a model or the definition of a source. The diagram is also dynamic, as you can drag around the boxes to arrange it in a way that makes more sense for you and eventually copy it or print it out to communicate with your colleagues or stakeholders better.

Deploying the first dbt model

Until now, we have just created the file, saved it a couple of times after each change, and run it using the **Preview** button feature on dbt Cloud – anyway, no table exists in our database yet and no code has been saved in our repository. Let's fix it.

To deploy our code in our DEV environment, we must manually execute the desired dbt commands using the command line at the bottom of the IDE.

Execute the following command to run all the models (even if for now, we have only one!) and deploy them to SF:

```
dbt run
```

After a few seconds, the command completes successfully and your model is created in the database, but where?

It will be created in the schema that you named in the wizard when you did the Snowflake configuration when creating this project. I used RZ and we suggested using your initials.

It also is the same schema where the initial default project was created when we used dbt run to test that everything was configured correctly.

To deploy the code in your DEV environment, you will run the commands manually, as it is common to add one model at a time and change it a few or many times before being happy with it, not wanting to run everything at every change. By running manually, you can run and test what you feel is right at any moment.

We will see that to deploy in a deployment environment, you will use a job – that is, a sequence of dbt commands. You will define it once and run it every time that you want to deploy and run that environment.

The nice thing is that you can define multiple jobs for each environment so that you can have a job that runs everything and another one that just loads the data that changes hourly and only refreshes whatever depends on that data.

Committing the first dbt model

We have now generated the model in our database by running the needed dbt command, but the code of the model only exists on the dbt Cloud server and is not in our Git repository.

To add the current version of the code to our Git repository, we must commit the changes.

You can do that very easily in dbt Cloud, as it has a guided Git workflow that allows you to easily create a Git branch, then commit the changes while you develop and finally, open a **Pull Request** (**PR**) to merge that development into the main or master branch.

To commit the current code for the project, models, and configs, click on the green **commit …** button in the top-left-hand corner of the dbt IDE and then enter a commit message in the popup that will open up. Clicking on the **commit** button will send the code to Git as a new commit.

Remember to save all your open models and config files before completing a commit, as only what is saved will be committed. In any case, rest assured that the dbt IDE will warn you if you have unsaved files.

Now that you have committed them, your changes are saved also to your Git repository, and most importantly, are now available for everyone else that can access the repository.

After each commit, while the code on your IDE is not changed since the last commit, you can open a PR to share the code with your colleagues and start to gather feedback or request a final approval to merge it back into the main branch. We will come back to collaboration in later chapters.

Configuring our project and where we store data

The schema that you define in your dev credentials is the schema where your development environment will exist and, if we do nothing, everything we create will be generated in that schema.

Note that the schema for our DEV environment or a deployment environment is often referred to in the dbt documentation as target schema and it is available in the code as `{{ target.schema }}`.

Over time, having everything generated in the same single schema will become chaotic, and because one of our main goals is to create and maintain an environment that makes life easier for the developers, let's fix it and start creating a bit more order by configuring different parts of the dbt project to be created in different schemata in our environment.

The problem is that our environment is defined as a schema and, in a database, you cannot have a schema nested into another schema, so we cannot create multiple schemata inside the target schema for our DEV environment.

To overcome this problem, dbt will generate the tables and views in multiple schemata that have the name composed by the name of our target schema followed by the name of the custom schema that we have defined for the specific content, with the final name of the schema having the following layout: `<target_schema>_<custom_schema>`.

As an example, if my target schema is `RZ` and the content is configured to go into a custom schema named `REFINED`, then the actual schema name when the content is deployed in my environment will be `RZ_REFINED`. The same content deployed to an environment that has a target schema of `PROD` will be created in the `PROD_REFINED` schema.

To recap, remember that you define the target schema where you define the environment, usually along with the connection details, while you configure the custom schema in the main dbt `config` file, or you override it along the project, as with any other configuration.

The main configuration file

The main element that we use to define and configure the dbt project, including where resources are created, is the main configuration file, `dbt_project.yml`.

dbt defines the folder that contains the `dbt_project.yml` file as the dbt project folder and this file contains the essential and general configuration for the project, which can be eventually overridden at more specific levels.

Open it and follow along with our description and changes.

In the first lines, usually 5 to 7, you will find the following:

```
name: 'my_new_project'
version: '1.0.0'
config-version: 2
```

It is a good practice to change the name to something meaningful, so we will name it 'portfolio_ tracking'.

You can change the version to '0.1.0' and update it when you do minor releases or leave it as it is and just update it when you do major releases. We will leave it unchanged.

Do not change config-version, as that specifies the version of the definition of the configuration to use and version 2 is the one in use now.

Moving down, you find the profile name to use around line 10, as shown here:

```
profile: 'default'
```

This is not used in dbt Cloud, but it is used in dbt Core to select which connection profile to use from the many that can be defined in the connection configuration file.

After this, there are the definitions of the paths where dbt finds the different types of objects, puts the generated code, and what to clean up if you run a dbt clean command.

This is usually in lines 15 to 25, as shown here:

```
model-paths: ["models"]
analysis-paths: ["analyses"]
test-paths: ["tests"]
seed-paths: ["seeds"]
macro-paths: ["macros"]
snapshot-paths: ["snapshots"]
target-path: "target"  # directory for compiled SQL files
clean-targets:          # directories to be removed by `dbt clean`
  - «target»
  - «dbt_packages"
```

Do not change these, as they are fine unless you have very special needs.

The last part in the default config file is about configuring models and other dbt objects, as we will see in a second. Over time, we might add configurations for other elements such as seeds, snapshots, variables, sources, tests, and any other feature that we want to configure globally for the project.

The model configuration still reflects the old name and the example project, so let's change it to suit our current needs, as exemplified here:

```
models:
  portfolio_tracking:
    +materialized: view
    refined:    # Applies to all files under models/refined/
      +materialized: table
      +schema: REFINED
```

You can find the initial version of this source file in our repository in the `05_05_v1__dbt_project.yml` file inside the materials for *Chapter 5* in the `dbt` folder.

Let's review what we have configured:

- Under the general `models:`, a label that applies to all models from all projects, we have nested the name of our project, `portfolio_tracking:`, to only configure the models of this project.

- Under our project, we have added the model-specific `materialized` configuration with a value of `view`, as we want that our models to be created as views by default.

  We have added a + symbol in front of the configuration keywords, like `schema`, to make it easier to distinguish between them and folder names that are used to hierarchically apply the configurations. Note that + is optional and used only for better readability.

- Under our project, we have then named the `refined` folder, which does not yet exist, but we can already declare configurations for it and its subfolders.

- Under the `refined` folder, we have declared the model-specific `materialized` configuration again with a value of `table`, as we want the models that are placed under it to be materialized as tables.

- Under the `refined` folder, we have also declared the `schema` configuration with a value of `REFINED`, as we want that the models under it to be created in a schema with the custom schema part of `REFINED`.

To recapitulate, if we do not define any custom schema for our models, they will be created in the target schema, which is the one that we have defined in the connection configuration. If we define a custom schema, the models will be created in a schema with the name composed by the target schema and the defined custom schema; this ensures that each developer or environment will have its database objects created in schemata with different, unique names.

Re-deploying our environment to the desired schema

After our first deployment, we added the configuration to be able to generate *refined models* into a custom `refined` schema.

If we now run the `dbt run` command again… nothing changes.

Why? Because we have configured models in the `refined` folder to go to the `refined` schema, and our `POSITION_ABC_BANK` model is in the `model` folder, not in the `model/refined` folder.

Let's create the folder, move the model, and re-run the project:

Figure 5.10: Menus to create the folder and the result with the file moved

If you hover over the **models** folder in the dbt IDE, it will be highlighted and at the right end, you will see a menu appear indicated by three dots. Click the three dots and then the **New Folder** menu entry.

Type `refined` in lowercase, as done in the configuration file, for the folder name. Please remember that in dbt, file and folder names are case-sensitive.

To move the **POSITION_ABC_BANK** model, hover over its name, click the three dots for the menu, and select the **Rename** entry.

Add `refined/` before the filename so that the full path reads `models/refined/POSITION_ABC_BANK.sql` and click the **Save** button.

You will see that the file now appears under the `refined` folder.

We can now run the project again to create the model where we configured it.

Execute the usual command on the command line of the dbt IDE:

```
dbt run
```

You can now go to your Snowflake database and check that the **POSITION_ABC_BANK** table has been created under the **RZ_REFINED** schema (replace **RZ** with your target schema). Please also note that the schema has also been created for you without the need for any extra action on your part:

Figure 5.11: The content of our Snowflake database before and after re-running the project

While you expect to find the new table where it is, you might be surprised that the old **POSITION_ABC_BANK** view in the **RZ** schema (replace **RZ** with your target schema) is still there.

This is the general behavior for dbt: it will never delete tables or views unless strictly necessary (as an example, it is necessary for a model change materialization from a view to a table or the other way around, as you cannot have two database objects with the same name in the same database schema).

This behavior is in place to safeguard your data, as in many databases, it will be impossible to recover deleted tables. dbt leaves the responsibility to you to take a possibly destructive action that can be avoided by dbt and delegates to your superior judgment.

The consequence is that old models can pile up and clutter your environment if you do not clean them up. So, let's do that.

In your Snowflake UI, run the following command to drop the old view:

```
DROP VIEW "PORTFOLIO_TRACKING"."RZ"."POSITION_ABC_BANK";
```

Replace **RZ** with your target schema and the names with ones you choose.

Thinking better, do we really need the **RZ** schema? No – let's drop it then.

In your Snowflake UI, run the following command to drop the **RZ** schema:

```
DROP SCHEMA "PORTFOLIO_TRACKING"."RZ";
```

Very well, we have easily cleaned up our DEV environment, and this is the way to go to keep it clean while you are developing and changing ideas on model names (frequent) and places (rare after the initial models).

Would that be a good way to manage a common QA or TEST environment or a PROD environment? No, manually managing an environment is advisable only for your own DEV environment and only for models that have not yet been released to another environment. As they only exist in your environment, we advise keeping the management lightweight and managing them directly with manual commands on the database.

For models that have been released to other environments, we need the changes to be applied consistently and at the right moment in every environment, so it cannot be done by hand – it must be automated.

Automated changes to databases are often called **database migrations**, as they migrate the database from one state to another and can be applied by specialized software such as Flyway or Liquibase.

We will see in the following chapters that the same approach can be used with dbt by using trivially simple dbt macros to hold the SQL code and the `run-operation` command to execute them.

To recap the concept: before you release a model, it is private to you and you can manage it by hand, but once it is released to the world, a consistent approach is needed and we will use the concept of database migrations to apply these changes in all the needed environments.

Configuring the layers for our architecture

Now that we have talked about where we want our models to be generated, it is a good time to think about the overall architecture that we have discussed and start to put in place the configuration to make it happen.

Let's see how we will organize the three layers that we have defined:

- **Data storage layer**: We will teach you to implement this layer in two ways – with *dbt snapshot* and with *insert-only ingestion into history tables*. In both cases, we will configure the snapshots or models to go into their own schema; the main difference is that snapshots are global, meaning that every environment uses the same snapshot, and will be stored in the `snapshots` folder, while the history tables are implemented with normal models stored in a `staging` folder and are therefore individual to each environment, allowing more freedom and scalability.

- **Refined data layer**: We have already configured the `refined` folder so that the model under it will be generated in the `refined` schema.

- **Data delivery layer**: The data delivery layer is implemented with one or more data marts. The models for each data mart are created in their own folder under the `marts` folder and each mart is created in its own schema in the database.

Let's prepare our configuration to have all the layers set up.

Both model and snapshot configurations can be stored in the main configuration file, dbt_project. yml, so open and update it as follows:

```
models:
  portfolio_tracking:
    +materialized: view
    staging:     # Data storage layer
      +materialized: view
      +schema: STAGING
    refined:     # Refined data layer
      +materialized: view
      +schema: REFINED
    marts:       # Data delivery layer
      portfolio:      # one specific data mart
        +materialized: table
        +schema: MART_PORTFOLIO
snapshots:
  portfolio_tracking:
    +target_schema: SNAPSHOTS
```

You can find the updated version of this source file in our repository in the 05_05_v2__dbt_ project.yml file inside the materials for *Chapter 5* in the dbt folder.

Let's review the configuration:

- The contents of the staging folder are now created in the STAGING schema, as views by default.

    This configuration will be used for the incremental-only ingestion using staging views, configured at the folder level, and history tables that will be incrementally loaded and individually configured for that.

- The contents of the refined folder are now created in the REFINED schema, as views by default.

- The contents of the portfolio folder, nested under the mart folder, will be created in the MART_PORTFOLIO schema, as tables by default.

- The snapshots of this project, organized under the snapshot folder, will be created in the SNAPSHOTS schema. They are always generated as tables, loaded incrementally.

Generating views or tables for the different layers is mostly a performance choice, as they are functionally equivalent. Tables are slower to create and take up space on storage, but they are much quicker to query.

Therefore, it makes sense to materialize models that are queried multiple times during the ELT as tables so that the calculations are performed only once, as well as for models queried by end users in interactive mode so that the query executes in the shortest time possible.

In the previous section, we configured the refined layer to be generated as tables; that is a sensible choice when we do not have a data mart layer yet and the refined layer is also our delivery layer.

The delivery layer is usually materialized at tables, but if you are using a BI tool that stores the data from your data mart layer internally, such as Power BI, it is a sensible choice to generate the layer as views, because each view will be queried once to load the data in the tool.

Ensuring data quality with tests

Until now, we have loaded data from a CSV into a landing table and created a model to read the data out of it, but how can we ensure that our data is sound?

How can we deliver real data quality?

The best way is to make data quality a real thing and not just hope it defines exactly what we expect as input and output and then check that the data adheres to these requirements. This is the essence of being able to define runnable tests on our data.

In dbt, we can define two types of tests:

- **Generic tests**, once called schema tests, are tests that are generic in nature and are therefore codified in a parametrized query, which can be applied to any model or any column in any model by naming them in a YAML configuration file.

  Examples of generic tests defined by default in dbt are tests that a column is not `null` or has unique values, but we can define our own tests, such as testing whether a hash column does not incur a hash conflict.

- **Singular tests** are the most generic form of test, as you can test everything that you can express in SQL. You just need to write a SQL query that returns the rows that do not pass your test, no matter what you would like to test, whether individual calculations, full table matches, or subsets of columns in multiple tables.

Generic tests are configured in YAML configuration files and allow us to easily test common requirements in a large number of tables and columns by just defining the requirement – no other effort is needed.

dbt comes with four types of generic tests already implemented:

- `not_null`: Tests that a column is never `null` in the table.

- `unique`: Tests that the values in a column are unique.

- `relationships`: Tests the referential integrity between two tables, meaning that each value of the foreign key in the table exists in the named column of the named table. Said in another way, you test that there are no *orphans* in the tested table.

- `accepted_values`: Tests that the values in the column are one of the listed values.

You can easily write your own tests (and we will do so) or use libraries that provide more ready-to-use tests, such as `expression_is_true` or `accepted_range`, which are provided by the `dbt_utils` library.

Singular tests are written for specific cases when a generic test is not available and creating one does not make sense.

The singular tests are like normal models, but they are stored under the `test` folder, and they are executed when you run the `dbt test` command, not when we use `dbt run`. Of course they are also run when you execute `dbt build`, that puts `run` and `test` together.

Testing that we have good source data

Let's make use of dbt capabilities to make sure that we get sound data as input.

Logically, we start from a list of our expectations on the incoming data and then we declare (if we have a suitable generic test) or write (if we need a singular test) the dbt tests to confirm or deny our expectations.

Open the file named `source_abc_bank.yml`, which describes our source, so that we can add the tests that describe our assumptions about the data.

Go to the definition of the source table and start to modify it as follows, adding a description for the table and the first test declaration:

```
tables:
  - name: ABC_BANK_POSITION
    description: >
        The landing table holding the data imported
        from the CSV extracted by ABC Bank.
    columns:
      - name: ACCOUNTID
        description: The code for the account at  ABC Bank.
        tests:
          - not_null
```

In the sample code here, we have added a description of the table, introducing the notation that allows you to enter multi-line text in YAML. Using the > character, you declare that the following block of text is all a single string to be fetched into the declared field.

We have also introduced `columns:`, the declaration that allows us to describe test-specific, individual columns of the table.

Under the `columns:` declaration, we have introduced the first column, declared using the `name` attribute, followed by the column `description` and the `tests` attribute, which will hold a list of tests.

We have then declared our first test, not_null, requiring that no row of the table contains the null value for the ACCOUNTID column. Note that this is independent of the database column being declared nullable or not.

The not_null test is by large the most used test, as it is very common that we want to be sure that the data that we get, or produce, always have not null data in the tested columns.

Practical tip

Before we move to the other tests that we want to introduce for this data source, here's a bit of practical advice for dealing with YAML files.

Please note how in YAML files, the alignment is key to defining the structure, so try to be precise with it or you will experience compilation errors, as the YAML interpreter will not be able to correctly parse your configuration files.

After you add the new piece of configuration, check that it says **ready** in green in the bottom-right-hand corner of the dbt IDE to be sure the project compiles correctly. To ensure that you do not introduce compilation errors, you can glance at it when you save more changes.

When this happens and you do not have a clue even after reading the error message, we suggest removing the block that you changed so that the compilation is correct again and then adding back one bit at a time to understand where the problem that blocks the compilation is.

Let's continue adding and commenting on the desired tests for the other columns of the table:

```
- name: SYMBOL
  description: The symbol of the security at ABC Bank.
  tests:
    - unique
    - not_null
```

Next, we are configuring the description and the tests for the SYMBOL column, which we assume to be a good natural key for a position in a bank.

For this reason, we have declared both the not_null and unique tests, which are the signature of a unicity constraint such as a key, whether natural or surrogate.

```
- name: DESCRIPTION
  description: The name of the security at ABC Bank.
  tests:
    - not_null
```

In the preceding piece of configuration, we are configuring the description and the tests for the DESCRIPTION column, which we want to be not_null, as it has the name of the security.

```
- name: EXCHANGE
  description: >
```

```
                    The short name or code of the exchange
                    where the security is traded.
            tests:
            - not_null
```

In the preceding piece of configuration, we are configuring the description and the tests for the EXCHANGE column, which we want to be not_null, as it has the name or code of the exchange where the security has been purchased. We will talk about naming in greater depth in reference to the STG model.

We might also consider expressing that the exchanges values should be limited to a list of known values with the accepted_values test, but as we do not have any reason to limit the values, such a test would just generate a false positive when it fails, prompting us to maintain the list to add new values.

Note that this could be a sensible strategy if we need to be alerted on new exchanges being used due to any regulations or to be sure that other data or authorizations are in place.

We would then add the authorized or configured exchanges to the list accepted by the test and would get errors if others are used that we have not named as accepted.

```
            - name: REPORT_DATE
              description: >
                The date of the report was extracted by ABC Bank.
                We consider this position to be the effective
        from this date forward, until a change is seen.
              tests:
                - not_null
```

For the REPORT_DATE column, we want it to be not_null, as we need to be able to know on what date the information in the position was referred to. Time matters a lot in reality and, in terms of data warehousing, this could be the subject of entire books. We will talk about it often.

```
            - name: QUANTITY
              description: >
                The number of securities we hold in the
                portfolio at ABC Bank at the Report Date.
              tests:
                - not_null
```

For the QUANTITY column, we want it to be not_null, as we need to know how many securities we have. It does not help at all just to know "the portfolio has some of this security" without knowing the actual number of shares or titles that are owned.

```
            - name: COST_BASE
              description: >
                The cost we paid for the securities that
```

```
            we hold in the portfolio at
            ABC Bank at the Report Date.
        tests:
          - not_null
```

For the COST_BASE column, we would like it to be not_null, as we can then use the value to calculate the position profit. We could probably survive without this piece of info, but as we are going to use it, assuming we have the value, let's put the test in place, and if at some point it fails, we will have to evaluate what to do.

Now, we would not be able to replace it, but down the line, we might have a position open date, changes made to it, and historical quotations related to it, allowing us to calculate a rolling value of the cost base. We understand that calculating it would be less accurate and more complex than just knowing it, but if we are unable to get that info from certain banks, there are not many alternatives.

For the moment being, as we are going to use this piece of data, let's ask dbt to keep an eye on it for us.

```
      - name: POSITION_VALUE
        description: >
        The value of the securities  in the portfolio
        at ABC Bank on the Report Date.
        tests:
          - not_null
```

For the POSITION_VALUE column, we would like it to be not_null so that we can calculate the position profit. Our considerations as to whether this would become null are analogous to the ones related to the COST_BASE column. As we are using it, let's have the test.

```
      - name: CURRENCY
        description: >

  The currency for the monetary amounts of the position.
        tests:
          - not_null
```

For the CURRENCY column, we would like it to be not_null, as we need to know in what currency the monetary amounts are expressed, and it would be a huge limitation to assume that all the amounts are already expressed in a single currency.

We already use the amounts, and in the future, we will need to be able to convert all the amounts into a single currency to be able to calculate totals. Let's have the test in place so we know that our plan is not in jeopardy.

Putting together all the individual pieces of configuration that we have gone through, we now have the contents of the new source_abc_bank.yml file.

You can find the updated version of this source file in our repository in the 05_03_v2__source_abc_bank.yml file inside the materials for *Chapter 5* in the dbt folder.

> **Important note**
>
> Tests are very useful throughout the data life cycle.
>
> Here, our discussion introduced them after we had created the source and the first model, to avoid overloading you with too many new topics. In the reality of projects, it is useful to write tests while you write the sources and models.
>
> Tests are especially useful when getting started with data that we do not fully know, as they allow the data engineer to express and verify his assumptions easily and quickly.
>
> Knowing whether the expected unicity constraints and nullability of fields, especially foreign key and relational integrity constraints, are fulfilled is very important when designing the ELT transformations on the data.
>
> Tests allow us to initially analyze, then fully describe, and finally, constantly monitor the quality of the incoming data, making our ELT much more reliable and the results trustworthy.

Running the test

Now that we have added our first tests, how do we use them?

In dbt, you execute the tests with the dbt test command, in a very similar manner as we have seen for running the dbt models.

Go to the dbt Cloud command line and run the following command:

```
dbt test
```

The preceding command will execute all the tests in the dbt project and you will see that the command-line area opens to show the execution first and then the results of the tests:

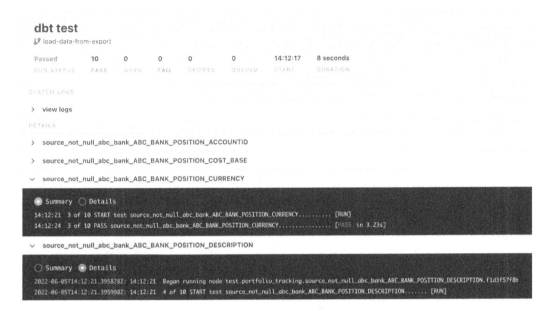

Figure 5.12: Test results

You will see that your tests are run and once completed, they have a green checkmark on the right if they pass, an orange exclamation mark if they produce a warning, and a red "x" sign if they fail.

You can open the line for each test to access the summary result, detailing the test result and its duration, and the details where you can also see the exact query that is run on your Snowflake database.

Right now, we have only defined tests for a single source table, so running all the tests is perfectly fine, but thinking about the future, it is important to be able to just run the tests for the source or models that you want.

The following commands provide you with alternatives for controlling the tests you run better:

- Run the tests on all the sources:

  ```
  dbt test -s source:*
  ```

- Run the tests on all the tables in the abc_bank source:

  ```
  dbt test -s source:abc_bank.*
  ```

- Run the tests on the ABC_BANK_POSITION table of the abc_bank source:

  ```
  dbt test -s source:abc_bank.ABC_BANK_POSITION
  ```

In the following chapters, we will look more into the model selection syntax that dbt provides to allow you to build commands that run or test exactly which models you want.

Testing that we deliver sound information

Now that we are sure that the incoming data fulfills our expectations, it is time to make sure that what we deliver does the same.

Writing tests that verify what we want to deliver will serve us well in many ways:

- To make sure that we got it right when we are writing the code the first time.

- It provides a clear and very valuable piece of documentation, which will stay up to date with our code or fail and call our attention if the code or the data does stop abiding by it.

  In this regard, it is important to note that the tests provide such valuable information for documenting the project that dbt uses them to enrich the project documentation.

- It will keep monitoring that every future change that we or someone else makes to our code will still fulfill our expectations and the contract that our clients have taken into use.

We have created our model in the `refined` folder, so let's create a YAML file named `refined.yml` in the `refined` folder to host our tests and a description of the transformations that we have implemented in the `refined` folder.

As always, in our YAML files, let's start with the version and the type of entities that we are going to describe in the file. Start the file with these two lines:

```
version: 2
models:
```

The version is always 2, as this is the current definition of the YAML file in use – then, we use the `models` keyword to declare that we are going to describe some models.

As we have done with the source too, first, we identify the model that we want to describe and test using the `name` entry, and then we can enter a description that, besides helping us developers, will be used in the documentation:

```
- name: POSITION_ABC_BANK
  description: The positions we have in the ABC Bank portfolio.
```

Nested inside a model, `columns` allows us to name the columns that we want to describe and test:

```
columns:
  - name: UNREALIZED_PROFIT
    description: The unrealized profit on the position.
    tests:
      - not_null
```

In the preceding code, we have identified the UNREALIZED_PROFIT column of the POSITION_ ABC_BANK model and we have declared the test as not_null, as we expect to always have data in that column.

```
- name: UNREALIZED_PROFIT_PCT
      description: >
        The unrealized profit percentage on the position.
      tests:
        - not_null
```

Also, for the UNREALIZED_PROFIT_PCT column, we have declared that we expect it to contain data by using the not_null test.

Both tests will be executed when we run the tests on the model or all the models of the project.

To run all the tests, go to the dbt Cloud command line and run the following command:

```
dbt test
```

The preceding command will execute all the tests in the dbt project and you will see that the command line area opens to show the execution first and then the results of the tests.

To just run the tests on the POSITION_ABC_BANK model, run the following command:

```
dbt test -s POSITION_ABC_BANK
```

We have now created tests that verify that we get good data as input and that we deliver good data at the end of our still trivial transformations.

Generating the documentation

The next thing that is important to get familiar with is the documentation that is automatically generated by dbt based on our code.

To generate the documentation, run the following command:

```
dbt docs generate
```

You will notice that once the generation is finished, in a few seconds, there will be a small popup in the upper-left-hand part of your DEV environment telling you that your docs are ready to view, as shown in the following screenshot:

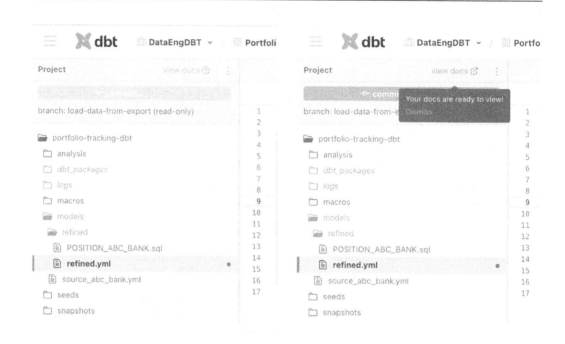

Figure 5.13: The development environment during the doc generation and at the end

Click on the **view docs** link and a new browser tab will open with the dbt-generated documentation. It will look like the following screenshot:

Figure 5.14: The dbt documentation home page

You can browse around, even if there is not very much there yet for now.

Click on the blue round button in the bottom-right-hand corner of the page to open the lineage graph:

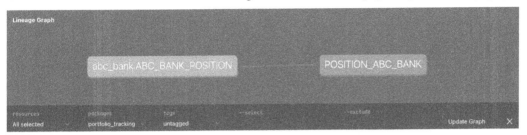

Figure 5.15: dbt lineage graph of our first model

The lineage graph will be very simple for now, as it only has to show that we have the ABC_BANK_POSITION source table from the abc_bank source system (shown in green in the lineage graph), which is used by (as in, the data flows to) the POSITION_ABC_BANK dbt model (shown in light blue in the lineage graph).

Summary

Congratulations – your first data application is running!

In this chapter, we started to develop our example application in dbt and followed all the steps to create, deploy, test, and document a data application, even if this one is still very simple.

In the next chapter, we will introduce more real-life requirements for this data application and we will have to adapt our code to consider them, so we will start to learn how to refactor our models and write maintainable code.

Part 2: Agile Data Engineering with dbt

In this section, you will learn how to implement data platforms using a solid engineering process and working in an agile way, writing readable and maintainable code, and producing data that the business can trust.

This section includes the following chapters:

Writing Maintainable Code

In this chapter, we will continue the example that we started in the previous chapter, and we will guide you to configure dbt and write some basic, but functionally complete, code to build the three layers of our reference architecture – staging/storage, refined data, and delivery with data marts.

We will begin by introducing you to some core principles to reach the goal of building a data platform that is easy to understand and maintain, and then we will start to put the principles into practice to build and configure the layers of our reference architecture.

At each step, we will analyze the key elements of the models that we write to transform the raw source data into usable information in a data mart with facts and dimensions. Facts tell us about what happened, while dimensions provide extra descriptive information about the entities involved in a fact. First, we will build the pipeline for a fact table, and then, in the following chapter, we will build it for a dimension, discussing the difference between them.

We will also introduce the Snapshots dbt feature that allows you to easily save the changes of an entity, storing it in a form called **slowly changing dimension of type two**. This allows our platform to capture the source data and its changes, becoming self-sufficient.

By the end of this chapter and the following one, you will be able to build a working data platform, with a sound architecture and clear organization, using only the basic features of dbt.

This chapter will explore the following topics:

- Writing code for humans
- Creating the architectural layers
- Why saving history is crucial

Technical requirements

This chapter builds on and continues the example we started in *Chapter 5*, so you need to be familiar with it to follow and have the code from it to continue with the hands-on examples.

All code samples of this chapter are available on GitHub at `https://github.com/PacktPublishing/Data-engineering-with-dbt/tree/main/Chapter_06`.

Writing code for humans

In the previous chapter, we loaded our first data and built our first model to transform it.

With so little code developed in our project, there is no risk of making any confusion or calling the same things with different names, yet these are real concerns in any real project, and they matter so much more than most people think.

Most people believe that when coding, you just write new code, but the reality is that to write one row of new code, you often must go back and check what you have done in a few other places, which means reading tens of rows again and again in existing code.

This becomes truer and more evident the older a project becomes, and the more people become involved in the project.

We have seen in previous chapters that there are some patterns to minimize and keep in check this issue, but remember that size is one dimension of complexity, and we can only do so much to manage it.

Removing duplicated or copied and pasted code is the top priority, as it limits the size of the project and makes evolution possible and maintenance much easier.

The other most important things that we can do to keep complexity in check are as follows:

- *Reduce the need to re-read*, applying the **Least Surprise Principle (LSP)**.

  To do so, it is beneficial to use meaningful model names, prefixes, and suffixes; use a good, layered architecture and apply patterns in a consistent way (and as few as you can) so that models behave and fields mean as you would expect from their name.

- *Make the code that you write easy to re-read/understand.*

  To achieve this, it is beneficial to use good **Common Table Expression (CTE)** names and column names and put everything not standard at the top of the file, so that every "deviation from expected" is as easy to spot as possible.

- *Keep the models that we write focused and limited in dimension.*

  One model should do one thing, do it well, and communicate it well with its name. This is the **Single Responsibility Principle** (**SRP**), which takes advantage of intermediate steps and builds simpler concepts to be used inside more complex ones, while refraining from creating a single model that does everything.

  Here, low model complexity and low project size are at odds, so err on the side of keeping your models simple and focused, but have them do meaningful work.

- *Keep the dependencies ordered and going only in one direction*, from one layer to the next in the architecture.

  The expected flow of data and direction of dependencies is as follows: `source systems => staging => refined => presentation (marts)`.

  Avoid at all costs jumping across multiple layers or, even worse, creating dependencies in the wrong direction. Luckily, dbt will most probably error out, as you will create a circular dependency; in any case, it would be a major issue in making your project understandeable.

- When you see an improvement, *refactor your models to keep them current.*

  Consistency is a key factor to keep a big project and multiple people working well together.

  If you have the right tests and the correct architecture in place, you will be able to apply refactoring at a small cost, even in data warehousing. This will keep your project workable pretty much forever, instead of having to rebuild every few years – does this ring any bells? Have you ever done evolution, revolution, and re-evolution projects?

Refactoring our initial model to be human-readable

If you open the code of the initial model that we have done, you have in front of you the definition of just two out of eleven columns produced by that model. That might not be an issue at all, as you have the lineage graph, and you can double-click on its predecessor to go and see what those columns are and how are they defined.

The problem is that the upstream model is a source and is just made of a metadata definition in a YAML file.

Luckily, if we have been good project citizens, we can get a human-readable, meaningful description of the columns that we have documented in the YAML file. You should list and describe at least the important ones – business keys, foreign keys, important metrics, and categories, especially the ones used in business rules that you expect to be there (and then test they actually are there).

Furthermore, we have no control over the source column names; they come from the source system that we do not control.

This could pose two important problems:

- Source names are a threat to the stability of our own project. If there is a change in the source, we would need to change all the code that uses this model and any test that uses the changed names.

- In general, the names from the sources are not the best names in our project, because often they are not as clear to us, they come from a different domain, or in our project we use a different term or even a totally different language, and we want to call one thing with the same name everywhere it appears. That is the only way to allow everyone in the project to clearly assume that it is the same thing, and if it has a different name, it is not.

> **Tip**
>
> We know that it will be very difficult to have a 100% rate of naming one thing in the same way in every place in a big project, but the benefit is already worthwhile if we get close to it.
>
> The closer the better, as it will reduce the risk of using data in the wrong way.

Let's try to fix all these problems in our first model using a combination of strategies:

- We will split the model into a "dumb" adaptation model that we will place in the staging layer. Here, we will choose the columns that we want to bring forward, and the names, and the data types for them.

- We will move the "intelligence" from the current model to the refined layer.

  The intelligence is also often referred to as business rules, and it belongs to the refined layer, which is applied on top of the securely stored data from the staging/storage layer.

Note that in this chapter, we will focus on providing you with an explanation of the key concepts and a sequence of practical steps to build the overall architecture and implement the transformations, from raw data to usable information.

The resulting code will not be the end of our journey, as we will still miss some key features and improvements, such as proper tests, hashing for hash keys, or refactoring of code into macros, because of page constraints or because we have not yet introduced a relevant feature.

In the following chapters, we will refactor the code to use the new features that we introduce.

Creating the architectural layers

In this section, we will complete the layers of the **Pragmatic Data Platform** (PDP) architecture – staging/storage, refined, and the marts for delivery.

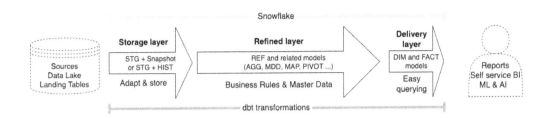

Figure 6.1: The layers that make up the Pragmatic Data Platform

Creating the Staging layer

In *Chapter 4*, we created the refined layer by adding the relevant configuration to the main configuration file, `dbt_project.yml`. Let's do the same for the staging layer.

Add at the end of the main config file the configuration for the staging layer, as exemplified here:

```
staging:    #Applies to all files under models/staging/
  +materialized: view
  +schema: STAGING
```

You can add it above or below the configuration for the refined layer, as you prefer, as long as it is indented correctly and at the same level as the refined config.

You can find the version of the main config file for this chapter in our repository, with the filename `06_01_v2__dbt_project.yml`. It is inside the materials for `Chapter 6`, in the dbt folder.

Note that it already contains other additions, which we will explain later.

Let's review what we have configured:

- Under our project, we have named the `staging` folder, which does not yet exist, but we can already declare configurations for it and its subfolders

- Under the `staging` folder, we have declared the `materialized` configuration with a value of `view`, as we want the models under that folder to be materialized as views

- Under the `staging` folder, we have declared the `schema` configuration with a value of `STAGING`, as we want the models under the `staging` folder to be created in a schema with the custom schema part of `STAGING`, generating full names such as `RZ_STAGING`

Note that contrary to the refined layer, we want the staging layer to be generated, by default, as views. Also, we want the models in a schema having the `STAGING` suffix.

To complete the staging layer creation, create a folder named `staging` under the `model` folder. Once you have done so, you have a place to create staging models.

Creating our first staging model

In the `models/staging` folder, create a new model named `STG_ABC_BANK_POSITION.sql` that will have the following content:

```sql
SELECT
        ACCOUNTID         as ACCOUNT_CODE      -- TEXT
      , SYMBOL            as SECURITY_CODE     -- TEXT
      , DESCRIPTION       as SECURITY_NAME     -- TEXT
      , EXCHANGE          as EXCHANGE_CODE     -- TEXT
      , REPORT_DATE       as REPORT_DATE       -- DATE
      , QUANTITY          as QUANTITY          -- NUMBER
      , COST_BASE         as COST_BASE         -- NUMBER
      , POSITION_VALUE    as POSITION_VALUE    -- NUMBER
      , CURRENCY          as CURRENCY_CODE     -- TEXT
FROM {{ source('abc_bank', 'ABC_BANK_POSITION') }}
```

You might type the code from scratch, or you might generate 90% of it and just do the required changes – a smart engineer puts the tools he has to good use. You can find out how to generate the skeleton for every staging model in the next section, just after the explanation of this code.

You can find this file in the Git repository in the materials for *Chapter 6*, in the dbt folder, with the filename `06_02_v1__STG_ABC_BANK_POSITION.sql`.

Let's discuss the code for the `STG_ABC_BANK_POSITION` model:

- The name starts with the `STG` prefix to make it crystal clear that this model performs the adaptation step of the staging layer for the `ABC_BANK_POSITION` source.

- We have decided to keep all the columns from the source model.

  This is often the best choice, especially when we start to store the history of a source, as it is easy to have it ready to use, while it is more complicated (if at all possible) to add history from the past. Read on for a few reasons to leave some data out.

- We have renamed a few columns to make clearer what their content is.

  We have added the _CODE suffix to columns that contain… well, code.

  We have renamed `SYMBOL` and `DESCRIPTION` to have names that work better in this domain and are clear for all people on the project. It would be hard to know what the `DESCRIPTION` column contains when we are two models down the line.

The result is that now we have a staging model with the source table expressed in our preferred terms, but it has not yet been deployed to the underlying database.

Run the model from your dbt Cloud command line so that it can be used downstream:

```
dbt run -s STG_ABC_BANK_POSITION
```

You can then check that you have in Snowflake the new schema for the staging layer, and that you have the view for this model in it.

While you are coding a model, you can run a preview to see the results, but please remember to do dbt run when the model is final to generate the view in your DB so that we can use it in other models.

Generating the staging models

When we introduced the code for this STG model, we teased you that you will not need to write it by hand and will be able to generate most of the code in the STG models.

Every modern database comes with an information schema – that is, a generated schema that you can use to query the database about itself. This is fantastic.

In Snowflake, and some other databases as well, that schema is aptly named INFORMATION_SCHEMA, ensuring that you will find the schema for the PORTFOLIO_TRACKING database with the fully qualified name of PORTFOLIO_TRACKING.INFORMATION_SCHEMA.

We can, therefore, use the information that our database already has about the source table to generate most of the code that we need to have in the STG model. Sounds brilliant!

The basic idea is that the core operation of an STG model is picking the desired columns, usually all of them, renaming some of them, and eventually, handling type or time-zone conversions.

Furthermore, most of the new names will not differ too much from the old names, unless we are talking about very old names (limited to eight characters), names in a different language, or weird naming strategies, such as the ones found in some proprietary or purpose-built systems.

As a result, the following SQL query will generate a result very close to the SQL that we want to have in our STG model, for the column definition part of the SELECT clause:

```
-- Generate STG query
SELECT
        ', ' || COLUMN_NAME || ' as '|| COLUMN_NAME
                || ' -- ' || DATA_TYPE as SQL_TEXT
FROM PORTFOLIO_TRACKING.INFORMATION_SCHEMA.COLUMNS
WHERE TABLE_SCHEMA = 'SOURCE_DATA'
  and TABLE_NAME = 'ABC_BANK_POSITION'
ORDER BY ORDINAL_POSITION
```

The first three rows of the result of running that query would be the following:

```
, ACCOUNTID as ACCOUNTID - TEXT
, SYMBOL as SYMBOL - TEXT
, DESCRIPTION as DESCRIPTION -- TEXT
```

Let's analyze the code and the result:

- The FROM clause shows us that we are querying the COLUMNS view of the info schema, so we can use the information about the columns of one or more tables. Each column of each table in the database is described in one row of the COLUMNS view. The WHERE clause will limit our query to the single table of interest.

- The SELECT clause creates one row for each column in the source, producing a text like `, col_name as col_name -- data_type_name`, which is a typical row in the SELECT clause in the STG model we want to create.

  The column name is repeated twice, as we need the first one unchanged to read from the source, which uses that original column name, while the second one is the basis for our editing, but it will work out of the box if left unchanged.

- The WHERE clause uses the schema and table names to select the table that we want to read the information from. Point it to the source table that you want to create the STG model for.

- The ORDER BY clause is there to produce results in a predictable way, respecting the order of the fields in the source table. Nothing stops you from changing the order in the STG model.

  It is actually a very common practice to reorganize the order of the columns, placing natural and surrogate key columns at the beginning and keeping related columns that might not be close in the source table close together.

- Note that all the rows start with a comma, but we need to remove the comma from the row that we will keep as first after the SELECT clause in the STG model.

We can then apply the following very simple pattern to produce the initial part of our STG models, with a more complete pattern presented in the next section:

```
SELECT
    <generated column block>
FROM {{ source('source_system', 'SOURCE_TABLE') }}
```

From this pattern, you can easily see the following:

- We pretty much avoid surprises. When you see an STG model, you know what to expect, as all STG models will have a simple consistent format.

- We run a query to produce the body of the model, and we enter the source table information once in the model and once in the query to generate the SQL code.

- We reduce our editing to the minimum required, and changing a good, working piece of code is easier and quicker than writing from scratch. Starting from the generated code, you also avoid the risk of forgetting about some columns.

The great thing about managing the STG layer in this way is that it allows us huge flexibility in adapting the incoming data to our needs, while requiring a minimal amount of effort from us. It's really not rocket science, just the conscientious application of some agreed-upon naming conventions.

Goals and contents of the staging models

The goal of the STG model is to adapt external data to how we want to see and use it in our project. This includes preparing it for change tracking and for storage in the most usable way for our future needs.

To achieve this, we have a few actions that we can perform in the STG model:

- Pick the desired columns, usually all of them

- Rename the columns to follow our conventions and use our project-designated names

- Manage data types, performing conversions to desired data types

- Apply "hard rules" with non-destructive transformations, such as time-zone conversions

- Add the default record but only for dimensions; it is not needed for facts/events

- Add the desired/available metadata, based on the input specifics

- Make keys and change tracking explicit by adding hash-based keys and diff fields

The list is long, and to apply the previous principles, we would need to apply most of these steps in their own piece of code, contained in a CTE, making the pattern for an STG model a well-defined sequence of CTEs that builds on the previous ones.

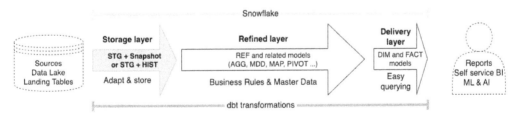

Figure 6.2: The staging layer highlighted in the Pragmatic Data Platform

The staging/storage layer is the interface we build to make the external data as usable as possible by us, without changing its meaning.

A general pattern for your staging models

The following is the simple skeleton code that orders all the preceding steps:

```
WITH
src_data as ( … ),
default_record as ( … ),
with_default_record as(
    SELECT * FROM src_data
    UNION ALL
    SELECT * FROM default_record
),
hashed as ( … )
SELECT * FROM hashed
```

Using the preceding pattern, the operations would be divided in this way:

- The `src_data` CTE will deal with all operations that directly work on the incoming data, such as picking the columns and their names, managing the data types, applying hard rules, and extracting the metadata that can be found in the source system (such as an export timestamp)

- The `default_record` CTE will do what its name implies – define one row with the values of the default record for the dimension, to be eventually used in the delivery layer

- The `with_default_record` CTE will just combine the two previous CTEs to get the full data

- The `hashed` CTE will add the hashes with the Key and Diff definitions, plus the eventual metadata that you want to add that does not come from the source data, such as the time of load of the data

You can decide to divide the code in more steps, but remember that programming is almost always about keeping a balance between opposing constraints – in this case, the SRP and conciseness.

In the next sections, let's go through the individual points listed as goals of a STG model.

Picking columns in an STG model

In general, we keep all the columns from a source table, but sometimes, there are valid reasons to leave out some columns:

- *Security or compliance needs or other legal or business requirements.*

   Sometimes, we do not want some types of data, such as personal information, health data, or other sensitive data on a system. This could be mandated by regulation or just a decision to simplify the compliance needs of one system.

- **When**, after also interrogating the business, *we cannot make any sense of some data.*

  If nobody knows nor cares about some data, it can be fine to leave it out. Consider the cost of asking to business VS just adding the data VS leaving the data out now, adding it later (recalculating the hash values, adaptations down the line, …).

In many cases, we will also add new columns, as we do for metadata or calculated fields. The suggestion, when you add calculated data, is to also keep the original data unless data volumes make that impractical.

Naming columns

Names are somewhat arbitrary things, so it's hard to have a strong rule. The best suggestion is to agree with the project team on some naming guidelines, and then pick the name that satisfies the majority of people that will have to work with it.

That said, it is important that you can quickly assign names that people will understand and recognize, so establishing good guidelines is key.

As an example, when you have a customer identifier, you can use many possible names, such as CUSTOMER_CODE, CUSTOMER_ID, CUSTOMER_NUM(BER), and CUSTOMER_KEY. The best that you can do is to decide to always use the same suffix, such as _CODE or _ID, for all columns that have the same role.

To achieve all this, it is useful to make your own list with your own definitions, like the following one:

- _CODE: An identifier that is used/known to business, also called a business key, and generally represented as a string, even if it is just made up of digits. This does not need to be a unique key for a table, as it can be something such as MARKET_CODE or COUNTRY_CODE.

- _ID: Generally, this is a single field acting as a unique identifier, often started as an internal number with a technical function. However, it might have migrated into business use (CUSTOMER_ID is widely used), and now it might not be a number anymore.

- _KEY: This is generally a technical field, not used for business or shown to business. There is a slight preference for the string type as of generic use.

- _NUMBER: This feels like it was a number at some point in time, but we have seen so many "number" fields containing text that it is better to just avoid such a suffix.

The most useful thing to do, once you have got your list done, is to decide which ones to use and which ones to always avoid, as they often overlap. Remember that the goal is to give all of your people (developers and business alike) an easy time when figuring out names.

When writing code, you will have to think, is the name CUSTOMER_ID or CUSTOMER_CODE or something else, at least tens or hundreds of times a day. Therefore, which one you pick matters way less than deciding to always use _CODE (or _ID) for all code-like things, and always making them strings.

Whenever possible, we should try to just use _CODE for "code-like" fields that will be exposed to business and _KEY for "developer-only" fields, such as the keys generated by hashing.

Managing data types

Quite often, you get data that is not represented with the correct data type, such as when you get a date or a timestamp represented as a string or an integer.

Other common cases are when timestamps are split in time and date, or when you get strings that just represent a part of a date, usually just a month and a year.

Other less frequent cases involve monetary amounts being represented with the wrong number of decimals (too many or too little) or even being converted to cents.

Modern databases and reporting tools work perfectly fine and are adept at dealing with dates, timestamps, and fixed precision numbers, so you should convert incoming data to the most appropriate data type, as that will make everything simpler and faster.

The suggestion here is that, whenever possible, it is better to keep both the original value, which will just stay stored in the history table, and the converted one, which will be used throughout the models.

This is for both auditing requirements and protection against bugs, and also weird data that might exist in small enough numbers that you will not notice or fix it in the first version of your models.

Applying hard rules

Applying hard rules is useful to increase the interoperability of data and, in some cases, is very close to data type management.

A hard rule is a rule that is always applied to data to make it acceptable in the format that we want to use, so data type transformations are a special and simple kind of hard rule.

Hard rules are not meant to change the meaning of data, just its format or representation.

A few examples of other kinds of hard rules are as follows:

- Trimming strings to remove useless spaces or clip out redundant parts
- Padding numbers into desired length strings, and the opposite – un-padding a string into a number or a string without useless, padding zeros
- Fixing cases, dealing with characters in character sets that are not supported, or other cases that need special treatment
- Extracting data from hierarchical sources, such as AVRO, Parquet, or JSON sources, into individual fields

The list is, of course, infinite, and sometimes, the classification of a rule as a hard rule (not business-driven, to be implemented in STG) or soft rule (business-driven, to be implemented in REF) is not so clear-cut, and you will have to do your own evaluation about where to put it.

If you see no risk of the rule changing and find value in storing in the history the result of the rule, go for STG, but if you think that you might change the rule or you would prefer flexibility, then definitely implement the rule in the refined layer, where it's easy to change.

Adding a default record

The default record is a record that your reporting tool will be pointed to when there is no match in the primary key of the dimension for a foreign key in the fact.

The lack of a match can be because there is no foreign key in the fact, or because the provided foreign key does not exist (yet) in the final dimension.

In any case, a default key enables us to properly handle all the cases where there is no data to show. We will show in the following chapters a couple of ways that it can be used.

We consider it useful and transparent to define the default record in the same model where the source data comes in, because it puts in a single place all the relevant info about the entity.

Having the default record defined as code in the STG model also allows you to track eventual changes that you want to apply to it. These changes will show in the code repository and will also be found and correctly handled in the history table.

Furthermore, the source data could already contain some form of default record and you want to manage that data to some extent.

We generally implement the default record as a very simple SELECT without any FROM clause, and we can use the following query to generate most of the code, as we saw for the src_data CTE.

You can adapt the following code to your preferences:

```
SELECT
    CASE DATA_TYPE
        WHEN 'TEXT' THEN IFF(ENDSWITH(COLUMN_NAME,'_CODE'), ', ''-
1''', ', ''Missing''')
        WHEN 'NUMBER' THEN ', -1'
        WHEN 'DATE' THEN ', ''2000-01-01'''
        WHEN 'TIMESTAMP_NTZ' THEN ', ''2000-01-01'''
        ELSE ', ''Missing'''
    END  || ' as ' || COLUMN_NAME as SQL_TEXT
FROM "PORTFOLIO_TRACKING"."INFORMATION_SCHEMA"."COLUMNS"
WHERE TABLE_SCHEMA = 'RZ_STAGING'
  and TABLE_NAME = 'STG_ABC_BANK_POSITION'
ORDER BY ORDINAL_POSITION;
```

The preceding code should be run on the STG model after you have implemented the `src_data` CTE to produce quite stable column names, data types, and order of the fields for the model.

The following screenshot shows the result of running this query on the STG model for the ABC Bank position entity:

Row	SQL_TEXT
1	, '-1' as ACCOUNT_CODE
2	, '-1' as SECURITY_CODE
3	, 'Missing' as SECURITY_NAME
4	, '-1' as EXCHANGE_CODE
5	, '2000-01-01' as REPORT_DATE
6	, -1 as QUANTITY
7	, -1 as COST_BASE
8	, -1 as POSITION_VALUE
9	, '-1' as CURRENCY_CODE

Figure 6.3: Generated code for the default record

Also, in this case, you can take the generated code, add `SELECT` before the first row, remove the extra initial comma, and have a working definition for your default record that you can keep as is or manually improve upon.

Adding metadata

Another common task is to record metadata that comes from the source system and add other metadata that we can generate.

Some of the "metadata" fields will come from normal fields of our source systems, while other will be added by the loading pipeline. By defining a metadata field, we copy the relevant information under the metadata name, preserving the original field, if it is useful also by itself. Because the same metadata can be called in many ways in different source systems, it is useful to always get the metadata into a field with the same name.

The following are some forms of metadata that might be added:

- LOAD_TS: This is the time when the data is loaded into our data platform. This is a must and does not depend on the source system. We usually add it as the last field.

- RECORD_SOURCE: This is the place the data comes from. This might be available from the data movement pipeline (for example, the filename of the CSV we are reading from) or not, so you can make up a description for it, such as the view/source table name. This is also a must, as it allows you to audit/understand where your data is coming from.

- EXTRACTION_TIME: This is the time when the data was extracted from the source system. Often, we do not read the source directly, so it might be quite different from LOAD_TS.

- CREATION_TIME: This is the time when the information was first created. Many systems record this information, and if this is generally available, it is useful to create such a metadata field.

- EFFECTIVE_FROM: This is the time when the information becomes effective for business purposes.

  This is purely a business field that allows you to handle multi-temporality – that is, multiple timelines. It is very important in all cases to distinguish between when you received some information and when you need to consider the information to be in use.

Of course, you can come up with your own metadata to describe any aspect of the source system and data platform processes as needed.

Identity and change detection fields

The last thing that we add in the STG model is three fields that will help in the storage of the entity:

- HASH_KEY: This is a single field with all the columns that make up the primary key of the entity chained together. The result is usually hashed, hence the name HASH_KEY.

  Its primary use is to provide a primary key in a single field, to standardize and simplify the loading of the history. By defining the HASH_KEY in your code, you give a clear, explicit definition of what the primary key is for the entity.

- HASH_DIFF: This is a single field with all the fields that we want to test for changes chained together. The result is usually hashed, hence the name HASH_DIFF.

  This field is used to simplify and standardize the loading of the history and provides an explicit definition of what is considered a change. It usually contains all fields except for the metadata ones.

- LOAD_TS: This is a timestamp that provides a timeline of the changes of the entity as they are received and stored by the data platform. This is metadata that we add as part of the loading process.

Using the HASH_KEY field, we are able to pick all the versions of a specific entity, whereas by using LOAD_TS, we are able to know what version is current or was current at some specific moment in time.

The HASH_DIFF field is a purely technical field that can be considered a version identifier, but be aware that it is perfectly normal for an entity to go back to the same set of values it had at some point in the past. Therefore, it might very well be that we have two equal hash diff values separated in the history table by one or more different ones.

In some cases, we will add more than one HASH_KEY, as the entities that we are storing might be viewed in more than one way (for example, an account can be looked at as a local or as a global account).

At times we will also add hashed keys for composite foreign keys that we want to store in the history table. This can be a common situation if you build hierarchies or dirty dimensions that use a hash made of multiple fields as a key. It is anyway more common to add such calculated keys in the REF layer.

Completing the STG model

Previously in this chapter, we have created an initial version of the STG model for the ABC Bank's positions. Let's complete it by adding the sections and following the pattern described in the previous section.

You can find the second version in full in the 06_02_v2__STG_ABC_BANK_POSITION.sql file in the dbt folder, under the Chapter_06 materials of the book's repository. Here, we will describe each section by itself.

Let's start by moving the current version into the src_data CTE and adding some metadata:

```
WITH
src_data as (
    SELECT
          ACCOUNTID            as ACCOUNT_CODE       -- TEXT
        , SYMBOL               as SECURITY_CODE      -- TEXT
        , DESCRIPTION          as SECURITY_NAME      -- TEXT
        , EXCHANGE             as EXCHANGE_CODE       -- TEXT
        , REPORT_DATE          as REPORT_DATE        -- DATE
        , QUANTITY             as QUANTITY            -- NUMBER
        , COST_BASE            as COST_BASE           -- NUMBER
        , POSITION_VALUE       as POSITION_VALUE      -- NUMBER
        , CURRENCY             as CURRENCY_CODE       -- TEXT

        , 'SOURCE_DATA.ABC_BANK_POSITION' as RECORD_SOURCE

    FROM {{ source('abc_bank', 'ABC_BANK_POSITION') }}
),
```

The only real addition in the preceding code is the RECORD_SOURCE metadata.

We do not have any real data incoming to tell us where the data is coming from, so a common solution is to use a string with the name of the view/table that we are reading.

The next section would be the default record CTE, if this was a dimension, but as this is a fact – that is, a table listing events that happened or describing the state of a system, and not descriptive information about an entity – we do not need a default record.

As we do not have a default record, the `with_default_record` CTE is not needed.

The last part of the STG model is the `hashed` CTE, which you can see in the following code block. Currently, we will not have any hashing, as we have not yet introduced the feature that we will use for hashing. Chaining the fields will work well enough anyway:

```
hashed as (
  SELECT
      concat_ws('|', ACCOUNT_CODE, SECURITY_CODE) as POSITION_HKEY
    , concat_ws('|', ACCOUNT_CODE, SECURITY_CODE,
        SECURITY_NAME, EXCHANGE_CODE, REPORT_DATE,
        QUANTITY, COST_BASE, POSITION_VALUE, CURRENCY_CODE )
        as POSITION_HDIFF
    , *
    , '{{ run_started_at }}' as LOAD_TS_UTC
  FROM src_data
)
SELECT * FROM hashed
```

This part of the code does the following:

- Defines the composite primary key, POSITION_HKEY, as the concatenation (without hash for now) of the ACCOUNT_CODE and SECURITY_CODE fields.

   This is one of the potential choices; as always when picking keys, the important consideration is that they reflect the reality of the situation. In theory, we could have in one account the same security quoted on different markets, and the quote of the security depends on the market you are looking at.

   We will start with this definition and eventually will change it later, if needed. Changing a key is never easy, so it's better to think well about it, but on the other hand, we should not get paralyzed by doubts and potential pros and cons. If you really have two good alternatives, find two names and define them in a consistent way, and then make extremely evident the one you use to store the history.

- Similarly, we have defined the change control field, POSITION_HDIFF, as the concatenation of all the non-metadata fields of our Position entity.

   Including all fields, key fields included, is a standard process that makes it possible to check with a single comparison, if even a huge record with tens or hundreds of fields has changed since a previous version.

- We have used the star symbol, *, to bring forward all the fields from the source data and the metadata that we have added in the previous CTEs.

- Last, but not least, we have added the most important piece of metadata, the LOAD_TS_UTC field, which records when the platform has received and stored the data.

  With our code, we have decided to use the same load timestamp for all the instances of all entities that are loaded during the same ETL load run. This way, it will be possible to investigate the history that we loaded and understand what data arrived in the same run.

While, in all STG models, there are many things going on, it is important to note that we have managed to keep them well separated, and most importantly, each CTE is concerned with one topic only:

- In the src_data CTE, you are concerned with the incoming data.

  You want to adapt it and extract the metadata that you get from the loading process.

- In the default_record CTE, you are concerned with providing a default record. You want to pick the most meaningful values to present when you have no data.

- In the hashed CTE, you are concerned with saving the history.

  You want to define what the identity of the entity is, what changes you want to react to, and also define the moment when you consider the data added to the platform, which is also the default order for the versions in the history table.

Now that you have completed the STG model, you want to try it by running it with the **Preview** button, and, especially if you are curious about the dbt functions that we have used, you can look at the generated code by using the **Compiled SQL** tab.

Once the model is running correctly and you have committed the code in your repo, do not forget to deploy it in your development environment by running the dbt run command.

Before moving on in a real-world scenario, you must make sure that you have added the tests that give you peace of mind about the incoming data, and your selection of the primary key. In this chapter, we will not look at the tests, as we want to focus on building the models and their content.

Connecting the REF model to the STG

We have added to our dbt project the STG model to adapt the data to how we want to see it, and it is working great, producing the results we want under the names that we have picked.

That's great; however, the new names and fields are not showing in the REF model – how come?

Well, we have not changed the model, so it is still reading directly from the source table.

Reading across multiple layers is a very bad way to code our models and a recipe to build a spaghetti ball with our SQL code, which, after a while, nobody will want to have anything to do with.

Let's fix that by making our model in the refined layer read from the STG model.

Open up the POSITION_ABC_BANK.sql file and change the FROM clause to read, as shown in the following block of code:

```
SELECT
    *
    , POSITION_VALUE - COST_BASE as UNREALIZED_PROFIT
    , ROUND(UNREALIZED_PROFIT / COST_BASE, 5)
        as UNREALIZED_PROFIT_PCT
FROM {{ ref('STG_ABC_BANK_POSITION') }}
```

You can run the preview to see that the model now keeps producing the same results as before, but with new column names.

Deploy the change to the database by running the changed model, one layer, or the full project:

```
dbt run -s refined
```

Executing the preceding command in your dbt Cloud command line will run all the models in your refined layer, which currently is just our initial model.

Go to Snowflake and verify that the table now has the new names.

We have then completed this first refactoring of our code, as we now have the same functionality as before, but with much better names and usability. Now, you can look at the lineage graph, and by clicking on the STG model, you can have a clear idea of what's what and a simple mapping to the source system.

We have also clearly divided the responsibilities between the two models – the STG model will be just concerned with receiving and adapting the data, without changing its meaning, while the model in the refined layer will use the names from the STG model and will add the needed business rules to perform any required calculation.

Goals and contents of the refined layer

The goal of the refined layer is clear – take the "adapted" data served from the staging layer and by applying business rules, including combining multiple sources, produce "refined" data that can be used in the data marts to provide useful information for the platform users.

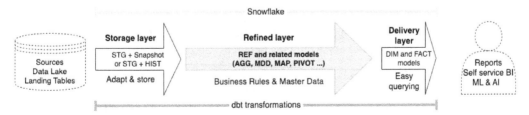

Figure 6.4: The refined layer highlighted in the Pragmatic Data Platform

The fact is that "*business rule*" is a very general term, and it can mean something as simple as a sum or product, or it can involve the use of multiple models and quite complicated logic.

Pretty much every operation that changes or combines data to produce other data is a business rule, so contrary to what we have seen for the staging layer, we cannot say much about what we will see inside each model of the refined layer.

What we can say is that we expect the transformation from *raw* to *refined* data to happen in steps.

We will have some semi-refined models that are built directly on top of the raw source data, coming from the STG layer, that will deal with business logic specific to that set of data, and they do not yet represent a fully refined business concept.

These "semi-refined" models can be seen as intermediate transformations that are used in turn to produce the final models that represent the final, fully refined business concepts. How each final concept will be built might be different, but generally, it will happen with the eventual help of a few intermediate models, according to the complexity of the final concept, and quite often with the contribution of other specialized models.

It is also useful to note that it might not always be immediate what to call a refined model, as one model could be a refined model on its own terms, such as "EMEA customer", which is a full-fledged concept for the EMEA reporting data mart and also a component of a more general concept such as "global customer".

As always in programming, naming is not always easy, and the best way to provide consistent naming is to have a few general guidelines and apply them with some consensus.

Types of models in the refined layer

In this section, we present a few common types of models that you will deal with in refined layers.

This is not a definitive list, as you might have other needs, and you can also dislike the names, but if you can make your own list that covers the kind of models that you use over and over, giving anyone on the project a clear idea of its content, then you will be going in the right direction:

- **Intermediate transformation (TR):** This is a catch-all type for models that you create for intermediate calculations that do not represent a proper business concept or that cannot exist by themselves, in the sense that you will not expect other developers to use such a model without knowing the specific caveats.

  You can consider these as an approximation of "private" intermediate models that you do not expect to be of general use or easily reusable in other contexts.

- **Refined model (REF):** This is the type for models that represent a recognizable business concept, at any level, with the level needing to be clear from the name if it is not for general use. We expect that anyone needing this concept at that level should reuse this model and not build their own.

The implication here is that the identity and semantic of the concept must be well defined, and the key must be the correct one for the level and for the systems as defined in the name.

- **Mapping model (MAP)**: This is the type for models that support conversion from one reference system to another, by providing the mapping for keys in one system to the equivalent key in the other system.

  These models are generally derived from master data management systems and should be clearly named to state what they help to map, indicating both the from and to systems and concepts.

  As an example, a model that maps inventory positions from logistics to organizational warehouses could be named `MAP_LOG_INVENTORY_TO_ORG_WAREHOUSE`.

- **Master Data Dimension (MDD) model**: This is the type for models that implement dimensions provided directly from the master data management system.

  These models could be as well named as REF models, but when they are available, we prefer to use MDD models to highlight that the data has not been calculated by the data platform but is instead data that is provided – with as few changes as possible – directly from the MDM system, which is generally the most authoritative system to produce dimensions.

- **Aggregated (AGG) model**: This is the type for models that contain aggregated or summarized data.

  These models are often the final transformation step that takes data from a complete REF model and produces a summarized fact, by aggregating on a subset of the available foreign keys. The AGG model is then referenced in the data mart when it is possible to use the compact and, therefore, quicker summarized data in place of the REF model, which remains available for cases when full, detailed granularity is needed.

- **Pivoted (PIVOT) model**: This is the type for models that contain pivoted data. This is a specialized model type that you can use if you happen to deal with pivoted data. It is listed here to make clear that you can create new model types according to your needs. The goal should always be to provide clear communication of what the model does.

We expect that most of the models in your REF layer will be TR and REF models, with few or many MAP models, according to your needs, being required to perform conversion from one key system to another.

Renaming the refined model

Now that we have provided a proper name for the model in the staging layer with the STG prefix, we should also pick a proper name for our model in the refined layer, considering the information from the previous section.

While the staging layer has a simple role and quite schematic names, leaving less room for doubt, the refined layer is a place of doubt, because end names should reflect roles, which depend on what you are building and what the team is feeling about the concepts that you are building.

To pick a name for the positions at the ABC Bank, you must consider what the model represents for your project:

- If you consider this the model that represents the positions at the ABC Bank so that is ready to be reused whenever you need those positions, then it makes sense to consider this the refined model for the concept, and name it with the REF prefix

- If, instead, you consider this an intermediate step in the process to make that data available in a more reusable way, then you should use the TR prefix

As often occurs in IT, you might have good considerations that argue for both directions, such as the following ones:

- We know that security symbols and exchange codes are different for each broker, so we will need some master data layer to be able to combine and reuse data in a general way.

- Currently, this is the best representation that we have of such data, and this is the best data that we can expose and use in reporting.

- In reporting, we want to expose only refined data, which can be used with little or no caveats and possibly reused and combined with other data. As a general pattern, we prefer data mart models to depend only on REF or equivalent models, such as AGG or MDD, and only from the refined layer.

We have pros and cons in both directions, and I am sure that you can find more yourself, but the important thing is to make a choice.

I urge you to consider that a project, and especially an agile project, is always changing, and moving forward with a good enough, generally accepted name is better than stalling and not moving forward. Luckily, the dbt tool and our way of working make changing names and code simpler than it was in the past, especially in the REF layer.

In this case, the model is the "most refined" that we have for the moment, even if we think that we will change it in the future, so our choice is to use the REF prefix.

Please go to your dbt Cloud IDE and rename the POSITION_ABC_BANK model to REF_POSITION_ABC_BANK, and then update the model's name in the refined.yml YAML file so that the description and tests keep working as expected.

Once you have tried the model and tested it, you can commit your change and run the model to deploy it in the database, using the following command:

```
dbt run --select REF_POSITION_ABC_BANK
```

Now, you have deployed the new model in the refined layer, which is connected to the STG model.

> **Tip**
> Please remember that dbt will not remove the table or view that you might have created with the old name. As we are in our development environment, you can just delete the old object with a DROP command to keep your project clean.

One possible alternative is to also create a TR model with the current code and a REF model that, for now, just reads everything from the TR model but, in the future, will evolve to apply the desired MD transformations. This is a good way to lay out practically and tangibly the future architecture for all to see, but it also risks introducing complexity with an extra step that will not be used for a while and potentially forever.

Applying the **You Aint Gonna Need It (YAGNI)** principle, you should not introduce things (features, models, and any other complication) until they are really needed. Following this principle is essential in big projects, and for this reason, we think that adding a temporary or skeleton REF model would only be a good idea when you already have a good plan on how to develop it, you are ready to do that development in a short time frame, and splitting the model in two would ease the work of the development team.

Creating the first data mart

In this section, we want to complete our initial architecture by creating the first model in the first data mart of this project. Data marts make up the delivery layer.

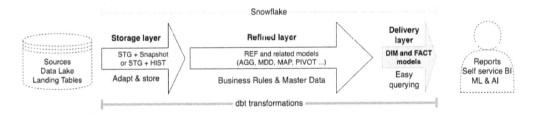

Figure 6.5: The delivery layer highlighted in the Pragmatic Data Platform

The general plan is to have one data mart for each domain that will use the platform's data so that we can provide the best dataset for each of them, using the right names, the correct depth and granularity of the data, and making available only the concepts that matter for that domain.

In the context of our simple example, we do not need multiple data marts, so we have decided to create a data mart with the name of portfolio, which we have already set up in the main configuration file, dbt_project.yml.

To create the data mart in practice, we have to create the `marts` and `portfolio` folders and then put the desired models inside the data mart folder.

Let's do it:

1. Create the `marts` folder under the `models` folder. You can do this by clicking on the three dots menu of the **models** folder and then picking the **New Folder** entry. You can enter only the `marts` name after `models/`, or do both steps in a single command by entering both levels as `models/marts/portfolio`.

2. Create the `portfolio` folder under the `marts` folder.

3. Create the first data mart model with the name `FACT_POSITION`. You can do it by picking the **New File** entry from the three dots menu of the `portfolio` folder and adding the model's name at the end of the path, with the `.sql` extension, producing the full name `models/marts/portfolio/FACT_POSITION.sql`.

    Our first version of the model will just read all data from the model in the refined layer, as seen in the following code:

    ```
    SELECT * FROM {{ ref('REF_POSITION_ABC_BANK') }}
    ```

4. Once you have saved the model, you can deploy it with the following command:

    ```
    dbt run --select FACT_POSITION
    ```

5. Once you have deployed the model, you can check in your Snowflake database that you now have a new schema named `XX_MART_PORTFOLIO` (replace XX with your personal schema) and, inside that schema, a table named `FACT_POSITION`.

With these steps, we have just created the first table, a fact, in our data mart.

A data mart with a single table is not very interesting, but in this case, our fact is the bare minimum we need to start building some basic reporting, and for us, the path that took us here has been more important than the current final result. Building the report is out of our scope.

For now, our data platform just reflects the latest content of our input.

In the next section, we will add to our platform the ability to store its input and changes over time.

Saving history is crucial

A data platform that does not store its input is a very fragile platform, as it needs all the input systems to be available at the same time of each run to be able to produce its results.

An even bigger limitation is that a platform without history cannot fulfill many of the requirements that are otherwise possible and expected today by a modern data platform, such as auditing, time travel, bi-temporality, and supporting the analysis and improvement of operational systems and practices.

To us, anyway, the core reason why you should always save the history of your entities is to build a simpler, more resilient data platform. When you split your platform into one part that just adapts and saves the history (the storage layer) and another that uses the saved data to apply the desired business rules (the refined layer), you apply the principles that we have discussed and achieve a great simplification of your data platform.

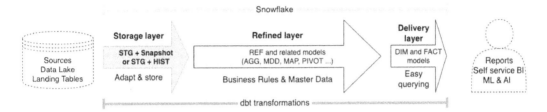

Figure 6.6: The storage layer highlighted in the Pragmatic Data Platform

The question you might have in mind is, "*OK, that's the pros, but what about the cons*"?

This is a fair question, and surprisingly the answer is that there are no real cons!

All the topics that I will list here are, ultimately, a net positive for the data platform, even if someone might initially see them as cons because they require "extra work":

- Your people (tech and business together) MUST understand the data they ingest and be very clear about the IDENTITY of the entities they store.

  Being forced to decide/discover a primary key might feel like a pain, but the result is much-improved use and interoperability of the data across all the data platforms.

- You will store the good, the bad, and the ugly. While you might care only about the good, having it all and being forced to explicitly manage the bad and the ugly will tell your people, especially the business ones, a lot about your operational systems and processes.

- Storing history takes up more room for your data. That is true, but in most cases, the rate of change is very low, as only a few of the entities in bigger tables have more than one version, so the amount of extra data is little. Furthermore, the columnar storage of a modern cloud platform greatly reduces the amount of room used.

  In any case, the value that you get from the simplification of the data platform, and the extra features that the history enables, is much more than the tiny cost of the extra storage. INSERT is by far the best-performing operation on cloud platforms, so in the advanced section, we will move to insert only history, as snapshots use updates, are shared across environments, and become a deployment issue when you want to change them.

- Dealing with source system exports and understanding well how each system provides its data for loading allows you to assess whether you can capture deletions of data or not, and it will tell you at what resolution you will be able to capture the changes.

- Separating source system identity management (to store history) from master data management (to produce integrated information) will show you where you are missing information and will surface the need to actively manage the connections between systems.

We feel that being compelled to deal with these topics early, one entity at a time, is a big positive, as it saves you from having to continue with ambiguous entities that are not clearly understood.

Without such clarity, you might produce something that initially works, until you have a small project with a single developer being consistent with his implicit assumptions, but it is extremely improbable that you might achieve any positive result in a medium-to-complex project with a few developers, let alone create an easy-to-maintain, long-lasting platform.

As an example, in our sample project, we have the position entity, and when we picked a key for it, we saw that its identity was not set in stone and that we could pick a primary key that we feel comfortable with, but we might change that later. This is often the case with facts.

The point here is that we are in a sample project, and there is no real business in the background to discuss and evaluate the different possibilities or just to provide us with some business context, so we must go with gut feelings and experience, which might prove sub-optimal and different for each developer.

In a real use case, the business will be able to answer your questions about the implications of picking one key or another, to better point you toward an appropriate decision.

Saving history with dbt

When working with dbt, we have two main avenues to pick up and save the changes to the instances of our entities:

- *Using the standard functionality of dbt snapshots*: This allows you to easily capture changes as a **Slowly Changing Dimension of type 2 (SCD2)** without writing any code for that purpose, as the logic is implemented by dbt itself using `merge` or `delete/insert` statements. If we get reliable full exports from the source, the snapshot can also capture deletions.

  This works very well for normal-size datasets (up to millions of rows), and it's the simplest way to go, but it comes with its own cons, so we generally prefer to store changes using insert only history, as explained in the second point.

  One of the major cons of snapshots is that they are global objects, so you only have one copy and one version active for all environments. Another one is that you cannot preview or test the `SELECT` query that feeds the data to the snapshot.

As you can imagine, these are not big issues if you have a simple query such as SELECT *
FROM <source>, but it is a limitation if you want to apply the best practices that we have
discussed for the staging layer before storing the history.

* *Using incremental models to save the new or changed data from each run*: We prefer to use this
  approach, applying set-based operations to capture changes in insert-only mode, as this is the
  most effective way to manage and store even huge amounts of data, and it can be tailored to
  work in all cases, even when you have multiple sources for a single table, such as a near-real-
  time feed and a periodic control feed.

  It requires writing your own macro, or adopting our own, to implement the logic to store the
  history – that is, to check whether the version of one instance present in the staging model is
  a new instance or a change relating to the last stored version of that instance.

  This is harder to explain than do in SQL, and we already have the macro ready, so for us,
  this method will amount to less work and allow us to store the changes exactly how we want.
  We will present the macro and this method in the final chapters, together with the more
  ingestion-related topics.

In the next section, we will introduce you to the use of snapshots to store changes and, eventually,
also record deletions.

Saving history using snapshots

dbt provides the snapshot functionality to save incoming data. The best use of it is to capture incoming
source data very close to how the source is, that is with the least changes possible.

In a snapshot, it is perfectly possible to apply all the transformations that we have discussed for the
staging model. Doing that in a snapshot works well in most cases, but it is just a bit less transparent
than doing it in a STG model, as we will see in the next chapter.

The snapshot functionality

A snapshot is a dbt-managed table that will store the data from a SELECT statement in the form of
a slowing changing dimension.

A snapshot is created by the special snapshot block that you create in a .sql file in dbt.

Snapshots are not normal models, in the sense that they are not run with the dbt run command,
but they must be run with the specific dbt snapshot command or with the catch-all dbt
build command.

The snapshot tables are usually generated in their own specific schema, as they are the only tables that
cannot be recreated at every run, so you do not want to drop them by accident. Because of that, they
are stored in the snapshots folder and not in the models folder.

It is important to note that a snapshot table is a global object, shared by all environments that use the same database, including all developer environments. This poses substantial limitations for teamwork because when you change a snapshot, all the environments sharing the snapshot need to be updated at the same time.

The general layout of a snapshot definition is as follows:

```
{% snapshot snapshot_name %}
{{ config(…) }}
select … from {{ source / ref }}
{% endsnapshot %}
```

From the definition, you can see that you do the following:

- Declare a snapshot with the `{% snapshot %}` block and by providing a name
- Configure the snapshot inside the `{{ config(…) }}` function
- Provide the data to be snapshotted by writing a SQL `SELECT` statement

Central to the operations of a snapshot are the following concepts:

- **Identity** or how to distinguish between two different instances of one entity, versus two versions of the same instance. Identity is expressed by a unicity constraint that is often called a *primary key*, *natural key*, or a similar name.

  To create a snapshot, you must configure the `unique_key` parameter for the entity that you are storing. It can be a single field or multiple fields. In the latter case, your entity has a composite key, and the best course of action is to define a single field as the desired combination of fields, using a SQL expression in your `SELECT` query.

  It is of paramount importance that, in any case, the unique key is really unique, and only different versions of the same instance will ever use the same unique key.

- **A strategy to identify changes** – that is, how you decide whether two rows with the same key are the same row or two different versions of that specific instance of the entity.

  In dbt, you can choose between two strategies. The **timestamp** strategy is simpler and quicker and should be preferred when you have a field that reliably tells you whether a record has changed, such as when you have an `updated_at` timestamp or an `ID` field with an ever-increasing sequence number. In these cases, you can just compare the key and the `updated_at` field to decide whether a row is new data or not.

The **check** strategy is the one that you use when you do not have a good high-watermark indicator, and instead, you must look at the data to check whether each row presented by the SELECT statement is the same or a different instance from the most recent one stored in the snapshot under the specified unique key. With this strategy, you must configure the columns to be checked to decide whether two rows are the same instance or not, using the check_cols configuration. You do not have to list all columns from SELECT but only the ones you want to compare; in any case, all columns from SELECT will be stored in the snapshot.

Once you have defined one or more snapshots, you run them with the dbt snapshot command, and you can reference the data in the snapshot in other models using the normal ref function, by using the snapshot name as the referenced model, as in ref('snapshot_name').

The intended usage of snapshots is as starting point of your ETL process to capture and store the source data, so that the general ETL would follow the following pattern:

1. Run the snapshots command to capture the source data – dbt snapshot.

2. Run the models to read the data out of the snapshots and calculate the desired transformations – dbt run.

3. Run the tests to verify the results – dbt test.

A recent version of dbt has introduced the dbt build command, which can replace the three preceding commands, as it will run in the correct order all the commands to build all kinds of models, including seeds and snapshots, and the tests defined on them.

Running a snapshot will cause the following:

-   The creation of a snapshot table from the result of the SELECT statement, which happens the first time that you run the snapshot

-   The snapshot table to be updated, with the changes coming from the SELECT statement relating to the contents of the snapshot table, which happens any other time that you run the snapshot after the first

Coding the SELECT query in a snapshot

In a snapshot, you can opt to just read the source unchanged and apply the changes we have seen in the STG model after the snapshot, but that will mean that every transformation has to be rerun every time that you read the data.

We prefer to put the transformation from the STG model in the snapshot so that we can run the transformations only once, and store the data transformed into the right data types, including the extra data that we have calculated (such as dates extracted from file names).

Putting the code from our STG model inside the snapshot slightly sacrifices the ease of building and maintaining the ELT, as you cannot preview the results of the `SELECT` statement inside the snapshot block.

This lack of ease in building the `SELECT` query without a preview is at odds with the goal of easily maintaining our models, especially if they implement most of the functionalities that we have been talking about with the STG layer.

We can alleviate this issue by keeping our STG model and declaring it to be an `ephemeral` model, which is a model that will not generate any persistence (no view or table is created) but only a named query definition. This way, we have an STG model that we can use to preview the results of the query, but we do not need to run it to make it available for the snapshot.

Layout of a snapshot tables

When you use the snapshot functionality, the snapshot table will contain one row for each new version of each instance that the `SELECT` statement has produced over time. Each time, the most recent version that is (still) active is the current value for the instance identified by the unique key.

The snapshot table will contain the following metadata fields in addition to the fields produced by the `SELECT` statement:

- `dbt_valid_from`: The timestamp when the row is inserted in the snapshot. It provides an order for the different "versions" of an instance.

- `dbt_valid_to`: The timestamp since the row stopped being active. The most recent version of an instance will have `dbt_valid_to` set to `null` if it's still active, or to the highest timestamp for the instance, if it's not active anymore.

- `dbt_scd_id`: A unique key generated for each row in the snapshot. This is internal to dbt.

- `dbt_updated_at`: The timestamp when the row was inserted. This is internal to dbt.

Here are some snapshot best practices:

- Snapshot source data as the first thing in your ETL, declaring a source as appropriate, and make the rest of the ETL depend only on the snapshot.

- Include all the source columns in your snapshot, as you cannot go back in time and backfill information that you do not have, and even if you have it, the backfilling of data is a complicated and time-consuming task.

- Do not add any business logic in the query that feeds data to the snapshot; use only hard rules that do not change the data. If you apply soft business rules and they will change, most probably you will not be able to go back to the original data and apply the new business rule, and even if it's possible, it would be a complex and slow manual process.

- Avoid joins in your SELECT query, as it is not always easy to establish when the result of a join is a new version, and even more difficult to absorb the changes into two tables. Snapshot the two tables to be joined independently, and then do the join in the downstream models where you apply the business logic.

Multiple ways to take into use the snapshots

We discussed that there are a few ways to take snapshots into use; here is a quick recap:

- **A snapshot as a first step**: Taking a snapshot as the first thing in the flow is what dbt suggests, but it means either preserving the source names by using the trivial SELECT * FROM {{ source(...) }} query or writing a query that is not simple to preview/debug.

    If you use this method, we suggest staying close to the trivial select-star query and then putting a full-fledged STG model just after the snapshot, ensuring that everything else will use the good names and data types, even if the snapshot will not.

- **A snapshot after the STG model**: Taking the snapshot out of an STG model solves the maintainability issue, but it is a bit clumsy if you use a normal model, as you need first to run only the STG models for the snapshots, take the snapshot, and then run all the models except the snapshot ones. The clumsiness is removed if you use ephemereal models for the STG models, as you do not need to run them before.

    If you use this method, you will have the ability to easily write, debug, and test at every run the query that you will use to feed the data to be stored by the snapshot.

Now that we have a good idea of the snapshot functionality, let's use it.

Introducing history in our sample project

In our sample project, we get data for the security positions that we have in the fictional ABC Bank.

We have already designed a simple pipeline that allows us to present the data as we prefer and calculate some new information from the input data that we get.

Let's use the snapshot functionality to store the data that we get and make the overall process more resilient, allowing us to do more with the data that we get over time.

The simple, straightforward way to introduce the snapshot functionality would be to copy and paste the code that we have in the STG model to become the SELECT query in the snapshot. This is possible, but we have already discussed that it would make the development and future management of such a query and the resulting snapshot more complicated, as you cannot preview or test that query in isolation.

To remove that issue, we will change the current STG model to use `ephemeral` materialization and use it to feed the content of the STG view to the snapshot:

1. First, let's change our staging model to use an `ephemeral` materialization – that is, to not produce a database object, but just define a model name for our STG query.

    We just need to add the configuration to make the model use `ephemeral`:

    ```
    {{ config(materialized='ephemeral') }}
    ```

2. Drop the view created by the STG model before we turned it into `ephemeral`:

    ```
    DROP VIEW <DB>.<SCHEMA>.STG_ABC_BANK_POSITION;
    ```

    It is better to remove the old view; otherwise, in the future, you or others on the project might think it's still connected to the STG model and even use it, but the view is not connected to the model anymore and will not be updated if there are changes.

3. Create the snapshot to store the incoming data and its evolution, by entering its configuration and using the STG model as the source of the data. Inside the `snapshot` folder, create a file named `SNSH_ABC_BANK_POSITION.sql`, and enter the following code for the snapshot:

    ```
    {% snapshot SNSH_ABC_BANK_POSITION %}
    {{
        config(
          unique_key= 'POSITION_HKEY',
          strategy='check',
          check_cols=['POSITION_HDIFF'],
          invalidate_hard_deletes=True,
        )
    }}
    select * from {{ ref('STG_ABC_BANK_POSITION') }}
    {% endsnapshot %}
    ```

In the preceding code of the snapshot, we have the following:

*   The snapshot block that defines the snapshot and its name:

    ```
    {% snapshot SNSH_ABC_BANK_POSITION %} … {% endsnapshot %}
    ```

*   The configuration block that defines the behavior of the snapshot. In this case, we have used the following configs:

    *   The definition of the field to use as primary key, to identify the instances of the entity that we want to track changes:

        ```
        unique_key= 'POSITION_HKEY'
        ```

- The definition of the strategy to be used to look for changes – that is, to identify new instances or new versions of a tracked instance:

```
strategy='check',
```

- `check_cols=['POSITION_HDIFF'],`

We have used the check strategy, as we do not trust the REPORT_DATE column to work as a good timestamp for the timestamp strategy.

- The configuration to enable tracking of deletions from the source:

```
invalidate_hard_deletes=True,
```

Note that to be able to track deletions, you need to have a reliable full export from the source, as any key that is not in the source is considered deleted.

- The query that is executed to fetch the data to update the snapshot:

```
select * from {{ ref('STG_ABC_BANK_POSITION') }}
```

As we have discussed previously in this section, to work around the impossibility of previewing the query used in a snapshot, we have coded our query in an STG model, configured as `ephemeral`.

Now that we have created our first snapshot, let's run it with the following command:

```
dbt snapshot
```

After the run completes in a few seconds, you should find a new table with the name of your snapshot in the database, and the schema that we have configured in the main dbt configuration file, `dbt_project.yml`.

It is important to remember that snapshots are a global, shared resource, as they end up in the same schema for all the developers and environments that share the same database.

Now that we have the snapshot containing our the data, it's time to connect the REF model with the snapshot in place of the STG model.

Connecting the REF layer with the snapshot

The `REF_POSITION_ABC_BANK` model that we wrote before is still reading data from the STG model that we made `ephemeral`. It still works, but it's now time to make it read from the snapshot so that our ELT will keep working even if the external source is not available.

If you just change the name of model inside the `ref()` function in your REF model, the effect would be to read everything out of the history – that is, all the versions that you encountered in the history of the snapshot. This is not what we want.

To report on the current portfolio, we want to read only the active positions.

To achieve this, we need to select from the snapshot only the rows that have not been closed – that is, where the DBT_VALID_TO field is null – as the old versions are the ones with a timestamp in this column.

The REF_POSITION_ABC_BANK model will now look like this:

```
WITH
current_from_snapshot as (
    SELECT *
    FROM {{ ref('SNSH_ABC_BANK_POSITION') }}
    WHERE DBT_VALID_TO is null
)
SELECT
    *
    , POSITION_VALUE - COST_BASE as UNREALIZED_PROFIT
    , ROUND(UNREALIZED_PROFIT / COST_BASE, 5)*100
        as UNREALIZED_PROFIT_PCT
FROM current_from_snapshot
```

You can see that in the current_from_snapshot CTE, we have added the WHERE clause to read from the snapshot only the rows that are not closed.

Now that we have changed the REF model, we can rebuild it and its predecessors with the following dbt command:

```
dbt build -s +FACT_POSITION
```

This command will run the tests on the source, refresh the snapshot, and rebuild the REF and data mart models.

We have now refactored our code to make it more resilient, maintainable, and easier to understand and evolve.

The fact that we have built is the minimum data model to output some reports, but in those reports, we would not even be able to get the name of the account owner.

To improve that situation, we need to start adding dimensional data, which we will do in the next chapter.

Summary

Good job!

In this chapter you have built a working data platform, with a sound architecture and clear organization, using only the basic features of dbt.

You now understand all the layers of our architecture, and you can build the appropriate models for each layer and save the changes to your data using dbt snapshots.

In the next chapter, we will learn all about incorporating dimensional data in our architecture and reinforcing everything we learned in this chapter.

> **Important note**
>
> Note that, in this chapter, we have been focused on giving you the basics of proper architecture and model organization in each architectural layer. To limit the page count and retain focus, we have deliberately disregarded some important activities, such as adding tests to verify the input source data and the data that we publish in the data mart. Do not assume they are not important.
>
> We have also used some basic functionality, as we have not yet introduced the features to implement more advanced solutions. We will introduce them in the upcoming chapters and refactor our solution to put them to use.

7

Working with Dimensional Data

In the previous chapter, we explored the core principles behind building a data platform from the ground up and implemented them in our reference architecture.

In this chapter, we will learn how to incorporate dimensional data in our data models and utilize it to extend the facts that tell what happens in the business. Dimensional data makes our fact information useful and easy to use for business users.

With the term **dimensional data**, we are referring to descriptive data that provides human-readable information for an entity, such as the name or country of a customer or account.

We will explore how to create data models to plan our work, and build the dbt models for all layers of the *Pragmatic Data Platform* architecture to deliver the dimensional data in data marts.

In the end, we will also recap everything we learned in the previous chapter and this chapter with the help of an exercise.

This chapter covers the following topics:

- Adding dimensional data
- Loading the data of the first dimension
- Building the STG model for the first dimension
- Saving history for the dimensional data
- Building the REF layer with the dimensional data
- Adding the dimensional data to the data mart
- Exercise – adding a few more hand-maintained dimensions

Adding dimensional data

In general, dimensional data is used to provide descriptive information about a fact by using the code of the dimension entity that is stored in the facts to join on the dimension table to retrieve the descriptive information.

The position fact that we loaded in the previous section has four explicit foreign keys, which we have aptly named with the _CODE suffix: the account code, the security code, the exchange code, and the currency code.

These four codes are the references, or foreign keys, to the four dimensions that we can directly connect to this fact.

There is also one extra implicit dimension, the bank dimension, which is implied in the names of the models.

Creating clear data models for the refined and data mart layers

To be able to finalize the dimensions and the fact design, we need to have a clear picture of the data model that we want to use in our reports (the data mart layer), which is often a star schema or, rarely, a wide table.

That in turn is strictly connected to and influenced by the data model of the data that we have and that we can represent in full in the refined layer.

Let's start by having a quick look at a simplified conceptual data model of the entities that we have named and want to report about in relation to the position fact:

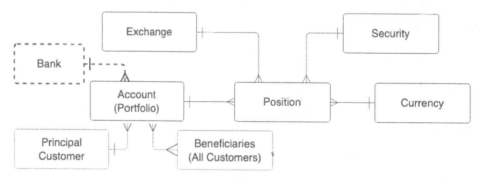

Figure 7.1: Conceptual data model of our sample project

In this data model, we see the four dimensions that we named before, plus the implied bank dimension we discussed.

We are also showing some possible relations with the bank customers/beneficiaries of the accounts, showing both that an account can have more than one beneficiary, which in turn can have more than one account, and that one of the beneficiaries is named the principal beneficiary/customer. Beneficiaries are also customers.

The accounts-to-beneficiaries relation allows us to show a common way to resolve the problem of many-to-many relationships in reporting data marts. Because it's impossible to represent a many-to-many relationship in a proper star schema, they are often reduced to many-to-one (like a normal dimension) by somehow picking the most representative element of the many on the dimension side or by making a (limited) text representation of the many.

This might be the star schema derived from the preceding data model used in the refined layer:

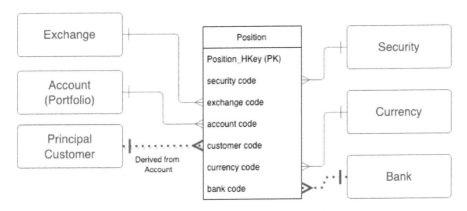

Figure 7.2: Star schema data model for our sample project

In the star schema model, we see that the four dimensions for which we have foreign keys in the fact are directly connected with the fact.

We also see that the **Bank** and **Principal Customer** relations are now directly connected with the fact as the star schema requires. The heavy dotted line is used here to signal that the relationship between the fact and these two dimensions has been "calculated" and added to the fact by following the relationships existing in the source data model (and preserved in the refined layer).

We have not added a dimension for the eventual text representation of the many, as it can be added as a column to the fact, and it's uncommon to build a real dimension to describe the set of elements matching the fact (the beneficiaries in this example) as a single element with compound/aggregated values.

We have clarified the target data model for our reporting and how it is connected to the data model that we will build in the refined layer from the sources. So, we can move on to building it.

Loading the data of the first dimension

In this section, we will see how to create (if you do not have the data from some external source system) and load the dimensional data for the security dimension, which is the one describing the securities that are contained in the positions of the accounts.

At the end of this section, we will invite you to add other dimensions as an exercise.

Creating and loading a CSV as a seed

In a real banking data platform, the security dimension will easily get to many tens of columns, with some columns being informational values that do not change often, while most would be calculated values from trading activity.

In this section, we will create a simple CSV file with some basic columns: `Security_Code`, `Security_Name`, `Sector`, `Industry`, `Country`, and `Exchange`.

	A	B	C	D	E	F
1	SECURITY_CODE	SECURITY_NAME	SECTOR	INDUSTRY	COUNTRY	EXCHANGE
2	TTD	The Trading Desc, Inc.	Technology	EDP Services	US	NASDAQ
3	GCM	GRAN COLOMBIA GOLD CORP	Basic Materials	GOLD	CA	TSE
4	STAR	ISTAR INC	Real Estate	REIT - Diversified	US	NYSE
5						

Figure 7.3: Excel table representing the content of the ABC_BANK_SECURITY_INFO CSV file

The content of the CSV file is shown here:

```
SECURITY_CODE,SECURITY_NAME,SECTOR,INDUSTRY,COUNTRY,EXCHANGE
TTD,"The Trading Desc, Inc.",Technology,EDP Services,US,NASDAQ
GCM,GRAN COLOMBIA GOLD CORP,Basic Materials,GOLD,CA,TSE
STAR,ISTAR INC,Real Estate,REIT - Diversified,US,NYSE
```

You can create your own CSV file in a spreadsheet such as Excel, as shown in the previous screenshot, and then export it to CSV or make it directly by creating a CSV file in dbt and typing or copying and pasting the content (beware of the new lines).

If you do not want to type the content, you can download it from our GitHub repository in the `chapter 6` folder with the name `06_05_v1__ABC_Bank_SECURITY_INFO.csv`.

Let's create the CSV file:

1. Open the `seeds` folder in the dbt Cloud **File Explorer**.

2. Open the menu on the right (three dots) and click **Create File**.

3. Enter the filename `ABC_Bank_SECURITY_INFO.csv` in the pop-up window.

4. Open the new file and edit its content to be like that shown in this section (the preceding code and the following screenshot):

ABC_Bank_SECURITY_INF... ✕

seeds 〉 ABC_Bank_SECURITY_INFO.csv

```
1    SECURITY_CODE,SECURITY_NAME,SECTOR,INDUSTRY,COUNTRY,EXCHANGE
2    TTD,"The Trading Desc, Inc.",Technology,EDP Services,US,NASDAQ
3    GCM,GRAN COLOMBIA GOLD CORP,Basic Materials,GOLD,CA,TSE
4    STAR,ISTAR INC,Real Estate,REIT - Diversified,US,NYSE
```

Figure 7.4: The ABC_BANK_SECURITY_INFO CSV file in the dbt Cloud IDE editor

Configuring the seeds and loading them

Once you have created the CSV file in the seeds folder, it's time to configure where you want your seed data to be loaded and then execute the load.

Let's do it:

1. Open the main configuration file, dbt_project.yml, and add the following code at the end:

   ```
   # Configuring Seeds
   seeds:
     +schema: seed_data
   ```

   This configuration instructs dbt to load all seeds in a schema named seed_data.

2. Once you have configured where you want dbt to create the table containing the data from the CSV, you can run the command to load the data. Execute the following command in the dbt command line:

   ```
   dbt seed
   ```

Once you have run the dbt seed command, you will find that dbt has created a table named the same as the CSV file in the schema that you have configured, with the usual prefix for your development environment.

Adding data types and a load timestamp to your seed

In the seed load, we have been lucky that all the data was of string type, and we had no nulls, so all went well even without specifying the data types of the columns.

After loading the table, we also noticed that we have no clue when we loaded the data.

Let's add a LOAD_TS column of timestamp type and fill it using a post_hook:

1. Open the CSV file and add , LOAD_TS at the end of the first row by adding a colon and the new column name at the end, without spaces, as shown in the following screenshot. Save the file.

    This adds the LOAD_TS column to the file, without any data in other rows, which will be filled by null values.

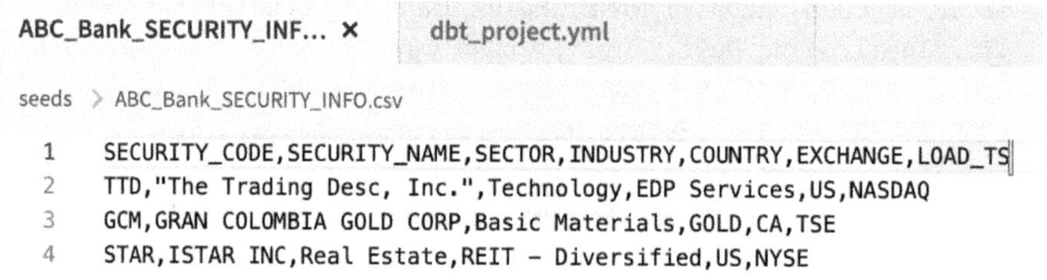

    ```
    ABC_Bank_SECURITY_INF... ✕        dbt_project.yml

    seeds  >  ABC_Bank_SECURITY_INFO.csv
    1    SECURITY_CODE,SECURITY_NAME,SECTOR,INDUSTRY,COUNTRY,EXCHANGE,LOAD_TS
    2    TTD,"The Trading Desc, Inc.",Technology,EDP Services,US,NASDAQ
    3    GCM,GRAN COLOMBIA GOLD CORP,Basic Materials,GOLD,CA,TSE
    4    STAR,ISTAR INC,Real Estate,REIT - Diversified,US,NYSE
    ```

    Figure 7.5: CSV file with the addition of the LOAD_TS column

2. Add to the main dbt configuration file the config to declare the LOAD_TS column of timestamp data type.

    To configure the data types, you need to add the column_types configuration under the seed that you want to configure, and inside it, map the columns that you want to the data type that you want to specify for them, as in the following code:

    ```
    portfolio_tracking:
      ABC_Bank_SECURITY_INFO:
        +column_types:
          LOAD_TS: TIMESTAMP
    ```

    Note that we have first listed our project name, and under it, the seed name.

    You do not need to specify all the columns. The ones that you do not name will be guessed by Snowflake based on the content of the column in the CSV file.

3. Add to the main dbt configuration file the config to run a SQL query after the creation of the table to hold the CSV files.

    To achieve that add the post-hook config under the CSV name to define the query, and then the line with the query to execute:

    ```
    ABC_Bank_SECURITY_INFO:
      +post-hook:
        - "UPDATE {{ this }} SET LOAD_TS = '{{ run_started_at
    }}' WHERE LOAD_TS is null"
    ```

Pre-hooks and **post-hooks** are dbt features that allow you to execute one or more SQL queries before or after the creation of a model, including seed tables.

Note that we put the full SQL query inside double quotes so that we can use single quotes as part of the query. Also, note the use of dbt scripting inside the query, and in particular the `this` and `run_started_at` variables.

The first one will be replaced by the fully qualified name of the model being built, while the latter will be replaced by the timestamp of the start of the dbt execution expressed in the UTC time zone.

The following screenshot provides the final configuration of the CSV seed:

```
ABC_Bank_SECURITY_INFO.csv       dbt_project.yml              ×

dbt_project.yml

58     # Configuring Seeds
59     # Full documentation: https://next.docs.getdbt.com/reference/seed-configs
60     seeds:
61       +schema: seed_data
62       portfolio_tracking:
63         ABC_Bank_SECURITY_INFO:
64           +post-hook:
65           - "UPDATE {{ this }} SET LOAD_TS = '{{ run_started_at }}' WHERE LOAD_TS is null"
66           +column_types:
67             LOAD_TS: TIMESTAMP
```

Figure 7.6: CSV data type and post-hook configuration in the dbt main configuration file

Note that defining the destination schema at line 61, under the `seed:` declaration, means that it will be applied to all seeds, including the ones imported by other libraries. If you want it to be applied only to seeds from our project, move it under our project name and indent it accordingly.

Now that we have added the column and completed the configuration, let's re-create the seed table from scratch so that the new column can be created. Run the following command:

```
dbt seed --full-refresh
```

We have added the `--full-refresh` option as we want to drop and re-create the seed table.

Now, you can go to Snowflake and check that the seed table has the LOAD_TS column and it contains the timestamp of when you run the command.

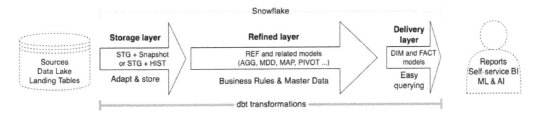

Figure 7.7: The layers of the Pragmatic Data Platform

In the previous section, we created the source to read from because in this example, we did not have a place to read from. In the next sections, we will build the dbt models for all the layers of our Pragmatic Data Platform, as shown in the preceding diagram.

Building the STG model for the first dimension

We have instructed dbt to load our CSV data in a table and we can use that as we would any other model through the `ref (…)` function.

That would work, but when we consider the CSV under the seed folder could be a temporary solution only, like in this case, we prefer to take the data loaded as a seed in use through sources, as we do with any external data.

Defining the external data source for seeds

We will define an external data source to read our seeds in a metadata-driven way so that we can easily adapt if the data would stop coming from a seed and start to come from a different place, such as a table from a master data system or a file from a data lake.

Let's define a YAML file to define the sources for the seeds, and then add the config for the seed that we have just created:

1. Create a new file named `source_seed.yml` in the `models` folder.

2. Add the configuration for the `seed` external source, as in the following code:

   ```
   version: 2
   sources:
     - name: seeds
       schema: "{{target.schema}}_SEED_DATA"
   ```

   Note that we are using the `schema` property of the `target` object to compose the actual name of the schema that will contain the table with our seed data.

3. Add the configuration for the CSV file after the code from *step 2*, as follows:

   ```
   tables:
     - name: ABC_Bank_SECURITY_INFO
   ```

The final YAML file will look as follows:

source_seed.yml   ✕

models > source_seed.yml

```yaml
1   version: 2
2   sources:
3     - name: seeds
4       schema: "{{target.schema}}_SEED_DATA"
5       tables:
6         - name: ABC_Bank_SECURITY_INFO
```

Figure 7.8: The definition of a source system to read our seed files

Now, we can also refer to the seed table with the `source()` function.

Creating an STG model for the security dimension

Now, we have loaded the data from a CSV that we have created, so hopefully we will be fine with the names and data types. But in a real setting, we might get that data from a source outside of our control, so the STG model will be useful to adapt the incoming data as usual.

Furthermore, from the general pattern of STG models, which you can find in the `06_06_v1__STG_Model.sql` file in the `patterns` folder of `Chapter_06` in our repository, you will remember that for dimensions, we want to also have a default record.

Let's start by building the skeleton STG model:

1. Create a new file, named `STG_ABC_BANK_SECURITY_INFO.sql`, in the `models/staging` folder.

2. Add the following code for the config and the `src_data` CTE:

```sql
{{ config(materialized='ephemeral') }}
WITH
src_data as (
    SELECT
      SECURITY_CODE      as SECURITY_CODE    -- TEXT
    , SECURITY_NAME      as SECURITY_NAME    -- TEXT
    , SECTOR             as SECTOR_NAME      -- TEXT
    , INDUSTRY           as INDUSTRY_NAME    -- TEXT
    , COUNTRY            as COUNTRY_CODE     -- TEXT
```

```
    , EXCHANGE              as EXCHANGE_CODE      -- TEXT
    , LOAD_TS               as LOAD_TS            -- TIMESTAMP_NTZ
    , 'SEED.ABC_Bank_SECURITY_INFO' as RECORD_SOURCE

    FROM {{ source('seeds', 'ABC_Bank_SECURITY_INFO') }}
),
```

You can see that we have configured the model to be materialized as `ephemeral`. We have added the `RECORD_SOURCE` field and made very few changes in the names of other fields. Lastly, we are referencing the seed table using the `source()` function.

3. Add the following code for the `hashed` CTE:

```
hashed as (
    SELECT
            concat_ws('|', SECURITY_CODE) as SECURITY_HKEY
        , concat_ws('|', SECURITY_CODE,
                         SECURITY_NAME, SECTOR_NAME,
                         INDUSTRY_NAME, COUNTRY_CODE,
                         EXCHANGE_CODE )
                as SECURITY_HDIFF


        , * EXCLUDE LOAD_TS
        , LOAD_TS as LOAD_TS_UTC
    FROM src_data
)
SELECT * FROM hashed
```

We have defined `HKEY` as the security code and added all the columns to HDIFF except for `LOAD_TS` and `RECORD_SOURCE` metadata columns.

There is an important point to note about the definition of the `LOAD_TS_UTC` column.

Normally, we define it as `'{{ run_started_at }}' as LOAD_TS_UTC`, which provides the timestamp of the start of the dbt run, but in this case, we have decided to use the time when the seed data has been loaded as the timestamp, mostly to introduce you to the new Snowflake syntax, `SELECT * EXCLUDE <columns>`.

This Snowflake syntax is very handy when you want to leave out some columns from the output or redefine the values for one column of one of the queried tables, avoiding listing all the other columns, as you would have to do in standard SQL. This is very handy for tables with a lot of columns.

A more conservative choice would be to rename the `LOAD_TS` field `INGESTION_TS` and keep the usual definition of the `LOAD_TS_UTC` column.

We have created the core of our STG model. In the next section, let's see how to add a default record to this model.

Adding the default record to the STG

The next section that we add is the default record CTE, reported as follows:

```
default_record as (
  SELECT
        '-1'       as SECURITY_CODE
      , 'Missing' as SECURITY_NAME
      , 'Missing' as SECTOR_NAME
      , 'Missing' as INDUSTRY_NAME
      , '-1'       as COUNTRY_CODE
      , '-1'       as EXCHANGE_CODE
      , '2020-01-01'       as LOAD_TS_UTC
      , 'System.DefaultKey'  as RECORD_SOURCE
),
```

In the preceding code, you can see the following:

- All CODE fields have the -1 string as the default value. This is a very common value used in data warehousing to indicate the entry that corresponds to the absence of a value in the dimension related to the code column.

- We have also added the RECORD_SOURCE field to the default record, with the System. DefaultKey value, which is important to distinguish the fact that this is data that is added by our system as a default value, and it is not coming from the original system.

  This is also a good reason to have the field added in the src_data CTE and here so that we can distinguish the origin of the default record from the rest of the data.

- Other fields have standard default values according to their types: string fields have Missing as the default value and number fields would have the -1 number, but you could choose whatever value makes sense for each field in this specific entity.

The with_default_record CTE is unchanged with respect to the pattern.

Saving history for the dimensional data

In the previous chapter, we saved the history of our first table, which was about positions. That is a FACT table, as it records information about facts that have happened or the state of a system at some point in time.

Facts may be subject to change. If they are, we need a business key to recognize the different instances of the fact, as we did for the positions. Alternatively, facts may be immutable, and then we do not need a business key, as is the case with web views.

Now we are going to save the history of our first DIMENSION.

Dimensions store descriptive information that allows us to fully comprehend a fact, such as information about a customer or, in our case, about securities.

The entities described by dimensions are long lived, often referenced by multiple facts at different times, and can generally change during their lifetime. Because of this, correctly defining the identity of the entity, hopefully with a business key, is of paramount importance. That is also the key to capturing the history of the instances of the entity.

Saving the history with a snapshot

In this chapter, we will capture the history of our dimensions with dbt snapshots, while in *Chapter 13*, we will see how we can do the same in a more efficient way using simple SQL to save history at scale.

Let's build our snapshot:

1. Create a file named SNSH_ABC_BANK_SECURITY_INFO.sql in the snapshot folder, like the other snapshot we created before.

2. Enter the following code in the file:

    ```
    {% snapshot SNSH_ABC_BANK_SECURITY_INFO %}
    {{
        config(
            unique_key= 'SECURITY_HKEY',
            strategy='check',
            check_cols=['SECURITY_HDIFF'],
        )
    }}
    select * from {{ ref('STG_ABC_BANK_SECURITY_INFO') }}
    {% endsnapshot %}
    ```

    You have probably noticed that the code is very much like the previous snapshot, with the only differences being the STG model referenced in the query and the HKEY and HDIFF fields.

Another difference is that we have removed the invalidate_hard_deletes parameter, as generally, for dimensions, it is more important to keep old entries than to capture deletions, as these old entries are referenced by old facts. Eventually, we might be interested to know whether an entry is still active or not. In that case, we would enable the parameter to track hard deletions, but then keep both the active and deleted rows in the REF model derived from the snapshot.

One important note to consider is how we have defined the HDIFF column: we have left out the LOAD_TS column from the seed, as it will change every time that we reload the seed, but we do not care about storing a new version if the actual data has not changed.

Please always consider with great care what you want to track as a change and build the HDIFF column accordingly.

Now that we have created the second snapshot, let's deploy it with the following command:

```
dbt snapshot
```

This will run and refresh both of the snapshots that we have defined, so you will find both in your Snowflake database.

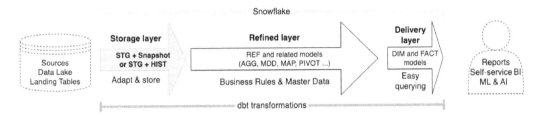

Figure 7.9: The storage layer highlighted in the Pragmatic Data Platform

Now that we have added the storage layer, we are ready to work on the refined layer.

Building the REF layer with the dimensional data

Let's continue building the security info dimension by building the REF model for it.

Let's do it:

1. Create a new file named REF_ABC_BANK_SECURITY_INFO.sql in the models/ refined folder

2. Enter the following code in the file:

```
WITH
current_from_snapshot as (
    SELECT *
    FROM {{ ref('SNSH_ABC_BANK_SECURITY_INFO') }}
    WHERE DBT_VALID_TO is null
)
SELECT *
FROM current_from_snapshot
```

You can see that the content of this file is pretty much the same as the REF model we created earlier for the REF model of the position fact.

We have created our REF model, so build it with the following code:

```
dbt build -s REF_ABC_BANK_SECURITY_INFO
```

Looking at the columns in the model, we can see that there are the DBT_SCD_ID, DBT_UPDATED_AT, DBT_VALID_FROM, and DBT_VALID_TO technical columns, which are not so useful outside of the snapshot.

We can easily remove them from the result using the Snowflake SELECT * EXCLUDE syntax. Change the current_from_snapshot CTE to look like the following:

```
current_from_snapshot as (
    SELECT * EXCLUDE (DBT_SCD_ID, DBT_UPDATED_AT,
                          DBT_VALID_FROM, DBT_VALID_TO)
    FROM {{ ref('SNSH_ABC_BANK_SECURITY_INFO') }}
    WHERE DBT_VALID_TO is null
)
```

Save and run the build command again to see that now, those fields are not in the output.

Very well, this looks much better!

It makes sense to bring this improvement also the other REF model that is implemented with similar code. You might think to open it up and copy and paste the code, like you probably have done when building this model.

ATTENTION! Copying and pasting should raise a *red alert* from your software engineering third sense!

Copying and pasting code is one of the safest ways to quickly reach maintenance hell. It wastes time and is error prone and maintenance will quickly get out of scale, as every change will need to be made manually in all the places that you have copied and pasted the code, but good luck finding them all!

In this case, you can easily understand that most models derived from snapshotted data will have the same code as previously to read the current data out of snapshots. If you have 100 tables, copying and pasting would expose you to the possibility of having to apply the same change in 100 places.

One of the most important features of dbt, macros, is the solution to this problem. In the next chapter, we will introduce macros and fix this problem, so we can leave it as it is for now.

Adding the dimensional data to the data mart

Now that we have the refined model for our dimension, we can publish it to our data mart.

Let's build the security dimension:

1. Create the DIM_SECURITY.sql file in the models/marts/portfolio folder.
2. Enter the following code in the file:

   ```
   SELECT * FROM {{ ref('REF_ABC_BANK_SECURITY_INFO') }}
   ```

As was the case for the position fact, we do not have special requirements now, so we are just publishing everything as it is in the REF model.

As usual, to deploy the model, run the following command:

```
dbt build -s DIM_SECURITY
```

And if you want to be sure that everything is deployed in the most recent form, run the following:

```
dbt build
```

After running one of the commands, you will have the two tables in the data mart, FACT_POSITION and DIM_SECURITY. You are now ready to start doing your analysis.

Exercise – adding a few more hand-maintained dimensions

In this chapter, we have shown you how to go from the source data, including creating a CSV when the data is not available elsewhere, through the storage and refined layers to produce data marts that you can use to power your analysis.

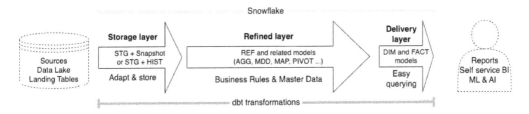

Figure 7.10: The layers of the Pragmatic Data Platform

Here, we propose you add a few dimensions to the project to provide more useful info on the fact that we have loaded.

For each dimension, you will create the dbt models for all the layers of the data platform and you will start to see how you keep applying the same patterns over and over.

Potential candidates and columns for each are as follows:

- **Exchange**: A dimension describing the exchanges where securities are exchanged, with code, name, country, city, trading hours, and time zone

- **Account**: A dimension describing the accounts holding the positions with code, nickname, primary beneficiary name, all beneficiaries' names, accounting currency, broker name or broker code

- **Currency**: A dimension that links the currency name with its alphabetic code, and eventually other info, such as symbol, number of decimals to use, and emitting country/entity

- **Country**: A dimension that has both the two-letter and three-letter country codes, country name, region, sub-region, and so on

This is just an example list; you can probably find more depending on your interest.

We suggest that you pick one or more and implement all the steps yourself to have them in use in your data mart:

1. Load the CSV as a seed, including the generation of LOAD_TS.
2. Define the source for the CSV as another seed data table.
3. Create the STG model to adapt the incoming data.
4. Create the snapshot to store the changes in the dimension data.
5. Create the refined model, reading the current data out of the snapshot.
6. Create the DIM model in the data mart.

In the book's Git repository, under the folder for this chapter, you will find a csv folder that contains three CSV files with data about currencies, countries, and exchanges.

Summary

In this chapter, we learned about dimensional data and how it enhances the usability of data platforms and data marts. We learned how to incorporate dimensional data in our data platform, using the basic features of dbt.

We reinforced our understanding of the layers of our Pragmatic Data Platform that we learned about in the previous chapters and applied those principles to work with dimensional data.

In the next chapter, we will start exploring more advanced features that will allow us to replace some of the basic code to produce a more resilient and easier-to-write and easier-to-maintain data platform.

8

Delivering Consistency in Your Data

In previous chapters, we saw how to use the basic dbt functionalities to build an end-to-end data platform that transforms source data into usable information.

In this chapter and the next one, you will learn how to add consistency and reliability to your transformations. These are two key benefits that only dbt makes so simple to achieve by having functions and tests as first-class citizens of the development process.

In this chapter, you will learn how to go beyond basic SQL and bring the power of scripting into your code, write your first macros, and learn how to use external libraries in your projects.

In this chapter, you will learn about the following topics:

- Keeping consistency by reusing code – macros
- Building on the shoulders of giants – dbt packages

Technical requirements

This chapter builds on the example that we have been developing in the previous two chapters.

You can read and understand this chapter without the previous ones as long as you know the basics of dbt, but for a better understanding, we suggest exploring the sample project.

All code samples of this chapter are available on GitHub at `https://github.com/ PacktPublishing/Data-engineering-with-dbt/tree/main/Chapter_08`.

Keeping consistency by reusing code – macros

In the previous chapters, we used dbt to chain simple SQL-based transformations to produce refined information for our reports. That works fine and offers a good way of working with SQL code, but it would not be a momentous improvement over the previous tools available for the job.

One main difference that sets dbt apart from other tools in transforming data lies in its ability to easily define macros, which are very similar to functions in programing languages and allow us to reuse logic and pieces of SQL code to produce the final SQL code to be executed in the database.

The other huge difference is the simplicity of incorporating testing while writing code and running the tests along with the code to keep data quality in check, as we will see later in the next chapter.

You write dbt macros in a scripting language called Jinja, which is based on Python and used in many other Python-based projects.

Using macros, you can apply the DRY and KISS software engineering principles, reducing duplication of code, and making complex tasks simple, allowing general solutions such as patterns to be widely adopted, as the complexity can be hidden away from most coders.

Repetition is inherent in data projects

While building a data platform is normal that you will be doing the same things over and over, sometimes hundreds of times. This is generally driven by two main reasons – applying column-specific transformations and applying general use patterns.

The first case, repeated field transformations, comes from the fact that you deal with data that is produced by some software, and it always comes with the specific quirks of that software.

Every time that you read from a system, you need to deal with its quirks, such as converting from a specific date format or removing empty strings in place of `null`, or getting rid of padding zeros in front of short numbers.

Whatever the needed treatment is, it is likely that it will be applied many times – potentially very many times – as there are fields that need to be treated in the data source.

The second type of common repetition comes from applying the same logic, aka a pattern, over and over. It might be how to store history, how to apply master data mapping using a mapping table, or any other simple or complex behavior that you end up doing over and over in your code.

In both these cases, the temptation to use copy and paste is strong, as the code needed is pretty much always the same, with the only change often being one field name or some other parameter.

We already have a case in our code.

Look at the `current_from_snapshot` **Common Table Expression (CTE)** in our two REF models – we have two "lookalike" models, done by copying and pasting. That's bad!

Why copy and paste kills your future self

We now have two REF models, and we have two copies of "the same code" that differ in the name of the snapshot we are reading from, but also in excluding or not some technical fields.

You can already see that if we are going to have 100 source tables, we are going to have 100 snapshots and 100 times the same code to extract the current data from them.

Copying and pasting the code 100 times seems like a good gain, as you do not have to think too much and you get the data that you need, but what if you want to make any changes?

With copy and paste, you must go and change the 100 times that your code repeats itself. That's a bummer! You saved a little effort at the beginning of the project, just to be screwed later.

What about having our code produced by a function, aka a macro?

In that case, you can just change the macro once and all the 100 uses get updated at once.

This saves a huge amount of time.

The only constant in projects is change and bugs. Bugs require even more changes than business changes. Every time that you write something a few times, start thinking about how you would be affected if you needed to change it.

The second, and in many cases more important, consideration is that when you change the function that produces the code, you are 100% sure that all the instances are updated. There's no need to go around looking for them.

I wish you good luck if you need to find all the occurrences of a pattern or a specific format that you have applied just 20 or 30 times in a medium-sized project. Besides the time spent, it is the uncertainty of the result and the consequences of incomplete changes that would make your developers scared of the proposed change. That is not a nice place to be, even if it's unfortunately quite normal.

Inconsistent application of patterns and formulas is one of the most common causes of bugs in data platforms built with tools that encourage copying and pasting, instead of making the creation of functions almost as simple as using copy and paste.

Macros in dbt give you the definitive weapon to forget about this problem, making you comfortable with repetitions instead of being scared by them.

How to write a macro

Writing a macro is as simple as writing your SQL inside a macro declaration in a SQL file inside the `macro` folder, and it would look like the following:

```
{% macro this_with_filter(arg1, arg2='XXXX') %}
  SELECT * FROM {{this}}
  {% if arg1 %}
```

```
    WHERE {{arg1}} = {{arg2}}
  {% endif %}
{% endmacro %}
```

In the preceding piece of code, we have the following:

- A macro named `this_with_filter` declared with two arguments.

- An `arg1` argument, which is mandatory, as it does not have a default value.

- An `arg2` argument, which is optional, as it does have the default value of the string XXXX.

- The body of the macro, which is made of four lines that mix normal SQL and Jinja code, which looks very much like Python.

  The macro will be run before the query is sent to the database to produce the final text to be sent to the database by running the logic in the macro.

  The text to produce, generally SQL, is "augmented" by Jinja expressions that print out values when run, such as `{{this}}` or `{{arg1}}`, and Jinja statements that control the flow, such as `{% if arg1 %}`. Later, we will see more constructs.

Please note that while the preceding macro is not helpful in any meaningful way, it allows us to appreciate that the macro and argument definitions look very much like Python, and the same goes for the Jinja statements.

Jinja, in fact, is a Python-based scripting language that is very easy to pick up and use if you have any idea of programming, not just Python. This also means that you can already do wonders with simple variable substitution and very simple logic based on `if` statements and `for` loops as shown in our simple example.

You can define multiple macros inside the same SQL file so that you can keep multiple related functions defined together, as you would do in many programming languages.

In the next two sections, we will improve our code with two sample macros, and then we will conclude the main section on macros with some basics of macro writing.

Refactoring the "current" CTE into a macro

We noted before that our two REF models have a CTE named `current_from_snapshot` that should achieve the same result, but if you look closely, they are similar but not equal.

Let's create a macro for that purpose and then replace the CTE code with a call to the macro:

1. Create a file named `current_from_snapshot.sql` in the `macros` folder.

2. Enter the following code in the `current_from_snapshot.sql` file:

    ```
    {% macro current_from_snapshot(snsh_ref) %}
    ```

```
        SELECT
              * EXCLUDE (DBT_SCD_ID, DBT_VALID_FROM, DBT_VALID_TO)
                RENAME (DBT_UPDATED_AT as SNSH_LOAD_TS_UTC )
        FROM {{ snsh_ref }}
        WHERE DBT_VALID_TO is null
    {% endmacro %}
```

3. Edit the CTE in the `REF_POSITION_ABC_BANK.sql` file by replacing the current SQL with a call to the macro that we created in the previous step:

```
    WITH
    current_from_snapshot as (
        {{ current_from_snapshot(
            snsh_ref = ref('SNSH_ABC_BANK_POSITION')
          ) }}
    )
    SELECT
        *
        , POSITION_VALUE - COST_BASE as UNREALIZED_PROFIT
        , ROUND(UNREALIZED_PROFIT / COST_BASE, 5)*100
                as UNREALIZED_PROFIT_PCT
    FROM current_from_snapshot
```

Note that you can decide whether you want to keep the parameter name and assign it a value, or just put the values in the correct order when calling a macro, just like you can do when calling a function in Python. Leaving the parameter makes the call easier to read and helps a lot when you have a few parameters and not all are as straightforward as here.

The following call without a parameter name would work as well:

```
    {{ current_from_snapshot(ref('SNSH_ABC_BANK_POSITION')) }}
```

After you have saved the file, with the macro taking the place of the CTE, you can see what the macro compiles to by clicking the </> **Compile** button. You will find the compiled code under the tab aptly named **Compiled Code**. Click the **Preview** button to run the query.

4. Edit the CTE in the `REF_ABC_BANK_SECURITY_INFO.sql` file also, as in step number 3, replacing the current SQL with a call to the macro:

```
    WITH
    current_from_snapshot as (
      {{ current_from_snapshot(
            snsh_ref=ref('SNSH_ABC_BANK_SECURITY_INFO')
          ) }}
    )
    SELECT *
    FROM current_from_snapshot
```

Note that in the preceding code, as it was already in the previous formulation, you could just keep the content of the CTE and remove the rest of the code to keep just what you see in the following code block. We prefer to keep this longer format with the CTE, as it makes it simpler to add logic while keeping the structure very clear and consistent across models:

```
{{ current_from_snapshot(
    snsh_ref = ref('SNSH_ABC_BANK_SECURITY_INFO')
) }}
```

As a good practice, after editing the model, run the preview to check that it works.

5. Now that we have created our macro, placed it in our code, and checked that our models keep working, you can deploy the updated code with the following command:

```
dbt build
```

If you look back at the macro that you have coded, you can see that with a very simple macro with just one parameter and no logic, we have improved the quality and maintainability of our project very much.

The only piece of Jinja coding in our macro is the `{{ snsh_ref }}` expression that will print out the value corresponding to the object, referenced by the `snsh_ref` variable.

In this particular case, you can see that in each of the models where we used the macro, we initialized the variable with a call to the `ref()` function:

`{{current_from_snapshot(snsh_ref = ref('SNSH_ABC_BANK_POSITION'))}}`.

If you look up the `ref()` function in the dbt reference under the dbt Jinja functions page, you will discover that it returns a `Relation` object "that has the same `table`, `schema`, and `name` attributes as the `{{ this }}` variable".

The `{{ this }}` variable represents a Relation object pointing at the model being compiled, and it is especially useful to reference the model itself in incremental models or hooks.

It is also useful to note that when called in an expression, such as `{{ snsh_ref }}`, the `Relation` object will return the string with the fully qualified name of the database object that it refers to, generally a view or a table.

Adding a conditional behavior to our macro

You might have noticed that since using the macro, our REF models got a new field named SNSH_LOAD_TS_UTC. This is because the macro excludes most of the technical fields from the snapshot and renames DBT_UPDATED_AT into SNSH_LOAD_TS_UTC.

Our REF models already have a LOAD_TS_UTC field coming from the STG models, so we might consider it overkill to have both timestamps, and we want to make the macro more flexible, offering the ability to choose whether we want to have that extra field or not.

Let's update the macro to add such flexibility:

1. Change the macro code as follows:

```
{% macro current_from_snapshot(snsh_ref,
                               output_load_ts = true) %}
    SELECT
        * EXCLUDE (DBT_SCD_ID, DBT_VALID_FROM, DBT_VALID_TO,
                   DBT_UPDATED_AT)
        {% if output_load_ts %}
        , DBT_UPDATED_AT as SNSH_LOAD_TS_UTC
        {% endif%}
    FROM {{ snsh_ref }}
    WHERE DBT_VALID_TO is null
{% endmacro %}
```

    In the preceding code, we have made three changes.

    First, we have added a new parameter, `output_load_ts`, with a default value.

    We added a default to make the parameter optional so that users of the macro do not need to make any changes in their code, and we picked a value of `true` so that the behavior will remain unchanged.

    Second, we have always excluded the `DBT_UPDATED_AT` column so that it is not returned unless we request it with the `output_load_ts` parameter.

    Third, we have added a conditional (the `if` statement) to allow the macro user to control whether the `SNSH_LOAD_TS_UTC` column is output or not.

2. To see the use of the new parameter, let's assume that we do not want the `SNSH_LOAD_TS_UTC` column in the `REF_POSITION_ABC_BANK` model anymore.

    You would then change the `current_from_snapshot` CTE to look as follows:

```
current_from_snapshot as (
    {{ current_from_snapshot(
          snsh_ref = ref('SNSH_ABC_BANK_POSITION'),
          output_load_ts = false
    ) }}
)
```

Here, you can see that we have added the second parameter and specified a value of `false` for it; running the model, you will see that the `SNSH_LOAD_TS_UTC` column is not part of the result anymore. You can find the full file in the book's Git repo.

In this section, we have added a macro to implement a pattern and make it simple for model developers to use its logic – in our case, how to get the current data out of a snapshot. The model developer now needs only to know from which snapshot they want to read the data and, eventually, whether they also want the SNSH_LOAD_TS_UTC column or not.

I am sure that you can understand the power of being able to produce, with such simplicity, macros that implement a project's opinionated way of working and let the model developers just use it, instead of developing or copying the code each time.

In the next section, we will see another common case that involves applying the same format, formula, or data fix over and over.

Fixing data loaded from our CSV file

Looking at the data that we have loaded for our positions at ABC BANK, you might have noticed that the dates are a bit off, as they refer to the first century and not to the 21st.

Damn! We have been victims of a very common issue – when exporting, importing, and moving data across systems, it is common that the format of the data is somehow imperfect and the data at the end will be different from that at the beginning.

In our case, the export from Excel to the CSV file has produced dates with only two digits for the year. Here, I've reproduced a line from the file, and you can see that the date is represented as 4/9/21. Snowflake has been able to interpret them as dates in the US format and has produced the date 0021-04-09, or April 9 in the year 21:

```
ABC000123,STAR,ISTAR INC,NYSE,4/9/21,150,2444,2725.5,USD
```

Now that we are wiser about the issue, we have the usual two ways forward that we have in any project:

- Fix the issue at the source and reload the data.

  This is the better option, as the data will be correct at all steps and your project will not need to have code to fix the issue, and less code means fewer bugs and less maintenance. Unfortunately, in many cases, we do not control the source or cannot ask for it to be fixed, or we need to preserve the history that we have collected, so fixing the source would just fix half of the problem.

- Live with it, at least for a while, and then fix it.

  This is often the solution that we are left with, even if it's inferior to the previous one.

  Even when we are able to request a fix in the data, the timeline of the fix and the expected release of our work might not match, or we might not want to depend on an external action, so we are left with the need to fix the data, even if just for a while.

If you want you can go and fix the CSV, reimport it, and run everything so that the latest version in the snapshot will be the correct one.

We will go with the fix path instead, as this is the path you will have to take often when you can't really choose because you cannot affect the issue at the source.

Our source is a table with the data already in the date data type, so we cannot fix the parsing of the CSV; our fix will entail bringing dates from the 1st century to the 21st century.

As we are ingesting the CSV as a seed, we could also force the column to be of text data type and then parse it from text to date providing the correct format. That could be implemented as a macro in a similar way to the one shown here. You could take that as an exercise.

We could just write the SQL directly in the STG model, but to make it reusable, we will create a macro with the SQL and a parameter and show you how to use it in the STG model.

Let's do it:

1. Create a to_21st_century_date.sql file in the macros folder with the following code:

    ```
    {% macro to_21st_century_date(date_column_name) -%}
         CASE
             WHEN {{ date_column_name }} >= '0100-01-01'::date
             THEN {{ date_column_name }}
             ELSE DATEADD(year, 2000, {{ date_column_name }})
         END
    {%- endmacro %}
    ```

    In the preceding code, we have created the to_21st_century_date macro with a single date_column_name parameter. The code is pure SQL, with just the column name replaced by the parameter that will hold the column name.

    Please note that the macro will be run in dbt to create the SQL to be sent to the database; therefore, the value of the parameter that we pass in is just a string with the column name, not the column values.

2. Open the STG_ABC_BANK_POSITION.sql file and edit the src_data CTE, editing the row for the REPORT_DATE column to look like this:

    ```
    src_data as (
        SELECT
               ACCOUNTID    as ACCOUNT_CODE     -- TEXT
             , SYMBOL       as SECURITY_CODE     -- TEXT
             , DESCRIPTION as SECURITY_NAME    -- TEXT
             , EXCHANGE     as EXCHANGE_CODE    -- TEXT
             , {{to_21st_century_date('REPORT_DATE')}}
                 as REPORT_DATE       -- DATE
             , QUANTITY     as QUANTITY         -- NUMBER
             , COST_BASE    as COST_BASE        -- NUMBER
             , POSITION_VALUE    as POSITION_VALUE
    ```

```
         , CURRENCY     as CURRENCY_CODE    -- TEXT
         , 'SOURCE_DATA.ABC_BANK_POSITION' as RECORD_SOURCE
    FROM {{ source('abc_bank', 'ABC_BANK_POSITION') }}
),
```

You can see that the only change has been to replace the REPORT_DATE column name with the `{{to_21st_century_date('REPORT_DATE')}}` macro call, passing the column name as a string (which is enclosed in single or double quotes).

When running the dbt model, the macro will be run and replaced with the code resulting from the execution. You can see the result by clicking the </> **Compile** button. You can preview the result and check that the dates are now in the 21st century by clicking the **Preview** button.

3. Run the model and the ones downstream with the following command:

```
dbt build -s STG_ABC_BANK_POSITION+
```

4. Once the run is completed, verify that you now have the new entries in the snapshot for the rows that have been fixed and the old rows are closed off, with the timestamp of our run in the DBT_VALID_TO column.

    You can also verify that the REF model is now serving out the current values, which are the ones with the 21st-century dates.

In this section, we created a macro that hides a longer piece of SQL code and makes it available under a simple name and easy to be applied to different columns.

While it would make no sense to make a macro for use only once, as in our case, in real-life projects, if you need to apply a fix or transformation, it is often the case that you need to apply it multiple times, so making a macro might be a good solution.

Before going all in with replacing SQL with macros, remember that the readability of code is one of the most important goals that we have, and introducing too many macros, especially if you cannot find a proper name, might make your code difficult to understand.

The basics of macro writing

In the previous sections, we saw a couple of simple examples of how you can use macros to empower junior colleagues to apply patterns and consistent transformations, improve your projects, and make your code easier to read and maintain.

In this section, we will see some basic elements that will get you started with writing useful macros, but to get a complete overview, we suggest that you start from the dbt Jinja reference at https://next.docs.getdbt.com/reference/dbt-jinja-functions and then the Jinja *Template Designer Documentation* at https://jinja.palletsprojects.com/en/3.1.x/templates/.

Jinja delimiters

The first and most important thing to understand when working with Jinja is how to move from the output context – where the code is output as is – to the Jinja context, where logic controls the flow and output, and how to produce output from Jinja that becomes part of the code that will be sent to the database.

The text that you write in a dbt model is considered the SQL code to be sent to a database, unless you enter the Jinja context by using the delimiters described here:

- `{% ... %}` start and end **Jinja statements**.

  Statements are the control structures that you can use in Jinja to control how an execution will flow. Examples are `if` conditionals, `for` loops, `macro` definitions, `set` assignments, and filters.

- `{{ ... }}` surround **Jinja expressions** and indicate to print the result out.

  Jinja expressions are very similar to Python ones and include literals for many types, math operations, comparison and logic operations, and a few other operators, including the ability to call Python methods.

- `{# ... #}` surround **Jinja comments**, which are useful to exclude some Jinja code from evaluation/output.

- It's important to note that once inside the Jinja context, you do not need the delimiter anymore, and you can just use expressions without extra curly braces.

Let's describe in a bit more detail some of the most used elements in the next sections.

Jinja expressions

Expressions, like in Python, allow you to use literals, variables, functions, and operators to calculate values. You can then use the result of an expression to store the result in a variable, as input to a function, or just print it out.

Here, we can see some examples in the different categories:

- **Examples of Jinja literals**:

```
'Hello World' or "Hello World"   -- String literals
42 or 42.24 or 42E3              -- Numeric literals
true / false                     -- Boolean literal
['list', 'of', 'objects']        -- List literal
('tuple', 'of', 'values')        -- Tuple literal
{'dict': 'of', 'key': 'and', 'value': 'pairs'}
        -- Dictionary literal
```

You can print them out by surrounding them with double curly brackets, such as {{ 'Hello World' }} or {{ 42.24 }}, which would just print out the values.

- **Examples of using math operators**:

```
{{ 1 + 1 }} or {{3-1}} or {{7 // 3}}   -- all print 2
{{ 2 / 1 }}                             -- prints out 0.5
{{ 3*2 }} or {{ 20 % 7 }}              -- all print out 6
{{ 2**3 }}                              -- prints out 8
```

The math operators are the usual four arithmetic operators (+, -, *, and /) that do floating point operations, plus the // integer division, the % modulus or remainder, and the ** power operators.

- **Examples of using comparison operators**:

```
{{ 42 == 42 }} or {{ 42 != 24 }}       -- both return true
{{ 42 > 24 }} or {{ 42 >= 24 }}        -- both return true
{{ 24 < 42 }} or {{ 24 <= 42 }}        -- both return true
```

As you can see in the preceding example, we have the usual comparison operators: == – equal, != – not equal, > – greater, >= – greater or equal, > – lower, and >= – lower or equal.

- **Examples of using logic operators**:

```
{{ true and true }} or {{ not false }}-- will return true
{{ false or (42 > 24) }}               -- will return true
```

You can use the logic operators (and, or, not, and () grouping) to combine Boolean expressions and control if statements, or any other place where a Boolean is useful.

- **Examples of using other operators**: The in operator performs a containment test, returning true if the tested element is included in the sequence or mapping after the in operator:

```
{{1 in [1, 2, 3]}} or {{'bc' in ['bc', 'a']}} -- in operator
```

The is operator performs a test, using one of the Jinja tests, on the variable or expression. You write the expression, then the is operator, and then the test name, eventually with the other parameters for the test following the test:

```
{{ (expr) is integer }}                 -- is operator
```

The ~ operator converts the operands to a string and concatenates them:

```
{{ 1 ~ " string" ~ ' !' }}             -- ~ operator
```

The () operator allows us to call a callable and pass eventual parameters:

```
{{ "Welcome {}!".format(name) }}        -- () operator
```

The | operator, called a pipe or vertical bar, is used to apply a filter. A filter modifies the value to which it is applied. Filters can be chained and are applied one after the other, with the output of the first modified by the second, and so on:

```
{{ "to uppercase"|upper }}          -- | operator (pipe)
```

The . or [] operator gives access to an attribute of the object stored in the variable to which you apply the operator, with a syntax similar to Java or Python:

```
{{ obj.attr }} or {{ obj[attr] }}      -- . / [] operator
```

Combining the different types of expressions, you can produce complex expressions that allow you to express pretty much any calculation or test, as you would do in Python.

The If statement (if… then…, and else)

The if statement, also called a conditional statement, works in the same way as in Python and allows you to decide in which branch to continue execution, depending on one or more tests.

The main difference is that the notation is slightly different, as it is started by a {% if value_to_test %} block and is always closed by an {% endif %} block.

In its simplest version, the if statement continues the flow if the value of the test is true, as in the following example:

```
{% if value_to_test %}
some output
{% endif %}
```

You can also write the preceding example all on a single line, if you prefer:

```
{% if value_to_test %}some output{% endif %}
```

If the test is true, then the code inside the if statement will be executed – in this case, returning the text. You could have other statements and expressions inside the if statement.

The general form of the if statement is the following:

```
{% if test1 %}
    Test 1 is true. Do something …
{% elif test2 %}
    Test 2 is true, but not test 1. Do second thing…
{% else %}
    Both test1 and test2 did not return true. Do something else…
{% endif %}
```

Looking at the preceding example, you see that you can chain as many elif blocks as you need, and you can use an else block to catch all the cases that did not fulfill one of the previous tests.

for loop statements

`for` loops are the other main control structure, together with `if-else` statements, and are very close to Python `for` loops. The main difference is that you cannot `break` or `continue` out of a Jinja `for` loop, but you can apply a filters and tests.

You can use a `for` loop to iterate over a sequence, like in this example:

```
{% for item in sequence %}
    {{item}} {% if not loop.last %},{% endif %}
{% endfor %}
```

Here, we have exemplified the use of the `last` property of the `loop` special variable.

The `sequence` variable in the example could be a list of any type of content, usually a list of column names or values. Another common use case is using the `range` function to produce a list of numbers – for example, to generate a list from 1 to 10, you can use the `range(1, 11)` expression.

You can also use a `for` statement to loop over the content of a dictionary:

```
{% for key, value in a_dict | dictsort %}
{{ key }}, {{ value }} is the same as {{ key ~ ', ' ~ value}}
{% endfor %}
```

In the preceding example, we have also applied the `dictsort` filter to sort the dictionary before looping through it.

The set statement

In Jinja, you use the `set` statement to perform variable assignments.

There are two formats for assignments; the first one is the inline assignment, which resembles the assignment in Python, like in the following examples:

```
{% set var = "some value" %}
{% set a_mixed_list = ['one', 2, three] %}
{% set var1, var2 = my_function() %}
```

As you can see, you can assign multiple variables in the same assignment used in Python.

Note that `for` loops introduce a different scope (while `if` conditionals do not); the consequence is that outside the `for` loop, you cannot see the effect of an assignment done inside, even if the variable was declared/initialized outside the `for` loop. You should use namespaces for that purpose, or a different construct.

The second type of assignment is the block assignment, where you just declare the variable name in the set statement, and the variable then gets assigned the result of the elaboration of the code inside the set block:

```
{% set date_filter %}
   DATE between {{ start_date }} and {{ end_date }}
{% endset %}
```

This second type of assignment is very handy to assign longer texts, especially if you want them properly formatted, as the block will keep the correct new lines.

We tend to use this kind of assignment when we want to incorporate variables inside a text, as inside a block, you can just type the text normally and output the variable or the result of a calculation, using the usual expression format with the two curly braces.

This is a simple and readable way to assign a variable with the text of a SQL query, or a filter to be passed in a macro.

run_sql() function

The run_sql() Jinja function provided by dbt allows us to execute a piece of SQL toward a database that is configured for the environment in which we are executing the call.

You do not need to use this function until you start writing more complex functions, where the behavior depends on the content of the database or when you want to execute SQL commands outside of the normal dbt run cycle.

The following sample code from the dbt reference of the function gives us two useful inputs to discuss:

```
{% set results = run_query('select 42 as the_answer') %}
{% do run_query('DROP TABLE IF EXISTS PUBLIC.MY_USELESS_TABLE') %}
```

- The first line shows that you can use an assignment to execute a function and get the result in a variable, if you want to store the result in a variable.
- The second line shows that, as an alternative, you can use the expression statement that uses the do tag to execute an expression without printing out any result.

  This is useful to execute expressions or functions with side effects if you do not want to store the result; examples include changing a list or running some DDL or DML SQL code.

We will generally use the run_query function only when we want to perform some operation – that is, no SELECT queries – and we do not want to use the result of the query as the result is an Agate table – that is, a complex object that is not so easy to manipulate.

When you want to use the results of your query in a macro, we suggest using the get_query_results_as_dict() macro from the dbt_utils library, which we will introduce in the next section. That macro will return an easy-to-use Python dictionary.

We will use the `run_query` function in conjunction with the `run-operation` dbt command when we want to run DDL or DML commands in an automated way, such as when we want to define external tables, create landing tables, or ingest data directly from files using the `COPY INTO` command.

The return() function

We will use the `return()` function only in more advanced macros that don't directly produce the final output, instead returning a data structure for further use, typically a list or a dictionary, as shown in the following example macro:

```
{% macro get_user_dictionary() -%}
{% set users_dict_yaml -%}
developers:
  - MY_SF_USER
  - ANOTHER_SF_USER
readers:
  - PBI_USER
{%- endset %}
{% do return(fromyaml(users_dict_yaml)) %}
{%- endmacro %}
```

The preceding macro allows you to create and maintain a dictionary using the YAML format, by writing it inside the block that is assigned to the `users_dict_yaml` variable.

The variable is then passed to the dbt `fromyaml` function that parses the text and builds the corresponding data structure. A similar function, `fromjson`, exists to parse the JSON format.

Finally, the `return()` function returns the data structure to the caller.

Here, we saw an example that returns a manually maintained configuration; the other common use of the return function is to return data that you have loaded through the `run_query()` function (or the other more usable variations provided by libraries).

Until now, we have been writing our models and macros from scratch – that is, by writing all the code without any help besides the base dbt functionality. In the next section, we will see that we can get a lot of help from dbt libraries, called packages, that we can import into our projects.

Building on the shoulders of giants – dbt packages

We have been writing our models and macros using only the base dbt functionality. In this section, we will see some existing libraries, called packages in dbt, and how we can import them to increase our productivity.

Using only dbt or Java or Python standard functionalities, you can build everything that you need. Doing everything by yourself does not pose an absolute limitation, but in all languages, the availability of libraries, collections of well-tested code to do frequent or complex tasks that you can easily download and use to accomplish complex tasks, has greatly augmented the productivity of programmers and their ability to solve more complex problems.

Using libraries, you can concentrate on the core of your problem and rely on a lot of other smart people's knowledge and experience to reduce the complexity of your project, saving a lot of time.

You can reuse the code written by experts in areas that your team is not expert in, use proven solutions that you might otherwise be unable to create yourself, or just use quick and standard solutions to implement everyday needs with proven solutions instead of reinventing the wheel.

Creating dbt packages

Maybe you are wondering how to create a dbt package.

You may be surprised to hear that you have already done it!

A dbt **package** is just a normal dbt project, like any other, and is usually stored in a git repository.

What makes a dbt project a package? Nothing really – just the fact of being imported by another package. The *package* name refers to the fact that the imported project packages some functionalities together that other projects can reuse.

A package can contain everything that a dbt project contains – models, macros, sources, tests, and so on – that will become part of the importing project, so you will be able to reference those elements as usual.

Therefore, you can reference an imported model with the ref() function and call a macro with its name, prefixed with the imported package name to avoid name clashes.

When you import a package, all dbt commands will work both on your code and the code that you have imported. As an example, when you run the dbt run command, the eventual models from the imported packages will also be run.

You can generally find or create packages to solve common problems such as the following:

- Transforming data from standard interfaces, such as SaaS and common products
- Libraries of macros to perform common tasks or tasks related to a specific domain
- Managing or auditing specific tools

How to import a package in dbt

To add a package to your dbt project, you must follow these two simple steps:

1. Add the package information to the `packages.yml` file under a `packages:` declaration.

   These couple of lines tell dbt where to find the package and what version to import.

   Please note that each package version generally works well with a range of dbt versions.

2. Run the `dbt deps` command.

   This executes the actual import or refreshes the package to the selected version.

Once you have added the entry for a package in the `packages.yml` file and run the `dbt deps` command, dbt will download the version of the package that you have pointed it to.

You will find the source code of the package in a folder with the package name, under the `dbt_packages` folder.

Methods to add dbt packages to your projects

There are a few slightly different ways to add a package to the `packages.yml` file:

- **From the dbt Hub registry, with the following syntax:**

  ```
  packages:
    - package: dbt-labs/dbt_utils
      version: 0.8.6    # version number or range
  ```

  A version must be specified but it can be a range, such as `version: [">=0.8.0", "<0.9.0"]`, allowing you to get the latest minor release when it becomes available. Please remember that you need to run the `dbt deps` command to check for upgrades and get a new release.

  This is the simplest and best way to install packages that are available in dbt Hub, as dbt can handle cross dependencies and download each dependency only once.

- **From Git public repositories, with the following syntax:**

  ```
  packages:
    - git: "https://github.com/dbt-labs/dbt-utils.git" # git URL
      revision: 0.9.2    # tag or branch name or commit hash
  ```

  With the `git` base syntax, you can add any package located in a git-compliant repository that dbt can access anonymously. By pinning to a specific `revision`, you control what version of the package dbt downloads, avoiding unexpected changes.

  Providing `revision` is optional but strongly recommended; otherwise, you will get master, in whatever state is when you run `dbt deps`. For `revision`, you can provide anything that Git would understand – a branch name, a release tag, or a full commit hash.

- **Using local folders, with the following syntax**:

```
packages:
  - local: /your/local/folder   # a local path
```

This is a special way to import packages and is very useful for packages that you are developing, as the changes will take effect as soon as you save the files of the package, without the need to run dbt deps at every change.

This feature is available only in dbt Core and not in dbt Cloud, as you have no access to the local filesystem of your dbt Cloud projects.

- **From Git private repositories**: The exact syntax is slightly different, depending on the Git service provider that you are using, as you need to use the correct HTTP URL format to provide the **access token** and, eventually, the username, as required by your service provider:

```
packages:
  # github format
  - git: "https://<application token>@github.com/..."
  - git: "https://<user_name>:<personal token>@github.com/..."
  # Azure format
  - git: "https://<personal access token>@dev.azure.com/..."

  # BitBucket format
  - git: "https://<user>:<pers token>@bitbucketserver.com/..."
  # GitLab format
  - git: "https://<user>:<personal token>@gitlab.xxx.com/..."
```

As you can see in the preceding examples, you provide the access information before an @ sign and the usual full repository URL.

The formats to provide the access information are essentially twofold – one with just an access token and another with a username and access token, separated by a colon.

To avoid putting secrets in clear into your repository, you should not write usernames and tokens directly in your YML file. Instead, you should use environment variables to store the actual values and use the env_var function in the YML file.

Looking at the preceding examples, you can make the following substitutions:

Replace <user_name> with {{env_var('DBT_ENV_SECRET_GIT_USERNAME')}}.

Replace <token> with {{env_var('DBT_ENV_SECRET_GIT_CREDENTIAL')}}.

Remember that in dbt Cloud, the environment variables have strict names that must start with DBT_ or DBT_ENV_SECRET_. The difference between the two is the ability of dbt Cloud to remove its printed values from logs and not show or print out the secret ones in the UI.

Now that we have seen how to import a package, let's discuss when to use each method.

Using dbt package import methods

Looking at these four ways to import packages, you might have guessed what their common use case is, but let's discuss it briefly:

- Importing packages from dbt Hub is the go-to method to import common, open source packages that are of general use. This is by far the most frequent, if not the only, method that you will use to import packages in your projects, or at least to bring in functionalities built by third parties.

- Importing from git public repos is a convenient way to import less known or niche packages that an author makes available to the community, without the effort of registering it with the dbt Hub. You can also use it for your own libraries if you are fine with making the code public.

- The local import is a specialized functionality mostly used by package developers. The main advantage is that any change is taken immediately into use, without the need to call the dbt deps command to refresh the package.

- Importing from private repositories offers the ability to have **private packages** so that you can build your own library of dbt macros and models to reuse in all of your projects, without the need to make your code public.

- Importing from private repositories can also be used to build **nested project architectures**, where common parts to be used in multiple projects, such as the ingestion and/or initial transformations from a common data source, are factored into a common package included in all the projects that need the same data.

  This can be achieved in two ways; the first is importing the code for the common package, duplicating the processing, and producing an independent copy of the data for each project, without managing multiple copies of the code and providing a continuous lineage graph. The drawback here is the duplication of the processing and the data.

  The second way is to have one project that does the common import/processing, which is run only once and on a single copy of the data, and then create a second "interface-only" project to define the results of the first project as sources. This second project can be imported into all the other projects that need to read the transformed data. The drawback of this setup is that the lineage is divided across the common project and the imported ones.

- Another use of a private import is to segment a bigger project into sub-projects, but the risk here is the increased complexity of the final, global project and a reduction of the benefits of working within smaller projects. This use might be needed when some data or code must not be shared with some third parties, which can instead work on less sensitive parts of the overall project.

We have discussed some common ways to import dbt packages, as well as some more advanced possibilities that you most probably won't need to consider until your project becomes quite big (hundreds of models) and you have accumulated significant experience.

It is perfectly normal that, most of the time, you will import the usual packages from dbt Hub; nevertheless, we believe that is useful to know some advanced possibilities for eventual future use.

Using packages to build internal shared libraries

If your company has multiple dbt projects, there is a good chance that you are applying the same best practices and patterns in all of them. As a consequence, a substantial number of macros and utility models are used with little to no changes in all or many of these projects.

Examples of shared macros might involve ingesting data (using macros, which we will see in the following chapters), generic tests that you keep using (such as against hash conflicts), or format conversion that you need to apply often (such as removing or adding padding zeros on strings).

Examples of shared models can include monitoring performance and resources in on-site deployments or consumption in SaaS platforms, providing reporting on security, such as users and role access, or providing audits on activity, such as queries run by a user or users accessing some info.

In these cases, the temptation to use copy and paste and reuse models or macros is strong, but if you go back to the beginning of this chapter and read again the *Why copy and paste kills your future self* section, you will be reminded that is not a good idea inside a project and, as you can guess, even across projects.

The solution is to refactor the common macros and models into a standalone dbt project that will become the first version of your shared library. You will then evolve it according to the needs that you will have across your projects, such as when we extended our `current_from_snapshot` macro when the need for an extra feature arose.

Designing a library is not a simple thing, as you need to balance the flexibility that you want to give to users with the simplicity of use. The following guidelines will help you to get started:

- Prefer small, focused packages to a catch-all package. It's easy to import three or five different packages, but you cannot import just half of one.

- Especially when including models that will be materialized at every run of your project, err on the side of making multiple, small packages with high cohesion so that your users can pick the functionalities they want without any extra baggage.

  Provide a simple way to configure the models, using dbt variables or environment variables, and document how to do the configuration.

- When you are making a package that consists only of macros or tests, you can err on the side of making fewer, bigger packages, as unused macros and tests just sit there without bothering anyone. A good example is the `dbt_utils` package that provides a set of quite different macros, with the common denominator being their general use.

The bigger the library, the more important is to organize your macros by domain and functionality, provide examples of their usage, clarify well what data type you expect for your parameters and the data structure that you expect to work with, and clarify whether there are any special requirements, such as the key field being the first in a column list.

- As always in software engineering, avoid circular references between your libraries, so consider their level of abstraction when you are building them, and eventually split a library to keep objects that are used by many libraries from the ones that use other libraries.

Now, by using macros, generic tests, and packages, you know how to avoid duplication inside a project and across projects. In the next section, we will browse through some useful packages that provide you with a host of new functionalities.

Browsing through noteworthy packages for dbt

You now know how to import packages to add functionalities to your projects, and that there is a dbt Hub repository that contains the most commonly used, open source packages, which you can easily add to your projects.

You can access the dbt Hub repository at the `https://hub.getdbt.com/` URL.

In the next sections, we will present some noteworthy packages that you can find in dbt Hub.

dbt_utils package

This is without any doubt the most common and generally used dbt package, as it provides a wide range of common functionalities that go from more generic tests to macros in different domains, such as loading data from a database, extending SQL, providing unified cross-database functionalities, and more specific needs, such as extracting parameters from URLs or helpers for Jinja.

Here is a list of a few generic tests and macros that we will find especially useful with this package:

- `expression_is_true`: This is a model level test that asserts that the SQL predicate (and expression evaluating to true or false) that you provide is true for all the records in the table. This macro allows you to test pretty much everything that you can express with a SQL predicate, but if you keep using in the same way we suggest you define your own generic test with an appropriate name.

- `not_empty_string`: This is a column-level test that verifies that there are no empty strings (`''`) in a column, after eventually trimming the content of the column.

  Together with the `not_null` test, you can verify that a text column actually contains real text values, without `null` and `''`:

  ```
  - name: column_name
    tests:
  ```

```
    - not_null
    - dbt_utils.not_empty_string
```

- `mutually_exclusive_ranges`: This model-level macro tests that the rows create correct date ranges when partitioned by a column, allowing you to verify that ranges do not overlap, have or don't have gaps, and that the range size is greater than zero.

- `get_column_values`: This macro loads the values from a specific column of a model as a Python list, without having to deal with Agate tables.

- `get_query_results_as_dict`: This macro loads the results from a SQL query as a Python dictionary so that you do not have to deal with Agate tables.

- `date_spine`: This macro generates the SQL code to generate a continuous sequence of dates in an interval, according to a desired granularity (day, month, and so on).

- `union_relations`: This macro allows you to unite two or more relations (tables or views), aligning fields with the same name and adding null columns for the missing ones, making it simple to UNION tables that are similar but do not have the same columns in the same order.

- `star`: The basic behavior of this macro produces a comma-separated list of columns from a relation, eventually with an alias, with the ability to exclude some columns. This can be used in place of the usual SELECT * code to better control what columns you want to select, even in databases that do not have the SELECT * EXCLUDE (...) constrct.

  More advanced uses allow you to add a prefix or suffix to the column names.

- `generate_surrogate_key`: This macro provides a cross-database way to calculate a hash for a list of columns. This can be used as a surrogate key or for any other hash common use.

  We will use this often in our macros to store the history of a table.

We have just provided a very short list of the useful macros that you can find in the dbt_utils package, and we urge you to have a peek at it at https://hub.getdbt.com/dbt-labs/dbt_utils/.

Codegen package

This package, also from *dbt-labs*, provides many useful macros to generate an initial version of commonly written pieces of code so that you can minimize the need to type information already available in your database, especially names.

With these macros, you can generate the source definition for the tables in a schema, which you can copy and paste into a source YAML file, or you can generate a skeleton staging model or the YAML code to document and test a set of models.

Previewing the following code will generate the YAML for a source file to import the relations from a schema in the selected database:

```
{{ codegen.generate_source('<schema>',database_name = '<database>') }}
```

You can also run the macro using a `run-operation` command, as shown here:

```
dbt run-operation generate_source --args '{"schema_name": "<schema>",
"database_name": "<database>", "table_names":["table_1", "table_2"]}'
```

The following code can instead be used to generate the YAML to describe and test a model:

```
{{ codegen.generate_model_yaml(model_name='<model>') }}
```

We strongly suggest using these macros or building your own to minimize useless typing, reduce the errors in typing column and relation names, and concentrate on the logic that you need to add to transform data into information.

In *Chapter 6*, we provided examples of SQL queries that you can run to the same effect to generate the code you need in your models from the metadata information that the database already has about your source tables.

dbt_expectations package

This package extends the testing abilities of dbt by defining many test macros, inspired by the Great Expectations package that tests Python programs.

The available tests go from simple ones such as `expect_table_row_count_to_equal_other_table` to more complex ones that can test the values of your data, such as `expect_column_values_to_be_within_n_moving_stdevs`.

The dbt_external_tables package

This package allows you to create external tables as sources in a database-independent way, by configuring the tables that you want in YAML.

The metrics package

This dbt-lab-created package uses the `metrics` definition introduced in dbt V1.0.0 to produce data tables, providing data according to the metrics definition.

This package allows you to materialize the metrics that you have defined and also take advantage of secondary calculations, such as period over period, period to date, rolling, and so on.

dbt_vault package

This is the first dbt package to help build a data platform according to the **Data Vault 2.0 (DV2)** principles and is produced by Data Vault, a UK-based company that specializes in DV2 consulting, run by the well-known DV2 expert Neil Strange.

datavault4dbt package

This is a package to build a data platform according to the DV2 principles, produced by Scalefree International, a company closely connected to the Data Vault creator Dan Lindstedt.

dbt Model Usage package

This dbt package provides tests to let you know whether your models are still relevant to your users. These tests scan your database's query logs to check whether users are still selecting from the tables that dbt produces. Test failures can let you know when it might be time to retire unused models.

dbt_profiler package

This package provides macros to profile the content of your relations, providing many measures for each column, such as the proportion of not null, min, max, and the number of distinct values.

This package can be used for initial data exploration, to create detailed documentation, or to write profiling queries, which can be useful to monitor tables that require special attention.

dbt_artifacts package

This dbt package builds a data mart to analyze the executions and usage of dbt components, such as models, tests, and exposures, ultimately describing the dbt project where you install the package.

snowflake_spend package

This package, provided by GitLab, allows you to collect and analyze the cost that your Snowflake database is accruing. It also provides queries to build the dashboard they use.

In this section, we have listed a few useful packages that you might be interested in adding to your dbt projects. In the next section, we will add the `dbt_util` package to our example project and use one of its macros to calculate hashes for our models.

Adding the dbt-utils package to our project

We have seen that the `dbt-utils` package has many useful functionalities, so let's add it to our project and then use it to refactor our code to produce better surrogate keys, replacing the simple field concatenation that we have used so far.

Let's add the dbt-utils package to our project:

1. Create a packages.yml file in the root of the project, alongside with the main configuration file, dbt_project.yml.

2. Add to the packages.yml file the following code:

```
packages:
  - package: dbt-labs/dbt_utils
    version: 0.8.6
```

When you save the file, your project will not compile anymore, as the dependency that you have just declared has not yet been downloaded. However, do not worry, as you will fix it in the next step.

Note that the 0.8.6 version of the dbt-utils package is compatible with all the dbt releases with major 1 – that is, version 1.0.0 and above, but lower than 2.0.0.

3. Run the dbt deps command to download the package.

Now that you have installed the dbt_utils package, your error should be fixed, and you should find the code of the package under the dbt_packages folder.

In the next section, we will start to use it.

Calculating the hashes for the STG model

In our STG models, we have been creating both our surrogate key and change detection key using simple string concatenation.

This method works perfectly well regarding functionality, but it is not the best overall way, as the resulting field might become very long, wasting space, and having a human-readable surrogate key is generally not a great idea.

A better way to create a computable surrogate key is to use a hashing algorithm to combine the information and always produce keys of the desired length and always the same key for the same inputs.

Using a hash key in place of the string concatenation introduces a small risk, as it is possible that two different inputs will produce the same output of the hashing algorithm, but using a hash with a big enough size makes the chance so little that we can use it without any real risk.

We will use the MD5 hashing algorithm, which produces a 128-bit digest, generally represented by 16 bytes or 32 hexadecimal characters. Using MD5, the collision risk is so low that in a table with 200 billion hashes, the chance of collision is negligible ($p=10^{-18}$) being 10,000 times less probable than the odds of a meteorite landing on the data center holding your data ($p=10^{-14}$). In any case, we can easily test that we do not have collisions.

To calculate the hash, we will use the surrogate_key function from the dbt_utils package at version 0.8.6.

This is the precursor of the `generate_surrogate_key` function that you will find in future releases of the package. The difference is in how the two manage `null` values, so be mindful that moving to the new function will change your hashes when there are `null` values. If you can, start by using the newer version.

Let's change our STG models, starting from the `STG_ABC_BANK_POSITION` model.

Change the `hashed` CTE in the `STG_ABC_BANK_POSITION` model as follows:

```
hashed as (
    SELECT
      {{ dbt_utils.surrogate_key([
            'ACCOUNT_CODE', 'SECURITY_CODE'])
      }} as POSITION_HKEY
    , {{ dbt_utils.surrogate_key([
            'ACCOUNT_CODE', 'SECURITY_CODE',
            'SECURITY_NAME', 'EXCHANGE_CODE', 'REPORT_DATE',
            'QUANTITY', 'COST_BASE', 'POSITION_VALUE',
            'CURRENCY_CODE' ])
      }} as POSITION_HDIFF
    , *
    , '{{ run_started_at }}' as LOAD_TS_UTC
    FROM src_data
)
```

As you can see, the `surrogate_key` function takes the place of the `concat` function, and we transform the list of columns into a list of strings with the column names.

You can preview the model with the new code and see that the hash codes are now in place of the string with the key values.

Let's also change the second STG model by changing the `hashed` CTE in the `STG_ABC_BANK_SECURITY_INFO` model as follows:

```
hashed as (
    SELECT
          {{ dbt_utils.surrogate_key([ 'SECURITY_CODE' ])
          }} as SECURITY_HKEY
    , {{ dbt_utils.surrogate_key([
            'SECURITY_CODE', 'SECURITY_NAME', 'SECTOR_NAME',
            'INDUSTRY_NAME', 'COUNTRY_CODE', 'EXCHANGE_CODE' ])
          }} as SECURITY_HDIFF
    , * EXCLUDE LOAD_TS
    , LOAD_TS as LOAD_TS_UTC
    FROM with_default_record
)
```

Also, preview this model to be sure that all is working as expected.

We do not have to deploy our STG models, as they are ephemeral, so let's update the snapshot that collects the data coming out of the STG model.

We have not changed the schema of the STG models, so we can just run the snapshot, and the effect would be that all the old rows are replaced by the rows with the new hash codes.

This does not make much sense anyway, as we would have the same entity represented in the table with two different keys. The solution to continue using the old history would be to rename the current table or the snapshot so that there is only one active snapshot table that uses the current keys. Then, you reference in the proper way both tables in the REF model.

In our case, as the snapshot does not contain any precious history, we will just drop the snapshot table so that running the snapshots will create new tables, with the keys based on hash codes.

Let's do it:

1. Let's drop the old snapshot tables:

    ```
    DROP TABLE
      PORTFOLIO_TRACKING.SNAPSHOTS.SNSH_ABC_BANK_POSITION;
    DROP TABLE
      PORTFOLIO_TRACKING.SNAPSHOTS.SNSH_ABC_BANK_SECURITY_INFO;
    ```

2. Run the snapshot to create the new tables:

    ```
    dbt snapshot
    ```

We have used the first function from a package, and you have seen where to find more packages and how to install them.

Summary

Congratulations! In this chapter, you learned how dbt makes it very simple to add consistency to your transformations.

You can now create your own macros and, even better, use macros provided by others in packages to speed up your development and consistently implement patterns and transformations.

In the next chapter, you will learn how to make your development and transformations reliable and ensure data quality with the help of tests.

Tests are the other great improvement that dbt brought to the world of data management – making testing part of a normal, expected development cycle, as it is normal to expect modern software to be developed with a robust test suite.

9

Delivering Reliability in Your Data

In the previous chapter, we learned how to ensure that your code behaves consistently and how to use macros and external libraries in the code.

In this chapter, you will learn how to ensure the reliability of your data by adding tests that verify your expectations and check the results of your transformations.

Finally, you will learn which tests make the most sense in each layer, and we will add many tests and macros to our sample project.

This chapter covers the following topics:

- Testing to provide reliability
- Testing the right things in the right places

Testing to provide reliability

If you take away only one thing from this section, please be it this: "*Tests are going to be your sleep-well-at-night superpower.*"

Tests ensure that things go as you wish them to go and alert you when that's not true.

They are your army, protecting your work and time from the evil influences of broken data sources and the inevitable code bugs (yours and from your colleagues).

That's real power.

Lack of testing compounded with development without rigor, as people writing SQL queries often lack a software engineering background, makes firefighting issues the most common activity in too many data teams, and the idea of changing some heavily used part of the data pipelines (think customers or orders) can make a whole team sweat. Ever been there?

We want you to be free of these nightmares. In the previous chapters, we provided sound guidelines on how to organize your code and make it easy to read and maintain. In this section, we will show you how you can also post guards at key points of the transformations that you deploy to check that everything goes as expected.

We introduced dbt out-of-the-box generic tests in *Chapter 5*, showing you how to use them in YAML files; in this chapter, we will discuss all types of tests and their usage in greater detail.

Types of tests

Each test checks that some expectation on a dbt resource is fulfilled.

In dbt, tests are implemented as SQL queries, and you can write them as SQL queries, but most of the time, you will just apply them to a dbt resource (a model, source, snapshot, or seed) or one of their columns in a declarative way inside a YAML file.

A dbt test runs a `SELECT` statement that returns the rows that do not fulfill the expectation that you are testing, so an empty result set is a passing test, while each row returned is a test failure. These failing rows can be automatically saved for your inspection.

As an example, the query for the `not-null` test looks like `SELECT column FROM model WHERE column is null`. You can see that if there are rows where `column` has the `null` value, then they are returned, while if there are no rows with the `null` value, the query has no resulting rows.

In dbt, you can express a test in two ways:

- By writing a plain SQL query that tests your assumption.

    This is called a **singular test**, as it is used in a single case. You will generally use only a few of these tests to cover the rare cases not covered by the available generic tests.

- By writing or using a parametrized SQL query and passing the required arguments; this is called a **generic test**, as in principle, you can use it to test any dbt resource.

    This kind of test will be your bread and butter, and you will get most tests from packages, as in general, you will be testing over and over the same kind of assumptions that other people also test in other projects.

Let's look at the two ways of writing tests before looking at what kind of test to write.

Singular tests

This is the simplest form of testing, and its power to test is only limited by your ability to express the assumption to be tested in SQL.

Writing a singular test is as simple as writing a SQL SELECT query that returns the rows that do not satisfy your expectation and putting it into a .sql file inside the tests directory. The filename will become the test name.

Each SQL file in the tests folder defines a test that is run when you test the models used in the test's SELECT statement. To write your test SQL, you can reference models, seeds, macros, and sources, as you would in any dbt model.

Creating a singular test

Let's make an example singular test for our sample project:

1. Create a new file in the test folder. We picked the following filename – STG_ABC_BANK_ SECURITY_INFO__NO_CLASH_DEFAULT_RECORD.

2. In the file, enter the following SQL code for the test:

```
SELECT *
FROM {{ ref('STG_ABC_BANK_SECURITY_INFO') }}
WHERE SECURITY_CODE = '-1'
    and RECORD_SOURCE != 'System.DefaultKey'
```

This test will check that the security code that we have used for our default record ('-1') does not clash with a value coming from the data source.

3. Run the test with the dbt test -s STG_ABC_BANK_SECURITY_INFO command.

This test is not needed, as testing that the SECURITY_CODE is unique would be enough to avoid the clash, but we wanted to show that any query works well as a singular test if it returns only the rows that break the expectation.

In this case, the RECORD_SOURCE field did its job by allowing us to distinguish between the data coming from the data source and the data that we added.

In this section, we showed you that you can be assured that whatever you want to assert about your data, you can always do with a singular test if you cannot find an existing generic test that fits the bill.

In the next section, we will see how a SQL query like this might become a generic test so that if you end up doing multiple similar singular tests, you can replace them with a singular test and maintain less code, while improving the consistency of the testing.

Generic tests

A generic test is a parametrized SQL query defined in a test block that is like a macro, which you either write or get from a package, and you can use it in any YAML file to invoke as one instance of the test applied with the parameters from the YAML file.

Given the fact that we end up testing similar assumptions on most dbt resources and that, once written, the generic tests are stupidly simple to use, you should not be surprised that this is the most common type of test.

In most cases, you will just use a generic test in a purely declarative way by adding the generic tests that you want to apply to a resource as elements of a list, under the `tests` property of your dbt resources in YAML files, as we did in *Chapter 5*.

Out-of-the-box generic tests

As you may recall from *Chapter 5*, dbt comes with the following four types of generic tests:

- `not_null`: This tests that a column is never `null` in a table.

- `unique`: This tests that the values in a column are unique.

- `relationships`: This tests the referential integrity between two tables, meaning that each value of a foreign key in a table exists in the named column of the named table. To put it another way, you test that there are no *orphans* in the tested table.

- `accepted_values`: This tests that the values in the column are one of the listed values.

Using these base tests, you can already strengthen your project and cover the basic assumptions that we make when building pipelines, such as having primary keys and business keys that are unique and not null, foreign keys that do not have orphans, and categories that have values in the expected set.

The generic tests provided by dbt cover the most common testing needs and can be further configured to tailor to a specific case – for example, demanding that a column such as `email` is unique but only for active users, or recognizing that a single customer with an empty name is not a big enough deal to block the ELT and should just raise a warning, while over 10 errors might justify stopping the pipeline.

Applying generic tests

You will apply generic tests to models using YAML files, as we have done earlier in the book with sources.

As an example, the following is the `refined.yml` file that provides a description and tests on the `REF_POSITION_ABC_BANK` model in the refined layer:

```
version: 2
models:
  - name: REF_POSITION_ABC_BANK
    description: The positions we have in the ABC Bank portfolio.
    columns:
      - name: UNREALIZED_PROFIT
        description: The unrealized profit on the position.
        tests:
          - not_null
```

```
      - name: UNREALIZED_PROFIT_PCT
        description: The unrealized profit % on the position.
        tests:
          - not_null
```

The preceding snippet demonstrates the basic use of the not_null test on two different columns. Later, you will see how to add additional configurations to better tailor test behavior, such as making a test return a warning, erroring out only above a certain threshold, or applying it with a condition.

The default tests provided by dbt are applied at the column level, but tests can also be applied at the resource level, without the need to nest them under a column.

The following syntax is used to apply the has_default_record test to the REF_SECURITY_ INFO_ABC_BANK table:

```
version: 2
models:
  - name: REF_SECURITY_INFO_ABC_BANK
    tests:
      - has_default_record
```

This is common for tests that are applied to a table and no specific column, as would be the case of a hypothetical table_is_not_empty test.

Generic tests from packages

You can supplement out-of-the-box generic tests with many others provided by open source or private packages, extending projects with generic tests written by others or even yourself.

In fact, in the previous section on packages, we named two packages that provide a trove of tests – dbt_utils and dbt_expectations.

The dbt_utils package provides a good selection of generic tests that complement the four provided out of the box by dbt Core, allowing you to cover the normal testing requirements so that you will seldom need to write generic tests, and you might just use it for readability or ease of configuration.

Please review the tests that we have described in the previous section and the remaining ones in the dbt_utils page on dbt Hub at https://hub.getdbt.com/dbt-labs/dbt_utils/.

The dbt_expectations package greatly extends the available generic tests and allows you to add tests to your projects, using the same test style as the Great Expectations test suite for Python.

To give you an idea of the extension of the available tests, here is a list of the test categories from version 0.8.0 of the dbt_expectations package: table shape, missing values, unique values and types, sets and ranges, string matching, aggregate functions, and multi-column and distributional functions.

You can review the definitions at `https://hub.getdbt.com/calogica/dbt_expectations/` on dbt Hub. Each test comes with usage examples, and you can look at the test source code.

Defining a generic test

To define a generic test, or to override one of the out-of-the-box ones, you can write a `test` Jinja block, containing the SQL for your test in a SQL file.

Test blocks are very similar to macros, as generic tests used to be macros with a name starting with `test_`, and they still work pretty much the same as macros – defining a function that takes arguments and whose result is evaluated as a test result.

The SQL for generic tests must be written to return the rows that fail the test, using the same logic that we saw for the singular tests. If you test for a column that is equal to 42, then your SQL should select all rows where the column value is not 42.

Generic tests are applied using YAML files and must always define at least two arguments, `model` and `column_name`, which are automatically used to pass to each test invocation the reference to the resource and, eventually, the name of the column on which the test is applied in the YAML file.

You can add other parameters in a test definition, with or without default values, as you can do with macros. You can then pass values for those extra parameters in the YAML file, as we will see shortly when developing our first generic test.

Since dbt version 1.0.0, you can place your generic tests in two places:

- In the `macro` folder, where you also define macros. This is a heritage of the original way to define generic tests as macros, and it turns out to be handy when you want to use other ad hoc macros to define complex logic in a generic test.

- In the `tests/generic` folder, close to the singular tests. This special folder was introduced in dbt 1.0.0 and allows you to place all tests under the same folder, with generic ones in the `generic` folder and the singular ones organized as you see fit.

We suggest you pick one of the two locations to organize your generic tests.

We will use a `tests` subfolder under the `macro` folder so that we can define macros along with tests if we need to, keeping the `tests` folder only for singular tests.

Generic test pattern

The SQL that you write for a generic test uses the `model` and `column_name` parameters to test the resource and column that you have configured the test for, but your test can use more arguments.

The following is a pattern for generic tests:

```
{% test my_test(model, column_name, more_params…) %}
WITH
model_data as (
    SELECT * FROM {{model}}
)
, validation_errors as (
    -- return the rows failing the test using model, column_name
    -- and eventual other parameters that you can add
)
SELECT * FROM validation_errors
{% endtest %}
```

Here, you can see that we first get the data for the resource to test, then we apply the test logic to find the rows that fail the test, and finally, we select the failing rows.

Writing your first generic test

In our project, we are using hash values as keys and to check when the content of a row is changed. The probability of having hash collision – that is, two different sets of values producing the same hash – is really minuscule, and it is very safe to use hashes for such purposes.

In any case, we will write a generic test that allows us to check whether we get unlucky and have a collision, so we can manage it and re-hash the table to avoid missing even a single row of data.

Let's write the generic test:

1. Create a new file named no_hash_collisions in the macro/tests folder, creating the folder if it does not exist.

2. Enter the SQL code for the generic test in the file:

    ```
    {% test no_hash_collisions(model,column_name,hashed_fields) %}
    WITH
    all_tuples as (
        SELECT distinct {{column_name}} as HASH, {{ hashed_fields }}
        FROM {{ model }}
    ),
    validation_errors as (
        SELECT HASH, count(*)
        FROM all_tuples
        GROUP BY HASH
        HAVING count(*) > 1
    )
    ```

```
SELECT * FROM validation_errors
{%- endtest %}
```

In the test block declaration for the `no_hash_collisions` generic test, we have declared three parameters, adding `hashed_fields` to the mandatory `model` and `column_name` parameters.

We have renamed the `model_data` CTE `all_tuples` to underline that we are taking all distinct tuples made by the `hash` field and all the fields used to build `hash`.

We have then selected all the hashes that exist with more than one tuple of the fields, as this would be a case of collision – the same hash generated by two distinct sets of values.

3. Create a `snapshots.yml` YAML file to describe and test snapshots:

```
version: 2
snapshots:
  - name: SNSH_ABC_BANK_POSITION
    columns:
      - name: POSITION_HKEY
        tests:
          - no_hash_collisions:
              hashed_fields: ACCOUNT_CODE, SECURITY_CODE
```

The `model` and `column_name` parameters are managed automatically by dbt, so we do not need to pass them to the test, but we need to provide a value for any other parameter of the generic test that does not have a default value, such as `hashed_fields`. We have omitted the descriptions, but they should be there.

You provide parameter values as properties of the test that you declare. In practice, this means that you add a `:` (colon) after the test name, and in the next row, indented with respect to the test name, you write the parameter name, `:` (colon), and the parameter value, as we did for the `hashed_fields` argument in the previous example.

The parameter value can be a Jinja expression, but then it should be properly quoted.

4. Run the tests on the snapshot to see your shiny new test in action:

```
dbt test -s SNSH_ABC_BANK_POSITION
```

We have easily defined a generic test by writing some SQL inside a `test` Jinja block and using some conventions for the mandatory argument names.

Let's see how we can add a macro that supports the use of this test so that we can use the same code for the test that we use to define the hash, instead of having to provide the same list of fields, but in not quoted form.

If you look at your STG models, you will see that to build the hash key and hash diff, we pass a list of field names to the `dbt_utils.surrogate_key` macro.

By using the `join` filter, it is very easy to produce the list of names separated by commas, so let's do it:

1. Add to the `no_hash_collisions` file the macro to produce the field list:

    ```
    {% macro as_sql_list(hashed_fields_list ) -%}
    {{ hashed_fields_list|join(', ') }}
    {%- endmacro %}
    ```

    This macro is simple; it uses the Jinja `join` filter to concatenate the field names separated by commas but makes it simple by quickly reusing the same list we used to define the hash fields, making it quick to write the test and reducing errors.

2. Add to the `snapshots.yml` file the `no_hash_collisions` test for the `POSITION_HDIFF` field that uses a long list of fields:

    ```
    - name: POSITION_HDIFF
      tests:
        - no_hash_collisions:
            hashed_fields: "{{ as_sql_list(
                ['ACCOUNT_CODE', 'SECURITY_CODE',
                'SECURITY_NAME', 'EXCHANGE_CODE',
                'REPORT_DATE', 'QUANTITY', 'COST_BASE',
                'POSITION_VALUE', 'CURRENCY_CODE'
                ] ) }}"
    ```

    You can see that in the parameter definition, we use a macro called inside curly braces to produce a string with the desired content, by passing in a list of strings. The macro will work well in the YAML file if it is properly enclosed in quotes. In this case, we use double quotes, as we want to use single quotes for the list of strings.

With this simple example, we have demonstrated to you a few important processes – defining a generic test with extra parameters, passing the extra parameters, adding a macro to simplify the use of a generic test, and finally, calling a macro to provide values inside a YAML file.

Configuring tests

Like with most dbt resources also for tests, there are some configurations that you can use to control test behavior, besides passing arguments.

You can configure tests at different hierarchical levels, with the most general having lower priority and the most specialized having higher priority:

*   In the global configuration file, `dbt_project.yml`, you can configure all tests using the `tests:` property, as shown in the following example:

    ```
    tests:
      portfolio_tracking:
    ```

```
+enabled: true
+severity: warn
```

This will enable all tests and configure them at the warning level. Of course you can always disable or reconfigure them at the error level with a more specific config.

- In a `config()` block inside the test SQL definition you can configure the default for a generic test:

```
{% test no_hash_collisions(model,column_name,hashed_fields) %}
{{ config(severity='warn') }}
...
```

In the preceding example, we configure the generic test to have, by default, a `warn` severity, which for generic tests can be redefined at the specific use case level in the YAML files. Singular tests are only configured with `config()` blocks along with SQL, as they cannot be configured using a YAML file.

- Generic tests can be fine-tuned at the specific use case level, with the desired value assigned to the configuration properties in the same place, where the tests are defined, placing them in a `config` property:

```
- name: POSITION_HKEY
  tests:
    - no_hash_collisions:
        hashed_fields: ACCOUNT_CODE, SECURITY_CODE
        config:
          severity: error
```

The preceding example configures the test to have an `error` severity, even if someone had included a `config()` block with a `warn` severity in the test definition.

Test configurations

Tests have the following specific configurations that can be applied:

```
- <test_name>:
    <argument_name>: <argument_value>
    config:
      where: <string>
      severity: error | warn
      error_if: <string>
      warn_if: <string>
      fail_calc: <string>
      store_failures: true | false
      limit: <integer>
```

The preceding code shows how to apply the configs as properties in a YAML file for a generic test, but they can be applied to any tests with a `config()` block or, generally, in the main config file.

The following is a brief description of them:

- `where`: This limits the test to the rows that satisfy the `where` clause passed as a string. This is often used to limit a test to active rows, where some columns are not null, or data in some time frame.

- `severity`: This sets the severity in case of test failures to be `error` or `warn`. The default value is `error`.

- `error_if` and `warn_if`: These configure a SQL condition that can be compared with the number of failures to fine-tune the severity, allowing you to apply a threshold to produce an error or a warning. The default is `!= 0` for both configs.

  The configs are checked, starting from the `severity` and `error_if` conditions, to evaluate whether an error must be raised, with the `warn_if` condition checked if an error is not triggered.

- `fail_calc`: This configures the aggregation function applied to the test query to report the errors. The default is `count(*)`, giving the number of rows failing the test.

  As an example, you can use `sum(n_records)` to see the total number of rows that have duplicates, or `max(n_records)` to see the maximum number of duplicates found. You need to know the test SQL code well to apply the right aggregation expression.

- `limit`: This configures the maximum number of failing rows to be returned by the test. This is generally not set, and it is useful only when storing errors on big tables.

- `store_failures`: This is a configuration to enable or disable the storage of the rows failing a test. The default is `false`, meaning that failing rows are not stored.

  When test failures are configured to be stored, dbt will save the results of the test query – that is, the failing rows – into a table with the same name as the test in the schema, with the default `dbt_test__audit` suffix. This allows you to easily analyze the failing rows.

Besides the test-specific configurations mentioned here, it is possible to apply to tests other general-purpose configurations, such as `enabled`, `tags`, and `meta`, plus `database`, `schema`, and a table `alias` to configure where to store failures.

Testing the right things in the right places

In the previous sections, we saw how easy is to add tests in dbt; most of the time, you just add a `tests:` property with a few test names under a table or column in a YAML file.

Adding tests is so simple that it is easy to go overboard and start testing everything and everywhere, but please refrain from doing that, and remember that tests are code and, therefore, bring with them their fair share of errors (wrong application or configuration of generic tests from libraries and coding errors in our own singular tests), maintenance (false positives, errors without business value that can just be ignored, and constant test refactoring), and consequences (ignoring important tests because of constant test failure fatigue).

Tests also take time and money to execute, so waiting for useless tests to complete is a total waste of money, and of a developer's time when they run tests in their development environments. It's also not particularly fun, so it would be great to find a good balance.

The real questions then are, *What do we test?* and *Where do we do the testing to get the best value for our time and money?*

Let's start by setting apart one unexpected and special use case for dbt tests – data exploration.

Writing dbt tests on sources is so simple and quick that it is often the single best way to get acquainted with some new data that you do not know well enough. In this situation, you can use dbt tests to explore your expectations and better understand the data.

One common case is to try out different potential primary and business keys to verify whether they are unique or not and whether their columns are always not null. Other common cases include verifying that relationships from a fact to a dimension do not have orphans (or that the dimension is complete), that categories and measures are present, and in what proportions.

Of course, one ideal way to do such explorations is to use the `dbt_profiler` package, but if you do not have that installed, using tests is a quick and commonplace way to check your initial expectations and document your findings with the rest of your team.

What do we test?

Once this initial flurry of testing to better understand data is over, we must concentrate on having the tests that matter in our projects. The following section will address it.

We must always start with what drives value and, therefore, what problems would impair value the most, or enough to matter.

Let's go through the major categories of data that we can find in our models:

- The **Primary Key (PK)** and the **Business Key (BK)**: Getting the PK/BK right is essential to be able to identify an entity and store their history of changes. They enable us to join facts and dimensions, and the BK is essential to be able to identify the same entity across different systems.

  While immutable facts can be fine without PK/BK, the keys are essential for all the other entities that we might want to use in our platform: mutable facts, dimensions, reference tables, mapping tables, and configurations.

- **Foreign Keys (FKs)**: FKs are the essential element of relational systems, as they store the relations between tables and entities by pointing to the PK/BK of another table that completes the information. In the case of a many-to-many relationship, the FK of each side is stored in the mapping table that defines the relation, instead of being directly inside a table.

  The most common case of FK is when a fact has FK that creates a relationship with a dimension. In this case, if the relationship is mandatory, we want to be sure that no FK in the fact is `null`. In any case, we also want that for each FK in the fact the equivalent PK exists in the dimension.

  It is also extremely commonplace and important to correctly represent the relationships between dimensions to create hierarchies, like a city inside a country inside a region inside a continent, and between facts that represent business processes, such as the invoice line or the return line related to a sales order line.

  A core topic running across the correct identification of a PK and an FK is correctly understanding the multiplicity of the relationships.

- **Business rules (BRs)**: BRs come in many flavors and are the spice that gives most of the value to our data platform. It is impossible to make a complete list of BR types, as they can range from calculations to ways of connecting entities to ways of formatting data.

  Whatever type they are, we need to get them right if we want to correctly represent our business.

- **Measures**: Measures are numeric types of data that can be used for calculations. Some measures are extremely important, as they are needed for calculations, and their absence can make data almost useless, such as a sales order without the amount sold.

- **Categories**: Categories are textual data that is not purely descriptive, such as a name or any free text, but they are used to group or somehow organize data, such as a type of product, the industry of a customer, or any value that our users use to slice reports, but is not a full fledged dimension.

- **Descriptive data**: Everything else can pretty much fall under the descriptive data category, which contains things such as names, freeform text, and generally, all kinds of textual data that does not fall into the other category types.

Looking at these categories of data, it is clear that some of them will cause a lot of problems if we get them wrong, while others might be considered a mere nuisance:

- PKs and BKs are essential, and we must do all that we can to get them right; otherwise, we will be unable to properly join data or store the history of changes, and we will likely generate duplicates.

  In short, if we get PKs/BKs wrong, there is no chance that our data model will work; therefore, we must test that what we pick to be the PK/BK is a good key.

- At a similar level of importance, there is the correct understanding of the multiplicity of the relationships identified by the FKs (including the optional or mandatory status). We must test that the FK for a mandatory relationship we use is there (not `null`); otherwise, our data model will not work as expected.

- When we get to BRs, it is also very important to test that we have all the pieces we need to calculate them and, if possible, to test that our calculations are correct. This last part requires support from the business users to provide usable test cases with the expected results.

- Getting into lower priority data categories such as measures, categories, or descriptive data, the importance should be considered case by case.

   The person responsible for sales, the sales team, or the customer's name can be of secondary importance in some contexts, while it might be crucial in others.

   You need to consider adding tests for these data categories while balancing the pros and cons.

Now that we have a clear picture of what to test, let's move on to analyze where it is best to perform our tests.

Where to test what?

The general idea of where to do tests looks simple; the earlier we catch a problem, the better it is, so we should do a test as soon as a test is doable.

You also want to test what you are delivering, to be sure that despite all the intermediate transformations you have done, the result conforms to your expected data model.

The golden rules are as follows:

- Test your expectations about inputs on sources or as soon as possible

- Test your expectations about outputs when you deliver them

- In the intermediate transformations of the ELT pipelines, test the important things that might create a lot of problems or that you do not totally trust to always work as planned, such as BRs or complex joins

In the following sections, let's discuss the typical tests for every layer of our data platform.

Tests on the sources (input layer)

This is the entry point of the data, which you have not touched yet, so you can only test assumptions that do not need any change on incoming data.

Here, you have some of the most important tests:

- Test PKs and BKs to be not null and unique. This is a top priority that ensures that you correctly understand and store your entities.

   If you have a source with a full history or even a partial history with multiple versions, you must move the unicity test to another layer, usually the STG layer (where you can filter to keep the latest version to be stored).

You can test the PK and that the update timestamp is unique, but this is more to explore your input data model than to ensure consistent data quality.

Remember that it's fine for an immutable fact to not have a PK/BK.

- Test FKs to check that mandatory one-to-many relationships are not null. This is a high priority that ensures that the FKs are in place and are as you expect them. A relationship is mandatory if it must always be there; therefore, the FK must not be null.

- Test relationships to check that they don't have an orphan FK. This is a low priority. Knowing that the relationship is complete is good, but you just have what you have been provided by the input data.

  Knowing that you have orphans in a fact (the dimension or lookup table does not have a PK for one or more FKs of the fact) might be a good input for the operational people to know about the issue, especially if they can add the missing primary keys, and otherwise to make yourself sure to manage the orphans, but it does not give structural info and you must live with the data you have.

- Categories and measures we depend upon are of mid to low priority, meaning that you must ensure that you have important pieces of data, but not everything is necessary.

  For example, it is difficult to report on sales if you do not have sales amounts or to split data by country if some customers do not have a country code. You must decide how important this is, based on eventual alternatives that you have and on actions that you can take if a test fails.

- Test the source freshness. This is of high priority. You must be sure that the data is as fresh as expected.

  Take advantage of the dbt functionality that allows you to enter the desired freshness threshold for each source table and automatically run the test, producing an easy-to-read report.

Tests on the storage layer – the STG and HIST models

Here, we filter and transform data in its basic usable format that we want to store, and we are able to test everything that we are interested in but we could not test directly on the source data.

This is the most important layer for your data quality, as here is where you put your data when is it in the proper shape to be used and store its history. You must be sure of what you are storing:

- Test that the PK and BK (that you could not test on sources) are not null and unique. This is a top priority. You need to be sure that the keys are valid keys, as you will depend on them.

  In most real-world cases, even when your sources contain more than one version, it is fine to add to the history only the most recent version at each run, filtering the data in the STG model to the version to be stored in the HIST model.

At this stage, you must test that PK/BK at the output of your STG model is unique and that, in the HIST model, the combination of PK/BK and LOAD_TS is also unique, as we want to store one change at each run.

- Test that HKEY and HDIFF have no hash collision (in the HIST model).

This is low-priority. The collision risk is tiny, especially if you do not have billions of rows.

The collision risk increases the more hashes you have in a table; therefore, it makes sense to check the hashes in the HIST model, as it contains all the hashes for one entity. The risk is always very small, and one collision would eventually compromise only one row of data, but it would be irresponsible to not test for it.

When tables have billions of rows, the test starts to be more useful but also slower, so it might make sense to run the hash collision test with a lower frequency.

- Create all the tests that you would have done in the source layer but that were impractical because they needed some data transformation.

It is quite common that some input data needs cleanup or transformation before working as expected. Common examples are dates and timestamps that are parsed from text (you want to be sure that you can parse them from their textual format, before being able to test what is expected by them), or text fields normalized by removing extra spaces or meaningless zeros, or changed to uppercase or lowercase.

Tests on the refined layer

This is the business rules layer that depends on stored data being correct.

In this layer, we should assume that the data that comes from the storage layer is sound, and we must test only where we can introduce errors by doing transformations:

- Test the results of the BRs that calculate values. This is of high priority. We must be sure that we have a result and that it's correct.

The minimum expectation is that you check that the calculated values produce a result and not null values (unless the value is optional), and if control data is available, test that the result is correct. The correctness of the BR is often tested using singular tests, with reference to well-known test cases.

- Test the PK/FK after risky or complex joins (to implement the BRs).

This is a top priority. Make sure that the data conforms to the data model of the BR.

Another big category of BRs is enrichments, where you join tables to bring in measures or descriptive values. We dealt with having the value and its use in a calculation in the previous bullet point.

Note that obtaining the correct cardinality for the resulting table is extremely important, and you should test that the chain of joins to implement a BR does not produce duplicates or leave out data.

Tests on the delivery layer

The delivery layer makes the data available for our consumers, our "customers."

We need to test that what we deliver fulfills our data models and the industry standards:

- **Test that the dimensions are well-formed**: Test that the PK or BK is unique and not null, and that there is one and only one default record.

- **Test that facts are well-formed**: Test that the PK (if it exists) is unique and not null, the FK to dimensions are not null (having a business value or a default value if it is an optional relation), and there are no orphans (the FK from the fact exists as a PK in the dimension, eventually as the default record).

- **Test the values in facts and dimensions**: Test that mandatory categories and measures are not null, and that categories have values in the expected set of values.

- **Test that well-known expected output is produced correctly**: Using a small set of well-known cases, check that the calculated values match the expected values. This is easily achieved with singular tests.

- **Run statistical, quantitative tests to ensure that data is flowing and in a reasonable range**: We know that a certain number of events or values should be flowing. Test that we are inside a range for the number of events or the values of a measure in a specific time frame, eventually based on data from the past, accounting also for seasonality. As an example, we should have a reasonable number of orders for every week/month, and the total amount of orders should be in a reasonable range.

These kinds of tests complement the source freshness, adding control to the quantity of data and ensuring that its values are reasonable.

Testing our models to ensure good quality

Looking back at our project, we have been quite good at adding tests for the ABC_BANK_POSITION source, as we are checking that the columns that we care about are not null.

We have devoted less effort to adding tests to the other layers, as we concentrated on building the models themselves; in this section, we will go through the layers of our sample and add some important tests to be sure that our application works as expected.

Testing the uniqueness of composite keys

In the `ABC_BANK_POSITION` source, we are checking that the `SYMBOL` column is unique. However, is that really the case?

Well, if we consider only a single portfolio for a single person, yes, but if we consider that one person can have more than one account at the same bank, then we should probably concede that this is too strict.

When we look at the STG layer, we can see that `POSITION_HKEY` is defined by the two fields, `ACCOUNT_CODE` and `SECURITY_CODE`, so we have a composite key, which is a common case.

As it also looks like a more realistic requirement, let's see how we can test this composite key on the source.

The suggested solution would be to create a column with their concatenation using a separator (to avoid 'ab'||'c' being equal to 'a'||'bc' and also equal to ''||'abc' or 'abc'||'') and do the test on it, but we cannot change the source, so this solution is a no-go.

We could move the test to the next layer, where we already have the `POSITION_HKEY` column defined as the combination of these columns, plus hashing. That works, but if we can test on the sources, it is better, so we know that the problem is not in our code but in our assumptions, which are at odds with the incoming data.

To keep the test in the source layer, we have two alternatives – creating an anonymous concatenation of the columns in the source YAML file or using the `unique_combination_of_columns` test from the `dbt_utils` package.

The first one is straightforward but might have performance issues, while the second is a test to be applied to the table, and it is an efficient solution.

Let's look at both ways and then you can decide which one you like more. Open the `source_abc_bank` file and add the following code for the `ABC_BANK_POSITION` table:

```
- name: ABC_BANK_POSITION
  tests:
    - dbt_utils.unique_combination_of_columns:
        combination_of_columns:
          - ACCOUNTID
          - SYMBOL
  columns:
    - name: CONCAT_WS('-', ACCOUNTID, SYMBOL)
      tests:
        - not_null
        - unique
    - name: SYMBOL
      tests:
        - not_null
```

In the preceding code, we have done the following:

- Added the `test:` property under the table name and the `unique_combination_of_columns` test, passing the two columns that we want (`ACCOUNTID` and `SYMBOL`) as a YAML list.

- Added a pseudo-column that in place of the name has a valid SQL expression.

  This is always valid, and by using the `CONCAT_WS` function, you can concatenate as many columns as you want using a separator. As you can see, this has the advantage of being quick and easy to read and places the test in the same place as the other column tests. Just be aware that the concatenation is not strictly needed and might add a lot of overhead, with big tables. The table test just does a `group by` of the columns to test, which is the minimum required and fast. It also places the test directly under the table making it to stand out and avoiding to mix the PK test with the tests on the other columns.

- Removed the `unique` test from the `SYMBOL` column.

To recap, we can say that it is fine to use the `CONCAT_WS` function on small tables while using the test from `dbt_utils` package when tables are big (100 million+ rows). We should consider moving such important tests to the next layer only when we need to edit or extract the columns involved or filter the source.

Testing a CSV seed

Our second input is a CSV file that we load as `seed`.

In this case, we have the possibility of doing our tests in three places:

- **On the CSV seed**: We would place a test here if the requirement or importance of the test relates to the source being a CSV file. An example could be parsing dates or numbers, or in our case, correctly applying a post-hook query.

- **On the seed source table**: We would place a test here if the test was important independent of the type of input. In other words, it relates to the semantics of the data.

- As always, we could pass the test forward in the STG model, but we should prefer to test earlier if possible.

To show you both ways, let's add a `not null` test for the `LOAD_TS` column on the seed and any other tests as we see fit on the source, which we have defined to read the CSV.

Let's start with the seeds:

1. Create a `seeds.yml` file under the `seeds` folder
2. Add the following code:

```
version: 2
seeds:
```

```
    - name: ABC_Bank_SECURITY_INFO
      columns:
        - name: LOAD_TS
          tests:
            - not_null
```

As usual, note that we have first defined the version of the file and the type of dbt object that we are describing, then we add a first element using the name property, and under it, we use the columns property to describe its columns, each introduced with the name property, and under that, we use a tests property to list the tests that we want to perform.

In the preceding case, we have added a not_null test for the LOAD_TS column, which we had declared as our intent.

Before moving to the tests under the seed definition, we need to add a simple generic test to test that a column is not empty. Note that this test is going to be available in the dbt_utils 1.0.0 package, but we are not yet using it in our sample project:

1. Let's create a not_empty.sql file in the tests folder.

2. Add the following code to the file:

```
{% test not_empty( model, column_name ) -%}
WITH
validation_errors as (
    SELECT {{column_name}}
    FROM {{ model }}
    WHERE LEN({{column_name}}) = 0
)
SELECT * FROM validation_errors
{%- endtest %}
```

We have created a test that is not only working for strings but also for other data types that might be susceptible to being empty, such as arrays.

Now that we have the test that we need, let's move to the tests under the seed definition:

1. Open the source_seed.yml file in the models folder.

2. Edit the file for the ABC_Bank_SECURITY_INFO table to look like this:

```
    - name: ABC_Bank_SECURITY_INFO
      columns:
        - name: SECURITY_CODE
          tests:
            - not_null
            - unique
        - name: SECURITY_NAME
```

```
tests:
  - not_null
  - not_empty
```

In the preceding code, we have done the following:

- Tested that the SECURITY_CODE column is unique and not null, implicitly defining it as a business key

- Tested that the SECURITY_NAME column is not null and not empty; we will use the security name very often, and we cannot accept that it is empty

We leave it to you as an exercise to add more not_null and/or not_empty tests for other columns of the ABC_Bank_SECURITY_INFO table if you consider this to be important.

Adding a test to avoid a regression

If we look at our STG layer, we do not have much left to test, as we have managed to do the important tests (unicity and mandatory not null fields) on the source and seed.

There has been only one field that we needed to transform, the report date that was stored with only two digits in the CSV file and was loaded as a date in the 1st century.

We have decided to keep the load unchanged (getting a date) and to "fix" the date in our STG model, creating a macro. We could have changed the load to load a string from the CSV and parse it correctly as a two-digit year in the STG model.

Both work, and we cannot exclude that someone down the line will dislike our solution and change the load or find another way, including getting the data from a different source. What we can do now to improve the quality and trust in our load is to put in place a test to avoid regressing to a problem that we have already solved.

Let's add a test to check that the REPORT_DATE column is in the 21st century:

1. Create a staging.yml file in the models/staging folder.

2. Add the following code to the file:

```
version: 2
models:
  - name: STG_ABC_BANK_POSITION
    tests:
      - dbt_utils.expression_is_true:
          expression: " YEAR(REPORT_DATE) >= 2000 "
```

We will use the expression_is_true test from the dbt_utils package to express the table-wide condition that the year of the REPORT_DATE column is greater than 2000, or any value that's right for you (maybe 1970 or 1900 if you have older data).

Now, we are sure that the data coming out of the STG model has dates that we are comfortable with, but are we sure that the date conversion works as expected?

To be sure about the macro correctness, we can add a singular test to unit-test the macro that we wrote to do the conversion. This is what we will do in the next section.

Testing a macro

In one of our STG models, we had the problem that some dates that should have been in the 21st century were incorrectly saved in the CSV file, with only two digits for the year when exporting them from Excel, and now we are getting them interpreted as 1st-century dates.

We wrote the to_21st_century_date macro to do a conversion of the dates that have the issue, while keeping modern dates unchanged.

Now, we will see how easy is to unit-test our macro and gain confidence in its correctness:

1. Create the to_21st_century_date.sql file in the tests/macros folder.

2. Add the following code in the file:

```
WITH
test_data as (
  SELECT '0021-09-23'::date as src_date,
            '2021-09-23'::date as expected_date
  UNION
  SELECT '1021-09-24', '1021-09-24'
  UNION
  SELECT '2021-09-25', '2021-09-25'
  UNION
  SELECT '-0021-09-26', '1979-09-26'
)
SELECT
    {{to_21st_century_date('src_date')}} as ok_date,
    expected_date,
    ok_date = expected_date as matching
FROM test_data
WHERE not matching
```

In the preceding code, we have created some test data that contains, in each row, the input data for the macro to be tested and the expected result. This way, it is very easy to apply the macro to the inputs and verify that the output is as expected.

3. To run the singular tests, run the following command:

```
dbt test --select test_type:singular
```

This is a very simple and efficient way to perform unit tests of your macros, but it is only one way, and many variations of this pattern can be used, depending on the test to be performed.

You can provide the input data in multiple ways, with a simple `SELECT` and `UNION ALL` as we did, but if you plan to provide a bigger amount of data, you might want to move to a `SELECT FROM VALUES` SQL clause or even have the data in a proper table, either loaded as `CSV seed` or as `source` provided to you and accessed for the test.

In some cases, it might be enough to verify that the results satisfy a rule instead of expressing the expectation with a value for each input, so you might not have the expected data, as it will be replaced by a calculation following the given rule.

In other cases, the expected data might not be tied to an individual row, but you will have an expected result set. In such a case, you will get two tables, one for the input data and one for the expected data, and you can use the `MINUS` (same as `EXCEPT`) set operator:

```
SELECT results
MINUS
SELECT expectations
UNION
SELECT expectations
MINUS
SELECT results
```

The first part of the preceding query verifies that all the rows in the results are expected rows from the expectation table, while the second part verifies that only the expected rows from the expectation table are produced in the results. The two parts together verify that the result produces the same rows as in the expectations.

We have already applied the `no_hash_collisions` test to our HIST models when we introduced the generic tests, so we do not need any more tests on them.

Avoiding orphan keys in fact tables

Moving to the refined layer, we have already in place a couple of tests that ensure that our calculated values, our BRs, are not null.

Our two REF models are also so simple that they do not do any join, so the only useful thing that we have left to test is that the relationship between the position fact and the security dimension is well formed and that the fact does not have orphans.

Let's use the relationship test provided by dbt to ensure that:

1. Open the `refined.yml` file in the `refined` folder.

2.   Add the following code:

```
- name: REF_POSITION_ABC_BANK
  columns:
  ...

    - name: SECURITY_CODE
      description: The code of the security in the position.
      tests:
        - relationships:
            to: ref('REF_ABC_BANK_SECURITY_INFO')
            field: SECURITY_CODE
```

We have added a `relationships` test to the `SECURITY_CODE` column of our fact.

The test declares that the column in the fact is a foreign key for a relationship with the security dimension, where the `SECURITY_CODE` field is the PK.

The test passes, so we can move on comforted by the knowledge that we do not have orphans, even if we know that sooner or later, we will have some orphans and will need to manage them. We will do that when we talk about refactoring our models.

Testing that the relationships that we expect between our models work as expected is extremely important to guarantee that our data models keep being appropriate.

It is also worth noting that, in general, we have one relational data model in the refined layer, between the REF models, that tries to broadly represent the real world and the processes of our domain, but we also have a Kimball (or star schema) model for each data mart that we create. They are related but not equal. Where should we test the relationships?

The golden rule is, as soon as possible! Therefore, we should test the relationships that are part of the REF layer data model in the REF layer, and then we should test the eventual relationship that is created only for the data mart in the data mart layer.

Testing the delivery layer

Looking at our models in the delivery layer, we can see that they are both a very simple `SELECT *` `FROM aRefModel` type, so we will just make sure that the PKs are respected and that the dimension has a default key.

Let's start with the PKs:

1.   Create the `_portfolio.yml` file in the data mart folder.

2.   Add the following code to the file:

```
version: 2
models:
  - name: FACT_POSITION
```

```
    tests:
        - dbt_utils.unique_combination_of_columns:
            combination_of_columns:
                - ACCOUNT_CODE
                - SECURITY_CODE
  - name: DIM_SECURITY
    columns:
        - name: SECURITY_CODE
          tests:
              - not_null
              - unique
```

In the preceding code, we have tested the PKs of the two models. We remind you that the two columns tested with the `unique_combination_of_columns` macro are not being tested to see whether they are null, so you should add the required column-level tests.

To be able to test that the dimension has a default record and only one default record key, we need to create the relevant generic tests, so let's do that.

3. Create a `has_default_key.sql` file in the `macros/tests` folder and add the code:

```
{% test has_default_key ( model, column_name
   , default_key_value = '-1'
   , record_source_field_name = 'RECORD_SOURCE'
   , default_key_record_source = 'System.DefaultKey'
) -%}
{{ config(severity = 'error') }}
WITH
default_key_rows as (
    SELECT distinct {{column_name}},
                    {{record_source_field_name}}
    FROM {{ model }}
    WHERE {{column_name}} = '{{default_key_value}}'
        and {{record_source_field_name}} = '{{default_key_record_
source}}'
),
validation_errors as (
    SELECT '{{default_key_value}}' as {{column_name}},
'{{default_key_record_source}}' as {{record_source_field_name}}
    EXCEPT
    SELECT {{column_name}}, {{record_source_field_name}}
    FROM default_key_rows
)
SELECT * FROM validation_errors
{%- endtest %}
```

This test verifies that there is one row with the correct value and record source.

4. Create the `warn_on_multiple_default_key.sql` file in the `macros/test` folder and add the code:

```
{% test warn_on_multiple_default_key ( model, column_name
  , default_key_value = '-1'
  , record_source_field_name = 'RECORD_SOURCE'
  , default_key_record_source = 'System.DefaultKey'
) -%}
{{ config(severity = 'warn') }}
WITH
validation_errors as (
    SELECT distinct {{column_name}},
                    {{record_source_field_name}}
    FROM {{ model }}
    WHERE {{column_name}} != '{{default_key_value}}'
      and {{record_source_field_name}} = '{{default_key_record_
source}}'
)
SELECT * FROM validation_errors
{%- endtest %}
```

This test raises a warning if there are rows with the default record's record source, and a key that is not the one expected for the default record. This might be a valid case if you want to distinguish different reasons for not having an FK in the fact, as in the following example: data is missing (-1), in the future/no data yet (-2), a bad/wrong value (-3), and intentionally empty/not applicable (-4). If this is the case, we suggest removing the test once you know that the multiple keys are intentional.

5. Let's apply both tests by editing the `_portfolio.yml` file.

    Add the two tests under the PK of the dimension (`SECURITY_CODE`):

```
- name: DIM_SECURITY
  columns:
    - name: SECURITY_CODE
      tests:
        - not_null
        - unique
        - has_default_key
        - warn_on_multiple_default_key
```

Now that we have defined the two tests, `has_default_key` and `warn_on_multiple_default_key`, you can see how easy it is to test each dimension.

We have gone through the layers of our sample project and added the test that we consider useful, eventually creating the needed generic test macros.

Summary

In this chapter, you saw multiple ways to test that incoming and resulting data conforms to your expectations, how to add more tests, and how to unit-test macros or your own code.

We have discussed what tests to apply in what layer of your projects, and we have applied such tests in the sample project.

In the next chapter, you will learn how to use dbt to work better as part of a team and automate the deployment and execution of your platform.

10

Agile Development

In the previous chapter, we completed the basics of coding with dbt, explained how to write macros and tests, and completed an MVP of our target architecture.

In this chapter, you will learn to develop with agility by mixing philosophy and practical hints, see how to keep a backlog agile through the phases of your projects, and take a deep dive into building data marts.

In this chapter, you will learn about the following topics:

- Agile development and collaboration
- Applying agile to data engineering
- Building reports in an agile way

Technical requirements

You can read and understand this chapter without reading the previous ones as long as you know the basics of dbt.

There are no code samples for this chapter.

Agile development and collaboration

In this chapter, we will touch on probably the most important part of the development cycle, the one that contributes the most to project success and delivery time – enabling your people to be productive and eager to work on a project as a team by helping each other.

With over two decades of experience working in different countries, companies, sectors, and functions, I can say that developers love their work, and they hate doing nothing or, even worse, stupid, pointless things.

You can be assured that as long as your developers have a clear picture of what to build and small enough incremental goals to achieve, they will build your project, as this is what brings them satisfaction.

The agile development part of this chapter concentrates on making your people work on what matters most, reducing useless work as much as possible. The collaboration part ensures that they do not work isolated but are aligned, and they help and coach each other.

There is huge power to be unleashed by moving from individual developers to an agile team.

Developers have pride in their work and care about what their peers think about them, so they will try to do their best job if you create the right atmosphere. They will not fear asking for help when needed, and their colleagues will be happy to help and coach them whenever needed.

The key is to create the right atmosphere where people do not fear exposing their limits, and others take pride and feel compelled to help the team, as a well-working team is the utmost goal.

Defining agile development

To set the stage, we will start by citing the **Agile Manifesto**, which you can find at `https://agilemanifesto.org/`. The following is the text of the manifesto:

Manifesto for Agile Software Development

We are uncovering better ways of developing software

by doing it and helping others do it.

Through this work we have come to value:

- **Individuals and interactions** over processes and tools
- **Working software** over comprehensive documentation
- **Customer collaboration** over contract negotiation
- **Responding to change** over following a plan

That is, while there is value in the items on the right,

we value the items on the left more.

© 2001 by Kent Beck, Mike Beedle, Arie van Bennekum, Alistair Cockburn, Ward Cunningham, Martin Fowler, James Grenning, Jim Highsmith, Andrew Hunt, Ron Jeffries, Jon Kern, Brian Marick, Robert C. Martin, Steve Mellor, Ken Schwaber, Jeff Sutherland, Dave Thomas

The message of this manifesto is that the creation of software is not like industrial serial production, done by robot-like workers, using frozen specifications according to a plan written in a contract.

It just does not work that way. Building software and creating a data platform is very much about writing new code in an organized way. It is a creative process, where different competencies, experiences, and points of view are important. It is much closer to the process of inventing a new product in a known industry.

Companies and needs can change as a data platform is built; the data and processes at the base of the data platform keep changing with the world and are not frozen. After the first line of code is written, even before the first release, evolution to keep up with the changing requirements is part of the development.

I suggest that you also read the *12 Principles behind the Agile Manifesto*, which is available at `https://agilemanifesto.org/principles.html`.

They offer invaluable and evergreen insight about working in an agile way, and most of these principles have become cornerstones of agile teams, such as the one that says, "*Working software is the primary measure of progress.*" Working software is what you want; everything else is useful only in how much it gets you closer to having (and keeping) working software.

Applying agile to data engineering

Looking at the four statements of the Agile Manifesto, the key message is that people, results, and following real-world concerns are more important than plans and papers. This does not mean that the other elements are bad per se, just that they are not the most important ones, and their importance is in contributing to the other elements.

Here are a few general considerations that apply to the data engineering domain:

- Agile is not improvising. Having a plan is important, as it is the understanding that any plan is not set in stone, and it will keep changing. The point of the plan is to keep track of where we are, the current desired goal, and the knowledge that we have accumulated about the surrounding areas of the domain. Quick failures are important to learn blocked roads as soon as possible .

- Pick a direction in collaboration with the people who know the domain (aka business) and the ones who know the technology. Deliver and verify the intermediate results constantly, and at every step, you will just need to make small course adjustments. The further you go, the smaller the changes in direction and the clearer the goal. When you have a failure, incorporate what you learn from it as soon as possible in your plan, and adjust the direction as needed.

- An important corollary to the previous point is to improve the detail of your goal while you go. It is an iterative process. You start afar with a clear scope but also a general goal and, possibly, little knowledge of the available data. By working on it and delivering the first results, you eventually clarify what you want and what you don't. You also understand better what you have in your data and what is not there. Keep discussing with the business what they want and adjust their expectations/your project accordingly. Keep the info flowing and the ideas flexible.

- A general goal is to keep your plan as flexible as possible, taking decisions (especially the ones that are difficult to change) at the last responsible moment so that the decision can be taken using as much knowledge and experience as possible. That does not mean procrastinating forever; it means that you should refrain from freezing decisions early if you can wait and do not keep doing things in one way just because of a plan. If you have a better idea, use it.

- Verify the biggest questions at the beginning so that the risk of a big change of direction decreases as you move forward. Examples might be checking that you can process some essential data that you cannot do without, that you can read a format or access a system, or that the time it takes to manage the amount of expected data is reasonable.

- Try to cut the work into small work increments, often referred to as a **story**, that can be completed with little risk of them having to stop. Just before starting the work on a story, split it into small tasks that can be completed in 1 day or less. Note that the set of work increments planned to be done in a set period, aka **development iteration**, is often called **product increment**.

- Don't try boiling the ocean or getting lost in too many different things. Try to focus the team on the most important topics of the moment so that they can collaborate on the solution. One working piece of software completed every week in a collaborative way is better than five or six in a month done in siloes. The quality will be better, the team will be happier, and the knowledge will be in many heads instead of only one.

- *Start completing and stop starting* – focus on closing open work before you start more work. Too many things up in the air create a huge mental drain on people, the project loses steam, it becomes impossible to focus, and it becomes difficult to understand how much progress is done if little work is completed.

- Agility is not only about flexibility but also about avoiding waste and removing things that are outdated or of little or uncertain value. This applies to all topics, from code to documentation to planning.

If I could summarize the agile concepts in one phrase, I would say that agile is about keeping an initially blurred but ever-clarifying big picture up to date, doing some work to produce the desired results, and shedding some light to further clarify the big picture and what you want to work on next.

Starting a project in an agile way

We have said that it is important to start by having a good understanding of the scope of your project and what the main goals that you want to achieve are, but that only means that you know what you want in general terms, not with all the implementation details.

At this stage, knowing what you do not want is as important as knowing what you do want. You should start by creating a good understanding of the scope of your project.

Picking the right scope and building a team to first find out the right direction and later how to get to the goal (business needs and technical abilities) are the most important things at this stage.

Let the team form an initial high-level plan that business and technology agree upon, and identify the starting point and the big questions that you are not sure about and that might derail the plan or considerably change its shape. These are the higher risks you have. Clarify them first.

Make a story for each risk to check that you can do what you planned in the way you planned, or in some alternative way. You do not need to develop the final deliverable, just concretely verify that what you plan to do is doable and how. This is sometimes called making a **Proof of Concept** (**POC**).

After this initial ideation/orientation phase, you will have a better picture of where you are and what you want to achieve, and with the main risks clarified, you should be able to pick a good direction to start actual work with enough confidence.

This initial phase should be short – ideally, one sprint only for run-of-the-mill projects and a few sprints at most if you are doing completely new things and need to make a lot of POCs.

To use a holiday as an analogy, you start by deciding whether you want to go to Spain for some beach time, France for some chateau hopping, Poland for some trekking, or Finland for fishing. It should also be clear who is in charge of the destination, budget, and operational decisions.

It is also useful to have an idea of the activity that you want to do, as it will affect packaging and transportation needs. You will not need fishing gear when tasting wine. Once you know your destination, you need to know how to get there and how to move around, especially if you plan to do a lot of it. If you are not sure about it, you might want to check whether there are planes and car rentals and verify the prices, the times and costs for going by car, or maybe the availability and prices for accommodation so that if you need to switch to camping, you know it before packing.

In this initial phase, you create an initial plan that will certainly change in many details but has been agreed upon by the parties involved and that the team understands, so when changes small or big are needed, they will know the implications and can act quicker and better.

Thinking about our Pragmatic Data Platform approach and its architecture, you want to be sure that you have picked a data platform for your project (we picked Snowflake and dbt), that you have a clear scope, that you will have access to the data that you expect to use, that you can use it on the selected data platform, and that you do not have big technical questions left open.

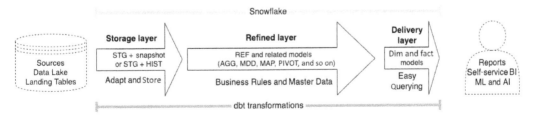

Figure 10.1: Pragmatic Data Platform architecture

You might want to apply a POC to the technical setup or some part of it if you have never tried it before.

A few examples of technical questions that I checked with a POC are the ability to load Avro files every minute into a landing table using internal stages, the ability to convert geospatial coordinates between reference systems, and the ability to undertake in a reasonable time some potentially slow operations with tables of sizes in the billions of rows.

Organizing work the agile way

Now that you have a clear scope and a direction to follow, it is time to start churning out results that add value and bring you closer to the final goal.

The agile principles suggest that frequent delivery of working software is preferable. This is a key agile concept and one of the hallmarks of a good working agile team – completion and demonstration of work done at the end of each development iteration or product increment.

In the widely used **Scrum** methodology, a development iteration is called a **sprint**.

Scrum is a fine methodology, but the term "sprint" is not really a great choice, as it evokes the image of someone running as quickly as possible. That is possible only for a short time before having to stop due to exhaustion. This is not what we want to achieve in our development iterations!

The goal of an agile team is to work in a sustainable way. A development iteration, even if called a sprint, must be planned for work to be done at a good pace that can be sustained for an indefinite period of time. This is the real secret of an agile team – distributing load across the team and not getting overloaded as an individual or as a team.

This starts with being honest about how much time each person can focus on project work and then on picking an amount of work that is likely to be completed during the iteration and that the team feels committed to do, accounting for the inevitable issues that will arise for the items being worked on and the parts of the project already delivered, aka maintenance work or bug fixing.

If you are in doubt, err on the side of committing to less work. This is because morale is much higher in a team that achieves its goals than in one that doesn't, and because most of the great improvements happen when a team has some wiggle room and can experiment with new ways of doing things or cleaning up old technical debt that is dragging them down.

Remember that software engineers like their work and are proud of doing their best if recognized.

Another cornerstone of agile development, mostly known as DevOps culture, is to provide a team with the tools, expertise, authority, and responsibility to perform all tasks that are needed to develop a project, from inception and analysis to execution in production.

Empower and trust the team, praise them for their successes, and be accountable for their results.

Managing the backlog in an agile way

What then should be in the **backlog**, or make up the list of work to be done?

The backlog must contain the description of the work to be done, but it does not mean that everything should be at the same level of detail or that the work to be done will not change.

The golden rule is that it should describe the work to be done in the next iteration with the most detail, containing enough information for the developers to fully understand what to do. It can also contain the description of other work to be done in the future in decreasing detail, as it is expected to be done further away in time. Future work should be in few and progressively more general stories.

At every iteration, aka sprint, you will get rid of the many small stories that you have developed, and you will split down into small, detailed stories and tasks the biger stories that you pick from the backlog and plan to work on next.

> **Tip**
> There is a common conflict about what to put in the backlog. For the development team, it is better to have just enough stories to fill a bit more than the current iteration, and any more is a burden, while the product owner is interested in keeping track of features to be developed further down the line and longer-term plans and ideas.

If reading through all the stories in your backlog takes too much, it is an indication that you have too many stories in your backlog. We strongly suggest grouping the ones that are far away into bigger, general stories. If the scope of the project is large, it makes sense to keep separated the backlog of the product owner, which is more a list of ideas and features considered for development, from the backlog of the development team, which should contain only the features that need to be developed in the next few iterations, as things further away are uncertain and likely to change.

This is just a basic principle of work environment hygiene – keep your backlog clean as you keep your desks and your offices. Nobody works well in offices full of dusty boxes or on tables overflowing with long-forgotten piles of paper. Why would you keep your backlog in such a shape?

As an example, you know that to develop report *XYZ*, you will need to load 10 tables and calculate a few more intermediate tables and so on. This is valuable information, but if you do not plan to do that work in the next sprint or so, it is much better to have that information as a piece of text and bullet points inside a single feature than having many individual stories. Until it is almost time for its development, it is easier to manage a single item with the `develop report xyz` title and then split it down into individual stories when you are about to work on it, splitting it into tasks that can be completed in less than 1 day once you put them into a sprint. This general story should be moved to the development team backlog when it is almost time to develop it, while it can stay in the product owner backlog when it is just one potential feature to be developed somewhere in the future.

Putting it in a more practical way, using a common terminology to identify work to be done at different levels of granularity, the backlog should contain the following:

- One or two sprints' worth of **stories** that are ready to be developed. These stories must be described at an implementation detail level so that everyone in the team understands what needs to be done. The stories taken into development must be split into **tasks** before starting work on them. Initially, the tasks can be a bullet list of to-dos in the story description. When you split them, you should make sure that each task can be done in less than a day.

- A handful of **features** that describe the work that is planned and potentially ready to be done but is still being analyzed in detail and split into individual stories. These should provide work for another couple of sprints or so, and no more.

- Eventually, a few very general **epics** that list the next areas of development that are not yet planned or planned further away than a handful of sprints. These are a few, high-level descriptions of future work, mostly of interest to the product owner. It is perfectly fine if they contain text or documents, such as presentations with the expected content as it was understood at the time of their preparation. Review them critically before starting the work based on old plans.

This seems so simple to do, but I can assure you that in the vast majority of projects, the backlog hygiene is dissatisfying at best, with a lot of festering stories that will never be done, left there to consume everybody's attention for nothing.

Sifting through hundreds of stories to find the handful of ones to be done in the next sprint or to update with your findings is more complicated, takes longer, and reduces focus than doing the same with a dozen or two stories.

What is the value of a "make report X" or "load table Y" story with no extra content? None! It just clutters your backlog and kills your productivity when planning work or using the backlog.

Ask yourself why it should be worth keeping stories if they are untouched for months. Delete them and keep your backlog short and focused. You will remember those stories if you need them later, and if you do not remember them, it means that they were not important. If there is truly valuable information in an old story, you can save it into a higher-level story, but if all that you have is a title, just get rid of it.

An initial backlog for our sample project

In the rest of this section, we will give you a practical example of managing the backlog, along with a tried and tested way of doing one of the most common tasks in data engineering – building reports.

We will describe our architecture following the way that data flows, so we have sources, then the storage layer with STG and SNAPSHOT or HIST models, then the refined layer with many specialized models, and finally, the delivery layer, where you have one data mart for each domain that powers the reports for the domain.

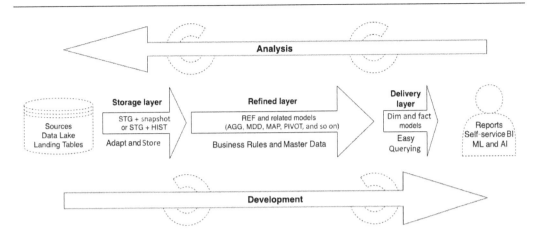

Figure 10.2: Pragmatic Data Platform architecture and iterative analysis and development

When building reports, as often in agile methods, we start from the end of the flow to identify the goal and work our way back to identify the minimum work required to achieve the goal.

The previous diagram visually shows the main direction of the analysis and development work, with the dotted loopback circles recalling that, in both cases, these are iterative processes, and whenever we find a blocker or a problem, we can go back and change the results of the previous steps.

As an iterative process, we mean that in each iteration (or set of iterations), we try to analyze and develop a small horizontal slice of our scope, covering all layers, to then move to another slice.

Thinking about the sample project that we have used in previous chapters, we could say that the initial overview produced the following epics:

- E1 – setting up the platform
- E2 – building customer reports
- E3 – building backlog reports

The first epic, E1, would cover the work that we did in the first few chapters to set up the platform. It would have been sliced into features such as "set up a Snowflake account," "set up a dbt account," and "set up a GitHub account."

The Snowflake feature could have been divided into stories such as "create aSnowflake account," "create a database for the dbt project," "create roles for the dbt project," "create a user for dbt to execute," "create users for developers," and so on. Each of these stories would be split into tasks if we thought that it could take more than 1 day for them to be completed.

There's no need to split a story if it is already small enough. Remember that agility is also about avoiding useless work.

The second epic (E2) might be sliced into features such as the following:

- F1 – building a customer current position report

- F2 – building a customer historical position report

- F3 – building a customer transaction report

- F4 – other customer reports

We have willingly named the F4 feature "other customer reports" to show that it makes more sense to have a single feature with a potentially long list of desired reports inside, rather than producing a long list by already creating one feature for each report when, now, we would be many sprints away before they would be considered to be worked on.

> **Tip**
> Keep the backlog short by putting faraway work at all levels in an "all the rest" item or in a separate product owner backlog. The meaning of "faraway" depends on sprint duration and the amount of work completed during a sprint.

A good rule of thumb is to have stories ready for a sprint or two and identified features split into stories to provide work for a handful of sprints. Everything else should be in the product owner's backlog or with the "all the rest" type items.

Building reports in an agile way

In this section, we will decompose in stories a feature to build a report in a very general way that you can use for any report and, pretty much, for any other result deliverable in a data mart.

The "F1 – building a customer current position report" feature can be split into stories of these five types:

- S1 – designing a light data model for the data mart to power the F1 report.

- S2 – designing a light data model for the REF layer to power the data mart for the F1 report.

- S3.x – developing with dbt models the pipeline for the `DIM_x` / `FACT_x` / `REF_x` table. This is not one story but a story for each table in the data mart, plus each necessary support table in the REF layer. We will discuss more details later.

- S4 – an acceptance test of the data produced in the data mart.

- S5 – development and verification of the report in the BI application.

These five types of stories are designed to be developed in the proposed order, as the stories of each type build on the results of the stories of the preceding type.

It is obvious that there is some overlapping of contiguous stories and that stories of the following type can sometimes start before the preceding is complete.

Stories S1 and S2 have so much overlapping and are so central to defining the work to build the report that it is strongly suggested they are developed by the same senior person, and that the person developing the models will be responsible for the delivery of the report by distributing the following stories to the team and overseeing and coordinating their development.

This set of stories can be used to collect requirements (S1 and S2) and develop (S3.x and S4) any report and, with minor adjustments, anything that can be delivered as a set of tables in a data mart.

In the following sections, we will delve into each story.

S1 – designing a light data model for the data mart

The report, AI model, or API that we want to build as the goal of the feature will read its data from the data mart that we are going to design in this story.

Designing a data model is a requirement collection exercise that produces as output the data model, aka the design of a set of tables expressed in a simple yet formal way, which will answer the queries of the report (or AI model or API reads).

Designing such a data model means being able to understand the data mart client-side needs, what queries will come in to satisfy those needs, and therefore, designing the tables and columns needed to answer such queries. This is typically what a data modeler or a senior analytical engineer can do by talking to the business and understanding what they want to achieve.

Building the data mart data model provides the deliverables that the REF layer needs to satisfy, allowing us to develop its requirements in story S2.

Keep the model simple

We talk about a lightweight data model, as the goal of building this data model is to provide a clear and unequivocal blueprint of what we will need to find in the data mart once the feature is developed. We need a blueprint that our analytical engineer can follow to build the data mart; we do not need a complete model detailing all the columns, all the relationships, and eventually, not even all tables.

We want to try to keep the visual model as simple to read as possible.

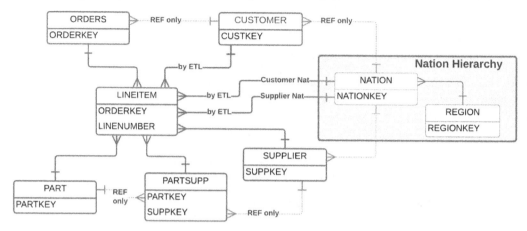

Figure 10.3: The lightweight data mart data model for TPCH

The preceding model is a pure star schema if you do not consider the dotted relations. It is as simple as it gets, having only the PK for each entity. The relations with no label are already existing in the source data, while the ones labeled **by ETL** are the ones that need to be added to the fact by following the relations that exist in the refined layer. These are labeled **REF only**, as they cannot be used by reporting tools expecting a star schema but provide the information to build the star schema.

An important point is that we do not need to have all the columns for all tables in the data model. We just need the columns with some importance, the ones that we want to be sure are there. We will assume that also the other information for dimensions and facts will be there, but we have no special interest in them. If you want to exclude some columns, add a note in the story.

As an example, if you have the classical customer dimension, you know that it can have many dozens of columns and sometimes hundreds of them. For our goals, it is enough to put the PK and only the columns that have some special meaning or requirement – for example, categories that we want to filter on in the report, such as CUSTOMER_CLASSIFICATION_CODE or CUSTOMER_SECTOR.

Similarly, in the fact table, we are going to put just what is important, such as the FK to the dimensions, or what needs special attention, such as measures or categories that we want to be sure are there or must be calculated. The obvious keys that exist in both the fact and the dimension, such as CUSTOMER_CODE, can be left out of the fact if we think there is no risk of mistakes.

Conversely, what is the benefit of listing all the 80+ or 200+ columns of a customer dimension in the data model – that is, a schematic representation of what we want to build?

I cannot see any benefit, only downsides – it will take a long time to enter the column names, it will make the model huge, cluttered, and impossible to keep on the screen at a readable size, it will be error-prone to maintain, and difficult to check that the columns that are there are the ones we really want and that are really in the data mart dimension. All in all, it will drown the useful information about a few columns that we need to have there in a sea of useless column names, which we just happen to have from the data sources.

If you want to check that a list of columns is in a dimension, it is much easier to just make a list of those columns and then add a test to the dimension to check that they are there:

```
- name: concat(SECURITY_NAME, SECTOR_NAME, INDUSTRY_NAME)
  tests:
    - not_null:
        where: "false"
```

The preceding test, added to any table, just checks that the SECURITY_NAME, SECTOR_NAME, and INDUSTRY_NAME columns are in the table, as the query with the WHERE condition set to false will never return any single row, so if the columns exist, the test will always pass.

Remember that with dbt, it is easier to let all the columns to flow forward in the ELT than to remove some from the flow, and the drawback of that in a columnar database is pretty much only the cost of cheap storage, so the common scenario is that a model has all the columns from the models that it is derived from.

The data models that we draw are a communication tool and the simpler they are, the easier to understand them. Here, less is more. Put only what you would point out when talking to a colleague.

Another important way to keep a model simple is to use only one example of multiple similar tables. As an example, if, in a data mart, you need to have 10 dimensions that are just 10 different groupings of data in a fact, it's enough to have a single dimension, Grouping X x10, with a PK in the dimension and an FK in the fact named Grouping_X_CODE. Then, you add a list of the 10 grouping names with the 10 keys in the story, maybe as an Excel attachment if you find it easier to manage.

Star schema data model

In most cases when we build reports with BI tools, we want to produce a Kimball architecture or star schema because this is what the BI tools expect and can use effectively.

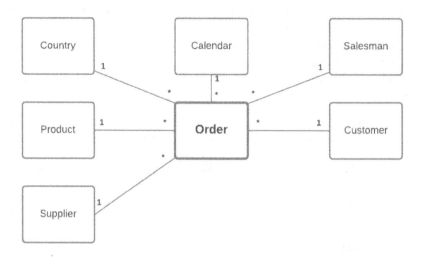

Figure 10.4: An example of a generic star schema

In these cases, the layout of the data model for the data mart is already designed with one fact in the center and dimensions connected to the fact, with many-to-one relationships.

If the layout of the data model is already decided, what remains to be designed then?

Quite a lot, actually. The most important part of the design is obviously the fact table, but the dimensions, even the simple flat dimensions that already have an FK in the fact, will prompt you to take decisions between alternatives, taking into consideration the simplicity of use, the simplicity of development, and the resilience of the solution.

Entire books have been written on how to design star schemas. The following is just a quick introduction to the main alternatives that you will face. This list is short and not complete, but it can help you a lot to design star schemas for your data marts:

- **Simple dimensions**: These are dimensions that simply list descriptive information for an entity with a PK that it is already, or it is very easy to have, in the fact.

  If you are lucky, most of your dimensions are like this. Draw the dimension with its name and PK, plus the eventual columns that are important.

- **Hierarchical dimensions**: These are dimensions that can be decomposed as a series of nested dimensions with different grains. One example is a geography dimension that can be composed of `city < province < region < state < country < continent`.

  Another common hierarchy is the calendar, with `date < week < month < quarter < year`.

The peculiarity of these dimensions is that there is a chain of many-to-one relationships between the different layers of the hierarchy, so it is very easy to think about and build a single complete dimension, "expanding" all the many-to-one relationships.

The hierarchy dimension resulting from this expansion has one row for each row in the dimension with the finer grain (`city` or `date`, in our examples), and the PK of that finer dimension also works as the key for the hierarchy.

The solution of building a single dimension for a hierarchy is common when, for each level of the hierarchy, we are interested only in a few descriptive columns, often a name or so. In this case, it is also enough to just name the layers in the data model.

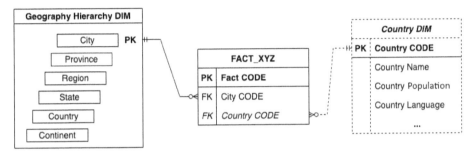

Figure 10.5: Hierarchical dimension modeling, with extra country dimension

When one or more levels in the hierarchy have many columns, and maybe also measures in which we are interested, it is more common to make an independent dimension for that level and connect it directly with the fact, navigating the relationship from the FK in the fact to the FK of the desired level when we build the fact.

It is not uncommon to have in the data mart both the **Hierarchy** dimension with a few columns for each level (enough for most analysis) and independent dimensions for one or two levels that need extra measures or details (as exemplified by the **Country** dimension in the preceding diagram).

- Composite or **Snowflaked dimensions**: These dimensions are a more general case of a dimension directly connected with the fact providing connection to other dimensions that are not directly connected with the fact. In these cases we do not have a neat chain of nested many-to-one relationships that go from the finer grain dimension to the coarser grain dimension, as we have in the hierarchical dimensions.

One example can be tracking course lessons at a university. The course dimension has a many-to-one relation to the department and a relation to the lecturer. The relation to the lecturer can be many-to-many in general, but we might find a many-to-one relationship with the "responsible lecturer" if we care only about the single lecturer responsible for the course.

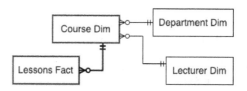

Figure 10.6: The modeling of department and course information

In this case, it would be strange to call a course-lecturer-department dimension a hierarchy. Nevertheless, one solution is to denormalize the descriptive columns of the department and of the responsible lecturer inside the course dimension by expanding the relationship, as we do for hierarchies. This works well and makes a lot of sense if we are not individually interested in the lecturer and department dimensions and we denormalize a few columns.

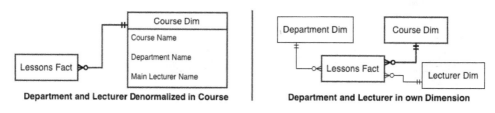

Figure 10.7: An alternative modeling of department and lecturer information

The alternative solution is to create the individual dimensions and bring the key for each of these dimensions into the fact when we build it, using the relationships between the fact, the first dimension, and the other snowflaked dimensions to enrich the fact in the REF layer.

- **Fact**: The fact is the table at the center of the star schema, providing the numbers that describe what has happened in the organization that is what we want to analyze. These numbers are called **measures**.

  We must have only one fact in one star schema, but the interesting answers often come from putting together different base facts, so in most cases, we have composite facts at the center of star schema that power analytical data marts, as we will discuss now.

Keep in mind that there is very little black and white here, with most cases having different shades of gray according to different stakeholders. It is important to understand that building the data model of a data mart is a design exercise to produce something that answers well to your current needs, not trying to replicate reality or building something that will work in all circumstances.

Most of the information in a domain is somehow connected and can be expanded to have a lot of data – for example, in most contexts, you can consider the lecturer from our previous example just having a name, an email, and maybe a category, as this is the necessary information in the reports in that domain, but when we go to the HR domain, we will definitely have more information, including a start date, position, salary, and so on. In some domains, it will be normal to denormalize the lecturer's info into some other dimension, while in others, it will be its own dimension.

The exact point of having data marts is to provide a clear and simple-to-use model for the different domains that we have in a complex organization. Embrace this ability to choose instead of pushing against it by trying to do everything in a similar way.

We will see in the next story, S2, that the REF layer is where we try to be as close to reality as we feel useful and try to build one single truth about every entity, which can then be looked at in different ways in the data marts.

Using multiple facts in a star schema

One of the most common issues in designing data marts is the constraint that in a star schema, according to the Kimball architecture and for most BI tools, you must have only one fact table.

This is often a non-issue when people realize that a composite or complex fact is a perfectly valid fact to have at the center of a star schema.

People correctly think of facts as the documents, events, and results of processes that describe the life of an organization, such as sales orders, production orders, invoices, additions or removal of stock, the amount in stock for every item, returned orders, or the payment of salaries.

For the sake of the following discussion, I will define **base fact** as the native information that an organization produces. These are often the facts that are named by the business when they make their requests, and this is what we usually get from the organization's systems.

The reality is that, almost always, interesting information for an organization to analyze is obtained by putting together data from multiple base facts. We could almost say that the more base facts you put together, the more valuable the information is.

How do we combine the need for a single fact in a star schema and the reality that putting together multiple facts is what provides a lot of value to an organization?

Enter the **composite fact**. A composite fact is created by putting together information from multiple base facts, using the relations that exist naturally between the base facts. These relations cannot be taken "as is" in a star schema, but they are used in the REF layer to produce the composite fact used in the star schema. The composite fact is just a simple table, like all facts.

To make a simple example, if our business wants invoiced amounts net of returns. The first option is, of course, to ask whether there is such a value already available in one of the native facts, but if that is not the case and we only have the invoices and the returns as base facts, then we know that we will need to build a composite fact using information from the two base facts that we have.

The question then becomes *how* to connect these two base facts, and how to get the correct granularity and multiplicity. That work is the core of the S2 story, as that is what gets done in the REF layer.

For the data mart, which is the context of the S1 story, our job is to identify a fact named something such as "invoices with returns," where we have columns such as "invoiced amount" and "returned amount," and maybe the calculated "invoiced amount net of returns."

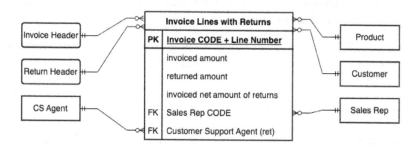

Figure 10.8: The data mart for invoices with returns

In the preceding model, we have not detailed the keys or fields for the product, the customer, the invoice, or return headers, as we considered them obvious, and we expect them to be already in the fact. We have instead pointed out the columns that we want to calculate and the FK to the sales representative and the customer support agent that we expect not to be in the fact, and they need to be enriched in the REF layer.

When we put together different base facts, it comes naturally to have one driving fact – usually, the one with the coarser granularity, and the other facts that are connected to it provide the additional measures that are required. All the measures become part of the composite fact, and they are aggregated to the correct granularity.

We need to also decide how to handle the descriptive data from the facts that are merged into the composite fact. As we have already seen, the choices are between denormalizing the columns into the fact or "creating a dimension out of a (base) fact." The choice is often driven by multiplicities.

As an example, in the "invoices with returns" case, if we want to analyze the data at the product level, we need to have the fact at invoice line granularity, composed with return lines. In both cases, we have an invoice header and a return header that are not only facts but also contain a lot of interesting descriptive information, such as dates, addresses, and who took the order or authorized the return.

If you want to analyze invoices or returns by city or zip code, which usually belong in the header, you could denormalize that information into the composite fact. This works well in columnar databases, but you need to code the ELT to bring it in the fact, and you usually do only that for a handful of columns.

A more general approach is to recognize the many-to-one multiplicity between the fact and the header and create a dimension out of it. By taking this approach, you might then decide that you want to bring into the "invoice header dimension" the name of the salesperson, which is more readable than the code you have in the header, and the same for the person that authorized the return, or the description of the problem category stated in the return header.

By now, it should be clear to you that while we have a fixed, forced layout for the star schema, we are free to reshape the data that we have available in terms of one fact connected to many dimensions, making it information that can be used easily by people and tools that expect a star schema.

You just need a bit of creativity to place the information in the star schema and be able to follow the relations already in the data. This is designed in the data mart layer and realized in the REF layer.

Can we have two separate fact tables used together for a single report? Even if we consider a report to be a set of visuals and queries that uses the same data model (that is, a star schema), having more than one fact table is risky at best (see the *Common problems in data models* section in *Chapter 3*) and often not even accepted by BI tools, which will complain about loops or other issues in the data model.

A case where we think that two fact tables might be used in the same visual report is when we compose independent queries/models in the same visual layout. You are actually using a single data model at a time, but you will see them used on the same page.

To clarify this with an example, consider that, along with the report for our "invoices with returns," we want to also have a visual showing the weather in the same period. You could have the average temperature, the number of sunny/rainy days, and the amount of rain or snow for a week or month so that your people might consider eventual correlations.

If you keep the two facts independent, by not using columns from one fact together with the ones from the other fact, everything should work (after all, it also depends on the smartness of the BI tool).

You might think that if you want to use the weather information together with your fact, you can denormalize the weather information into the fact or enrich the fact with the key of the weather information dimension (such as date, week, or month), as we saw with dimensions. That is a risky path.

It is important to remember that, in the first case, you can denormalize into the fact if they are at the same granularity – that is, if you pick totals by date, week, or month from both sides. In the second case, you cannot use the measures in a dimension, as we saw in *Chapter 3*, because you will have a fan trap if you do.

In the second case, you might manage the issue of using the measures by picking the appropriate aggregation function, such as using the average of the number of rainy days from the weather dimension in place of the default sum, but as mentioned before, this is a slippery slope.

Such ability should be limited to experienced people that are conscious of the possible issues. It is a recipe for disaster if it is available in a self-service setting, in the hands of people not aware of the criticality of the data model.

At the end of this discussion it is important to remember that the S1 story will provide us with the design of the star schema that we need to power the desired reporting. Next, we look at the S2 story that we will use to find out how to build the start schema designed in the S1 story.

S2 – designing a light data model for the REF layer

Someone could argue that designing the data model of the data mart and the data model of the REF layer that effectively powers the data mart is the same process. That is, in large part, true, as the two are inextricably connected, and that's why we suggest that they are done by the same person.

We have decided to divide the two parts and have one story for each data model because the two models provide value in themselves, are often created in different contexts by talking to different people, and can also change at different times and for different reasons.

We reiterate the suggestion that the same senior person should drive both these stories (S1 and S2) and have the overall responsibility to support the end-to-end creation of the report.

The main reason for the modeler being responsible from end to end is that building a proper understanding of the requirements, of the data mart, and of the sources that will be combined in the REF layer is a slow and complex process that involves discussion with many people, and it is quite difficult to communicate to others with all the necessary nuances while the building process is ongoing.

Once the development is done, especially with dbt, we have the SQL, the lineage graph, and the data models, which provide very good material that describes the requirements that, in the meantime, have also become familiar to the team.

Having multiple people in the team collaborating on the development is the best way to have them internalize a good part of the knowledge about the report while, at the same time, contributing to improving the quality of the solution. The role of the modeler is to guide colleagues and ensure that even the nuances that are complex to communicate are satisfied.

The development of this S2 story generally happens as a dialogue between the modeler and the people with knowledge of the source systems that will provide the data for the report, as tentatively identified during the story analyzing the data mart (S1).

In S1, the businesspeople generally express themselves using the base facts handled by the operational systems or other concepts built in previous or local versions of the reports they have.

Between S1 and S2, the modeler designs and refines, in successive steps, the fact and dimensions with their enrichments to satisfy the requirements, while dealing with the available sources.

The work to be performed in this story is as follows:

- Learn how to combine the data from the base facts and dimensions built in the refined layer to produce the composite fact and the enriched dimensions that the story S1 has identified

- Identify what the needed tables in the refined layer are – base facts and dimensions, plus the supporting tables that represent additional relations or are needed to convert between systems

- Identify from which source systems to collect data for the preceding tables most simply or easily, and how to load and store it in the data platform

The general progression of this S2 story, which generally overlaps with the final part of the S1 story, is a kind of recursive process to find where is and how to connect the required information that is not yet available to produce the desired refined models.

Once the required information has been accounted for, it is time to check that the data provides the information as expected and start to think about special cases that can be different from the simple/general case. This part is usually a strict collaboration with the source system experts and with the business to verify or adapt the requirements to the reality of the data.

The following is a quick description of the typical cases that you will be handling over and over.

The definition of a REF model from sources

The following diagram describes how a table, **XYZ**, from a source, **S1**, is ingested, stored, enriched, and then mapped to the master data system to provide a fully refined **REF_XYZ** model that can be related to other REF models, as they are all expressed in master data code.

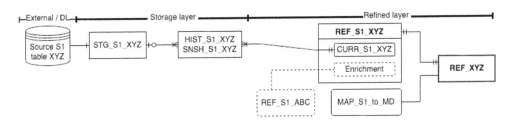

Figure 10.9: An example data model for a final master data REF model

As explained in the previous chapters when working with dbt in our Pragmatic Data Platform approach, we make extensive use of the preceding loading pattern:

1. We bring data from the source system table, **XYZ**, into a staging model, **STG_S1_XYZ**, which is used to adapt the data without adding any **business rules** (**BRs**). The **S1** in the name clarifies that all the codes and conventions are still the ones from the S1 system.

2. We store the output of the STG model using a dbt snapshot or our insert-only history macro in the only incremental model, which stores all the versions that a single instance of the entity has shown us. For one PK in the STG, there can be multiple rows in the storage table.

3. When it is time to use the **XYZ** data in the REF layer, we take out the current version for each instance using our current macro, making the **CURR_S1_XYZ** CTE or table.

4. The current instances are eventually joined with other tables from the same S1 system to enrich the entity and produce a "locally refined" version, **REF_S1_XYZ**, still limited to the S1 system. In this step, we enrich the entity with the data from the same system that we want to carry forward.

The enrichment operation might be done in a single step between models that are pretty much just a shell around the CURR CTE, or as the result of multiple transformations of all the entities contributing to the final REF model. That depends on the BRs to be applied.

5.   The last step to build a generally reusable refined model for the **XYZ** entity is to apply a master data mapping to convert the codes and conventions from the system S1 ones to the ones of the selected master data system.

    The various **REF_XYZ** models directly derived from source system tables, but converted to the master data system, are the base to build more complex REF models, which combine the information of multiple systems.

    The combination of data from multiple systems can provide enrichment (such as bringing in the salesperson's name from the HR system), the extension of scope (such as making available invoices from multiple countries), or generate new, higher-level concepts that do not exist in a single system.

This pattern is repeated so often and consistently named that, in most cases, it is redundant to draw all of it, as this would add no value and just clutter the REF layer data model.

For this reason, it is often enough to identify the final REF model in the REF layer data model. You can start from the CURR model if you feel it is important to identify the other entities that contribute to the REF model by performing important enrichment steps.

Note that in the rare cases where we need to work with all the versions (often referred to as *slowly changing dimension type two*), the logic is similar but more complex, as it needs to account for the version timeline from all entities to perform the operations.

Dimension enrichment

This is one of the most common cases, when in the S1 story you opted to denormalize the data from a snowflaked dimension or a reference table into a target dimension connected to the fact.

To model this, you identify the join clause between the target dimension and the related REF models (dimensions) from which you want to bring values, checking the multiplicities to be sure that you can bring in a single value of the snowflaked dimension for each row of the target dimension, without generating duplicates.

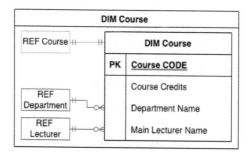

Figure 10.10: An example of an enriched dimension

In the preceding data model, we have identified the two REF models and their relations with the **REF Course** model that is used to enrich the course and produce the **DIM Course** table. Here, we have also identified the **REF Course** model, which is the base for **DIM Course**, but it is often so obvious that you can leave it out.

In the `DIM` table, we have also identified the attributes that we want to be sure to have or that we need to calculate:

```
SELECT
  c.*,
  d.Department_Name,
  c.Lecturer_Name
FROM REF_Course as c
LEFT OUTER JOIN REF_Dept as d on d.Dept_CODE = c.Dept_CODE
LEFT OUTER JOIN REF_Lect as l on l.Lect_CODE = c.Main_Lect_CODE
```

Remember that we draw these data models to collect information, communicate with stakeholders and colleagues, and remember what is not obvious to us. We are not going to generate code from these models, so they need to be useful for humans and don't need to be totally complete.

Connecting to a fact a snowflaked dimension

The classical alternative to denormalization of data into a dimension already connected to a fact is to connect to a fact table more dimensions that, in turn, contain the desired data. This is obtained by enriching the fact with the relevant FKs taken from the connected dimension.

The base process is the same in both cases – using the relationships between the connected dimension and the other sources of information to either collect the data in the dimension or bring the FK into the fact by joining through the connected dimension.

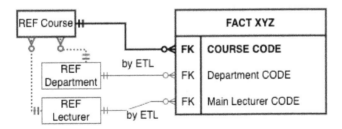

Figure 10.11: The data model for a fact enriched with an FK to additional dimensions

In the data model, we can see in the thicker line the relationship between the fact and the course table and the two relationships between the course, the department, and the main lecturer. These last two are dotted, as they are not part of the final data mart, but they play a key role, as they mean that **REF Course** has the FK to these models.

The data model shows also, in the thin line with a **by ETL** description, the two relationships that are created by adding to the fact the FK of the department and main lecturer dimensions:

```
SELECT
  f.*,
  c.Department_CODE,
  c.Main_Lecturer_CODE
FROM FACT_XWZ as f
LEFT OUTER JOIN REF_Course as c on f.Course_Code = c. Course_Code
```

The preceding code, which would be part of the FACT_XYZ model, shows how such enrichment can be done by following the join from the fact to the course and picking the FK for these two tables, which are in the **REF Course** table.

The application of master data

The other common task that you need to consider in the REF layer is the master data mapping needed to convert data from the coding and conventions of the original source to the ones in use in the master data system, if there is one, or at least into a common system to be used for the specified data mart.

This is so common that we have already added this step, in the diagram of the data model of the normal transformation chain to build a REF model at the beginning of this story's description.

A definition of the composite fact

In most cases, the fact at the center of the star schema for your report is a composite fact that needs to be created from base facts and supporting tables, including mappings and many-to-many relation tables

It is important that during stories S1 and S2, you cover well how to build the composite fact, with S1 more focused on what the desired content is, and S2 more focused on how to build it and apply the correct BRs to provide correct values.

We cannot cover all the possible situations that you will face, but we want to point out that you should carefully consider the nature of the relationships of the facts and intermediate tables that you need to compose, as cases where you have many-to-many relationships are very difficult to deal with.

The solution for such cases can be specific BRs that reduce the complexity of the relationships and/or aggregate the different parts to such a level that the relationship becomes easier to handle.

S3.x – developing with dbt models the pipeline for the XYZ table

Once the S1 and S2 stories have been completed or are at least in the advanced stage of completion, you will have a list of tables that you need to build in the refined and delivery layers.

You will create an S3 story for each table that generally includes the following:

- Refined tables (local or master data refined), used directly in the data mart or to build more complex models: These include the support tables, such as master data mappings and many-to-many relationship tables, that need to be loaded from a source system and made available in the ref layer.

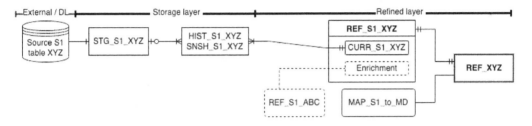

Figure 10.12: A general layout of the pipeline to build a REF model

For each table in this category, the preceding diagram gives a general plan of what happens. It is up to you to define clearly in the story where the data comes from (source) and what is needed, especially past the CURR model.

- The complex models to be built on top of refined tables: Each story should specify how the model should be built and the BRs involved.

- The final facts and dimensions used in the data mart: If a dimension is built directly on a REF model without any specific rule (pretty much with a SELECT * query), you can add the creation of the dimension to the story to create the REF table, as the work is minimal.

The important points to know for each of these stores are as follows:

- Whether the source provides a full export (all instances) or only a partial export.

- Whether the source provides only one version or provides multiple versions.

- If there are deletions in the source and how they are handled.

- What is the natural key for the entity and the primary key of the source table?

- Decide what you want to store in the storage. Generally, you want to store only the different changes when they are received, but in some cases, it is easier for later use to store a snapshot for every day (or another interval of time).

- Specify the eventual BRs for enrichment and master data mapping in the REF layer.

Do not be surprised if many of these stories are run-of-the-mill "import table XYZ from source SX to REF layer" types, without any special BR and maybe not even MD mapping, as the final REF model might just be used to enrich another model.

These are excellent stories that can be built in parallel by less experienced colleagues, who can start to learn the complexities of correctly ingesting data with the initial help of an experienced colleague.

Few of the stories will be related to the construction of the composite fact and of dimensions that incorporate complex BRs or must overcome a lot of problems in the data. These are better suited for the most experienced colleagues or should be done in direct collaboration with the modeler, to avoid being bogged down by unexpected issues in data and corner cases in the BRs.

As always, remember that working in an agile way means that we do not want to spend a lot of time collecting all the detailed requirements (waterfall style), but we need to have a quick and continuous connection with the business and experts to be able to overcome the issues that arise.

The set of these stories is pretty independent until you reach the REF layer, so they can be delivered in parallel, but then you need to start completing the preceding stories to start the stories for the complex models and the data mart tables.

S4 – an acceptance test of the data produced in the data mart

Once you start to have the final tables that you are going to use in the data mart, it is time to verify that the data that you are delivering is sound.

There are two main approaches to this:

- **Automated acceptance/integration tests**: In some cases, it is possible to have the expected output for all or at least part of the data that you must produce. This is the case when there is (or was) a previous system in operation that we are going to replace, but it is also possible that the business has produced the desired output for a limited set of data.

  In these cases, just set up singular tests in dbt to verify that the output is as expected.

- **Manual acceptance test**: This is still the most common case where you ask the business or colleagues from another team to verify that the data that you produced is correct.

  In these cases, we suggest preparing temporary reports that support the effort of your colleagues. We also suggest keeping a channel open during the testing and having a quick turnaround time to fix one issue as soon as it is found, rather than batching up the changes.

The point and the detail of this story change a lot from place to place, with some needing detailed and formal verification and acceptance, and others being happy with a few manual checks.

The story is done when the data is considered good enough to go to production.

S5 – development and verification of the report in the BI application

This is the final story, where you will use the data mart verified in S4 to build the report using the BI application.

The starting point is the data model for the data mart designed in the S1 story, which was developed with the BI tool needs in mind and will, therefore, provide the correct model for your BI tool, whether it is a star schema or a wide table.

We will not go into further details for this story, as this work is done outside of dbt and your data platform, depending very much on the BI tool at hand.

> **Agility tip**
> We have just discussed the usual steps, codified in stories, that are needed to build a report backed by a data platform.
>
> The process applied is general (know what you want, find out how to build it, build it, verify the data, and deliver the visuals to your audience), but it is important to remember that in an agile team, you do not interpret these steps in a waterfall-like mindset, completing (and signing off) one step before moving to the next. The right approach is to have them overlap and clarify more details as you get closer to the implementation, circling back and rethinking if the data says a different story to what you were thinking.
>
> Keep the goal in mind – delivering to the customer, not building documentation.

In this section, we have discussed how to work in an agile way and taken a deep dive into building star schema data marts to power your reports, as this is one of the most common uses of dbt and data warehousing in general.

Summary

In this chapter, you learned some agile philosophy and practical hints, starting from the commencement of your project, managing the backlog, and finally, taking a deep dive into how to organize your work to build reporting data marts. Good job!

In the next chapter, you will learn about collaboration and using Git alongside dbt Cloud to coallborate.

11

Team Collaboration

In the previous chapter about agile development, we discussed the development process, often referring to how it impacts teamwork.

In this chapter, we will touch on a few practices that help developers work as a team and the support that dbt provides for this.

This chapter covers the following topics:

- Enabling collaboration
- Working with branches and pull requests
- Working with Git in dbt Cloud
- Making your first pull request

Enabling collaboration

The most important aspect for a team to be able to work together is **alignment**, which I will simply define as the ability and desire of team members to go in the same direction. It is important to reflect on both dimensions – ability and desire.

Team members must be able to work in the same direction; they must know and clearly understand the expected common direction (that must be the same of the management), and they should not have conflicting priorities or assignments. This is especially important for teams where not all the people depend on the same organization/manager.

Team members must be willing to work in the same direction; they must have knowledge and competence that allows them to work effectively in the team, and they must actively participate in the creation of the team direction to have a real buy-in in the team's work.

A cornerstone of agile is "self-organizing" teams, as this is the best way to ensure that a direction is known and agreed upon by all the teammates, and that everyone in the team has a saying proportional to their competence on the subject. The 11th principle of the Agile Manifesto says, "*The best architectures, requirements, and designs emerge from self-organizing teams.*"

Core collaboration practices

To collaborate, you need shared goals, achieved by writing and choosing development features and stories together, and ways of working, so that all tasks, even the ones usually associated with individual work such as writing code or designing a data model, are looked at from a team perspective and performed in a team-friendly/usable way.

This means that there must be common practices and tools.

The following is a list of important practices that help teamwork:

1. **Common code ownership**: The development must be open and transparent, with the team having ownership of code, not the individual writing it. It must be encouraged that everyone can change every part of the code base, with the goal of improving quality, not just to change code according to the preferences of the code developer.

   This is probably the most important step for many teams – breaking down the mental walled gardens of "my code" versus "your code" and settling for "our code".

   Once we agree that the code that we write belongs to the entire team, then collaboration becomes possible.

2. **Clean code and technical excellence**: To enable the team to grow and collaborate, code must be the best that the team can write and as easy to read as prose.

   The 9th principle of the Agile Manifesto says *"Continuous attention to technical excellence and good design enhances agility."* The *least surprise principle* is very important for collaboration as it makes code easier to understand, avoiding unexpected code behavior.

   The key question here is, *"Who are you writing for?"*. The answer is, *"For you, and for your colleagues,"* as the code that you write will be read tens if not hundreds of times. Minimizing the time needed to understand it, and the chances of it being misunderstood, are key.

   Good professionals want to have pride in their work, and that is only possible when the code that they work on is clear and works well. The team must be encouraged to increase the average quality of code daily, not lessen it, and this can also be done by coaching colleagues.

3. **Trust, but challenge**: Freedom is only possible together with responsibility. The collective ownership and the high quality of code (and of the process) are a continuous process, not only when actively writing it but also when evaluating or reviewing any piece of it.

   Each person on a team is welcome to challenge and request or propose the improvement of every piece of code. This must be done to provide real value and communicated in a constructive manner, not with the intention of shaming, controlling, or micromanaging.

   Usually, this happens during development – remember the "boy scout rule" – and during reviews of new code, but any moment is fine if there is enough value to be added.

4. **An open door policy**: Transparency and contribution must be encouraged not only in code but also in all deliverables and activities, including meetings.

In every activity, every team member must feel welcome if they can contribute, but they should also feel free and compelled to leave if they cannot contribute.

Freedom and responsibility are the keys.

The preceding practices provide a good base for teamwork to flourish, but paying only lip service to them is not enough. All team members must understand them and feel safe working according to them, so management has the responsibility to coach the team to absorb them.

These common practices and tools should cover all work, from goal and work management (writing and picking stories) to development (database access and coding) and collaboration (communication, version control, and code reviewing).

Collaboration with dbt Cloud

The use of dbt Cloud provides many benefits in the common tool category:

- A web-based, system-independent **Integrated Development Environment** (IDE) that provides the same access, tools, and working processes to all the members of the team.

  Individual choice of working tools is encouraged in agile teams, as it improves individual well-being and productivity, but the availability of an easy-to-use, equal-for-all environment is very important to enable common ways of working.

  This is especially important for data team members that do not come from a programming background and instead have experience as a BI or analyst, where they might not be used to coding practices such as version control, testing, or releasing to multiple environments.

- Easy and transparent access to databases and code, without the need to manage manual connections or access to a Git repository.

- An opinionated, simple, and effective Git-based process to work with version control, development branches, and pull requests, enabling people with little understanding of Git to develop code following Git branching best practices.

  Working with version control, and with development branches in particular, is a key enabler for collaboration in the form of code reviews and **Pull Requests** (PRs).

  We will look at the collaboration related to Git, branches, and PRs later in this section.

- A simple way to manage a team member's development environment, as well as the team deployment environments (such as QA and PROD) and the jobs to deploy and run code on them.

  This dbt Cloud part, which we will look at in the last section of this chapter, automates most of the work and reduces the burden on teams, empowers more members to deal with deployment, and provides more transparency in a process than typical home-brew tooling.

When you put together common goals, ways of working, and tools, you provide an environment that is conducive to good teamwork. Culture is the secret sauce that makes good teamwork real.

When working with dbt, the following practices are great ways to collaborate on writing code, build a common way of coding, and coach or share knowledge between colleagues:

- **Pairing**: Working together on the same piece of code. It is the most powerful way to coach colleagues, build a common way of working, and spread knowledge of the domain.

  Whether you do it traditionally with two (or even more) people in front of a single PC with one keyboard or online, pairing is always very effective. The code that comes out of pairing sessions is constantly better than code done alone, and if colleagues are satisfied with the code, it is ready to be merged into `master`. Furthermore, knowledge now resides in two heads.

- **Code walkthrough**: The developer of one piece of code walks the team around their code. The team asks clarification questions and can challenge, in a collaborative way, the solutions adopted by the developer.

  A positive, honest, and friendly attitude is central to this practice, as the goal of questions must be a better understanding of the code, the reasons beyond choices, and to provide a tangible improvement of the quality.

  This technique is extremely useful to bring a large group of people up to speed concerning a piece of code, whether it is an important part of an application or the use of a common pattern or library that is recurrent in the domain.

  The downside of using only this technique is that the walkthrough will be made when the code is at least in a very advanced state, if not almost complete. Having critically useful feedback at this time means that a lot has to be redone, and therefore, the bar is raised for what changes/improvements the team can do.

- **Pull request (PR) and a code review**: A PR is the request to bring code from one development branch into another branch, usually the main one containing the current integrated version of the changes. This branch is often called `master` or `main`.

  The code review is the act of colleagues reviewing the changes proposed by the dev branch and asking questions/proposing suggestions. We will see more about this in the next section.

Culture is the strongest factor to enable a team to collaborate and ultimately work effectively. You have a good team culture when developers and managers put the team's well-being and result before the individual ones, while, of course, keeping individual needs and interests in mind.

Tools and practices enable and support collaboration and are part of a team culture, but ultimately, it is the mindset that makes or breaks a team's culture.

After all, the fifth principle of the Agile Manifesto says, *"Build projects around motivated individuals. Give them the environment and support they need and trust them to get the job done."*

As an example, a bonus organized in quartiles, where the top quarter of colleagues takes much more and the lower quarter less, fosters competition more than collaboration. A bonus based on team results is more likely to incentivize collaboration and coaching.

Effective collaboration in software development often relies on efficient use of version control, with branches and PRs being powerful tools in managing code changes and team alignment, which is the topic of our next section.

Working with branches and PRs

The most important and disruptive moment in software development is the integration of new code into an existing code base. At this time, you have to make sure that the new code does what the developer expects it to do and that it fits in well with the existing code, especially with the other recent changes that have just been developed by other developers.

Experience has shown that the integration of small increments is much quicker and easier to perform than so-called "big bang" releases, with huge amounts of code.

It is, in fact, much easier to be sure of what a small piece of code does, and as developing a small change takes a short time, there are very few changes that have been delivered since the development started and that the new piece of code must integrate well with.

Modern software engineering has adopted as a standard the use of **version control systems** (**VCSs**) for code, as it allows controlled and predictable steps in the evolution of software.

The use of branches is the technical way to allow the aforementioned quick development and frequent integration of new code into an existing code base.

The creation of a branch is like making a named copy of the code, which can then be modified and developed independently from the original. This allows a developer to work on a specific feature isolated from the changes created in parallel by other developers in other branches.

When the development done inside a branch is ready to be integrated, the code from the branch is merged into the `master` branch, or another long-lived branch of the code that symbolizes the current version of the product.

The merge process applies the changes from the branch that is merged on top of the current version of the code in the target branch. The process to apply changes is usually handled automatically by the VCS. It requires human intervention, called **conflict resolution**, only in rare occasions when two parallel changes try to change the same file.

The conflict can arise when a proposed change would touch the same part of a file that has been changed after that the branch proposing the change was created from the original branch and the conflicting change has already been incorporated in the target branch by a previous merge operation from another branch.

In the last decade, **Git** – an open source VCS created in 2005 by Linus Torvalds, the author of the Linux operating system – has become the de facto standard version control system, and a few online services have emerged that complement Git with the critical feature called a PR.

The PR process is innovative in that it provides a guided process for a team, even if it is distributed and doesn't have constant communication, to propose the merging of one branch into another branch, allowing simple inspection and collaboration of the code to be merged. This provides a great way to improve code quality and inform/coach colleagues.

The PR process is implemented slightly differently by each online Git repository provider, but the signature elements are providing reviewers with easy access to the changed code and a simple way to communicate with the developer, usually using comments or tags, to request information and propose alternative solutions. This becomes an asynchronous discussion that continues with answers and changes provided by the developer in response to questions and suggestions, until an agreement is reached to either complete the PR by merging the changes from the branch or close the PR without merging the changes, leaving the branch open for more work and a future PR.

dbt Cloud uses Git as a VCS to implement an opinionated "branching and merging" way of working that simplifies the process for users and guides them to use the best practices developed in the last decades, including the use of PRs to improve the quality of the resulting code.

Working with Git in dbt Cloud

When working with dbt Cloud, you must have a Git repository to store your code.

You can use your own Git providers, such as GitHub, GitLab, Azure DevOps, Bitbucket, or others that implement the standard HTTPS or SSH Git communication interfaces. If you do not have a Git provider, dbt Cloud can use and internally manage the open source Git implementation.

It is important to note that branch and merge are Git concepts and are, therefore, always available, while PRs are totally external to Git and are a collaborative tool developed and powered by the individual Git provider.

If you use one of the Git providers that dbt Cloud has developed an integration for, (currently GitHub, GitLab, and Azure DevOps), you will already have PRs configured and a **Continuous Integration** (**CI**) process available when you open or propose a change to a PR.

In all other cases, to use PRs you just need to configure the correct URL so that dbt Cloud allows you to open a PR at the right moment in the process.

The dbt Cloud Git process

The common strategy that dbt Cloud implements is commonly referred to as **feature branching workflow**, as it postulates that all feature development should happen in a dedicated branch and not on the `master`/`main` branch.

Developers make changes in their own branch until everything works as expected, and the code is merged back into main. This has the advantage that the main branch should only receive well-tested, working code and move from one meaningful set of features to another one.

When you work on code in the dbt Cloud IDE, you can be either on the master branch, which after the first commit is considered read-only, or on a branch with a different name, which is considered a feature development branch that can be deployed to your own development environment.

In *Chapter 2*, we saw how to initialize a project from an empty repository, and in the previous chapters, we often used Git-related commands, but let's describe what the full process of development for a feature looks like, with reference to Git-related commands:

1. Start from the main branch. Note that it is marked as read-only. This is a best practice to prevent unexpected and unsupervised changes entering the main branch without following the proper process.

    As you see from the following screenshot, dbt Cloud features related to Git are grouped in the top-left area of the window, with the name of the branch that you are inside on the first line and the commands and changed files (there are none in the following screenshot) in the **Version Control** area.

    If you are not on main, click **Change branch** and select main in the popup to go there.

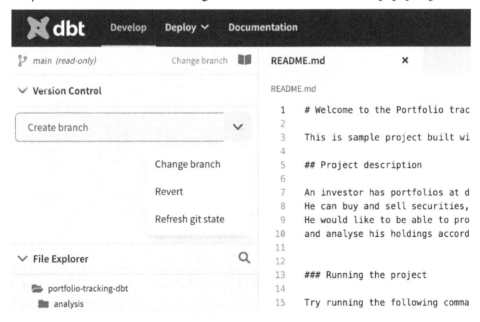

Figure 11.1: Available Git actions on the master branch

You can click **Refresh Git state** at any time to check for any changes.

2.   Create a new feature branch to work on code by clicking the **Create branch** button and providing a name for the branch in the popup that appears.

3.   After a few seconds, you will find yourself in the new branch (in the following screenshot, named **chapter08**) that will not be read-only anymore.

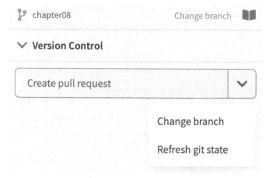

Figure 11.2: Available Git actions in a clean state development branch

When a branch has no changes still to be committed, it is in a clean state, as the working directory is in sync with the Git repo, and you have the option to create a new PR.

4.   You can now edit and develop the feature as required.

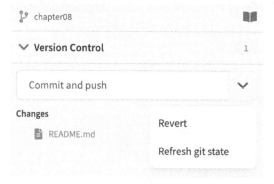

Figure 11.3: The available Git actions in a dirty state branch

Once you edit one file, your branch will be in a dirty state, as the working directory is not in sync with the Git repo. Changed files will be listed in the **Version Control** area, and you can click on the filenames there to see what the changes are, with respect to the previous version.

If you want to abandon all the changes since the last commit and go back to the state as of the last commit of the branch, you can click **Revert** and confirm.

Keep developing by adding files and tests, until you reach a consistent state that you want to save by committing it to the Git repository. By clicking on **Commit and push**, you will get a popup asking for a commit message. Provide the message and continue to send the open changes to the Git repository as a new commit.

5. While developing, it is common for someone to have completed some PR and merged new code into the `main` branch.

    The code that you are writing will need to integrate with the new version of the main branch, so after each commit on your branch, if there are changes on `main`, you will be given the possibility to bring them in by the Git button changing to **Pull from "main"**.

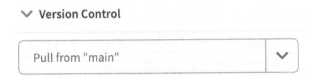

Figure 11.4: The pull action button

The best course is to accept importing the changes so that you can already adapt your code to them. Note that the incoming changes are not shown to you, as they come from a recently merged PR, which you should already know about. In any case, running the code and tests should give you good confidence that all is working fine without the need for changes, while errors would point you to areas that need checking/fixing.

You should realize that nothing substitutes good communication in a team, so you must be aware of the open PRs and, especially, the ones that are ready to be merged, so the fact that they are merged and you get a change in the master branch should not come as a surprise.

If you want to see the changes, you can always go to your Git provider and review what has been recently merged into `master`. This is one more reason to import changes as soon as they are available, so you have fewer to review if you need to understand what has changed.

6. Continue developing and adding small increments to the feature as commits, until *you have an initial version of the feature that you can share with your colleagues to start getting feedback and suggestions. This is the right time to open a PR.*

    Do not wait until your feature is complete to open a PR, as your colleagues will have much more code to review in a single go, and any suggestion or request for a change would require more rework, possibly leading to a lot of wasted work.

    To be able to open a PR, you need to have the branch in a clean state, so complete what you are doing, make a commit, and if you have configured the PR URL for the project, you will have the **Create pull request** button to click.

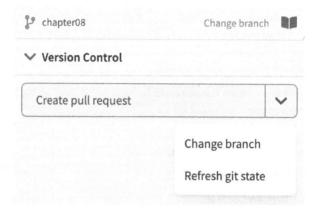

Figure 11.5: The Create pull request button

By clicking this button, you will be redirected to your online Git provider to follow the steps to create a PR in that product. All the collaboration on the PR happens in the Git provider product, not on dbt.

The only interaction between the two products is through Git commands, as even after you have opened a PR on a branch, you can continue developing on that branch in dbt, and each time that you make a new commit, the changes will be added to the open PR.

7. Once you have completed the development, you will merge the PR in the Git provider product and the code will be added to the `master` branch.

    It is then time to go back to *step 1*, returning to the `main` branch and importing the changes shown in *step 5*. You are then ready to start a new feature.

We have seen the steps that you will go through when working with dbt Cloud and how the development of other features happening in parallel influences your own development.

> **Tip**
> Please remember that opening the PR as early as possible (when there is something to be discussed) is crucial to have early feedback, offer less work for reviewers, and limit rework, while producing high-quality code that some of your colleagues are already familiar with. This also helps a lot in avoiding siloes.

Keeping your development environment healthy

One thing that you can do every time that your branch is in a clean state is change the branch and go and see or execute the code of another branch, potentially the one from another branch that you are commenting on in a PR.

Even if you are not actively moving between branches but you develop in your branch, go back to main, and then start on another branch; you are bound to import changes to existing tables that you have not made in your branch.

When you switch or progress through branches, the code will reflect the branch that you are on, while the database of your development environment will accumulate changes according to what you are running.

In general, to be sure that the database of your development environment reflects the code that you are working on, you can run the dbt project with a --full-refresh switch. This recreates all the tables, including the ones with incremental load, so while you will lose some history (which should not matter in the development environment), you will make sure that you have the up-to-date table definitions.

A simple alternative is to just drop one or more schema or individual tables in your development environments so that they can be recreated at the next dbt run.

There is another thing to note about switching between branches – it is perfectly fine to do so, as it can be used to inspect and run the code of a PR or to do coaching or pairing in remote settings, but you should never make changes in someone else's branch without prior agreement.

If you want to propose changes to an existing feature branch, you should start another branch from the feature branch that you want to modify, using your Git provider, then work on the new branch in dbt Cloud, and then open a PR, picking the feature branch as the target.

The dbt Cloud managed workflow only allows you to create branches from master, as that is what you would normally do, and prevents people without enough understanding of Git to put themselves in complex situations. But you can start a branch from a branch that is not master and all that is allowed by Git in your Git provider, and once you have created a branch, you can work on it normally in dbt Cloud.

Suggested Git branch naming

In the workflow that we have presented, we have just considered the existence of a main or master branch and feature branches, with the implicit understanding of main being a long-lived branch providing the current version of our product and the feature branches being throwaway, short-lived branches.

That is perfectly fine for the development branches, but the reality is more complex than that, and often, you do not just have a development environment and a production environment.

In the next chapter, which is about automation, you will see that in dbt Cloud, you can create environments and associate them with one branch, usually a long-lived branch.

A very common situation is to have three environments: the development environment for your developers, an intermediate integration environment, and the final production environment.

Let's see how to match branches to environments and how to do releases:

1. In the development environment, every developer will switch between the feature branches as needed and will maintain their database in sync, as we saw in the previous section.

2. It is then convenient to use the `main` branch as the integration branch, which we often name `CI` for **Continuous Integration** or `QA` for **Quality Assurance**. The name is a function of the organization's culture, but the function is the same – all the changes from the features are merged into this branch, which is used to ensure that the features that are working well individually keep working together.

    While it should not happen if the code of every PR is properly tested and executed with all the tests, real-life experience shows that, for one reason or another, a few bugs can pass through at the PR revision phase.

    You can consider the integration branch to be the low-maintenance canary in the mine that helps you catch most of the bugs that pass through the PR process.

    Being always very close to or a bit ahead of the final production environment helps to start early development of reports or external integrations while the details are still being ironed out.

3. Finally, you can create another branch, which we usually name `PROD`, to contain the code that you promote from the integration environment to the production environment.

    The promotion of code from integration to production is done by using your Git provider to merge the selected code into the `PROD` branch.

In most cases, this three-branch setup is effective, as it allows you to control the release process to production while being efficient, as you must maintain only one intermediate environment.

This works very well in typical internal projects, as the organization usually wants to bring to production every feature as it becomes available.

In very structured organizations or when production changes need to be strictly monitored and communicated, as in the case of formal versioning or periodic releases with only agreed-upon features, you might add extra environments as needed. A couple of examples are a "release candidate" to accumulate the changes ready to go out in one version and a "hot-fix" to test quick fixes to be applied on top of production.

In some rare cases where there are no real integration needs/risks, it is possible to avoid the intermediate environment and use `main` for production. This can be the case when there is only one developer, or when all the developments are independent (such as ingesting and publishing data as is). When going straight to production, you should also be fine with the occasional hiccup in your production environment.

Adopting frequent releases

The third principle of the Agile Manifesto says, *"Deliver working software frequently, from a couple of weeks to a couple of months, with a preference for the shorter timescale."*

I would say that given the productivity enhancement that we have had in the 20+ years since the Agile Manifesto and the release simplification brought by dbt Cloud, we can move the shorter release timescale to be under a week, even when we keep iteration duration to a couple of weeks.

When working with dbt, it is quite common that in a team, you complete a PR and get new features in the integration environment every day or so. This is normal, as when a developer has completed the work for an open PR, it is standard to complete and merge it into main.

Sometimes, we do not see the same pace for releases to production, and we use this section to advocate for releases to production made as frequently as possible.

The normal pattern of releasing projects that use the three environments discussed in the previous section should be to open a PR from the main branch to the PROD branch, which means promoting all the code that is in the integration environment to the production environment.

The rationale is threefold – first and foremost, we want to try to keep integration and production aligned so that releases are small and not risky. Secondly, only by releasing to production what we have tested together in the integration environment, we can assume that the released features will work well together. Third, promoting main to production is the simpler and safer way to release new features to production.

Because of the nature of working with dbt, it is most often the case that multiple features can be released independently and put into production when ready, even if they are just part of a bigger feature that will be used in production only when complete.

A typical example is building data mart components for a new report, where the individual features that are worked on are the pipelines to take the base entities to the REF layer, then the implementation of the master data transformations and the business rules, and lastly, the views that release to the data mart.

Given the preceding considerations, we suggest as a modus operandi that approved PRs should be released to production, at the latest, the day after their merge into main.

A good schedule is to promote main to PROD once the full cycle of load and testing, which is generally at least daily, has been completed and before merging any new PR.

This ensures that all the PRs that have been merged the day before properly work, together with the rest of the code base on a full load.

To be able to proceed in such a way, it is important to recognize eventual PRs that need a special timing to be released and complete them only when it is time to put them into production. Keeping a PR open for a long time or accumulating the PRs to be released later in a "release candidate" branch exposes the team to the risk of this code needing to be updated because of other PRs being merged into main, but it is important to prevent merging PRs into main that would block its promotion to PROD.

The alternative to the promotion of main to PROD is merging individual development branches or cherry-picking commits into production, but that is manual, complex, error-prone, and removes the benefits of the integration environment.

This manual selection process can be used when something urgent, such as a fix, must be released but something else prevents the promotion of main. Ultimately, you should release the fix to main and aim to be able to restart the normal release, based on the promotion of main when possible.

Now that we have discussed PRs, it is time to make one.

Making your first PR

To complete this chapter, let's see how we can create a PR in our setup with GitHub as our Git provider.

Remember that you can open a PR only when your working environment is clean – that is, when you have no pending changes after the last commit. Therefore, to create a PR, commit, or revert, all the changes.

Once you have a clean working environment, follow these steps:

1. To start the process to create a PR on the service provider, click on the **Create pull request** button.

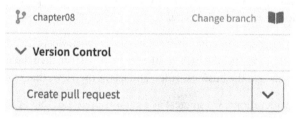

Figure 11.6: The PR creation option

2. You will be directed to the site of your Git provider on the page to start the PR creation and confirm the start and target branch. The branches will already be set from the branch you had open in dbt, as **main** or **master**. Each Git provider has a slightly different process, but you always have to confirm the start and target branch.

Comparing changes

Choose two branches to see what's changed or to start a new pull request. If you need to, you can also compare across forks.

base: main ▾ ← compare: chapter08 ▾	✓ Able to merge. These branches can be automatically merged.

Discuss and review the changes in this comparison with others. Learn about pull requests   **Create pull request**

-○- 1 commit	1 file changed	൛ 1 contributor

-○- Commits on Jan 9, 2023

Adding tests for the delivery layer   ┌┐   c2efb40   <>
RobMcZag committed last week

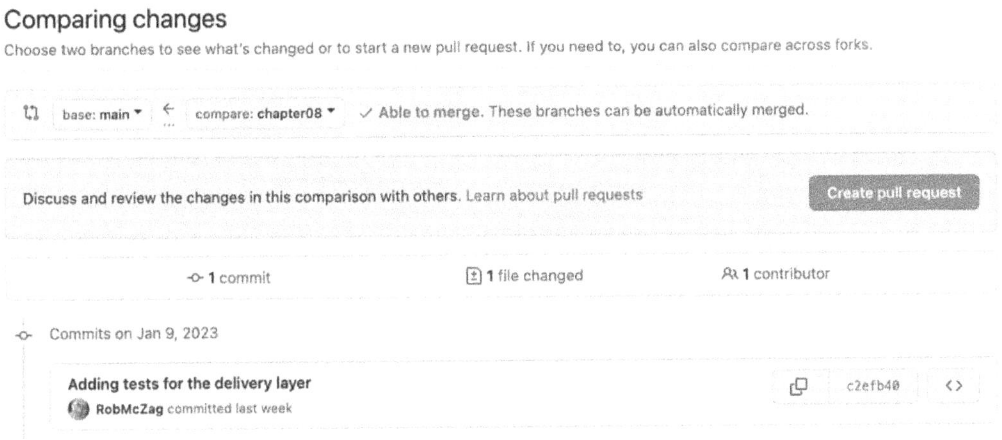

Figure 11.7: Confirming the start and target branch

As merging our development branch into **main** is what we want, click the **Create pull request** button.

3. The next step is to provide a title for the PR and write a good description of the content of the PR. Another step that you can take when opening a PR is to name one or more reviewers, who will be notified of the new PR and invited to comment on it.

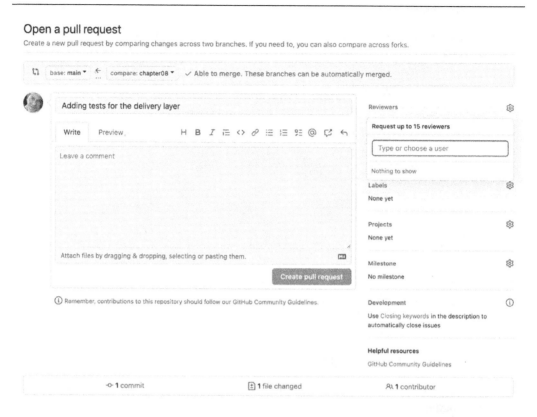

Figure 11.8: The PR window

Once you have entered the title and description and invited the reviewers, you can click the **Create pull request** button, and this time, the PR is created.

4.   Now that the PR is created, it is time to collaborate with your team.

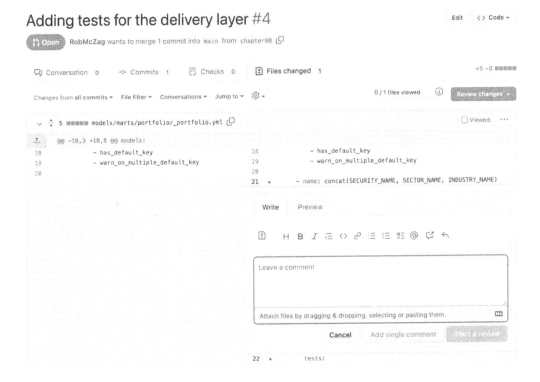

Figure 11.9: Finalizing the PR

The main collaboration feature of PRs is that reviewers and all the colleagues that have access to the PR can read the code with the changes highlighted (what has been added is in green and what was deleted is in red) and comment on it, asking questions and proposing alternatives.

Here, in the interactions on the PR, is where a lot of magic can happen – code becomes better, people are coached, and the knowledge of the project is disseminated to the team instead of being siloed. However, you have to use PR honestly, reading the code and commenting on it, not just clicking **Approve**.

Of course, PR reviewers can also approve the PR when it is considered ready for merging, but that should be seen as an indication that everything is ready, not as a sign-off or some kind of approval by a superior authority.

5.   Once you are ready to complete the PR and merge its code, click the **Merge pull request** button.

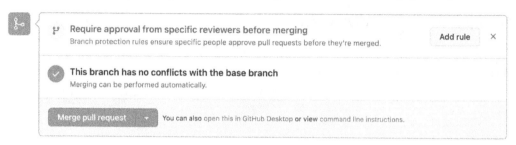

Figure 11.10: Merging the PR

6.   The previous form will be replaced by a new one, where you can edit the commit message and its description, but we advise leaving the message as is.

Figure 11.11: Confirming the merge

If you did not change idea, click the **Confirm merge** button.

7.   Once you confirm the merge, the form will be replaced with a message that confirms that the code has been merged and the PR closed.

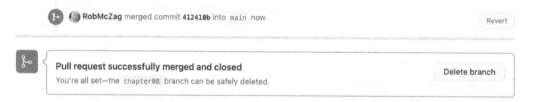

Figure 11.12: Final status after merging the PR

8.   Once the PR is merged, the changes are available in main, so you can refresh the branch you are in and click **Pull from "main"** to bring the changes in, or you can go back to main and click **Pull from remote** to bring the changes into the local working directory for the **main** branch.

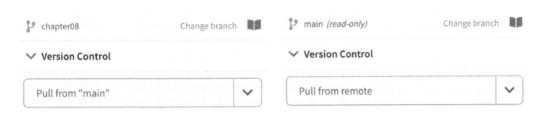

Figure 11.13: Checking the version control for branches

> Note that bringing the changes into the branch that you just merged is useful only if you plan to continue working in that branch to further develop that feature. In general, we suggest creating new branches.

Now that you have opened, completed, and merged your first PR, you can see that the process in itself is just a bit of bureaucracy that requires a few clicks to put your changes up for review, complete the review, and then merge it into the main branch. The process in itself has little value besides notarizing what changes have been proposed and then merged at a certain time.

The value of the PR process is in the collaboration of the team. If you do PRs but you have no comments and no participation from the team, you are not collaborating, and the PR process is close to meaningless.

Summary

Collaboration is an essential part of software development, and version control tools such as Git make it easier to work on code collaboratively and spread knowledge in a team.

This chapter covered how to streamline collaborative workflows using Git and dbt Cloud, with a focus on branches and PRs. You also learned how to make your first PR in a step by step guide.

In the next chapter, we will learn how to automate our data platform operations using environments and jobs.

Further reading

Using dbt, you will not need to become a Git pro, but if you want to know more about the de facto standard, you can read the *Pro Git* book, written by Scott Chacon and Ben Straub and published by Apress, which is available online for free at `https://git-scm.com/book/en/v2`.

If you want to explore all the available features of GitHub, you can explore the *GitHub docs* at `https://docs.github.com/en`.

There are plenty of books and web resources about Agile, but I liked the practical style of Henrik Kniberg in his "from the trenches" books about Scrum, XP, and Lean development.

Part 3:
Hands-On Best Practices
for Simple, Future-Proof
Data Platforms

In this section, we will put to use the software engineering and dbt skills learned in the first two parts when looking at the full scale of a data platform. We will discuss realistic use cases and practice on sample data. We will analyze different data warehousing architectures and delve deeper into two of the key aspects of managing information: managing identities and dealing with the history of changes.

We'll close by looking into patterns for special use cases and suggestions to publish dependable datasets.

This section includes the following chapters:

- *Chapter 12, Deployment, Execution, and Documentation Automation*
- *Chapter 13, Moving beyond Basics*
- *Chapter 14, Enhancing Software Quality*
- *Chapter 15, Patterns for Frequent Use Cases*

12

Deployment, Execution, and Documentation Automation

In this chapter, you will learn how to automate the operation of your data platform by setting up environments and jobs that automate the release and execution of your code following your deployment design.

You will learn about the notification system to alert the relevant people when a job is canceled or fails, either because of an error or a test not passing and providing an error.

You will also learn about the documentation, lineage graph, and source data freshness dashboard, which is automatically generated from the metadata provided in the YAML files of the project.

In this chapter, you will learn about the following topics:

- Designing your deployment automation
- Advanced automation – hooks and run-operations
- Documentation

Technical requirements

This chapter uses the sample project that we built in the second part of this book as the setting to create environments and jobs.

All the code samples for this chapter are available on GitHub at https://github.com/PacktPublishing/Data-engineering-with-dbt/tree/main/Chapter_12.

Designing your deployment automation

In the previous chapter, we discussed how to work with Git in dbt.

The process promoted by the dbt user interface balances speed of delivery, control over the quality, and the ability to disseminate code knowledge and coach less experienced colleagues.

The basic process uses the `main` branch to receive all the changes from the short-lived feature branches used to develop the changes.

Developers work on feature branches in their personal development environment, where they can deploy and run the code from any branch.

The most basic setup, suitable only for the simplest use cases, is made by two environments only: a common production environment, created by deploying the code from the `main` branch, and the individual development environments of the developers.

Working with dbt environments

To design your deployment strategy you can use the two types of environment that are available in dbt Cloud:

1. **Development environment**, where the connection and deployment schema are delegated to the developer's credentials, generating one environment for each developer where dbt commands are run in the IDE by the developer in first person. The code that is executed is the one from the branch selected in the IDE.

2. **Deployment environment**, where the connection, deployment schema, and code branch to use is configured in the environment definition, producing a single environment where dbt commands are executed by jobs, using the code from the configured branch.

We generally configure only one development environment, as defined by default, as it already produces one development environment for each developer. We use as many deployment environments as we need to design our deployment strategy.

Development environment

The development environment's definition is created automatically at project creation and is used to instantiate one physical environment for each developer, using the developer's credentials.

The connection details (database, role, and compute warehouse for Snowflake) in the developer's credentials are the same as the project's connection by default. We suggest that, during the project's creation, you set it up to suit the development environments.

In this way, the developers just need to provide their access credentials and pick a personal schema name to have a fully working development environment.

Deployment environments

We use deployment environments to create the common environments that are maintained through automation, using jobs.

In very simple realities, you can define only one deployment environment pointing to the main branch's code. If you do not specify a custom branch, main will be used.

This is very simple but is only suitable when you have only one or two developers, making a few changes with no overlapping work and an eventual downtime in the data platform is acceptable as you will need to rely only on the testing done in the individual developer's development environment, without any integration testing.

In this simple setup, once you merge a PR, the code is immediately deployed and your users will see the changes after the next project run.

In general, you will want to create more environments, with our common setup being the one presented in the previous chapter – that is, with one QA environment connected to the main branch and a production environment connected to a PROD branch.

In more structured setups using many long-lived branches, such as a full Git Flow with release branches, it will be natural to create more environments.

In dbt, you can create as many environments as you wish – there is no limit. However, in general, an environment is created by association with a long-lived branch that has a specific semantic in the organization, such as the PROD branch, which represents the production environment in our sample project.

You can have multiple environments associated with the same code branch. It can serve special cases where you want to freeze a branch at some point in time without blocking another environment defined on the same branch or you want to deploy the same code in different places. As an example, this can be used to serve audits or stress tests as you do not want your reports/results to change halfway through the process, but you do not want to stop development either.

Creating our QA and PROD environments

In this section, we will use our sample project to create two deployment environments. The QA environment will be associated with the main branch, while our production environment will be named PROD and it will be associated with a PROD branch that we will create with GitHub.

Let's create our QA environment:

1. From the main menu on the top of the dbt Cloud pages, under **Deploy**, select the **Environments** entry. You will land on the **Environments** page:

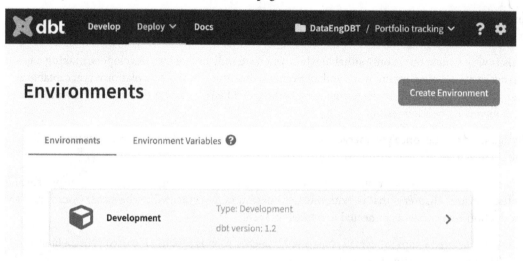

Figure 12.1: The initial Environments configuration page

Here, all the defined environments are listed. For now, we just have the **Development** environment, which was created automatically at setup.

Click the **Create Environment** button to start creating a new environment.

2. The page to create a new deployment environment is divided into three parts: **General Settings**, **Deployment Connection**, and **Deployment Credentials**.

Once you have created an environment, the **Semantic Layer** part will be added so that you can configure this dbt functionality:

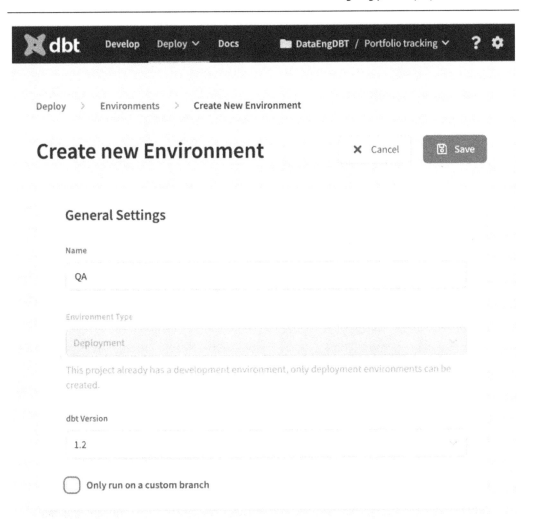

Figure 12.2: General Settings part of the Create new Environment page

In the **General Settings** part, you must pick a name, what dbt core version to use, and optionally what code branch, if you do not want to use main/master.

3.   Scrolling down, you will find the **Deployment Connection** part:

Deployment Connection

Override connection settings for this environment, only certain fields are able to be overriden.

Account

op36091.north-europe.azure

Role

DBT_EXECUTOR_ROLE

Database

PORTFOLIO_TRACKING

Warehouse

COMPUTE_WH

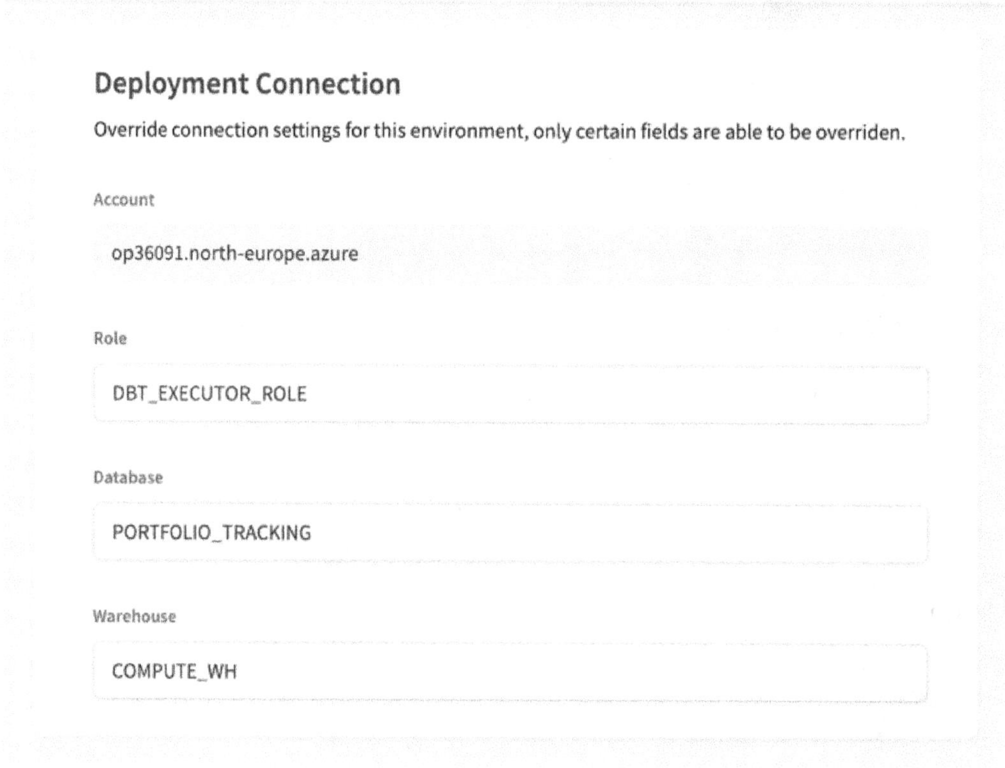

Figure 12.3: Deployment Connection part of the Create new Environment page

Here, you can override the parameters configured in the project connection.

Configure the name of the database where you want to deploy this environment and pick the database role that provides the right access to dbt in such a database.

You can also select what Snowflake warehouse to use to run this environment. This allows you to eventually divide the load of different environments between different warehouses. Our suggestion is to start with one warehouse for all environments and move out the most sensitive environment, which is usually production, if you need better performance.

4. Scroll further down and you will find the **Deployment Credentials** part:

Deployment Credentials

Enter your deployment credentials here. dbt will use these credentials to connect to your database and run scheduled jobs in this environment.

Auth Method

Username & Password

Username

DBT_PORTFOLIO_TRACKING_SVC

Password

Schema

QA

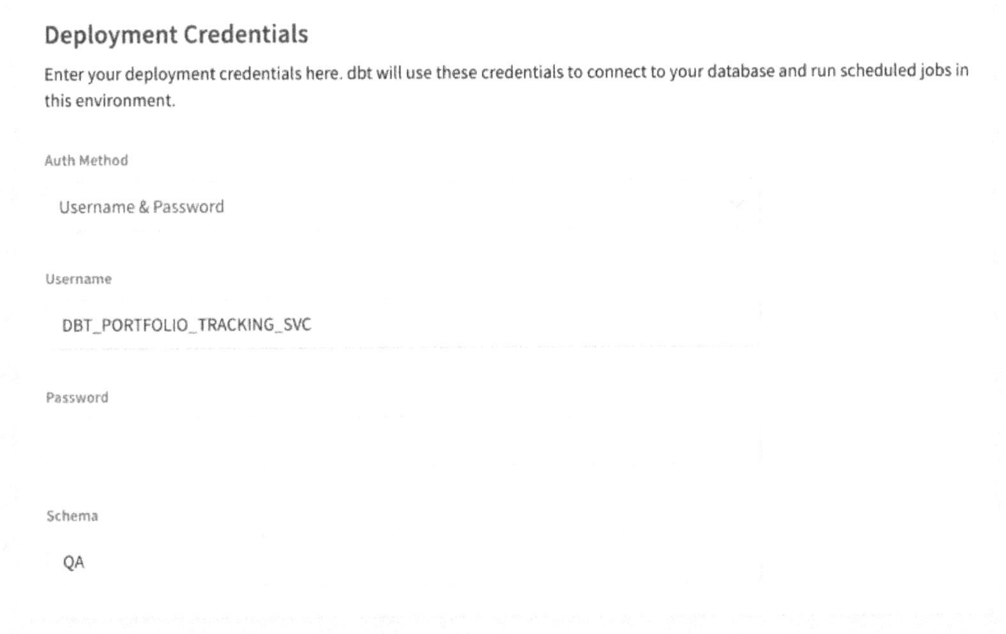

Figure 12.4: Deployment Credentials part of the Create new Environment page

Here, you must configure the service user that dbt will use to deploy and execute the environment and its password. Alternatively, you can provide a username and key pair.

You must enter the **target schema** for the environment. This is the name of the schema when a custom schema is not specified in the code configuration, and it is the prefix of the actual schema name when a custom schema is specified for a dbt object.

5. When you are done configuring the new environment, click the **Save** button at the top of the page.

With that, we have created the QA environment that will deploy the code from the main branch on the selected database, which is the same as the DEV environment since we have not changed it, using the QA schema name when we have no custom schema and the QA prefix where we have one.

Even if it is overkill for our sample case, let's create an environment for production that we will call PROD and that will deploy the code from the PROD branch:

1. Again, go to the **Environments** page by selecting the **Environments** entry from the **Deploy** menu of the main menu at the top of the dbt Cloud page:

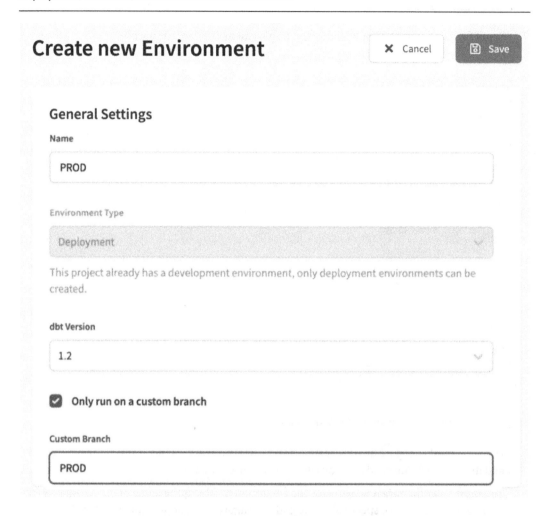

Figure 12.5: General Settings part of the Create new Environment page

Enter PROD as the name of the environment, select one version of dbt to run, activate the **Only run on a custom branch** checkbox, then enter PROD as the custom branch name.

2. Scroll through the **Deployment Connection** part of the page and make changes as you want. For this sample project, we think it's fine to deploy all the environments in the same database using the same role and warehouse, so we won't make any changes, leaving the values as configured in the project connection.

3. Scroll further down to the **Deployment Credentials** part of the page and enter the username and password for the service user used by dbt or a key pair.

At the bottom of the section, enter PROD as the target schema for this environment:

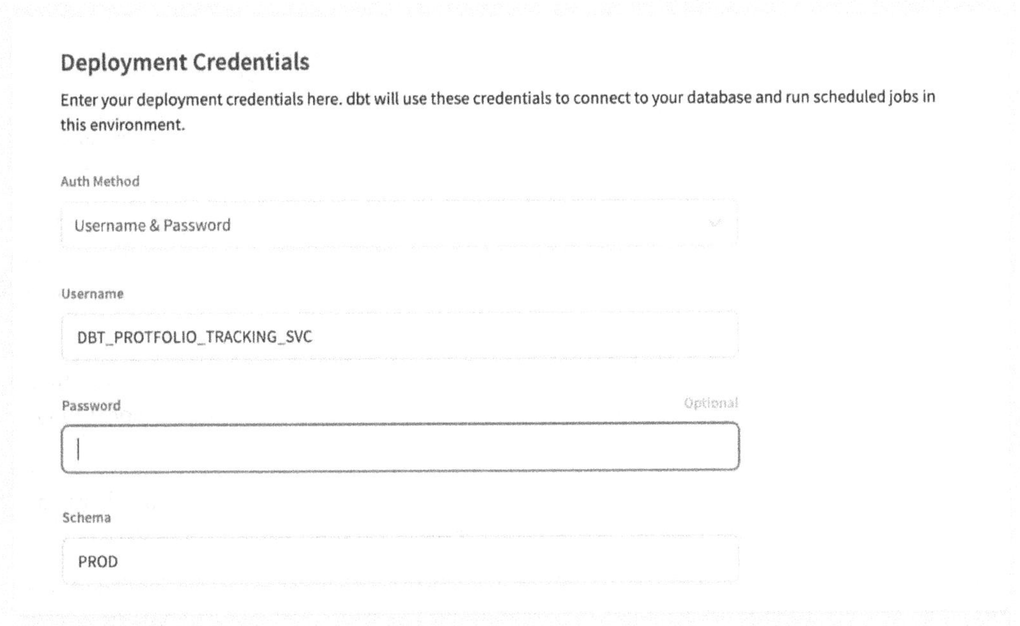

Deployment Credentials

Enter your deployment credentials here. dbt will use these credentials to connect to your database and run scheduled jobs in this environment.

Auth Method

Username & Password

Username

DBT_PROTFOLIO_TRACKING_SVC

Password   Optional

Schema

PROD

Figure 12.6: Deployment Credentials part of the Create new Environment page

4. When you are done, click the **Save** button at the top of the page.

You will now find yourself on the **Environments** page, with three environments defined:

- **Development**: The default development environment created by dbt
- **QA**: The first deployment environment that we have created, which will deploy the main branch
- **PROD**: The second deployment environment that we have created, which will deploy the PROD branch

So far, we have configured some things (listed) in the environments, but not the dbt commands to be executed. These are set into jobs that operate in a specific environment. We will do that in the following section about jobs.

Deciding where to deploy

Before talking about jobs, let's recap your options regarding two of the main decisions in a data platform design: where to deploy each environment and what code to run.

dbt allows you to deploy any environment to a database and target schema of your choice, giving you the freedom to arrange your environments.

The main decision is if you want to have one database for each environment or if you want to host some or all in the same database and differentiate them based on the target schema.

In the case of Snowflake, the difference is minimal as you can easily query across databases and the same role can have privileges across multiple databases. However, in other cases, the difference can be much bigger.

If you decide to have the QA and PROD environments in two different DBs, we suggest using the same target schema for both environments so that the schema and table names will be the same in the two environments.

This will make it very simple to switch clients, such as BI applications, so that they use QA and PROD by just changing the connection string. As an example, this allows you to easily test a report in QA and then switch it to PROD by changing the database you point to.

In terms of what code to run when using the dbt Cloud IDE, this is straightforward as you either name a specific custom branch to be used for the environment or the environment will use the `main` branch.

As a note, consider that you can start jobs on any deployment environment using the dbt Cloud API. In that case, you can override most of the environment settings by providing the optional values in the REST call.

Creating jobs

Now that we have created the environments, it is time to see how we can effectively deploy our code. This is done by creating dbt jobs that run dbt commands.

In essence, a **dbt job** is a set of commands that you want to run on an environment.

You use jobs to organize the operation of your data platform by selecting the commands that you run and deciding on what part of your project each command is applied to by using the dbt node selection syntax (see `https://docs.getdbt.com/reference/node-selection/syntax` for all the details).

Jobs can be scheduled, and they will be triggered by the internal dbt Cloud scheduler, or they can be triggered through an API call. You can also have a job triggered by a webhook when a **Pull Request** (**PR**)is created or updated if you are using one of the Git provider dbt integrations (currently GitHub, GitLab, or Azure DevOps).

Designing your platform execution

Jobs are the base components for designing how your data platform is executed.

You decide where to deploy using the environments and inside one environment, you design what to deploy and its orchestration with jobs.

Orchestration in dbt is a combination of selecting what nodes to run by using the dbt selection syntax in the commands inside your jobs and scheduling the jobs by timer or REST invocation.

The dbt selection syntax leverages the graph of dependencies of the dbt resources, visible as the **lineage graph** in dbt, and other model metadata to select which nodes to run. Then, dbt will run them while respecting their dependencies.

Remember that dbt will always execute the commands while properly orchestrating the execution of the nodes that have been selected by the command, from all the nodes in your project to a single line of dependencies.

> **Tip**
>
> When we talk about dbt commands and the dependency graph, we should use the term nodes or (dbt) resources to identify all types of dbt resources, such as sources, seeds, snapshots, models, tests, analyses, and exposures.
>
> Sometimes, we use the term *models* as they make up most of the nodes, and developers are familiar with the term, but please consider that most of the commands and configuration apply to most node types and we use the term with a general meaning.

Therefore, designing the orchestration of your platform is an act of high-level resource selection. It involves picking the nodes to execute using the high-level selection syntax and then letting dbt do the actual low-level orchestration to run the nodes according to their dependencies.

In practice, you write the commands, pick the nodes the command applies, and then put them in the correct order in a job so that you can run the jobs according to your design and let dbt do the low-level orchestration inside each command's execution.

Our suggestion to keep the resiliency high is to go for the simplest orchestration that works for you, often letting dbt run everything according to their dependencies. Having a default job that executes (almost) everything is a good starting point.

In the next section on advanced automation, we will see that the dbt run-operation command can add any operation on the data platform to our jobs, coded as a dbt macro. This allows us to perform any task, even outside of the normal dbt resource execution, by adding the relevant SQL in the macro called by run-operation.

Such tasks are part of the normal operation of a data platform, such as database maintenance, data ingestion or extraction, and other routine operations.

These commands are generally added at the start or end of a job that is executed with the right periodicity or that needs to use the newly ingested data. In some cases, you can create a job just to run routine operations coded as dbt macros at the right times.

dbt build versus low-level commands

When you are coding in your development environment, it is normal to run the classical, low-level dbt commands that execute one specific type of dbt resource, such as `dbt run`, `dbt test`, or `dbt seed`, as you are just focusing on the small area where you are working.

The recent changes in the dbt IDE that provide a **build** button might change this habit for many developers, making the `build` command the most used.

You can use these low-level commands when you write the jobs to have all the nodes of one type executed together and to have the test run when you decide. They give you full control, which comes with more responsibility and longer job definitions.

As a generally better alternative, you can use the dbt **build** command, which is a high-level command that encapsulates the `snapshot`, `seed`, `run`, and `test` commands and will execute the resources connected to them: snapshots, seeds, and models, along with their tests.

The main difference when using the `build` command is that it will execute and immediately test each node so that nodes that depend on a resource that fails to execute or have a failing test will not be executed.

This is a major improvement for our data quality because when an error occurs, the data from that node is not propagated in our platform, giving us the ability to inspect and fix the problem.

The `build` command makes our life easier, our data better, and our job definition shorter and less error-prone as you pass the eventual selection to only one command.

Therefore, we suggest always using the `build` command in your job definition, unless you want to use the full control provided by the lower-level, type-specific commands.

If you want to stop the execution of the commands in a job when the first error is found, you can add the *global* `--fail-fast` flag to your commands so that they will stop immediately instead of continuing to execute the nodes that do not depend on the node that produced the error.

We will now create a few sample jobs that are useful in most projects and provide you with a sample blueprint for your jobs.

Default job for base operations

In most cases, having a job that builds all the resources daily is a good baseline to provide up-to-date reports that follow the data export cycle from the company data sources.

If you have very expensive nodes that would take a lot to build every day and just change every week or month, it makes sense to exclude them from this "normal day" run and have a specific job to execute such resources when needed.

Similarly, if you have resources that should be run more often or upon specific events, you can create a job for them and schedule them as needed or have them started by a REST API call when the event happens.

In this base job, we want to execute all the resources. So, if we were to use the old-style, low-level dbt commands, the list may look like this:

```
dbt seed
dbt source freshness
dbt test -select source:*
dbt snapshot
dbt run
dbt test -exclude source:*
dbt docs generate
```

In the preceding code, we load the seeds. Then, we test the source data to be sure the input data is fresh (according to the SLA we have defined) and fulfills our expectations.

Once we know that the sources are fine, we run the snapshots and the models, and we complete the run with tests on everything but the sources.

We finish by generating the documentation for our project. Before and after these commands, we might have run-operation commands that run other SQL-based operations.

Let's create the baseline job for our project, using the modern dbt build command:

1. From the main menu, at the top, open the **Deploy** menu and click on the **Jobs** entry:

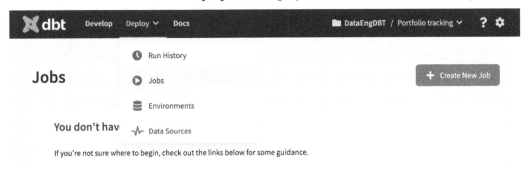

Figure 12.7: The Jobs page and the Deploy menu

Once you're on the **Jobs** page, click the **Create New Job** button at the top right.

2. Start creating a new job by entering its name:

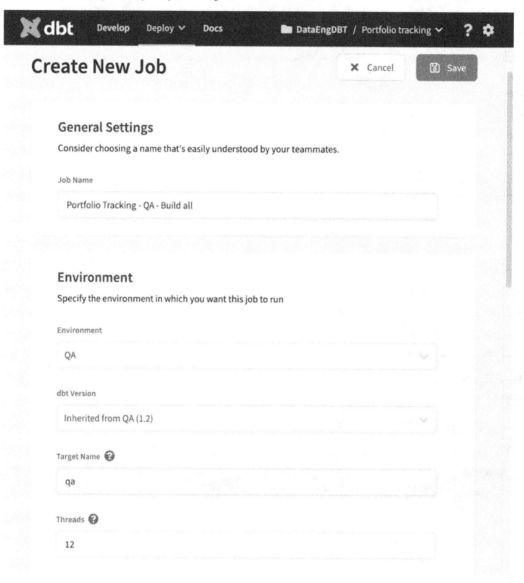

Figure 12.8: The Create New Job page

We suggest starting the job name with the project's name or acronym, the environment acronym, and then a description of the job. This will make it immediately clear which job has failed when you receive a notification once you have multiple dbt projects.

Continue by picking the deployment environment on which to run the job and configure the dbt version to be used (keep the same as the environment).

Then, set a target name that can be used in your code to act differently based on different targets set in different jobs. We set it as the environment name in lowercase.

Finally, pick the number of parallel threads to run. The higher the number, the faster the run will be, as more queries can be executed in parallel. However, once the queries start to compete for resources, there will be contention. dbt will always respect the dependencies, so, at every moment, there are only so many queries that can be run. We usually pick a number around 8 to 12, but it is worth experimenting with this a bit and seeing the effect of different values on your data platform execution time.

3. If your project defines any environment variable, you have a chance to enter a job-specific value for each variable:

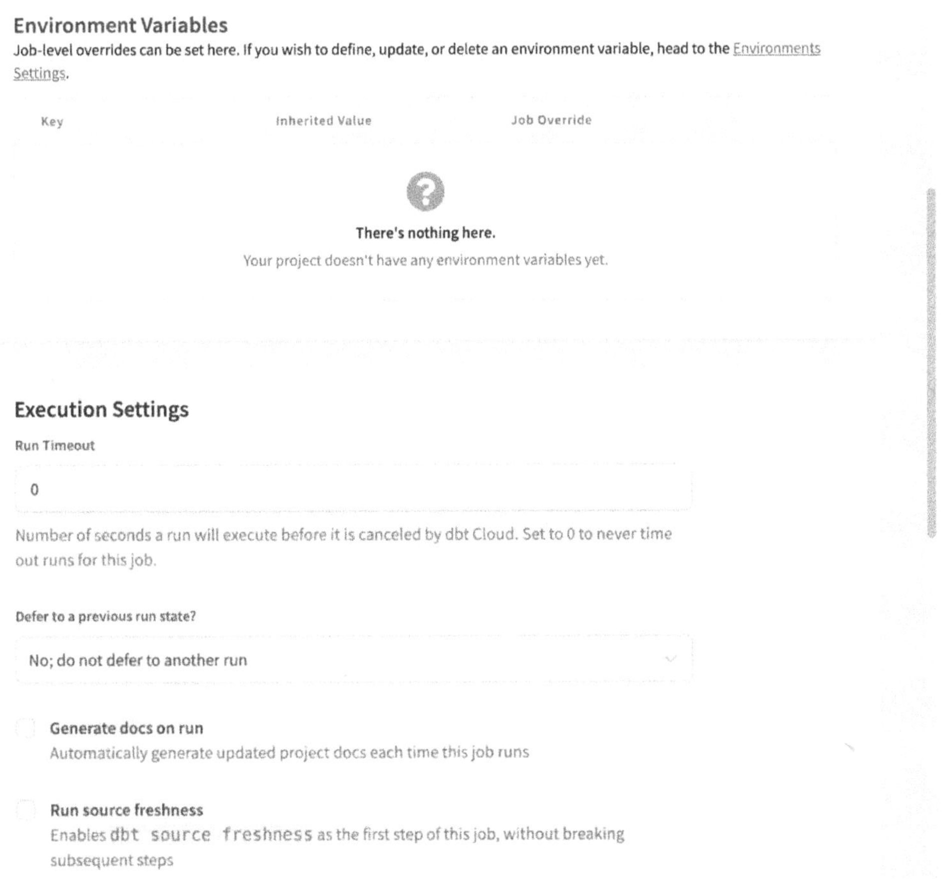

Environment Variables

Job-level overrides can be set here. If you wish to define, update, or delete an environment variable, head to the Environments Settings.

Key	Inherited Value	Job Override

There's nothing here.

Your project doesn't have any environment variables yet.

Execution Settings

Run Timeout

```
0
```

Number of seconds a run will execute before it is canceled by dbt Cloud. Set to 0 to never time out runs for this job.

Defer to a previous run state?

```
No; do not defer to another run
```

☐ **Generate docs on run**
Automatically generate updated project docs each time this job runs

☐ **Run source freshness**
Enables dbt source freshness as the first step of this job, without breaking subsequent steps

Figure 12.9: The Environment Variables section of the Create New Job page

4. In the next section, you can control a few execution settings.

    You can enter a maximum execution time after which the job is canceled by dbt Cloud, but we generally leave it to 0 for daily runs.

    We do not defer to another job execution as we want to compile and build everything at every run:

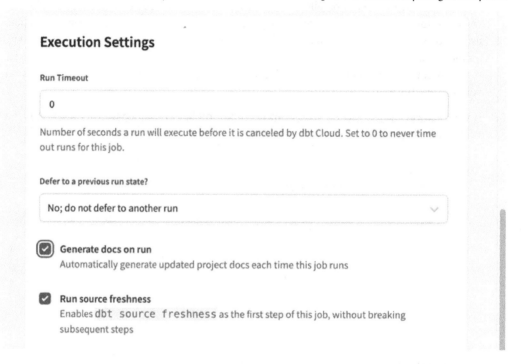

Figure 12.10: The Execution Settings section of the Create New Job page

Finally, we activate the checkboxes to generate the documentation and collect the source freshness data when running the job. In the next section, we will learn how to tell dbt which job to use to publish docs and freshness.

5. The next section is the heart of any job as it is where you list the dbt commands in the order that you want dbt to execute them:

Figure 12.11: The Commands section of the Create New Job page

Since the introduction of the `build` command, this section is much more concise, and the variations are mostly about the selection of what to build and the `run-operation` commands that are added before and after the build.

We have a neat `dbt build` command that will execute everything in the right order and test each node right away.

6. The last step is optional, and it is about setting a schedule to execute the job.

    By activating the **Run on schedule** switch, you can create a schedule with the simplified **Schedule Days** dbt UI by picking on which days and at what hours to run the job, as shown in the following screenshot:

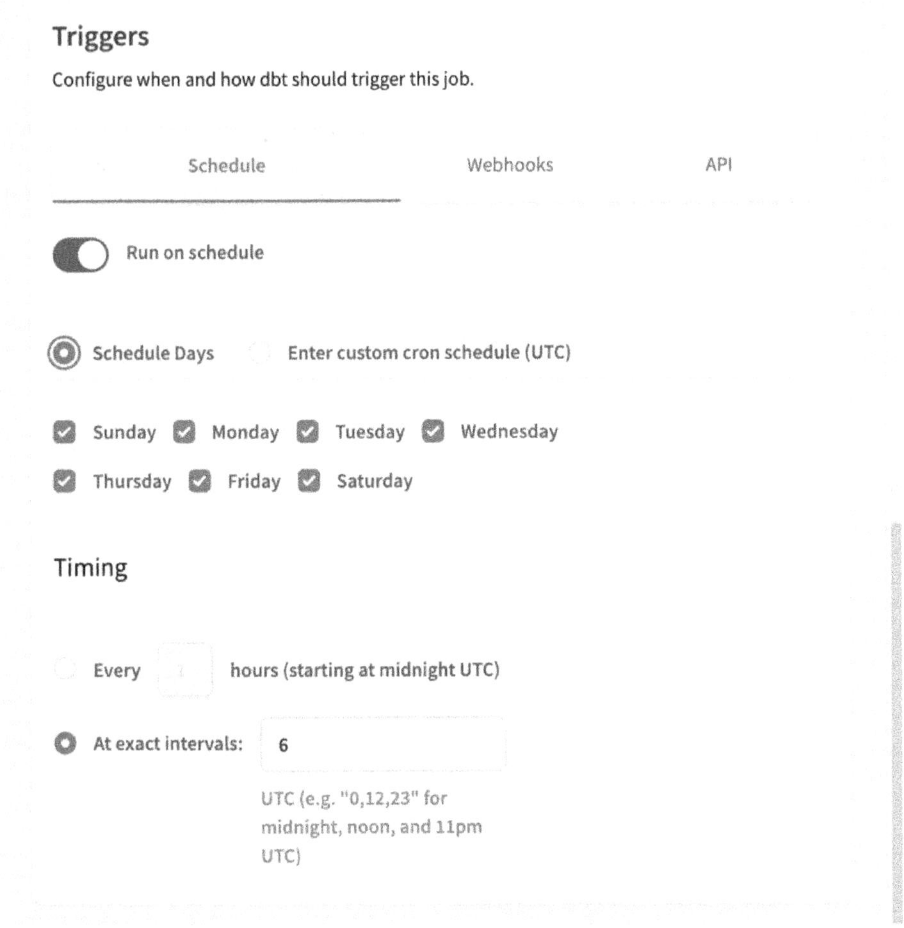

Triggers

Configure when and how dbt should trigger this job.

Schedule	Webhooks	API

Run on schedule

⊙ Schedule Days   ○ Enter custom cron schedule (UTC)

☑ Sunday ☑ Monday ☑ Tuesday ☑ Wednesday
☑ Thursday ☑ Friday ☑ Saturday

Timing

○ Every ⬚ hours (starting at midnight UTC)

● At exact intervals: 6

UTC (e.g. "0,12,23" for midnight, noon, and 11pm UTC)

Figure 12.12: The Triggers section of the Create New Job page

Here, we have configured the job to run every day at 6 A.M. UTC.

As an alternative, you can set a schedule using the **Enter custom cron schedule (UTC)** dbt UI, which allows you to enter a **cron** configuration string:

Figure 12.13: Details about cron scheduling on the Create New Job page

To help yourself, set a cron string that does exactly what you want. You can try it out and tweak it at `https://crontab.guru/`.

Once you have completed the setup, click on the **Save** button at the top right.

With that, we have created a new job that will build all dbt resources according to our schedule, but of course, you can always run any job manually by clicking the **Run now** button on the job's specific page, which you can reach by clicking on the job name on the **Jobs** page. You can reach it from the **Jobs** entry under **Deploy** in the main menu:

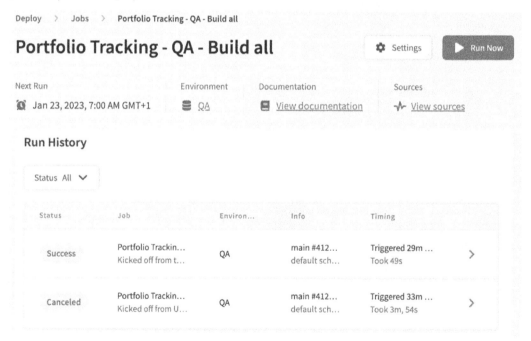

Figure 12.14: A specific job's page

The job's page provides the **Settings** button so that you can edit the job and the **Run Now** button so that you can immediately enqueue one execution of the job. It also lists some information about the job, such as the timestamp of the next run, the deployment environment used, and a link to the source freshness report. Lower on the page, you can find the full run history for the job.

Click the **Run Now** button to start a new instance of the job. Click on the new line that appears in the **Run History** area to go to the **Run Overview** page:

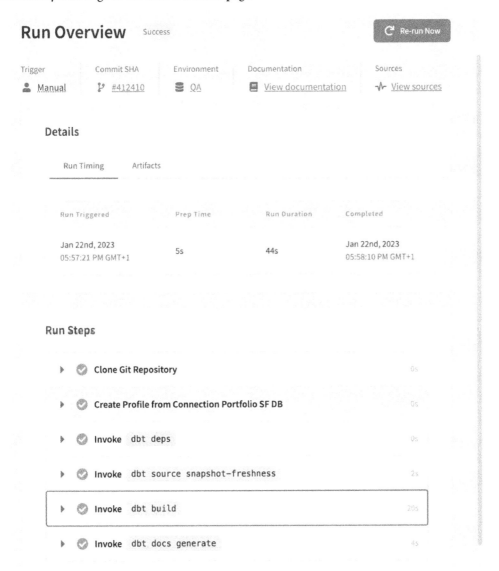

Figure 12.15: A job's Run Overview page

Now that our job has run and been completed nicely, collecting the source freshness and generating the automatic documentation in the process, let's see how to use them.

Setting the job that builds documentation and the freshness report

In dbt Cloud, you can browse the documentation that is automatically generated by the project structure, the content of the data platform, and also the developer's input in the YAML files.

Later in this chapter, we will look in more detail at producing good documentation for your project.

Similarly, dbt can produce a very useful report about the freshness of the project's source data.

Here, we will concentrate on how to configure from which job to pick the generated documentation and source freshness data.

These are project-wide configurations, so you have to go to the **Project Details** page by selecting **Account Settings** from the cog menu in the top right: ✿

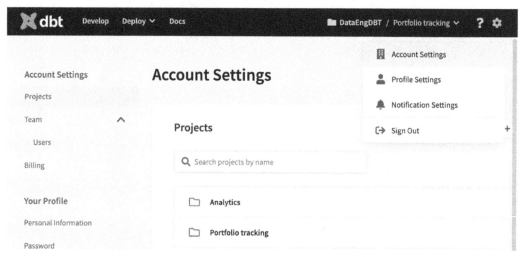

Figure 12.16: The top of the Account Settings page and the open settings menu

Then, select the **Projects** entry in the menu on the left and click on your project in the **Projects** section of the **Account Settings** page.

Once on the **Project Details** page, scroll down to the bottom of the page to find the **Artifacts** section.

Open the dropdown under **Documentation** to select the job to use for the documentation artifacts:

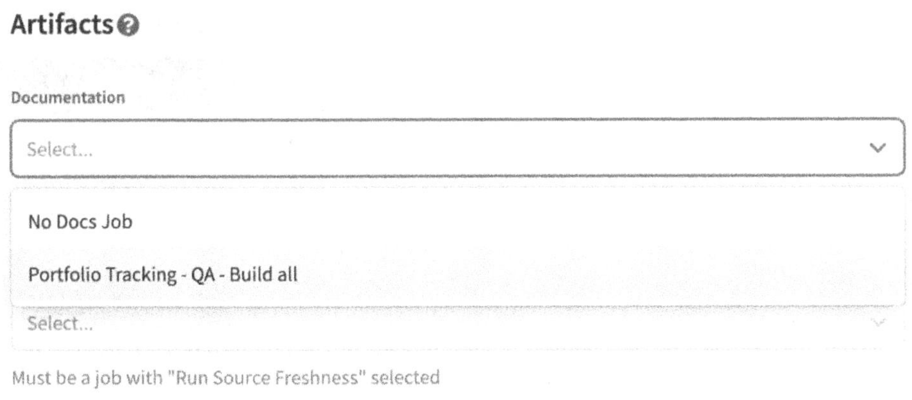

Artifacts ❓

Documentation

Select...	⌄

No Docs Job

Portfolio Tracking - QA - Build all

Select...	⌄

Must be a job with "Run Source Freshness" selected

Figure 12.17: The Documentation dropdown in the Artifacts section of the Project Details page

Open the dropdown under **Source Freshness** to select the job to use for the source freshness artifacts:

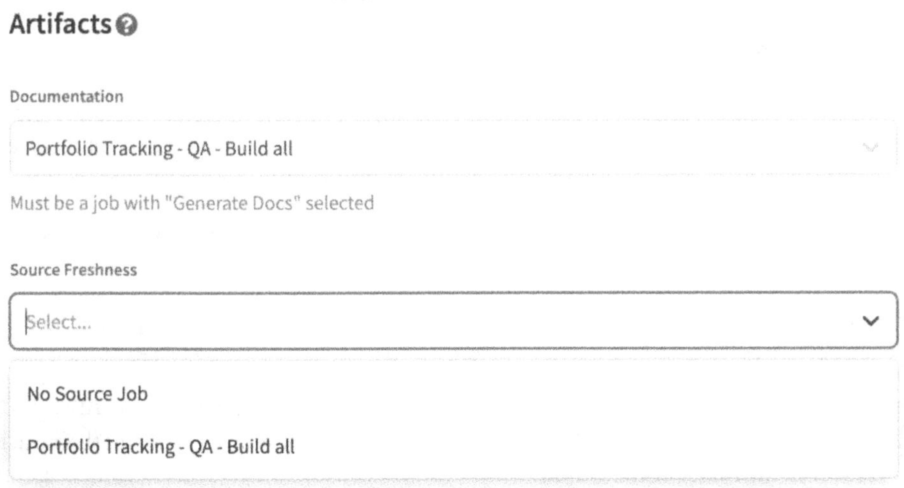

Artifacts ❓

Documentation

Portfolio Tracking - QA - Build all	⌄

Must be a job with "Generate Docs" selected

Source Freshness

Select...	⌄

No Source Job

Portfolio Tracking - QA - Build all

Figure 12.18: The Source Freshness dropdown in the Artifacts section of the Project Details page

Once you've selected the jobs to provide the artifacts, click the **Save** button at the bottom:

Figure 12.19: The open Deploy entry in the main menu

Once you have selected the jobs to provide the artifacts, the menus to access the documentation (**Docs** in the main menu) and the freshness report (**Data Sources** under the **Deploy** menu) become active.

After the jobs you have selected have run at least once, with the checkbox to generate the artifacts active, the freshness report and documentation will be available.

Special job – loading more frequent data

One of the great features of dbt is its ability to understand the graph of relationships between the models and use it to execute the needed commands in the correct order to complete all or even just part of our project.

This means that we do not need to explicitly maintain the orchestration as dbt will generate the correct orchestration automatically based on the selectors that we apply to the commands.

dbt offers a simple yet powerful node selection syntax that allows us to direct dbt to apply the commands to exactly the part of the lineage graph that we want.

In this section, we will use this to make a job that executes only what depends on the ABC_BANK_ POSITION source. We will then be able to schedule this job to run more frequently than the base job that executes all the nodes of the graph.

The + graph operator allows you to instruct dbt to also apply the command to the parents of the model if you place the + operator to the left of the model name, and to the children of the model if you place the + operator to the right of the model name.

By applying the + operator to the right of a source model, we can build everything that depends on it.

A single command can have multiple model specifications. They are unioned if they are separated by a space and intersected if separated by a comma (with no spaces around). Space and comma are set graph operators.

As an example, +MODEL will apply to MODEL and its parents, MODEL+ will apply to MODEL and its children, and +MODEL+ will apply to MODEL parents and children.

The dbt cmd +mod_A mod_B+ command would apply to mod_A with its parents, and mod_B with its children, in the correct dependency order and without duplicates.

Let's make a job that executes what depends on the ABC_BANK_POSITION source:

1. Select **Deploy | Jobs** from the main menu to go to the **Jobs** page. Then, click the **Create New Job** button to start the job creation wizard, as we did in the previous section for the baseline job.

2. In the **Create New Job** page, enter Portfolio Tracking - QA - Load new position data as the job's name in the **General Settings** section.

    Select QA as the environment, qa as the target name, and 12 as the number of threads in the **Environment** section.

3. Move to the **Execution Settings** section and change the command, as follows:

    ```
    dbt build -s source:abc_bank.ABC_BANK_POSITION+
    ```

    The preceding command will apply the build command to all models that depend on the ABC_BANK_POSITION source:

Figure 12.20: Lineage graph of nodes depending on the ABC_BANK_POSITION source

    You can visualize the graph for each dbt resource by opening the resource and looking at the lineage graph in the IDE or by looking at the graph in the generated docs for the resource. The preceding screenshot shows the lineage graph in the IDE.

4. If you want, you can add a schedule to run this specific job and then click the **Save** button.

5. If you want, you can click the **Run Now** button on the job page to confirm that all works as expected.

You have now added a second job to your project to perform the specialized task of refreshing the data, depending on one source.

Similarly, you could create a job that refreshes a full data mart by building all the predecessors, with a syntax such as dbt build -s +marts.portfolio.

Designing the orchestration of your data platform with dbt means planning what sets of resources to execute at the right frequency or following a REST call.

The suggestion is, as always, to keep it as simple as possible, grouping the resources that have the same frequency and using the selection syntax to write resilient commands, using source systems (or specific sources) and data marts as the high-level logical specification of what to run (independent by specific model names), and working with the graph operators to include what is needed.

This often boils down to building all that is needed for a data mart or everything that depends on a certain data source or a specific set of source tables. Your mileage may vary and there are good reasons to craft other kinds of selections.

Last but not least, remember that you can apply the selection syntax to any dbt command, so you can create jobs that just test specific models, sources, or data marts and use them to notify people of eventual issues.

Special job – full refreshes and ad hoc commands

Another type of job that we want to introduce is a job that you could see as the equivalent of the command line of the IDE: a job to execute specific one-off commands on a specific environment.

Some reasons to have such a job are as follows:

- To maintain alignment between the different environments, we do not want to allow developers to execute manual, unaudited SQL commands on any environment that is not their dev environment. Experience shows that manual commands are the recipe for divergent environments, which, in turn, defeats the purpose of having them. Without full alignment, something that works well in one environment is not guaranteed to work in another.

- We need a way to perform maintenance operations. In general, we can perform them using `run-operation`, which we will see in the next section, but in some cases, it is simpler and safer to just run a dbt command.

- If you use variables or environment variables to drive your process, you will have default values set in YAML files or in the periodic jobs that run the processes. Sometimes, you might want to do a limited, special run with different parameters without editing the main periodic job. Consider, as an example, re-running only a subset of the graph reading the last month of ingested data instead of the last couple of days, as done in the usual job.

- Doing special runs to reset some incremental tables (using the `-full-refresh` option) when you want to purge the old data or apply changes to the schema (also purging the old data). The alternative is to write a migration, which is a set of SQL commands to alter the table or its content, as we will see in the next section.

Having a single job that you use to do all these special, one-off runs makes it very easy to look back to find details of such special runs and gives you the peace of mind that the execution and its logs are stored and well documented, contrary to the alternative of temporarily changing some periodic job.

In our sample project, we do not have incremental tables yet as the changes in the incoming data are handled using the dbt snapshot feature. However, in the next chapter, we will show you how using insert-only incremental models provides more flexibility and much better performance on cloud platforms, allowing you to handle big volumes of frequently changing data.

Let's make another job for these special runs:

1. Select **Deploy** | **Jobs** from the main menu to go to the **Jobs** page. Then, click the **Create New Job** button to start the job creation wizard, as we did in the previous section for the baseline job.

2. On the **Create New Job** page, enter `Portfolio Tracking - QA - manual runs` as the job name in the **General Settings** section.

    Select QA as the environment, qa as the target name, and 12 as the number of threads in the **Environment** section.

3. Move to the **Execution Settings** section and change the command as follows:

    ```
    dbt build -s REF_POSITION_ABC_BANK --full-refresh
    ```

    The preceding command will apply the build command with the `full-refresh` flag, which recreates incremental tables, to the `REF_POSITION_ABC_BANK` model. As this is not an incremental model, the `full-refresh` option will have no special effect, but it is introduced here to illustrate how it can be used.

4. Do not add a schedule to this job as it will always be run once and manually after editing the commands. Click the **Save** button to save the job. There's no sense in running it now.

We have created this job, so if you need to run a one-off command on the QA environment, you now have a convenient way to do so. Also, remember that the goal is to keep the environments aligned, and that is much easier if we just run dbt commands. We suggest to create a similar job for each environment.

Designing the architecture of your data platform

By now, you have seen the main dbt elements that delineate the architecture of your platform by deciding what is deployed, where it is deployed, and how everything is orchestrated.

Let's recap the main elements that influence the architecture:

*   The **environment** is used to select the main part of where your platform is deployed by picking the database to use, the target schema (the prefix used for all schemata in the environment), the user and role used to connect to the database, and the warehouse used to run the dbt commands.

*   The **job** is used to select what to run and when. Using jobs, you can orchestrate the execution of your data platform

- The **main configuration file**, `dbt_project.yml`, used together with the file structure to organize your models, is used to add custom schemata to the target schema provided by the environment, allowing you to divide and organize the tables and views of an environment into multiple schemata.

- In the case of very big data platforms or approaches where you prefer to compose the final architecture using loosely coupled domains instead of a monolithic platform, such as in a **data mesh,** you can develop each domain in its own dbt project and use sources to declare dependencies clearly.

You should now be able to use the preceding elements to design the architecture of your projects and deploy the dbt-generated objects according to your wishes.

In any case, consider that most of the settings provided by these elements can be overridden by using the `config()` macro or configurations embedded in YAML files, so some discipline is useful to avoid surprises and puzzled colleagues.

Notifications

Effective alerting allows your data team to stay on top of issues that are bound to happen proactively and be ahead of your (internal) customers, allowing you to react and service them professionally, instead of firefighting when caught red-handed.

dbt allows you to send notifications via email or on a Slack channel.

In this section, we will show you how to set up email notifications that are available for all and can be tailored for each dbt user, project, and job. We will leave out Slack notifications as they need a Slack subscription and they are set up at the account level, sending the notification in the desired Slack channel.

Let's set up the notifications for our sample project:

1. To set up the notifications, select **Notifications Settings** from the cog menu in the top-right area of dbt Cloud:

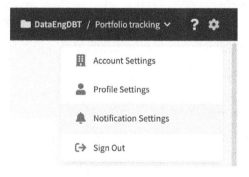

Figure 12.21: The open settings menu

2. Select the user, as well as the environment for which you want to set up the alerts, then click the **Edit** button.

3. On the **Email Notifications** page, you can now select, using the checkboxes, for which jobs of the selected environment the user will receive notifications based on the three available events: job succeeds, job fails, or job is canceled:

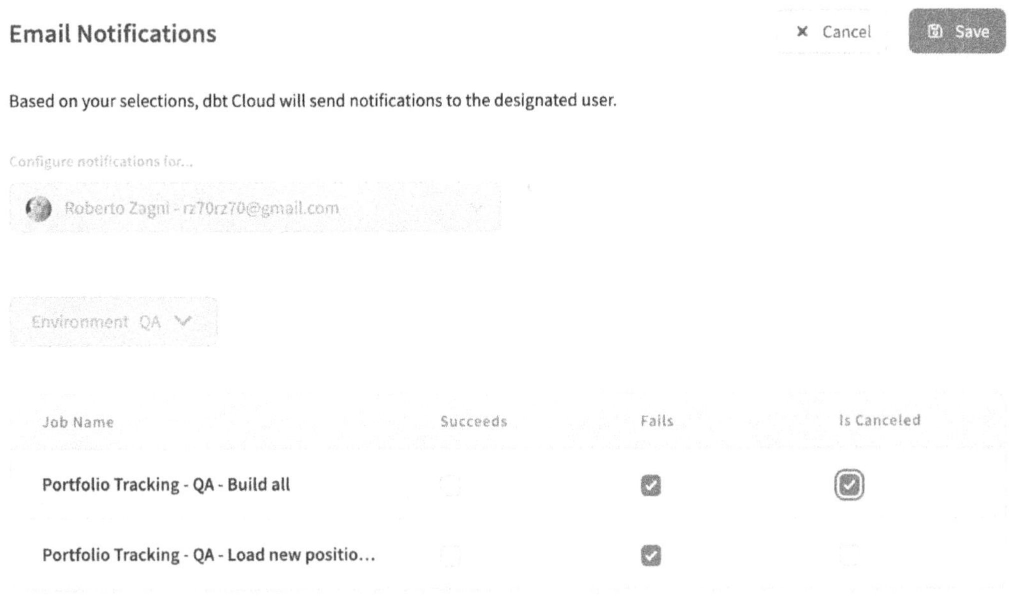

Email Notifications   ✕ Cancel   🖫 Save

Based on your selections, dbt Cloud will send notifications to the designated user.

Configure notifications for...

🔵 Roberto Zagni - rz70rz70@gmail.com   ⌄

Environment QA ⌄

Job Name	Succeeds	Fails	Is Canceled
Portfolio Tracking - QA - Build all	☐	☑	☑
Portfolio Tracking - QA - Load new positio...	☐	☑	

Figure 12.22: Details of the Email Notifications page

4. Once you have made your selection, you can click the **Save** button.

This is all that you need to do to set up email alerts for you or any of your colleagues added to your dbt account.

If you have too many notifications, you can reset all of them with a single button, as shown in the following screenshot:

Don't want to receive any of these emails? You can unsubscribe from all email notifications by clicking the button below.

Unsubscribe from all email notifications

Figure 12.23: Email notification unsubscribe button

In the next section, we will look into some advanced automation features.

Advanced automation – hooks and run-operations

With environments, jobs, and configuration, you can design your architecture and deploy and run your data platform using one or more dbt projects, but other activities are needed to keep a data platform up and running beyond data transformations.

In this chapter, we will look at two advanced functionalities, `hook` and `run-operation` commands, and the use of the latter to handle the database migrations that are not handled by dbt.

Both these functionalities allow you to execute the arbitrary SQL that you need to complement dbt transformations. It could be from creating user functions to managing grants or doing database-specific operations such as cloning or vacuuming or creating shares or running any other command besides creating tables/views and transforming data.

The main difference between the two functionalities lies in when the SQL must be activated: connected to some model life cycle or independent of it.

Hooks

The **hook** feature allows you to attach the execution of arbitrary SQL to specific moments in the life cycle of models and project runs.

You can put a piece of SQL into a hook directly or call a macro that will return the SQL to be executed and dbt will execute the SQL at the right time.

The available hooks are as follows:

- **pre-hook**: The SQL will be run before building the dbt node it is attached to
- **post-hook**: The SQL will be run after building the dbt node it is attached to
- **on-run-start**: The SQL will be run at the beginning of the dbt command
- **on-run-end**: The SQL will be run at the end of the dbt command

Hooks allow you to run arbitrary SQL, but the most common use has been to apply grants to models when they are built. This is still a way to achieve the level of control on grants that you wish, even if the new dbt grant feature that's been available since dbt 1.2 now allows you to configure grants in a declarative way.

With a touch of creativity, we have used a post-hook configured in the main project's config file to set the runtime timestamp as the LOAD_TS column in our seed:

```
ABC_Bank_SECURITY_INFO:
  +post-hook:
    - "UPDATE {{ this }} SET LOAD_TS =
      '{{ run_started_at }}' WHERE LOAD_TS is null"
```

```
        +column_types:
          LOAD_TS: TIMESTAMP
```

The preceding snippet updates the seed table after it has been loaded by replacing the null values in the LOAD_TS column with the run timestamp. All rows have null as we did not provide any timestamp in the seed file. Note that we need to configure the column to be of the right type; otherwise, Snowflake would infer it to be of the Number type, which is the default when all values are null.

To generate the SQL for a hook with a macro, use syntax like the following:

```
    some_model:
      +post-hook: "{{ my_macro(this, 'a string') }}"
```

The preceding snippet calls the my_macro macro while passing two arguments: the this variable, which represents the current model, and the a string string. The macro will produce a SQL command that will be executed after the some_model node is built.

Note that while you can attach pre and post-hooks to individual models, you can also attach them to an entire folder in the dbt_project.yml config file; the hooks will be executed for each model in the folder (and its subfolders).

We have seen pre-hooks used to delete the records for the current period that was being re-written by the model from an incremental table. While this is a well-known practice when using transactional DBs for data warehousing, it conflicts both with dbt and modern columnar cloud database's way of working. We encourage you to find a different pattern, avoiding deletions and updates, which are much more expensive than inserts in cloud platforms.

While all hooks can access the context available in the model, consider that the

on-run-end hook has some extra context variables:

- The schemas variable contains the list of schemas that contain models that have been built by dbt in the current run

- The database_schemas variable is like the schemas variable but contains tuples (database, schema) in place of schema names

- The results variable contains a list with a result object for each node that has been built by dbt in the current run. This corresponds to the data that will populate the result's JSON artifact.

You can leverage the context available to a hook to write direct SQL commands or macros that use this information to produce the SQL or just to save the context information.

Run-operations

The **run-operation** command allows you to activate a macro from the command line or as part of a job, giving you the ability to extend dbt functionality by executing arbitrary SQL commands available in your platform coupled with business logic.

Some examples of common operations are as follows:

- **Data ingestion**: Using macros to configure external tables, or to ingest data from files residing in data lakes. We will look more into this topic in chapter 15 where we will talk about ingestion patterns.

- **Migrations**: Perform the evolutionary changes to your database objects that are not handled by dbt, such as dropping unused tables or managing individual fields. The following section introduces the migration concept and how to use them.

- **Post-run operations**: Once your transformations are done, there are extra things that you might want to do, such as managing grants, writing audit information, profiling tables, producing extra documentation, and so on.

You can run a macro using a hook, but then you need to attach it to a node being run. The `run-operation` command allows you to run macros independently from models. You might have a job that just uses `run-operation` commands to run macros and no model.

The syntax to invoke a macro using `run-operation` is as follows:

```
dbt run-operation {macro} --args {args}
```

At a minimum, you must pass the macro name without any parameter. This makes it very easy to run any macro that does not require any parameter with the `dbt run-operation macro_name` command.

If you need to pass or override the default value for any argument, you can do so by passing a dictionary while providing the argument's name and argument value as a YAML string – for example, `--args '{arg_name: arg_value, arg_name2: arg_value2}'`.

Note the quotes surrounding the braces as this must be a YAML string.

An important difference between `hook` and `run-operation` commands is that, with a hook, you have to pass the SQL, while with a `run-operation`, your macro is executed and it must explicitly do all the needed actions. So, if you want to run any SQL, you must do so using *statement blocks* or the `run_query` macro.

The latter is much easier to use as you pass the SQL as a string and you get a result, with a common pattern of use being the following:

```
{% set sql %}
  -- write some SQL or generate it with logic
```

```
{% endset %}
{% do run_sql(sql) %}   -- if you do not need the results
{% set results = run_query(sql) %}     -- if you need them
```

In the preceding snippet, you use a set Jinja block to write or generate the SQL that you want to execute as text, then you call the run_sql macro while passing the sql string. You can use the do operator if you do not need the result of your query or the set operator if you want to get hold of the result object.

Table migrations

Dbt manages most of the DDL and DML commands needed to create and maintain the schemata, tables, and views in your data platform, but in some cases, you might want to do things that dbt does not do for you.

The most common things that you need to manage by yourself are as follows:

- **Deleting tables and views that are not in use anymore.**

  As an example, when you rename a model after running it, the object with the old name will not be deleted by dbt because it cannot know if it is safe to delete it or not. A table could contain useful data or can still be used by other systems.

- **Evolving incremental tables.**

  While normal tables and views are recreated at every run, and therefore any change can be easily applied, the incremental tables are the ones that retain data across executions. Whether you want to rename them or operate on their columns, often, you cannot just drop and recreate them; instead, you have to manually evolve them.

- **Performing bulk operations on data.**

  While editing/tampering with data in a data warehouse should not happen often, there are cases when you will want to edit/fix or delete data. One example might be changing the end-of-time date from 2100-12-31 to 9999-9-9 in a table.

All these operations can be done by writing simple SQL statements, such as drop table or alter table, which developers should be allowed to run in their development environment, but should not run in shared environments such as QA and PROD.

Once a resource has been published in a shared environment, it becomes part of the public API of your data platform, so you have to manage its evolution and its eventual deletion explicitly, guaranteeing that the changes are aligned across environments and released in sync with the code of each environment.

By using some conventions and some scripting inside macros activated by a run-operation, you can create a simple setup that allows you to quickly write the migrations that you need.

A **database migration** is a set of SQL commands that take your database from one version to another. The concept is widely used in application development, where the database has to stay strictly in sync with the code of the application, and database changes are usually associated with application releases.

In data warehousing with dbt our database is constantly changing because of dbt running code from an environment's branch. As discussed previously we do need a way to apply changes that dbt will not run by himself so that they are synchronized with the code being run by dbt.

We can achieve this by having a `run-operation` executed as the first step of our jobs and running the SQL to apply the changes that our code requires, such as changing the name of a column or changing the value of a reference value.

The macro with the SQL code will be merged into `master`, together with the code requiring the change, so that they will both be applied in QA together. They will stay there for a while until they are promoted to PROD and any other environment that you have where the change and the new code should be applied.

One key requirement of the macros running and applying the changes is idempotency, which is the ability to run the macro an arbitrary number of times, always obtaining the same final result and no errors.

Luckily, most SQL commands have clauses such as `IF NOT EXISTS` or `IF EXISTS`, which simplify our task of writing idempotent commands. In other cases, we must be creative and resort to querying the information schema to check if we need to apply a change or not.

As an example, if we have renamed the `REF_POSITION_ABC_BANK` model from its previous name of `REF_ABC_BANK_POSITIONS`, the old table would still be around in all the environments where we had released it. To remove it, we could write the following migration macro:

```
{% macro drop_REF_ABC_BANK_POSITIONS() -%}
DROP TABLE IF EXISTS {{target.database}}.{{target.schema}}_REFINED.
REF_ABC_BANK_POSITIONS;
{%- endmacro %}
```

By adding the `IF EXISTS` clause, we are sure that we can run the macro as many times as we wish and at the end, the `REF_ABC_BANK_POSITIONS` table will be gone.

We have used the `target` object so that the macro will operate on the database and schema of the environment where it is being run, ensuring that the action is performed where it is needed.

To perform the migration in our DEV environment, we can run the following dbt command in our IDE command line:

```
dbt run-operation drop_REF_ABC_BANK_POSITIONS
```

To have the migration applied in QA, PROD, or any other environment, we have to add the preceding command line at the beginning of the main job, or add to the ad hoc job and run it immediately if it does not require synchronization with the code.

Organizing migrations

Whenever we need to run a migration, we could write a new macro for it and add an ad hoc
run-operation command to our jobs to call it, but that would be a lot of manual work every time
and it would also be error-prone.

We propose a better setup where we have a macro named run_migrations that is always called at
the beginning of the main job so that it is synchronized with code runs, and it will call the individual
migration macros as needed.

We also suggest organizing the migration macros by creating a migrations folder under the
macros folder to hold the migrations in active use and an ARCHIVE folder inside it, to hold the
migration used in the past, as shown in the following screenshot:

Figure 12.24: Sample organization for migration macros

The run_migrations macro would look like this:

```
{% macro run_migrations(
        database = target.database,
        schema_prefix = target.schema
) -%}
{% do log(
"Running V001_drop_example_table migration with database = "
~ database ~ ", schema_prefix = " ~ schema_prefix,
        info=True) %}
{% do run_query(V001_drop_example_table(
                    database, schema_prefix) ) %}
{#% do log("No migrations to run.", info=True) %#}
-- Remove # to uncomment if no migration to run
{%- endmacro %}
```

Let's look at the preceding run_migrations macro:

- It has database and schema_prefix arguments that have the default values that we want
  for them, so we do not need to pass the values unless we want to override them for some reason.

- For each migration to run, there is a `log` and a `run` statement. The log is useful to show in the log the migration being run and the database and schema used.

- There is a commented-out `log` statement to use when there are no migrations.

We have also created a sample migration, named `V001_drop_example_table`, to show the naming convention and how simple it becomes to write additional migrations and add them to the `run_migrations` macro:

```
{% macro V001_drop_example_table(
        database = target.database,
        schema_prefix = target.schema
) -%}
DROP TABLE IF EXISTS
{{database}}.{{schema_prefix}}_STAGING.TABLE_XXX ;
{%- endmacro %}
```

The preceding sample migration has the same arguments as the `run_migrations` macro and exemplifies the use of the arguments to run the SQL command in the correct database and schema according to the environment in use.

By using this simple setup, all your developers can add migrations that will evolve the tables in sync with the release of the code that uses the new names of tables and columns, keeping the release process very smooth.

Once a migration has done what it was written for in all the needed environments it can be removed from the `run_migrations` macro and the file can be moved to the `ARCHIVED` folder.

Documentation

A great advantage of working with dbt is the documentation that is produced automatically or with minimal effort by the developers.

In this section, we will touch on the following documentation-related features:

- **Lineage graph**: This is the graph of dependencies between the models in our project that dbt presents us with in the IDE and the generated documentation

- **Generated documentation**: This is an automatically generated website describing all the models using human-provided and generated metadata

- **Source freshness report**: This is a web page that checks how fresh the data in the sources is and verifies it against the SLA set in the YAML files

- **Exposures**: This feature allows us to describe the dependencies of external objects such as dashboards or ML models on dbt-managed models

- **Markdown documentation**: This allows us to use Markdown in all description fields to produce neatly formatted documentation

By using and combining these features, we can provide our developers, business, and power users with a simple way to navigate and understand our project and the models that we have created.

Lineage graph

We briefly introduced the lineage graph at the end of *Chapter 2* when looking at the IDE, the default dbt project, and the introduction of the `ref` and `source` functions.

The lineage graph shows, in an easy-to-use way, the **Directed Acyclic Graph** (**DAG**) of your project. The fact that your models must be organized in a directed graph that cannot have a cycle is a key feature of dbt. This promotes good development practices and allows dbt to manage the execution simply and predictably.

In the context of documentation, we feel that it's important to note that having the lineage graph available in real time while coding is a huge saver of mental effort as you can use it not only to quickly jump to other models by double-clicking them, without the need to search for them, but it allows you to visually see the structure of your transformations without the need to keep it in mind or to create and maintain such documentation:

Figure 12.25: Real-time lineage in the dbt Cloud IDE

In the preceding screenshot, you can see that seeds and snapshots have different icons than models and that we have dragged the node representation to show the organization in layers, with, as an example, the STG and SNSH making the staging or storage layer.

The lineage graph is also available in the generated documentation, with the difference that, in the IDE, you always have the lineage of the models connected with the model you have opened, while in the docs, you can explore the full lineage graph of the project, as well as focus on a single node to show the same view that you have in the IDE.

If you are using dbt Core, you will not have the real-time lineage when editing, which is a serious limitation to your ease of work, but you will have the same access to the lineage in the generated documentation:

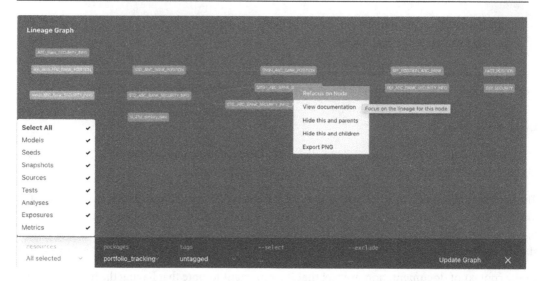

Figure 12.26: Full lineage of the project in the generated documentation

One useful feature of the lineage graph in the documentation is the right-click contextual menu, which allows you to quickly refocus on one node or jump to the documentation for a node and hide part of the graph.

Another useful feature is the ability to enable and disable the different types of nodes that make up the dbt lineage graph. Enabling and disabling the changed nodes are colored in gray, showing them.

Last, but not least, in the **tags**, **--select**, and **--exclude** boxes, you can try out selection syntax expressions and visually see what nodes get selected. This is a handy way to try out and see the effect of complex selections that you plan to use in commands.

dbt-generated documentation

One of the hallmark differences of dbt versus any other tool to transform data is the ease to produce useful documentation with little effort, making your data platform more valuable as it can be better understood and used by a wider range of users.

Automatic generation of web-based documentation is not new, as Java already had it in the nineties.

The merit of dbt is making the creation of useful, up-to-date, and easy-to-read documentation simple by collecting metadata and information from your code, your tests, your database, and naturally from the doc-oriented features such as exposures and description properties:

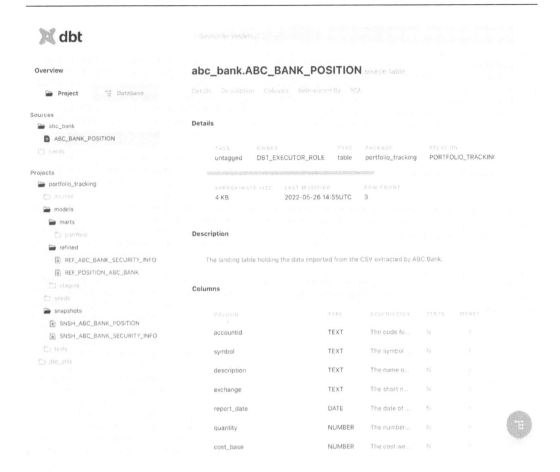

Figure 12.27: Doc page for a source node – project view

The simplicity of the navigation and the automatically generated doc site makes dbt docs accessible also by non-developers that just need a reader account.

dbt allows you to complement the information that's automatically generated with manually provided descriptions that can be simple strings or even consist of Markdown docklets, contained in .md files.

On the left pane of the doc site, you have a navigation area that gives you access to both the project layout, as shown in the previous screenshot, and the database layout, shown in the following screenshot, making it easy for you to find the node that you want:

Figure 12.28: Doc page for a model node with a relation test – database view

The bulk of the information used in the generated docs is provided by the following:

- The `ref` and `source` functions, which provide the dependencies of the nodes.

- The *tests* applied to the tables and columns in YAML files.

  Tests are your main line of defense for data quality, but they also produce extremely valuable information in docs as they make data assumptions explicit.

- The *manual descriptions* provided by the description property of nodes in YAML files.

  Whether you just use strings or you produce well-formatted and visually pleasing Markdown descriptions for tables, columns, and exposures, the manually entered information allows you to empower your data users by letting them know valuable information such as the definition, the semantic, or the unit of measure of columns in your tables.

- The *source declarations* in YAML files.

  You can use tests and descriptions to describe your input data declared as sources, making input requirements/expectations explicit.

- The information collected by querying the *database*.

  This provides quantitative information about your tables.

- The *exposures* defined in YAML files.

  They allow you to describe how your models are used outside of dbt, and provide rich descriptions of your dataset for the users of such external reports/tools/ML models.

On the doc site, you can access the overall or a specific model's lineage graph, as shown in the previous section, by clicking the round icon in the lower-right corner. You can use the lineage graph as a third option to navigate the docs.

Source freshness report

Would your users be happy if your platform is running perfectly and all the tests passed but the data is a few days, weeks, or months old?

Are you checking that all your inputs are fresh every day? Or are you at risk of receiving a not-so-nice email asking you why there is no data for the last week in some report? Can you quickly find what data gets into such a report and what source is stale?

dbt allows you to stop firefighting against such problems and act proactively.

With the use of the lineage graph, you can quickly see what sources are used in any data mart, or are ancestors to any model, and with the exposure feature that we will look at next, you will be able to define the tables that power a dashboard or an ML model.

The source freshness report allows you to define a **Service-Level Agreement** (**SLA**) to consider the content of a table fresh enough, and to raise a warning or an error if the SLA is not respected:

Figure 12.29: Data source freshness report, by system

The source freshness report provides a quick and easy way to check if there are issues with the incoming data and, coupled with the ability of dbt to send alerts if a job fails, send an alert when the SLA for a table is not met, raising an error to the responsible person/team. It's as simple as creating a job that only does the freshness check and configures who needs to be alerted upon failure:

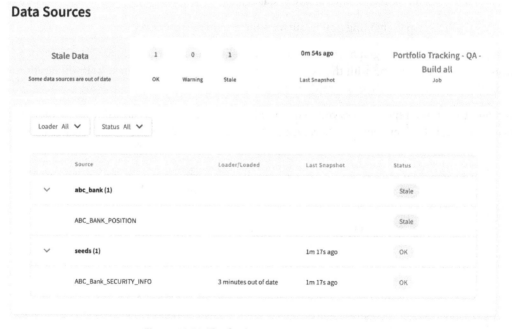

Figure 12.30: The freshness report per system

The report for our sample project shows that we have two systems defined and each has a table defined. The **abc_bank** system has some stale data, while for the **seeds** system, all data is fresh.

You can set the SLA in the YAML file where you declare the source system by setting the threshold level and naming the timestamp column:

```
sources:
  - name: seeds
    freshness:
      warn_after: {count: 3, period: day}
      error_after: {count: 5, period: day}
    loaded_at_field: LOAD_TS
```

As shown in the preceding code, you can provide a warning level and an error level, and you have to name the timestamp column to check against the current time.

Like most dbt configurations, you can set the general SLA at the system level and override both the threshold and timestamp column for each source table.

If you set a system-wide SLA you can disable the freshness check for the tables that do not need it (think reference tables that change seldom) by setting the freshness to `null`, as we did for the `t2` table in the following snippet:

```
    tables:
      - name: t1
      - name: t2
        freshness: null    # no freshness for this table
```

The data source freshness report is accessed as the last entry in the **Deploy** menu.

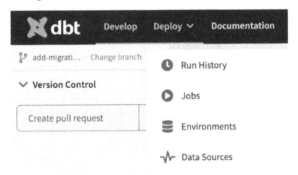

Figure 12.31: The Deploy menu with the Data Sources entry

The freshness report is also available to non-developer users that access dbt with a reader license, making it available to business users, together with the generated documentation.

Exposures

Exposure adds a terminal node in the dependency graph to describe an external dependency upon some specific dbt models.

At the core of an exposure, there is a list of the dbt models that the exposed dependency depends upon.

The main benefits of exposures are as follows:

- A clear name to select the listed models that the external feature depends upon, to apply dbt commands simply and consistently

- The ability to add manually curated documentation to the doc site for the report and direct access to the models upon which the exposure depends

The following code creates an exposure for our simple report made by our only fact and our only dimension:

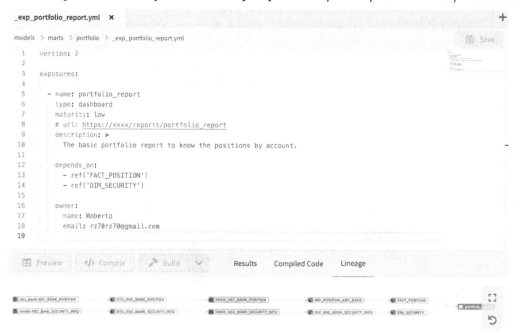

Figure 12.32: Code to define an exposure for our sample project

Let's analyze it:

- You create an exposure by providing a name, which is therefore mandatory.

  The name must be in camel case, as it can be used as any dbt node name.

- You also need to provide the type of external dependency.

  The external dependency can be anything, but the available types are `analysis`, `application`, `dashboard`, `ml`, and `notebook`.

  The type is used to organize the exposures in the documentation site, where they are grouped by type.

- The last mandatory field is the `email` field of the report `owner`, while `name` is optional.

- The most important thing to provide is the `depends_on` list.

  While optional, it is the main reason to create an exposure, unless you just want a page in the docs that you can manually edit.

  You can use both the `ref` and `source` functions to build the list, but you will rarely need the `source` function.

  In the list, you should just list the final models that the external feature depends on; the other models that are needed to build them will be known to dbt thanks to the node's DAG. In the preceding screenshot, we listed two models in the data mart layer and dbt shows the full lineage graph.

- Another key component of an exposure can be the description.

  While you can just enter some simple text, it becomes a very powerful way of providing easy-to-use and visually compelling documentation when used with Markdown doc blocks.

- The exposure node will now appear in all the lineage graphs, both in the IDE and in the doc site with the generated documentation.

The result of the previous exposure definition is shown in the following screenshot, which has been enhanced by the use of a Markdown doc block to provide a nicer description of the report's content:

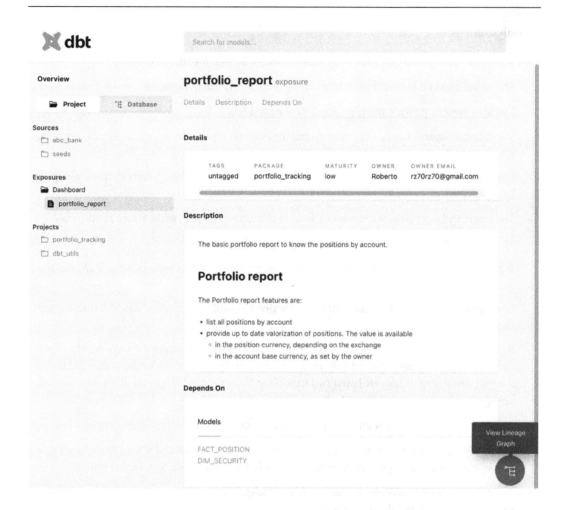

Figure 12.33: Generated documentation for an exposure

In the documentation page generated for the exposure, you can see the details that point to the owner, the description that has been enhanced in its appearance by the use of a Markdown doc block, and the list of models, which are one click away.

The lineage graph is also just one click away, showing the same layout as seen in the screenshot of the IDE.

The exposures have a dedicated menu in the left navigation, with the exposures grouped by type.

Markdown documentation

When talking about exposures, we showed the result of using a Markdown doc block. What are we talking about?

In dbt, you can declare a description field in most elements described in YAML files. Whenever you can enter a description, you can also define all or part of it using a doc bloc.

A doc block is the definition of a docs Jinja object with a unique name, which contains text that is interpreted as Markdown when visualized in the doc site:

```
{% docs exp_portfolio_report %}
# Portfolio report
The Portfolio report features are:
* list all positions by account
* provide up to date valorization of positions.
  The value is available
  * in the position currency, depending on the exchange
  * in the account base currency, as set by the owner
{% enddocs %}
```

The preceding doc bloc that we used in the exposure example must be inside a file ending with .md. It can be in the same folder as your models, with the name that you prefer. More than one doc block can be in the same file.

To use a doc block, you can use the doc function, along with the block's name:

```
description: |
    The basic portfolio report. Positions by account.
    {{ doc('exp_portfolio_report') }}
```

The preceding description mixes and matches normal text with the doc function, using the | YAML block notation that stands for "literal" interpretation of the multiline YAML string.

This is important as the empty line matters in Markdown, and if you would instead use the > YAML folded style, the new line would be replaced with a space, changing your Markdown and therefore the rendered output.

You can also use the doc function directly in a description field for a table, a column, or anywhere possible, but in that case, you might have to quote the doc function:

```
description: "{{ doc('exp_portfolio_report') }}"
```

Whenever you quote a Jinja block, use the opposite type of quotes concerning the ones that you use for the string with the name of the doc block.

Consider that you can use Markdown directly in the description, without the need to create a doc block. This is useful when you want to include links, as shown in the following example:

```
description: "See [the docs](http://www.docs.com)"
```

Providing easy-to-use and pleasant-to-read documentation improves the ability of your power users to make the most out of the dataset that you will prepare. dbt allows you to provide the documentation as you see fit.

Summary

Congratulations, you have completed the second part of this book and now know all the core dbt functionalities and how to use them!

In this chapter, you learned how to deploy and run your projects and how to use the advanced automation features that allow you to extend dbt to perform all the tasks that you need.

You are now familiar with dbt functionalities and their extensive documentation features, and you can use them to improve the value of your projects.

In the next chapter, *Moving Beyond Basics*, we will start introducing more advanced data engineering topics, such as identity and master data management or saving the changes of your entities, and the dbt functionality that we use to handle them.

13
Moving Beyond the Basics

In the previous chapters, we discussed the basic tenets of data engineering, our opinionated approach to the **Pragmatic Data Platform** (**PDP**), and we used basic and advanced dbt functionalities to implement it in its basic form.

In this chapter, you will review the best practices to apply modularity in your pipelines to simplify their evolution and maintenance.

Next you will learn how to manage the identity of your entities as it is central to store changes to them and to apply master data management to combine data from different systems.

We will also use macros, the most powerful dbt functionality, to implement the first pattern to store and retrieve the changes in our data according to our discussion of identity management. This allows all developers to use the best practices that senior colleagues have developed.

In this chapter, you will learn about the following topics:

- Building for modularity
- Managing identity
- Master data management
- Saving history at scale

Technical requirements

This chapter builds on the concepts from the previous chapters, including the basic dbt functions, the description of our target architecture, and the sample project.

All the code samples for this chapter are available on GitHub at

```
https://github.com/PacktPublishing/Data-engineering-with-dbt/tree/
main/Chapter_13.
```

Building for modularity

By now, you should be familiar with the layers of our *Pragmatic Data Platform* (PDP) and the core principles of each layer:

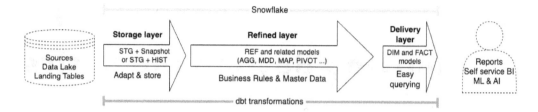

Figure 13.1: The layers of the Pragmatic Data Platform

Let's quickly recap them:

- **Storage layer**: Here, we adapt incoming data to how we want to use it without changing its semantics and store all the data: the good, the bad, and the ugly.

  The core principle is to isolate here the platform state – that is, models that depend on previous runs such as snapshots or incremental models – so that the next layers can be rebuilt from scratch on top of the storage layer.

  The perspective is source centric, with one load pipeline for each source table.

- **Refined layer**: Here, we apply master data and implement business rules.

  The core principle here is to apply modularity while building more abstract and general-use concepts on top of the simpler, source-centric ones from storage.

  No state, patterns, and clear names that avoid surprises keep us nimble and allow us to add and evolve business rules with minimal effort.

  The perspective is business-centric, or better, the final goal is to have business concepts – and eventually intermediate ones – that are expressed in business terms, even if they're built out of the source-specific inputs from the storage layer.

- **Delivery layer**: Here, we organize the data to be easy to use, depending on the user.

  The core principle here is to provide datasets well-tailored to the audience.

  Providing only useful and tested content – exposed with business names and in the desired format and delivery architecture, such as a star schema or wide table – allows simple adoption by the client users or applications.

Building lightly on top of the refined layer allows us to easily provide the same data cut in different ways for different audiences, such as marketing or operations.

The perspective is business-centric, with a focus on content, naming, and architecture for a specific audience or business domain.

Looking back at the layers and their content, we can say that modularity is achieved by providing components that you can use to build your pipelines in a modular system.

These components can be provided in the form of simple patterns that provide a clear semantic with a consistent name so that it is clear what to expect from the model and identify its role in the pipeline without doubts.

Patterns can often be implemented as macros, but in some cases, in the interest of readability, it might be better to just use a tried and tested layout and avoid the indirection of calling a macro.

By composing the simple components that guide the implementation of the core needs, you can build your pipelines and create a complete architecture.

In the following sections, we'll recap some of the components that we have already seen and introduce a few ones that we will see later.

Modularity in the storage layer

The storage layer benefits from great predictability, and we have a big array of components that allow us to follow clear patterns to build this part of the pipeline, automate most of the code creation, and implement the layer in multiple different ways by swapping interchangeable components such as HIST models versus snapshots.

Let's review the available components:

- **Seed**: A seed's role is to easily load the small reference or hand-maintained data that is not coming from a specific system and is stored in small CSV files.

  If you plan to use them directly with the `ref ()` function, we suggest naming them SEED_xxx so that their function is crystal clear. If you plan to access them indirectly using the `source ()` function, the CSV name is less important.

- **Source definition**: The source definition's role is to reference external data in a way that's easy and flexible to manage, adding semantics by naming groups of inputs and flexibility through a layer of indirection.

  You can organize the external data – that is, data that is not managed by dbt models – by naming the sources after a system or logical subsystem while keeping the names of the tables unchanged for ease of auditing/testing.

- **Snapshot**: The snapshot's role is to store changes in an input entity when you receive periodic snapshots from the source. It is a core dbt component.

  One key limitation is that it's a resource shared by all the environments; another one is the need for full exports to track deletions.

- **STG model**: We present the STG model when incorporating multiple components and patterns, each divided in its CTE, but you can choose what components to use or even chain the components as individual models:

  - **Adaptation**: This component makes the incoming data as usable as possible by adapting the data types, renaming columns, extracting nested objects, and applying hard data fixes.

  - **Default record**: The default record provides dimensions with a record with default values for all the fields, including the primary key, and the description columns to be used when a fact has an orphan foreign key. If it appears before the change storage component, the changes in the defaults are captured too.

  - **Hashed**: This component defines and calculates the HKEY and HDIFF columns and generates the LOAD_TS metadata column when needed.

    The HKEY and HDIFF columns provide a clear definition of what the key used for storage is and what defines a version change for the entity. Because of this, they play a crucial role in multiple patterns.

  For simplicity, we have presented the STG model as a single model that implements all our desired components by reading out of the source (since our reference implementation uses the HIST component in place of the snapshot) for performance, scalability, and, most importantly, greater freedom of evolution between the environments.

- **HIST model**: The HIST model's role is to store the changes of an entity. It uses an insert-only strategy that builds a slowly changing dimension type two table with a row for each version of each instance of the entity.

  This is our default implementation to store changes as it is high-performance and serves both the current state of a table and all its changes well.

  By using delete-aware HIST variants, you can track deletions effectively and produce the same storage layout, making no difference in downstream use.

- **PII model**: The role of this highly specialized model is to store the actual **Personally Identifiable Information** (**PII**) data apart from the normal transformations so that it can be replaced in the delivery layer where needed, to authorized people and while still available (think of, for example, the **GDPR** right to be forgotten).

In the storage layer, it is very clear what needs to be done, and this inventory of components and model roles allows us to achieve the layer objectives in different ways, organizing these logical components in the most appropriate way for our case.

In the previous chapters, we arranged all the components we intended to use in a single STG model as this is the best setup when using the insert-only HIST model, which is what our target architecture uses. It offers great flexibility, ease of development, and better performance compared to the default dbt snapshots.

If you are planning to use snapshot models to store changes, it makes sense to keep what you store the same as the input to minimize the chances of change in the snapshot code. This is because a snapshot is a shared component across all environments.

In such a case, you might calculate the hash and even add the default record before the snapshot. However, if you fear a higher rate of change in the adaptation component, you could move it after the snapshot, even if doing so might incur some performance penalty by complex or slow transformations that would be applied at every read.

Modularity in the refined layer

The refined layer does not have the same level of predictability as the storage layer, but the general playbook is pretty clear and goes trough these stages:

1. **Refined individual system**: The initial process is to compose and transform the data from each individual source system, including the use of locally specific business rules, up to an abstraction level comparable with the other systems. In the process, it replaces local surrogate keys with business keys whenever possible.

2. **Master data mapping**: This process involves applying master data transformations to convert the codes from one system to make them interoperable with a wider range of systems.

3. **Master data refined layer**: This is the "holy grail" that we are looking for. The final process is to compose and transform the results of the master data mapping to produce a set of business concepts, expressed with master data codes, that allow us to calculate company-wide business metrics and apply company business rules.

It is important to note that if you have a lot of legacy systems or systems resulting from multiple integrations, *steps 1* and *2* can be repeated a few times, incrementally building domains of homogeneous master data codes that increase in size (the left-hand side of *Figure 13.2*). This is generally the result of progressive and often partial efforts to build some level of common reporting across organizational entities such as plants, countries, or regions:

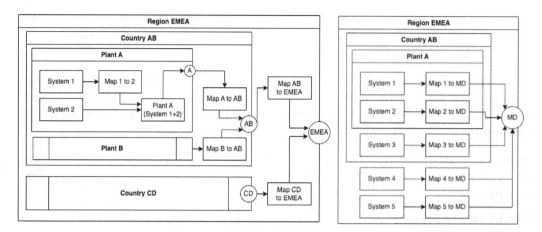

Figure 13.2: Progressive MD code conversion versus direct MD code conversion

When there have been corporate-wide Master Data initiatives to bring all/most of the data to some interoperability level, the result can be closer to the right-hand side of *Figure 13.2*, with a direct conversion from each source system to the agreed master data codes.

In both cases, it is common to have multiple nested domains and business rules that need to be applied inside each domain to make the data interoperable by representing the same concept. As an example, think about accounting for different taxes or cost structures in different countries to build a "cost of labor" concept.

In the preceding figure, we have highlighted the source systems that produce the data and the mapping tables used to convert from one "master data" perimeter into the next. However, most of the transformations are usually related to the business rules, as we discussed earlier.

The variability of the transformation in the REF layer is maximal as it is the place where master data conversion and the different levels of business rules are applied. Nevertheless, we can identify the following components with clear roles:

- **REF model**: The REF model's role is to represent a refined entity in a certain context, something that you expect to be generally reusable in that context because it represents a concept that is useful and fairly complete in the context.

  Before building the corporate-level REF entity, it is common to build the REF entities of the lower domains; then, using business rules and mapping tables, these concepts are used to compose the higher-level REF model.

  As an example, it is common to build multiple REF_<country>_CUSTOMER models that then are used to build the final corporate-wide REF_CUSTOMER. The country-level entities are useful beyond the use to build the wider entity.

- **AGG model**: The AGG model's role is to represent an aggregated refined model.

  It is quite common that different systems provide the same concepts at different levels of detail, and to be able to compose them, they need to be brought to the same granularity by aggregating on the common dimensions.

  Another driver of AGG models is the desire to reduce the number of rows fed into the reporting tool by aggregating fact tables to the desired granularity.

- **MDD model**: The MDD model's role is to represent a dimension coming directly from master data, therefore a kind of "authoritative" list of entities.

- **MAP model**: The MAP model's role is to represent a mapping table that allows code conversions between one system/context and another.

  This can come from master data tools or be calculated or even manually created. The idea is that it supports some kind of conversion/translation.

  A key aspect of these models is to clearly express in the name what mapping they do, with names such as `MAP_US_ITEM_TO_MD_PRODUCT` to express both the contexts and the entities that are mapped.

- **TR model**: The TR model's role is to represent an intermediate transformation.

  The main difference with a REF model is that a TR model is considered an intermediate step that has no real meaning by itself and would be hardly reused as it does not represent some generally useful concept.

  A TR model is the closest thing to a private model. Caution should be posed when reusing a TR model because of potential limitations that might not be evident from the name or the starting selection.

- **PIVOT model**: The PIVOT model's role is to obtain models by pivoting other models.

  It is a very specialized role, like the AGG one, and it provides the same data as other models but reorganizes it by pivoting it.

While we can hardly predict what transformations will be needed in the REF layer, we can easily identify the roles of most of the models that we will create.

This list is probably not complete, as the naming is something that the team has to agree upon and decide what aspect to emphasize. As an example, you will have associative or join tables that you will use to represent many-to-many relations.

You might name the table that puts in relation customer and purchased products as `JOIN_PRODUCT_PURCHASED_BY_CUSTOMER` (hey, this relation is generally called invoice or order) or even `REF_JOIN_xxx`, but in many cases, these relations have a business name, and it will be natural to call it `REF_ORDER` or `REF_INVOICE`.

The most important thing for the usability of the REF layer is to adopt a clear naming convention so that everyone can understand not only the role of a model but also the context where it belongs.

This is important as the context identifies the other models with which it can readily be joined as the codes and semantics of the fields are interoperable.

Modularity in the delivery layer

When we move to the delivery layer, we have one or more data marts.

The role of each data mart is to deliver a dataset related to a specific subject, such as marketing, finance, or operations, at the level of a domain that often matches one organization boundary, such as a plant, country, region, or corporation-wide.

All the business rules that transform the data must be applied in the REF layer to produce the refined representation of a concept in a domain. After the REF layer, all the business rules that have a semantic meaning for the domain have been applied.

Therefore, in each data mart, we rely on the models created in the REF layer and on their modularity to access the concepts we want at the right domain level.

In a data mart, we shouldn't need any business rules to produce correct results, but it might be useful, and it is common to have business rules that deal with the presentation of the results, from column names to their format, and filtering to only present the data that is relevant for the data mart.

As an example, you can think of having a REF or AGG model representing the general ledger for a country, but if you are building a data mart for a plant or marketing, you might not need all the data. Therefore, you may only want to put in the facts of the data mart only the cost and profit centres that are useful in that context.

In the delivery layer, we generally find models that fulfill the roles of the desired reporting style. So, if we deliver Kimball star schemas, we will mostly have facts and dimensions, while if we deliver wide tables, we will mostly have such tables. This might be another reason to expose similar data in two different data marts.

Let's look at some common models found in data marts:

- **FACT model**: The FACT model's role is to represent a Kimball-style fact.

  It is imperative to remember that, for the Kimball architecture, each report must be based on a single fact. So, if you need data from two "base facts", you should build the "composite fact" that puts together the data that you need.

  You build the "composite fact" in the REF layer by applying the required business rules. Then, you expose it all, in part, or aggregated, in the data marts.

- **DIM model**: The DIM model's role is to represent a Kimball-style dimension or hierarchy.

  For dimensions, or hierarchies compressed in a dimension with the granularity of the lowest element of the hierarchy, the most important aspect is to have the right codes to match the facts in the data mart.

  The other key feature of a dimension is to have all the entries being referenced by the codes of the facts in the data mart, so that the fact does not have orphan codes.

- **REPORT model**: The REPORT model's role is to represent a table that can power a report.

  This type of model is used to deliver wide tables that can power a report or an AI/ML use case. The name can also vary a lot as there is not a common way of naming as it is for facts and dimensions.

  Generally, it is not used in Kimball-style data marts but can live in a parallel data mart for use with other tools or just to exchange disk space for performance. A wide table is a pre-joined data mart where the fact is already joined with all dimensions. This is less efficient in terms of storage, but it is much more efficient in terms of querying, so it can pay off when you write once and query many times.

- **FILTER model**: This is a specialized model whose role is to make it extremely clear how one or more facts are filtered based on requirements that exist only in the specific data mart where the filter model lives.

  If the filtering would be of general use, the filter should be moved to the REF layer and applied to the fact there to build a new fact model that's aptly named while considering the filtering that's been applied.

  The use of such a model serves two main purposes. The first is to modularize the code and improve the visibility of the filtering, providing an independent DB object that can be used in the reporting tools.

  The second purpose is to make maintaining the filtering logic simple and explicit. This is even more important when the filter is applied to more than just one fact in the data mart.

In this section, we saw how important is to recognize why we are writing some piece of SQL and to build our models with a logical flow and names that make the role of the SQL we wrote concerning that flow clear.

The lack of such organization and modularity is one of the key reasons why data warehouse projects start to become hard to manage when they become big.

We offer our set of model types and roles as a solid starting point, giving you our blessing to change them and adopt your own names and roles, or even develop new ones. Just be very clear about them inside your organization.

Now that we have a better understanding of how to build our architecture in a modular way, in the next section, we'll discuss how to identify instances of an entity in more detail. This is central to selecting them or tracking their changes.

Managing identity

Identity is probably the single most important concept in data management, even if, at its core, it is extremely simple: being able to identify to what instance of an entity some data refers.

The problems with identity arise from the fact that we humans are very flexible in using the available information and we can easily put information in the right bucket, even if it is presented to us in the wrong way.

We are not good at being consistent in the real world but that is not a problem for us as we are very flexible in our data processing. We can easily recognize that two names are referring to the same person, even if they are in uppercase or lowercase, or that it is still the same person with or without the middle name initial, even if we invert the name and surname.

Machines are fast, but not as good at coping with the variability of information as we are, so indicating how to identify instances of an entity, whether they are people, products, documents, or fully abstract information, is essential in every data project.

Identity and semantics – defining your concepts

Because of our inherent inability of being consistent with descriptions, the data industry has created the concept of **key** or **code**, which is intended to be a simple and concise piece of information that can be used to easily identify instances of an entity.

If you think about people, companies create an employee code or customer code, depending on the role a person plays; states create tax codes or social security numbers. For most use cases that involve a computer, these codes, and not our names, become the major or even only way to identify ourselves in such organizations.

The purpose of a key is to identify one instance of an entity, such as a specific employee of a company, or a specific car in traffic.

Those are simple cases where the semantic of the identity is clear, but if we are identifying a car in the catalog of a producer versus a specific car in traffic?

In the first case, we are referring to the "car's model", while in the second case, we are referring to a specific "car instance". Again, our flexibility in understanding the semantics of what we talk about can be a misleading force in designing our data transformations.

The only way to avoid confusion and errors is to be very explicit in naming entities and their keys, maybe to the point of being pedantic.

In the case of the catalog, we should probably name the entity/table CAR_MODEL and its key CAR_MODEL_CODE or CAR_MODEL_KEY, while in the traffic case, we could name the entity CAR and its key CAR_CODE or CAR_KEY.

Yes, CAR_INSTANCE seems a bit too pedantic, even to us.

Time series semantics

Another case when we can easily be fooled by not having a clear semantic is when we want to track something that changes over time.

In such cases, we need to be crystal clear about what we want to track: the changes that happen to the instances of the entity, independently of when they happen, or whether we want to track the values at certain times, even if no change has happened.

The first case is a normal process of tracking the entity changes, using its key, while in the second case, we are building a time series of the values. Here, the key would be composed of the entity key plus the key for the time, according to the desired periodicity.

One such common case is tracking the inventory of goods.

In some cases, you want to know how much (and many other metrics) of a product you have and track its changes only when there are changes. In this case, you would track changes using the entity key.

In other cases, you might want to track the values of the metrics for a product with a given periodicity (day, week, month) independently if the metric changes or not. In this case, you would track changes by building a composite key using the entity and period keys.

These two are connected, and you can go from one representation to the other, but if you have already cleared your use case, it is much better to name your table according to the semantics that you want and use the correct key for it.

Different types of keys

In this section, we will complement and extend the description of keys that we provided in *Chapter 3* while talking about entity-relationship diagrams.

When talking about the field names of keys, terms such as CODE and KEY are used, but also ID (short for identifier) and NUMBER.

Consistently with human lack of consistency, but with the ability to cope with it, it is common to find all of them in use with the same meaning, so you can find columns named CUSTOMER_CODE, CUSTOMER_KEY, CUSTOMER_ID, or CUSTOMER_NUMBER.

The first and most important distinction concerns the visibility of keys:

- **Surrogate key (SK)**: This is a key that exists only for technical needs and is usually limited to the internals of a system. `Hash_Key` is an example of a surrogate key.

- **Natural key (NK)** or **business key (BK)**: This is a key that fulfills its technical role but is also in public use. It is printed on documents and is referred to in business conversations and documents. `Invoice_code` is an example of a natural key.

In our discussions and in the names that we use, we prefer to use the term `CODE` for natural keys, while we prefer `SK` (short of `SURROGATE_KEY`) or the generic `KEY` for surrogate keys.

In many cases, we have keys that have an `ID` or `NUMBER` as part of their names. While there is nothing inherently wrong with them, often, the `XXX_NUMBER` fields are not numbers anymore, and the `XXX_ID` suffix that started as an internal identifier has become a well-known business key, so we suggest using only one name to identify its visibility. As mentioned previously, in such cases, we tend to use `CODE` and `KEY` as general terms.

Interestingly the `NUMBER` suffix is reminiscent of past technology requirements that made using numbers, generated by sequences or autoincrement, a common way of generating codes that were also efficient for database handling. This is not the case anymore, but the field names have survived through multiple system migrations.

The second very important distinction is based on the role of a key in a table:

- **Primary key (PK)**: This key is tasked with uniquely identifying an instance of the entity. Rows that have the same PK in a table describe the same instance.

  Most of the data modeling is done for operational systems, where you keep updating the values of an instance so that it always has up-to-date values in the table. In such cases, the PK must be unique in the table to guarantee that you have only one row describing the current values for an instance of the entity.

  Instead, when a table stores multiple versions of an instance, as we do in snapshots and HIST tables, the PK alone will not be unique. It will be unique the combination of the PK and the timestamp of each version.

  Please pay attention to the semantics you use for PK: what we have described here is the meaning of "PK of an entity" – as identifying the one specific instance of the entity, which is what matters for information management. Often, people will say PK using the semantics of "PK of the table" that means a unique constraint on a table.

  If we have a `CUSTOMER` entity where `CUSTOMER_CODE` is the PK of the entity, then it will also be the PK of the `CUSTOMER` table in the operational system and in all the data platform tables where you just have the current customers. However, the PK of the `HIST_CUSTOMER` or `CUSTOMER_SNSH` tables will be the composition of `CUSTOMER_CODE` and `LOAD_TS`.

- **Foreign key (FK)**: This is a key that matches the PK of another entity.

  FKs are the fundamental way to connect information, making it possible to express that two or more entities are in some relationship. If the relationship is optional, the FK can be null, but if it is mandatory, the FK must not be null.

  As an example, when we create an invoice line, it will contain one FK for each entity that we want to connect, such as `CUSTOMER_CODE` and `PRODUCT_CODE`, but also `PROMOTION_CODE` and so on.

  While customer and product are mandatory and their codes must be not null, promotion is optional, and the code can therefore be null.

So far, we have talked about keys. We have always used examples where the key is a single field, but it is perfectly fine to have keys that are composed of multiple columns. In that case, we often create a single-column surrogate key, by hashing the multiple fields, to make our work simpler.

The most common case when we must deal with compound keys is facts. These facts are documents, such as orders or invoices, or business events, and they often have a business key or at least a surrogate key attached. Many other facts do not have a PK, but it is often possible to build one using all the FKs in the fact and eventually some time information that allows us to distinguish between multiple instances of the same FK.

In some cases, such as when tracking page views from users, it might be too hard or impossible to distinguish between two identical actions done in a short time because we cannot build a stable key to identify each instance of the "page view" action.

If we are not able to build a good, stable PK for an entity, we will not be able to track changes for such an entity and we must accept that we must just store all the instances that we receive as independent, immutable instances.

Another case when we are confronted by compound keys is when we have to deal with dimensions that were not designed for the domain where we are using them, and we do not have master data to perform the proper conversion. In such cases, the original key might not be enough to ensure proper identification, so we must add a second column indicating the domain.

As an example, if we have two `PRODUCT` dimensions that have been independently developed in two plants or two countries, and no master data mapping to convert the codes into common MD codes, we can create a common `PRODUCT` dimension by putting the two together. However, since `PRODUCT_CODE` alone might have a conflict, we need to add in the key a second column for the source. This is *not* a good solution, as we might have the same product twice with two different codes (one per source), but in some cases, that is the only thing that we can do, and we must accept the technical debt.

Main uses of keys

In the previous section, we saw that the PK of an entity is used to identify the instances of the entity and that FKs are used to put in relation the instances of the entities.

These are the most common operations where the keys are central:

- **Tracking and applying changes**: The PK is used to identify the instance that the incoming data belongs to so that we can compare if anything has changed compared to what we have already stored.

- **Extracting the current or historical version**: The PK is used to collect all the versions that are stored and extract the most recent one or the one that was active at some point in time.

- **Joining data**: Joining tables by equating the FK in a table with the PK of another table is the main operation that we do in the REF layer to put together the data that we need across the existing relations.

  Creating relations between tables by putting the PK of another table as the FK in a table is the most powerful thing that relational DBs exist for. It is the most important ability for understanding and designing data models.

  You should only join tables while following the direct FK-PK relationships or the associative tables that are used to implement many-to-many relations. In the latter case, you should expect to potentially have multiple rows returned by the join for each row o fthe starting table.

  Beware of blindly joining two tables on a common foreign key as this is what brings you directly to the *chasm trap* data problem we described in *Chapter 3*.

- **Referential integrity**: When we have an FK in a table, we should ensure that the instance referenced by the FK exists in the parent table hosting the PK. If there is no PK to match an FK, we are missing some information. In such cases, we say that the FK is an orphan as there is no entry in the parent table.

  Ensuring proper referential integrity is very important to guarantee that we can query our tables and retrieve all the expected information.

  This is the common case of fact tables that store multiple FKs, each pointing to a parent table that is a dimension.

Now that we've learned about keys and what they are used for, let's delve into how to use master data management to extend our ability to identify entities beyond their initial domain.

Master Data management

When we refer to Master Data, we are talking about the descriptive data that is at the core of an organization and the processes to ensure that we can understand when different units are referring to the same instance of a concept.

To many extents, Master Data in the data platform realm overlaps with the dimensions that describe the organization concepts, such as customer, product, employee, and so on.

The rare times when we have a Master Data dimension, it adds the semantic of containing the "golden records" selected to represent the instances of the business concept (that is, the entity) represented by the dimension.

As an example, the product MD dimension (MDD_PRODUCT for us in the REF layer) contains the golden records of the products, starting from the codes used as the PK of the entity and continuing with the values of the columns.

Quite often, we will have only a list of MD codes, eventually with names, and mapping tables that allow us to transform local dimensions into MD codes and produce an MD-coded dimension using data from local dimensions, thanks to business rules.

When we talk about Master Data management, we are talking about the processes and data (MDD and MAP tables) for managing Master Data entities across domains.

Data for Master Data management

In Master Data management, we rely on two types of data:

- **Master Data Dimensions** (**MDDs**): This is the dimension that contains the "gold records" of the business concept. Often, there is not a full dimension but only a list of master data codes, maybe with a name or description for human use.

  Its validity can be limited to a specific domain, such as US products only.

- **Mapping tables** (**MAPs**): This is a table that allows us to convert the codes from one domain into another – for example, converting Italian product codes into EMEA codes.

  These mapping tables are at the heart of every MD initiative as they are the tools for making data interoperable.

  They can be used to convert the codes of a dimension, but their power is to also convert the codes into facts, opening the use of facts across domains.

  Mapping tables are generally expressed in terms of business keys and not surrogate keys since they have no business meaning.

  A key element to be aware of for each mapping table is the *directionality of mapping*. It is quite common that the cardinality of a concept is different across domains, and therefore the mapping cannot be one-to-one and bidirectional.

  If, in a local domain, multiple codes have been used to identify a single code in the Master Data dimension over time, then all these codes will map to the same MD code and the mapping will be many-to-one and unidirectional from the local domain to the MD domain.

This would be the case if a country has multiple codes to represent a "generic box 30x30x5 cm" product because they are sourcing them from different vendors or producing them in different plants, but the MDD has only one such product.

This also shows that a mapping table might use multiple columns to map one code across domains. Using the box as an example, we would need the MD code and the production plant code to map an MD code to the local domain.

It might be surprising to you, but the mapping tables are the ones that are needed, whereas having the master data dimension for all or even most concepts is not common. It is very welcome, but not a must.

Even when we just have the mapping table, we implicitly have also a minimal MDD that's made by all the MD codes that are present in the mapping table. In such cases, the dimension used in data marts is derived from the local dimensions, along with some business rules to decide what data to collect from each local dimension and the eventual precedence when data can be alternatively sourced by multiple dimensions.

A light MDM approach with DBT

When we discussed modularity earlier in this chapter, we introduced the two possible extreme situations that we will find when making data interoperable across domains.

One possibility is to progressively convert the data from one domain to the next, while the other extreme is to convert everything directly to the higher-level domain, which is often considered the target master data system of reference.

Reality is hardly black and white, and you will find yourself in situations where, for some data, you have to go through a few conversion steps, while for others, you just have to take a single step. This mixed approach is often the case as some entities do not have the same semantics. Besides this, with master data code conversions, some rules are needed to have the same definition and build a more widely applicable version of the concept.

Let's make a simple graphical example to better clarify one step of the MD conversion process. In our example, we have two systems that have Order LINES data to be converted into some master data domain to make it interoperable:

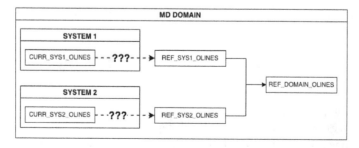

Figure 13.3: Desired result of the master data conversion – interoperable Order LINES from SYS1 and SYS2

Here, we start our conversion from data that is encoded with SYS1 and SYS2 keys (business or surrogate keys, which will be discussed next), making them not interoperable. Our goal is to produce one model coded in the desired MD domain and then be able to combine them to provide a domain-level model.

When we start looking into the Order Lines from system 1, we can see that they do not have business keys, only surrogate keys (SK).

The problem is that SKs are only valid inside one specific environment, so the SK for the same instance is different in DEV, QA, and PROD and it will change if one environment or a dimension is recreated:

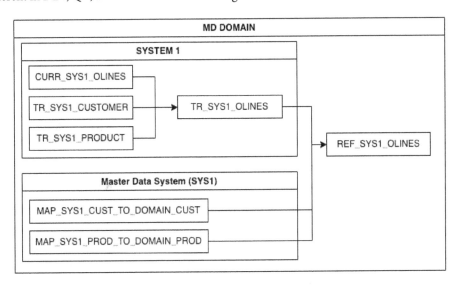

Figure 13.4: Transformations to apply MD when the source data uses surrogate keys

Because of their nature, SKs do not have any meaning for anyone and could change at any time, so they are not used in master data systems.

The master data system uses the BKs of the entities as they are meaningful to people and stable over time to identify instances of the entity.

To retrieve the BK of an entity, we can join its dimension using the SK provided.

Therefore, our first action is to replace the surrogate keys that we have in our source with the corresponding business keys.

In the preceding figure, we joined our source data in CURR_SYS1_OLINES with the dimensions of system one (TR_SYS1_CUSTOMER and TR_SYS1_PRODUCT) to produce the TR_SYS1_OLINES model that has the SYS1 BKs in place of SKs.

The next step is to join the `TR_SYS1_OLINES` model with the mapping table for each BK that we have to convert from SYS1 into the desired MD domain to produce the `REF_SYS1_OLINES` model, which has the MD domain BKs in place.

In this example, we have assumed that we only had customer and product keys that needed to be converted, first from SK to SYS1 BK and then to MD domain BK. It might well be that you have a different number of SKs to convert. As an example, consider that you have a country key. First, you would need to convert from SK to SYS1 BK, but if SYS1 already uses international country codes, then you might already be using the desired BKs, which means you do not need a further MD conversion for the country BK.

We also want you to note how subjective and depending on the expected usage of our models the naming of them can be.

We have used the `TR_` prefix for the dimensions because they are expressed in terms of the SKs and therefore are not of general use outside SYS1. Then, we named `TR_` the Order Lines model. This is where we put the SYS1 BKs as we only plan to build reporting using the domain codes, so we don't consider it reusable. For the same reason, we named `REF_` the next model that will contain the SYS1 data with DOMAIN BK.

In a way, our assumption to always do reports using MD domain BKs made us call `REF_` the only model that uses such a code reference system, so we do not need to be explicit about in what domain it is a REF model.

If we had plans to produce reporting data marts that use SYS1 BKs, then we should name the `TR_SYS1_OLINES` model `REF_SYS1_OLINES`, and the next one that contains the same data but uses DOMAIN BKs `REF_DOMxxx__SYS1_OLINES`, to make clear what BKs are used in each model and where the data is coming from.

This last convention is a bit verbose but is more clear overall. Please be aware of your assumptions and make them public when you decide how to name your models.

Now that we've converted system one, let's look at what we need to do for system two:

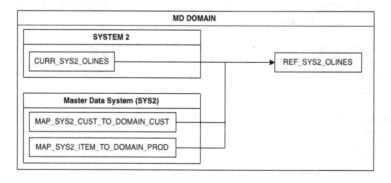

Figure 13.5: Transformations to apply MD when the source data uses business keys

In our example, we have assumed that system two is already using its own BK, so we do not need a first step to replace the internal SK with the system BKs.

In this case, we just have to apply the MD part of the transformation to convert the SYS2 BKs into the MD domain BKs.

We have named one of the mapping tables `MAP_SYS2_ITEM_TO_DOMAIN_PROD` so that we can when the concepts in the two domains are not aligned.

In our example, we assumed that, in SYS2, we have the concept of `ITEM`, which has to be converted into a `PRODUCT` in the MD domain. The difference and the business rules needed to do this conversion can be whatever, so we haven't made any special assumptions. However, in such situations, a lookup on the mapping table might not be enough and you will need to implement more complex business rules and eventually use intermediate models to simplify the computation and make it clear for other developers what transformations are being done and why.

Once you have transformed the data from both source systems so that we can use the desired MD domain BK, you can put them together by selecting the common fields and applying eventual business rules to produce the columns that are not immediately available in all the inputs. In some cases, you might add intermediate steps to perform this adaptation.

One simple example is that some inputs might already have amounts in the local currency and the desired accounting currency, while others might need one extra transformation to calculate the amounts in the accounting currency from the ones in the local currency. Here, we are back to normal business rules and not something specific to MD conversions.

In this section, we discussed how to apply Master Data transformations to make data from different systems interoperable. Having data interoperability across sources is by far the most important goal that we have when we build a data platform that has as input a plurality of data sources that use different BKs for some of the data.

In the next section, we will look at an advanced way to store the input data that we use in all our projects running on cloud databases such as Snowflake or BigQuery.

Saving history at scale

In *Chapter 6*, we saw that storing the data that we work on gives us many benefits, with the biggest being the ability to build a simple platform where the state is limited to the data storage and the refined and delivery layers are stateless.

Back then, we introduced the dbt feature of snapshots and showed you a second way of storing change history based on incremental models that is simple, quick, and does not have the architectural limit of being shared across environments:

Figure 13.6: Storage layer highlighted in the context of the Pragmatic Data Platform

While looking at the three-layer architecture of our Pragmatic Data Platform in this section, we are going to discuss our preferred way to store incoming data: HIST models that store all the versions of your data using the most efficient features of Snowflake.

We will create HIST models as they are simple, efficient, flexible, and resilient and they are the best solution, whether you wish to store the changes, if you want to be able to audit the data that you ingest, or even if you just want to have the current data.

Later in this section, we will introduce you to a macro that implements the pattern of saving your incoming data and how to use it to create a HIST model.

Now, let's start by discussing the main advantages of this storage pattern:

- HIST models save version changes using insert-only operations and offer the most simple and scalable way to save your data while keeping all the versions that your data has gone through. You get two for the price of one!

    Insert is the most efficient operation on modern cloud databases, while updates or deletes used by Snapshot have poor performances.

    The columnar format is quite good at compressing data, especially for columns with low variability, so your versions will be stored effectively.

- HIST tables implement idempotent loads, allowing you to run and re-run your dbt project. This provides resilience and ease of work for your team.

- HIST tables store the changes in a common and flexible way as slowly changing dimensions, allowing you to start by using only the current versions, and move to use all the changes in case you need them. There's no need to reload the data or change how you load/store data if you want to use the stored changes.

- Even the simplest implementation of the save_history macro provides full auditability of the changes if you receive one change per key per load. There are other versions you can use to ingest multiple changes per key and track hard deletions.

    They all store the data in the same way, so you can use them easily.

- The history is saved in normal incremental models, with all the logic delegated to the save_ history macro. This makes working with them as simple as with the other models and you can preview them as any model.

- The implementation of the loading pattern in the save_history macro makes it usable in the most effective way by all levels of developers.

- The save_history macro provides multiple parameters to greatly improve the performance of the load in special cases, such as when you have a good column for the role of a high watermark.

We suggest that you replace the snapshots in your project with HIST models. This will make your project more flexible and it will be ready to scale to huge tables.

Understanding the save_history macro

To understand how we store history using the save_history macro, which implements our general loading pattern, let's see how it is generally used in our code and then analyze the code in the macro.

Creating HIST models

The normal use of the macro is to create HIST models that read data from our STG models and save it.

The following is the full code of the HIST_ABC_BANK_POSITION model:

```
{{ save_history(
    input_rel = ref('STG_ABC_BANK_POSITION'),
    key_column = 'POSITION_HKEY',
    diff_column = 'POSITION_HDIFF',
) }}
```

Yes, you understood it right – these four rows are all that you need to save the full history of the data coming in from a source.

You might want to use some of the other parameters that are available in the macro, but the vast majority of the HIST models are perfectly fine with just this basic setup.

All the other parameters are available to improve the performance of the macro in different situations, but it makes sense to start using them only for tables that are big enough. This is usually when tables have many million rows and many GB of storage.

By using this pattern to load our HIST tables, we will have the following logical and physical layout of the data in the table:

	Storage of the data by LOAD_TS			Current data		Logical view of the data by KEY		
1								
2	**HKEY**	**HDIFF**	**LOAD_TS**			**HKEY**	**HDIFF**	**LOAD_TS**
3	key01	ghi	2023-02-23 17:25	<=	=>	key01	ghi	2023-02-23 17:25
4	key01	def	2023-02-22 16:15			key01	def	2023-02-22 16:15
5	key02	**bbb**	2023-02-22 16:15	<=		key01	abc	2023-02-21 15:11
6	key01	abc	2023-02-21 15:11		=>	key02	**bbb**	2023-02-22 16:15
7	key02	aaa	2023-02-21 15:11			key02	aaa	2023-02-21 15:11

Figure 13.7: Storage view and logical view of the data in a HIST table

The preceding tables only show the three columns that are needed to understand the working of a HIST table, leaving out the actual payload of the input.

These tables exemplify the result after the loads on February 21, 22, and 23 2023 of data for two instances with the key01 and key02 keys.

On the left, you can see the data split by load timestamp, one per daily run, while on the right, you can see the logical view by ordering by key and load time, with the current data at the top of the section for each key.

In both tables, the HDIFF is in bold for the row that contains the current value for each key. The pointers in the **Current data** columnhelp locating the current rows.

General analysis of the macro

Let's start analyzing the macro, which you can go and read in one piece in the /Chapter_13/dbt/ macros/13_01_v1__save_history.sql file in the repository associated with this book. For the full URL to the repository, see the *Technical requirements* section at the beginning of this chapter.

First, we will analyze the overall strategy by looking at the layout of the macro and discussing the CTEs it employs, without looking at the code. Next, we will analyze the code of each CTE on its own.

Let's start with the basic macro declaration, with its mandatory parameters:

```
{% macro save_history(
    input_rel,
    key_column,
    diff_column,
) -%}    # ... the other params are to improve performance
```

Here, we only listed the three mandatory parameters, which are the model providing the input data, the name of the key column, and the name of the HDIFF column – this is the most common way to use this macro. Now that we've provided an overview, we can delve into all the details.

Then, we have a config line to make the model incremental:

```
{{ config(materialized='incremental') }}
```

Please note that by not providing a `unique_key` parameter to the config, we instruct dbt to append all the rows returned by our SQL code to the incremental model.

The macro's design is based on the dbt `is_incremental()` macro to run the right code depending if we already have the underlying table or if we are creating it.

The macro returns `true` if the incremental table already exists and the run of the model is a normal run for an incremental model; it returns `false` when the target table does not exist (yet) or when the run is a `full-refresh` run. This can be achieved by passing the `--full-refresh` argument to recreate the table from scratch.

```
WITH
{%- if is_incremental() %}
```

If we already have the target table, for each key, we need to compare only the latest version stored in the HIST table with the incoming data, to see what is unchanged and does not need to be saved and what is new or changed and needs to be saved.

```
current_from_history as (
-- get the current HDIFF for each HKEY
),
```

By ensuring that the HDIFF column contains the source payload, including the business key of the entity, and excluding only the metadata (and any other field that we do not want to track changes on), it acts like a unique content identifier.

Therefore, we can do an equijoin on the HDIFF column alone, to achieve the most efficient comparison in a columnar database.

```
load_from_input as (
-- join the input with the HIST on the HDIFF columns
-- and keep the rows where there is no match
)
```

When the HDIFF from the input and the HIST are the same, it means that we already have that version of the data stored as the most recent version. Then, we need to load from the input only the rows where the HKEY does not match between the input and HIST table. These are the rows where the input is different from the current or new.

A crucial step of this load pattern is to be sure that, in both the input and the `current_from_history`, we only have one row for each key. If we have multiple rows, one HDIFF can never match two different ones, so the load will be incorrect. The `current_from_history` macro satisfies this requirement by design, so you need to ensure that the input is unique by HKEY.

Unless you need perfect auditability, you can easily filter the incoming data to keep in the input only the most recent version for each key, making this requirement hardly a limitation in real-world cases.

If you need to store multiple input versions at the same time, there is a pattern version to handle that too, which is slightly more complex and has inferior performance on big tables as it needs to run a window function on all the input. We will see it, along with the other variants that also allow us to detect deletions, in chapter 15.

```
{%- else %}  -- not an incremental run
```

We use the following code if we do not have the HIST table or we want to recreate it from scratch:

```
load_from_input as (
-- load all from the input
)
```

In this case, we just want to load all the data that is arriving from the input.

```
{%- endif %}
```

In both cases, be it an incremental or non-incremental run, we have prepared the data to be saved in the `load_from_input` CTE, so the final step is just to read everything from it:

```
SELECT * FROM load_from_input
-- ORDER BY option to optimize writes
{%- endmacro %}
```

The last option that we are presenting is to add an ORDER BY clause when reading from the `load_from_input` CTE so that the data will be output and then written to disk in the desired order to take advantage of Snowflake micro-partitions.

Now that we have looked at the general flow of the macro, let's delve into each section in detail to analyze the actual code.

Analyzing the parameters of the save_history macro

The following code is the full declaration of the macro, including the optional parameters:

```
{% macro save_history(
    input_rel,
    key_column,
    diff_column,
    load_ts_column = 'LOAD_TS_UTC',
    input_filter_expr = 'true',
    history_filter_expr = 'true',
    high_watermark_column = none,
```

```
    high_watermark_test = '>=',
    order_by_expr = none
) -%}
```

Let's analyze them one at a time:

- The `input_rel` parameter is an object of the `Relation` type, as returned by the `ref()` or `source()` functions, that provides the input data to be saved.

  In our PDP architecture, this is generally an STG model, which, in turn, is reading from a source, but any valid relation would work.

- The `key_column` parameter is a string with the name of the column to be used as a key to determine the most recent version of an instance.

  This parameter is essential for reading data out of the HIST table as it allows us to identify instances of the entity stored in the table, and therefore select the most recent version – that is, the "current" version.

- The `diff_column` parameter is a string that specifies the name of the column that holds the HASH DIFF column. This can be used to compare different versions of the entities stored in the table. It must include the entity key.

- The `load_ts_column` parameter is an optional string with at least the name of the column to be used to order the data to understand what's current.

  By default, its value is LOAD_TS_UTC and points to the field that contains the time when the data was added to the data platform. It can be any column that increases when a new, more recent, version is added.

- The `input_filter_expr` parameter is an optional string with a SQL expression to be used to filter the input data.

  By default, its value is TRUE, which means no filtering of the input. This filter is applied both in incremental and non-incremental runs.

  For efficient operations, filtering is applied to the input model, but the parameter also allows us to filter using data coming from the HIST table itself.

  Another use case is when multiple models depend on the same input model, which means the filtering cannot be pushed back to the input model, as in the case of real-time Lambda architectures.

- The `history_filter_expr` parameter is an optional string with a SQL expression to be used to filter the HIST data.

  By default, its value is TRUE, which means no filtering of the HIST table. This filter is only applied in incremental runs since it applies to the HIST table.

  This parameter is seldom used as, normally, you want to compare the input data with the current version for all the contents of the HIST table, even if it's very old.

If you know that changes cannot go too far in the past, such as in some accounting setups, or only affect a few categories of the data, you can limit the current rows so that they're only in the relevant subset of the HIST table.

When ingesting fact tables, commonly, changes arrive only for the most recent dates, while changes in the far past are extremely rare. In such cases, we can exchange a daily great benefit that's achieved by not loading the current rows from the past with a long history, in exchange for the possibility to add again a row that would have matched a very old version. The data that we read from the HIST table would anyway be perfectly correct.

This filter, used in the same way on the input, gives us a neat solution when we must not accept changes too far in the past, such as in old, already closed exercises where we do not want to see any more changes. This works well but voids the auditability of the HIST versus the source for older data.

- The `high_watermark_column` parameter is an optional string that specifies the name of a column to be used to filter the input based on the max value of the column in the HIST table. It does not limit the current values from the HIST table.

  By default, its value is `none`, which means no filtering of the input. This filter is applied only in incremental runs.

  This column is often a timestamp column pointing to a `LAST_UPDATED` type of column from the table payload or an `EXPORTED_AT` or `INGESTED_TS` type of column from the transport and ingestion pipeline.

  Any column that increases over time and based on which we do not risk having late arrivals is a good candidate, independent of the data type.

- The `high_watermark_test` parameter is an optional string that specifies the comparison operator to be used, along with the `high_watermark_column` parameter.

  By default, its value is `>=`, which means that the data with the same value as the max in the HIST is kept in the input and compared with the HDIFF.

  This is a conservative assumption that makes sense when the high watermark is a date or a week number or a column with quite coarse values, as you might have new data with the same value that arrived after the last ingestion.

  When using a timestamp column or some kind of batch ingestion ID as a high watermark, it is advised that you use `>` for testing if there is no risk of new data with the same value as the last platform run.

- The `order_by_expr` parameter is an optional string that can hold a SQL expression to order the data flowing into the HIST table.

  By default, its value is `none`, which means no ordering to the data.

  This parameter is useful for organizing the data saved in the HIST table to take advantage of Snowflake micro-partitions when reading data out of the table.

As an example, if our data contains rows from a few countries and if we often filter data by country when reading from the HIST model, then ordering the data by country will ensure that the rows for each country appear only in a fraction of the partitions written. This, in turn, will enable SF to prune away the partitions that do not have data on a country if we are filtering on that column.

The sample usage of the `save_history` macro and the preceding discussion of it should give you the perspective that, most of the time, you will just use the three-field basic version that gives you ease of use and a full guarantee of correctness.

In the remaining few cases (maybe 1% to 5%) where the table is big enough (number of rows, number of columns, and size of the data in the column) that there is some performance to gain by better analyzing the load and applying some knowledge of how the data is flowing, then there is ample possibility to achieve excellent performance. In the really big tables putting together the STG and HIST model is the only way to use all the available information to achieve the best performance gains.

This behavior is consistent with the goals of our PDP: making the platform as resilient and easy to use as possible, while allowing the ability to intervene where more complexity/effort brings considerable advantage.

Continuing with the analysis of the macro, we have the `current_from_history` CTE, but as its code is just a call to the `current_from_history` macro, we have deferred its detailed explanation to the next section, where we'll explain the macro.

The core of this pattern is to determine what rows from the input need to be inserted into the HIST table. This job is performed by the two versions of the `load_from_input` CTE – one for the incremental runs and one for the non-incremental ones.

Analyzing the load_from_input CTE – incremental run

If we are in an incremental load, after retrieving the HDIFF columns of the most recent versions from the HIST table, the next operation is to join the incoming data with the HDIFF from the HIST to determine which rows need to be inserted into the HIST table.

The rest of the rows are already there, so we do not need to do anything with them:

```
load_from_input as (
  SELECT i.*
  FROM {{input_rel}} as i
  LEFT OUTER JOIN current_from_history as h
    ON h.{{diff_column}} = i.{{diff_column}}
  WHERE h.{{diff_column}} is null
    and {{input_filter_expr}}
{%- if high_watermark_column %}
  and {{high_watermark_column}} {{high_watermark_test}}
```

```
    (select max({{high_watermark_column}}) from {{ this }})
{%- endif %}
)
```

Let's analyze the code of this CTE in detail:

- The first three clauses of this CTE (SELECT, FROM, and JOIN) select all the columns from the input model and join it with the HDIFF column from the HIST table.

  The main thing to notice here is that only data from the input model is returned and that JOIN is a LEFT OUTER JOIN, potentially keeping all the rows from the input.

- The rest of the CTE is all about the WHERE clause.

  The first filter is the most important and the only one that's needed:

  ```
  WHERE h.{{diff_column}} is null
  ```

  When the JOIN column on the HIST side is not null, this means that there was a match between an input HDIFF and a HIST HDIFF. This means that the two rows represent the same version and the HIST already has it.

  When the JOIN column on the HIST side is null, it means that the row is either a new key or it is a different version of an old key and we need to store it.

  The first part of the WHERE clause just keeps the rows that we want to store.

- The second filter allows us to unconditionally filter the incoming data:

  ```
  and {{input_filter_expr}}
  ```

  This filter allows us to remove data that we do not want to save in the history but cannot be filtered out directly in the input model.

- The third filter is used to apply the high watermark logic:

  ```
  {%- if high_watermark_column %}
   and {{high_watermark_column}} {{high_watermark_test}}
      (select max({{high_watermark_column}})
        from {{ this }} )
  {%- endif %}
  ```

  The if conditional ensures that the filter is added when a high watermark column name is passed since the code would not make sense without one.

  The actual SQL code would generate a simple expression that filters the desired column based on the MAX() value found in the HIST table, as shown in the following example:

  ```
  and LAST_UPDATED >=
      (select MAX(LAST_UPDATED) from HIST_TABLE)
  ```

In the preceding example, I used `LAST_UPDATED` as the value of the `high_watermark_column` parameter and `>=` as the value of the `high_watermark_test` parameter.

To recap, the work of this CTE is very focused: join the input with the HDIFF to only keep the lines that need to be added to the HIST table.

It also provides two extra options to improve the `JOIN` performance by filtering the input table, which means there are fewer rows to compare.

Analyzing the load_from_input CTE – non-incremental run

If we are in a non-incremental load, it means that we either do not yet have the HIST table or that we want to recreate it from scratch.

In both cases, all the rows from the input model need to be inserted in the HIST table, so our code is very simple:

```
load_from_input as (
    SELECT *
    FROM {{input_rel}}
    WHERE {{input_filter_expr}}
)
```

The only option that we have is to filter the incoming data to remove data that we do not want to save in the history but cannot be filtered out directly in the input model.

In this section, we discussed the `save_history` macro. In the next section, we will discuss the `current_from_history` macro, which is the interface for getting the current data from the HIST table. It is used in downstream REF models as well as in the saving macro itself.

Understanding the current_from_history macro

In the previous section, we analyzed the inner workings of the basic macro, which is used to store history of changes for an entity. The `current_from_history` macro is used to read the current data out of such history tables.

In all cases, when we refer to a HIST table, we are referring to a table that stores multiple versions (distinguished by HDIFF) as per the BK (hashed in HKEY), tracking the order in which the versions have been added to the table (LOAD_TS).

The following table provides the two main views of a HIST table – storage by load time and logical by key – using the fields used to control the table's contents:

	Storage of the data by LOAD_TS			Current data		Logical view of the data by KEY		
1								
2	**HKEY**	**HDIFF**	**LOAD_TS**			**HKEY**	**HDIFF**	**LOAD_TS**
3	key01	**ghi**	2023-02-23 17:25	<=	=>	key01	**ghi**	2023-02-23 17:25
4	key01	def	2023-02-22 16:15			key01	def	2023-02-22 16:15
5	key02	**bbb**	2023-02-22 16:15	<=		key01	abc	2023-02-21 15:11
6	key01	abc	2023-02-21 15:11		=>	key02	**bbb**	2023-02-22 16:15
7	key02	aaa	2023-02-21 15:11			key02	aaa	2023-02-21 15:11

Figure 13.8: Storage view and logical view of the data in a HIST table

The `current_from_history` macro is pretty simple – all it does is order the data by key and load timestamp and get the top value for each key.

As an example, to read the current rows out of the `HIST_ABC_BANK_POSITION` model that we created in the previous section, you just need four rows:

```
{{ current_from_history(
    history_rel = ref('HIST_ABC_BANK_POSITION'),
    key_column = 'POSITION_HKEY',
) }}
```

Let's analyze the code of the `current_from_history` macro:

```
{% macro current_from_history(
    history_rel,
    key_column,
    selection_expr = '*',
    load_ts_column = 'LOAD_TS_UTC',
    history_filter_expr = 'true',
    qualify_function = 'row_number'
) -%}
SELECT {{selection_expr}}
FROM {{history_rel}}
WHERE {{history_filter_expr}}
QUALIFY {{qualify_function}}()
    OVER( PARTITION BY {{key_column}}
        ORDER BY {{load_ts_column}} desc ) = 1
{%- endmacro %}
```

Looking at the preceding code, we can see that the heavy lifting is done by the `QUALIFY` clause, where we partition the data by the desired key and order it by the desired column, in descending order, so that the first row that we keep is the most recent.

Looking at the macro declaration, we can see that the only mandatory parameters are the relation to the HIST model and the name of the `HKEY` column.

The other parameters provide flexibility by replacing the default values. Let's discuss them:

- The `history_rel` parameter is an object of the `Relation` type, as returned by the `ref()` or `source()` functions, that points to a HIST table.

- The `key_column` parameter is a string with the name of the column to be used as a key to partition the data and get the current value.

  This parameter provides the granularity at which to get the latest version. It is almost always the same key that's used to store the history, but any key with a coarser grain than the one used to store the data would work.

- The `selection_expr` parameter is an optional string that lists the columns to retrieve from the HIST table.

  The default value is `*`, which means that all columns are retrieved.

- The `load_ts_column` parameter is an optional string that provides the name of the column to order the partitioned data.

  The default value is `LOAD_TS_UTC`, which is the default name in our project.

  When the HIST table also has an effectivity date, this parameter can be used to get the current version according to both the effectivity and load time.

  A value of `load_ts_column='EFFECTIVITY desc, LOAD_TS '` would do the trick to order the partitioning on both columns.

- The `history_filter_expr` parameter is an optional string that provides an expression to filter the data and tell it where to look for the current version in the HIST table.

  The default value is `true`, which means that all data is retrieved.

- The `qualify_function` parameter is an optional string that designates the window function used to filter the HIST table.

  The default value is `row_number`, which means that the most recent row is returned, based on the key used to partition and the column used to order.

  When we use a key with a coarser grain than the data stored in the HIST table, we can use other functions to control what data is retrieved.

  As an example, by using the `rank()` function together with a `MONTH(LOAD_TS_UTC)` order column, you can retrieve all the changes that were made in the month with the most recent data by each key.

Following the usual way of working in our PDP, the `current_from_history` macro makes reading data out of HIST tables a very simple task that you can accomplish with 4 lines of code, but it also provides the flexibility to accommodate more advanced needs.

By chaining an STG model, a HIST model, and the `current_from_history` macro, you now have all the pieces of the puzzle to build a simple, highly resilient load pipeline that allows you to adjust, store, and serve the full range of incoming data for business use in an efficient and highly scalable way.

In the last chapter, we will look at patterns for ingesting data and storing history with more advanced needs such as tracking deletion and multiple changes per load run.

But before that, in the next chapter, we will use our newfound knowledge to refactor our sample project and use the `save_history` macro to create HIST models, add more data, and implement some business rules.

Summary

In this chapter, you learned how to build modular pipelines based on well-thought-out keys that reflect the desired semantics of entities.

You learned how to combine entities from different systems and how to store their changes simply and effectively, according to their semantics.

With the knowledge you've gained in this chapter, you are now able to build modern, maintainable, and scalable data platforms with hundreds of entities and hundreds of millions, or even billions, of rows in the major tables.

In the next chapter, we will wrap up our sample project and use it to discuss a few more topics that come in handy when delivering a real-life project.

Enhancing Software Quality

In this chapter, you will discover and apply more advanced patterns that provide high-quality results in real-life projects, and you will experiment with how to evolve your code with confidence through refactoring.

Through the selection of small use cases around our sample project, you will learn how to save the history of changes of your entities in a very efficient way, how to detect deleted rows from a source, and how to use window functions to leverage the data stored in HIST tables to analyze data evolution over time.

In the last section of this chapter, you will create and apply a macro to properly handle the orphans keys in your facts using self-completing dimensions to produce better quality facts and dimensions for your data marts.

In this chapter, you will learn about the following topics:

- Refactoring and evolving models
- Implementing real-world code and business rules
- Publishing dependable datasets

Technical requirements

This chapter builds on the concepts, the sample project, and the macros discussed in the previous chapters.

The code samples for this chapter are available on GitHub at `https://github.com/PacktPublishing/Data-engineering-with-dbt/tree/main/Chapter_14`.

Refactoring and evolving models

One central idea of our Pragmatic Data Platform is to produce clean code with a clean structure, according to the least surprise principle, which, in turn, promotes quicker development, high maintainability, and reduces developer stress.

Why? Because databases are the longest-lived applications in any company, and they need to be managed for a long time. Therefore, our pipelines will need to change and adapt to business changes and changes in the source systems, and sometimes to changes for compliance or other legal reasons.

Maybe counterintuitively, the more success our data product has, the more requests we will get to add more functionalities. The time and cost of all the changes are directly affected by the quality of the code where the change must be applied.

In this long journey, we will have two activities that will keep our project relevant:

- **Evolution**: This involves adding new functionalities and keeping the existing ones working as expected. Don't take the last part of this sentence for granted.

   Evolution should take advantage of modularity, building new concepts on top of what already exists, and consistently providing only one truth for each concept.

- **Refactoring**: Refactoring *"is a disciplined technique for restructuring an existing body of code, altering its internal structure without changing its external behavior"* as stated on the `Refactoring.` `com` home page, by Martin Fowler, one of my coding heroes.

   The core of refactoring is to do multiple small changes that keep the project working, test after each small change, and in the end replace the initial code with better code that keeps working as desired.

In this chapter, we will start by refactoring the existing code to replace our initial implementation that was using snapshots with the one that uses the HIST tables that we have introduced in the previous chapter and that we prefer to have as a long-term solution.

Later in this chapter, we will add a few more functionalities that have all gone through a first working but rough version, then refactored into a better solution.

You now know all the core concepts that we need to use to start transforming our sample project into a simple, tiny, incomplete, but realistic project. It will never get close to the real thing, but we would like that what we have is well done.

Dealing with technical debt

When evolving the code, the first objective and normal procedure is to create a solution that works, and that includes the core tests that check what we deliver.

Normally, the first solution that we develop is not clean, performant, or both. All the imperfections that we see and that we would like to get rid of go under the name of technical debt.

A bit more formally, **technical debt** can be defined as the cost of future work needed to transform the current solution into a cleaner one that improves (maximizes) our ability to maintain and evolve the project.

Our working, but imperfect, solution now gives us the value of the added functionality, but it has incurred some technical debt that makes it harder to work on the project.

The analogy with the finance world is that of a company that has a limited amount of money that it can borrow before having to repay the debt, so a dev team has limited capacity to deal with complexity before grinding to a halt and having to only fix code.

Continuing with the analogy, it is normal for a company to take some debt to build new capabilities that bring in more revenue, but then it needs to pay it back to keep debt in control. This is because borrowing with a lot of debt becomes more and more expensive, to the point where a company might lose the ability to pay it back.

Similarly, it is normal to have some technical debt, but every team must keep it in check to be sure that they can keep delivering new functionalities at a good pace, and that technical debt does not cause the team to lose effectiveness.

The best strategy to handle technical debt is to try to incur as little as you can in normal times, but to have the flexibility for it to be used in special times.

This means that when we add functionalities, we do not immediately settle for the first working solution; instead, we try to take it to a good level while that area of the code is still in the works, and we have its workings well in our minds.

The natural flow of work is to make an initial version, and then, with the feedback from the team, clean it up by applying one or more rounds of refactoring. Our work is not done until we have a good enough version. *Refactoring is part of the normal work, not extra.*

Think of the first working version as a starting draft and stop when the final, acceptable one is good enough to be seen and worked on every day, even if it's not perfect.

The right attitude is that refactoring the initial version into the acceptable one is not a separate job from delivering the functionality, but the work needed to deliver it sustainably.

This attitude will allow your team to keep debt in check, but the reality is that some debt will trickle through and accumulate anyway. So, how do we deal with it?

Stopping the delivery of new functionalities to concentrate on removing debt makes sense only if you have so much debt that your work is jeopardized by it.

In normal circumstances, the best solution is to keep removing small bits of debt during the normal development work, having a normal attitude to keep or make the code that we happen to work on in good order. This is often called the *"boy scout rule,"* which states that you should leave the place where you stopped better than you found it if you can.

In this section, we learned that refactoring is an essential part of delivering our projects. So, what should be the goals of your refactoring? We think that easy-to-read code, clean architecture, and performant-enough queries are the important ones.

Tools for refactoring in dbt projects

Let's look at the basic tools for refactoring in our projects:

- **Code readability and organization**: We make our code easier to maintain by providing good names for columns, CTEs, and models, and we improve its organization by introducing a CTE that does a single step at a time and splitting big models into smaller models that achieve one goal at a time.

- **Tests**: A generic test provides the first line of defense to guarantee that the data that we receive and produce is of good quality and fulfills expectations.

  Singular tests can provide punctual verification of business rule correctness, checking that the results of a transformation are the expected ones.

  The tests passing on the initial solution must keep passing on each refactoring.

- **Data auditing**: Once we have the initial solution working, we can save the validated results and then, while we keep the input frozen in our dev environment, compare with them the results of each step of the refactoring.

  The process of auditing the changes is greatly simplified by the `audit helper` package: `https://hub.getdbt.com/dbt-labs/audit_helper/latest/`.

We have seen that to keep your project healthy, you have to keep evolving it to provide new functionalities and at the same time constantly refactor it to keep the code clean.

In the next section, we will make a few enhancements to the code in our sample project, including refactoring, where we will start with a solution that can be improved.

Implementing real-world code and business rules

In this section, we will provide many samples of real-life code, replacing the initial sample code with real project code and implementing some business logic, known as business rules, and adding some extra data, showing you how the changes are stored.

Replacing snapshots with HIST tables

The first thing that we want to do is replace the snapshots that we used to store the changes in the incoming data with the HIST tables that we introduced in the previous chapter.

First, we will replace the SNSH_ABC_BANK_POSITION snapshot with the HIST_ABC_BANK_POSITION table in the REF_POSITION_ABC_BANK model:

1. Create a new file named HIST_ABC_BANK_POSITION in the staging folder and add the following code:

    ```
    {{ save_history(
        input_rel = ref('STG_ABC_BANK_POSITION'),
        key_column = 'POSITION_HKEY',
        diff_column = 'POSITION_HDIFF',
    ) }}
    ```

    We presented this code in the previous chapter, where you can learn more about the use of the save_history macro.

    Enter the code and click the **Save** button. Then, click the **Build** button or run the dbt build -s HIST_ABC_BANK_POSITION command.

2. Edit the REF_POSITION_ABC_BANK model so that it uses the HIST table as input in place of the snapshot.

    Here is the current_from_snapshot CTE:

    ```
    current_from_snapshot as (
        {{ current_from_snapshot(
                snsh_ref = ref('SNSH ABC_BANK_POSITION'),
                output_load_ts = false
        ) }}
    )
    ```

    Replace it with the current_from_history CTE, as shown here:

    ```
    current_from_history as (
        {{ current_from_history(
            history_rel = ref('HIST_ABC_BANK_POSITION'),
            key_column = 'POSITION_HKEY',
        ) }}
    )
    ```

    You can immediately see that the two CTE are very similar, with the difference being that to read the current version from the HIST table, we need to specify the key we want to use to retrieve the current version.

    To make the change effective, save the file and build the model.

Second, we will replace the SNSH_ABC_BANK_SECURITY_INFO snapshot with the HIST_ABC_BANK_SECURITY_INFO table in the REF_ABC_BANK_SECURITY_INFO model:

1. Create a new file named HIST_ABC_BANK_SECURITY_INFO in the staging folder and add the following code:

```
{{ save_history(
    input_rel = ref('STG_ABC_BANK_SECURITY_INFO'),
    key_column = 'SECURITY_HKEY',
    diff_column = 'SECURITY_HDIFF',
) }}
```

Enter the code and click the **Save** button. Then, click the **Build** button or run the dbt build -s HIST_ABC_BANK_SECURITY_INFO command.

2. Edit the REF_ABC_BANK_SECURITY_INFO model so that it uses the HIST table as input in place of the snapshot.

Here is the current_from_snapshot CTE:

```
current_from_snapshot as (
  {{ current_from_snapshot(
      snsh_ref = ref(SNSH_ABC_BANK_SECURITY_INFO'),
  ) }}
)
```

Replace it with the current_from_history CTE, as shown here:

```
current_from_history as (
  {{ current_from_history(
      history_rel = ref('HIST_ABC_BANK_SECURITY_INFO'),
      key_column = 'SECURITY_HKEY',
  ) }}
)
```

When you are done, save and build the models.

You can find the full REF files with the code to use the HIST models in the *Chapter 14* materials in the repository associated with this book.

We have now created and deployed the two HIST models and refactored the REF models to use the data coming from the HIST models. Now, the lineage graph looks like this:

Figure 14.1: Lineage graph after the last refactoring

We can now delete or disable the snapshots that are not in use anymore.

To disable the snapshot, add the `{{ config(enabled=false) }}` line inside the snapshot declaration. You could just add the `enabled=false` parameter to the existing `config` definition, but we think that adding it in its own `config` is clearer.

You can now remove the snapshot table from the database.

Note that as you can write it, you do not need any extra privilege to drop the only existing copy of the snapshot, shared by all environments, and potentially wipe away important production data, killing the production environment.

Having the different environments owned and writable by different roles is a common strategy to ensure QA and PROD stay safe and are changed in a controlled way, using dbt commands or migrations. This is another reason why having a HIST table per environment is a better solution. No dev user can wipe away the HIST tables of QA and PROD, which will keep working undisturbed.

Adding the tests to the HIST tables

When we use the HIST tables, there are three tests that we want to put in place:

1. The unicity of the HIST table primary key, which is made by the HKEY property of the entity stored in the HIST table and LOAD_TS_UTC.

    Unless we use an advanced HIST macro to ingest multiple versions of the same key in a single ingestion run, we want to have one version per key per load timestamp.

2. Check that HKEY does not produce a hash collision.

3. Check that HDIFF does not produce a hash collision.

    Let's see the tests for the HIST_ABC_BANK_POSITION model:

    ```
    - name: HIST_ABC_BANK_POSITION
      tests:
        - dbt_utils.unique_combination_of_columns:
            combination_of_columns:
              - POSITION_HKEY
              - LOAD_TS_UTC
    columns:
      - name: POSITION_HKEY
        tests:
          - no_hash_collisions:
              hashed_fields: ACCOUNT_CODE, SECURITY_CODE
      - name: POSITION_HDIFF
        tests:
          - no_hash_collisions:
              hashed_fields: "{{ as_sql_list(
    ```

```
[ 'ACCOUNT_CODE', 'SECURITY_CODE',
  'SECURITY_NAME', 'EXCHANGE_CODE', 'REPORT_DATE',
  'QUANTITY','COST_BASE','POSITION_VALUE','CURRENCY_CODE'
  ] ) }}"
```

You can find the full `staging.yml` file, along with the tests for both HIST models, in the *Chapter 14* materials in the repository associated with this book.

An important consideration is that for this to be a good refactoring the behavior of our project should not change, so the tests on the REF models that we changed to read from the new HIST models should keep passing as before, together with the tests on downstream models.

Renaming the REF_ABC_BANK_SECURITY_INFO model

Looking at the names of our two models in the REF layer, we can see that the `REF_POSITION_ABC_BANK` model has a name that is more business-oriented as it puts the concept first, and the source/master data code universe name after.

The `REF_ABC_BANK_SECURITY_INFO` model, on the other hand, is still more source/MD universe-centric by having it first in the name.

Both ways of naming make sense and in some cases, you might use both because you might need to start with a source-centric REF model, and then apply MD and some rules to transform it into a more business-oriented REF model.

In our sample case, we are dealing with only one bank/source system and neither of our REF models has a surrogate key, only business keys. We do not have an MD set of keys, so we decided to lean on names with the concept first.

So, let's rename the `REF_ABC_BANK_SECURITY_INFO` model and clean up the old table by creating a migration:

1. Rename the `REF_ABC_BANK_SECURITY_INFO` model as `REF_SECURITY_INFO_ABC_BANK` by selecting **Rename** in the IDE.

2. Rename the table in the YAML file where you have the tests and descriptions.

3. Change the reference to the renamed table in the `DIM_SECURITY` model.

    You can use the lineage graph to see the dependencies.

4. Click on the **Build** button to run and deploy the table with the new name.

    All the models and tests should execute correctly, confirming that our refactoring is done and working well.

5. Create a file named `V003_drop_table_with_old_name` in the `macros/migrations` folder to hold the migration code to remove the table with the old name.

Add the following code to the migration file:

```
{% macro V003_drop_table(
        database = target.database,
        schema_prefix = target.schema
) -%}
DROP TABLE IF EXISTS {{database}}.{{schema_prefix
        }}_REFINED.REF_ABC_BANK_SECURITY_INFO;
{%- endmacro %}
```

This macro will produce the code to drop the table.

6.   Add the migration to the `run_migrations` macro by adding the following code to it:

```
{% do log("Running V003_drop_table migration with database = " ~
database ~ ", schema_prefix = " ~ schema_prefix, info=True) %}
{% do run_query(V003_drop_table(database, schema_prefix)) %}
```

This macro will run the code of all active migrations on the database.

You can now run the active migrations in your dev environment by executing dbt `run-operation`
`run_migration`.

To be sure that it is also run in *QA* and *PROD*, verify that the main job ("Build all") contains dbt
`run-operation run_migrations` as the first command.

Refactoring the run_migrations macro

Looking at the `run_migrations` macro, we can see that when we want to add one new migration
to be run, we need to add two lines: one for the log and one for the actual call to the `run_query()`
macro, which will run the SQL code produced by our migration macro.

The driving factor of these two lines is the migration macro's name, and the other parameters, so it
makes sense to consider refactoring all that code inside a macro that would just take the parameters,
producing a call like the following:

```
 run_migration("V003_drop_table", database, schema_prefix)
```

The main problem is that the migration macro's name is used twice, first as a string in the logging,
and a second to call the macro:

- The first use is easy to refactor as we get the string with the macro name, and it is easy to pass
  it forward and use it in the logging.

- The second use of the name is the macro call. Luckily in Jinja, we can assign, pass, and call
  macro objects as we can with functions in Python.

Now, the problem is to go from the macro name as a string to the macro object that we can pass and call.

We can solve this by accessing the `context` variable, which is available in every macro. However, it is an undocumented feature, so there is a potential risk of this stopping working at any time without notice.

If we accept that risk, we can create the following macro that provides the same functionality of the two lines that we want to refactor:

```
{% macro run_migration(migration_name, database,
          schema_prefix) %}
{% if execute %}
{% do log(" * Running " ~ migration_name ~ " migration with database =
" ~ database ~ ", schema_prefix = " ~ schema_prefix, info=True) %}
{% set migration_macro = context.get(migration_name, none)%}
{% do run_query(migration_macro(database, schema_prefix))
          if migration_macro
      else log("!! Macro " ~ migration_name ~ " not found.
            Skipping call.", info=True) %}
{% endif %}
{% endmacro %}
```

Then, we can refactor the two line call and log for the individual migration inside the `run_migrations` macro with a single call to the preceding macro where we pass the name of the migration macro to call:

```
{% do run_migration('V003_drop_table', database,
                schema_prefix) %}
```

You can find both versions of the `run_migrations.sql` file containing these macros in the *Chapter 14* materials in the repository associated with this book.

Handling orphans in facts

In our first version, we have just loaded our fact and our only dimension as they are, pretty much hoping that they would match correctly.

In the real world, when you produce a data mart, you would like that all the foreign keys that you have in a fact exist in the related dimensions.

This is important as we want to be sure that, even when using use equi-joins in our analytics, we do not lose any piece of data. Said in another way, we do not want the FK of the fact to be an orphan of the PK in the dimension.

An equi-join between `fact` and `dim` looks like this:

```
SELECT * FROM fact JOIN dim on fact.FK = dim.PK
```

It will leave out the rows of the fact that do not have a match in the dim.

For this reason, we have a relationship test in our `refined.yml` file between the `REF_POSITION_ABC_BANK` fact and the `REF_SECURITY_INFO_ABC_BANK` dimension. Until the test passes, we are safe, but our safety depends on the inputs.

Another important reason is that `null` values make our metrics unreliable/unpredictable. As an example, SQL queries containing `DISTINCT`, which are very often created by BI tools, will have unexpected behavior.

Look at the following two queries:

```
SELECT DISTINCT c1, c2 FROM t1
-- Select all rows with distinct tuples
-- The presence of null makes a tuple distinct
SELECT COUNT(DISTINCT c1, c2) FROM t1
-- Select the count of distinct combinations of values
-- null is not a value, tuples with null are not counted
```

If you have `null` values in `c1` or `c2`, then the number of rows returned by the first query will be different from the count returned by the second query. This is contrary to common expectations by most SQL developers.

As an example, this can easily happen if you want to analyze promo codes used in orders, if you have a `null` promo code when no promo was used.

You might use a query like the first and correctly get all the combinations of customer code and promo code or all promo codes used in all orders, `null` included, but if you or your BI tool would use something like the second in a calculation (such as to make a percentage of total), you would only count the cases when a promo was used, making your calculation wrong.

In the next section, we will review the reasons why we might have no match between the fact and dimension and then two ways to make sure we are always safe.

Understanding when fact and dimension do not match

In most cases, we expect that an FK will match a PK in the related dimension, but there are cases when this does not happen.

Let's look at the possible situations:

1. Error 1 – not found/data is missing in the dimension.

   This is the typical case where you have an orphan in the fact – that is, the fact has a proper FK that is not found in the dimension.

   Later in this section, we will present two ways to handle this case.

2. Error 2 – missing/data is missing in the fact.

    This happens when you have an FK or a piece of a composite FK that is `null` in a mandatory relation. The mandatory data is missing in the fact.

    In our pipelines, this should be checked by the tests on the source or at least on the STG model if we need to fix some `null` values. In such a case, it's better to introduce a specific default record to highlight that the data is missing from the fact and replace `null` with the default record key in the STG model. If the missing data will be fixed in the future, the newer version of the fact will be the current one in the HIST table.

3. N/A yet – temporarily missing/not yet available.

    In some cases, we have facts that change over time, and some of the data in the fact is not yet available, such as the shipping company or shipping date for an order that is still being prepared for shipping.

    This happens when an FK is `null` while the fact is in some known state. This is a special case of what would otherwise be an Error 2, which is instead valid for a part of the life cycle of the fact. To differentiate this from Error 2, you can create a separate default record.

4. N/A – optional, no data provided/not applicable.

    This happens when we do not have data in an optional relation. This is usually seen as an FK that equals `null` in an optional relation.

    You can handle this during the load in the STG model by replacing the `null` value with the key for the "not applicable" default record.

The preceding discussion presented compelling reasons why there can be multiple **default records** in a dimension.

The number of different default records in a dimension depends on how precise you want to be in recording the reasons why we do not have a match between the fact and the dimension.

The simple solution is to have a single default record, usually with PK = -1, that will be used for all the cases, but in organizations that want to be more precise, this is done at least in some cases (some extra codes for some tables).

Replacing orphans with default records

Cases *2*, *3*, and *4* in the previous list are normally handled directly in the STG model or early in the REF layer as soon as all the data to apply the business rule to distinguish cases 2 and 3 is available.

The classical way to handle case one from the previous list – that is, orphans in the fact – is to replace the orphan FKs with an FK pointing to the right default record. This makes sure that all the FKs in the fact point to an entry in the dimension.

This can easily be achieved by joining the fact with the dimension and replacing the fact FK with the dim PK or the default record PK when the dim PK is null.

The code to achieve this is very simple and is the reason why it is often used:

```
SELECT
    ...
    , coalesce(dim.PK, '-1') as FK
    ...
FROM fact LEFT OUTER JOIN dim ON (dim.PK = fact.FK)
```

In the pseudocode, we assumed `'-1'` to be the PK of the desired default record.

Let's see how we can do this for the REF_POSITION_ABC_BANK fact concerning the REF_SECURITY_INFO_ABC_BANK dimension.

First, let's get the inputs as CTEs:

```
WITH
position as (
    {{ current_from_history(
        history_rel = ref('HIST_ABC_BANK_POSITION'),
        key_column = 'POSITION_HKEY',
    ) }}
)
, security as (
    SELECT * FROM {{ ref('REF_SECURITY_INFO_ABC_BANK') }}
)
```

Now, let's add the new SECURITY_CODE calculation to the calculated fields:

```
SELECT
    p.* exclude (SECURITY_CODE)
    , coalesce(s.SECURITY_CODE, '-1') as SECURITY_CODE
    , POSITION_VALUE - COST_BASE as UNREALIZED_PROFIT
    , ROUND(UNREALIZED_PROFIT / COST_BASE, 5)*100
        as UNREALIZED_PROFIT_PCT
FROM position as p
LEFT OUTER JOIN security as s
    ON(s.SECURITY_CODE = p.SECURITY_CODE)
```

Now, we can be sure that either our fact has an FK that can be found in the dimension, or we have replaced the original FK with the PK of the desired default record.

> **Important note**
>
> Permanently replacing the original FK found in the fact with the PK of one default record, despite being very common, is quite problematic as it amounts to losing information. Missing keys for major dimensions looks bad.
>
> We can afford to do it in our REF models as they are stateless, being re-created at every run. The original FK is safely stored in the HIST table and at every run, it is replaced only if the original FK is not present in the current dimension.
>
> It still looks bad, and you cannot use the lost keys until you fix the dimension.

Contrary to most legacy data platforms built on incremental load in all layers, we can use this simple solution for all the facts that are not loaded incrementally without the risk of permanently losing data, and we can be confident that we will always use the most recent data both from the fact and dimension. We will deliver less usable data in our data marts anyway.

Another problem with this kind of load is performance. It limits the parallelism of the process by forcing all the REF models for the dimensions to be built before the fact that they will be joined on. This wastes some performance from modern architectures that can perform massively parallel computations.

Consider that, despite the fantastic performances of Snowflake on joins, the data size has a quality of its own, and facts tend to be the biggest tables around. If we do an incremental load, we cannot use this load pattern as we would lose data, and if we do the normal full load, joining very large tables would take time.

What are our solutions, then?

The simple but inferior solution is to keep this FK replacement in the REF layer and accept that we will have eventual consistency on our incrementally loaded facts by doing a `full-refresh` run of these fact tables at acceptable time intervals. Hopefully the full refresh run will fix the problem by finding the late arrivals in the dimension when joining the full fact table with the most recent data from the dimension and our data loss will be only temporary.

The far superior solution, called **self-completing dimension**, is to keep the correct data in the facts, loading them independently of each dimension, and instead add the orphan FKs from the facts in the dimensions, completing them with a copy of a default record for each orphan FK from the facts.

This second loading pattern better preserves parallelism as it can be applied on top of REF models of the fact and dimension, even if they are loaded incrementally, and can leverage the exceptional ability of Snowflake (and other columnar databases) to extract the list of distinct values from one column without scanning all the data.

When building the dimension in the data mart, which is generally much smaller than a fact and can be recreated every day, we can take the list of distinct FKs from the facts that join on the dimension and create new entries in the dimension for the FKs that do not (yet) exist in the dimension. The added FKs will have the same values as the desired default record.

Later in this chapter, we will present the macro to automatically create a self-completing dim from the REF models of the dim and the facts using it.

Calculating closed positions

Now that we have brought our existing models up to speed with the patterns we prefer to use, it's time to look at an important business rule that we have not managed.

We have assumed that, in a portfolio, you have one row for each position.

This statement is correct but misses one key point: positions in a portfolio are opened when you buy a security and closed when you sell all of it. The amount of each security that you have can vary up and down. Over time, you can open a new position on a security that you had in the past.

If the account can sell shares short, then you can also open a position by selling one security (going into a negative amount) and close the position by buying it back to have a final amount of zero of that security.

If our source of data is so nice and smart to provide us with the position that has been closed by providing an input row with an amount of zero, then we are fine – there's no need to change our pipeline.

Unfortunately, if we are getting our input from reports of our banking system, either by exporting the positions in the account or by querying them via an API, it is much more likely that we will just get listed the open positions.

In many operational systems and APIs built on top of them, it is common that the focus is to manage the active entities, so the ones that become inactive are either deleted or archived and often are not reported by APIs that are made to work on active entities and not to transfer data between systems.

The problem is that if we do not get any input when a position is closed, we will keep it open at its last value forever, or at least until another position is open on the same security in the same account.

This is a big problem as the value of our portfolio will be wrong, and it will become even more wrong over time as never-closed positions accumulate.

Detecting closed positions from deleted rows

Let's see how we can keep our portfolio correct even if, once we close a position, it is not visible anymore in our portfolio, which means we cannot export it and it is not available anymore in the API that we read from.

This is a very clear case where tracking deletions is needed for the correctness of our pipeline, and it is a quite common situation with facts.

If we are lucky, we get to know that an entity has been closed, deactivated, or deleted as a change to a status column. In this case, we can just use the normal STG and HIST models.

If we are almost lucky, we do not get the information as a change in a status column, but we somehow get a list of entities that have been deleted. We will look at the load pattern for this case in the next chapter.

If we are not lucky and we stop getting data about inactive data, as it happens when they are deleted, we are left with the option to detect their change of status from their absence in the input.

A fundamental requirement to be able to detect the deletion of an entity from its absence in the input is that we always get a full export from the input source, so we can assume that every entity that exists in the HIST table but not in the input has been deleted from the input.

This condition is fundamental and sets a limit on the performance for this loading pattern as we always need to compare the full input with all the current entities.

Dealing with the change in the HIST table

To be able to detect the deletions in the input, we need to act in the load when we have the incoming data and can read the current data from the history.

This means that if we want to track deletions, we need to change the basic loading pattern of the HIST model to detect and save the deleted rows.

In this specific case for the closed positions, when we detect a row that has been deleted from the input, we can also apply a business rule that let us recognize a deleted row as a closed position and set some position values to zero.

While there is no discussion that detecting the deletion belongs to the HIST model, you could argue that applying a business rule in the storage layer is a violation of our PDP design principles.

Let's discuss it and check out the pros and cons:

- We could argue that a deleted position being considered a closed position is more of a hard business rule, something that is in the nature of the data more than a business interpretation.

- Similarly, there is not much interpretation concerning the values of fields such as quantity (of security owned), cost of the current position, and the current value of the position. We think that there are no real alternatives than setting those values to zero. Furthermore, we are not changing any data from a source; we are creating data that is not directly observable to us.

- If we are going to set suitable values for the fields that represent the closed position, we will always have the "correct values" in the HIST model for everyone to read without extra effort.

- If, instead, we detect the deletion in the HIST model and delegate the setting of these values to a model in the REF layer, we would need some extra processing and one more model for it.

- To evaluate the opportunity of implementing the business rule, whether hard or not, it is also worth considering how hard it would be to recognize and change the data affected by the BR. In this case, it is very easy to isolate the data affected by the BR as it is all the positions that are in a closed state.

Given this discussion, we feel that it makes sense to recognize the deleted position and implement the hard BR to set the desired values for the closed positions.

Therefore, in this section, we will show and discuss the code for recognizing and valorizing closed positions.

An alternative path would be to use the generic load pattern of the history with deletions, which we will cover in the next chapter, to generalize the code that we will discuss here, and then set the values of the closed positions.

This last operation can be done by creating a ref model that depends on the HIST table with deletions or by using a post-hook to set the desired values for the newly entered closed position of which we know the state and LOAD_TS, which is the time of the start of the current dbt run.

Implementing the recognition of closed positions

Let's create and discuss the new HIST model that tracks the closed positions:

1. In the staging folder, create a new model file named HIST_ABC_BANK_POSITION_ WITH_CLOSING.sql

2. Start by configuring the incremental materialization:

    ```
    {{ config(materialized='incremental') }}
    ```

3. Then, redefine the shape of the HIST table so that we know the position of the columns that we want to handle in our code:

    ```
    WITH
    stg_input as (
        SELECT
            i.* EXCLUDE (REPORT_DATE, QUANTITY, COST_BASE,
                         POSITION_VALUE, LOAD_TS_UTC)
            , REPORT_DATE
            , QUANTITY
            , COST_BASE
            , POSITION_VALUE
            , LOAD_TS_UTC
            , false as CLOSED
        FROM {{ ref('STG_ABC_BANK_POSITION') }} as i
    ```

    Note that we first exclude the columns that we want to position manually and then we lay them out the way we like.

4. Start the branch when we are in an incremental run:

    ```
    {% if is_incremental() %}-- in an incremental run …
    ```

5. Read the current values from the HIST table with the usual macro:

```
, current_from_history as (
    {{ current_from_history(
        history_rel = this,
        key_column = 'POSITION_HKEY',
    ) }}
),
```

6. Select the data to be loaded in the HIST from the input, as usual:

```
load_from_input as (
    SELECT i.*
    FROM stg_input as i
    LEFT OUTER JOIN current_from_history curr
    ON (not curr.closed
        and i.POSITION_HDIFF = curr.POSITION_HDIFF)
    WHERE curr.POSITION_HDIFF is null
),
```

7. Select the data that has been deleted – that is, the active rows in the HIST table that are not in the input – and set the values to represent a closed position:

```
closed_from_hist as (
  SELECT
    curr.* EXCLUDE (REPORT_DATE, QUANTITY, COST_BASE,
                    POSITION_VALUE, LOAD_TS_UTC, CLOSED)
    , (SELECT MAX(REPORT_DATE) FROM stg_input)
            as REPORT_DATE
    , 0 as QUANTITY
    , 0 as COST_BASE
    , 0 as POSITION_VALUE
    , '{{ run_started_at }}' as LOAD_TS_UTC
    , true as CLOSED
  FROM current_from_history curr
  LEFT OUTER JOIN stg_input as i
    ON (i.POSITION_HKEY = curr.POSITION_HKEY)
  WHERE not curr.closed
    and i.POSITION_HKEY is null
),
```

Note that we keep most of the columns for a closed position with the same values that the position had in the last version before being closed. This is something that you need to decide and act on according to your definition.

8. Build the changes to be stored in an incremental run by putting together the new data from the input and the closed positions that were identified:

```
changes_to_store as (
    SELECT * FROM load_from_input
    UNION ALL
    SELECT * FROM closed_from_hist
)
```

This is the last CTE of the incremental branch.

9. If this is not an incremental run – that is, we are creating the table from scratch – we get all the data from the reshaped input and we have no deletions:

```
{%- else %}-- not an incremental run …
, changes_to_store as (
    SELECT *
    FROM stg_input
)
```

10. Last, but not least, let's select the changes to be stored:

```
{%- endif %}
SELECT * FROM changes_to_store
```

If you compare this loading pattern with the one from the `save_history` macro, you will notice two changes: initially, we re-shape the input data so that we leave the columns to handle at the end, and during the incremental run, we detect and add the deleted rows to the HIST table.

Now, if you run the new model, it will just store the data from the input as it is doing the normal, old HIST model, as we do not have any deletions.

In the next section, we will modify the content of the table that mimics the external source so that we can see what will be stored by the new model when positions are added or closed.

Adding new data to the position fact

So far, we have always had the same data in the `ABC_BANK_POSITION` table that we use as a source and that we initially loaded directly into Snowflake from a CSV file exported from an Excel spreadsheet.

Now, we want to make changes in that table to simulate the arrival of different inputs at the start of our pipeline.

The changes that we want to simulate in our portfolio are as follows:

1. Create a new position in the `'SAFE'` stock. The stock will not be listed in the stock info dimension.
2. Change the position in the `'STAR'` stock.
3. Close the position in the `'GCM'` stock.

To change the content of the source table, we can reload it from a new CSV. This would be logical if we were to export the data from a real portfolio, but to keep the example quick and easy to replicate, we will alter the content of the table by using a few SQL statements that we will store in an analysis, from where we can easily run the SQL.

To apply these three changes, you can run the following SQL code:

```
DELETE FROM PORTFOLIO_TRACKING.SOURCE_DATA.ABC_BANK_POSITION
WHERE ACCOUNTID='ABC000123'
    and SYMBOL IN ('GCM', 'SAFE', 'STAR');
```

The previous code removes the old positions in 'GCM', 'SAFE', and 'STAR', while the following code inserts the new positions in 'SAFE' and 'STAR':

```
INSERT INTO PORTFOLIO_TRACKING.SOURCE_DATA.ABC_BANK_POSITION
        (ACCOUNTID, SYMBOL, DESCRIPTION, EXCHANGE, REPORT_DATE, QUANTITY,
    COST_BASE, POSITION_VALUE, CURRENCY)
    VALUES
        ('ABC000123', 'SAFE', 'SAFEHOLD INC', 'NYSE', '2022-04-23', 100,
    4015.00000, 4389.50000, 'USD')
        , ('ABC000123', 'STAR', 'ISTAR INC', 'NYSE', '2022-04-23', 200,
    3125.00000, 2950.50000, 'USD');
```

Once you have run that code, your source table should contain the following data:

Row	ACCOUNTID	SYMBOL	DESCRIPTION	EXCHANGE	REPORT_DATE	QUANTITY	COST_BASE	POSITION_VALU	CURRENCY
1	ABC000123	TTD	TRADE DES...	NASDAQ	0021-04-09	10	5310.45000	6925.60000	USD
2	ABC000123	SAFE	SAFEHOLD I...	NYSE	2022-04-23	100	4015.00000	4389.50000	USD
3	ABC000123	STAR	ISTAR INC	NYSE	2022-04-23	200	3125.00000	2950.50000	USD

Figure 14.2: Indicative content of the source position table

You can find the preceding SQL code in the `analysis` folder in the accompanying repository under the materials for this chapter.

Understanding how closed positions are stored

Let's run the pipeline and see what will be in the HIST tables.

Once we have the source table with the new portfolio situation, we can run our pipeline with the following command:

```
dbt build -s staging
```

This will run and test all the models in the staging folder, including the old and new HIST tables:

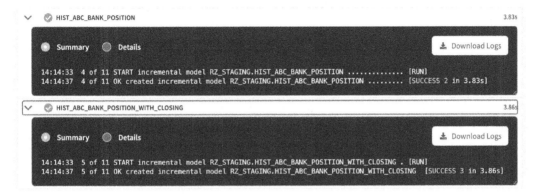

Figure 14.3: Results of the run with the new portfolio as input

Looking at the result of the run, you can see that two rows have been inserted into the normal HIST table. They are the row for the new position in 'SAFE', and for the changed position in 'STAR':

Row	ACCOUNT_CODE	SECURITY_CODE	REPORT_DATE	QUANTITY	COST_BASE	POSITION_VALUE	LOAD_TS_UTC
1	ABC000123	GCM	2021-04-09	100	559.00000	678.00000	2023-03-08 14:12:32....
2	ABC000123	SAFE	2022-04-23	100	4015.00000	4389.50000	2023-03-08 14:14:29....
3	ABC000123	STAR	2021-04-09	150	2444.00000	2725.50000	2023-03-08 14:12:32....
4	ABC000123	STAR	2022-04-23	200	3125.00000	2950.50000	2023-03-08 14:14:29....
5	ABC000123	TTD	2021-04-09	10	5310.45000	6925.60000	2023-03-08 14:12:32....

Figure 14.4: Selected contents of the normal HIST table

Note that the position in 'GCM' is still open, and only two rows have been updated by the run at **14:14** with the new contents of the portfolio.

On the other hand, the new HIST table with the closed position has three new entries. Two are the same as the old HIST table, while the third is the closed position in 'GCM':

Row	ACCOUNT_CODE	SECURITY_CODE	REPORT_DATE	QUANTITY	COST_BASE	POSITION_VALUE	LOAD_TS_UTC	CLOSED
1	ABC000123	GCM	2021-04-09	100	559.00000	678.00000	2023-03-08 14:12:32....	FALSE
2	ABC000123	GCM	2022-04-23	0	0.00000	0.00000	2023-03-08 14:14:29....	TRUE
3	ABC000123	SAFE	2022-04-23	100	4015.00000	4389.50000	2023-03-08 14:14:29....	FALSE
4	ABC000123	STAR	2021-04-09	150	2444.00000	2725.50000	2023-03-08 14:12:32....	FALSE
5	ABC000123	STAR	2022-04-23	200	3125.00000	2950.5000	2023-03-08 14:14:29....	FALSE
6	ABC000123	TTD	2021-04-09	10	5310.45000	6925.60000	2023-03-08 14:12:32....	FALSE

Figure 14.5: Selected contents of the HIST table with closed positions

Note that now, three rows have been updated by the run at **14:14** with the new contents of the portfolio. The third row that was inserted is the one with `quantity` = 0 to close the position in the `'GCM'` stock.

Picking the right loading pattern to load history

Now that you have two HIST tables with different data for the same input, you might wonder which one is correct.

Both tables are correct, as they both correctly record what they set out to record.

The question you should have is not about correctness, but about how to choose the right pattern. It is us, the analytics engineers, that must choose the right loading pattern based on the data to be loaded and how the data is exported from the source system.

In general, you can load with the basic history loading pattern all the dimensions, whose entries we must keep in use even after they are deleted, and the facts that are not deleted, but eventually disabled or deactivated. We can also use this pattern when we have Change Tracking or Change Data Capture enabled to get the data from the source, along with the column telling us when the entries of the table are deleted.

In all cases where we have facts where rows are deleted and we do not get the information of the deletion as part of the source data, we must use the load pattern which recognizes and stores the deletions, even if it is not as performant as the other.

Getting the closed position in the flow

Now that we have created the new HIST table that detects the closed positions, let's get this better data into use in place of the old HIST table.

Open the `REF_POSITION_ABC_BANK` model and replace the reference to the old HIST table in the `current_from_history` macro:

```
history_rel = ref('HIST_ABC_BANK_POSITION'),
```

Apply the following reference to the new HIST table:

```
history_rel = ref('HIST_ABC_BANK_POSITION_WITH_CLOSING'),
```

Now, if you try to run the REF model, you will receive an error. This is because we have a division by zero in correspondence with the closed position as the cost basis is now zero.

To remove the error and output a value of zero when we have a cost basis value of zero, we must replace the normal division with the SF `DIV0` function:

```
, ROUND(DIV0(UNREALIZED_PROFIT, COST_BASE), 5)*100
    as UNREALIZED_PROFIT_PCT
```

Consider that another possible alternative would be to set the UNREALIZED_PROFIT_PCT column to null. While it might make a lot of sense from the SQL and theoretical points of view, it would probably make the presentation in your BI tool not so nice.

A compromise might be to set it null in the REF model and change it to 0 in the data mart. Beware that too many of these cosmetic rules would make you data mart code less clear to read.

Now, running the REF model will give you a truthful representation of your portfolio, with the closed position showing up as closed:

Row	ACCOUNT_CODE	SECURITY_CODE	QUANTITY	COST_BASE	POSITION_VALUE	LOAD_TS_UTC	CLOSED	UNREALIZED_PR	UNREALIZED_PR
1	ABC000123	-1	100	4015.00000	4389.50000	2023-03-08 ...	FALSE	374.50000	9.32800
2	ABC000123	GCM	0	0.00000	0.00000	2023-03-08 ...	TRUE	0.00000	0.00000
3	ABC000123	STAR	200	3125.00000	2950.50000	2023-03-08 ...	FALSE	-174.50000	-5.58400
4	ABC000123	TTD	10	5310.45000	6925.60000	2023-03-08 ...	FALSE	1615.15000	30.41500

Figure 14.6: REF model for the positions with the closed positions

Please note SECURITY_CODE = -1 in the first row and how bad it looks. We have it because we do not (yet) have the row for the SAFE security in the Security Info dimension and our code to remove the orphan key replaced it with the default key (-1).

In the next section, we'll learn about publishing dependable datasets and how to use self-completing dimensions to avoid this issue.

For now, let's think about FACT_POSITION, which we publish in our data mart.

Do we want it to also show the closed positions, all the closed positions since the beginning of time? Or we do prefer to just have the open positions?

In the first case, you have nothing to do, as all the closed positions are what you are now getting in the REF model. We think that this is the appropriate behavior for the REF model as it is very easy to filter out the closed positions in all cases where you do not want to have them.

As an example, if you want your FACT_POSITION to not show the closed positions, you can just add a simple WHERE clause to make it look as follows:

```
SELECT * FROM {{ ref('REF_POSITION_ABC_BANK') }}
WHERE NOT CLOSED
```

By choosing appropriate naming conventions for our columns, the SQL that we write turns out to be very simple to understand.

Calculating transactions

Now that we have the closing of the positions, we can use that to infer the transactions that generate the changes in the position we observe.

From an observability point of view, it would be much better the other way around – that is, having the transactions as the provided input (along with an initial state). That would easily allow us to calculate the changes in positions.

The basic idea that we want to implement is that when we have a change in a position, we will calculate a transaction that will bridge the gap between the two positions that we observe.

The transactions that we will generate will have the accurate number of securities bought or sold and should have a good estimation of the cost incurred in buying, because the cost basis should change only when buying securities. We will have a low precision of the proceeds obtained by selling the stock as the value of the position is based on the day when we get the export of the position. This might be far from when the sale happened. Lastly, we do not get a value of the position when the position is closed, so we must use the value from the previuos transaction. In this case, having daily quotes for the stock would improve our situation very much.

We have created a new model named `REF_POSITION_TX__ABC_BANK` in the REF folder. Let's have a look at the code to calculate the buy/sell transactions that we have in the model:

```
WITH
position_history as (
    SELECT *
    FROM {{ ref('HIST_ABC_BANK_POSITION_WITH_CLOSING') }}
)
```

The first thing we need to do is read all the data from the HIST table with the closed positions, not only the current data.

Next, we must use the `LAG()` window function to bring into each row some values from the previous row in the window, partitioned by position and ordered by time:

```
, position_with_lead as (
    SELECT
        p.*
    , LAG(QUANTITY) OVER(PARTITION BY POSITION_HKEY
            ORDER BY LOAD_TS_UTC) as PREV_QUANTITY
    , LAG(COST_BASE) OVER(PARTITION BY POSITION_HKEY
            ORDER BY LOAD_TS_UTC) as PREV_COST_BASE
    , LAG(POSITION_VALUE) OVER(PARTITION BY POSITION_HKEY
            ORDER BY LOAD_TS_UTC) as PREV_POSITION_VALUE
    FROM position_history as p
)
```

In this way, every row contains the values from the previous position in the PREV_xxx columns and null if there was no previous position.

Then, we must take some data from the position to create a key from the position key and the data of the report of the change in the position:

```
, tx_calculation as (
    SELECT
            {{ dbt_utils.surrogate_key(['ACCOUNT_CODE',
                'SECURITY_CODE', 'REPORT_DATE']) }}
                as TX_HKEY
      , ACCOUNT_CODE
      , SECURITY_CODE
      , REPORT_DATE
```

We created an HKEY mostly to identify the intended Business Key and make testing and joining easier.

Next, we must take a few more columns from the position to describe the transaction:

```
      , SECURITY_NAME
      , EXCHANGE_CODE
      , CURRENCY_CODE
      , RECORD_SOURCE
      , LOAD_TS_UTC
```

Then, we must calculate the new metrics for the transaction:

```
    , COALESCE(QUANTITY - PREV_QUANTITY, QUANTITY)
        as QUANTITY_PURCHASED
    , CASE
      WHEN QUANTITY_PURCHASED > 0 THEN 'BUY'
      WHEN QUANTITY_PURCHASED < 0 THEN 'SELL'
      ELSE 'UNCHANGED'
    END as TX_TYPE
    ,CASE
      WHEN QUANTITY_PURCHASED > 0
        THEN -1 * COALESCE(COST_BASE - PREV_COST_BASE,
                            COST_BASE)
      WHEN QUANTITY_PURCHASED < 0
        THEN IFF(QUANTITY = 0, PREV_POSITION_VALUE,
              POSITION_VALUE / QUANTITY * QUANTITY_PURCHASED)
      ELSE 0
    END as ESTIMATED_TX_PROCEEDS
```

The QUANTITY_PURCHASED metric is the difference between the current quantity and the previous one unless the previous was null as we are opening the position. In such cases, the variation is the quantity itself.

This value should be correct, or at least correctly represent all the transactions that happened between the two different positions that we have observed.

The TX_TYPE metric provides an easy-to-understand semantic regarding the direction of the transaction.

The *ESTIMATED_TX_PROCEEDS* metric, as the name implies, is an estimation of the monetary flow associated with the transaction (negative for buy, positive for sell). As explained previously, the cost of buying should be accurate, while the proceeds for the sale are only an estimation (based on the last change of the position before selling).

We will close this CTE with the metrics that describe the position after the transaction:

```
    , QUANTITY            as FINAL_QUANTITY
    , COST_BASE           as FINAL_COST_BASE
    , POSITION_VALUE      as FINAL_POSITION_VALUE
FROM position_with_lead as p
)
```

Finally, we will close the model by returning the columns from the previous CTE with the data ordered by the transaction key:

```
SELECT * FROM tx_calculation
ORDER BY ACCOUNT_CODE, SECURITY_CODE, REPORT_DATE
```

If we would like to use this new fact in our data mart, along with the security info dimension, we might add a CTE to join it with the dimension to remove orphans, but we prefer not to remove the missing key and use the self-completing dimension pattern. In this case, completing the dimension for the position fact will also complete the transactions as the list of securities involved is the same.

Publishing dependable datasets

The role of the delivery layer is to make our data, built in the REF layer, accessible to our users, who will use them in a variety of ways.

One thing that we can be sure about is that the more often we change the layout of our data in the delivery layer, the less happy our customers will be as they must react to all our changes.

Unexpected changes are another good way to anger your customers.

What should we learn from this?

Managing data marts like APIs

The tables and views that you publish in your data marts are the public APIs of your data platform, so you should handle them as such.

These are the basic starting points to make the life of your clients better:

- Provide clear and consistent naming for columns and tables.

  As an example, do not call the same thing PRODUCT_ID in one place and PRODUCT_CODE in another. Always use the same term for the same concept, and do not mix synonyms (PRODUCT, ITEM, MERCHANDISE, and so on).

- Use a consistent naming convention.

  As an example, name all the PKs in a similar way – for example, <ENTITY>_CODE.

- Use correct and predictable data types.

  Are you going to do math on PKs and FKs? No, so you better have them as text rather than numbers, even if they look like numbers.

- Decide on the set of default records that you want to use and consistently apply them.

- Right-size your data marts. Small data marts are easier to understand and use than huge ones with hundreds of tables, but if you have too many data marts, it's difficult to name them in a good descriptive way, and it becomes difficult for your users to find the right data mart.

- Once you publish a fact or dimension, refrain from renaming it, renaming the columns inside, or changing the data types.

- When you want/need to change your API, do so in a controlled and communicated way. Provide a timeframe for the change and if the change would break the clients, consider leaving the old version available (at least for a transition period), and provide the new one under a new name.

To ease your work in keeping the external API constant, you can try to deliver your data marts as views on top of the final tables with the data so that, if for some reason you have to change the underlying tables, you can keep the external interface unchanged, trying to absorb the change in the view publishing the data.

What shape should you use for your data mart?

Different uses of the data call for different ways to deliver the dataset for optimal usability.

As an example, for most AI/ML workloads, it is preferable to provide a wide table with all the interesting data cleaned up and pre-joined to the desired granularity, while most BI tools expect to have data models provided in Kimball style – that is, in the shape of a star schema.

Do not think that all cases should use the same data mart; instead, look at what could be the best solution for each use case.

As an example, if you have to power a REST API, it is better to provide tables that are cut along the data that the API is serving. You should try to use *Hybrid Tables* from *Snowflake Unistore*'s new functionality.

When you are looking into operational activities and you want to analyze error situations or when processes do not complete as expected or are left halfway, it might be useful to build a few composite facts using full outer joins so that, besides the usual matching data from the normal (inner) join, you can also observe the data that is not matching from both sides.

If you recall our discussion of the *Unified Star Schema* from *Chapter 3*, you can leverage the UNION ALL operator to build wide tables with many FKs built by following the relations in the data to report on seemingly disparate objects that instead have some common FK in their chain of relations.

In most cases, you will have at least some data mart prepared for power reporting with BI tools, providing a Kimball star schema.

In *Chapter 10*, we discussed how to build star schema in an agile way, but let's recap the key points here:

- Your data marts will contain many facts, as they will power multiple related reports that use the same dimensions.

- You should provide the needed composite facts, joining multiple individual base facts from the REF layer using the existing relationships, so that each report can be built using one single fact.

- Provide dimensions and hierarchies so that your facts have no orphans. We will see how to do that with the self-completing dimensions next.

- Avoid putting metrics in the dimensions as much as possible as they open up the possibility of getting wildly wrong numbers because of fan traps.

- Decide for which fields that might also be available in a dimension you want to provide as part of a fact with the historical value. As an example, the address at the time of delivery, because the normal dimension (SCD type one) will contain the current value, which might be different.

- Decide what dimensions should (also) be available with all the history of changes, and put the right version FK (the HDIFF from the version in the dimension is a great candidate) in the facts that want to use these *SCDs of type two*.

Please go back to *Chapter 10* for more details on this, as well as the huge number of books published on this topic for all the nitty gritty details.

In the next section, we will learn how to build self-completing dimensions.

Self-completing dimensions

The SAFE stock is now missing from the stock info dimension.

This causes the POSITION fact to be missing the SAFE security code as it has been replaced by -1, which is the key for the default record.

In this section, we will learn how to replace this old way of handling orphans with a more modern one that takes advantage of modern cloud platforms.

We will do this by following these steps:

1. Create the self_completing_dimension macro that encapsulates this delivery pattern, making it easy to use by all developers.

2. Create a new DIM_SECURITY_INFO dimension using this macro. You can also change the existing DIM_SECURITY to use the macro.

3. Remove the join on the REF model of the SECURITY dimension to remove the orphans from the fact from the POSITION fact in the REF layer.

4. Move the relationship test from the models in the REF layer to the FACT toward the DIMENSION in the delivery layer, as it should be.

At the end of these steps, you will have a POSITION fact that is not altered and keeps the correct values of its FKs, and a SECURITY dimension that can join on all the FKs of this and eventually other facts that relate to it.

Creating the self_completing_dimension macro

This macro is used in the delivery layer, so let's create a folder named delivery in the macros folder and create a self_completing_dimension.sql file to hold the code of the macro.

Let's analyze the macro one block/CTE at a time:

```
{%- macro self_completing_dimension(
    dim_rel,
    dim_key_column,
    dim_default_key_value = '-1',
    rel_columns_to_exclude = [],
    fact_defs = []
) -%}
```

First, we declare the macro with the following parameters:

*   dim_rel is a relation pointing to the model containing the base data for the dimension. Generally, this is the REF model for the dimension.

*   dim_key_column is the name of the PK column of the dimension.

- `dim_default_key_value` is the string value of the PK of the default record to be used to populate the rows for the orphan keys.

- `rel_columns_to_exclude` is a list of the columns of the given relationship that we do not want to expose in the final dimension. This generally contains the HKEY, HDIFF, and other columns that are not needed in the data mart.

- `fact_defs` is a list of fact definition objects, with each object in the form of a dictionary that has the two fields `model` and `key` – for example, `[ {'model': 'REF_POSITION_ABC_BANK', 'key': 'SECURITY_CODE'} ]`.

  If the list is empty, the DIM is a normal dim from the REF model.

Next, we must add the key for the dimension to the list of fields to be excluded:

```
{% do rel_columns_to_exclude.append(dim_key_column) -%}
```

This is because we want to make sure that the key is in the first position in the dim.

The first CTE selects the base data that we want to have in the dimension:

```
WITH
dim_base as (
  SELECT
    {{ dim_key_column }}
    , d.* EXCLUDE( {{rel_columns_to_exclude|join(', ')}} )
  FROM {{ dim_rel }} as d
),
```

As you can see, we exclude all the columns that we do not want, as well as the key of the dimension, so that we can position it manually where we want.

The following CTE builds the list of values that appear in the FK of all the facts related to this dimension:

```
fact_key_list as (
  {% if fact_defs|length > 0 %} -- If some FACT passed
    {%- for fact_model_key in fact_defs %}
      SELECT DISTINCT
        {{fact_model_key['key']}} as FOREIGN_KEY
      FROM {{ ref(fact_model_key['model']) }}
      WHERE {{fact_model_key['key']}} is not null
      {% if not loop.last %} union {% endif %}
    {%- endfor -%}
  {%- else %} -- If NO FACT, list is empty.
    select null as FOREIGN_KEY WHERE false
  {%- endif%}
),
```

We just need to extract the list of distinct values from each fact. Then, we can UNION the result from each fact so that we do not have duplicates. Contrary to normal transactional databases, the select distinct operation is very quick on Snowflake.

If no fact is passed, the list is empty and the CTE returns no rows.

The following CTE joins the list of keys from the facts with the dimension base and keeps only the ones that do not exist in the dimension:

```
missing_keys as (
    SELECT fkl.FOREIGN_KEY
    FROM fact_key_list fkl
    LEFT OUTER JOIN dim_base
      ON dim_base.{{dim_key_column}} = fkl.FOREIGN_KEY
    WHERE dim_base.{{dim_key_column}} is null
),
```

The following CTE extracts the row of the desired default key from the dimension:

```
default_record as (
    SELECT *
    FROM dim_base
    WHERE {{dim_key_column}} = '{{dim_default_key_value}}'
    LIMIT 1
),
```

If you have multiple versions of the desired default record and you want to ensure you pick the latest, you can replace the simple LIMIT 1 with a QUALIFY expression, but you also need to provide the column to sort on.

The following CTE puts together the list of missing keys with the values of the default record to produce the new rows to be added to complete the dimension:

```
dim_missing_entries as (
    SELECT
        mk.FOREIGN_KEY,
        dr.* EXCLUDE( {{ dim_key_column }} )
    FROM missing_keys as mk
    JOIN default_record dr
),
```

This CTE replicates the row of the default record for each missing key.

Note that this is a CROSS JOIN because we do not have an ON clause to limit what row from one side is joined with the rows on the other side. This works well as we have a few rows of missing keys joined with a single row with the default record.

The final CTE builds the final dimension by putting together the content of the dimension properly with the new rows for the missing entries:

```
dim as (
    SELECT * FROM dim_base
    UNION ALL
    SELECT * FROM dim_missing_entries
)
SELECT * FROM dim
{% endmacro %}
```

The last line returns the contents of the completed dimension. Now, the macro is ready to be used.

Creating the self-completing security dimension

Now, let's use this macro to create the self-completing version of the security dimension.

You can create a new file in your data mart, or you can modify the existing DIM_SECURITY model with the following content:

```
{{ self_completing_dimension(
    dim_rel = ref('REF_SECURITY_INFO_ABC_BANK'),
    dim_key_column   = 'SECURITY_CODE',
    dim_default_key_value = '-1',
    rel_columns_to_exclude =
        ['SECURITY_HKEY','SECURITY_HDIFF'],
    fact_defs = [ {'model': 'REF_POSITION_ABC_BANK',
                   'key': 'SECURITY_CODE'} ]
) }}
```

As explained alongside the code of the macro, we just pass the relation to the model with the data for the dimension, the name of the PK column, and the value of the PK for the default record that we want to use for the line that we created to complete the dimension.

The rel_columns_to_exclude parameter is a utility that allows us to easily remove from the published dimension the columns that we do not need in the data mart.

It is important to note that you can pass the definition of each fact that might introduce orphans into the fact_defs parameter. A fact definition is made of the fact model name and the name of the FK to the dimension.

In our case, since the transactions are calculated out of the positions, the set of securities named is the same, so there's no need to pass both, but it would not hurt.

The following screenshot shows the content of the self-completing dimension after introducing the SAFE position in our portfolio:

Row	SECURITY_CODE	SECURITY_NAME	SECTOR_NAME	INDUSTRY_NAME	COUNTRY_CODE	EXCHANGE_CODE	RECORD_SOURCE	LOAD_TS_UTC
1	TTD	The Trading De...	Technology	EDP Services	US	NASDAQ	SEED.ABC_Ban...	2023-01-21 17:...
2	STAR	ISTAR INC	Real Estate	REIT - Diversifi...	US	NYSE	SEED.ABC_Ban...	2023-01-21 17:...
3	GCM	GRAN COLOM...	Basic Materials	GOLD	CA	TSE	SEED.ABC_Ban...	2023-01-21 17:...
4	-1	Missing	Missing	Missing	-1	-1	System.Default...	2020-01-01 00:...
5	SAFE	Missing	Missing	Missing	-1	-1	System.Default...	2020-01-01 00:...

Figure 14.7: Content of the self-completing security dimension

As you can see, the dimension now has an entry for PK = SAFE, and the content of the row is the same as the default record.

This, together with the discussion about the multiple default records that we had previously, allows you to choose the right values of the columns for your reports.

Restoring the position fact to keep its data unchanged

If you previewed the self-completing dimension and you do not see the row with the SAFE PK, chances are that you have forgotten to restore the position fact to its completeness.

To fix this, open the REF_POSITION_ABC_BANK model and change the final query to its original form, as shown here:

```
SELECT
    p.*
    , POSITION_VALUE - COST_BASE as UNREALIZED_PROFIT
    , ROUND(DIV0(UNREALIZED_PROFIT, COST_BASE), 5)*100
        as UNREALIZED_PROFIT_PCT
FROM position as p
```

By removing the join on the security dimension and using the fact's own FK, we remove the dependency from the REF layer and we have the SAFE FK back in our fact, which will, in turn, become available in the self-completing dimension.

Moving the test on the orphan PK of the position fact

Last but not least, we must move to the delivery layer the test on the relationship between the position fact and the security model, which is now in the REF layer.

By removing the join in the REF model, the test could fail, but what we care about is that the relationship is valid and doesn't have orphans in the delivery layer, where our BI tool will try to do the equi-joins.

To move the test to the delivery layer, start by removing it from the section of the REF_POSITION_ABC_BANK table in the refined.yml file.

Then, you can add it to the _portfolio.yml file, as follows:

```
- name: FACT_POSITION
  columns:
    - name: SECURITY_CODE
      description: The code of the security
      tests:
        - relationships:
            to: ref('DIM_SECURITY')
            field: SECURITY_CODE
```

The preceding code will test that the position fact does not have orphans in the relationship with the security dimension.

Now, our position fact is intact, our security dimension is complete, and all the tests should pass flawlessly.

History in reports – that is, slowly changing dimensions type two

Most reports are based on the current values of the dimensions as businesses want to see the current name of companies, the current contact, the current phone/email, and the current name of the product – not how it was 3 months or 3 years ago when the order/contract was done.

What we have done until now, by extracting the current data from the history tables in the REF layer, is geared to this kind of reporting, but our approach to storing the history with all the changes allows us to serve those cases when you need to look at how the data was back in time.

In our history tables, we already have all the versions of the data that we have seen and by creating the HDIFF column in the STG, we have also created a unique key for these versions.

Our history tables efficiently store the data that you need to produce what is more formally called a **slowly changing dimension** of type two.

By extracting the data from the HIST table and taking only one copy for each HDIFF (remember that you might see and store the same content multiple times), you can build an SCD2 dimension with all the versions of an entity.

To be able to use such a dimension, you must enrich the facts that you want to join to it with the correct HDIFF based on the fact date and the validity period of the different HDIFF for a specific HKEY.

You can calculate the validity period for each HDIFF using the LAG function in a similar way to what we did to calculate the transactions from the positions.

To enrich the HDIFF, you start with the fact that gives you the dimension FK and some relevant date that you can use to look up the HDIFF in the SCD2 dimension based on the PK and the validity ranges.

A detailed discussion of this topic is beyond the scope of this chapter, but once you recognize that all the data is in the HIST table and that you can easily build the validity range of each record in the HIST table, then you are well on track to building your first SCD2.

Summary

Congratulations!

In this chapter, you discovered and applied more advanced patterns to improve the quality of your projects and experimented with how to evolve your code through refactoring.

You also learned how to save the history of changes of your entities, how to detect deletion from a source, how to better handle the orphans of your facts using self-completing dimensions, and how to use window functions to leverage the data stored in the HIST tables to analyze data evolution over time.

In the next chapter, *Patterns for Common Use Cases*, you will find a small library of common use patterns for ingesting data in Snowflake to extend the range of history tables, as well as a few more specialized patterns.

Further reading

In this chapter, we introduced and experimented with the concept of refactoring, which is key for each professional code developer and every real-life project.

If you are serious about this profession, I want to recommend Martin's book because it has been exceptionally important in my education as a developer.

It shaped my views that software is an ever-evolving body of knowledge expressed as code that you must keep in good shape to keep evolving it. Because of that core need, the goal of good developers is to express that knowledge as clearly as possible for colleagues that will come, including your future self, who will read that code again and again.

It also cemented my belief that tests are the superpower that allows developers to sleep well at night and be able to confidently go to the office day after day.

While SQL code and its use together with Jinja in dbt are different from pure Python or Java coding, the basics behind producing good working software are the same. Even if you won't be able to adopt the refactoring techniques exactly as presented for Java (in the first edition) or JavaScript (in the second edition), you will be able to absorb the ideas and techniques because the book was written not for a specific language, but with the explicit goal to be of general use:

- *Refactoring, Improving the Design of Existing Code*, 2nd edition, 2018, by Martin Fowler, with Kent Beck: `https://martinfowler.com/books/refactoring.html`

PS: In the first chapter, you will find a suggestion that I quote in many of my social profiles, to tell you how important this book and Martin's work have been to me. Good hunting!

Patterns for Frequent Use Cases

In this last chapter, we want to present you with a small library of patterns that are frequently used for ingesting data from external files and storing this ingested data in what we call history tables.

We will start this chapter from the key task of the automation of data ingestion. We will discuss alternative approaches and their pros and cons, and provide you with our opinionated insights and code to ingest data in Snowflake.

Next we will extend the basic pattern for storing the history of changes in an entity that we presented in previous chapters. We will provide you with a set of frequent use cases for storing incoming data and the code and conditions to deal with all these different needs.

In this chapter, you will learn about the following topics:

- Ingestion patterns
- History patterns

Technical requirements

This chapter is more technical than the previous ones, so a good understanding of SQL and knowledge of how dbt and Snowflake work is needed to fully understand all the topics. However, for many of the topics that will be covered, having an understanding of SQL might be enough to get the basics.

All the code samples for this chapter are available on GitHub at `https://github.com/ PacktPublishing/Data-engineering-with-dbt/tree/main/Chapter_15`.

Ingestion patterns

Ingesting data into the platform is still one of the key aspects of building any data platform – without data, there is no data platform.

It is a topic with a big range of possibilities as ingesting data depends on the data platform, the storage service, the file format, and many more big and small details.

In this chapter, we will concentrate on Snowflake, where it is possible to load data in multiple ways. However, the most efficient way to ingest decent amounts of data is through files. The concepts that we described for Snowflake apply, with some adaptations, to other platforms.

As an example, it is possible to use SQL insert statements, but the throughput is orders of magnitude lower than file-based ingestion or reading data from external tables (that, under the hood, read from files), but that also has its drawbacks, as we will see in a second.

In this section, we will present some of the most common use cases for ingesting data into Snowflake using dbt and one possible way to solve them, using code that implements tried and tested best practices, and should be simple to use.

Let's look at the different ways we can load data into Snowflake:

- **SQL INSERT**: This is the standard `SQL INSERT` command that you know from the transactional databases. It works well for inserting a few rows, but it does not scale.

  dbt uses the `SQL INSERT` command to load the rows from the CSV files that you place in the `seed/data` folder into Snowflake. It is a way to limit the size of what you can load. Good luck loading 10K or 100K rows…

  This is not a viable way to ingest any decent amount of data.

- **EXTERNAL TABLE**: In Snowflake, it is possible to define external tables that point to a folder in a container on an external storage service and the table will parse the files according to the provided file format and expression for the fields.

  This is a very flexible way to access external data, structured or semi-structured. Snowflake can exploit the schema information stored in semi-structured files, making the creation very simple.

  The major downside of using external tables is that every time that you query the table, and you do not hit the cache, all the files that back it must be loaded, parsed, and eventually filtered to answer your query.

  Some improvement can be achieved by adding partitioning based on the file/path name, but they help only if you query with a filter on a partitioning column. In the special case of Delta Lake-based tables, Snowflake can use the metadata in the Delta Lake log files to just parse the files that make up the current state of the table. However, they still must be parsed at every query (that does not hit the cache).

- **COPY INTO**: The `COPY INTO` command is the most important for loading data in Snowflake because all high-performance ingestion methods rely on ingesting files through this command in one way or the other.

You can do it actively by issuing the COPY INTO command directly (manually or with a script, as we will do) or indirectly by having a Snowpipe issue it. Even when ingesting data through the Snowflake Kafka Connector, you end up writing temp files that are then ingested through a COPY INTO command.

The main advantage of using COPY INTO is that files are parsed only once. This is because Snowflake tracks the files loaded in the destination table, which is often called a "landing table," so that at every COPY INTO query, Snowflake will only load new or modified files in the landing table.

A further advantage is that at the end of the COPY INTO command, the data is in a normal Snowflake table and every query that you issue on it takes advantage of micro-partitions and the associated metadata to reduce the data that's queried.

Another advantage is that you could transform the data while loading it, using almost all normal SQL expressions and functions, even though we will not do that.

As a final note, consider that, with COPY INTO, you can write from Snowflake tables into files of compatible formats, allowing you to feed data back into a data lake.

The effort to create a SQL expression to generate the columns of an external table is comparable to that of writing a SELECT statement to do the same as part of a COPY INTO command to load the data into a landing table.

Considering the similar effort, we generally prefer to use the landing table approach so that data is parsed only once and then is immediately ready to be queried with the best possible performance. This makes little difference for small tables but is a noticeable difference when you have millions of rows in a table or GBs of data in files.

Now that we have discussed the possible way to ingest data, let's see what techniques we will present to load different types of data:

1. Ingestion of **structured data**, which is typically done by loading CSV files.

    We will ingest the data by using the COPY INTO command inside a script that will be using the position of each column in the files. Column names and data types will be put in place by the CREATE TABLE statement for the landing table.

    In the special case that we are reading from a Delta Lake, then we would consider the external table approach for small to mid-sized tables, as the performance penalty is reduced sensibly because Snowflake will just parse the Parquet files that make up the current table.

2. Ingestion of **semi-structured data** in the file formats that Snowflake supports, such as JSON, Parquet, AVRO, and ORC.

    In this case, we will use the landing table approach, but we will show how Snowflake can use the schema information embedded in some of these file formats to make our life easier and type little or nothing.

In the next section, we will look at the common setup that we will need for any ingestion approach that includes reading from files.

Basic setup for ingestion

Whenever you need to ingest data coming from files into Snowflake, you have three basic problems: describing how to parse the file, telling where the files are, and authorizing access to these files.

In the next few sections, we'll describe the objects that Snowflake provides for these needs.

Describing where your files are

The first thing that comes to mind when you want to ingest data from files is to have a convenient way to point Snowflake to your files. This is the role of a **stage**.

You can think of a stage as an abstract container of files, with the ability to enable a Directory Table on it to query the files contained.

If you create an internal stage, then Snowflake will create a container for files in the cloud platform you are using, while to create an external stage, you have to provide Snowflake the URL to the files in one of the supported cloud platforms and the authentication.

Internal stages are handy if you have an application, such as a microservice, that's handling data that you want to load in Snowflake. You load the temporary local files with the data directly in the stage and once loaded, you do not have to deal with security as it is handled by the app connecting to Snowflake with a Snowflake driver. You cannot share with the world the files loaded in an internal share, but you can download then using a Snowflake driver.

The most common kind of stage for mature companies is the external stage pointing to the cloud provider that you already use to store your data files, such as in a data lake. You can reuse these files, or you can have specialized containers for Snowflake ingestion.

If you look at the syntax for the CREATE STAGE command in Snowflake, you might feel overwhelmed by the never-ending options, but the typical command that we use to create a stage looks like this:

```
CREATE STAGE IF NOT EXISTS stage_name
  URL = 'cloud_provider_specific_url'
  STORAGE_INTEGRATION = integration_name
  FILE_FORMAT = file_format_name;
```

The URL describes where the files are, and its format is dependent on the cloud provider where the files are located; as an example, for an Azure container, it looks like 'azure://account.blob.core.windows.net/container/path/'.

The storage integration, which we will see next, encapsulates the authorization and it is done once and forever between the file service and the Snowflake account.

The file format, as you can guess, encapsulates all that is needed to read the files in the stage and is optional. If we provide it with the stage, we do not need to provide the file format when we are reading from the stage and the format set in the stage is fine.

The **Directory Table** feature was recently added to Snowflake stages to allow us to query the file metadata of staged files like we do when listing a directory.

To add the directory service to a stage, add the following to the stage definition:

```
DIRECTORY = ( ENABLE = TRUE
              REFRESH_ON_CREATE =  TRUE )
```

Once you have added the directory table to a stage, you can run queries on it with the following syntax while using the DIRECTORY function on the stage name:

```
SELECT * FROM DIRECTORY(@mystage)
WHERE SIZE > 100000;
```

The preceding code makes it possible to query the metadata fields of the files, such as FILE_URL, LAST_MODIFIED, or RELATIVE_PATH.

When you use the Directory Table feature, you have to refresh the file list either by providing Snowflake with integration from the underlying cloud provider or by issuing a manual request before querying it.

While planning your file containers, consider that when you have many files in a stage, numbered in the many hundred thousand or millions, the file access operations, including filtering the files to ingest and refreshing the directory, become slower.

In our ingestion automation, we do not need to use a Directory Table as we rely on the ability of Snowflake to track the files that have been already processed and loaded into a landing table by the COPY INTO command.

Authorizing access to your files

Now that you understand that a stage describes where the files are, we have the problem of providing the authorization information to access such files.

In Snowflake, it is possible to do this in multiple ways, depending on the cloud provider where the files are, including providing the credentials when creating a stage or loading or unloading data.

We prefer to use **Storage Integration**, a Snowflake object that stores the identity and the authorization received by the external cloud provider, along with some metadata, that can be used to create multiple stages or loads/unloads without the need to know the credentials. This provides both extra security and ease of use.

Unless you have special security needs, we suggest creating one storage integration for each bucket/storage account, dividing it with top folders/containers by source system, and then pairing the stages with the top folders/containers that give access to the files for the tables of one specific system. Under the system level folder a folder for each table or topic or message type from that system is a good initial organization.

If you have some tables that require special security, we suggest hosting their data in a different bucket/account and creating separate integrations and stages for each group of people that can access such data. This allows you to provide their roles with the usage of the integration (if they have to manage the stages) or of the stages to read the files.

Creating a storage integration is a different process for each cloud provider, so we suggest that you look up the process for your cloud provider on the page for the CREATE STORAGE INTEGRATION command in the Snowflake documentation at https://docs.snowflake.com/en.

How to parse your files

Once we know where the files are and we are authorized to read them, we still have to tell Snowflake how to read them.

For many of the semi-structured formats such as Parquet, AVRO, and ORC, there are just a few options as the formats both have schema descriptions of the content and a clear way to read and write the content.

For the CSV and, to a minor level, JSON formats, we have a bit more variability, and when creating a format, it is important to provide the needed options so that Snowflake can correctly read and represent the data.

For each file type supported by Snowflake, there is a default file format implicitly defined by the defaults of the CREATE_FILE_FORMAT command. So, to define a format, you only need to provide the values for the options that do not align with the default value.

Options that often need to be specified are the number of rows to skip as a header, the field delimiter, the file encoding, the escape character, and the date and time formats.

Here is an example of a file format definition with some basic options defined:

```
CREATE FILE FORMAT IF NOT EXISTS file_format_name
  TYPE = 'csv'
  FIELD_DELIMITER = '|'                     -- default ','
  SKIP_HEADER = 1                           -- default 0
  ENCODING = 'ISO-8859-1'                   -- default 'UTF8'
  FIELD_OPTIONALLY_ENCLOSED_BY = '"'  -- default NONE
;
```

We consider it a good practice to always specify at least these common options, even when their values align with the default values.

Having them defined explicitly makes it easier for everybody involved to know the actual values, even if they do not remember the default value from Snowflake, and even easier to change them or create a different file format for the files that require it.

Loading data from files

Once you have access to the files and you can parse them, the last but most important thing you need to do is understand how the data is organized in the file so that you can read it, as well as understand how you want to organize the data if you are loading it into a landing table.

The organization of the fields in a file or table is called the **schema** of the file/table and it includes the name, type, and eventual organization (nesting) of columns. The name "schema" is overused in data, but this is the most common use.

Let's have a quick overview of schema issues based on the type of data:

- **Structured data in CSV files**: In this case, the schema is flat by design, and the fields appear in the same order in each row, so we must provide the name and data type for each field.

- **Semi-structured data**: The two main differences with semi-structured data are that data can be nested into objects or arrays and that entities do not have the same fixed schema.

  In Snowflake, you have three alternative ways to ingest semi-structured data: load all in one VARIANT column (leaving it to Snowflake to parse and infer the structure), explicitly transform the data while loading it to provide the desired organization, and the ability to automatically infer the column definitions for some formats (Parquet, AVRO, and ORC). The latter feature is in preview at the time of writing.

- **Unstructured data**: This is data that does not benefit from a column-based schema, such as images, videos, social media feeds, or formats that need application-based processing outside of the database to deliver their information.

  Snowflake can access the files in internal or external storage through stages, and then store and serve the URL and metadata that points to the files to provide shared access. Discussing unstructured data is beyond our scope.

The process of loading data, be it structured or semi-structured, into a table can be done in two steps:

1. Create the landing table to hold the loaded data:

   ```
   CREATE TABLE my_table (the_only_column VARIANT);
   ```

   Doing in this way it is very simple, but we delegated the schema decisions to Snowflake and we will have to deal with them when we read the data out.

Instead, we prefer to create a table with the schema that matches how we want to organize the data, including the metadata from the load process. In this way when we want to read the data there are no unresolved issues to deal with.

2. Use the COPY command to load the data into the table:

```
COPY INTO my_table ...
   FROM @my_stage        -- stage can include format
   PATTERN = '.*xxx.*.json'
```

With this basic command, we instruct Snowflake to load all new files into the stage whose name matches the pattern in the table.

When loading a CSV, the fields must be in the correct order, but for semi-structured formats, you can use the MATCH_BY_COLUMN_NAME option of the COPY command if the file and the table have the same schema.

In general, however, we replace the FROM @my_stage clause with a FROM (SELECT ... FROM @my_stage) clause that allows us to transform the data and add available metadata when loading the data from files.

Loading structured and semi-structured data in Snowflake works similarly, but what is different is how to build the SELECT statement to transform the data while loading.

Let's look at how to deal with the schema needs for CSV and semi-structured data.

Providing a schema to load CSV data

For CSV files, not much needs to be provided. Since the schema is flat, we only need to provide the names and data types of the columns, considering that the order matters.

This can be done once with a CREATE TABLE statement that lists the columns in the same order as they appear in the CSV file to be loaded in the table.

Once we have a landing table that matches the order of the columns in the file, we can ingest the data in a very simple way, like so:

```
COPY INTO {{ full_table_name }}
FROM (
    SELECT
        $1, $2, … $n,        -- one for each column in file
        METADATA$FILENAME as FROM_FILE,
        METADATA$FILE_ROW_NUMBER as FILE_ROW_NUMBER,
        '{{ run_started_at }}' as INGESTION_TS_UTC

    FROM @{{ full_stage_name }}/
)
PATTERN = '{{file_pattern}}'
```

The preceding code is from the macro for loading the CSV files, which we'll discuss later.

Please note that the only information we need to load from the file is the number of columns as we can reference them by their number. The data type is set in the landing table, which is created once with the CREATE TABLE command, which references the file columns in the right order.

Interpolating the schema for semi-structured data

If you think that it is simple to count how many fields you have in a CSV file, you still have to know the latest functions provided by Snowflake to manage semi-structured data.

Together, the INFER_SCHEMA and GENERATE_COLUMN_DESCRIPTION functions allow you to point Snowflake to a file (Parquet, Avro, or ORC formats) and do most or all the work to generate the landing table and the SELECT command for you.

The command to read the metadata from supported files in a stage looks like this:

```
INFER_SCHEMA(
  LOCATION => '@mystage/path/folder/'
  , FILE_FORMAT => 'my_parquet_format'
  , FILES => '<file_name.parquet>' [, …]
  )
```

The FILE_FORMAT parameter is mandatory, and we suggest using the FILES parameter to limit the sampling to one or a few files that are known to contain good payload data. Pay particular attention to support files, such as the checkpoint files of Delta Lake, which could contain other columns used for metadata or tooling.

Between LOCATION and the names in FILES, they must produce the full path of a file, so it is a good practice to set LOCATION to the folder where your files are.

You can look at the paths of files in a folder in a stage using the LIST command:

```
list '@mystage/path/folder/'
  PATTERN = '.*[.]parquet';
```

By pointing the INFER_SCHEMA function to a set of files, you will get this information for each column that appears in the source files: COLUMN_NAME, TYPE, NULLABLE, EXPRESSION, FILENAMES, and ORDER_ID.

You can query the output of the INFER_SCHEMA function by wrapping it in the table() function and selecting from it, as shown in this example:

```
SELECT *
FROM table( INFER_SCHEMA(…) )
```

This would produce an output like the following (first line column header):

COLUMN_NAME	TYPE	NULLABLE	EXPRESSION	FILENAMES	ORDER_ID
continent	TEXT	True	$1: continent::TEXT	xxx.parquet	0
country	VARIANT	True	$1: continent::VARIANT	xxx.parquet	1

Please note that the EXPRESSION column provides the code to select the column out of the parsed Parquet file, which is useful for both defining the external tables and for use in the SELECT queries used in the COPY INTO commands.

You can use the GENERATE_COLUMN_DESCRIPTION function to produce useful output for three use cases: create a table, create an external table, and create a view by passing the table, external_table, or view string value, respectively.

The following code shows how to use the GENERATE_COLUMN_DESCRIPTION function to output the list of columns and data types needed for a create table:

```
SELECT GENERATE_COLUMN_DESCRIPTION
          ( ARRAY_AGG(OBJECT_CONSTRUCT(*)), 'table')
FROM table( INFER_SCHEMA(…) )
```

The result would be something like the following:

```
"country" VARIANT,
"continent" TEXT
```

To generate the desired code from the inferred schema, we prefer to use normal SQL that we can control.

The following SELECT query produces similar column definitions for a create table:

```
SELECT
  COLUMN_NAME || ' ' || type || ' ,' as sql_create_table
FROM table( INFER_SCHEMA(…) )
```

On the other hand, the following query produces the columns for a SELECT query to read the data:

```
SELECT EXPRESSION as sql_select
FROM table( INFER_SCHEMA(…) )
```

The result looks as follows:

```
$1:country::VARIANT,
$1:continent::TEXT
```

The following SELECT query produces the column definitions for an external table:

```
SELECT
   COLUMN_NAME || ' ' || TYPE
      || ' as (' || EXPRESSION|| ') ,'   as sql_ext_table
FROM table( INFER_SCHEMA(…) )
```

The result looks like this:

```
country VARIANT AS ($1:country::VARIANT),
continent TEXT AS ($1:continent::TEXT)
```

In this section, we saw how easy it is to have Snowflake sample our data files in modern semi-structured formats and produce the schema definition of the data from the definitions stored in the files.

In the next few sections, we will learn how to use these pieces of code to create external tables or ingest our data into landing tables.

External tables

We have already hinted that using external tables is not our favorite option, but it is a possible way to ingest data into Snowflake. So, why not load data by querying directly from storage?

The short answer is performance, cost, and having to deal with duplicates.

The main explanation is that reading from an external table, unless you actively filter on the filename/ path of files, means parsing each file at every query that does not hit the cache. This is slow and expensive (you pay for the time).

A second reason is that when you read all the files in a folder where you have been accumulating full or incremental exports for some days, let alone years, at every load you get a huge number of old versions, which are duplicates on the primary key – again, unless you actively filter on the filename/path of files.

The third reason is that, as we will see, the complexity of creating an external table is comparable to ingesting the data into a landing table, without the benefits.

The last reason is that, unless you configure the underlying filesystem to notify Snowflake of each file change, you must refresh the external table before querying it so that it can check what files are now available under the table definition. In dbt, it is very easy to do this just before querying, so it's not a big problem, but it's one more thing we need to do.

The code to refresh the files underlying an external table is as follows:

```
ALTER EXTERNAL TABLE my_ext_table REFRESH;
```

In short, these are non-issues for small tables where you end up loading a few million rows. It is a slow death sentence for tables of any meaningful size and velocity unless you resort to incremental loads and tight filtering.

The only exception to this is when your data is stored in Delta Lake format. In this case, Snowflake can read and leverage the format to only parse the Parquet files that make up the current state of the table, allowing you to query the latest snapshot of the source table.

You still have to wait and pay for parsing the needed Parquet files every time you query the table, but at least you do not need to filter and manage the incremental loads.

To create an external table, you need to have created a stage and a file format. Then, you can create an external table with code similar to this:

```
CREATE EXTERNAL TABLE my_ext_table
(
    file_part as (<expression on metadata$filename>)
    col1 varchar AS (value:col1::varchar)
    ...
)
    PARTITION BY (file_part)
    LOCATION=@mystage/daily/           -- @stage/path
    FILE_FORMAT = my_file_format
    AUTO_REFRESH = FALSE;
```

In the preceding pseudocode, you define the VIRTUAL columns in the external table in a slightly different way from a normal table.

After the virtual column name and type, we need to provide an expression to extract the column from the underlying files. It has to be an expression based on the VALUE column, of the VARIANT type, that you get when you ask Snowflake to parse semi-structured data.

To set up the stage and file format, you can use the setup_XXX file, as described in the next section on landing tables, as they are set up in the same way.

In the previous section, we provided a SQL expression to produce the definitions of the virtual columns from INFER_SCHEMA. The following snippet of code creates an external table using the same information from the INFER_SCHEMA function:

```
CREATE EXTERNAL TABLE my_ext_table
  USING TEMPLATE (
    SELECT ARRAY_AGG(OBJECT_CONSTRUCT(*))
      FROM TABLE(
        INFER_SCHEMA(
          LOCATION=>'@mystage',
          FILE_FORMAT=>'my_ file _format'
```

```
        )
      )
    )
  ...
```

While this is a very handy way to create a table for some extemporary data reading or exploration work, it is not the most stable way to create a long-term external table to be the base of an ETL, as the columns would depend on the current files in the stage.

Therefore, we prefer to run the SQL from the previous section and store the resulting CREATE TABLE statement so that we can reproduce it whenever needed.

A reasonable use case for external tables is when the underlying data is hosted in DELTA LAKE format.

To instruct Snowflake to use the Delta format, add TABLE_FORMAT = DELTA to the command to create the external table, as shown here:

```
CREATE EXTERNAL TABLE my_ext_table
   ...
   TABLE_FORMAT = DELTA;
```

For such a table, Snowflake will look for and use the log files to determine what Parquet files to parse to serve the queries.

Landing tables

Finally, we are at the landing tables, our preferred way to load data into Snowflake as they provide the most benefits for the effort.

This approach works well and scales up for big tables and high-velocity data.

In the previous sections, we saw that to load the data, we need to follow three steps:

1. Set up the database objects, such as the stage, file format, and schema.
2. Create the landing table to hold the loaded data.
3. Write a COPY INTO command to load the data into the landing table.

In this section, we will capitalize on the description from the previous sections to present you with an opinionated collection of macros to automate the creation and loading of your landing table that is easy to understand, resilient, and low maintenance.

The code that we will present to automate the ingestion is made up of macros, so the files that contain the necessary code must be located under the macros folder.

Generally, we create an `ingestion_lib` folder to hold the macros that implement the general patterns and the support functions and a second `ingestion_code` folder that contains one sub-folder for each source system, with the code to set up the objects for the specific system and ingest the individual tables from that system.

Before jumping into the code, a note about the frequency of loads: loading data in Snowflake is inherently a batch process, and using Snowpipe is no different.

The good thing is that it is a quick process that can ingest big amounts of data in seconds and can therefore accommodate near-real time loading with micro-batches. This is because you can run the `COPY INTO` command on a landing at short intervals, down to minutes.

Setting up the objects for landing and external tables

First, we want to set up a single file, named `_setup_XXX.sql`, that encapsulates the naming and creation of the needed common objects to ingest from one source system.

We will create one setup file for each source system that we want to ingest as that is generally a domain that requires a different file format/stage or that we want to keep separated in a different schema, but of course, your mileage might vary.

The high-level layout of a `_setup_XXX.sql` file is as follows:

- Utility macros to generate and eventually run all the SQL for the setup

- Getter macros to define and make the names of the objects available

- Creation macros to generate the SQL of each needed object

Let's describe the macros that are contained in the file in more detail.

We start the file with a helper macro that allows us to generate all the required SQL to run all the setup:

```
{% macro setup_XXX_sql() %}
  {{ create_XXX_ingestion_schema_sql() }}
  {{ create_XXX_ingestion__ff_sql() }}
  {{ create_XXX_ingestion__stage_sql() }}
{%- endmacro %}
```

Note that we name all these macros with a final `_sql` as they create the required SQL without running it. The `setup_XXX` macro invokes the three individual macros that generate the SQL for each of the setup elements that we need.

To run the SQL, we must pass the result of the `_sql` macro to the `run_query` macro:

```
{% macro run_setup_XXX() %}
    {{ log('**  Setting up the LANDING / EXTERNAL tables,
         schema, FF and STAGE for XXX system **', true) }}
```

```
      {% do run_query(setup_XXX_sql()) %}
{%- endmacro %}
```

You can add a helper macro like this to be able to run the setup, without loading the data in the tables. To run it, use dbt run-operation run_setup_XXX. This is also the first call in the load_XXX_... macro that runs all the ingestion.

Next, we have the macros that define the names and locations (DB and schema) of the objects that we create for the ingestion and landing tables.

The first macro, shown here, defines the database for the objects and the landing tables:

```
/* DEFINE Names   */
{%  macro get_XXX_db_name() %}
  {% do return( target.database ) %}
{%- endmacro %}
```

Usually, we return target.database to use the same database as the environment where we are running the code, but it is possible to return a fixed name so that we always use that database. In such cases, all your environments will depend on the same tables (which is bad for incremental evolution) and you need to provide access to that database to the roles used in all environments.

The second macro, shown here, defines the schema name for the objects and landing tables:

```
{%  macro get_XXX_schema_name() %}
  {% do return( 'LAND_XXX' ) %}
{%- endmacro %}
```

We usually return a fixed string, mostly for simplicity, but you could use a variable to use the same definition here and in the source definition that we will use to read from the landing tables.

The following macro produces the fully qualified name of the file format:

```
{%  macro get_XXX_ff_name() %}
  {% do return( get_XXX_db_name()
                ~'.'~ get_XXX_schema_name()
                ~ '.XXX__FF' ) %}
{%- endmacro %}
```

In most cases, it is enough to have one file format for one source since all the data from one source is generally exported in one way, but you can create more names if needed.

The last naming macro produces the fully qualified name of the stage:

```
{%  macro get_XXX_stage_name() %}
  {% do return( get_XXX_db_name()
                ~ '.' ~ get_XXX_schema_name()
```

```
                          ~ '.XXX_STAGE' ) %}
    {%- endmacro %}
```

In general, one stage – and one name – is enough for one source system.

The last part of the file contains the macros that create the SQL to be executed.

An important point is that these macros must produce SQL code that is idempotent and can be run every day with the objects existing or not without producing errors, and not changing the existing definitions if the objects exist.

The first macro creates the schema to hold the objects and landing tables:

```
{% macro create_XXX_schema_sql() %}
CREATE SCHEMA IF NOT EXISTS
   {{ get_XXX_db_name() }}.{{ get_XXX_schema_name() }}
   COMMENT = 'The Landing Schema for XXX data.';
{%- endmacro %}
```

It simply creates the schema using the database and schema names returned by the macros.

The second macro creates the file format:

```
{% macro create_XXX__ff_sql() %}
CREATE FILE FORMAT IF NOT EXISTS {{ get_XXX_ff_name() }}
     TYPE = 'csv'
     FIELD_DELIMITER = ','
     SKIP_HEADER = 1
     FIELD_OPTIONALLY_ENCLOSED_BY = '"'
     ESCAPE = '\\'
     -- ENCODING = 'ISO-8859-1'  -- For nordic languages
     ;
{%- endmacro %}
```

This macro creates a file format for CSV files since more parameters need to be provided, but the creation is similar, albeit shorter, for other formats.

In this example, we have selected some of the most common options that often need to be specified. A special mention goes to UTF-8 encoding that is the default. You need to specify the encoding if the files are created with a different one than UTF8.

Using formats such as Parquet, Avro, or ORC removes most of these format issues.

The third macro that we need creates the stage to access the files:

```
{% macro create_XXX__stage_sql() %}
CREATE STAGE IF NOT EXISTS {{ get_XXX_stage_name() }}
```

```
    STORAGE_INTEGRATION = <STORAGE_INTEGRATION_NAME>
    URL = 'azure://strg_account.blob.core.windows.net/XYZ-container/
XXXpath/'
    FILE_FORMAT = {{ get_XXX_ff_name() }};
{%- endmacro %}
```

This macro creates a stage using a storage integration that encapsulates the authorization between Snowflake and the platform containing the files.

In this example, we are providing an Azure-based URL that is pointing to the XXXpath path in a container named XYZ-container in the strg_account storage account.

We have also provided a file format so that it is used by default in most cases (not by external tables) when reading data from the stage.

This first setup file can be considered useful for creating ingestion based on external tables and landing tables since the schema, the file format, and the stage can be shared.

Loading from CSV files

Now that we have the technical objects needed to ingest our data set up, let's look at the code to do the ingestion.

For each table that we want to ingest, we will create a file that will achieve the two remaining steps: creating the landing table and invoking the COPY INTO command.

The file to ingest each table will contain the following:

- A macro to create the landing table for the data of the table to be ingested
- A master macro that accepts the necessary parameters and orchestrates the two steps – that is, calling the macro to create the landing table and calling a library macro to run the COPY INTO command based on the input parameters

Let's analyze the table-specific file, leaving the library macro for the end of this section.

We will open the file with the master macro that is named after the table to ingest:

```
{%  macro load_<tableYYYYYY>(
        db_name = get_XXX_ingestion_db_name(),
        schema_name = get_XXX_ingestion_schema_name(),
        stage_name = get_XXX_ingestion_stage_name(),
        format_name = None,
        table_name = 'YYYYYY',
        pattern = '.*YYYYYY:*[.]csv',
        field_count = 12
) %}
```

```
    {% set full_table_name =
        db_name ~ '.' ~ schema_name ~ '.' ~ table_name %}
    {% do run_query(X_Y__create_table_sql(full_table_name)) %}
    {% do run_query(ingest_into_landing_sql(
            full_table_name,
            field_count = field_count,
            file_pattern = pattern,
            full_stage_name = stage_name,
            full_format_name = format_name
        ) ) %}
{%- endmacro %}
```

The first thing to note is that we name the main macro with `load`, plus the table name.

Then, we use the parameters' declaration to set them either using the getters defined in the setup file or by providing the values specific to this table.

They are the name of the table, which will be the name of the landing table, the pattern to select the files to be loaded from the stage, and the number of columns in the CSV file.

Note that we do not need the names of the columns here as we define them in the CREATE TABLE macro.

To select the files to load, you can provide a simple regular expression; Snowflake will just load the files that have not been loaded in the table referenced by the COPY INTO command or have been modified since being loaded.

Then, we must build the fully qualified name of the landing table and use it to invoke the create table-specific macro, passing the result to the run_query() function to execute the generated SQL code.

Please note that, for brevity, we have removed the logging instructions from the macro.

The last operation invokes the ingest_into_landing_sql library macro by passing the needed parameters, set in the declaration of the main macro for ease of use.

The create table macro is very simple and does what its name suggests:

```
{% macro X_Y__create_table_sql(full_table_name) %}
CREATE TRANSIENT TABLE {{ full_table_name }} IF NOT EXISTS
(
        -- Add declaration for table columns
        --   column type [[NOT] NULL],
        YYY_CODE string NOT NULL,
        YYY_NAME string NULL,

        -- metadata
        FROM_FILE string,
        FILE_ROW_NUMBER integer,
```

```
            INGESTION_TS_UTC TIMESTAMP_NTZ(9)
    )
    COMMENT = '...';
{%- endmacro %}
```

As you can see, there is only so much to say here as this macro just encapsulates a normal CREATE TABLE SQL command.

The interesting point is that you should declare all the columns that are present in the CSV in the initial part of the table, leaving the three metadata fields at the end, as they are created automatically by the ingestion macro in the last three positions.

As a note, you can define the nullability of the fields, with the default being nullable. Unless you want to have a very strict and inflexible loading setup, we suggest leaving all columns as nullable and checking the ones that you want to be not null with tests on the source that you will define to read from the landing table.

Finally, let's look into the `ingest_into_landing_sql` library macro, which implements the call of the COPY INTO command:

```
{% macro ingest_into_landing_sql(
            full_table_name,
            field_count,
            file_pattern,
            full_stage_name,
            full_format_name
) %}
BEGIN TRANSACTION;
COPY INTO {{ full_table_name }}
FROM (
  SELECT
  {% for i in range(1, field_count+1) %}${{i}},{% endfor %}

    METADATA$FILENAME as FROM_FILE,
    METADATA$FILE_ROW_NUMBER as FILE_ROW_NUMBER,
    '{{ run_started_at }}' as INGESTION_TS_UTC
  FROM @{{ full_stage_name }}/
)
PATTERN = '{{ file_pattern }}'
{%- if full_format_name %}
FILE_FORMAT = (FORMAT_NAME = '{{ full_format_name }}')
{%- endif %}
;
```

```
COMMIT;
{%- endmacro %}
```

As you can see, the ingestion itself is very simple – it involves calling the COPY INTO command inside a transaction and passing the right names for the landing table, the stage, the file pattern, and eventually a file format to override the one from the stage.

The macro for the CSV ingestion generates the $1, $2... positional column names to load the payload of the CSV and then adds the metadata columns: the filename, the row number in the file, and the time of the load (when we started the dbt run).

Loading from semi-structured files

Ingesting semi-structured files works pretty much the same as ingesting CSV files, with the only difference that instead of just using the list of positional columns ($1, ... $n), we need to have one expression for each column that we want to read out of the file.

The expression must provide the path to the information in the schema of the semi-structured file and also cast the expression to the desired SQL type.

We saw how we can get the expressions to read the data out of the semi-structured files with the INFER_SCHEMA function previously.

Considering that the only difference with the CSV ingestion is the need to provide the expressions to read the fields, the changes in our macros will be as follows:

*   Replacing the number of fields with the definition of the field expressions
*   Using the field definitions instead of generating the positional column names

Let's look at the two macros that we have in the file that are named after the table that we want to ingest, starting with the loading macro:

The macro declaration is like the CSV one but without the number of fields. Now, we need to provide the full expression to read the fields, not just specify how many they are:

```
{%  macro load_ZZZ(
        db_name = get_XXX_ingestion_db_name(),
        schema_name = get_XXX_ingestion_schema_name(),
        stage_name = get_XXX_ingestion_stage_name(),
        format_name = None,
        table_name = 'ZZZ',
        pattern = '.*ZZZ[.]parquet'
) %}
```

The full table name creation and the call to the macro to create the landing table are the same as they are for the CSV ingestion:

```
{% set full_table_name =
            db_name ~ '.' ~ schema_name ~ '.' ~ table_name %}

{% do run_query(X_Z__create_table_sql(full_table_name)) %}
{% set field_expressions %}
    $1 as src_data,
    $1:ZZZ_CODE::string as ZZZ_CODE,
    $1:ZZZ_NAME::string as ZZZ_NAME,
    $1:ZZZ_VALUE::double as ZZZ_VALUE
{% endset %}
```

Next, we used a set bloc to create a variable with the expressions to read the fields out of the semi-structured data. Note that you can write it yourself or have it generated by the INFER_SCHEMA and GENERATE_COLUMN_DESCRIPTION functions or some SQL, as we have shown in the preceding section of this chapter.

We finish by calling the ingest_semi_structured_into_landing_sql macro and passing the field expressions in place of the number of fields:

```
{% do run_query(ingest_semi_structured_into_landing_sql(
            full_table_name,
            field_expressions,
            file_pattern = pattern,
            full_stage_name = stage_name,
            full_format_name = format_name
        ) ) %}
{%- endmacro %}
```

The second macro is the macro to create the landing table – it is the same as in the CSV case, but remember that now, you have to define the columns with the same names and data types as in the field_expressions variable.

The only peculiarity is that if you want to store the source data in its variant form, as we have done in this example by having $1 as src_data as the first expression. Then, you need to create the first field for such a column with a variant data type:

```
-- Add declaration for table columns
    SRC_DATA variant,
    ZZZ_CODE string NOT NULL,
    ZZZ_NAME string,
    ZZZ_VALUE double,
```

The preceding snippet exemplifies the field declarations for the fields defined in the `field_expressions` variable example in this section.

Please be aware that by storing `$1` in the source data in variant form, you are duplicating the size of the data that you are storing, so it only makes sense in the first development phase if you are having trouble with extracting data from the variant or if you have decided to extract very few fields and keep most of the data stored as variants as your main storage.

Note that this can be a sensible solution when unpacking and flattening the schema of the semi-structured entity is either very complex or will bring problems with the object-relational conversion.

One typical example is when unpacking documents with headers and rows. This is a common example of **nested hierarchical data** stored in semi-structured files.

If the rows do not have a stable, unique identifier and are just identified by the header ID plus the row number, which is often done with orders or invoices, then it is impossible to track the rows by themselves (think of what to do if a row gets deleted, with no changes in the other rows), so it is better to track the versions of the document as a single thing and then unpack it in the ref layer.

One alternative is to flatten headers and rows but create a `HDIFF` of the rows so that if any changes occur (in the header or rows), all existing rows will be saved with the same `LOAD_TS` as the changed header and can all be retrieved using a `QUALIFY` clause with a `rank` function partitioned on the `HKEY` header and sorted on decreasing `LOAD_TS`. `rank=1` will retrieve all the rows written at the last `LOAD_TS`.

Now that we have seen the loading macro for the semi-structured data, let's have a quick look at the macro that implements the loading pattern – the `ingest_semi_structured_into_landing_sql` macro:

```
{% macro ingest_semi_structured_into_landing_sql(
        full_table_name, field_expressions,
        file_pattern, full_stage_name, full_format_name
) %}
BEGIN TRANSACTION;
COPY INTO {{ full_table_name }}
FROM (
    SELECT
        {{ field_expressions }},

        METADATA$FILENAME as FROM_FILE,
        METADATA$FILE_ROW_NUMBER as FILE_ROW_NUMBER,
        '{{ run_started_at }}' as INGESTION_TS_UTC
    FROM @{{ full_stage_name }}/
)
```

```
PATTERN = '{{ file_pattern }}'
{%- if full_format_name %}
, FILE_FORMAT = (FORMAT_NAME = '{{ full_format_name }}')
{%- endif %}
;
COMMIT;
{%- endmacro %}
```

Unsurprisingly, this is almost the same as the macro for ingesting from CSV files, but it replaces the for loop that generates the numbered columns ($1, … $n) with the provided field_expressions that we have highlighted in the preceding code.

In theory, by moving the for loop into a macro that generates the numbered columns ($1, … $n) and using that as an argument, you could always use this pattern with a call like the following:

```
field_expressions = positional_columns(field_count)
```

We prefer to have two patterns to keep the process simple for developers.

Using the landing tables loading pattern

At this point, you know how to set up the needed object, create the landing tables, and ingest the data into the landing tables.

To do this simply and reliably, create a load_all_XXX macro that will call the setup macro and then all the load_YYY macros to load the individual tables.

The content of the load_all XXX macro looks like this:

```
{% macro load_all_XXX() %}
{{ log('*** Load for XXX system ***', true) }}

{{ log('**   Setting up for XXX system **', true) }}
{% do run_query(setup_XXX_sql()) %}

{{ log('*    load_YYYYYY *', true) }}
{% do load_YYYYYY() %}
    --
{{ log('*** DONE loading for XXX system ***', true) }}
{%- endmacro %}
```

First, you must call the setup macro, then add the call to each table's load macro.

Once you've done this, you can schedule the execution by adding the following command to a job:

```
dbt run-operation load_all_XXX
```

You can either schedule the ingestion of each source system, each with a `load_all_XXX` macro, one after the other, or you can do them in parallel and then schedule the transformations.

In any case, you will read from the landing tables by defining them as the sources for your staging models.

Another practical consideration, especially if you have everyday full exports from your sources, is to remove the old data that has been loaded from the landing tables.

To achieve this, you can simply add a `DELETE` query after the `COPY INTO` command. The `DELETE` query would look like this:

```
DELETE FROM landing_table
WHERE <where_clause>
```

There are a few approaches that you can follow for the `WHERE` clause:

- Keep the last *N* ingestion batches. Every time we load data into the landing table, all the rows have the same `INGESTION_TS_UTC`, so you can write a clause like this:

```
WHERE INGESTION_TS_UTC NOT IN
   (SELECT DISTINCT INGESTION_TS_UTC
    FROM <landing>
    ORDER BY INGESTION_TS_UTC DESC
    LIMIT N)
```

- Delete the data that was ingested more than *N* days ago. Here, you can write a clause like this:

```
WHERE
   INGESTION_TS_UTC < DATEADD(DAY, -N, CURRENT_DATE)
```

- You could also write a `WHERE` clause that is referencing the `HIST` table where the data from the landing table will be stored and delete what was loaded before the max `INGESTION_TS_UTC` from the `HIST` table.

  While tempting and allowed by SQL, this is not a great idea you will create a cycle where the landing table depends on the `HIST` table and the `HIST` table on the landing table. This can complicate the process of running and maintaining the project.

Note that while deletions are quite slow in general in columnar databases, if you delete based on `INGESTION_TS_UTC`, you will pretty much delete according to the micro-partitions created during each daily load, so you will get very good performance.

History patterns

In the previous chapters, we have seen how to define proper `HKEY` and `HDIFF` fields, use the `save_history` macro to store the versions of the entities that we see over time, and use the `current_from_history` macro to read the current version for each instance of the entity out of the history table.

We have also seen how we can use the `HDIFF` field as a version identifier to be used in facts when we do not just care about the current version but we want to use dimensions with all the historical versions, also known as SCDT2 dimensions.

When talking about how to calculate the open positions in our portfolio from some periodic extract of the active portfolio, we introduced the problem of deletions from source data, and we created a solution to detect deletions to recognize closed positions.

One important caveat of the loading pattern of the `save_history` macro is that it can handle one version per key, per load. This is simple to achieve by using a `QUALIFY` clause in the STG model and let pass through only the most recent version we have in the inputs.

This solution is simple to code, very resilient, and easy to test, but it cannot be used when we need to keep a reliable audit of the changes as our `QUALIFY` clause might remove some intermediate versions.

In this chapter, we will discuss and provide usable code to extend the use of the history tables to cover those use cases when you want to track deletions in the incoming sources or when you need to keep a full audit of the changes that you receive.

We will also provide you with a solution to handle **Personally Identifiable Information** (**PII**) and follow **GDPR compliance** when saving your history tables.

To recap, let's look at a list of the use cases that we will cover:

- Storing history while recognizing deletions from full exports.
- Storing history while receiving explicit deletions. Here, we will distinguish when you receive the full record with a deleted flag or just the keys of deleted entities.
- Storing history while preserving multiple versions in input (full auditing).
- Storing history when you have PII, and you need to be GDPR-compliant.

By looking at this set of macros, we have covered most of the real use cases that you will face and have provided you with the competence to adapt these to other use cases where the proposed solutions cannot be applied directly.

Storing history with deletions – full load

The common case, that we have somehow introduced in our sample project, is to recognize deletions when you are not provided with information about them.

In this case, you can detect deletions only if you have a full, current export from the source system. By comparing that with the current (and active) entities in the history table, you can consider deleted the ones that appear in the history, but not in the full export from the source.

Handling deletions is especially important for fact tables, but getting full exports at every load can be problematic for big fact tables. This is one of the reasons why you might get the information about deletions from a fact table via a change data capture system. We will look at this scenario in the next section.

Let's look at the macro that implements this pattern, one block of code at a time.

The macro declaration, in this case, has fewer parameters than the normal save_history macro since there is no room to reduce the data to be used. We need the full export on one side and the current history on the other:

```
{% macro save_history_with_deletion(
    input_rel,
    key_column,
    diff_column,
    load_ts_column = 'LOAD_TS_UTC'
) -%}
```

You can configure the incremental materialization inside of the macro or leave it out and leave the responsibility of the correct configuration to the model using the macro:

```
{{ config(materialized='incremental') }}
```

Like in the normal save_history macro, we only have to apply the complex logic when the load is incremental; otherwise, we just initialize the table with all the input:

```
WITH
{% if is_incremental() %}-- in an incremental run
```

To start, we retrieve the current rows, deleted or not, from the history:

```
current_from_history as (
    {{- current_from_history(
        history_rel = this,
        key_column = key_column,
        load_ts_column = load_ts_column,
    ) }}
),
```

To decide what new rows will be loaded in the history table, we join the input with the current data from the history that is not deleted, using the HDIFF column to check for a new version, as explained for the normal save_history macro.

We keep the input rows that do not match the version from the current history.

For the rows to be added, we reshape the row layout so that we're in control of the two columns that we will modify during this load: the load timestamp and the DELETED column, which we set to false for new versions that we load from the input:

```
load_from_input as (
    SELECT
            i.* EXCLUDE ({{load_ts_column}})
          , i.{{load_ts_column}}
          , false as deleted
    FROM {{ input_rel }} as i
    LEFT OUTER JOIN current_from_history curr
     ON  (not curr.deleted
          and i.{{diff_column}} = curr.{{diff_column}})
    WHERE curr.{{diff_column}} is null
),
```

To detect the rows that have been deleted, we must join the non-deleted rows from the current history with the input data, on the HKEY entity, as we just want to know if there is any version of each entity.

The entities in the history that don't match the input are the ones that have been deleted. To record the deletion, we will create a new row in the hist table with the same content as the currently active row, but with this run's load timestamp and the DELETED column set to true:

```
deleted_from_hist as (
    SELECT
        curr.* EXCLUDE (deleted, {{load_ts_column}})
          , '{{ run_started_at }}' as {{load_ts_column}}
          , true as deleted
    FROM current_from_history curr
    LEFT OUTER JOIN {{ input_rel }} as i
     ON (i.{{key_column}} = curr.{{key_column}})
    WHERE not curr.deleted and i.{{key_column}} is null
),
```

The next step is to put the rows to be stored together – that is, the new and changed versions that we received from the input and the rows for the deletions that we have recognized:

```
changes_to_store as (
    SELECT * FROM load_from_input
    UNION ALL
    SELECT * FROM deleted_from_hist
)
```

If we are not in an incremental run, then we can store all the input that we receive in the history, reshaped as needed, with the load timestamp and DELETED columns last:

```
{%- else %}-- not an incremental run
changes_to_store as (
    SELECT
        i.* EXCLUDE ({{load_ts_column}})
        , {{load_ts_column}}
        , false as deleted
    FROM {{ input_rel }} as i
)
{%- endif %}
```

Finally, we select everything from the `changes_to_store` CTE to complete the macro:

```
SELECT * FROM changes_to_store
{% endmacro %}
```

The preceding code is not particularly complex, but there are a few subtleties, such as reshaping the table to be in control of the fields that we need to modify and applying filtering to the deleted rows from the history table.

Note that if you were to add a `WHERE not curr.deleted` clause to the initial CTE `current_from_history`, you would get the wrong results since the `WHERE` clause would be applied before the `QUALIFY` clause, which is used to keep the most recent version. This would exclude the deleted versions before any can be selected as the most recent version.

Storing history with deletion – deletion list

In the previous section, we saw that if you have a full export, you can recognize the deleted rows without further external help. It works well, but it can be quite slow for big tables as you are joining two tables of the same size twice.

To avoid big, expensive exports and even bigger joins, it is common for companies to configure their system to provide you with information about what columns have been deleted, even if that was not an original feature of the system.

You can configure many databases to keep track of the changes in a table (new rows, updates, and deletions) and make them available in some way.

In other cases, where a change data capture feature is not available (or it is too expensive for the organization), it is possible to use existing database features, such as triggers, to capture the change events in a table.

When we are provided information about deletions, we distinguish two cases: when we get the full table payload, along with the information about what entities have been deleted, and when we are provided with only the keys of the deleted entities.

Deletion with a full payload

The first case we discuss is when you receive all the normal columns with the payload for the table, plus another one that contains the state of the row (deleted VS active) or the operation that produces the row (creation, update, or deletion).

In this case, you can just consider the state/operation column like a normal payload column and load the table using the normal `save_history` macro, having that column as part of the HDIFF column of the table.

In this case, we suggest that, in the STG model, you add a Boolean DELETED column that encapsulates the specific rule to recognize if a row has been deleted or not. This helps in keeping the hard rules about the export and load encapsulated in the storage layer.

Handling deletion detection in this way is good because we are back to the normal case when we have only one source of truth for the content of the table.

One special case is when you have one initial or periodic reconciliation full exports without this extra state/operation column and more frequent delta loads that have this column instead.

The "trick" here is to consider that the full export provides you with rows that exist at some moment in time and that you can create the extra column in the STG model, all while designating such rows as active or with an operation code that could also have its own value.

In the next section we enter the realm of multiple sources of truth for the same table, so we need to establish a reliable timeline and eventually set some precedence rules in the STG model so that the right row for each entity is sent to the HIST table.

Deletion with deleted keys only

When we do not have the full payload for the deleted rows and only their keys, we find ourselves in a situation close to the deletion from the full export, but with knowledge of what rows have been deleted without the need to have a full export in the input and without the need to perform an expensive join operation.

Our solution will load the entities coming from the input as usual, while we generate the rows to record the deletions using the history and the list of deletions.

Let's discuss the code for this macro.

The macro declaration is pretty much the same as the normal `save_history` macro, with the addition of the `del_rel` and `del_key_column` parameters, which contain the relationship to the model with the list of deleted entities and the column with the key for the input entities, respectively:

```
{% macro save_history_with_deletion_from_list(
    input_rel,
    key_column,
    diff_column,

    del_rel,
    del_key_column,

    load_ts_column = 'LOAD_TS_UTC',
    input_filter_expr = 'true',
    high_watermark_column = none,
    high_watermark_test = '>=',
    order_by_expr = none
) -%}
```

Here, or in the model calling the macro, we need to have the incremental model configuration:

```
{{ config(materialized='incremental') }}
```

As we often do with incremental models, we start with the code for the incremental case.

First, we read the current data from the history table as usual:

```
WITH
{% if is_incremental() %}      -- in an incremental run
current_from_history as (
    {{- current_from_history(
        history_rel = this,
        key_column = key_column,
        load_ts_column = load_ts_column,
    ) }}
),
```

Next, we must keep the rows from the input that contain a new entity or a new row compared to the history. This is very similar to the normal `save_history` macro.

Note that now we filter the history to compare only against active entities.

We also reshape the layout of the input so that we know the position of the columns that we must manipulate – the `load` timestamp and the deleted columns:

```
load_from_input as (
    SELECT
        i.* EXCLUDE ({{load_ts_column}})
        , i.{{load_ts_column}}
        , false as deleted
    FROM {{ input_rel }} as i
    LEFT OUTER JOIN current_from_history curr
     ON   (not curr.deleted
            and i.{{diff_column}} = curr.{{diff_column}})
    WHERE curr.{{diff_column}} is null
      and {{input_filter_expr}}
    {%- if high_watermark_column %}
        and {{high_watermark_column}} {{high_watermark_test}} (select
max({{high_watermark_column}}) from {{ this }})
    {%- endif %}
),
```

After, we must generate the deleted rows for the entities that are active in the history and have their keys in the list of deleted entities.

For each entity, we use its last non-deleted version as the base for the deleted entry:

```
delete_from_hist as (
    SELECT
        curr.* EXCLUDE (deleted, {{load_ts_column}})
        , '{{ run_started_at }}' as {{load_ts_column}}
        , true as deleted
    FROM current_from_history curr
    WHERE not curr.deleted
      and curr.{{key_column}} IN
        ( SELECT {{del_key_column}} FROM {{del_rel}} )
),
```

Finally, we put together the rows to record the incoming data and the deleted rows:

```
changes_to_store as (
    SELECT * FROM load_from_input
    UNION ALL
    SELECT * FROM delete_from_hist
)
```

When we are not in an incremental run, we just store the input data as there are no rows in the history to be marked as deleted:

```
{%- else %}-- not an incremental run
changes_to_store as (
    SELECT
          i.* EXCLUDE ({{load_ts_column}})
        , {{load_ts_column}}
        , false as deleted
    FROM {{ input_rel }} as i
    WHERE {{ input_filter_expr }}
)
{%- endif %}
```

As usual, we close our macro by selecting all from the `changes_to_store` CTE:

```
SELECT * FROM changes_to_store
{%- if order_by_expr %}
ORDER BY {{order_by_expr}}
{%- endif %}
{% endmacro %}
```

You might have noticed that we have also added the ability to sort the data that we are going to save. This allows for some extra optimization based on Snowflake micro-partitions, besides having micro-partitions that have the same load timestamp.

The idea is that if you order the data when writing the table rows with the same values in the ordering columns, they will all end in one or a few micro-partitions. When you query the data, if you apply a filter on the ordering columns, Snowflake will be able to purge the micro partitions that do not contain values based on your filter.

While these extra details might provide better performance when you know the typical query pattern in advance, we suggest that you don't overthink it.

Dealing with conflicting sources of truth

An important topic when it comes to marking deleted rows from a deletion list is dealing with potential clashes between the two sources of truth for your history table: the input data and the deletion list.

What would be the correct behavior if you see that the same entity appears in both the input, meaning it is active, and in the deletion list, meaning it is deleted?

The answer is that it depends. It depends on the business rules of the system, it might depend on timestamps of the input and deletion list, and many other combinations.

You should either put tests in place that state you cannot have the same keys in both sources or handle that case in the desired way in the two STG models that provide the input and deletion list to the history table.

The macro has the following clear, but not idempotent, behavior:

- When an entity is marked as deleted in the HIST table, it will be added again if it's present in the input.

- When an entity is not marked as deleted in the HIST table, it will be marked as deleted if it's present in the DEL input.

  If the version in the input is different from the version in the history, then both the new version and the deletion will be added to the HIST table, breaking the contract of the history table to have one entry for each load timestamp.

  This could create problems and duplicates as two current versions would exist, but because one version would be marked as deleted, the most probable behavior is that the deletion would be practically ignored.

- The combined result of these two outputs is that if a key is present in both the input and the deletion list, the result will depend on its state and version in HIST: if the key has been deleted, it will be undeleted, while if it hasn't been deleted, the results will depend on the versions being equal or not.

As an example, to remove this, you can prioritize one of the inputs by putting one of the following pieces of logic in the STG models that feed the history table:

- To give priority to the input, the keys that appear in the input must be removed from the deletion list

- To give priority to the deletion list, the keys that appear in the deletion list must be removed from the input

With this final discussion, we have provided you with some tools to get the most out of this powerful pattern, which operates in a complex situation and needs to be understood well by the analytics engineer designing the models.

Storing history with multiple versions in the input

So far, we have only been adding one version at a time to the history – the "latest" from the input – so it is natural that it is either the same version that is already in the history or some more recent version.

In this section, we will look at a pattern you can use to load multiple versions in a single load round, making it possible to load data at any velocity and keep accurate audits for storing all the versions that can be observed in our input (the STG model on top of the source).

The pattern that we propose here uses the current version in the history as the baseline, comparing the current from history with the first (oldest) of the inputs for each instance (key) and then the remaining inputs in their order from the input.

This demands having a few easy-to-achieve but important conditions:

- The order of the versions must be stable. You need to provide a sorting expression to ensure that the versions are evaluated in the right order.

  The most common situation is to have some effectivity or last modified timestamp that provides the version order, but anything that produces a sort without multiple rows with the same rank will work, including sorting on the ingestion filename and row number.

  After all, if you cannot establish an order for the versions that you receive, how can you tell which one is the current/most recent? This might be a sign that you are missing something.

- To have a lean, well-ordered sequence of versions, the input must only contain versions that are aligned or more recent than the current version from the history.

  If your input contains versions older than the current from the history, the history will contain the full sequence of versions in the right order, but the versions before the current one from the history will be inserted again without any need, generating rows that are duplicates except for the load timestamp.

  The natural solution is to use a high watermark column to filter the data incoming from the STG model based on the content of the history table.

  This pattern is well suited for ingesting delta loads but can work equally well with full exports, so long as you can have a high watermark that is part of the business information, such as a last modified or an effective timestamp, and not some loading metadata such as an ingestion timestamp.

  In this pattern, the high watermark is implemented at the table level, implemented as max of the given column. It is a common situation and provides good performance, but the pattern could be modified to have a per-key level.

- Another important consideration is late arrivals.

  Data is added to the history table considering the arrival timeline, so input data is considered arrived at the same time or after the previous load.

  Versions for each key will be compared with the "previous" version based on the provided sorting expression. The first input is compared to the current from history; the others are compared to their predecessor in the input.

  In many cases, it is possible to architect the HDIFF column, the sort expression, and the load timeline to store data arriving late with the acceptance that some data might be stored twice, but you can read data out of the history table correctly.

  If you have multiple timelines and for your use case, it is not good enough to compare the input with the most current record in the history table based on one timeline (load timestamp or another), this pattern is not suitable for you.

So far, we have been ingesting the latest version from the input. Now, we can save all the new information that arrived after the last ingestion in one go if we can identify this starting point. Usually, that is done with the last updated column.

Before we jump into the code, we can already say that the ingestion mechanism is very similar to the other macros to save history. What makes this different is the ability to store multiple versions of an instance for a single load timestamp, and conversely, the ability to get the single-most current instance from the history despite having multiple versions with the same load timestamp.

As we mentioned previously, to achieve this we need a sorting expression to put the multiple versions of one instance in order.

To implement this pattern, we will implement two macros: one is an extension of `current_from_history` and is for selecting the last row from the multiple rows from the last load time; the other is an extension of `save_history`, which applies the correct comparison based on the order of the versions.

Let's start by discussing the `save_history_with_multiple_versions` macro.

You will immediately notice that the declaration here is the same as the one in the `save_history` macro, except for the addition of the `sort_expr` parameter, which is new and mandatory.

This new parameter needs to provide a SQL expression that, when combined with `ORDER BY`, produces stable sorting for the input, with the oldest version first and the newest last.

As an example, `LAST_UPDATED asc` or `FILE_NAME, ROW_NUMBER` would be two good expressions, the first working in all cases, including a full export, and the second suitable for incremental loads:

```
{% macro save_history_with_multiple_versions(
    input_rel,
    key_column,
    diff_column,
    sort_expr,
    history_rel = this,
    load_ts_column = 'LOAD_TS_UTC',
    input_filter_expr = 'true',
    history_filter_expr = 'true',
    high_watermark_column = none,
    high_watermark_test = '>='
) -%}
```

Then, we have the config to declare the incremental materialization:

```
{{- config(materialized='incremental') }}
```

We include the config in the macro as the macro makes no sense without incremental materialization, but you can take it out and have it in your models.

As usual, we start the code with the case for incremental materialization.

The first thing that we do, as in the other macro to save the history, is retrieve the last version that we have stored for each instance:

```
WITH
{% if is_incremental() %}
current_from_history as (
    {{current_from_history_with_multiple_versions(
        history_rel = history_rel,
        key_column = key_column,
        sort_expr = sort_expr,
        selection_expr = key_column ~ ', ' ~ diff_column,
        load_ts_column = load_ts_column,
        history_filter_expr = history_filter_expr
    ) }}
),
```

Here, we are using the `current_from_history_with_multiple_versions` macro, which, as the name implies, is a specialized macro for reading the most recent version when the history table can store more than one version for a single load timestamp. In this case, we also need `sort_expr`, a SQL expression, to order the versions that are presented when they are input/loaded at the same time.

For this macro, we need to retrieve both the `HKEY` and `HDIFF` columns for the most recent version, so we must build a SQL expression for this in the `selection_expr` parameter.

The following `load_from_input` CTE has the same functionality of selecting the rows to be saved as we have in the other `save_history` macros:

```
load_from_input as (
    SELECT
        i.*
        , LAG(i.{{diff_column}})
          OVER(PARTITION BY i.{{key_column}}
          ORDER BY {{sort_expr}}) as PREV_HDIFF
        , CASE
            WHEN PREV_HDIFF is null
            THEN COALESCE(i.{{diff_column}}
                            != h.{{diff_column}}, true)
            ELSE (i.{{diff_column}} != PREV_HDIFF)
          END as TO_BE_STORED
    FROM {{input_rel}} as i
    LEFT OUTER JOIN current_from_history as h
      ON h.{{key_column}} = i.{{key_column}}
    WHERE {{input_filter_expr}}
```

```
{%- if high_watermark_column %}
    and {{high_watermark_column}} {{high_watermark_test}}
    (select max({{high_watermark_column}})
    from {{ history_rel }})
{%- endif %}
)
```

The difference with the other implementations of the same CTE is that we use the LAG function to bring on one row the HDIFF column from the previous line according to the provided sort expression, sort_expr.

Then, for the first row, which has LAG() returning null, we compare the HDIFF column with the HDIFF column of the current version from the history. For the other rows, we compare the HDIFF column with the one from the previous row.

Also, note that we need to join the input and the history on the HKEY column. In the other save history macros, we have simply joined on the HDIFF column and avoided any other comparison as the one between the two HDIFF columns (input versus history) was all we needed.

After the code for the incremental runs, we have the code for the table creation runs:

```
{%- else %}
load_from_input as (
    SELECT
        i.*
        , LAG(i.{{diff_column}}) OVER(
                PARTITION BY i.{{key_column}}
                ORDER BY {{sort_expr}}  ) as PREV_HDIFF
        , CASE
            WHEN PREV_HDIFF is null THEN true
            ELSE (i.{{diff_column}} != PREV_HDIFF)
          END as TO_BE_STORED
    FROM {{input_rel}} as i
    WHERE {{input_filter_expr}}
)
{%- endif %}
```

What is different from the other save history macros is that here, we need to process the input without any contribution from the not-yet-existing history, to keep only the versions that represent a change concerning the previous row.

The only difference with the incremental run is that the first version is always stored.

We close with the usual query, which produces the desired results in all cases:

```
SELECT * EXCLUDE(PREV_HDIFF, TO_BE_STORED)
FROM load_from_input
WHERE TO_BE_STORED
ORDER BY {{key_column}}, {{sort_expr}}
{%- endmacro %}
```

Here, we have a few differences compared to the other save history macros.

The first is that we have an explicit filter on the TO_BE_STORED column. We could have used a QUALIFY predicate in the two cases, but we think that here we use a single predicate and it is more readable.

The second is that we remove the temporary PREV_HDIFF and TO_BE_STORED columns that we calculated to determine the rows to store from the final SELECT projection.

The third is that we put an ORDER BY at the end to facilitate the retrieval of data when reading from the history table.

Now that we know how we can store multiple versions in the history table, let's have a look at the current_from_history_with_multiple_versions macro, which retrieves the last version.

The macro declaration is like the one for the current_from_history macro, with the addition of the sort_expr parameter, which provides the order of the versions and the value of the default of the qualify_function parameter, which is used to filter the results:

```
{% macro current_from_history_with_multiple_versions(
    history_rel,
    key_column,
    sort_expr,
    selection_expr = '*',
    load_ts_column = 'LOAD_TS_UTC',
    history_filter_expr = 'true',
    qualify_function = '(rn = cnt) and rank'
) %}
```

After the macro's declaration, we create a new variable that extends the provided expression for the SELECT projection by adding the row_number and count window functions. These are used to determine the most recent version by load timestamp:

```
{%- set multiple_versions_selection_expression %}
    {{selection_expr}}
    , row_number() OVER( PARTITION BY
            {{key_column}}, {{load_ts_column}}
            ORDER BY {{sort_expr}}) as rn
```

```
      , count(*) OVER( PARTITION BY
             {{key_column}}, {{load_ts_column}}) as cnt
{%- endset -%}
```

The actual code creation is delegated to the usual `current_from_history` macro, which is called with the new `SELECT` expression and `QUALIFY` function:

```
{{current_from_history(
    history_rel = history_rel,
    key_column = key_column,
    selection_expr = multiple_versions_selection_expression,
    load_ts_column = load_ts_column,
    history_filter_expr = history_filter_expr,
    qualify_function = qualify_function
) }}
{% endmacro %}
```

Please note that the result of this macro does not suppress the `rn` and `cnt` temporary columns as they might be useful to the user that can decide to suppress them or not.

Storing history with PII and GDPR compliance

One common use case is to have data that contains **Personal Identifiable Information** (**PII**) that needs to be compliant with the GDPR, especially with the right to be forgotten.

This might be a tough requirement for a data platform as it is difficult to gather information about what data needs to be deleted or anonymized, compounded with the need to track all the places where that data has been propagated to.

If the source systems that feed your data platform are GDPR-compliant, then you can use their changes to anonymize the PII in the data platform, with the following results:

- Keep the PII segregated from long-term storage (history tables) but make it possible to visualize it whenever needed

- Make the PII impossible to retrieve after it is removed from the sources by keeping only its anonymized version

- After anonymization, maintain the ability to analyze the data, along with the individual actions, but without being able to assign an identity to the actor

The central idea is that instead of storing the actual PII in the history tables, we are going to store a surrogate of the PII, represented as S_{PII}, like the hash of the actual PII.

The surrogate will then be propagated everywhere the PII would have been.

In terms of history loading, we will also create a load to store the PII and its surrogate, S_{PII}, in a PII mapping table, with two columns called S_{PII} and PII.

Using this mapping table, it is possible to go from the surrogate to the actual PII at any moment if the mapping table contains the PII that corresponds with the surrogate.

The implementation of the mapping table is different if the PII data comes from a full export or an incremental export, as we will analyze later in this section.

The solution that we propose works well for dimensions and facts alike as it is equally simple to hash a field in the STG model, before it's going into the HIST table. However, the MAP table's implementation might be slightly different as the facts tend to have incremental loads, while dimensions are usually loaded with a full export.

Handling PII with full exports

Let's start with the solution for when your PII comes from a full export:

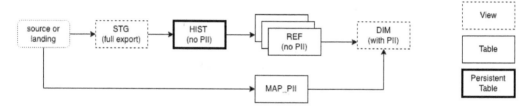

Figure 15.1: PII workflow for full exports

If your input is a full export, either only the last date or the last few dates from the landing table where the export is loaded, you can use the full export itself as the source of the PII, without storing it permanently in the data platform.

With a full export, the PII will disappear from the source system when the relevant data is either deleted or anonymized, until then the active PIIs will be present in the STG at every export.

By taking advantage of the fact that the PIIs are always available in the STG until we can use them, we can build the solution in three simple steps:

1. In the STG, substitute the PII with its surrogate by hashing it, for example. Build the HIST table and all the REF models as usual, but note that you will only have the surrogate in place of the PII.

2. Build the MAP table as a non-incremental table so that it is recreated at every run (use dbt "table" materialization). This table will contain the PII column and its surrogate version (S_{PII}) and can be created by using SELECT DISTINCT on the PII column.

3. In the delivery layer if/where you need to visualize the PII, you can simply join back from the surrogate S_{PII} to the PII value. If the surrogate is not found, this means that the PII is not available anymore and you should visualize the S_{PII}.

Using this approach, the PII information is naturally purged out of your data platform when it disappears from the source system. In the landing table, the PII remains only for the retention period that you have decided before deleting the imported data, and you can make as short as you need for tables with PII data; in the data platform it is only stored in tables that are recreated every day.

Another advantage is that by using the same surrogate everywhere, you can still join, count, and analyze the activity of each actor, even after you have "forgotten" their PII.

Handling PII with delta export

If the PII that we want to handle is part of a delta export, the solution requires a bit more logic as we cannot delegate the PII storage to the external source. This is because the export only contains the changed rows and most of the rows do not change for a long time.

In this case, the implementation differs from *step 2* of the previous one as we need to store the PII in a permanent table. To be able to remove the PII when the time comes, we need to receive a signal.

The signal can be of two types:

- We receive information that a PII is not in use anymore. This can come from the fact that the row containing the PII has been deleted or that the PII itself changed, creating a new version of the entity. If that version was the only occurrence of the old PII, we need to remove/anonymize it.

- We receive information that a certain PII needs to be anonymized/removed.

In any of these cases, we can use the signal to replace the value of the PII in the MAP table with its surrogate, making the two columns identical. This will ensure that, in the delivery layer, the join will automatically output the surrogate value.

The first use case is more complex as we need to put business rules in place to decide when a PII has to be anonymized.

Consider the case where, in one invoice, you have the name of a salesperson or operator. Just because you delete that invoice does not mean that you need to anonymize that value in all the invoices.

Similarly, when we receive a new version of a PII, let's call it PII_2, we need to decide what to do with the previous version, PII_1, and often, the correct action is doing nothing.

In this case, if the value of the operator's name is changed in one invoice, that does not mean that all the versions of the previous operator's name must be anonymized.

One solution for this case is to compare the list of surrogates in the MAP table with the list of the ones from the current versions from the HIST table.

All the surrogates that appear only in the MAP table should be anonymized as they are not in use anymore, either as they have changed or the record using it has been deleted.

History and schema evolution

The last topic we want to touch on before closing this book is managing changes in the schema of your data – that is, when the names, columns, or data types of tables change.

Some changes in the schema of your data, such as adding a new column with a default value, are considered nonbreaking changes, as existing clients as well as new ones can continue to use the table without disruption.

For this kind of change, you can use the migrations that we covered in *Chapter 12* to apply the desired changes to the existing tables, modify the SQL as needed, and just keep chugging along.

In most other cases, the change is a breaking change where you cannot continue to store the data in the same table.

The change in this case can also be logical, such as getting the output of a different model or some fields having a different semantic.

In these cases, our suggestion is to freeze the old STG and HIST tables and build a new version of them where you start loading the new data; then, in the REF layer, you put the business logic in place to merge the two (or more) inputs.

A key element in this context is the REF model built on top of the old HIST table, as it has to put the old data in a usable form that goes along with the new schema. As the HIST table is not going to change, that can be a static model too. And in the same way, if you need the current versions from the old history, you can also calculate that only once.

For dimensions, if you have a full export, you can calculate a static set of instances that exist in the old history and not in the new one – that is, the instances that have been deleted before the creation of the new HIST table and that you need to adapt to the new schema and add to the new history to have a complete history of that dimension to also cover the old facts.

For facts, which normally come as delta loads, you can have a cut-off date before which you take the current from the old history (adapted to the new schema) and after which you take data from the new one. Then, if old facts can change, you need to take the current out of the united histories.

In general, when you have delta loads and data can change arbitrarily, you can put together the existing versions by taking the current of each and keeping the most recent of each instance. Note that you can create a static table that does that for all the histories but the last, so you really have to take the current from this past histories recap table and the current HIST table.

To do that, you can use the following pseudocode:

```
WITH
current_from_old_histories as (
  SELECT * FROM {{ ref('REF_XXX_old_curr') }}
)
```

```
, current_from_history as (
  {{ current_from_history(
    history_rel = ref(' HIST_XXX_Vn'),
    key_column = 'XXX_HKEY'
  ) }}
)
, all_current as (
  SELECT * FROM current_from_history
  UNION ALL
  SELECT * FROM current_from_old_histories
)
{{ current_from_history(
    history_rel ='all_current',
    key_column = 'XXX_HKEY'
) }}
```

The preceding code takes the current entities from all the previous history tables – that is, a static table – as these history tables are not changing. Then, the current from the active history puts them together and takes the most recent entity from the united data.

As an alternative, depending on the number of changes in the table, you could add the current from all the previous history tables to the active history and take the current out of the union. In practice, this means replacing `current_from_history` in the pseudocode with a CTE named `active_history` containing a `select * from {{ ref('HIST_XXX_Vn') }}` query to get everything from the active history.

This example also shows you that the macros that we have seen can often be applied in similar cases, even if they're not identical to the ones for which we have introduced them.

By understanding what they do, you can apply them even in new contexts or derive a new macro that does something that you need often.

Summary

Congratulations, you made it to the end of this book!

In this chapter, we presented some more advanced patterns for ingesting data into Snowflake and multiple extensions of the `save_history` macro for dealing with different use cases, from detecting deleted rows to ingesting multiple versions at once to managing PII in our history tables.

As the author, first and foremost, I hope that I have passed on some of my passion for software engineering and the pleasure to put together a well-architected, simple-to-understand project that makes it possible to onboard new colleagues and maintain and evolve the functionalities without losing any sleep.

One of the key goals of the team working on this book was to discuss data engineering and data architecture while presenting how dbt works and how it can be used to solve the common problems that we all face when building a data platform.

After decades of dealing with data, I have my opinionated way of doing things, and this forms the bulk of the Pragmatic Data Platform, which is my attempt to balance simplicity with efficiency (of the developer and the platform) and generality.

Often, these goals conflict and sometimes, I presented different alternatives. This is because the best course of action can be subjective or depend on the actual use case.

In the end, I hope I have provided you with good insights into how data engineering and dbt work and the ability to learn more and adapt what I have shown to your real-life needs.

Further reading

Snowflake and dbt are two products that are evolving at the speed of light, introducing new features almost every quarter, so our principal suggestion is to become familiar with their documentation websites and get involved in their communities, which are great sources of information and support.

You can find them here:

- dbt Cloud documentation: `https://docs.getdbt.com/`
- Snowflake documentation: `https://docs.snowflake.com/`

Trying to capture such evolution in a static medium is difficult and there will always be important things that remain excluded, such as `EXCLUDE` for the `SELECT` command in Snowflake (which we started to use as soon as it was available) or metrics in dbt (which still have to mature and be supported to be used properly).

Index

H

I

W

Y

Packtpub.com

Subscribe to our online digital library for full access to over 7,000 books and videos, as well as industry leading tools to help you plan your personal development and advance your career. For more information, please visit our website.

Why subscribe?

- Spend less time learning and more time coding with practical eBooks and Videos from over 4,000 industry professionals
- Improve your learning with Skill Plans built especially for you
- Get a free eBook or video every month
- Fully searchable for easy access to vital information
- Copy and paste, print, and bookmark content

Did you know that Packt offers eBook versions of every book published, with PDF and ePub files available? You can upgrade to the eBook version at packtpub.com and as a print book customer, you are entitled to a discount on the eBook copy. Get in touch with us at customercare@packtpub.com for more details.

At www.packtpub.com, you can also read a collection of free technical articles, sign up for a range of free newsletters, and receive exclusive discounts and offers on Packt books and eBooks.

Other Books You May Enjoy

If you enjoyed this book, you may be interested in these other books by Packt:

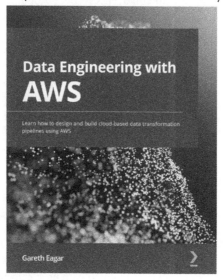

Data Engineering with AWS

Gareth Eagar

ISBN: 978-1-80056-041-3

- Understand data engineering concepts and emerging technologies
- Ingest streaming data with Amazon Kinesis Data Firehose
- Optimize, denormalize, and join datasets with AWS Glue Studio
- Use Amazon S3 events to trigger a Lambda process to transform a file
- Run complex SQL queries on data lake data using Amazon Athena
- Load data into a Redshift data warehouse and run queries
- Create a visualization of your data using Amazon QuickSight
- Extract sentiment data from a dataset using Amazon Comprehend

Data Engineering with Python

Paul Crickard

ISBN: 978-1-83921-418-9

- Understand how data engineering supports data science workflows
- Discover how to extract data from files and databases and then clean, transform, and enrich it
- Configure processors for handling different file formats as well as both relational and NoSQL databases
- Find out how to implement a data pipeline and dashboard to visualize results
- Use staging and validation to check data before landing in the warehouse
- Build real-time pipelines with staging areas that perform validation and handle failures
- Get to grips with deploying pipelines in the production environment

Packt is searching for authors like you

If you're interested in becoming an author for Packt, please visit authors.packtpub.com and apply today. We have worked with thousands of developers and tech professionals, just like you, to help them share their insight with the global tech community. You can make a general application, apply for a specific hot topic that we are recruiting an author for, or submit your own idea.

Share Your Thoughts

Now you've finished *Data Engineering with dbt*, we'd love to hear your thoughts! Scan the QR code below to go straight to the Amazon review page for this book and share your feedback or leave a review on the site that you purchased it from.

https://packt.link/r/1-803-24628-6

Your review is important to us and the tech community and will help us make sure we're delivering excellent quality content.

Download a free PDF copy of this book

Thanks for purchasing this book!

Do you like to read on the go but are unable to carry your print books everywhere? Is your eBook purchase not compatible with the device of your choice?

Don't worry, now with every Packt book you get a DRM-free PDF version of that book at no cost.

Read anywhere, any place, on any device. Search, copy, and paste code from your favorite technical books directly into your application.

The perks don't stop there, you can get exclusive access to discounts, newsletters, and great free content in your inbox daily

Follow these simple steps to get the benefits:

1. Scan the QR code or visit the link below

https://packt.link/free-ebook/9781803246284

2. Submit your proof of purchase
3. That's it! We'll send your free PDF and other benefits to your email directly

www.ingramcontent.com/pod-product-compliance
Lightning Source LLC
Chambersburg PA
CBHW081451050326
40690CB00015B/2752